Python®

for Programmers

Deitel® Series

For Computer Science and Data Science Series

Intro to Python for Computer Science and Data Science: Learning to Program with AI, Big Data and the Cloud

How To Program Series

Java™ How to Program, Early Objects Version, 11/E
Java™ How to Program, Late Objects Version, 11/E
C++ How to Program, 10/E
C How to Program, 8/E
Visual C#® How to Program, 6/E
Internet & World Wide Web How to Program, 5/E
Android™ How to Program, 3/E
Visual Basic® 2012 How to Program, 6/E

REVEL™ Interactive Multimedia

REVEL™ for Deitel Java™

VitalSource Web Books

http://bit.ly/DeitelOnVitalSource

Java™ How to Program, 10/E and 11/E
C++ How to Program, 9/E and 10/E
Visual C#® How to Program, 6/E
Android™ How to Program, 2/E and 3/E

Visual C#® 2012 How to Program, 5/E
Visual Basic® 2012 How to Program, 6/E
Simply Visual Basic® 2010: An App-Driven Approach, 4/E

Deitel® Developer Series

Python for Programmers
Java™ for Programmers, 4/E
C++11 for Programmers
C for Programmers with an Introduction to C11
C# 6 for Programmers
JavaScript for Programmers
Android™ 6 for Programmers: An App-Driven Approach, 3/E
Swift™ for Programmers

LiveLessons Video Training

http://deitel.com/books/LiveLessons/

Java SE 9™ Fundamentals, 3/E
C++ Fundamentals
C# 6 Fundamentals
JavaScript Fundamentals
Java SE 8™ Fundamentals, 2/E
Android™ 6 App Development Fundamentals, 3/E
C# 2012 Fundamentals
Swift™ Fundamentals

To receive updates on Deitel publications, Resource Centers, training courses, partner offers and more, please join the Deitel communities on

- Facebook®—http://facebook.com/DeitelFan
- Twitter®—@deitel
- LinkedIn®—http://linkedin.com/company/deitel-&-associates
- YouTube™—http://youtube.com/DeitelTV
- Instagram®—http://instagram.com/DeitelFan

To communicate with the authors, send e-mail to:

deitel@deitel.com

For information on programming-languages corporate training seminars offered by Deitel & Associates, Inc. worldwide, write to deitel@deitel.com or visit:

http://www.deitel.com/training/

For continuing updates on Pearson/Deitel publications visit:

http://www.deitel.com
http://www.pearson.com/deitel

python™

Python®

for Programmers

with **introductory AI case studies**

- ▶ **Natural Language Processing**
- ▶ **Data Mining Twitter®**
- ▶ **IBM® Watson™**
- ▶ **Machine Learning with scikit-learn®**
- ▶ **Deep Learning with Keras**
- ▶ **Big Data with Hadoop®, Spark™, NoSQL and the Cloud**
- ▶ **Internet of Things (IoT)**
- ▶ **Python Standard Library**
- ▶ **Data Science Libraries: NumPy, Pandas, SciPy, NLTK, TextBlob, Tweepy, Matplotlib, Seaborn, Folium and more**

PAUL DEITEL • HARVEY DEITEL

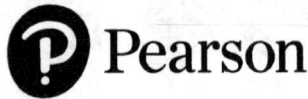

Library of Congress Control Number: 2019933267

ISBN-13: 978-0-13-522433-5
ISBN-10: 0-13-522433-0

2 2019

*In Memory of Marvin Minsky,
a founding father of
artificial intelligence*

*It was a privilege to be your student in two
artificial-intelligence graduate courses at M.I.T.
You inspired your students to think beyond limits.*

Harvey Deitel

Contents

6 Dictionaries and Sets   137

7 Array-Oriented Programming with NumPy   159

8 Strings: A Deeper Look   191

9 Files and Exceptions   217

10 Object-Oriented Programming   243

11 Natural Language Processing (NLP)   303

Preface

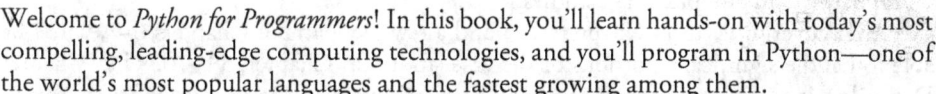

"There's gold in them thar hills!"[1]

Welcome to *Python for Programmers*! In this book, you'll learn hands-on with today's most compelling, leading-edge computing technologies, and you'll program in Python—one of the world's most popular languages and the fastest growing among them.

Developers often quickly discover that they like Python. They appreciate its expressive power, readability, conciseness and interactivity. They like the world of open-source software development that's generating a rapidly growing base of reusable software for an enormous range of application areas.

For many decades, some powerful trends have been in place. Computer hardware has rapidly been getting faster, cheaper and smaller. Internet bandwidth has rapidly been getting larger and cheaper. And quality computer software has become ever more abundant and essentially free or nearly free through the "open source" movement. Soon, the "Internet of Things" will connect tens of billions of devices of every imaginable type. These will generate enormous volumes of data at rapidly increasing speeds and quantities.

In computing today, the latest innovations are "all about the data"—*data* science, *data* analytics, big *data*, relational *data*bases (SQL), and NoSQL and NewSQL *data*bases, each of which we address along with an innovative treatment of Python programming.

Jobs Requiring Data Science Skills

In 2011, McKinsey Global Institute produced their report, "Big data: The next frontier for innovation, competition and productivity." In it, they said, "The United States alone faces a shortage of 140,000 to 190,000 people with deep analytical skills as well as 1.5 million managers and analysts to analyze big data and make decisions based on their findings."[2] This continues to be the case. The August 2018 "LinkedIn Workforce Report" says the United States has a shortage of over 150,000 people with data science skills.[3] A 2017 report from IBM, Burning Glass Technologies and the Business-Higher Education Forum, says that by 2020 in the United States there will be hundreds of thousands of new jobs requiring data science skills.[4]

---

1. Source unknown, frequently misattributed to Mark Twain.
2. `https://www.mckinsey.com/~/media/McKinsey/Business%20Functions/McKinsey%20Digi-tal/Our%20Insights/Big%20data%20The%20next%20frontier%20for%20innovation/MGI_big_data_full_report.ashx` (page 3).
3. `https://economicgraph.linkedin.com/resources/linkedin-workforce-report-august-2018`.
4. `https://www.burning-glass.com/wp-content/uploads/The_Quant_Crunch.pdf` (page 3).

Modular Architecture

The book's **modular architecture** (please see the **Table of Contents graphic** on the book's inside front cover) helps us meet the diverse needs of various professional audiences.

Chapters 1–10 cover Python programming. These chapters each include a brief **Intro to Data Science** section introducing artificial intelligence, basic descriptive statistics, measures of central tendency and dispersion, simulation, static and dynamic visualization, working with CSV files, pandas for data exploration and data wrangling, time series and simple linear regression. These help you prepare for the data science, AI, big data and cloud case studies in Chapters 11–16, which present opportunities for you to use **real-world datasets** in complete case studies.

After covering Python Chapters 1–5 and a few key parts of Chapters 6–7, you'll be able to handle significant portions of the case studies in Chapters 11–16. The "Chapter Dependencies" section of this Preface will help trainers plan their professional courses in the context of the book's unique architecture.

Chapters 11–16 are loaded with cool, powerful, contemporary examples. They present hands-on implementation case studies on topics such as **natural language processing, data mining Twitter, cognitive computing with IBM's Watson, supervised machine learning with classification and regression, unsupervised machine learning with clustering, deep learning with convolutional neural networks, deep learning with recurrent neural networks, big data with Hadoop, Spark and NoSQL databases**, the **Internet of Things** and more. Along the way, you'll acquire a **broad literacy** of data science terms and concepts, ranging from brief definitions to using concepts in small, medium and large programs. Browsing the book's detailed **Table of Contents** and Index will give you a sense of the breadth of coverage.

Key Features

KIS (Keep It Simple), KIS (Keep it Small), KIT (Keep it Topical)

- **Keep it simple**—In every aspect of the book, we strive for **simplicity and clarity**. For example, when we present natural language processing, we use the simple and intuitive **TextBlob** library rather than the more complex NLTK. In our deep learning presentation, we prefer **Keras** to TensorFlow. In general, when multiple libraries could be used to perform similar tasks, we use the simplest one.

- **Keep it small**—Most of the book's 538 examples are small—often just a few lines of code, with immediate interactive **IPython** feedback. We also include 40 larger scripts and in-depth case studies.

- **Keep it topical**—We read scores of recent Python-programming and data science books, and browsed, read or watched about 15,000 current articles, research papers, white papers, videos, blog posts, forum posts and documentation pieces. This enabled us to "take the pulse" of the Python, computer science, data science, AI, big data and cloud communities.

Immediate-Feedback: Exploring, Discovering and Experimenting with IPython

- The ideal way to learn from this book is to read it and run the code examples in parallel. Throughout the book, we use the **IPython interpreter**, which provides a friendly, immediate-feedback interactive mode for quickly exploring, discovering and experimenting with Python and its extensive libraries.

- Most of the code is presented in **small, interactive IPython sessions**. For each code snippet you write, IPython immediately reads it, evaluates it and prints the results. This **instant feedback** keeps your attention, boosts learning, facilitates rapid prototyping and speeds the software-development process.

- Our books always emphasize the **live-code approach**, focusing on complete, working programs with live inputs and outputs. IPython's "magic" is that it turns even snippets into code that "comes alive" as you enter each line. This promotes learning and encourages experimentation.

Python Programming Fundamentals

- First and foremost, this book provides rich Python coverage.

- We discuss Python's programming models—**procedural programming, functional-style programming** and **object-oriented programming**.

- We use best practices, emphasizing current idiom.

- **Functional-style programming** is used throughout the book as appropriate. A chart in Chapter 4 lists most of Python's key functional-style programming capabilities and the chapters in which we initially cover most of them.

538 Code Examples

- You'll get an engaging, challenging and entertaining introduction to Python with **538 real-world examples** ranging from individual snippets to substantial computer science, data science, artificial intelligence and big data case studies.

- You'll attack significant tasks with **AI, big data and cloud** technologies like **natural language processing, data mining Twitter, machine learning, deep learning, Hadoop, MapReduce, Spark, IBM Watson**, key data science libraries (**NumPy, pandas, SciPy, NLTK, TextBlob, spaCy, Textatistic, Tweepy, Scikit-learn, Keras**), key visualization libraries (**Matplotlib, Seaborn, Folium**) and more.

Avoid Heavy Math in Favor of English Explanations

- We capture the conceptual essence of the mathematics and put it to work in our examples. We do this by using libraries such as **statistics, NumPy, SciPy, pandas** and many others, which hide the mathematical complexity. So, it's straightforward for you to get many of the benefits of mathematical techniques like **linear regression** without having to know the mathematics behind them. In the **machine-learning** and **deep-learning** examples, we focus on creating objects that do the math for you "behind the scenes."

Visualizations

- 67 **static, dynamic, animated and interactive visualizations** (charts, graphs, pictures, animations etc.) help you understand concepts.

- Rather than including a treatment of low-level graphics programming, we focus on high-level visualizations produced by **Matplotlib**, **Seaborn**, **pandas** and **Folium** (for **interactive maps**).

- We use visualizations as a pedagogic tool. For example, we make the **law of large numbers** "come alive" in a dynamic **die-rolling simulation** and bar chart. As the number of rolls increases, you'll see each face's percentage of the total rolls gradually approach 16.667% (1/6th) and the sizes of the bars representing the percentages equalize.

- Visualizations are crucial in big data for **data exploration** and **communicating reproducible research results**, where the data items can number in the millions, billions or more. A common saying is that a picture is worth a thousand words[5]—in **big data**, a visualization could be worth billions, trillions or even more items in a database. Visualizations enable you to "fly 40,000 feet above the data" to see it "in the large" and to get to know your data. **Descriptive statistics** help but can be misleading. For example, Anscombe's quartet[6] demonstrates through visualizations that *significantly different* datasets can have *nearly identical* descriptive statistics.

- We show the visualization and animation code so you can implement your own. We also provide the animations in source-code files and as **Jupyter Notebooks**, so you can conveniently customize the code and animation parameters, re-execute the animations and see the effects of the changes.

Data Experiences

- Our **Intro to Data Science sections** and case studies in Chapters 11–16 provide rich data experiences.

- You'll work with many **real-world datasets and data sources**. There's an enormous variety of **free open datasets** available online for you to experiment with. Some of the sites we reference list hundreds or thousands of datasets.

- Many libraries you'll use come bundled with popular datasets for experimentation.

- You'll learn the steps required to obtain data and prepare it for analysis, analyze that data using many techniques, tune your models and communicate your results effectively, especially through visualization.

GitHub

- **GitHub** is an excellent venue for finding open-source code to incorporate into your projects (and to contribute your code to the open-source community). It's also a crucial element of the software developer's arsenal with version control tools that help teams of developers manage open-source (and private) projects.

- You'll use an extraordinary range of free and open-source Python and data science **libraries**, and **free**, **free-trial** and **freemium** offerings of software and cloud services. Many of the libraries are hosted on GitHub.

---

5. https://en.wikipedia.org/wiki/A_picture_is_worth_a_thousand_words.
6. https://en.wikipedia.org/wiki/Anscombe%27s_quartet.

Hands-On Cloud Computing

- Much of big data analytics occurs in the cloud, where it's easy to scale *dynamically* the amount of hardware and software your applications need. You'll work with various cloud-based services (some directly and some indirectly), including **Twitter, Google Translate, IBM Watson, Microsoft Azure, OpenMapQuest, geopy, Dweet.io** and **PubNub.**

- We encourage you to use free, free trial or freemium cloud services. We prefer those that don't require a credit card because you don't want to risk accidentally running up big bills. **If you decide to use a service that requires a credit card, ensure that the tier you're using for free will not automatically jump to a paid tier.**

Database, Big Data and Big Data Infrastructure

- According to IBM (Nov. 2016), 90% of the world's data was created in the last two years.[7] Evidence indicates that the speed of data creation is rapidly accelerating.

- According to a March 2016 *AnalyticsWeek* article, within five years there will be over 50 billion devices connected to the Internet and by 2020 we'll be producing 1.7 megabytes of new data every second *for every person on the planet!*[8]

- We include a treatment of **relational databases** and **SQL** with **SQLite.**

- Databases are critical **big data infrastructure** for storing and manipulating the massive amounts of data you'll process. Relational databases process *structured data*—they're not geared to the *unstructured* and *semi-structured data* in big data applications. So, as big data evolved, **NoSQL and NewSQL databases** were created to handle such data efficiently. We include a NoSQL and NewSQL overview and a hands-on case study with a **MongoDB JSON document database.** MongoDB is the most popular NoSQL database.

- We discuss **big data hardware** and **software infrastructure** in Chapter 16, "Big Data: Hadoop, Spark, NoSQL and IoT (Internet of Things)."

Artificial Intelligence Case Studies

- In case study Chapters 11–15, we present **artificial intelligence** topics, including **natural language processing, data mining Twitter to perform sentiment analysis, cognitive computing with IBM Watson, supervised machine learning, unsupervised machine learning** and **deep learning.** Chapter 16 presents the big data hardware and software infrastructure that enables computer scientists and data scientists to implement leading-edge AI-based solutions.

Built-In Collections: Lists, Tuples, Sets, Dictionaries

- There's little reason today for most application developers to build *custom* data structures. The book features a rich **two-chapter treatment of Python's built-in data structures**—lists, tuples, dictionaries and sets—with which most data-structuring tasks can be accomplished.

---

7. `https://public.dhe.ibm.com/common/ssi/ecm/wr/en/wrl12345usen/watson-customer-engagement-watson-marketing-wr-other-papers-and-reports-wrl12345usen-20170719.pdf`.

8. `https://analyticsweek.com/content/big-data-facts/`.

Array-Oriented Programming with NumPy Arrays and Pandas Series/DataFrames

- We also focus on three key data structures from open-source libraries—**NumPy arrays, pandas `Series`** and **pandas `DataFrames`**. These are used extensively in data science, computer science, artificial intelligence and big data. NumPy offers as much as two orders of magnitude higher performance than built-in Python lists.

- We include in Chapter 7 a rich treatment of NumPy arrays. Many libraries, such as pandas, are built on NumPy. The **Intro to Data Science sections** in Chapters 7–9 introduce pandas `Series` and `DataFrames`, which along with NumPy arrays are then used throughout the remaining chapters.

File Processing and Serialization

- Chapter 9 presents **text-file processing**, then demonstrates how to serialize objects using the popular **JSON (JavaScript Object Notation)** format. JSON is used frequently in the data science chapters.

- Many data science libraries provide built-in file-processing capabilities for loading datasets into your Python programs. In addition to plain text files, we process files in the popular **CSV (comma-separated values) format** using the Python Standard Library's `csv` module and capabilities of the pandas data science library.

Object-Based Programming

- We emphasize using the huge number of valuable classes that the **Python open-source community** has packaged into industry standard class libraries. You'll focus on knowing what libraries are out there, choosing the ones you'll need for your apps, creating objects from existing classes (usually in one or two lines of code) and making them "jump, dance and sing." This **object-*based* programming** enables you to build impressive applications quickly and concisely, which is a significant part of Python's appeal.

- With this approach, you'll be able to use machine learning, deep learning and other AI technologies to quickly solve a wide range of intriguing problems, including **cognitive computing** challenges like **speech recognition** and **computer vision**.

Object-Oriented Programming

- Developing *custom* classes is a crucial **object-oriented programming** skill, along with inheritance, polymorphism and duck typing. We discuss these in Chapter 10.

- Chapter 10 includes a discussion of **unit testing with `doctest`** and a fun card-shuffling-and-dealing simulation.

- Chapters 11–16 require only a few straightforward custom class definitions. In Python, you'll probably use more of an object-based programming approach than full-out object-oriented programming.

Reproducibility

- In the sciences in general, and data science in particular, there's a need to reproduce the results of experiments and studies, and to communicate those results effectively. **Jupyter Notebooks** are a preferred means for doing this.

- We discuss reproducibility throughout the book in the context of programming techniques and software such as Jupyter Notebooks and **Docker**.

Performance

- We use the `%timeit` **profiling tool** in several examples to compare the performance of different approaches to performing the same tasks. Other performance-related discussions include generator expressions, NumPy arrays vs. Python lists, performance of machine-learning and deep-learning models, and Hadoop and Spark distributed-computing performance.

Big Data and Parallelism

- In this book, rather than writing your own parallelization code, you'll let libraries like Keras running over TensorFlow, and big data tools like Hadoop and Spark parallelize operations for you. In this big data/AI era, the sheer processing requirements of massive data applications demand taking advantage of true parallelism provided by **multicore processors**, **graphics processing units (GPUs)**, **tensor processing units (TPUs)** and huge *clusters* **of computers in the cloud**. Some big data tasks could have thousands of processors working in parallel to analyze massive amounts of data expeditiously.

Chapter Dependencies

If you're a trainer planning your syllabus for a professional training course or a developer deciding which chapters to read, this section will help you make the best decisions. Please read the one-page color **Table of Contents** on the book's inside front cover—this will quickly familiarize you with the book's unique architecture. Teaching or reading the chapters in order is easiest. However, much of the content in the Intro to Data Science sections at the ends of Chapters 1–10 and the case studies in Chapters 11–16 requires only Chapters 1–5 and small portions of Chapters 6–10 as discussed below.

Part 1: Python Fundamentals Quickstart

We recommend that you read all the chapters in order:

- **Chapter 1, Introduction to Computers and Python**, introduces concepts that lay the groundwork for the Python programming in Chapters 2–10 and the big data, artificial-intelligence and cloud-based case studies in Chapters 11–16. The chapter also includes **test-drives** of the **IPython** interpreter and **Jupyter Notebooks**.

- **Chapter 2, Introduction to Python Programming**, presents Python programming fundamentals with code examples illustrating key language features.

- **Chapter 3, Control Statements**, presents Python's **control statements** and introduces **basic list processing**.

- **Chapter 4, Functions**, introduces custom functions, presents **simulation techniques** with **random-number generation** and introduces **tuple fundamentals**.

- **Chapter 5, Sequences: Lists and Tuples**, presents Python's built-in list and tuple collections in more detail and begins introducing **functional-style programming**.

Part 2: Python Data Structures, Strings and Files

The following summarizes inter-chapter dependencies for Python Chapters 6–9 and assumes that you've read Chapters 1–5.

- **Chapter 6, Dictionaries and Sets**—The Intro to Data Science section in this chapter is not dependent on the chapter's contents.

- **Chapter 7, Array-Oriented Programming with NumPy**—The Intro to Data Science section requires dictionaries (Chapter 6) and arrays (Chapter 7).

- **Chapter 8, Strings: A Deeper Look**—The Intro to Data Science section requires raw strings and regular expressions (Sections 8.11–8.12), and pandas Series and DataFrame features from Section 7.14's Intro to Data Science.

- **Chapter 9, Files and Exceptions**—For **JSON serialization**, it's useful to understand dictionary fundamentals (Section 6.2). Also, the Intro to Data Science section requires the built-in open function and the with statement (Section 9.3), and pandas DataFrame features from Section 7.14's Intro to Data Science.

Part 3: Python High-End Topics

The following summarizes inter-chapter dependencies for Python Chapter 10 and assumes that you've read Chapters 1–5.

- **Chapter 10, Object-Oriented Programming**—The Intro to Data Science section requires pandas DataFrame features from Intro to Data Science Section 7.14. Trainers wanting to cover only **classes and objects** can present Sections 10.1–10.6. Trainers wanting to cover more advanced topics like **inheritance, polymorphism and duck typing,** can present Sections 10.7–10.9. Sections 10.10–10.15 provide additional advanced perspectives.

Part 4: AI, Cloud and Big Data Case Studies

The following summary of inter-chapter dependencies for Chapters 11–16 assumes that you've read Chapters 1–5. Most of Chapters 11–16 also require dictionary fundamentals from Section 6.2.

- **Chapter 11, Natural Language Processing (NLP)**, uses pandas DataFrame features from Section 7.14's Intro to Data Science.

- **Chapter 12, Data Mining Twitter**, uses pandas DataFrame features from Section 7.14's Intro to Data Science, string method join (Section 8.9), JSON fundamentals (Section 9.5), TextBlob (Section 11.2) and Word clouds (Section 11.3). Several examples require defining a class via inheritance (Chapter 10).

- **Chapter 13, IBM Watson and Cognitive Computing**, uses built-in function open and the with statement (Section 9.3).

- **Chapter 14, Machine Learning: Classification, Regression and Clustering**, uses NumPy array fundamentals and method unique (Chapter 7), pandas DataFrame features from Section 7.14's Intro to Data Science and Matplotlib function subplots (Section 10.6).

- **Chapter 15, Deep Learning**, requires NumPy array fundamentals (Chapter 7), string method join (Section 8.9), general machine-learning concepts from

Chapter 14 and features from Chapter 14's Case Study: Classification with k-Nearest Neighbors and the Digits Dataset.

- **Chapter 16, Big Data: Hadoop, Spark, NoSQL and IoT**, uses string method `split` (Section 6.2.7), Matplotlib `FuncAnimation` from Section 6.4's Intro to Data Science, pandas `Series` and `DataFrame` features from Section 7.14's Intro to Data Science, string method `join` (Section 8.9), the `json` module (Section 9.5), NLTK stop words (Section 11.2.13) and from Chapter 12, Twitter authentication, Tweepy's `StreamListener` class for streaming tweets, and the geopy and `folium` libraries. A few examples require defining a class via inheritance (Chapter 10), but you can simply mimic the class definitions we provide without reading Chapter 10.

Jupyter Notebooks

For your convenience, we provide the book's code examples in **Python source code (.py) files** for use with the command-line IPython interpreter *and* as **Jupyter Notebooks (.ipynb) files** that you can load into your web browser and execute.

Jupyter Notebooks is a free, open-source project that enables you to combine text, graphics, audio, video, and interactive coding functionality for entering, editing, executing, debugging, and modifying code quickly and conveniently in a web browser. According to the article, "What Is Jupyter?":

> *Jupyter has become a standard for scientific research and data analysis. It packages computation and argument together, letting you build "computational narratives"; ... and it simplifies the problem of distributing working software to teammates and associates.*[9]

In our experience, it's a wonderful learning environment and **rapid prototyping tool**. For this reason, we use **Jupyter Notebooks** rather than a traditional IDE, such as **Eclipse**, **Visual Studio**, **PyCharm** or **Spyder**. Academics and professionals already use Jupyter extensively for sharing research results. Jupyter Notebooks support is provided through the traditional open-source community mechanisms[10] (see "Getting Jupyter Help" later in this Preface). See the Before You Begin section that follows this Preface for software installation details and see the test-drives in Section 1.5 for information on running the book's examples.

Collaboration and Sharing Results

Working in teams and communicating research results are both important for developers in or moving into data-analytics positions in industry, government or academia:

- The notebooks you create are **easy to share** among team members simply by copying the files or via **GitHub.**

- Research results, including code and insights, can be shared as static web pages via tools like **nbviewer** (`https://nbviewer.jupyter.org`) and **GitHub**—both automatically render notebooks as web pages.

---

9. `https://www.oreilly.com/ideas/what-is-jupyter`.
10. `https://jupyter.org/community`.

Reproducibility: A Strong Case for Jupyter Notebooks

In data science, and in the sciences in general, experiments and studies should be reproducible. This has been written about in the literature for many years, including

- Donald Knuth's 1992 computer science publication—*Literate Programming.*[11]

- The article "Language-Agnostic Reproducible Data Analysis Using Literate Programming,"[12] which says, "Lir (literate, reproducible computing) is based on the idea of literate programming as proposed by Donald Knuth."

Essentially, reproducibility captures the complete environment used to produce results—hardware, software, communications, algorithms (especially code), data and the **data's provenance** (origin and lineage).

Docker

In Chapter 16, we'll use **Docker**—a tool for packaging software into containers that bundle everything required to execute that software conveniently, reproducibly and portably across platforms. Some software packages we use in Chapter 16 require complicated setup and configuration. For many of these, you can download free preexisting **Docker containers**. These enable you to avoid complex installation issues and execute software locally on your desktop or notebook computers, making Docker a great way to help you get started with new technologies quickly and conveniently.

Docker also helps with reproducibility. You can create custom Docker containers that are configured with the versions of every piece of software and every library you used in your study. This would enable other developers to recreate the environment you used, then reproduce your work, and will help you reproduce your own results. In Chapter 16, you'll use Docker to download and execute a container that's preconfigured for you to code and run big data Spark applications using Jupyter Notebooks.

Special Feature: IBM Watson Analytics and Cognitive Computing

Early in our research for this book, we recognized the rapidly growing interest in **IBM's Watson**. We investigated competitive services and found Watson's "no credit card required" policy for its "free tiers" to be among the most friendly for our readers.

IBM Watson is a **cognitive-computing** platform being employed across a wide range of real-world scenarios. Cognitive-computing systems simulate the **pattern-recognition** and **decision-making** capabilities of the human brain to "learn" as they consume more data.[13,14,15] We include a significant hands-on Watson treatment. We use the free **Watson Developer Cloud: Python SDK**, which provides APIs that enable you to interact with Watson's services programmatically. Watson is fun to use and a great platform for letting your creative juices flow. You'll demo or use the following Watson APIs: **Conversation, Discovery, Language Translator, Natural Language Classifier, Natural Language**

---

11. Knuth, D., "Literate Programming" (PDF), *The Computer Journal*, British Computer Society, 1992.
12. http://journals.plos.org/plosone/article?id=10.1371/journal.pone.0164023.
13. http://whatis.techtarget.com/definition/cognitive-computing.
14. https://en.wikipedia.org/wiki/Cognitive_computing.
15. https://www.forbes.com/sites/bernardmarr/2016/03/23/what-everyone-should-know-about-cognitive-computing.

Understanding, Personality Insights, Speech to Text, Text to Speech, Tone Analyzer and **Visual Recognition**.

Watson's Lite Tier Services and a Cool Watson Case Study
IBM encourages learning and experimentation by providing *free lite tiers* for many of its APIs.[16] In Chapter 13, you'll try demos of many Watson services.[17] Then, you'll use the lite tiers of Watson's **Text to Speech**, **Speech to Text** and **Translate** services to implement a **"traveler's assistant" translation app**. You'll speak a question in English, then the app will transcribe your speech to English text, translate the text to Spanish and speak the Spanish text. Next, you'll speak a Spanish response (in case you don't speak Spanish, we provide an audio file you can use). Then, the app will quickly transcribe the speech to Spanish text, translate the text to English and speak the English response. Cool stuff!

Teaching Approach
Python for Programmers contains a rich collection of examples drawn from many fields. You'll work through interesting, real-world examples using **real-world datasets**. The book concentrates on the principles of good **software engineering** and stresses **program clarity**.

Using Fonts for Emphasis
We place the key terms and the index's page reference for each defining occurrence in **bold** text for easier reference. We refer to on-screen components in the **bold Helvetica** font (for example, the **File** menu) and use the Lucida font for Python code (for example, x = 5).

Syntax Shading
For readability, we syntax shade all the code. Our syntax-shading conventions are as follows:

```
comments appear like this
keywords appear like this
constants and literal values appear like this
all other code appears in this thin black font
```

538 Code Examples
The book's **538 examples** contain approximately **4000 lines of code**. This is a relatively small amount for a book this size and is due to the fact that Python is such an expressive language. Also, our coding style is to use powerful class libraries to do most of the work wherever possible.

160 Tables/Illustrations/Visualizations
We include abundant tables, line drawings, and static, dynamic and interactive visualizations.

---

16. Always check the latest terms on IBM's website, as the terms and services may change.
17. https://console.bluemix.net/catalog/.

Programming Wisdom

We *integrate* into the discussions programming wisdom from the authors' combined nine decades of programming and teaching experience, including:

- **Good programming practices** and preferred Python idioms that help you produce clearer, more understandable and more maintainable programs.

- **Common programming errors** to reduce the likelihood that you'll make them.

- **Error-prevention tips** with suggestions for exposing bugs and removing them from your programs. Many of these tips describe techniques for preventing bugs from getting into your programs in the first place.

- **Performance tips** that highlight opportunities to make your programs run faster or minimize the amount of memory they occupy.

- **Software engineering observations** that highlight architectural and design issues for proper software construction, especially for larger systems.

Software Used in the Book

The software we use is available for Windows, macOS and Linux and is free for download from the Internet. We wrote the book's examples using the free **Anaconda Python distribution**. It includes most of the Python, visualization and data science libraries you'll need, as well as the IPython interpreter, Jupyter Notebooks and Spyder, considered one of the best Python data science IDEs. We use only IPython and Jupyter Notebooks for program development in the book. The Before You Begin section following this Preface discusses installing Anaconda and a few other items you'll need for working with our examples.

Python Documentation

You'll find the following documentation especially helpful as you work through the book:

- The Python Language Reference:

    https://docs.python.org/3/reference/index.html

- The Python Standard Library:

    https://docs.python.org/3/library/index.html

- Python documentation list:

    https://docs.python.org/3/

Getting Your Questions Answered

Popular Python and general programming online forums include:

- python-forum.io

- https://www.dreamincode.net/forums/forum/29-python/

- StackOverflow.com

Also, many vendors provide forums for their tools and libraries. Many of the libraries you'll use in this book are managed and maintained at github.com. Some library maintainers provide support through the **Issues** tab on a given library's GitHub page. If you cannot find an answer to your questions online, please see our web page for the book at

http://www.deitel.com[18]

Getting Jupyter Help

Jupyter Notebooks support is provided through:

- Project Jupyter Google Group:

    https://groups.google.com/forum/#!forum/jupyter

- Jupyter real-time chat room:

    https://gitter.im/jupyter/jupyter

- GitHub

    https://github.com/jupyter/help

- StackOverflow:

    https://stackoverflow.com/questions/tagged/jupyter

- Jupyter for Education Google Group (for instructors teaching with Jupyter):

    https://groups.google.com/forum/#!forum/jupyter-education

Supplements

To get the most out of the presentation, you should execute each code example in parallel with reading the corresponding discussion in the book. On the book's web page at

http://www.deitel.com

we provide:

- **Downloadable Python source code** (.py files) and **Jupyter Notebooks** (.ipynb files) for the book's **code examples.**
- **Getting Started videos** showing how to use the code examples with IPython and Jupyter Notebooks. We also introduce these tools in Section 1.5.
- **Blog posts** and **book updates.**

For download instructions, see the Before You Begin section that follows this Preface.

Keeping in Touch with the Authors

For answers to questions or to report an error, send an e-mail to us at

deitel@deitel.com

or interact with us via **social media:**

- Facebook® (http://www.deitel.com/deitelfan)
- Twitter® (@deitel)
- LinkedIn® (http://linkedin.com/company/deitel-&-associates)
- YouTube® (http://youtube.com/DeitelTV)

---

18. Our website is undergoing a major upgrade. If you do not find something you need, please write to us directly at deitel@deitel.com.

Acknowledgments

We'd like to thank Barbara Deitel for long hours devoted to Internet research on this project. We're fortunate to have worked with the dedicated team of publishing professionals at Pearson. We appreciate the efforts and 25-year mentorship of our friend and colleague Mark L. Taub, Vice President of the Pearson IT Professional Group. Mark and his team publish our professional books, LiveLessons video products and Learning Paths in the Safari service (`https://learning.oreilly.com/`). They also sponsor our Safari live online training seminars. Julie Nahil managed the book's production. We selected the cover art and Chuti Prasertsith designed the cover.

We wish to acknowledge the efforts of our reviewers. Patricia Byron-Kimball and Meghan Jacoby recruited the reviewers and managed the review process. Adhering to a tight schedule, the reviewers scrutinized our work, providing countless suggestions for improving the accuracy, completeness and timeliness of the presentation.

Reviewers

Book Reviewers

Daniel Chen, Data Scientist, Lander Analytics

Garrett Dancik, Associate Professor of Computer Science/Bioinformatics, Eastern Connecticut State University

Pranshu Gupta, Assistant Professor, Computer Science, DeSales University

David Koop, Assistant Professor, Data Science Program Co-Director, U-Mass Dartmouth

Ramon Mata-Toledo, Professor, Computer Science, James Madison University

Shyamal Mitra, Senior Lecturer, Computer Science, University of Texas at Austin

Alison Sanchez, Assistant Professor in Economics, University of San Diego

José Antonio González Seco, IT Consultant

Jamie Whitacre, Independent Data Science Consultant

Elizabeth Wickes, Lecturer, School of Information Sciences, University of Illinois

Proposal Reviewers

Dr. Irene Bruno, Associate Professor in the Department of Information Sciences and Technology, George Mason University

Lance Bryant, Associate Professor, Department of Mathematics, Shippensburg University

Daniel Chen, Data Scientist, Lander Analytics

Garrett Dancik, Associate Professor of Computer Science/Bioinformatics Department of Computer Science, Eastern Connecticut State University

Dr. Marsha Davis, Department Chair of Mathematical Sciences, Eastern Connecticut State University

Roland DePratti, Adjunct Professor of Computer Science, Eastern Connecticut State University

Shyamal Mitra, Senior Lecturer, Computer Science, University of Texas at Austin

Dr. Mark Pauley, Senior Research Fellow, Bioinformatics, School of Interdisciplinary Informatics, University of Nebraska at Omaha

Sean Raleigh, Associate Professor of Mathematics, Chair of Data Science, Westminster College

Alison Sanchez, Assistant Professor in Economics, University of San Diego

Dr. Harvey Siy, Associate Professor of Computer Science, Information Science and Technology, University of Nebraska at Omaha

Jamie Whitacre, Independent Data Science Consultant

As you read the book, we'd appreciate your comments, criticisms, corrections and suggestions for improvement. Please send all correspondence to:

    deitel@deitel.com

We'll respond promptly.

Welcome again to the exciting open-source world of Python programming. We hope you enjoy this look at leading-edge computer-applications development with Python, IPython, Jupyter Notebooks, data science, AI, big data and the cloud. We wish you great success!

Paul and Harvey Deitel

About the Authors

Paul J. Deitel, CEO and Chief Technical Officer of Deitel & Associates, Inc., is an MIT graduate with 38 years of experience in computing. Paul is one of the world's most experienced programming-languages trainers, having taught professional courses to software developers since 1992. He has delivered hundreds of programming courses to industry clients internationally, including Cisco, IBM, Siemens, Sun Microsystems (now Oracle), Dell, Fidelity, NASA at the Kennedy Space Center, the National Severe Storm Laboratory, White Sands Missile Range, Rogue Wave Software, Boeing, Nortel Networks, Puma, iRobot and many more. He and his co-author, Dr. Harvey M. Deitel, are the world's best-selling programming-language textbook/professional book/video authors.

Dr. Harvey M. Deitel, Chairman and Chief Strategy Officer of Deitel & Associates, Inc., has 58 years of experience in computing. Dr. Deitel earned B.S. and M.S. degrees in Electrical Engineering from MIT and a Ph.D. in Mathematics from Boston University—he studied computing in each of these programs before they spun off Computer Science programs. He has extensive college teaching experience, including earning tenure and serving as the Chairman of the Computer Science Department at Boston College before founding Deitel & Associates, Inc., in 1991 with his son, Paul. The Deitels' publications have earned international recognition, with more than 100 translations published in Japanese, German, Russian, Spanish, French, Polish, Italian, Simplified Chinese, Traditional Chinese, Korean, Portuguese, Greek, Urdu and Turkish. Dr. Deitel has delivered hundreds of programming courses to academic, corporate, government and military clients.

About Deitel® & Associates, Inc.

Deitel & Associates, Inc., founded by Paul Deitel and Harvey Deitel, is an internationally recognized authoring and corporate training organization, specializing in computer programming languages, object technology, mobile app development and Internet and web software technology. The company's training clients include some of the world's largest companies, government agencies, branches of the military and academic institutions. The company offers instructor-led training courses delivered at client sites worldwide on major programming languages.

Through its 44-year publishing partnership with Pearson/Prentice Hall, Deitel & Associates, Inc., publishes leading-edge programming textbooks and professional books in print and e-book formats, **LiveLessons** video courses (available for purchase at https://www.informit.com), **Learning Paths** and live online training seminars in the Safari service (https://learning.oreilly.com) and **Revel**™ interactive multimedia courses.

To contact Deitel & Associates, Inc. and the authors, or to request a proposal on-site, instructor-led training, write to:

deitel@deitel.com

To learn more about Deitel on-site corporate training, visit

      `http://www.deitel.com/training`

Individuals wishing to purchase Deitel books can do so at

      `https://www.amazon.com`

Bulk orders by corporations, the government, the military and academic institutions should be placed directly with Pearson. For more information, visit

      `https://www.informit.com/store/sales.aspx`

Before You Begin

This section contains information you should review before using this book. We'll post updates at: http://www.deitel.com.

Font and Naming Conventions

We show Python code and commands and file and folder names in a sans-serif font, and on-screen components, such as menu names, in a **bold sans-serif font**. We use *italics for emphasis* and **bold occasionally for strong emphasis**.

Getting the Code Examples

You can download the examples.zip file containing the book's examples from our *Python for Programmers* web page at:

> http://www.deitel.com

Click the **Download Examples** link to save the file to your local computer. Most web browsers place the file in your user account's Downloads folder. When the download completes, locate it on your system, and extract its examples folder into your user account's Documents folder:

- Windows: C:\Users*YourAccount*\Documents\examples
- macOS or Linux: ~/Documents/examples

Most operating systems have a built-in extraction tool. You also may use an archive tool such as 7-Zip (www.7-zip.org) or WinZip (www.winzip.com).

Structure of the examples Folder

You'll execute three kinds of examples in this book:

- Individual code snippets in the IPython interactive environment.
- Complete applications, which are known as scripts.
- Jupyter Notebooks—a convenient interactive, web-browser-based environment in which you can write and execute code and intermix the code with text, images and video.

We demonstrate each in Section 1.5's test drives.

The examples folder contains one subfolder per chapter. These are named ch##, where ## is the two-digit chapter number 01 to 16—for example, ch01. Except for Chapters 13, 15 and 16, each chapter's folder contains the following items:

- snippets_ipynb—A folder containing the chapter's Jupyter Notebook files.

- snippets_py—A folder containing Python source code files in which each code snippet we present is separated from the next by a blank line. You can copy and paste these snippets into IPython or into new Jupyter Notebooks that you create.
- Script files and their supporting files.

Chapter 13 contains one application. Chapters 15 and 16 explain where to find the files you need in the ch15 and ch16 folders, respectively.

Installing Anaconda

We use the easy-to-install Anaconda Python distribution with this book. It comes with almost everything you'll need to work with our examples, including:

- the IPython interpreter,
- most of the Python and data science libraries we use,
- a local Jupyter Notebooks server so you can load and execute our notebooks, and
- various other software packages, such as the Spyder Integrated Development Environment (IDE)—we use only IPython and Jupyter Notebooks in this book.

Download the Python 3.x Anaconda installer for Windows, macOS or Linux from:

```
https://www.anaconda.com/download/
```

When the download completes, run the installer and follow the on-screen instructions. To ensure that Anaconda runs correctly, do not move its files after you install it.

Updating Anaconda

Next, ensure that Anaconda is up to date. Open a command-line window on your system as follows:

- On macOS, open a **Terminal** from the **Applications** folder's **Utilities** subfolder.
- On Windows, open the **Anaconda Prompt** from the start menu. When doing this to update Anaconda (as you'll do here) or to install new packages (discussed momentarily), execute the **Anaconda Prompt** as an *administrator* by right-clicking, then selecting **More > Run as administrator**. (If you cannot find the Anaconda Prompt in the start menu, simply search for it in the **Type here to search** field at the bottom of your screen.)
- On Linux, open your system's **Terminal** or shell (this varies by Linux distribution).

In your system's command-line window, execute the following commands to update Anaconda's installed packages to their latest versions:

1. `conda update conda`
2. `conda update --all`

Package Managers

The conda command used above invokes the **conda package manager**—one of the two key Python package managers you'll use in this book. The other is **pip**. Packages contain the files required to install a given Python library or tool. Throughout the book, you'll use conda to install additional packages, unless those packages are not available through conda, in which case you'll use `pip`. Some people prefer to use `pip` exclusively as it currently supports more packages. If you ever have trouble installing a package with conda, try `pip` instead.

Installing the Prospector Static Code Analysis Tool

You may want to analyze you Python code using the Prospector analysis tool, which checks your code for common errors and helps you improve it. To install Prospector and the Python libraries it uses, run the following command in the command-line window:

```
pip install prospector
```

Installing jupyter-matplotlib

We implement several animations using a visualization library called Matplotlib. To use them in Jupyter Notebooks, you must install a tool called `ipympl`. In the **Terminal, Anaconda Command Prompt** or shell you opened previously, execute the following commands[1] one at a time:

```
conda install -c conda-forge ipympl
conda install nodejs
jupyter labextension install @jupyter-widgets/jupyterlab-manager
jupyter labextension install jupyter-matplotlib
```

Installing the Other Packages

Anaconda comes with approximately 300 popular Python and data science packages for you, such as NumPy, Matplotlib, pandas, Regex, BeautifulSoup, requests, Bokeh, SciPy, SciKit-Learn, Seaborn, Spacy, sqlite, statsmodels and many more. The number of additional packages you'll need to install throughout the book will be small and we'll provide installation instructions as necessary. As you discover new packages, their documentation will explain how to install them.

Get a Twitter Developer Account

If you intend to use our "Data Mining Twitter" chapter and any Twitter-based examples in subsequent chapters, apply for a Twitter developer account. Twitter now requires registration for access to their APIs. To apply, fill out and submit the application at

```
https://developer.twitter.com/en/apply-for-access
```

Twitter reviews every application. At the time of this writing, personal developer accounts were being approved immediately and company-account applications were taking from several days to several weeks. Approval is not guaranteed.

Internet Connection Required in Some Chapters

While using this book, you'll need an Internet connection to install various additional Python libraries. In some chapters, you'll register for accounts with cloud-based services, mostly to use their free tiers. Some services require credit cards to verify your identity. In

---

1. `https://github.com/matplotlib/jupyter-matplotlib`.

a few cases, you'll use services that are not free. In these cases, you'll take advantage of monetary credits provided by the vendors so you can try their services without incurring charges. **Caution: Some cloud-based services incur costs once you set them up. When you complete our case studies using such services, be sure to promptly delete the resources you allocated.**

Slight Differences in Program Outputs

When you execute our examples, you might notice some differences between the results we show and your own results:

- Due to differences in how calculations are performed with floating-point numbers (like –123.45, 7.5 or 0.0236937) across operating systems, you might see minor variations in outputs—especially in digits far to the right of the decimal point.

- When we show outputs that appear in separate windows, we crop the windows to remove their borders.

Getting Your Questions Answered

Online forums enable you to interact with other Python programmers and get your Python questions answered. Popular Python and general programming forums include:

- `python-forum.io`

- `StackOverflow.com`

- `https://www.dreamincode.net/forums/forum/29-python/`

Also, many vendors provide forums for their tools and libraries. Most of the libraries you'll use in this book are managed and maintained at `github.com`. Some library maintainers provide support through the **Issues** tab on a given library's GitHub page. If you cannot find an answer to your questions online, please see our web page for the book at

> `http://www.deitel.com`[1]

You're now ready to begin reading *Python for Programmers*. We hope you enjoy the book!

---

1. Our website is undergoing a major upgrade. If you do not find something you need, please write to us directly at `deitel@deitel.com`.

Introduction to Computers and Python

Objectives

In this chapter you'll:

- Learn about exciting recent developments in computing.
- Review object-oriented programming basics.
- Understand the strengths of Python.
- Be introduced to key Python and data-science libraries you'll use in this book.
- Test-drive the IPython interpreter's interactive mode for executing Python code.
- Execute a Python script that animates a bar chart.
- Create and test-drive a web-browser-based Jupyter Notebook for executing Python code.
- Learn how big "big data" is and how quickly it's getting even bigger.
- Read a big-data case study on a popular mobile navigation app.
- Be introduced to artificial intelligence—at the intersection of computer science and data science.

1.1 Introduction

Welcome to Python—one of the world's most widely used computer programming languages and, according to the *Popularity of Programming Languages (PYPL) Index*, the world's most popular.[1]

Here, we introduce terminology and concepts that lay the groundwork for the Python programming you'll learn in Chapters 2–10 and the big-data, artificial-intelligence and cloud-based case studies we present in Chapters 11–16.

We'll review *object-oriented programming* terminology and concepts. You'll learn why Python has become so popular. We'll introduce the Python Standard Library and various data-science libraries that help you avoid "reinventing the wheel." You'll use these libraries to create software objects that you'll interact with to perform significant tasks with modest numbers of instructions.

Next, you'll work through three test-drives showing how to execute Python code:

- In the first, you'll use IPython to execute Python instructions interactively and immediately see their results.

- In the second, you'll execute a substantial Python application that will display an animated bar chart summarizing rolls of a six-sided die as they occur. You'll see the "Law of Large Numbers" in action. In Chapter 6, you'll build this application with the Matplotlib visualization library.

- In the last, we'll introduce Jupyter Notebooks using JupyterLab—an interactive, web-browser-based tool in which you can conveniently write and execute Python instructions. Jupyter Notebooks enable you to include text, images, audios, videos, animations and code.

In the past, most computer applications ran on standalone computers (that is, not networked together). Today's applications can be written with the aim of communicating among the world's billions of computers via the Internet. We'll introduce the Cloud and

---

1. `https://pypl.github.io/PYPL.html` (as of January 2019).

the Internet of Things (IoT), laying the groundwork for the contemporary applications you'll develop in Chapters 11–16.

You'll learn just how big "big data" is and how quickly it's getting even bigger. Next, we'll present a big-data case study on the Waze mobile navigation app, which uses many current technologies to provide dynamic driving directions that get you to your destination as quickly and as safely as possible. As we walk through those technologies, we'll mention where you'll use many of them in this book. The chapter closes with our first Intro to Data Science section in which we discuss a key intersection between computer science and data science—artificial intelligence.

1.2 A Quick Review of Object Technology Basics

As demands for new and more powerful software are soaring, building software quickly, correctly and economically is important. *Objects*, or more precisely, the *classes* objects come from, are essentially *reusable* software components. There are date objects, time objects, audio objects, video objects, automobile objects, people objects, etc. Almost any *noun* can be reasonably represented as a software object in terms of *attributes* (e.g., name, color and size) and *behaviors* (e.g., calculating, moving and communicating). Software-development groups can use a modular, object-oriented design-and-implementation approach to be much more productive than with earlier popular techniques like "structured programming." Object-oriented programs are often easier to understand, correct and modify.

Automobile as an Object

To help you understand objects and their contents, let's begin with a simple analogy. Suppose you want to *drive a car and make it go faster by pressing its accelerator pedal*. What must happen before you can do this? Well, before you can drive a car, someone has to *design* it. A car typically begins as engineering drawings, similar to the *blueprints* that describe the design of a house. These drawings include the design for an accelerator pedal. The pedal *hides* from the driver the complex mechanisms that make the car go faster, just as the brake pedal "hides" the mechanisms that slow the car, and the steering wheel "hides" the mechanisms that turn the car. This enables people with little or no knowledge of how engines, braking and steering mechanisms work to drive a car easily.

Just as you cannot cook meals in the blueprint of a kitchen, you cannot drive a car's engineering drawings. Before you can drive a car, it must be *built* from the engineering drawings that describe it. A completed car has an *actual* accelerator pedal to make it go faster, but even that's not enough—the car won't accelerate on its own (hopefully!), so the driver must *press* the pedal to accelerate the car.

Methods and Classes

Let's use our car example to introduce some key object-oriented programming concepts. Performing a task in a program requires a **method**. The method houses the program statements that perform its tasks. The method hides these statements from its user, just as the accelerator pedal of a car hides from the driver the mechanisms of making the car go faster. In Python, a program unit called a **class** houses the set of methods that perform the class's tasks. For example, a class that represents a bank account might contain one method to *deposit* money to an account, another to *withdraw* money from an account and a third to *inquire* what the account's balance is. A class is similar in concept to a car's engineering drawings, which house the design of an accelerator pedal, steering wheel, and so on.

Instantiation

Just as someone has to *build a car* from its engineering drawings before you can drive a car, you must *build an object* of a class before a program can perform the tasks that the class's methods define. The process of doing this is called *instantiation*. An object is then referred to as an **instance** of its class.

Reuse

Just as a car's engineering drawings can be *reused* many times to build many cars, you can *reuse* a class many times to build many objects. Reuse of existing classes when building new classes and programs saves time and effort. Reuse also helps you build more reliable and effective systems because existing classes and components often have undergone extensive *testing*, *debugging* and *performance tuning*. Just as the notion of *interchangeable parts* was crucial to the Industrial Revolution, reusable classes are crucial to the software revolution that has been spurred by object technology.

In Python, you'll typically use a *building-block approach* to create your programs. To avoid reinventing the wheel, you'll use existing high-quality pieces wherever possible. This software reuse is a key benefit of object-oriented programming.

Messages and Method Calls

When you drive a car, pressing its gas pedal sends a *message* to the car to perform a task—that is, to go faster. Similarly, you *send messages to an object*. Each message is implemented as a method call that tells a method of the object to perform its task. For example, a program might call a bank-account object's *deposit* method to increase the account's balance.

Attributes and Instance Variables

A car, besides having capabilities to accomplish tasks, also has *attributes*, such as its color, its number of doors, the amount of gas in its tank, its current speed and its record of total miles driven (i.e., its odometer reading). Like its capabilities, the car's attributes are represented as part of its design in its engineering diagrams (which, for example, include an odometer and a fuel gauge). As you drive an actual car, these attributes are carried along with the car. Every car maintains its *own* attributes. For example, each car knows how much gas is in its own gas tank, but *not* how much is in the tanks of *other* cars.

An object, similarly, has attributes that it carries along as it's used in a program. These attributes are specified as part of the object's class. For example, a bank-account object has a *balance attribute* that represents the amount of money in the account. Each bank-account object knows the balance in the account it represents, but *not* the balances of the *other* accounts in the bank. Attributes are specified by the class's **instance variables**. A class's (and its object's) attributes and methods are intimately related, so classes wrap together their attributes and methods.

Inheritance

A new class of objects can be created conveniently by **inheritance**—the new class (called the **subclass**) starts with the characteristics of an existing class (called the **superclass**), possibly customizing them and adding unique characteristics of its own. In our car analogy, an object of class "convertible" certainly *is an* object of the more *general* class "automobile," but more *specifically*, the roof can be raised or lowered.

Object-Oriented Analysis and Design (OOAD)

Soon you'll be writing programs in Python. How will you create the code for your programs? Perhaps, like many programmers, you'll simply turn on your computer and start typing. This approach may work for small programs (like the ones we present in the early chapters of the book), but what if you were asked to create a software system to control thousands of automated teller machines for a major bank? Or suppose you were asked to work on a team of 1,000 software developers building the next generation of the U.S. air traffic control system? For projects so large and complex, you should not simply sit down and start writing programs.

To create the best solutions, you should follow a detailed **analysis** process for determining your project's **requirements** (i.e., defining *what* the system is supposed to do), then develop a **design** that satisfies them (i.e., specifying *how* the system should do it). Ideally, you'd go through this process and carefully review the design (and have your design reviewed by other software professionals) before writing any code. If this process involves analyzing and designing your system from an object-oriented point of view, it's called an **object-oriented analysis-and-design (OOAD) process**. Languages like Python are object-oriented. Programming in such a language, called **object-oriented programming (OOP)**, allows you to implement an object-oriented design as a working system.

1.3 Python

Python is an object-oriented scripting language that was released publicly in 1991. It was developed by Guido van Rossum of the National Research Institute for Mathematics and Computer Science in Amsterdam.

Python has rapidly become one of the world's most popular programming languages. It's now particularly popular for educational and scientific computing,[2] and it recently surpassed the programming language R as the most popular data-science programming language.[3,4,5] Here are some reasons why Python is popular and everyone should consider learning it:[6,7,8]

- It's open source, free and widely available with a massive open-source community.

- It's easier to learn than languages like C, C++, C# and Java, enabling novices and professional developers to get up to speed quickly.

---

2. https://www.oreilly.com/ideas/5-things-to-watch-in-python-in-2017.
3. https://www.kdnuggets.com/2017/08/python-overtakes-r-leader-analytics-data-science.html.
4. https://www.r-bloggers.com/data-science-job-report-2017-r-passes-sas-but-python-leaves-them-both-behind/.
5. https://www.oreilly.com/ideas/5-things-to-watch-in-python-in-2017.
6. https://dbader.org/blog/why-learn-python.
7. https://simpleprogrammer.com/2017/01/18/7-reasons-why-you-should-learn-python/.
8. https://www.oreilly.com/ideas/5-things-to-watch-in-python-in-2017.

- It's easier to read than many other popular programming languages.

- It's widely used in education.[9]

- It enhances developer productivity with extensive standard libraries and third-party open-source libraries, so programmers can write code faster and perform complex tasks with minimal code. We'll say more about this in Section 1.4.

- There are massive numbers of free open-source Python applications.

- It's popular in web development (e.g., Django, Flask).

- It supports popular programming paradigms—procedural, functional-style and object-oriented.[10] We'll begin introducing functional-style programming features in Chapter 4 and use them in subsequent chapters.

- It simplifies concurrent programming—with asyncio and async/await, you're able to write single-threaded concurrent code[11], greatly simplifying the inherently complex processes of writing, debugging and maintaining that code.[12]

- There are lots of capabilities for enhancing Python performance.

- It's used to build anything from simple scripts to complex apps with massive numbers of users, such as Dropbox, YouTube, Reddit, Instagram and Quora.[13]

- It's popular in artificial intelligence, which is enjoying explosive growth, in part because of its special relationship with data science.

- It's widely used in the financial community.[14]

- There's an extensive job market for Python programmers across many disciplines, especially in data-science-oriented positions, and Python jobs are among the highest paid of all programming jobs.[15,16]

- R is a popular open-source programming language for statistical applications and visualization. Python and R are the two most widely used data-science languages.

Anaconda Python Distribution

We use the Anaconda Python distribution because it's easy to install on Windows, macOS and Linux and supports the latest versions of Python, the IPython interpreter (introduced in Section 1.5.1) and Jupyter Notebooks (introduced in Section 1.5.3). Anaconda also includes other software packages and libraries commonly used in Python programming and data science, allowing you to focus on Python and data science, rather than software

---

9. Tollervey, N., *Python in Education: Teach, Learn, Program* (O'Reilly Media, Inc., 2015).
10. https://en.wikipedia.org/wiki/Python_(programming_language).
11. https://docs.python.org/3/library/asyncio.html.
12. https://www.oreilly.com/ideas/5-things-to-watch-in-python-in-2017.
13. https://www.hartmannsoftware.com/Blog/Articles_from_Software_Fans/Most-Famous-Software-Programs-Written-in-Python.
14. Kolanovic, M. and R. Krishnamachari, *Big Data and AI Strategies: Machine Learning and Alternative Data Approach to Investing* (J.P. Morgan, 2017).
15. https://www.infoworld.com/article/3170838/developer/get-paid-10-programming-languages-to-learn-in-2017.html.
16. https://medium.com/@ChallengeRocket/top-10-of-programming-languages-with-the-highest-salaries-in-2017-4390f468256e.

installation issues. The IPython interpreter[17] has features that help you explore, discover and experiment with Python, the Python Standard Library and the extensive set of third-party libraries.

Zen of Python

We adhere to Tim Peters' *The Zen of Python*, which summarizes Python creator Guido van Rossum's design principles for the language. This list can be viewed in IPython with the command `import this`. The Zen of Python is defined in Python Enhancement Proposal (PEP) 20. "A PEP is a design document providing information to the Python community, or describing a new feature for Python or its processes or environment."[18]

1.4 It's the Libraries!

Throughout the book, we focus on using existing libraries to help you avoid "reinventing the wheel," thus leveraging your program-development efforts. Often, rather than developing lots of original code—a costly and time-consuming process—you can simply create an object of a pre-existing library class, which takes only a single Python statement. So, libraries will help you perform significant tasks with modest amounts of code. In this book, you'll use a broad range of Python standard libraries, data-science libraries and third-party libraries.

1.4.1 Python Standard Library

The **Python Standard Library** provides rich capabilities for text/binary data processing, mathematics, functional-style programming, file/directory access, data persistence, data compression/archiving, cryptography, operating-system services, concurrent programming, interprocess communication, networking protocols, JSON/XML/other Internet data formats, multimedia, internationalization, GUI, debugging, profiling and more. The following table lists some of the Python Standard Library modules that we use in examples.

Some of the Python Standard Library modules we use in the book	
collections—Additional data structures beyond lists, tuples, dictionaries and sets.	**os**—Interacting with the operating system.
csv—Processing comma-separated value files.	**queue**—First-in, first-out data structure.
datetime, time—Date and time manipulations.	**random**—Pseudorandom numbers.
decimal—Fixed-point and floating-point arithmetic, including monetary calculations.	**re**—Regular expressions for pattern matching.
doctest—Simple unit testing via validation tests and expected results embedded in docstrings.	**sqlite3**—SQLite relational database access.
json—JavaScript Object Notation (JSON) processing for use with web services and NoSQL document databases.	**statistics**—Mathematical statistics functions like mean, median, mode and variance.
	string—String processing.
	sys—Command-line argument processing; standard input, standard output and standard error streams.
math—Common math constants and operations.	**timeit**—Performance analysis.

---

17. https://ipython.org/.
18. https://www.python.org/dev/peps/pep-0001/.

1.4.2 Data-Science Libraries

Python has an enormous and rapidly growing community of open-source developers in many fields. One of the biggest reasons for Python's popularity is the extraordinary range of open-source libraries developed by its open-source community. One of our goals is to create examples and implementation case studies that give you an engaging, challenging and entertaining introduction to Python programming, while also involving you in hands-on data science, key data-science libraries and more. You'll be amazed at the substantial tasks you can accomplish in just a few lines of code. The following table lists various popular data-science libraries. You'll use many of these as you work through our data-science examples. For visualization, we'll use Matplotlib, Seaborn and Folium, but there are many more. For a nice summary of Python visualization libraries see `http://pyviz.org/`.

Popular Python libraries used in data science
Scientific Computing and Statistics *NumPy* (Numerical Python)—Python does not have a built-in array data structure. It uses lists, which are convenient but relatively slow. NumPy provides the high-performance ndarray data structure to represent lists and matrices, and it also provides routines for processing such data structures. *SciPy* (Scientific Python)—Built on NumPy, SciPy adds routines for scientific processing, such as integrals, differential equations, additional matrix processing and more. scipy.org controls SciPy and NumPy. *StatsModels*—Provides support for estimations of statistical models, statistical tests and statistical data exploration.
Data Manipulation and Analysis *Pandas*—An extremely popular library for data manipulations. Pandas makes abundant use of NumPy's ndarray. Its two key data structures are Series (one dimensional) and DataFrames (two dimensional).
Visualization *Matplotlib*—A highly customizable visualization and plotting library. Supported plots include regular, scatter, bar, contour, pie, quiver, grid, polar axis, 3D and text. *Seaborn*—A higher-level visualization library built on Matplotlib. Seaborn adds a nicer look-and-feel, additional visualizations and enables you to create visualizations with less code.
Machine Learning, Deep Learning and Reinforcement Learning *scikit-learn*—Top machine-learning library. Machine learning is a subset of AI. Deep learning is a subset of machine learning that focuses on neural networks. *Keras*—One of the easiest to use deep-learning libraries. Keras runs on top of TensorFlow (Google), CNTK (Microsoft's cognitive toolkit for deep learning) or Theano (Université de Montréal). *TensorFlow*—From Google, this is the most widely used deep learning library. TensorFlow works with GPUs (graphics processing units) or Google's custom TPUs (Tensor processing units) for performance. TensorFlow is important in AI and big data analytics—where processing demands are huge. You'll use the version of Keras that's built into TensorFlow. *OpenAI Gym*—A library and environment for developing, testing and comparing reinforcement-learning algorithms.

Popular Python libraries used in data science

Natural Language Processing (NLP)

NLTK (Natural Language Toolkit)—Used for natural language processing (NLP) tasks.

TextBlob—An object-oriented NLP text-processing library built on the NLTK and pattern NLP libraries. TextBlob simplifies many NLP tasks.

Gensim—Similar to NLTK. Commonly used to build an index for a collection of documents, then determine how similar another document is to each of those in the index.

1.5 Test-Drives: Using IPython and Jupyter Notebooks

In this section, you'll test-drive the IPython interpreter[19] in two modes:

- In **interactive mode**, you'll enter small bits of Python code called **snippets** and immediately see their results.

- In **script mode**, you'll execute code loaded from a file that has the .py extension (short for Python). Such files are called **scripts** or **programs**, and they're generally longer than the code snippets you'll use in interactive mode.

Then, you'll learn how to use the browser-based environment known as the Jupyter Notebook for writing and executing Python code.[20]

1.5.1 Using IPython Interactive Mode as a Calculator

Let's use IPython interactive mode to evaluate simple arithmetic expressions.

Entering IPython in Interactive Mode

First, open a command-line window on your system:

- On macOS, open a **Terminal** from the **Applications** folder's **Utilities** subfolder.

- On Windows, open the **Anaconda Command Prompt** from the start menu.

- On Linux, open your system's **Terminal** or shell (this varies by Linux distribution).

In the command-line window, type ipython, then press *Enter* (or *Return*). You'll see text like the following, this varies by platform and by IPython version:

```
Python 3.7.0 | packaged by conda-forge | (default, Jan 20 2019, 17:24:52)
Type 'copyright', 'credits' or 'license' for more information
IPython 6.5.0 -- An enhanced Interactive Python. Type '?' for help.

In [1]:
```

---

19. Before reading this section, follow the instructions in the Before You Begin section to install the Anaconda Python distribution, which contains the IPython interpreter.
20. Jupyter supports many programming languages by installing their "kernels." For more information see https://github.com/jupyter/jupyter/wiki/Jupyter-kernels.

The text "In [1]:" is a *prompt*, indicating that IPython is waiting for your input. You can type ? for help or begin entering snippets, as you'll do momentarily.

Evaluating Expressions
In interactive mode, you can evaluate expressions:

```
In [1]: 45 + 72
Out[1]: 117

In [2]:
```

After you type 45 + 72 and press *Enter*, IPython *reads* the snippet, *evaluates* it and *prints* its result in Out[1].[21] Then IPython displays the In [2] prompt to show that it's waiting for you to enter your second snippet. For each new snippet, IPython adds 1 to the number in the square brackets. Each In [1] prompt in the book indicates that we've started a new interactive session. We generally do that for each new section of a chapter.

Let's evaluate a more complex expression:

```
In [2]: 5 * (12.7 - 4) / 2
Out[2]: 21.75
```

Python uses the asterisk (*) for multiplication and the forward slash (/) for division. As in mathematics, parentheses force the evaluation order, so the parenthesized expression (12.7 - 4) evaluates first, giving 8.7. Next, 5 * 8.7 evaluates giving 43.5. Then, 43.5 / 2 evaluates, giving the result 21.75, which IPython displays in Out[2]. Whole numbers, like 5, 4 and 2, are called **integers**. Numbers with decimal points, like 12.7, 43.5 and 21.75, are called **floating-point numbers**.

Exiting Interactive Mode
To leave interactive mode, you can:

- Type the exit command at the current In [] prompt and press *Enter* to exit immediately.

- Type the key sequence *<Ctrl> + d* (or *<control> + d*). This displays the prompt "Do you really want to exit ([y]/n)?". The square brackets around y indicate that it's the default response—pressing *Enter* submits the default response and exits.

- Type *<Ctrl> + d* (or *<control> + d*) twice (macOS and Linux only).

1.5.2 Executing a Python Program Using the IPython Interpreter

In this section, you'll execute a script named RollDieDynamic.py that you'll write in Chapter 6. The **.py extension** indicates that the file contains Python source code. The script RollDieDynamic.py simulates rolling a six-sided die. It presents a colorful animated visualization that dynamically graphs the frequencies of each die face.

---

21. In the next chapter, you'll see that there are some cases in which Out[] is not displayed.

Changing to This Chapter's Examples Folder

You'll find the script in the book's ch01 source-code folder. In the Before You Begin section you extracted the examples folder to your user account's Documents folder. Each chapter has a folder containing that chapter's source code. The folder is named ch##, where ## is a two-digit chapter number from 01 to 17. First, open your system's command-line window. Next, use the cd ("change directory") command to change to the ch01 folder:

- On macOS/Linux, type cd ~/Documents/examples/ch01, then press *Enter*.

- On Windows, type cd C:\Users*YourAccount*\Documents\examples\ch01, then press *Enter*.

Executing the Script

To execute the script, type the following command at the command line, then press *Enter*:

```
ipython RollDieDynamic.py 6000 1
```

The script displays a window, showing the visualization. The numbers 6000 and 1 tell this script the number of times to roll dice and how many dice to roll each time. In this case, we'll update the chart 6000 times for 1 die at a time.

For a six-sided die, the values 1 through 6 should each occur with "equal likelihood"—the probability of each is $1/6^{th}$ or about 16.667%. If we roll a die 6000 times, we'd expect about 1000 of each face. Like coin tossing, die rolling is *random*, so there could be some faces with fewer than 1000, some with 1000 and some with more than 1000. We took the screen captures below during the script's execution. This script uses randomly generated die values, so your results will differ. Experiment with the script by changing the value 1 to 100, 1000 and 10000. Notice that as the number of die rolls gets larger, the frequencies zero in on 16.667%. This is a phenomenon of the "Law of Large Numbers."

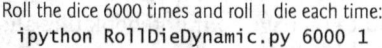

Roll the dice 6000 times and roll 1 die each time:
```
ipython RollDieDynamic.py 6000 1
```

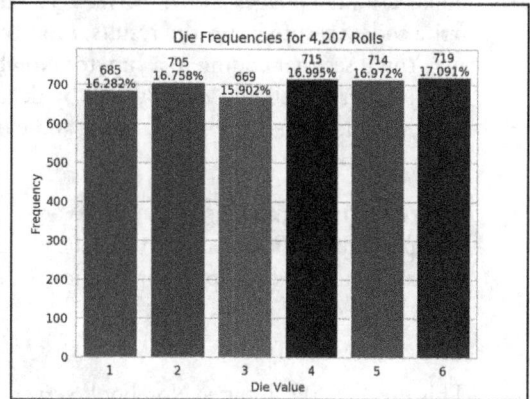

Creating Scripts

Typically, you create your Python source code in an editor that enables you to type text. Using the editor, you type a program, make any necessary corrections and save it to your computer. **Integrated development environments (IDEs)** provide tools that support the entire software-development process, such as editors, debuggers for locating logic errors that cause programs to execute incorrectly and more. Some popular Python IDEs include Spyder (which comes with Anaconda), PyCharm and Visual Studio Code.

Problems That May Occur at Execution Time

Programs often do not work on the first try. For example, an executing program might try to divide by zero (an illegal operation in Python). This would cause the program to display an error message. If this occurred in a script, you'd return to the editor, make the necessary corrections and re-execute the script to determine whether the corrections fixed the problem(s).

Errors such as division by zero occur as a program runs, so they're called **runtime errors** or **execution-time errors**. **Fatal runtime errors** cause programs to terminate immediately without having successfully performed their jobs. **Non-fatal runtime errors** allow programs to run to completion, often producing incorrect results.

1.5.3 Writing and Executing Code in a Jupyter Notebook

The Anaconda Python Distribution that you installed in the Before You Begin section comes with the **Jupyter Notebook**—an interactive, browser-based environment in which you can write and execute code and intermix the code with text, images and video. Jupyter Notebooks are broadly used in the data-science community in particular and the broader scientific community in general. They're the preferred means of doing Python-based data analytics studies and *reproducibly* communicating their results. The Jupyter Notebook environment supports a growing number of programming languages.

For your convenience, all of the book's source code also is provided in Jupyter Notebooks that you can simply load and execute. In this section, you'll use the **JupyterLab** interface, which enables you to manage your notebook files and other files that your notebooks use (like images and videos). As you'll see, JupyterLab also makes it convenient to write code, execute it, see the results, modify the code and execute it again.

You'll see that coding in a Jupyter Notebook is similar to working with IPython—in fact, Jupyter Notebooks use IPython by default. In this section, you'll create a notebook, add the code from Section 1.5.1 to it and execute that code.

Opening JupyterLab in Your Browser

To open JupyterLab, change to the ch01 examples folder in your Terminal, shell or Anaconda Command Prompt (as in Section 1.5.2), type the following command, then press *Enter* (or *Return*):

```
jupyter lab
```

This executes the Jupyter Notebook server on your computer and opens JupyterLab in your default web browser, showing the ch01 folder's contents in the **File Browser** tab

at the left side of the JupyterLab interface:

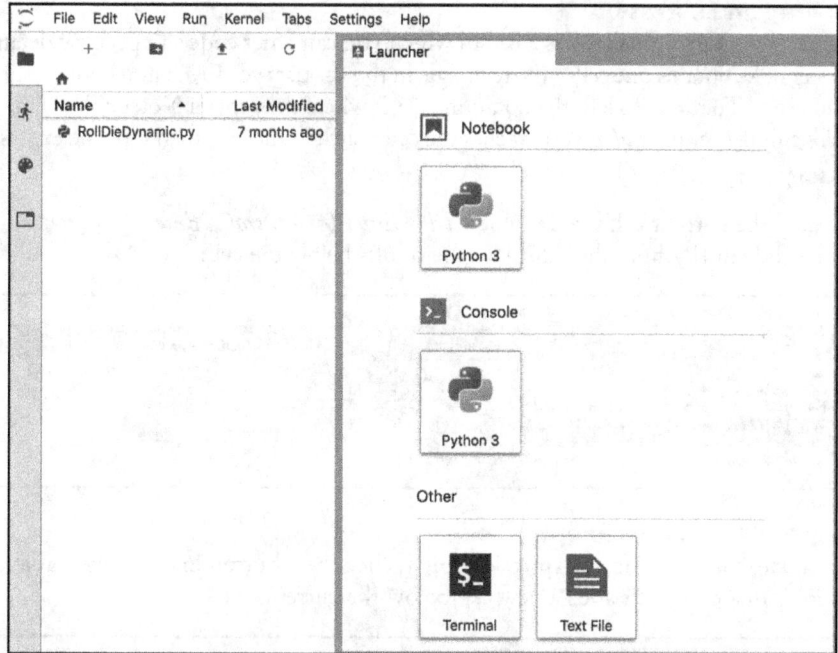

The Jupyter Notebook server enables you to load and run Jupyter Notebooks in your web browser. From the JupyterLab **Files** tab, you can double-click files to open them in the right side of the window where the **Launcher** tab is currently displayed. Each file you open appears as a separate tab in this part of the window. If you accidentally close your browser, you can reopen JupyterLab by entering the following address in your web browser

```
http://localhost:8888/lab
```

Creating a New Jupyter Notebook
In the **Launcher** tab under **Notebook**, click the **Python 3** button to create a new Jupyter Notebook named Untitled.ipynb in which you can enter and execute Python 3 code. The file extension **.ipynb** is short for IPython Notebook—the original name of the Jupyter Notebook.

Renaming the Notebook
Rename Untitled.ipynb as TestDrive.ipynb:

1. Right-click the Untitled.ipynb tab and select **Rename Notebook...**
2. Change the name to TestDrive.ipynb and click **RENAME**.

The top of JupyterLab should now appear as follows:

Evaluating an Expression

The unit of work in a notebook is a **cell** in which you can enter code snippets. By default, a new notebook contains one cell—the rectangle in the TestDrive.ipynb notebook—but you can add more. To the cell's left, the notation [ ]: is where the Jupyter Notebook will display the cell's snippet number *after* you execute the cell. Click in the cell, then type the expression

```
45 + 72
```

To execute the current cell's code, type *Ctrl + Enter* (or *control + Enter*). JupyterLab executes the code in IPython, then displays the results below the cell:

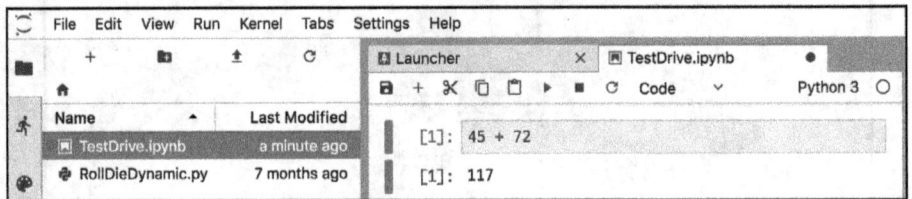

Adding and Executing Another Cell

Let's evaluate a more complex expression. First, click the **+** button in the toolbar above the notebook's first cell—this adds a new cell below the current one:

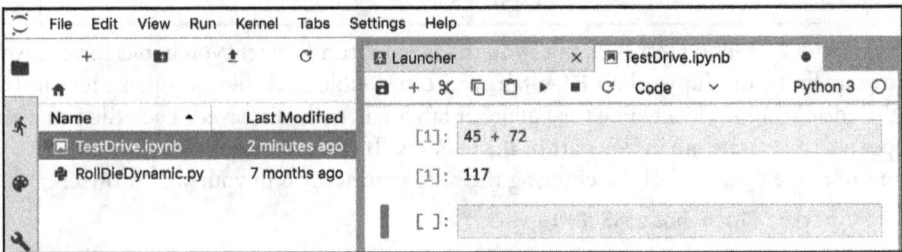

Click in the new cell, then type the expression

```
5 * (12.7 - 4) / 2
```

and execute the cell by typing *Ctrl + Enter* (or *control + Enter*):

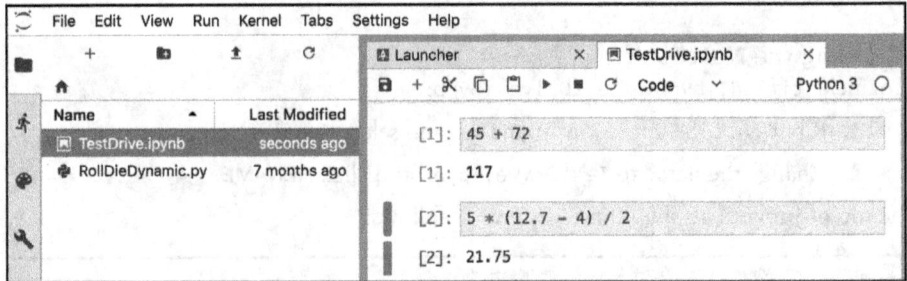

Saving the Notebook

If your notebook has unsaved changes, the **X** in the notebook's tab will change to • . To save the notebook, select the **File** menu in JupyterLab (not at the top of your browser's window), then select **Save Notebook**.

Notebooks Provided with Each Chapter's Examples

For your convenience, each chapter's examples also are provided as ready-to-execute note-books without their outputs. This enables you to work through them snippet-by-snippet and see the outputs appear as you execute each snippet.

So that we can show you how to load an existing notebook and execute its cells, let's reset the TestDrive.ipynb notebook to remove its output and snippet numbers. This will return it to a state like the notebooks we provide for the subsequent chapters' examples. From the **Kernel** menu select **Restart Kernel and Clear All Outputs...**, then click the **RESTART** button. The preceding command also is helpful whenever you wish to re-exe-cute a notebook's snippets. The notebook should now appear as follows:

From the **File** menu, select **Save Notebook**, then click the TestDrive.ipynb tab's **X** button to close the notebook.

Opening and Executing an Existing Notebook

When you launch JupyterLab from a given chapter's examples folder, you'll be able to open notebooks from that folder or any of its subfolders. Once you locate a specific notebook, double-click it to open it. Open the TestDrive.ipynb notebook again now. Once a note-book is open, you can execute each cell individually, as you did earlier in this section, or you can execute the entire notebook at once. To do so, from the **Run** menu select **Run All Cells**. The notebook will execute the cells in order, displaying each cell's output below that cell.

Closing JupyterLab

When you're done with JupyterLab, you can close its browser tab, then in the Terminal, shell or Anaconda Command Prompt from which you launched JupyterLab, type *Ctrl + c* (or *control + c*) twice.

JupyterLab Tips

While working in JupyterLab, you might find these tips helpful:

- If you need to enter and execute many snippets, you can execute the current cell *and* add a new one below it by typing *Shift + Enter*, rather than *Ctrl + Enter* (or *control + Enter*).

- As you get into the later chapters, some of the snippets you'll enter in Jupyter Notebooks will contain many lines of code. To display line numbers within each cell, select **Show line numbers** from JupyterLab's **View** menu.

More Information on Working with JupyterLab

JupyterLab has many more features that you'll find helpful. We recommend that you read the Jupyter team's introduction to JupyterLab at:

```
https://jupyterlab.readthedocs.io/en/stable/index.html
```

For a quick overview, click **Overview** under **GETTING STARTED**. Also, under **USER GUIDE** read the introductions to **The JupyterLab Interface**, **Working with Files**, **Text Editor** and **Notebooks** for many additional features.

1.6 The Cloud and the Internet of Things

1.6.1 The Cloud

More and more computing today is done "in the cloud"—that is, distributed across the Internet worldwide. Many apps you use daily are dependent on **cloud-based services** that use massive clusters of computing resources (computers, processors, memory, disk drives, etc.) and databases that communicate over the Internet with each other and the apps you use. A service that provides access to itself over the Internet is known as a **web service**. As you'll see, using cloud-based services in Python often is as simple as creating a software object and interacting with it. That object then uses web services that connect to the cloud on your behalf.

Throughout the Chapters 11–16 examples, you'll work with many cloud-based services:

- In Chapters 12 and 16, you'll use Twitter's web services (via the Python library Tweepy) to get information about specific Twitter users, search for tweets from the last seven days and receive streams of tweets as they occur—that is, in real time.

- In Chapters 11 and 12, you'll use the Python library TextBlob to translate text between languages. Behind the scenes, TextBlob uses the Google Translate web service to perform those translations.

- In Chapter 13, you'll use the IBM Watson's Text to Speech, Speech to Text and Translate services. You'll implement a traveler's assistant translation app that enables you to speak a question in English, transcribes the speech to text, translates the text to Spanish and speaks the Spanish text. The app then allows you to speak a Spanish response (in case you don't speak Spanish, we provide an audio file you can use), transcribes the speech to text, translates the text to English and speaks the English response. Via IBM Watson demos, you'll also experiment with many other Watson cloud-based services in Chapter 13.

- In Chapter 16, you'll work with Microsoft Azure's HDInsight service and other Azure web services as you implement big-data applications using Apache Hadoop and Spark. Azure is Microsoft's set of cloud-based services.

- In Chapter 16, you'll use the Dweet.io web service to simulate an Internet-connected thermostat that publishes temperature readings online. You'll also use a web-based service to create a "dashboard" that visualizes the temperature readings over time and warns you if the temperature gets too low or too high.

- In Chapter 16, you'll use a web-based dashboard to visualize a simulated stream of live sensor data from the PubNub web service. You'll also create a Python app that visualizes a PubNub simulated stream of live stock-price changes.

In most cases, you'll create Python objects that interact with web services on your behalf, hiding the details of how to access these services over the Internet.

Mashups

The applications-development methodology of *mashups* enables you to rapidly develop powerful software applications by combining (often free) complementary web services and other forms of information feeds—as you'll do in our IBM Watson traveler's assistant translation app. One of the first mashups combined the real-estate listings provided by http://www.craigslist.org with the mapping capabilities of Google Maps to offer maps that showed the locations of homes for sale or rent in a given area.

ProgrammableWeb (http://www.programmableweb.com/) provides a directory of over 20,750 web services and almost 8,000 mashups. They also provide how-to guides and sample code for working with web services and creating your own mashups. According to their website, some of the most widely used web services are Facebook, Google Maps, Twitter and YouTube.

1.6.2 Internet of Things

The Internet is no longer just a network of *computers*—it's an **Internet of Things (IoT)**. A *thing* is any object with an IP address and the ability to send, and in some cases receive, data automatically over the Internet. Such *things* include:

- a car with a transponder for paying tolls,
- monitors for parking-space availability in a garage,
- a heart monitor implanted in a human,
- water quality monitors,
- a smart meter that reports energy usage,
- radiation detectors,
- item trackers in a warehouse,
- mobile apps that can track your movement and location,
- smart thermostats that adjust room temperatures based on weather forecasts and activity in the home, and
- intelligent home appliances.

According to statista.com, there are already over 23 billion IoT devices in use today, and there could be over 75 billion IoT devices in 2025.[22]

1.7 How Big Is Big Data?

For computer scientists and data scientists, data is now as important as writing programs. According to IBM, approximately 2.5 quintillion bytes (2.5 *exabytes*) of data are created daily,[23] and 90% of the world's data was created in the last two years.[24] According to IDC,

---

22. https://www.statista.com/statistics/471264/iot-number-of-connected-devices-worldwide/.
23. https://www.ibm.com/blogs/watson/2016/06/welcome-to-the-world-of-a-i/.
24. https://public.dhe.ibm.com/common/ssi/ecm/wr/en/wrl12345usen/watson-customer-engagement-watson-marketing-wr-other-papers-and-reports-wrl12345usen-20170719.pdf.

the global data supply will reach 175 *zettabytes* (equal to 175 trillion gigabytes or 175 billion terabytes) annually by 2025.[25] Consider the following examples of various popular data measures.

Megabytes (MB)

One megabyte is about one million (actually 2^{20}) bytes. Many of the files we use on a daily basis require one or more MBs of storage. Some examples include:

- MP3 audio files—High-quality MP3s range from 1 to 2.4 MB per minute.[26]

- Photos—JPEG format photos taken on a digital camera can require about 8 to 10 MB per photo.

- Video—Smartphone cameras can record video at various resolutions. Each minute of video can require many megabytes of storage. For example, on one of our iPhones, the **Camera** settings app reports that 1080p video at 30 frames-per-second (FPS) requires 130 MB/minute and 4K video at 30 FPS requires 350 MB/minute.

Gigabytes (GB)

One gigabyte is about 1000 megabytes (actually 2^{30} bytes). A dual-layer DVD can store up to 8.5 GB[27], which translates to:

- as much as 141 hours of MP3 audio,

- approximately 1000 photos from a 16-megapixel camera,

- approximately 7.7 minutes of 1080p video at 30 FPS, or

- approximately 2.85 minutes of 4K video at 30 FPS.

The current highest-capacity Ultra HD Blu-ray discs can store up to 100 GB of video.[28] Streaming a 4K movie can use between 7 and 10 GB per hour (highly compressed).

Terabytes (TB)

One terabyte is about 1000 gigabytes (actually 2^{40} bytes). Recent disk drives for desktop computers come in sizes up to 15 TB,[29] which is equivalent to:

- approximately 28 years of MP3 audio,

- approximately 1.68 million photos from a 16-megapixel camera,

- approximately 226 hours of 1080p video at 30 FPS and

- approximately 84 hours of 4K video at 30 FPS.

---

25. https://www.networkworld.com/article/3325397/storage/idc-expect-175-zettabytes-of-data-worldwide-by-2025.html.

26. https://www.audiomountain.com/tech/audio-file-size.html.

27. https://en.wikipedia.org/wiki/DVD.

28. https://en.wikipedia.org/wiki/Ultra_HD_Blu-ray.

29. https://www.zdnet.com/article/worlds-biggest-hard-drive-meet-western-digitals-15tb-monster/.

Nimbus Data now has the largest solid-state drive (SSD) at 100 TB, which can store 6.67 times the 15-TB examples of audio, photos and video listed above.[30]

Petabytes, Exabytes and Zettabytes

There are nearly four billion people online creating about 2.5 quintillion bytes of data each day[31]—that's 2500 petabytes (each petabyte is about 1000 terabytes) or 2.5 exabytes (each exabyte is about 1000 petabytes). According to a March 2016 *Analytics Week* article, within five years there will be over 50 billion devices connected to the Internet (most of them through the Internet of Things, which we discuss in Sections 1.6.2 and 16.8) and by 2020 we'll be producing 1.7 megabytes of new data every second *for every person on the planet.*[32] At today's numbers (approximately 7.7 billion people[33]), that's about

- 13 petabytes of new data per second,
- 780 petabytes per minute,
- 46,800 petabytes (46.8 exabytes) per hour and
- 1,123 exabytes per day—that's 1.123 zettabytes (ZB) per day (each zettabyte is about 1000 exabytes).

That's the equivalent of over 5.5 million hours (over 600 years) of 4K video every day or approximately 116 billion photos every day!

Additional Big-Data Stats

For an entertaining real-time sense of big data, check out `https://www.internetlives-tats.com`, with various statistics, including the numbers so far today of

- Google searches.
- Tweets.
- Videos viewed on YouTube.
- Photos uploaded on Instagram.

You can click each statistic to drill down for more information. For instance, they say over 250 *billion* tweets were sent in 2018.

Some other interesting big-data facts:

- Every hour, YouTube users upload 24,000 hours of video, and almost 1 billion hours of video are watched on YouTube every day.[34]
- Every second, there are 51,773 GBs (or 51.773 TBs) of Internet traffic, 7894 tweets sent, 64,332 Google searches and 72,029 YouTube videos viewed.[35]

---

30. `https://www.cinema5d.com/nimbus-data-100tb-ssd-worlds-largest-ssd/`.
31. `https://public.dhe.ibm.com/common/ssi/ecm/wr/en/wrl12345usen/watson-customer-engagement-watson-marketing-wr-other-papers-and-reports-wrl12345usen-20170719.pdf`.
32. `https://analyticsweek.com/content/big-data-facts/`.
33. `https://en.wikipedia.org/wiki/World_population`.
34. `https://www.brandwatch.com/blog/youtube-stats/`.
35. `http://www.internetlivestats.com/one-second`.

- On Facebook each day there are 800 million "**likes**,"[36] 60 million emojis are sent,[37] and there are over two billion searches of the more than 2.5 trillion Facebook posts since the site's inception.[38]

- In June 2017, Will Marshall, CEO of Planet, said the company has 142 satellites that image the whole planet's land mass once per day. They add one million images and seven TBs of new data each day. Together with their partners, they're using machine learning on that data to improve crop yields, see how many ships are in a given port and track deforestation. With respect to Amazon deforestation, he said: "Used to be we'd wake up after a few years and there's a big hole in the Amazon. Now we can literally count every tree on the planet every day."[39]

Domo, Inc. has a nice infographic called "Data Never Sleeps 6.0" showing how much data is generated *every minute*, including:[40]

- 473,400 tweets sent.

- 2,083,333 Snapchat photos shared.

- 97,222 hours of Netflix video viewed.

- 12,986,111 million text messages sent.

- 49,380 Instagram posts.

- 176,220 Skype calls.

- 750,000 Spotify songs streamed.

- 3,877,140 Google searches.

- 4,333,560 YouTube videos watched.

Computing Power Over the Years

Data is getting more massive and so is the computing power for processing it. The performance of today's processors is often measured in terms of **FLOPS (floating-point operations per second)**. In the early to mid-1990s, the fastest supercomputer speeds were measured in gigaflops (10^9 FLOPS). By the late 1990s, Intel produced the first teraflop (10^{12} FLOPS) supercomputers. In the early-to-mid 2000s, speeds reached hundreds of teraflops, then in 2008, IBM released the first petaflop (10^{15} FLOPS) supercomputer. Currently, the fastest supercomputer—the IBM Summit, located at the Department of Energy's (DOE) Oak Ridge National Laboratory (ORNL)—is capable of 122.3 petaflops.[41]

Distributed computing can link thousands of personal computers via the Internet to produce even more FLOPS. In late 2016, the Folding@home network—a distributed network in which people volunteer their personal computers' resources for use in disease

---

36. https://newsroom.fb.com/news/2017/06/two-billion-people-coming-together-on-facebook.
37. https://mashable.com/2017/07/17/facebook-world-emoji-day/.
38. https://techcrunch.com/2016/07/27/facebook-will-make-you-talk/.
39. https://www.bloomberg.com/news/videos/2017-06-30/learning-from-planet-s-shoe-boxed-sized-satellites-video, June 30, 2017.
40. https://www.domo.com/learn/data-never-sleeps-6.
41. https://en.wikipedia.org/wiki/FLOPS.

research and drug design[42]—was capable of over 100 petaflops.[43] Companies like IBM are now working toward supercomputers capable of exaflops (10^{18} FLOPS).[44]

The **quantum computers** now under development theoretically could operate at 18,000,000,000,000,000,000 times the speed of today's "conventional computers"![45] This number is so extraordinary that in one second, a quantum computer theoretically could do staggeringly more calculations than the total that have been done by all computers since the world's first computer appeared. This almost unimaginable computing power could wreak havoc with blockchain-based cryptocurrencies like Bitcoin. Engineers are already rethinking blockchain to prepare for such massive increases in computing power.[46]

The history of supercomputing power is that it eventually works its way down from research labs, where extraordinary amounts of money have been spent to achieve those performance numbers, into "reasonably priced" commercial computer systems and even desktop computers, laptops, tablets and smartphones.

Computing power's cost continues to decline, especially with cloud computing. People used to ask the question, "How much computing power do I need on my system to deal with my *peak* processing needs?" Today, that thinking has shifted to "Can I quickly carve out on the cloud what I need *temporarily* for my most demanding computing chores?" You pay for only what you use to accomplish a given task.

Processing the World's Data Requires Lots of Electricity

Data from the world's Internet-connected devices is exploding, and processing that data requires tremendous amounts of energy. According to a recent article, energy use for processing data in 2015 was growing at 20% per year and consuming approximately three to five percent of the world's power. The article says that total data-processing power consumption could reach 20% by 2025.[47]

Another enormous electricity consumer is the blockchain-based cryptocurrency Bitcoin. Processing just one Bitcoin transaction uses approximately the same amount of energy as powering the average American home for a week! The energy use comes from the process Bitcoin "miners" use to prove that transaction data is valid.[48]

According to some estimates, a year of Bitcoin transactions consumes more energy than many countries.[49] Together, Bitcoin and Ethereum (another popular blockchain-based platform and cryptocurrency) consume more energy per year than Israel and almost as much as Greece.[50]

Morgan Stanley predicted in 2018 that "the electricity consumption required to create cryptocurrencies this year could actually outpace the firm's projected global electric

---

42. https://en.wikipedia.org/wiki/Folding@home.
43. https://en.wikipedia.org/wiki/FLOPS.
44. https://www.ibm.com/blogs/research/2017/06/supercomputing-weather-model-exascale/.
45. https://medium.com/@n.biedrzycki/only-god-can-count-that-fast-the-world-of-quantum-computing-406a0a91fcf4.
46. https://singularityhub.com/2017/11/05/is-quantum-computing-an-existential-threat-to-blockchain-technology/.
47. https://www.theguardian.com/environment/2017/dec/11/tsunami-of-data-could-consume-fifth-global-electricity-by-2025.
48. https://motherboard.vice.com/en_us/article/ywbbpm/bitcoin-mining-electricity-consumption-ethereum-energy-climate-change.
49. https://digiconomist.net/bitcoin-energy-consumption.
50. https://digiconomist.net/ethereum-energy-consumption.

vehicle demand—in 2025."[51] This situation is unsustainable, especially given the huge interest in blockchain-based applications, even beyond the cryptocurrency explosion. The blockchain community is working on fixes.[52,53]

Big-Data Opportunities

The big-data explosion is likely to continue exponentially for years to come. With 50 billion computing devices on the horizon, we can only imagine how many more there will be over the next few decades. It's crucial for businesses, governments, the military and even individuals to get a handle on all this data.

It's interesting that some of the best writings about big data, data science, artificial intelligence and more are coming out of distinguished business organizations, such as J.P. Morgan, McKinsey and more. Big data's appeal to big business is undeniable given the rapidly accelerating accomplishments. Many companies are making significant investments and getting valuable results through technologies in this book, such as big data, machine learning, deep learning and natural-language processing. This is forcing competitors to invest as well, rapidly increasing the need for computing professionals with data-science and computer science experience. This growth is likely to continue for many years.

1.7.1 Big Data Analytics

Data analytics is a mature and well-developed academic and professional discipline. The term "data analysis" was coined in 1962,[54] though people have been analyzing data using statistics for thousands of years going back to the ancient Egyptians.[55] Big data analytics is a more recent phenomenon—the term "big data" was coined around 2000.[56]

Consider four of the V's of big data[57,58]:

1. Volume—the amount of data the world is producing is growing exponentially.

2. Velocity—the speed at which that data is being produced, the speed at which it moves through organizations and the speed at which data changes are growing quickly.[59,60,61]

---

51. https://www.morganstanley.com/ideas/cryptocurrencies-global-utilities.
52. https://www.technologyreview.com/s/609480/bitcoin-uses-massive-amounts-of-energy-but-theres-a-plan-to-fix-it/.
53. http://mashable.com/2017/12/01/bitcoin-energy/.
54. https://www.forbes.com/sites/gilpress/2013/05/28/a-very-short-history-of-data-science/.
55. https://www.flydata.com/blog/a-brief-history-of-data-analysis/.
56. https://bits.blogs.nytimes.com/2013/02/01/the-origins-of-big-data-an-etymological-detective-story/.
57. https://www.ibmbigdatahub.com/infographic/four-vs-big-data.
58. There are lots of articles and papers that add many other "V-words" to this list.
59. https://www.zdnet.com/article/volume-velocity-and-variety-understanding-the-three-vs-of-big-data/.
60. https://whatis.techtarget.com/definition/3Vs.
61. https://www.forbes.com/sites/brentdykes/2017/06/28/big-data-forget-volume-and-variety-focus-on-velocity.

3. Variety—data used to be alphanumeric (that is, consisting of alphabetic characters, digits, punctuation and some special characters)—today it also includes images, audios, videos and data from an exploding number of Internet of Things sensors in our homes, businesses, vehicles, cities and more.

4. Veracity—the validity of the data—is it complete and accurate? Can we trust that data when making crucial decisions? Is it real?

Most data is now being created digitally in a *variety* of types, in extraordinary *volumes* and moving at astonishing *velocities*. Moore's Law and related observations have enabled us to store data economically and to process and move it faster—and all at rates growing exponentially over time. Digital data storage has become so vast in capacity, cheap and small that we can now conveniently and economically retain *all* the digital data we're creating.[62] That's big data.

The following Richard W. Hamming quote—although from 1962—sets the tone for the rest of this book:

"The purpose of computing is insight, not numbers."[63]

Data science is producing new, deeper, subtler and more valuable insights at a remarkable pace. It's truly making a difference. Big data analytics is an integral part of the answer. We address big data infrastructure in Chapter 16 with hands-on case studies on NoSQL databases, Hadoop MapReduce programming, Spark, real-time Internet of Things (IoT) stream programming and more.

To get a sense of big data's scope in industry, government and academia, check out the high-resolution graphic.[64] You can click to zoom for easier readability:

> http://mattturck.com/wp-content/uploads/2018/07/Matt_Turck_First-
> Mark_Big_Data_Landscape_2018_Final.png

1.7.2 Data Science and Big Data Are Making a Difference: Use Cases

The data-science field is growing rapidly because it's producing significant results that are making a difference. We enumerate data-science and big data use cases in the following table. We expect that the use cases and our examples throughout the book will inspire you to pursue new use cases in your career. Big-data analytics has resulted in improved profits, better customer relations, and even sports teams winning more games and championships while spending less on players.[65,66,67]

---

62. http://www.lesk.com/mlesk/ksg97/ksg.html. [The following article pointed us to this Michael Lesk article: https://www.forbes.com/sites/gilpress/2013/05/28/a-very-short-history-of-data-science/.]

63. Hamming, R. W., *Numerical Methods for Scientists and Engineers* (New York, NY., McGraw Hill, 1962). [The following article pointed us to Hamming's book and his quote that we cited: https://www.forbes.com/sites/gilpress/2013/05/28/a-very-short-history-of-data-science/.]

64. Turck, M., and J. Hao, "Great Power, Great Responsibility: The 2018 Big Data & AI Landscape," http://mattturck.com/bigdata2018/.

65. Sawchik, T., *Big Data Baseball: Math, Miracles, and the End of a 20-Year Losing Streak* (New York, Flat Iron Books, 2015).

66. Ayres, I., *Super Crunchers* (Bantam Books, 2007), pp. 7–10.

67. Lewis, M., *Moneyball: The Art of Winning an Unfair Game* (W. W. Norton & Company, 2004).

Data-science use cases

anomaly detection
assisting people with disabilities
auto-insurance risk prediction
automated closed captioning
automated image captions
automated investing
autonomous ships
brain mapping
caller identification
cancer diagnosis/treatment
carbon emissions reduction
classifying handwriting
computer vision
credit scoring
crime: predicting locations
crime: predicting recidivism
crime: predictive policing
crime: prevention
CRISPR gene editing
crop-yield improvement
customer churn
customer experience
customer retention
customer satisfaction
customer service
customer service agents
customized diets
cybersecurity
data mining
data visualization
detecting new viruses
diagnosing breast cancer
diagnosing heart disease
diagnostic medicine
disaster-victim identification
drones
dynamic driving routes
dynamic pricing
electronic health records
emotion detection
energy-consumption reduction

facial recognition
fitness tracking
fraud detection
game playing
genomics and healthcare
Geographic Information Systems (GIS)
GPS Systems
health outcome improvement
hospital readmission reduction
human genome sequencing
identity-theft prevention
immunotherapy
insurance pricing
intelligent assistants
Internet of Things (IoT) and medical device monitoring
Internet of Things and weather forecasting
inventory control
language translation
location-based services
loyalty programs
malware detection
mapping
marketing
marketing analytics
music generation
natural-language translation
new pharmaceuticals
opioid abuse prevention
personal assistants
personalized medicine
personalized shopping
phishing elimination
pollution reduction
precision medicine
predicting cancer survival
predicting disease outbreaks
predicting health outcomes
predicting student enrollments

predicting weather-sensitive product sales
predictive analytics
preventative medicine
preventing disease outbreaks
reading sign language
real-estate valuation
recommendation systems
reducing overbooking
ride sharing
risk minimization
robo financial advisors
security enhancements
self-driving cars
sentiment analysis
sharing economy
similarity detection
smart cities
smart homes
smart meters
smart thermostats
smart traffic control
social analytics
social graph analysis
spam detection
spatial data analysis
sports recruiting and coaching
stock market forecasting
student performance assessment
summarizing text
telemedicine
terrorist attack prevention
theft prevention
travel recommendations
trend spotting
visual product search
voice recognition
voice search
weather forecasting

1.8 Case Study—A Big-Data Mobile Application

Google's Waze GPS navigation app, with its 90 million monthly active users,[68] is one of the most successful big-data apps. Early GPS navigation devices and apps relied on static

---

68. https://www.waze.com/brands/drivers/.

maps and GPS coordinates to determine the best route to your destination. They could not adjust dynamically to changing traffic situations.

Waze processes massive amounts of **crowdsourced data**—that is, the data that's continuously supplied by their users and their users' devices worldwide. They analyze this data as it arrives to determine the best route to get you to your destination in the least amount of time. To accomplish this, Waze relies on your smartphone's Internet connection. The app automatically sends location updates to their servers (assuming you allow it to). They use that data to dynamically re-route you based on current traffic conditions and to tune their maps. Users report other information, such as roadblocks, construction, obstacles, vehicles in breakdown lanes, police locations, gas prices and more. Waze then alerts other drivers in those locations.

Waze uses many technologies to provide its services. We're not privy to how Waze is implemented, but we infer below a list of technologies they probably use. You'll use many of these in Chapters 11–16. For example,

- Most apps created today use at least some open-source software. You'll take advantage of many open-source libraries and tools throughout this book.

- Waze communicates information over the Internet between their servers and their users' mobile devices. Today, such data often is transmitted in JSON (JavaScript Object Notation) format, which we'll introduce in Chapter 9 and use in subsequent chapters. The JSON data is typically hidden from you by the libraries you use.

- Waze uses speech synthesis to speak driving directions and alerts to you, and speech recognition to understand your spoken commands. We use IBM Watson's speech-synthesis and speech-recognition capabilities in Chapter 13.

- Once Waze converts a spoken natural-language command to text, it must determine the correct action to perform, which requires natural language processing (NLP). We present NLP in Chapter 11 and use it in several subsequent chapters.

- Waze displays dynamically updated visualizations such as alerts and maps. Waze also enables you to interact with the maps by moving them or zooming in and out. We create dynamic visualizations with Matplotlib and Seaborn throughout the book, and we display interactive maps with Folium in Chapters 12 and 16.

- Waze uses your phone as a streaming Internet of Things (IoT) device. Each phone is a GPS sensor that continuously streams data over the Internet to Waze. In Chapter 16, we introduce IoT and work with simulated IoT streaming sensors.

- Waze receives IoT streams from millions of phones at once. It must process, store and analyze that data immediately to update your device's maps, to display and speak relevant alerts and possibly to update your driving directions. This requires massively parallel processing capabilities implemented with clusters of computers in the cloud. In Chapter 16, we'll introduce various big-data infrastructure technologies for receiving streaming data, storing that big data in appropriate databases and processing the data with software and hardware that provide massively parallel processing capabilities.

- Waze uses artificial-intelligence capabilities to perform the data-analysis tasks that enable it to predict the best routes based on the information it receives. In

Chapters 14 and 15 we use machine learning and deep learning, respectively, to analyze massive amounts of data and make predictions based on that data.

- Waze probably stores its routing information in a graph database. Such databases can efficiently calculate shortest routes. We introduce graph databases, such as Neo4J, in Chapter 16.

- Many cars are now equipped with devices that enable them to "see" cars and obstacles around them. These are used, for example, to help implement automated braking systems and are a key part of self-driving car technology. Rather than relying on users to report obstacles and stopped cars on the side of the road, navigation apps could take advantage of cameras and other sensors by using deep-learning computer-vision techniques to analyze images "on the fly" and automatically report those items. We introduce deep learning for computer vision in Chapter 15.

1.9 Intro to Data Science: Artificial Intelligence—at the Intersection of CS and Data Science

When a baby first opens its eyes, does it "see" its parent's faces? Does it understand any notion of what a face is—or even what a simple shape is? Babies must "learn" the world around them. That's what artificial intelligence (AI) is doing today. It's looking at massive amounts of data and learning from it. AI is being used to play games, implement a wide range of computer-vision applications, enable self-driving cars, enable robots to learn to perform new tasks, diagnose medical conditions, translate speech to other languages in near real time, create chatbots that can respond to arbitrary questions using massive databases of knowledge, and much more. Who'd have guessed just a few years ago that artificially intelligent self-driving cars would be allowed on our roads—or even become common? Yet, this is now a highly competitive area. The ultimate goal of all this learning is **artificial general intelligence**—an AI that can perform intelligence tasks as well as humans. This is a scary thought to many people.

Artificial-Intelligence Milestones

Several artificial-intelligence milestones, in particular, captured people's attention and imagination, made the general public start thinking that AI is real and made businesses think about commercializing AI:

- In a 1997 match between **IBM's DeepBlue** computer system and chess Grandmaster Gary Kasparov, DeepBlue became the first computer to beat a reigning world chess champion under tournament conditions.[69] IBM loaded DeepBlue with hundreds of thousands of grandmaster chess games.[70] DeepBlue was capable of using *brute force* to evaluate up to 200 million moves per second![71] This is big data at work. IBM received the Carnegie Mellon University Fredkin Prize, which

---

69. https://en.wikipedia.org/wiki/Deep_Blue_versus_Garry_Kasparov.
70. https://en.wikipedia.org/wiki/Deep_Blue_(chess_computer).
71. https://en.wikipedia.org/wiki/Deep_Blue_(chess_computer).

in 1980 offered \$100,000 to the creators of the first computer to beat a world chess champion.[72]

- In 2011, **IBM's Watson** beat the two best human Jeopardy! players in a \$1 million match. Watson simultaneously used hundreds of language-analysis techniques to locate correct answers in 200 million pages of content (including all of Wikipedia) requiring four terabytes of storage.[73,74] Watson was trained with **machine learning** and **reinforcement-learning techniques.**[75] Chapter 13 discusses IBM Watson and Chapter 14 discusses machine-learning.

- Go—a board game created in China thousands of years ago[76]—is widely considered to be one of the most complex games ever invented with 10^{170} possible board configurations.[77] To give you a sense of how large a number that is, it's believed that there are (only) between 10^{78} and 10^{87} atoms in the known universe![78,79] In 2015, **AlphaGo**—created by Google's DeepMind group—used *deep learning with two neural networks to beat the European Go champion Fan Hui.* Go is considered to be a far more complex game than chess. Chapter 15 discusses neural networks and deep learning.

- More recently, Google generalized its AlphaGo AI to create **AlphaZero**—a game-playing AI that *teaches itself to play other games.* In December 2017, AlphaZero learned the rules of and taught itself to play chess in less than four hours using reinforcement learning. It then beat the world champion chess program, Stockfish 8, in a 100-game match—winning or drawing every game. After *training itself* in Go for just eight hours, AlphaZero was able to play Go vs. its AlphaGo predecessor, winning 60 of 100 games.[80]

A Personal Anecdote

When one of the authors, Harvey Deitel, was an undergraduate student at MIT in the mid-1960s, he took a graduate-level artificial-intelligence course with Marvin Minsky (to whom this book is dedicated), one of the founders of artificial intelligence (AI). Harvey:

> *Professor Minsky required a major term project. He told us to think about what intelligence is and to make a computer do something intelligent. Our grade in the course would be almost solely dependent on the project. No pressure!*
>
> *I researched the standardized IQ tests that schools administer to help evaluate their students' intelligence capabilities. Being a mathematician at heart, I decided*

---

72. https://articles.latimes.com/1997/jul/30/news/mn-17696.
73. https://www.techrepublic.com/article/ibm-watson-the-inside-story-of-how-the-jeopardy-winning-supercomputer-was-born-and-what-it-wants-to-do-next/.
74. https://en.wikipedia.org/wiki/Watson_(computer).
75. https://www.aaai.org/Magazine/Watson/watson.php, *AI Magazine*, Fall 2010.
76. http://www.usgo.org/brief-history-go.
77. https://www.pbs.org/newshour/science/google-artificial-intelligence-beats-champion-at-worlds-most-complicated-board-game.
78. https://www.universetoday.com/36302/atoms-in-the-universe/.
79. https://en.wikipedia.org/wiki/Observable_universe#Matter_content.
80. https://www.theguardian.com/technology/2017/dec/07/alphazero-google-deepmind-ai-beats-champion-program-teaching-itself-to-play-four-hours.

to tackle the popular IQ-test problem of predicting the next number in a sequence of numbers of arbitrary length and complexity. I used interactive Lisp running on an early Digital Equipment Corporation PDP-1 and was able to get my sequence predictor running on some pretty complex stuff, handling challenges well beyond what I recalled seeing on IQ tests. Lisp's ability to manipulate arbitrarily long lists recursively was exactly what I needed to meet the project's requirements. Python offers recursion and generalized list processing (Chapter 5).

I tried the sequence predictor on many of my MIT classmates. They would make up number sequences and type them into my predictor. The PDP-1 would "think" for a while—often a long while—and almost always came up with the right answer.

Then I hit a snag. One of my classmates typed in the sequence 14, 23, 34 and 42. My predictor went to work on it, and the PDP-1 chugged away for a long time, failing to predict the next number. I couldn't get it either. My classmate told me to think about it overnight, and he'd reveal the answer the next day, claiming that it was a simple sequence. My efforts were to no avail.

The following day he told me the next number was 57, but I didn't understand why. So he told me to think about it overnight again, and the following day he said the next number was 125. That didn't help a bit—I was stumped. He said that the sequence was the numbers of the two-way crosstown streets of Manhattan. I cried, "foul," but he said it met my criterion of predicting the next number in a numerical sequence. My world view was mathematics—his was broader.

Over the years, I've tried that sequence on friends, relatives and professional colleagues. A few who spent time in Manhattan got it right. My sequence predictor needed a lot more than just mathematical knowledge to handle problems like this, requiring (a possibly vast) world knowledge.

Watson and Big Data Open New Possibilities
When Paul and I started working on this Python book, we were immediately drawn to IBM's Watson using big data and artificial-intelligence techniques like natural language processing (NLP) and machine learning to beat two of the world's best human Jeopardy! players. We realized that Watson could probably handle problems like the sequence predictor because it was loaded with the world's street maps and a whole lot more. That whet our appetite for digging in deep on big data and today's artificial-intelligence technologies, and helped shape Chapters 11–16 of this book.

It's notable that all of the data-science implementation case studies in Chapters 11–16 either are rooted in artificial intelligence technologies or discuss the big data hardware and software infrastructure that enables computer scientists and data scientists to implement leading-edge AI-based solutions effectively.

AI: A Field with Problems But No Solutions
For many decades, AI has been viewed as a field with problems but *no* solutions. That's because once a particular problem is solved people say, "Well, that's not intelligence, it's just a computer program that tells the computer exactly what to do." However, with machine learning (Chapter 14) and deep learning (Chapter 15) we're not pre-programming solutions

to *specific* problems. Instead, we're letting our computers solve problems by learning from data—and, typically, lots of it.

Many of the most interesting and challenging problems are being pursued with deep learning. Google alone has thousands of deep-learning projects underway and that number is growing quickly.[81, 82] As you work through this book, we'll introduce you to many edge-of-the-practice artificial intelligence, big data and cloud technologies.

1.10 Wrap-Up

In this chapter, we introduced terminology and concepts that lay the groundwork for the Python programming you'll learn in Chapters 2–10 and the big-data, artificial-intelligence and cloud-based case studies we present in Chapters 11–16.

We reviewed object-oriented programming concepts and discussed why Python has become so popular. We introduced the Python Standard Library and various data-science libraries that help you avoid "reinventing the wheel." In subsequent chapters, you'll use these libraries to create software objects that you'll interact with to perform significant tasks with modest numbers of instructions.

You worked through three test-drives showing how to execute Python code with the IPython interpreter and Jupyter Notebooks. We introduced the Cloud and the Internet of Things (IoT), laying the groundwork for the contemporary applications you'll develop in Chapters 11–16.

We discussed just how big "big data" is and how quickly it's getting even bigger, and presented a big-data case study on the Waze mobile navigation app, which uses many current technologies to provide dynamic driving directions that get you to your destination as quickly and as safely as possible. We mentioned where in this book you'll use many of those technologies. The chapter closed with our first Intro to Data Science section in which we discussed a key intersection between computer science and data science—artificial intelligence.

---

81. http://theweek.com/speedreads/654463/google-more-than-1000-artificial-intelli-gence-projects-works.
82. https://www.zdnet.com/article/google-says-exponential-growth-of-ai-is-changing-nature-of-compute/.

2

Introduction to Python Programming

Objectives

In this chapter, you'll:

- Continue using IPython interactive mode to enter code snippets and see their results immediately.
- Write simple Python statements and scripts.
- Create variables to store data for later use.
- Become familiar with built-in data types.
- Use arithmetic operators and comparison operators, and understand their precedence.
- Use single-, double- and triple-quoted strings.
- Use built-in function `print` to display text.
- Use built-in function `input` to prompt the user to enter data at the keyboard and get that data for use in the program.
- Convert text to integer values with built-in function `int`.
- Use comparison operators and the `if` statement to decide whether to execute a statement or group of statements.
- Learn about objects and Python's dynamic typing.
- Use built-in function `type` to get an object's type.

2.1 Introduction

In this chapter, we introduce Python programming and present examples illustrating key language features. We assume you've read the IPython Test-Drive in Chapter 1, which introduced the IPython interpreter and used it to evaluate simple arithmetic expressions.

2.2 Variables and Assignment Statements

You've used IPython's interactive mode as a calculator with expressions such as

```
In [1]: 45 + 72
Out[1]: 117
```

Let's create a variable named x that stores the integer 7:

```
In [2]: x = 7
```

Snippet [2] is a **statement**. Each statement specifies a task to perform. The preceding statement creates x and uses the **assignment symbol** (=) to give x a value. Most statements stop at the end of the line, though it's possible for statements to span more than one line. The following statement creates the variable y and assigns to it the value 3:

```
In [3]: y = 3
```

You can now use the values of x and y in expressions:

```
In [4]: x + y
Out[4]: 10
```

Calculations in Assignment Statements
The following statement adds the values of variables x and y and assigns the result to the variable total, which we then display:

```
In [5]: total = x + y

In [6]: total
Out[6]: 10
```

The = symbol is not an operator. The right side of the = symbol always executes first, then the result is assigned to the variable on the symbol's left side.

Python Style
The *Style Guide for Python Code*[1] helps you write code that conforms to Python's coding conventions. The style guide recommends inserting one space on each side of the assignment symbol = and binary operators like + to make programs more readable.

Variable Names

A variable name, such as x, is an **identifier**. Each identifier may consist of letters, digits and underscores (_) but may not begin with a digit. Python is *case sensitive*, so number and Number are *different* identifiers because one begins with a lowercase letter and the other begins with an uppercase letter.

Types

Each value in Python has a **type** that indicates the kind of data the value represents. You can view a value's type with Python's built-in **type function**, as in:

```
In [7]: type(x)
Out[7]: int

In [8]: type(10.5)
Out[8]: float
```

The variable x contains the integer value 7 (from snippet [2]), so Python displays int (short for integer). The value 10.5 is a floating-point number, so Python displays float.

2.3 Arithmetic

The following table summarizes the **arithmetic operators**, which include some symbols not used in algebra.

Python operation	Arithmetic operator	Algebraic expression	Python expression
Addition	+	$f + 7$	f + 7
Subtraction	−	$p - c$	p - c
Multiplication	*	$b \cdot m$	b * m
Exponentiation	**	x^y	x ** y
True division	/	x/y or $\frac{x}{y}$ or $x \div y$	x / y
Floor division	//	$\lfloor x/y \rfloor$ or $\left\lfloor \frac{x}{y} \right\rfloor$ or $\lfloor x \div y \rfloor$	x // y
Remainder (modulo)	%	$r \bmod s$	r % s

Multiplication (*)

Python uses the **asterisk (*) multiplication operator**:

```
In [1]: 7 * 4
Out[1]: 28
```

Exponentiation (**)

The **exponentiation (**) operator** raises one value to the power of another:

```
In [2]: 2 ** 10
Out[2]: 1024
```

---

1. https://www.python.org/dev/peps/pep-0008/.

To calculate the square root, you can use the exponent 1/2 (that is, 0.5):

```
In [3]: 9 ** (1 / 2)
Out[3]: 3.0
```

True Division (/) vs. Floor Division (//)

True division (/) divides a numerator by a denominator and yields a floating-point number with a decimal point, as in:

```
In [4]: 7 / 4
Out[4]: 1.75
```

Floor division (//) divides a numerator by a denominator, yielding the highest *integer* that's not greater than the result. Python **truncates** (discards) the fractional part:

```
In [5]: 7 // 4
Out[5]: 1

In [6]: 3 // 5
Out[6]: 0

In [7]: 14 // 7
Out[7]: 2
```

In true division, -13 divided by 4 gives -3.25:

```
In [8]: -13 / 4
Out[8]: -3.25
```

Floor division gives the closest integer that's *not greater than* -3.25—which is -4:

```
In [9]: -13 // 4
Out[9]: -4
```

Exceptions and Tracebacks

Dividing by zero with / or // is not allowed and results in an **exception**—a sign that a problem occurred:

```
In [10]: 123 / 0
---------------------------------------------------------------------------
ZeroDivisionError                         Traceback (most recent call last)
<ipython-input-10-cd759d3fcf39> in <module>()
----> 1 123 / 0

ZeroDivisionError: division by zero
```

Python reports an exception with a **traceback**. This traceback indicates that an exception of type ZeroDivisionError occurred—most exception names end with Error. In interactive mode, the snippet number that caused the exception is specified by the 10 in the line

```
<ipython-input-10-cd759d3fcf39> in <module>()
```

The line that begins with ----> shows the code that caused the exception. Sometimes snippets have more than one line of code—the 1 to the right of ----> indicates that line 1 within the snippet caused the exception. The last line shows the exception that occurred, followed by a colon (:) and an error message with more information about the exception:

```
ZeroDivisionError: division by zero
```

The "Files and Exceptions" chapter discusses exceptions in detail.

An exception also occurs if you try to use a variable that you have not yet created. The following snippet tries to add 7 to the undefined variable z, resulting in a `NameError`:

```
In [11]: z + 7
-----------------------------------------------------------------------
NameError                              Traceback (most recent call last)
<ipython-input-11-f2cdbf4fe75d> in <module>()
----> 1 z + 7

NameError: name 'z' is not defined
```

Remainder Operator
Python's **remainder operator (%)** yields the remainder after the left operand is divided by the right operand:

```
In [12]: 17 % 5
Out[12]: 2
```

In this case, 17 divided by 5 yields a quotient of 3 and a remainder of 2. This operator is most commonly used with integers, but also can be used with other numeric types:

```
In [13]: 7.5 % 3.5
Out[13]: 0.5
```

Straight-Line Form
Algebraic notations such as

$$\frac{a}{b}$$

generally are not acceptable to compilers or interpreters. For this reason, algebraic expressions must be typed in **straight-line form** using Python's operators. The expression above must be written as a / b (or a // b for floor division) so that all operators and operands appear in a horizontal straight line.

Grouping Expressions with Parentheses
Parentheses group Python expressions, as they do in algebraic expressions. For example, the following code multiplies 10 times the quantity 5 + 3:

```
In [14]: 10 * (5 + 3)
Out[14]: 80
```

Without these parentheses, the result is *different*:

```
In [15]: 10 * 5 + 3
Out[15]: 53
```

The parentheses are **redundant** (unnecessary) if removing them yields the *same* result.

Operator Precedence Rules
Python applies the operators in arithmetic expressions according to the following **rules of operator precedence**. These are generally the same as those in algebra:

1. **Expressions in parentheses evaluate first**, so parentheses may force the order of evaluation to occur in any sequence you desire. Parentheses have the highest level of precedence. In expressions with **nested parentheses**, such as (a / (b - c)), the expression in the *innermost* parentheses (that is, b - c) evaluates first.

2. Exponentiation operations evaluate next. If an expression contains several exponentiation operations, Python applies them from right to left.

3. Multiplication, division and modulus operations evaluate next. If an expression contains several multiplication, true-division, floor-division and modulus operations, Python applies them from left to right. Multiplication, division and modulus are "on the same level of precedence."

4. Addition and subtraction operations evaluate last. If an expression contains several addition and subtraction operations, Python applies them from left to right. Addition and subtraction also have the same level of precedence.

For the complete list of operators and their precedence (in lowest-to-highest order), see

```
https://docs.python.org/3/reference/expressions.html#operator-prece-
dence
```

Operator Grouping
When we say that Python applies certain operators from left to right, we are referring to the operators' **grouping**. For example, in the expression

```
a + b + c
```

the addition operators (+) group from left to right as if we parenthesized the expression as (a + b) + c. All Python operators of the same precedence group left-to-right except for the exponentiation operator (**), which groups right-to-left.

Redundant Parentheses
You can use redundant parentheses to group subexpressions to make the expression clearer. For example, the second-degree polynomial

```
y = a * x ** 2 + b * x + c
```

can be parenthesized, for clarity, as

```
y = (a * (x ** 2)) + (b * x) + c
```

Breaking a complex expression into a sequence of statements with shorter, simpler expressions also can promote clarity.

Operand Types
Each arithmetic operator may be used with integers and floating-point numbers. If both operands are integers, the result is an integer—except for the true-division (/) operator, which always yields a floating-point number. If both operands are floating-point numbers, the result is a floating-point number. Expressions containing an integer and a floating-point number are **mixed-type expressions**—these always produce floating-point results.

2.4 Function print and an Intro to Single- and Double-Quoted Strings
The built-in **print function** displays its argument(s) as a line of text:

```
In [1]: print('Welcome to Python!')
Welcome to Python!
```

In this case, the argument `'Welcome to Python!'` is a string—a sequence of characters enclosed in single quotes (`'`). Unlike when you evaluate expressions in interactive mode, the text that `print` displays here is not preceded by `Out[1]`. Also, `print` does not display a string's quotes, though we'll soon show how to display quotes in strings.

You also may enclose a string in double quotes (`"`), as in:

```
In [2]: print("Welcome to Python!")
Welcome to Python!
```

Python programmers generally prefer single quotes. When `print` completes its task, it positions the screen cursor at the beginning of the next line.

Printing a Comma-Separated List of Items

The `print` function can receive a comma-separated list of arguments, as in:

```
In [3]: print('Welcome', 'to', 'Python!')
Welcome to Python!
```

It displays each argument separated from the next by a space, producing the same output as in the two preceding snippets. Here we showed a comma-separated list of strings, but the values can be of any type. We'll show in the next chapter how to prevent automatic spacing between values or use a different separator than space.

Printing Many Lines of Text with One Statement

When a backslash (\) appears in a string, it's known as the **escape character**. The backslash and the character immediately following it form an **escape sequence**. For example, \n represents the **newline character** escape sequence, which tells `print` to move the output cursor to the next line. The following snippet uses three newline characters to create several lines of output:i

```
In [4]: print('Welcome\nto\n\nPython!')
Welcome
to

Python!
```

Other Escape Sequences

The following table shows some common escape sequences.

Escape sequence	Description
\n	Insert a newline character in a string. When the string is displayed, for each newline, move the screen cursor to the beginning of the next line.
\t	Insert a horizontal tab. When the string is displayed, for each tab, move the screen cursor to the next tab stop.
\\	Insert a backslash character in a string.
\"	Insert a double quote character in a string.
\'	Insert a single quote character in a string.

Ignoring a Line Break in a Long String

You may also split a long string (or a long statement) over several lines by using the \ **continuation character** as the last character on a line to ignore the line break:

```
In [5]: print('this is a longer string, so we \
   ...: split it over two lines')
this is a longer string, so we split it over two lines
```

The interpreter reassembles the string's parts into a single string with no line break. Though the backslash character in the preceding snippet is inside a string, it's not the escape character because another character does not follow it.

Printing the Value of an Expression

Calculations can be performed in `print` statements:

```
In [6]: print('Sum is', 7 + 3)
Sum is 10
```

2.5 Triple-Quoted Strings

Earlier, we introduced strings delimited by a pair of single quotes (') or a pair of double quotes ("). **Triple-quoted strings** begin and end with three double quotes (""") or three single quotes ('''). The *Style Guide for Python Code* recommends three double quotes ("""). Use these to create:

*   multiline strings,
*   strings containing single or double quotes and
*   **docstrings**, which are the recommended way to document the purposes of certain program components.

Including Quotes in Strings

In a string delimited by single quotes, you may include double-quote characters:

```
In [1]: print('Display "hi" in quotes')
Display "hi" in quotes
```

but not single quotes:

```
In [2]: print('Display 'hi' in quotes')
  File "<ipython-input-2-19bf596ccf72>", line 1
    print('Display 'hi' in quotes')
                     ^
SyntaxError: invalid syntax
```

unless you use the \' escape sequence:

```
In [3]: print('Display \'hi\' in quotes')
Display 'hi' in quotes
```

Snippet [2] displayed a syntax error due to a single quote inside a single-quoted string. IPython displays information about the line of code that caused the syntax error and points to the error with a ^ symbol. It also displays the message `SyntaxError: invalid syntax`.

A string delimited by double quotes may include single quote characters:

```
In [4]: print("Display the name O'Brien")
Display the name O'Brien
```

but not double quotes, unless you use the \" escape sequence:

```
In [5]: print("Display \"hi\" in quotes")
Display "hi" in quotes
```

To avoid using \' and \" inside strings, you can enclose such strings in triple quotes:

```
In [6]: print("""Display "hi" and 'bye' in quotes""")
Display "hi" and 'bye' in quotes
```

Multiline Strings

The following snippet assigns a multiline triple-quoted string to `triple_quoted_string`:

```
In [7]: triple_quoted_string = """This is a triple-quoted
   ...: string that spans two lines"""
```

IPython knows that the string is incomplete because we did not type the closing """ before we pressed *Enter*. So, IPython displays a **continuation prompt** ...: at which you can input the multiline string's next line. This continues until you enter the ending """ and press *Enter*. The following displays `triple_quoted_string`:

```
In [8]: print(triple_quoted_string)
This is a triple-quoted
string that spans two lines
```

Python stores multiline strings with embedded newline characters. When we evaluate `triple_quoted_string` rather than printing it, IPython displays it in single quotes with a \n character where you pressed *Enter* in snippet [7]. The quotes IPython displays indicate that `triple_quoted_string` is a string—they're not part of the string's contents:

```
In [9]: triple_quoted_string
Out[9]: 'This is a triple-quoted\nstring that spans two lines'
```

2.6 Getting Input from the User

The built-in **input function** requests and obtains user input:

```
In [1]: name = input("What's your name? ")
What's your name? Paul

In [2]: name
Out[2]: 'Paul'

In [3]: print(name)
Paul
```

The snippet executes as follows:

- First, `input` displays its string argument—a prompt—to tell the user what to type and waits for the user to respond. We typed Paul and pressed *Enter*. We use **bold** text to distinguish the user's input from the prompt text that `input` displays.

- Function `input` then returns those characters as a string that the program can use. Here we assigned that string to the variable name.

Snippet [2] shows name's value. Evaluating name displays its value in single quotes as 'Paul' because it's a string. Printing name (in snippet [3]) displays the string without the quotes. If you enter quotes, they're part of the string, as in:

```
In [4]: name = input("What's your name? ")
What's your name? 'Paul'

In [5]: name
Out[5]: "'Paul'"

In [6]: print(name)
'Paul'
```

Function input Always Returns a String

Consider the following snippets that attempt to read two numbers and add them:

```
In [7]: value1 = input('Enter first number: ')
Enter first number: 7

In [8]: value2 = input('Enter second number: ')
Enter second number: 3

In [9]: value1 + value2
Out[9]: '73'
```

Rather than adding the integers 7 and 3 to produce 10, Python "adds" the *string* values '7' and '3', producing the *string* '73'. This is known as **string concatenation**. It creates a new string containing the left operand's value followed by the right operand's value.

Getting an Integer from the User

If you need an integer, convert the string to an integer using the built-in **int function**:

```
In [10]: value = input('Enter an integer: ')
Enter an integer: 7

In [11]: value = int(value)

In [12]: value
Out[12]: 7
```

We could have combined the code in snippets [10] and [11]:

```
In [13]: another_value = int(input('Enter another integer: '))
Enter another integer: 13

In [14]: another_value
Out[14]: 13
```

Variables value and another_value now contain integers. Adding them produces an integer result (rather than concatenating them):

```
In [15]: value + another_value
Out[15]: 20
```

If the string passed to int cannot be converted to an integer, a ValueError occurs:

```
In [16]: bad_value = int(input('Enter another integer: '))
Enter another integer: hello
-------------------------------------------------------------------------
ValueError                                Traceback (most recent call last)
<ipython-input-16-cd36e6cf8911> in <module>()
----> 1 bad_value = int(input('Enter another integer: '))

ValueError: invalid literal for int() with base 10: 'hello'
```

Function int also can convert a floating-point value to an integer:

```
In [17]: int(10.5)
Out[17]: 10
```

To convert strings to floating-point numbers, use the built-in **float function**.

2.7 Decision Making: The if Statement and Comparison Operators

A **condition** is a Boolean expression with the value **True** or **False**. The following determines whether 7 is greater than 4 and whether 7 is less than 4:

```
In [1]: 7 > 4
Out[1]: True

In [2]: 7 < 4
Out[2]: False
```

True and False are Python keywords. Using a keyword as an identifier causes a SyntaxError. True and False are each capitalized.

You'll often create conditions using the **comparison operators** in the following table:

Algebraic operator	Python operator	Sample condition	Meaning
>	>	x > y	x is greater than y
<	<	x < y	x is less than y
≥	>=	x >= y	x is greater than or equal to y
≤	<=	x <= y	x is less than or equal to y
=	==	x == y	x is equal to y
≠	!=	x != y	x is not equal to y

Operators >, <, >= and <= all have the same precedence. Operators == and != both have the same precedence, which is lower than that of >, <, >= and <=. A syntax error occurs when any of the operators ==, !=, >= and <= contains spaces between its pair of symbols:

```
In [3]: 7 > = 4
  File "<ipython-input-3-5c6e2897f3b3>", line 1
    7 > = 4
        ^
SyntaxError: invalid syntax
```

Another syntax error occurs if you reverse the symbols in the operators !=, >= and <= (by writing them as =!, => and =<).

Making Decisions with the if Statement: Introducing Scripts

We now present a simple version of the **if statement**, which uses a condition to decide whether to execute a statement (or a group of statements). Here we'll read two integers from the user and compare them using six consecutive if statements, one for each comparison operator. If the condition in a given if statement is True, the corresponding print statement executes; otherwise, it's skipped.

IPython interactive mode is helpful for executing brief code snippets and seeing immediate results. When you have many statements to execute as a group, you typically write them as a **script** stored in a file with the .py (short for Python) extension—such as fig02_01.py for this example's script. Scripts are also called programs. For instructions on locating and executing the scripts in this book, see Chapter 1's IPython Test-Drive.

Each time you execute this script, three of the six conditions are True. To show this, we execute the script three times—once with the first integer *less than* the second, once with the *same* value for both integers and once with the first integer *greater than* the second. The three sample executions appear after the script

Each time we present a script like the one below, we introduce it before the figure, then explain the script's code after the figure. We show line numbers for your convenience—these are not part of Python. IDEs enable you to choose whether to display line numbers. To run this example, change to this chapter's ch02 examples folder, then enter:

```
ipython fig02_01.py
```

or, if you're in IPython already, you can use the command:

```
run fig02_01.py
```

```python
1   # fig02_01.py
2   """Comparing integers using if statements and comparison operators."""
3
4   print('Enter two integers, and I will tell you',
5         'the relationships they satisfy.')
6
7   # read first integer
8   number1 = int(input('Enter first integer: '))
9
10  # read second integer
11  number2 = int(input('Enter second integer: '))
12
13  if number1 == number2:
14      print(number1, 'is equal to', number2)
15
16  if number1 != number2:
17      print(number1, 'is not equal to', number2)
18
19  if number1 < number2:
20      print(number1, 'is less than', number2)
21
22  if number1 > number2:
23      print(number1, 'is greater than', number2)
24
25  if number1 <= number2:
26      print(number1, 'is less than or equal to', number2)
27
28  if number1 >= number2:
29      print(number1, 'is greater than or equal to', number2)
```

```
Enter two integers and I will tell you the relationships they satisfy.
Enter first integer: 37
Enter second integer: 42
37 is not equal to 42
37 is less than 42
37 is less than or equal to 42
```

```
Enter two integers and I will tell you the relationships they satisfy.
Enter first integer: 7
Enter second integer: 7
7 is equal to 7
7 is less than or equal to 7
7 is greater than or equal to 7
```

```
Enter two integers and I will tell you the relationships they satisfy.
Enter first integer: 54
Enter second integer: 17
54 is not equal to 17
54 is greater than 17
54 is greater than or equal to 17
```

Comments

Line 1 begins with the hash character (**#**), which indicates that the rest of the line is a **comment**:

```
# fig02_01.py
```

For easy reference, we begin each script with a comment indicating the script's file name. A comment also can begin to the right of the code on a given line and continue until the end of that line.

Docstrings

The *Style Guide for Python Code* states that each script should start with a docstring that explains the script's purpose, such as the one in line 2:

```
"""Comparing integers using if statements and comparison opera-
tors."""
```

For more complex scripts, the docstring often spans many lines. In later chapters, you'll use docstrings to describe script components you define, such as new functions and new types called classes. We'll also discuss how to access docstrings with the IPython help mechanism.

Blank Lines

Line 3 is a blank line. You use blank lines and space characters to make code easier to read. Together, blank lines, space characters and tab characters are known as **white space**. Python ignores most white space—you'll see that some indentation is required.

Splitting a Lengthy Statement Across Lines
Lines 4–5

```
print('Enter two integers, and I will tell you',
    'the relationships they satisfy.')
```

display instructions to the user. These are too long to fit on one line, so we broke them into two strings. Recall that you can display several values by passing to print a comma-separated list—print separates each value from the next with a space.

Typically, you write statements on one line. You may spread a lengthy statement over several lines with the \ continuation character. Python also allows you to split long code lines in parentheses without using continuation characters (as in lines 4–5). This is the preferred way to break long code lines according to the *Style Guide for Python Code*. Always choose breaking points that make sense, such as after a comma in the preceding call to print or before an operator in a lengthy expression.

Reading Integer Values from the User
Next, lines 8 and 11 use the built-in input and int functions to prompt for and read two integer values from the user.

if Statements
The if statement in lines 13–14

```
if number1 == number2:
    print(number1, 'is equal to', number2)
```

uses the == comparison operator to determine whether the values of variables number1 and number2 are equal. If so, the condition is True, and line 14 displays a line of text indicating that the values are equal. If any of the remaining if statements' conditions are True (lines 16, 19, 22, 25 and 28), the corresponding print displays a line of text.

Each if statement consists of the keyword if, the condition to test, and a colon (:) followed by an indented body called a **suite**. Each suite must contain one or more statements. Forgetting the colon (:) after the condition is a common syntax error.

Suite Indentation
Python requires you to indent the statements in suites. The *Style Guide for Python Code* recommends four-space indents—we use that convention throughout this book. You'll see in the next chapter that incorrect indentation can cause errors.

Confusing == and =
Using the assignment symbol (=) instead of the equality operator (==) in an if statement's condition is a common syntax error. To help avoid this, read == as "is equal to" and = as "is assigned." You'll see in the next chapter that using == in place of = in an assignment statement can lead to subtle problems.

Chaining Comparisons
You can chain comparisons to check whether a value is in a range. The following comparison determines whether x is in the range 1 through 5, inclusive:

```
In [1]: x = 3
```

```
In [2]: 1 <= x <= 5
Out[2]: True

In [3]: x = 10

In [4]: 1 <= x <= 5
Out[4]: False
```

Precedence of the Operators We've Presented So Far

The precedence of the operators introduced in this chapter is shown below:

Operators	Grouping	Type
()	left to right	parentheses
**	right to left	exponentiation
* / // %	left to right	multiplication, true division, floor division, remainder
+ -	left to right	addition, subtraction
> <= < >=	left to right	less than, less than or equal, greater than, greater than or equal
== !=	left to right	equal, not equal

The table lists the operators top-to-bottom in decreasing order of precedence. When writing expressions containing multiple operators, confirm that they evaluate in the order you expect by referring to the operator precedence chart at

> https://docs.python.org/3/reference/expressions.html#operator-precedence

2.8 Objects and Dynamic Typing

Values such as 7 (an integer), 4.1 (a floating-point number) and 'dog' are all objects. Every object has a type and a value:

```
In [1]: type(7)
Out[1]: int

In [2]: type(4.1)
Out[2]: float

In [3]: type('dog')
Out[3]: str
```

An object's value is the data stored in the object. The snippets above show objects of built-in types **int** (for integers), **float** (for floating-point numbers) and **str** (for strings).

Variables Refer to Objects

Assigning an object to a variable **binds** (associates) that variable's name to the object. As you've seen, you can then use the variable in your code to access the object's value:

```
In [4]: x = 7

In [5]: x + 10
Out[5]: 17
```

```
In [6]: x
Out[6]: 7
```

After snippet [4]'s assignment, the variable x **refers** to the integer object containing 7. As shown in snippet [6], snippet [5] does not change x's value. You can change x as follows:

```
In [7]: x = x + 10

In [8]: x
Out[8]: 17
```

Dynamic Typing
Python uses **dynamic typing**—it determines the type of the object a variable refers to while executing your code. We can show this by rebinding the variable x to different objects and checking their types:

```
In [9]: type(x)
Out[9]: int

In [10]: x = 4.1

In [11]: type(x)
Out[11]: float

In [12]: x = 'dog'

In [13]: type(x)
Out[13]: str
```

Garbage Collection
Python creates objects in memory and removes them from memory as necessary. After snippet [10], the variable x now refers to a float object. The integer object from snippet [7] is no longer bound to a variable. As we'll discuss in a later chapter, Python automatically removes such objects from memory. This process—called **garbage collection**—helps ensure that memory is available for new objects you create.

2.9 Intro to Data Science: Basic Descriptive Statistics

In data science, you'll often use statistics to describe and summarize your data. Here, we begin by introducing several such **descriptive statistics**, including:

- **minimum**—the smallest value in a collection of values.
- **maximum**—the largest value in a collection of values.
- **range**—the range of values from the minimum to the maximum.
- **count**—the number of values in a collection.
- **sum**—the total of the values in a collection.

We'll look at determining the *count* and *sum* in the next chapter. **Measures of dispersion** (also called **measures of variability**), such as *range*, help determine how spread out values are. Other measures of dispersion that we'll present in later chapters include *variance* and *standard deviation*.

Determining the Minimum of Three Values

First, let's show how to determine the minimum of three values manually. The following script prompts for and inputs three values, uses if statements to determine the minimum value, then displays it.

```
1   # fig02_02.py
2   """Find the minimum of three values."""
3
4   number1 = int(input('Enter first integer: '))
5   number2 = int(input('Enter second integer: '))
6   number3 = int(input('Enter third integer: '))
7
8   minimum = number1
9
10  if number2 < minimum:
11      minimum = number2
12
13  if number3 < minimum:
14      minimum = number3
15
16  print('Minimum value is', minimum)
```

```
Enter first integer: 12
Enter second integer: 27
Enter third integer: 36
Minimum value is 12
```

```
Enter first integer: 27
Enter second integer: 12
Enter third integer: 36
Minimum value is 12
```

```
Enter first integer: 36
Enter second integer: 27
Enter third integer: 12
Minimum value is 12
```

After inputting the three values, we process one value at a time:

- First, we assume that number1 contains the smallest value, so line 8 assigns it to the variable minimum. Of course, it's possible that number2 or number3 contains the actual smallest value, so we still must compare each of these with minimum.

- The first if statement (lines 10–11) then tests number2 < minimum and if this condition is True assigns number2 to minimum.

- The second if statement (lines 13–14) then tests number3 < minimum, and if this condition is True assigns number3 to minimum.

Now, minimum contains the smallest value, so we display it. We executed the script three times to show that it always finds the smallest value regardless of whether the user enters it first, second or third.

Determining the Minimum and Maximum with Built-In Functions `min` **and** `max`
Python has many built-in functions for performing common tasks. Built-in functions `min`
and `max` calculate the minimum and maximum, respectively, of a collection of values:

```
In [1]: min(36, 27, 12)
Out[1]: 12

In [2]: max(36, 27, 12)
Out[2]: 36
```

The functions `min` and `max` can receive any number of arguments.

Determining the Range of a Collection of Values
The *range* of values is simply the minimum through the maximum value. In this case, the
range is 12 through 36. Much data science is devoted to getting to know your data.
Descriptive statistics is a crucial part of that, but you also have to understand how to interpret the statistics. For example, if you have 100 numbers with a range of 12 through 36,
those numbers could be distributed evenly over that range. At the opposite extreme, you
could have clumping with 99 values of 12 and one 36, or one 12 and 99 values of 36.

Functional-Style Programming: Reduction
Throughout this book, we introduce various *functional-style programming* capabilities.
These enable you to write code that can be more concise, clearer and easier to **debug**—
that is, find and correct errors. The `min` and `max` functions are examples of a functional-
style programming concept called **reduction**. They reduce a collection of values to a *single*
value. Other reductions you'll see include the sum, average, variance and standard deviation of a collection of values. You'll also see how to define custom reductions.

Upcoming Intro to Data Science Sections
In the next two chapters, we'll continue our discussion of basic descriptive statistics with
measures of central tendency, including *mean*, *median* and *mode*, and *measures of dispersion*,
including *variance* and *standard deviation*.

2.10 Wrap-Up

This chapter continued our discussion of arithmetic. You used variables to store values for
later use. We introduced Python's arithmetic operators and showed that you must write
all expressions in straight-line form. You used the built-in function `print` to display data.
We created single-, double- and triple-quoted strings. You used triple-quoted strings to
create multiline strings and to embed single or double quotes in strings.

   You used the `input` function to prompt for and get input from the user at the keyboard. We used the functions `int` and `float` to convert strings to numeric values. We presented Python's comparison operators. Then, you used them in a script that read two
integers from the user and compared their values using a series of `if` statements.

   We discussed Python's dynamic typing and used the built-in function `type` to display
an object's type. Finally, we introduced the basic descriptive statistics minimum and maximum and used them to calculate the range of a collection of values. In the next chapter,
we present Python's control statements.

3

Control Statements

Objectives

In this chapter, you'll:

- Make decisions with if, if...else and if...elif...else.
- Execute statements repeatedly with while and for.
- Shorten assignment expressions with augmented assignments.
- Use the for statement and the built-in range function to repeat actions for a sequence of values.
- Perform sentinel-controlled iteration with while.
- Create compound conditions with the Boolean operators and, or and not.
- Stop looping with break.
- Force the next iteration of a loop with continue.
- Use functional-style programming features to write scripts that are more concise, clearer, easier to debug and easier to parallelize.

3.1 Introduction

In this chapter, we present Python's control statements—if, if...else, if...elif...else, while, for, break and continue. You'll use the for statement to perform sequence-controlled iteration—you'll see that the number of items in a sequence of item determines the for statement's number of iterations. You'll use the built-in function range to generate sequences of integers.

We'll show sentinel-controlled iteration with the while statement. You'll use the Python Standard Library's Decimal type for precise monetary calculations. We'll format data in f-strings (that is, format strings) using various format specifiers. We'll also show the Boolean operators and, or and not for creating compound conditions. In the Intro to Data Science section, we'll consider measures of central tendency—mean, median and mode—using the Python Standard Library's statistics module.

3.2 Control Statements

Python provides three selection statements that execute code based on a condition that evaluates to either True or False:

- The if statement performs an action if a condition is True or skips the action if the condition is False.

- The **if...else statement** performs an action if a condition is True or performs a *different* action if the condition is False.

- The **if...elif...else statement** performs one of many different actions, depending on the truth or falsity of *several* conditions.

Anywhere a single action can be placed, a group of actions can be placed.

Python provides two **iteration statements**—while and for:

- The **while statement** repeats an action (or a group of actions) as long as a condition remains True.

- The **for statement** repeats an action (or a group of actions) for every item in a sequence of items.

Keywords

The words if, elif, else, while, for, True and False are Python keywords. Using a keyword as an identifier such as a variable name is a syntax error. The following table lists Python's keywords.

Python keywords				
and	as	assert	async	await
break	class	continue	def	del
elif	else	except	False	finally
for	from	global	if	import
in	is	lambda	None	nonlocal
not	or	pass	raise	return
True	try	while	with	yield

3.3 if Statement

Let's execute a Python if statement:

```
In [1]: grade = 85

In [2]: if grade >= 60:
   ...:         print('Passed')
   ...:
Passed
```

The condition grade >= 60 is True, so the indented print statement in the if's suite displays 'Passed'.

Suite Indentation

Indenting a suite is required; otherwise, an IndentationError syntax error occurs:

```
In [3]: if grade >= 60:
   ...: print('Passed')  # statement is not indented properly
  File "<ipython-input-3-f42783904220>", line 2
    print('Passed')  # statement is not indented properly
        ^
IndentationError: expected an indented block
```

An IndentationError also occurs if you have more than one statement in a suite and those statements do not have the *same* indentation:

```
In [4]: if grade >= 60:
   ...:         print('Passed')  # indented 4 spaces
   ...:     print('Good job!')  # incorrectly indented only two spaces
  File <ipython-input-4-8c0d75c127bf>, line 3
    print('Good job!')  # incorrectly indented only two spaces
        ^
IndentationError: unindent does not match any outer indentation level
```

Sometimes error messages may not be clear. The fact that Python calls attention to the line is usually enough for you to figure out what's wrong. Apply indentation conventions uniformly throughout your code—programs that are not uniformly indented are hard to read.

Every Expression Can Be Interpreted as Either True or False
You can base decisions on *any* expression. A nonzero value is True. Zero is False:

```
In [5]: if 1:
   ...:        print('Nonzero values are true, so this will print')
   ...:
Nonzero values are true, so this will print

In [6]: if 0:
   ...:        print('Zero is false, so this will not print')

In [7]:
```

Strings containing characters are True and empty strings (`''`, `""` or `""""""`) are False.

Confusing == and =
Using the equality operator == instead of = in an assignment statement can lead to subtle problems. For example, in this session, snippet [1] defined grade with the assignment:

```
grade = 85
```

If instead we accidentally wrote:

```
grade == 85
```

then grade would be undefined and we'd get a NameError. If grade had been defined before the preceding statement, then grade == 85 would simply evaluate to True or False, and not perform an assignment. This is a logic error.

3.4 if...else and if...elif...else Statements

The if...else statement executes different suites, based on whether a condition is True or False:

```
In [1]: grade = 85

In [2]: if grade >= 60:
   ...:        print('Passed')
   ...: else:
   ...:        print('Failed')
   ...:
Passed
```

The condition above is True, so the if suite displays 'Passed'. Note that when you press *Enter* after typing print('Passed'), IPython indents the next line four spaces. You must delete those four spaces so that the else: suite correctly aligns under the i in if.

The following code assigns 57 to the variable grade, then shows the if...else statement again to demonstrate that only the else suite executes when the condition is False:

```
In [3]: grade = 57

In [4]: if grade >= 60:
   ...:        print('Passed')
   ...: else:
   ...:        print('Failed')
   ...:
Failed
```

Use the up and down arrow keys to navigate backwards and forwards through the current interactive session's snippets. Pressing *Enter* re-executes the snippet that's displayed. Let's set grade to 99, press the up arrow key twice to recall the code from snippet [4], then press *Enter* to re-execute that code as snippet [6]. Every recalled snippet that you execute gets a new ID:

```
In [5]: grade = 99

In [6]: if grade >= 60:
   ...:     print('Passed')
   ...: else:
   ...:     print('Failed')
   ...:
Passed
```

Conditional Expressions

Sometimes the suites in an if...else statement assign different values to a variable, based on a condition, as in:

```
In [7]: grade = 87

In [8]: if grade >= 60:
   ...:     result = 'Passed'
   ...: else:
   ...:     result = 'Failed'
   ...:
```

We can then print or evaluate that variable:

```
In [9]: result
Out[9]: 'Passed'
```

You can write statements like snippet [8] using a concise **conditional expression**:

```
In [10]: result = ('Passed' if grade >= 60 else 'Failed')

In [11]: result
Out[11]: 'Passed'
```

The parentheses are not required, but they make it clear that the statement assigns the conditional expression's value to result. First, Python evaluates the condition grade >= 60:

- If it's True, snippet [10] assigns to result the value of the expression to the *left* of if, namely 'Passed'. The else part does not execute.

- If it's False, snippet [10] assigns to result the value of the expression to the *right* of else, namely 'Failed'.

In interactive mode, you also can evaluate the conditional expression directly, as in:

```
In [12]: 'Passed' if grade >= 60 else 'Failed'
Out[12]: 'Passed'
```

Multiple Statements in a Suite

The following code shows two statements in the else suite of an if...else statement:

```
In [13]: grade = 49
```

```
In [14]: if grade >= 60:
    ...:      print('Passed')
    ...: else:
    ...:      print('Failed')
    ...:      print('You must take this course again')
    ...:
Failed
You must take this course again
```

In this case, grade is less than 60, so *both* statements in the else's suite execute.

If you do not indent the second print, then it's not in the else's suite. So, that statement *always* executes, possibly creating strange incorrect output:

```
In [15]: grade = 100

In [16]: if grade >= 60:
    ...:      print('Passed')
    ...: else:
    ...:      print('Failed')
    ...: print('You must take this course again')
    ...:
Passed
You must take this course again
```

if...elif...else Statement

You can test for many cases using the **if...elif...else statement**. The following code displays "A" for grades greater than or equal to 90, "B" for grades in the range 80–89, "C" for grades 70–79, "D" for grades 60–69 and "F" for all other grades. Only the action for the *first* True condition executes. Snippet [18] displays C, because grade is 77:

```
In [17]: grade = 77

In [18]: if grade >= 90:
    ...:      print('A')
    ...: elif grade >= 80:
    ...:      print('B')
    ...: elif grade >= 70:
    ...:      print('C')
    ...: elif grade >= 60:
    ...:      print('D')
    ...: else:
    ...:      print('F')
    ...:
C
```

The first condition—grade >= 90—is False, so print('A') is skipped. The second condition—grade >= 80—also is False, so print('B') is skipped. The third condition—grade >= 70—is True, so print('C') executes. Then all the remaining code in the if...elif...else statement is skipped. An if...elif...else is faster than separate if statements, because condition testing stops as soon as a condition is True.

else Is Optional

The else in the if...elif...else statement is optional. Including it enables you to handle values that do not satisfy *any* of the conditions. When an if...elif statement without an else tests a value that does not make any of its conditions True, the program does not execute any of the statement's suites—the next statement in sequence after the if...elif statement executes. If you specify the else, you must place it *after* the last elif; otherwise, a SyntaxError occurs.

Logic Errors

The incorrectly indented code segment in snippet [16] is an example of a *nonfatal logic error*. The code executes, but it produces incorrect results. For a *fatal logic error in a script*, an exception occurs (such as a ZeroDivisionError from an attempt to divide by 0), so Python displays a traceback, then terminates the script. A *fatal error in interactive mode* terminates only the current snippet—then IPython waits for your next input.

3.5 while Statement

The **while statement** allows you to *repeat* one or more actions while a condition remains True. Let's use a while statement to find the first power of 3 larger than 50:

```
In [1]: product = 3

In [2]: while product <= 50:
   ...:         product = product * 3
   ...:

In [3]: product
Out[3]: 81
```

Snippet [3] evaluates product to see its value, 81, which is the first power of 3 larger than 50.

Something in the while statement's suite must change product's value, so the condition eventually becomes False. Otherwise, an infinite loop occurs. In applications executed from a Terminal, Anaconda Command Prompt or shell, type *Ctrl + c* or *control + c* to terminate an infinite loop. IDEs typically have a toolbar button or menu option for stopping a program's execution.

3.6 for Statement

The **for statement** allows you to *repeat* an action or several actions for each item in a **sequence** of items. For example, a string is a sequence of individual characters. Let's display 'Programming' with its characters separated by two spaces:

```
In [1]: for character in 'Programming':
   ...:         print(character, end='  ')
   ...:
P  r  o  g  r  a  m  m  i  n  g
```

The for statement executes as follows:

- Upon entering the statement, it assigns the 'P' in 'Programming' to the **target** variable between keywords for and in—in this case, character.

- Next, the statement in the suite executes, displaying character's value followed by two spaces—we'll say more about this momentarily.

- After executing the suite, Python assigns to character the next item in the sequence (that is, the 'r' in 'Programming'), then executes the suite again.

- This continues while there are more items in the sequence to process. In this case, the statement terminates after displaying the letter 'g', followed by two spaces.

Using the target variable in the suite, as we did here to display its value, is common but not required.

Function print's end Keyword Argument

The built-in function print displays its argument(s), then moves the cursor to the next line. You can change this behavior with the argument **end**, as in

```
print(character, end=' ')
```

which displays character's value followed by two spaces. So, all the characters display horizontally on the *same* line. Python calls end a **keyword argument**, but end itself is not a Python keyword. Keyword arguments are sometimes called **named arguments**. The end keyword argument is optional. If you do not include it, print uses a newline ('\n') by default. The *Style Guide for Python Code* recommends placing no spaces around a keyword argument's =.

Function print's sep Keyword Argument

You can use the keyword argument **sep** (short for separator) to specify the string that appears *between* the items that print displays. When you do not specify this argument, print uses a space character by default. Let's display three numbers, each separated from the next by a comma and a space, rather than just a space:

```
In [2]: print(10, 20, 30, sep=', ')
10, 20, 30
```

To remove the default spaces, use sep='' (that is, an empty string).

3.6.1 Iterables, Lists and Iterators

The sequence to the right of the for statement's in keyword must be an **iterable**—that is, an object from which the for statement can take one item at a time until no more items remain. Python has other iterable sequence types besides strings. One of the most common is a **list**, which is a comma-separated collection of items enclosed in square brackets ([and]). The following code totals five integers in a list:

```
In [3]: total = 0

In [4]: for number in [2, -3, 0, 17, 9]:
   ...:     total = total + number
   ...:

In [5]: total
Out[5]: 25
```

Each sequence has an **iterator**. The for statement uses the iterator "behind the scenes" to get each consecutive item until there are no more to process. The iterator is like a bookmark—it always knows where it is in the sequence, so it can return the next item when it's called upon to do so. We cover lists in detail in the "Sequences: Lists and Tuples" chapter. There, you'll see that the order of the items in a list matters and that a list's items are **mutable** (that is, modifiable).

3.6.2 Built-In range Function

Let's use a for statement and the built-in **range function** to iterate precisely 10 times, displaying the values from 0 through 9:

```
In [6]: for counter in range(10):
   ...:     print(counter, end=' ')
   ...:
0 1 2 3 4 5 6 7 8 9
```

The function call range(10) creates an iterable object that represents a sequence of consecutive integers starting from 0 and continuing up to, but *not* including, the argument value (10)—in this case, 0, 1, 2, 3, 4, 5, 6, 7, 8, 9. The for statement exits when it finishes processing the last integer that range produces. Iterators and iterable objects are two of Python's *functional-style programming* features. We'll introduce more of these throughout the book.

Off-By-One Errors

A common type of off-by-one error occurs when you assume that range's argument value is included in the generated sequence. For example, if you provide 9 as range's argument when trying to produce the sequence 0 through 9, range generates only 0 through 8.

3.7 Augmented Assignments

Augmented assignments abbreviate assignment expressions in which the same variable name appears on the left and right of the assignment's =, as total does in:

```
for number in [1, 2, 3, 4, 5]:
    total = total + number
```

Snippet [2] reimplements this using an **addition augmented assignment (+=) statement**:

```
In [1]: total = 0

In [2]: for number in [1, 2, 3, 4, 5]:
   ...:     total += number  # add number to total
   ...:

In [3]: total
Out[3]: 15
```

The += expression in snippet [2] first adds number's value to the current total, then stores the new value in total. The table below shows sample augmented assignments:

Augmented assignment	Sample expression	Explanation	Assigns
Assume: c = 3, d = 5, e = 4, f = 2, g = 9, h = 12			
+=	c += 7	c = c + 7	10 to c
-=	d -= 4	d = d - 4	1 to d
*=	e *= 5	e = e * 5	20 to e
**=	f **= 3	f = f ** 3	8 to f
/=	g /= 2	g = g / 2	4.5 to g
//=	g //= 2	g = g // 2	4 to g
%=	h %= 9	h = h % 9	3 to h

3.8 Sequence-Controlled Iteration; Formatted Strings

This section and the next solve two class-averaging problems. Consider the following requirements statement:

> *A class of ten students took a quiz. Their grades (integers in the range 0 – 100) are 98, 76, 71, 87, 83, 90, 57, 79, 82, 94. Determine the class average on the quiz.*

The following script for solving this problem keeps a running total of the grades, calculates the average and displays the result. We placed the 10 grades in a list, but you could input the grades from a user at the keyboard (as we'll do in the next example) or read them from a file (as you'll see how to do in the "Files and Exceptions" chapter). We show how to read data from SQL and NoSQL databases in Chapter 16.

```
 1  # class_average.py
 2  """Class average program with sequence-controlled iteration."""
 3
 4  # initialization phase
 5  total = 0  # sum of grades
 6  grade_counter = 0
 7  grades = [98, 76, 71, 87, 83, 90, 57, 79, 82, 94]  # list of 10 grades
 8
 9  # processing phase
10  for grade in grades:
11      total += grade  # add current grade to the running total
12      grade_counter += 1  # indicate that one more grade was processed
13
14  # termination phase
15  average = total / grade_counter
16  print(f'Class average is {average}')
```

```
Class average is 81.7
```

Lines 5–6 create the variables total and grade_counter and initialize each to 0. Line 7

```
grades = [98, 76, 71, 87, 83, 90, 57, 79, 82, 94]  # list of 10 grades
```

creates the variable grades and initializes it with a list of 10 integer grades.

The for statement processes each grade in the list grades. Line 11 adds the current grade to the total. Then, line 12 adds 1 to the variable grade_counter to keep track of the number of grades processed so far. Iteration terminates when all 10 grades in the list have been processed. The *Style Guide for Python Code* recommends placing a blank line above and below each control statement (as in lines 8 and 13). When the for statement terminates, line 15 calculates the average and line 16 displays it. Later in this chapter, we use functional-style programming to calculate the average of a list's items more concisely.

Introduction to Formatted Strings

Line 16 uses the following simple **f-string** (short for **formatted string**) to format this script's result by inserting the value of average into a string:

```
f'Class average is {average}'
```

The letter f before the string's opening quote indicates it's an f-string. You specify where to insert values by using *placeholders* delimited by curly braces ({ and }). The placeholder

{average}

converts the variable average's value to a string representation, then replaces {average} with that **replacement text**. Replacement-text expressions may contain values, variables or other expressions, such as calculations or function calls. In line 16, we could have used total / grade_counter in place of average, eliminating the need for line 15.

3.9 **Sentinel-Controlled Iteration**

Let's generalize the class-average problem. Consider the following requirements statement:

> *Develop a class-averaging program that processes an arbitrary number of grades each time the program executes.*

The requirements statement does not state what the grades are or how many there are, so we're going to have the user enter the grades. The program processes an arbitrary number of grades. The user enters grades one at a time until all the grades have been entered, then enters a *sentinel value* (also called a *signal value*, a *dummy value* or a *flag value*) to indicate that there are no more grades.

Implementing Sentinel-Controlled Iteration

The following script solves the class average problem with sentinel-controlled iteration. Notice that we test for the possibility of division by zero. If undetected, this would cause a fatal logic error. In the "Files and Exceptions" chapter, we write programs that recognize such exceptions and take appropriate actions.

```
 1   # class_average_sentinel.py
 2   """Class average program with sentinel-controlled iteration."""
 3
 4   # initialization phase
 5   total = 0  # sum of grades
 6   grade_counter = 0  # number of grades entered
 7
 8   # processing phase
 9   grade = int(input('Enter grade, -1 to end: '))  # get one grade
10
11   while grade != -1:
12       total += grade
13       grade_counter += 1
14       grade = int(input('Enter grade, -1 to end: '))
15
16   # termination phase
17   if grade_counter != 0:
18       average = total / grade_counter
19       print(f'Class average is {average:.2f}')
20   else:
21       print('No grades were entered')
```

```
Enter grade, -1 to end: 97
Enter grade, -1 to end: 88
Enter grade, -1 to end: 72
Enter grade, -1 to end: -1
Class average is 85.67
```

Program Logic for Sentinel-Controlled Iteration

In sentinel-controlled iteration, the program reads the first value (line 9) before reaching the `while` statement. The value input in line 9 determines whether the program's flow of control should enter the `while`'s suite (lines 12–14). If the condition in line 11 is `False`, the user entered the sentinel value (-1), so the suite does not execute because the user did not enter any grades. If the condition is `True`, the suite executes, adding the `grade` value to the `total` and incrementing the `grade_counter`.

Next, line 14 inputs another grade from the user and the condition (line 11) is tested again, using the most recent `grade` entered by the user. The value of `grade` is always input immediately before the program tests the `while` condition, so we can determine whether the value just input is the sentinel before processing that value as a grade.

When the sentinel value is input, the loop terminates, and the program does not add −1 to `total`. In a sentinel-controlled loop that performs user input, any prompts (lines 9 and 14) should remind the user of the sentinel value.

Formatting the Class Average with Two Decimal Places

This example formatted the class average with two digits to the right of the decimal point. In an f-string, you can optionally follow a replacement-text expression with a colon (`:`) and a **format specifier** that describes how to format the replacement text. The format specifier `.2f` (line 19) formats the average as a floating-point number (`f`) with two digits to the right of the decimal point (`.2`). In this example, the sum of the grades was 257, which, when divided by 3, yields 85.666666666.... Formatting the average with `.2f` *rounds* it to the hundredths position, producing the replacement text `85.67`. An average with only one digit to the right of the decimal point would be formatted with a **trailing zero** (e.g., `85.50`). The chapter "Strings: A Deeper Look" discusses many more string-formatting features.

3.10 Built-In Function range: A Deeper Look

Function `range` also has two- and three-argument versions. As you've seen, `range`'s one-argument version produces a sequence of consecutive integers from 0 up to, but not including, the argument's value. Function `range`'s two-argument version produces a sequence of consecutive integers from its first argument's value up to, but not including, the second argument's value, as in:

```
In [1]: for number in range(5, 10):
   ...:     print(number, end=' ')
   ...:
5 6 7 8 9
```

Function `range`'s three-argument version produces a sequence of integers from its first argument's value up to, but not including, the second argument's value, *incrementing* by the third argument's value, which is known as the **step**:

```
In [2]: for number in range(0, 10, 2):
   ...:     print(number, end=' ')
   ...:
0 2 4 6 8
```

If the third argument is negative, the sequence progresses from the first argument's value *down* to, but not including, the second argument's value, *decrementing* by the third argument's value, as in:

```
In [3]: for number in range(10, 0, -2):
   ...:     print(number, end=' ')
   ...:
10 8 6 4 2
```

3.11 Using Type Decimal for Monetary Amounts

In this section, we introduce Decimal capabilities for precise monetary calculations. If you're in banking or other fields that require "to-the-penny" accuracy, you should investigate Decimal's capabilities in depth.

For most scientific and other mathematical applications that use numbers with decimal points, Python's built-in floating-point numbers work well. For example, when we speak of a "normal" body temperature of 98.6, we do not need to be precise to a large number of digits. When we view the temperature on a thermometer and read it as 98.6, the actual value may be 98.5999473210643. The point here is that calling this number 98.6 is adequate for most body-temperature applications.

Floating-point values are stored in binary format (we introduced binary in the first chapter and discuss it in depth in the online "Number Systems" appendix). Some floating-point values are represented only approximately when they're converted to binary. For example, consider the variable amount with the dollars-and-cents value 112.31. If you display amount, it appears to have the exact value you assigned to it:

```
In [1]: amount = 112.31
```

```
In [2]: print(amount)
112.31
```

However, if you print amount with 20 digits of precision to the right of the decimal point, you can see that the actual floating-point value in memory is not exactly 112.31—it's only an approximation:

```
In [3]: print(f'{amount:.20f}')
112.31000000000000227374
```

Many applications require *precise* representation of numbers with decimal points. Institutions like banks that deal with millions or even billions of transactions per day have to tie out their transactions "to the penny." Floating-point numbers can represent some but not all monetary amounts with to-the-penny precision.

The **Python Standard Library**[1] provides many predefined capabilities you can use in your Python code to avoid "reinventing the wheel." For monetary calculations and other applications that require precise representation and manipulation of numbers with decimal points, the Python Standard Library provides type **Decimal**, which uses a special coding scheme to solve the problem of to-the-penny precision. That scheme requires additional memory to hold the numbers and additional processing time to perform calculations but provides the precision required for monetary calculations. Banks also have to deal with other issues such as using a *fair rounding algorithm* when they're calculating daily interest on accounts. Type Decimal offers such capabilities.[2]

---

1. https://docs.python.org/3.7/library/index.html.
2. For more decimal module features, visit https://docs.python.org/3.7/library/decimal.html.

Importing Type Decimal from the decimal Module

We've used several *built-in types*—**int** (for integers, like 10), **float** (for floating-point numbers, like 7.5) and **str** (for strings like 'Python'). The Decimal type is not built into Python. Rather, it's part of the Python Standard Library, which is divided into groups of related capabilities called **modules**. The **decimal** module defines type Decimal and its capabilities.

To use type Decimal, you must first **import** the entire decimal module, as in

```
import decimal
```

and refer to the Decimal type as decimal.Decimal, or you must indicate a specific capability to import using **from...import**, as we do here:

```
In [4]: from decimal import Decimal
```

This imports only the type Decimal from the decimal module so that you can use it in your code. We'll discuss other import forms beginning in the next chapter.

Creating Decimals

You typically create a Decimal from a string:

```
In [5]: principal = Decimal('1000.00')

In [6]: principal
Out[6]: Decimal('1000.00')

In [7]: rate = Decimal('0.05')

In [8]: rate
Out[8]: Decimal('0.05')
```

We'll soon use these variables principal and rate in a compound-interest calculation.

Decimal Arithmetic

Decimals support the standard arithmetic operators +, -, *, /, //, ** and %, as well as the corresponding augmented assignments:

```
In [9]: x = Decimal('10.5')

In [10]: y = Decimal('2')

In [11]: x + y
Out[11]: Decimal('12.5')

In [12]: x // y
Out[12]: Decimal('5')

In [13]: x += y

In [14]: x
Out[14]: Decimal('12.5')
```

You may perform arithmetic between Decimals and integers, but *not* between Decimals and floating-point numbers.

Compound-Interest Problem Requirements Statement

Let's compute compound interest using the Decimal type for *precise* monetary calculations. Consider the following requirements statement:

> *A person invests $1000 in a savings account yielding 5% interest. Assuming that
> the person leaves all interest on deposit in the account, calculate and display the
> amount of money in the account at the end of each year for 10 years. Use the fol-
> lowing formula for determining these amounts:*
>
> $$a = p(1 + r)^n$$
>
> *where*
>
> > *p is the original amount invested (i.e., the principal),*
> > *r is the annual interest rate,*
> > *n is the number of years and*
> > *a is the amount on deposit at the end of the nth year.*

Calculating Compound Interest

To solve this problem, let's use variables principal and rate that we defined in snippets
[5] and [7], and a for statement that performs the interest calculation for each of the 10
years the money remains on deposit. For each year, the loop displays a formatted string
containing the year number and the amount on deposit at the end of that year:

```
In [15]: for year in range(1, 11):
   ...:         amount = principal * (1 + rate) ** year
   ...:         print(f'{year:>2}{amount:>10.2f}')
   ...:
 1    1050.00
 2    1102.50
 3    1157.62
 4    1215.51
 5    1276.28
 6    1340.10
 7    1407.10
 8    1477.46
 9    1551.33
10    1628.89
```

The algebraic expression $(1 + r)^n$ from the requirements statement is written as

```
(1 + rate) ** year
```

where variable rate represents *r* and variable year represents *n*.

Formatting the Year and Amount on Deposit

The statement

```
print(f'{year:>2}{amount:>10.2f}')
```

uses an f-string with two placeholders to format the loop's output.
    The placeholder

```
{year:>2}
```

uses the format specifier >2 to indicate that year's value should be **right aligned** (>) in a
field of width 2—the **field width** specifies the number of character positions to use when
displaying the value. For the single-digit year values 1–9, the format specifier >2 displays

a space character followed by the value, thus right aligning the years in the first column. The following diagram shows the numbers 1 and 10 each formatted in a field width of 2:

You can **left align** values with <.

The format specifier 10.2f in the placeholder

```
{amount:>10.2f}
```

formats amount as a floating-point number (f) right aligned (>) in a field width of 10 with a decimal point and two digits to the right of the decimal point (.2). Formatting the amounts this way *aligns their decimal points vertically*, as is typical with monetary amounts. In the 10 character positions, the three rightmost characters are the number's decimal point followed by the two digits to its right. The remaining seven character positions are the leading spaces and the digits to the decimal point's left. In this example, all the dollar amounts have four digits to the left of the decimal point, so each number is formatted with three *leading spaces*. The following diagram shows the formatting for the value 1050.00:

```
              field width 10

              | | | |1|0|5|0|.|0|0|

         leading spaces          two digits to right
              decimal point       of decimal point
```

3.12 break and continue Statements

The break and continue statements alter a loop's flow of control. Executing a **break** statement in a while or for immediately exits that statement. In the following code, range produces the integer sequence 0–99, but the loop terminates when number is 10:

```
In [1]: for number in range(100):
   ...:     if number == 10:
   ...:         break
   ...:     print(number, end=' ')
   ...:
0 1 2 3 4 5 6 7 8 9
```

In a script, execution would continue with the next statement after the for loop. The while and for statements each have an optional else clause that executes only if the loop terminates normally—that is, not as a result of a break.

Executing a **continue** statement in a while or for loop skips the remainder of the loop's suite. In a while, the condition is then tested to determine whether the loop should continue executing. In a for, the loop processes the next item in the sequence (if any):

```
In [2]: for number in range(10):
   ...:     if number == 5:
   ...:         continue
   ...:     print(number, end=' ')
   ...:
0 1 2 3 4 6 7 8 9
```

3.13 Boolean Operators and, or and not

The conditional operators >, <, >=, <=, == and != can be used to form simple conditions such as grade >= 60. To form more complex conditions that combine simple conditions, use the and, or and not Boolean operators.

Boolean Operator and

To ensure that two conditions are *both* True before executing a control statement's suite, use the **Boolean and operator** to combine the conditions. The following code defines two variables, then tests a condition that's True if and only if *both* simple conditions are True— if either (or both) of the simple conditions is False, the entire and expression is False:

```
In [1]: gender = 'Female'

In [2]: age = 70

In [3]: if gender == 'Female' and age >= 65:
   ...:         print('Senior female')
   ...:
Senior female
```

The if statement has two simple conditions:

- gender == 'Female' determines whether a person is a female and

- age >= 65 determines whether that person is a senior citizen.

The simple condition to the left of the and operator evaluates first because == has higher precedence than and. If necessary, the simple condition to the right of and evaluates next, because >= has higher precedence than and. (We'll discuss shortly why the right side of an and operator evaluates *only* if the left side is True.) The entire if statement condition is True if and only if *both* of the simple conditions are True. The combined condition can be made clearer by adding redundant parentheses

```
(gender == 'Female') and (age >= 65)
```

The table below summarizes the and operator by showing all four possible combinations of False and True values for *expression1* and *expression2*—such tables are called *truth tables*:

expression1	*expression2*	*expression1* and *expression2*
False	False	False
False	True	False
True	False	False
True	True	True

Boolean Operator or

Use the **Boolean or operator** to test whether one *or* both of two conditions are True. The following code tests a condition that's True if either *or* both simple conditions are True— the entire condition is False only if *both* simple conditions are False:

```
In [4]: semester_average = 83
```

```
In [5]: final_exam = 95

In [6]: if semester_average >= 90 or final_exam >= 90:
   ...:     print('Student gets an A')
   ...:
Student gets an A
```

Snippet [6] also contains two simple conditions:

- `semester_average >= 90` determines whether a student's average was an A (90 or above) during the semester, and

- `final_exam >= 90` determines whether a student's final-exam grade was an A.

The truth table below summarizes the Boolean or operator. Operator and has higher precedence than or.

expression1	expression2	expression1 or expression2
False	False	False
False	True	True
True	False	True
True	True	True

Improving Performance with Short-Circuit Evaluation

Python stops evaluating an and expression as soon as it knows whether the entire condition is False. Similarly, Python stops evaluating an or expression as soon as it knows whether the entire condition is True. This is called *short-circuit evaluation*. So the condition

```
gender == 'Female' and age >= 65
```

stops evaluating immediately if gender is not equal to 'Female' because the entire expression must be False. If gender is equal to 'Female', execution continues, because the entire expression will be True if the age is greater than or equal to 65.

Similarly, the condition

```
semester_average >= 90 or final_exam >= 90
```

stops evaluating immediately if semester_average is greater than or equal to 90 because the entire expression must be True. If semester_average is less than 90, execution continues, because the expression could still be True if the final_exam is greater than or equal to 90.

In expressions that use and, make the condition that's more likely to be False the leftmost condition. In or operator expressions, make the condition that's more likely to be True the leftmost condition. These techniques can reduce a program's execution time.

Boolean Operator not

The **Boolean operator not** "reverses" the meaning of a condition—True becomes False and False becomes True. This is a **unary operator**—it has only *one* operand. You place the not operator before a condition to choose a path of execution if the original condition (without the not operator) is False, such as in the following code:

```
In [7]: grade = 87

In [8]: if not grade == -1:
   ...:     print('The next grade is', grade)
   ...:
The next grade is 87
```

Often, you can avoid using not by expressing the condition in a more "natural" or convenient manner. For example, the preceding if statement can also be written as follows:

```
In [9]: if grade != -1:
   ...:     print('The next grade is', grade)
   ...:
The next grade is 87
```

The truth table below summarizes the not operator.

expression	not expression
False	True
True	False

The following table shows the precedence and grouping of the operators introduced so far, from top to bottom, in decreasing order of precedence.

Operators	Grouping
()	left to right
**	right to left
* / // %	left to right
+ -	left to right
< <= > >= == !=	left to right
not	left to right
and	left to right
or	left to right

3.14 Intro to Data Science: Measures of Central Tendency—Mean, Median and Mode

Here we continue our discussion of using statistics to analyze data with several additional descriptive statistics, including:

- **mean**—the *average value* in a set of values.
- **median**—the *middle value* when all the values are arranged in *sorted order*.
- **mode**—the *most frequently occurring value*.

These are **measures of central tendency**—each is a way of producing a single value that represents a "central" value in a set of values, i.e., a value which is in some sense typical of the others.

Let's calculate the mean, median and mode on a list of integers. The following session creates a list called `grades`, then uses the built-in **sum** and **len** functions to calculate the mean "by hand"—sum calculates the total of the grades (397) and len returns the number of grades (5):

```
In [1]: grades = [85, 93, 45, 89, 85]

In [2]: sum(grades) / len(grades)
Out[2]: 79.4
```

The previous chapter mentioned the *descriptive statistics* count and sum—implemented in Python as the built-in functions len and sum. Like functions min and max (introduced in the preceding chapter), sum and len are both examples of functional-style programming **reductions**—they reduce a collection of values to a single value—the sum of those values and the number of values, respectively. In Section 3.8's class-average example, we could have deleted lines 10–15 of the script and replaced average in line 16 with snippet [2]'s calculation.

The Python Standard Library's **statistics module** provides functions for calculating the mean, median and mode—these, too, are reductions. To use these capabilities, first import the statistics module:

```
In [3]: import statistics
```

Then, you can access the module's functions with "statistics." followed by the name of the function to call. The following calculates the grades list's mean, median and mode, using the statistics module's **mean**, **median** and **mode** functions:

```
In [4]: statistics.mean(grades)
Out[4]: 79.4

In [5]: statistics.median(grades)
Out[5]: 85

In [6]: statistics.mode(grades)
Out[6]: 85
```

Each function's argument must be an *iterable*—in this case, the list grades. To confirm that the median and mode are correct, you can use the built-in **sorted function** to get a copy of grades with its values arranged in increasing order:

```
In [7]: sorted(grades)
Out[7]: [45, 85, 85, 89, 93]
```

The grades list has an odd number of values (5), so median returns the *middle value* (85). If the list's number of values is even, median returns the *average* of the *two* middle values. Studying the sorted values, you can see that 85 is the mode because it occurs most frequently (twice). The mode function causes a StatisticsError for lists like

```
[85, 93, 45, 89, 85, 93]
```

in which there are two or more "most frequent" values. Such a set of values is said to be **bimodal**. Here, both 85 and 93 occur twice.

3.15 **Wrap-Up**

In this chapter, we discussed Python's control statements, including `if`, `if...else`, `if...elif...else`, `while`, `for`, `break` and `continue`. You saw that the `for` statement performs sequence-controlled iteration—it processes each item in an iterable, such as a range of integers, a string or a list. You used the built-in function `range` to generate sequences of integers from 0 up to, but not including, its argument, and to determine how many times a `for` statement iterates.

You used sentinel-controlled iteration with the `while` statement to create a loop that continues executing until a sentinel value is encountered. You used built-in function `range`'s two-argument version to generate sequences of integers from the first argument's value up to, but not including, the second argument's value. You also used the three-argument version in which the third argument indicated the step between integers in a range.

We introduced the `Decimal` type for precise monetary calculations and used it to calculate compound interest. You used f-strings and various format specifiers to create formatted output. We introduced the `break` and `continue` statements for altering the flow of control in loops. We discussed the Boolean operators `and`, `or` and `not` for creating conditions that combine simple conditions.

Finally, we continued our discussion of descriptive statistics by introducing measures of central tendency—mean, median and mode—and calculating them with functions from the Python Standard Library's `statistics` module.

In the next chapter, you'll create custom functions and use existing functions from Python's `math` and `random` modules. We show several predefined functional-programming reductions and you'll see additional functional-programming capabilities.

4

Functions

Objectives

In this chapter, you'll

- Create custom functions.
- Import and use Python Standard Library modules, such as random and math, to reuse code and avoid "reinventing the wheel."
- Pass data between functions.
- Generate a range of random numbers.
- See simulation techniques using random-number generation.
- Seed the random number generator to ensure reproducibility.
- Pack values into a tuple and unpack values from a tuple.
- Return multiple values from a function via a tuple.
- Understand how an identifier's scope determines where in your program you can use it.
- Create functions with default parameter values.
- Call functions with keyword arguments.
- Create functions that can receive any number of arguments.
- Use methods of an object.
- Write and use a recursive function.

4.1 Introduction

In this chapter, we continue our discussion of Python fundamentals with custom functions and related topics. We'll use the Python Standard Library's random module and random-number generation to simulate rolling a six-sided die. We'll combine custom functions and random-number generation in a script that implements the dice game craps. In that example, we'll also introduce Python's tuple sequence type and use tuples to return more than one value from a function. We'll discuss seeding the random number generator to ensure reproducibility.

You'll import the Python Standard Library's math module, then use it to learn about IPython tab completion, which speeds your coding and discovery processes. You'll create functions with default parameter values, call functions with keyword arguments and define functions with arbitrary argument lists. We'll demonstrate calling methods of objects. We'll also discuss how an identifier's scope determines where in your program you can use it.

We'll take a deeper look at importing modules. You'll see that arguments are passed-by-reference to functions. We'll also demonstrate a recursive function and begin presenting Python's functional-style programming capabilities.

In the Intro to Data Science section, we'll continue our discussion of descriptive statistics by introducing measures of dispersion—variance and standard deviation—and calculating them with functions from the Python Standard Library's statistics module.

4.2 Defining Functions

You've called many built-in functions (int, float, print, input, type, sum, len, min and max) and a few functions from the statistics module (mean, median and mode). Each performed a single, well-defined task. You'll often define and call *custom* functions. The following session defines a square function that calculates the square of its argument. Then it calls the function twice—once to square the int value 7 (producing the int value 49) and once to square the float value 2.5 (producing the float value 6.25):

```
In [1]: def square(number):
   ...:     """Calculate the square of number."""
   ...:     return number ** 2
   ...:

In [2]: square(7)
Out[2]: 49

In [3]: square(2.5)
Out[3]: 6.25
```

The statements defining the function in the first snippet are written only once, but may be called "to do their job" from many points throughout a program and as often as you like. Calling `square` with a non-numeric argument like `'hello'` causes a `TypeError` because the exponentiation operator (`**`) works only with numeric values.

Defining a Custom Function

A **function definition** (like `square` in snippet [1]) begins with the **def keyword**, followed by the function name (`square`), a set of parentheses and a colon (`:`). Like variable identifiers, by convention function names should begin with a lowercase letter and in multiword names underscores should separate each word.

The required parentheses contain the function's **parameter list**—a comma-separated list of **parameters** representing the data that the function needs to perform its task. Function `square` has only one parameter named `number`—the value to be squared. If the parentheses are empty, the function does not use parameters to perform its task.

The indented lines after the colon (`:`) are the function's **block**, which consists of an optional docstring followed by the statements that perform the function's task. We'll soon point out the difference between a function's block and a control statement's suite.

Specifying a Custom Function's Docstring

The *Style Guide for Python Code* says that the first line in a function's block should be a docstring that briefly explains the function's purpose:

```
"""Calculate the square of number."""
```

To provide more detail, you can use a multiline docstring—the style guide recommends starting with a brief explanation, followed by a blank line and the additional details.

Returning a Result to a Function's Caller

When a function finishes executing, it returns control to its caller—that is, the line of code that called the function. In `square`'s block, the **return** statement:

```
return number ** 2
```

first squares `number`, then terminates the function and gives the result back to the caller. In this example, the first caller is in snippet [2], so IPython displays the result in `Out[2]`. The second caller is in snippet [3], so IPython displays the result in `Out[3]`.

Function calls also can be embedded in expressions. The following code calls `square` first, then `print` displays the result:

```
In [4]: print('The square of 7 is', square(7))
The square of 7 is 49
```

There are two other ways to return control from a function to its caller:

- Executing a `return` statement without an expression terminates the function and *implicitly* returns the value **None** to the caller. The Python documentation states that None represents the absence of a value. None evaluates to `False` in conditions.

- When there's no `return` statement in a function, it *implicitly* returns the value None after executing the last statement in the function's block.

Local Variables

Though we did not define variables in `square`'s block, it is possible to do so. A function's parameters and variables defined in its block are all **local variables**—they can be used only inside the function and exist only while the function is executing. Trying to access a local variable outside its function's block causes a `NameError`, indicating that the variable is not defined.

Accessing a Function's Docstring via IPython's Help Mechanism

IPython can help you learn about the modules and functions you intend to use in your code, as well as IPython itself. For example, to view a function's docstring to learn how to use the function, type the function's name followed by a **question mark (?)**:

```
In [5]: square?
Signature: square(number)
Docstring: Calculate the square of number.
File:      ~/Documents/examples/ch04/<ipython-input-1-7268c8ff93a9>
Type:      function
```

For our `square` function, the information displayed includes:

- The function's name and parameter list—known as its **signature**.

- The function's docstring.

- The name of the file containing the function's definition. For a function in an interactive session, this line shows information for the snippet that defined the function—the 1 in `"<ipython-input-1-7268c8ff93a9>"` means snippet [1].

- The type of the item for which you accessed IPython's help mechanism—in this case, a function.

If the function's source code is accessible from IPython—such as a function defined in the current session or imported into the session from a `.py` file—you can use **??** to display the function's full source-code definition:

```
In [6]: square??
Signature: square(number)
Source:
def square(number):
    """Calculate the square of number."""
    return number ** 2
File:      ~/Documents/examples/ch04/<ipython-input-1-7268c8ff93a9>
Type:      function
```

If the source code is not accessible from IPython, ?? simply shows the docstring.

If the docstring fits in the window, IPython displays the next In [] prompt. If a docstring is too long to fit, IPython indicates that there's more by displaying a colon (:) at the bottom of the window—press the *Space* key to display the next screen. You can navigate backwards and forwards through the docstring with the up and down arrow keys, respectively. IPython displays (END) at the end of the docstring. Press *q* (for "quit") at any : or the (END) prompt to return to the next In [] prompt. To get a sense of IPython's features, type ? at any In [] prompt, press *Enter*, then read the help documentation overview.

4.3 Functions with Multiple Parameters

Let's define a maximum function that determines and returns the largest of three values— the following session calls the function three times with integers, floating-point numbers and strings, respectively.

```
In [1]: def maximum(value1, value2, value3):
   ...:     """Return the maximum of three values."""
   ...:     max_value = value1
   ...:     if value2 > max_value:
   ...:         max_value = value2
   ...:     if value3 > max_value:
   ...:         max_value = value3
   ...:     return max_value
   ...:

In [2]: maximum(12, 27, 36)
Out[2]: 36

In [3]: maximum(12.3, 45.6, 9.7)
Out[3]: 45.6

In [4]: maximum('yellow', 'red', 'orange')
Out[4]: 'yellow'
```

We did not place blank lines above and below the if statements, because pressing return on a blank line in interactive mode completes the function's definition.

You also may call maximum with mixed types, such as ints and floats:

```
In [5]: maximum(13.5, -3, 7)
Out[5]: 13.5
```

The call maximum(13.5, 'hello', 7) results in TypeError because strings and numbers cannot be compared to one another with the greater-than (>) operator.

Function maximum's Definition

Function maximum specifies three parameters in a comma-separated list. Snippet [2]'s arguments 12, 27 and 36 are assigned to the parameters value1, value2 and value3, respectively.

To determine the largest value, we process one value at a time:

- Initially, we assume that value1 contains the largest value, so we assign it to the local variable max_value. Of course, it's possible that value2 or value3 contains the actual largest value, so we still must compare each of these with max_value.

- The first if statement then tests value2 > max_value, and if this condition is True assigns value2 to max_value.

- The second if statement then tests value3 > max_value, and if this condition is True assigns value3 to max_value.

Now, max_value contains the largest value, so we return it. When control returns to the caller, the parameters value1, value2 and value3 and the variable max_value in the function's block—which are all *local variables*—no longer exist.

Python's Built-In max and min Functions

For many common tasks, the capabilities you need already exist in Python. For example, built-in **max** and **min** functions know how to determine the largest and smallest of their two or more arguments, respectively:

```
In [6]: max('yellow', 'red', 'orange', 'blue', 'green')
Out[6]: 'yellow'

In [7]: min(15, 9, 27, 14)
Out[7]: 9
```

Each of these functions also can receive an iterable argument, such as a list or a string. Using built-in functions or functions from the Python Standard Library's modules rather than writing your own can reduce development time and increase program reliability, portability and performance. For a list of Python's built-in functions and modules, see

```
https://docs.python.org/3/library/index.html
```

4.4 Random-Number Generation

We now take a brief diversion into a popular type of programming application—simulation and game playing. You can introduce the **element of chance** via the Python Standard Library's **random module**.

Rolling a Six-Sided Die

Let's produce 10 random integers in the range 1–6 to simulate rolling a six-sided die:

```
In [1]: import random

In [2]: for roll in range(10):
   ...:     print(random.randrange(1, 7), end=' ')
   ...:
4 2 5 5 4 6 4 6 1 5
```

First, we import random so we can use the module's capabilities. The **randrange** function generates an integer from the first argument value up to, but *not* including, the second argument value. Let's use the up arrow key to recall the for statement, then press *Enter* to re-execute it. Notice that *different* values are displayed:

```
In [3]: for roll in range(10):
   ...:     print(random.randrange(1, 7), end=' ')
   ...:
4 5 4 5 1 4 1 4 6 5
```

Sometimes, you may want to guarantee **reproducibility** of a random sequence—for debugging, for example. At the end of this section, we'll use the random module's seed function to do this.

Rolling a Six-Sided Die 6,000,000 Times

If randrange truly produces integers at random, every number in its range has an equal **probability** (or *chance* or *likelihood*) of being returned each time we call it. To show that the die faces 1–6 occur with equal likelihood, the following script simulates 6,000,000 die rolls. When you run the script, each die face should occur approximately 1,000,000 times, as in the sample output.

```python
1   # fig04_01.py
2   """Roll a six-sided die 6,000,000 times."""
3   import random
4
5   # face frequency counters
6   frequency1 = 0
7   frequency2 = 0
8   frequency3 = 0
9   frequency4 = 0
10  frequency5 = 0
11  frequency6 = 0
12
13  # 6,000,000 die rolls
14  for roll in range(6_000_000):  # note underscore separators
15      face = random.randrange(1, 7)
16
17      # increment appropriate face counter
18      if face == 1:
19          frequency1 += 1
20      elif face == 2:
21          frequency2 += 1
22      elif face == 3:
23          frequency3 += 1
24      elif face == 4:
25          frequency4 += 1
26      elif face == 5:
27          frequency5 += 1
28      elif face == 6:
29          frequency6 += 1
30
31  print(f'Face{"Frequency":>13}')
32  print(f'{1:>4}{frequency1:>13}')
33  print(f'{2:>4}{frequency2:>13}')
34  print(f'{3:>4}{frequency3:>13}')
35  print(f'{4:>4}{frequency4:>13}')
36  print(f'{5:>4}{frequency5:>13}')
37  print(f'{6:>4}{frequency6:>13}')
```

```
Face    Frequency
   1       998686
   2      1001481
   3       999900
   4      1000453
   5       999953
   6       999527
```

The script uses *nested* control statements (an if...elif statement nested in the for statement) to determine the number of times each die face appears. The for statement iterates 6,000,000 times. We used Python's underscore (_) digit separator to make the value 6000000 more readable. The expression range(6,000,000) would be incorrect.

Commas separate arguments in function calls, so Python would treat `range(6,000,000)` as a call to `range` with the *three* arguments 6, 0 and 0.

For each die roll, the script adds 1 to the appropriate counter variable. Run the program, and observe the results. This program might take a few seconds to complete execution. As you'll see, each execution produces *different* results. Note that we did not provide an `else` clause in the `if...elif` statement.

Seeding the Random-Number Generator for Reproducibility

Function `randrange` actually generates **pseudorandom numbers**, based on an internal calculation that begins with a numeric value known as a **seed**. Repeatedly calling `randrange` produces a sequence of numbers that *appear* to be random, because each time you start a new interactive session or execute a script that uses the `random` module's functions, Python internally uses a *different* seed value.[1] When you're debugging logic errors in programs that use randomly generated data, it can be helpful to use the *same* sequence of random numbers until you've eliminated the logic errors, before testing the program with other values. To do this, you can use the `random` module's **seed** function to **seed the random-number generator** yourself—this forces `randrange` to begin calculating its pseudorandom number sequence from the seed you specify. In the following session, snippets [5] and [8] produce the same results, because snippets [4] and [7] use the same seed (32):

```
In [4]: random.seed(32)

In [5]: for roll in range(10):
   ...:     print(random.randrange(1, 7), end=' ')
   ...:
1 2 2 3 6 2 4 1 6 1
In [6]: for roll in range(10):
   ...:     print(random.randrange(1, 7), end=' ')
   ...:
1 3 5 3 1 5 6 4 3 5
In [7]: random.seed(32)

In [8]: for roll in range(10):
   ...:     print(random.randrange(1, 7), end=' ')
   ...:
1 2 2 3 6 2 4 1 6 1
```

Snippet [6] generates *different* values because it simply continues the pseudorandom number sequence that began in snippet [5].

4.5 Case Study: A Game of Chance

In this section, we simulate the popular dice game known as "craps." Here is the requirements statement:

> *You roll two six-sided dice, each with faces containing one, two, three, four, five and six spots, respectively. When the dice come to rest, the sum of the spots on the two upward faces is calculated. If the sum is 7 or 11 on the first roll, you win. If*

---

1. According to the documentation, Python bases the seed value on the system clock or an operating-system-dependent randomness source. For applications requiring secure random numbers, such as cryptography, the documentation recommends using the `secrets` module, rather than the `random` module.

*the sum is 2, 3 or 12 on the first roll (called "craps"), you lose (i.e., the "house"
wins). If the sum is 4, 5, 6, 8, 9 or 10 on the first roll, that sum becomes your
"point." To win, you must continue rolling the dice until you "make your point"
(i.e., roll that same point value). You lose by rolling a 7 before making your point.*

The following script simulates the game and shows several sample executions, illustrating
winning on the first roll, losing on the first roll, winning on a subsequent roll and losing
on a subsequent roll.

```
 1  # fig04_02.py
 2  """Simulating the dice game Craps."""
 3  import random
 4
 5  def roll_dice():
 6      """Roll two dice and return their face values as a tuple."""
 7      die1 = random.randrange(1, 7)
 8      die2 = random.randrange(1, 7)
 9      return (die1, die2)  # pack die face values into a tuple
10
11  def display_dice(dice):
12      """Display one roll of the two dice."""
13      die1, die2 = dice  # unpack the tuple into variables die1 and die2
14      print(f'Player rolled {die1} + {die2} = {sum(dice)}')
15
16  die_values = roll_dice()  # first roll
17  display_dice(die_values)
18
19  # determine game status and point, based on first roll
20  sum_of_dice = sum(die_values)
21
22  if sum_of_dice in (7, 11):  # win
23      game_status = 'WON'
24  elif sum_of_dice in (2, 3, 12):  # lose
25      game_status = 'LOST'
26  else:  # remember point
27      game_status = 'CONTINUE'
28      my_point = sum_of_dice
29      print('Point is', my_point)
30
31  # continue rolling until player wins or loses
32  while game_status == 'CONTINUE':
33      die_values = roll_dice()
34      display_dice(die_values)
35      sum_of_dice = sum(die_values)
36
37      if sum_of_dice == my_point:  # win by making point
38          game_status = 'WON'
39      elif sum_of_dice == 7:  # lose by rolling 7
40          game_status = 'LOST'
41
42  # display "wins" or "loses" message
43  if game_status == 'WON':
44      print('Player wins')
45  else:
46      print('Player loses')
```

```
Player rolled 2 + 5 = 7
Player wins
```

```
Player rolled 1 + 2 = 3
Player loses
```

```
Player rolled 5 + 4 = 9
Point is 9
Player rolled 4 + 4 = 8
Player rolled 2 + 3 = 5
Player rolled 5 + 4 = 9
Player wins
```

```
Player rolled 1 + 5 = 6
Point is 6
Player rolled 1 + 6 = 7
Player loses
```

Function roll_dice—Returning Multiple Values Via a Tuple

Function roll_dice (lines 5–9) simulates rolling two dice on each roll. The function is defined once, then called from several places in the program (lines 16 and 33). The empty parameter list indicates that roll_dice does not require arguments to perform its task.

The built-in and custom functions you've called so far each return one value. Sometimes it's useful to return more than one value, as in roll_dice, which returns both die values (line 9) as a **tuple**—an **immutable** (that is, unmodifiable) sequences of values. To create a tuple, separate its values with commas, as in line 9:

    (die1, die2)

This is known as **packing a tuple**. The parentheses are optional, but we recommend using them for clarity. We discuss tuples in depth in the next chapter.

Function display_dice

To use a tuple's values, you can assign them to a comma-separated list of variables, which **unpacks** the tuple. To display each roll of the dice, the function display_dice (defined in lines 11–14 and called in lines 17 and 34) unpacks the tuple argument it receives (line 13). The number of variables to the left of = must match the number of elements in the tuple; otherwise, a ValueError occurs. Line 14 prints a formatted string containing both die values and their sum. We calculate the sum of the dice by passing the tuple to the built-in sum function—like a list, a tuple is a sequence.

Note that functions roll_dice and display_dice each begin their blocks with a docstring that states what the function does. Also, both functions contain local variables die1 and die2. These variables do not "collide," because they belong to different functions' blocks. Each local variable is accessible only in the block that defined it.

First Roll

When the script begins executing, lines 16–17 roll the dice and display the results. Line 20 calculates the sum of the dice for use in lines 22–29. You can win or lose on the first roll or any subsequent roll. The variable game_status keeps track of the win/loss status.

The **in operator** in line 22

```
sum_of_dice in (7, 11)
```

tests whether the tuple (7, 11) contains sum_of_dice's value. If this condition is True, you rolled a 7 or an 11. In this case, you won on the first roll, so the script sets game_status to 'WON'. The operator's right operand can be any iterable. There's also a **not in** operator to determine whether a value is *not* in an iterable. The preceding concise condition is equivalent to

```
(sum_of_dice == 7) or (sum_of_dice == 11)
```

Similarly, the condition in line 24

```
sum_of_dice in (2, 3, 12)
```

tests whether the tuple (2, 3, 12) contains sum_of_dice's value. If so, you lost on the first roll, so the script sets game_status to 'LOST'.

For any other sum of the dice (4, 5, 6, 8, 9 or 10):

- line 27 sets game_status to 'CONTINUE' so you can continue rolling
- line 28 stores the sum of the dice in my_point to keep track of what you must roll to win and
- line 29 displays my_point.

Subsequent Rolls

If game_status is equal to 'CONTINUE' (line 32), you did not win or lose, so the while statement's suite (lines 33–40) executes. Each loop iteration calls roll_dice, displays the die values and calculates their sum. If sum_of_dice is equal to my_point (line 37) or 7 (line 39), the script sets game_status to 'WON' or 'LOST', respectively, and the loop terminates. Otherwise, the while loop continues executing with the next roll.

Displaying the Final Results

When the loop terminates, the script proceeds to the if...else statement (lines 43–46), which prints 'Player wins' if game_status is 'WON', or 'Player loses' otherwise.

4.6 Python Standard Library

Typically, you write Python programs by combining functions and classes (that is, custom types) that you create with preexisting functions and classes defined in modules, such as those in the Python Standard Library and other libraries. A key programming goal is to avoid "reinventing the wheel."

A module is a file that groups related functions, data and classes. The type Decimal from the Python Standard Library's decimal module is actually a class. We introduced classes briefly in Chapter 1 and discuss them in detail in the "Object-Oriented Programming" chapter. A **package** groups related modules. In this book, you'll work with many preexisting modules and packages, and you'll create your own modules—in fact, every

Python source-code (.py) file you create is a module. Creating packages is beyond this book's scope. They're typically used to organize a large library's functionality into smaller subsets that are easier to maintain and can be imported separately for convenience. For example, the matplotlib visualization library that we use in Section 5.17 has extensive functionality (its documentation is over 2300 pages), so we'll import only the subsets we need in our examples (pyplot and animation).

The Python Standard Library is provided with the core Python language. Its packages and modules contain capabilities for a wide variety of everyday programming tasks.[2] You can see a complete list of the standard library modules at

> https://docs.python.org/3/library/

You've already used capabilities from the decimal, statistics and random modules. In the next section, you'll use mathematics capabilities from the math module. You'll see many other Python Standard Library modules throughout the book's examples, including many of those in the following table:

Some popular Python Standard Library modules	
collections—Data structures beyond lists, tuples, dictionaries and sets.	math—Common math constants and operations.
Cryptography modules—Encrypting data for secure transmission.	os—Interacting with the operating system.
	profile, pstats, timeit—Performance analysis.
csv—Processing comma-separated value files (like those in Excel).	random—Pseudorandom numbers.
	re—Regular expressions for pattern matching.
datetime—Date and time manipulations. Also modules time and calendar.	sqlite3—SQLite relational database access.
	statistics—Mathematical statistics functions such as mean, median, mode and variance.
decimal—Fixed-point and floating-point arithmetic, including monetary calculations.	string—String processing.
doctest—Embed validation tests and expected results in docstrings for simple unit testing.	sys—Command-line argument processing; standard input, standard output and standard error streams.
gettext and locale—Internationalization and localization modules.	tkinter—Graphical user interfaces (GUIs) and canvas-based graphics.
json—JavaScript Object Notation (JSON) processing used with web services and NoSQL document databases.	turtle—Turtle graphics.
	webbrowser—For conveniently displaying web pages in Python apps.

4.7 math Module Functions

The **math module** defines functions for performing various common mathematical calculations. Recall from the previous chapter that an import statement of the following form enables you to use a module's definitions via the module's name and a dot (.):

```
In [1]: import math
```

For example, the following snippet calculates the square root of 900 by calling the math module's **sqrt function**, which returns its result as a float value:

```
In [2]: math.sqrt(900)
Out[2]: 30.0
```

---

2. The Python Tutorial refers to this as the "batteries included" approach.

Similarly, the following snippet calculates the absolute value of -10 by calling the `math` module's **fabs function**, which returns its result as a `float` value:

```
In [3]: math.fabs(-10)
Out[3]: 10.0
```

Some math module functions are summarized below—you can view the complete list at

`https://docs.python.org/3/library/math.html`

Function	Description	Example
`ceil(x)`	Rounds x to the smallest integer not less than x	`ceil(9.2)` is 10.0 `ceil(-9.8)` is -9.0
`floor(x)`	Rounds x to the largest integer not greater than x	`floor(9.2)` is 9.0 `floor(-9.8)` is -10.0
`sin(x)`	Trigonometric sine of x (x in radians)	`sin(0.0)` is 0.0
`cos(x)`	Trigonometric cosine of x (x in radians)	`cos(0.0)` is 1.0
`tan(x)`	Trigonometric tangent of x (x in radians)	`tan(0.0)` is 0.0
`exp(x)`	Exponential function e^x	`exp(1.0)` is 2.718282 `exp(2.0)` is 7.389056
`log(x)`	Natural logarithm of x (base e)	`log(2.718282)` is 1.0 `log(7.389056)` is 2.0
`log10(x)`	Logarithm of x (base 10)	`log10(10.0)` is 1.0 `log10(100.0)` is 2.0
`pow(x, y)`	x raised to power y (x^y)	`pow(2.0, 7.0)` is 128.0 `pow(9.0, .5)` is 3.0
`sqrt(x)`	square root of x	`sqrt(900.0)` is 30.0 `sqrt(9.0)` is 3.0
`fabs(x)`	Absolute value of x—always returns a float. Python also has the built-in function `abs`, which returns an `int` or a `float`, based on its argument.	`fabs(5.1)` is 5.1 `fabs(-5.1)` is 5.1
`fmod(x, y)`	Remainder of x/y as a floating-point number	`fmod(9.8, 4.0)` is 1.8

4.8 Using IPython Tab Completion for Discovery

You can view a module's documentation in IPython interactive mode via **tab completion**—a **discovery** feature that speeds your coding and discovery processes. After you type a portion of an identifier and press *Tab*, IPython completes the identifier for you or provides a list of identifiers that begin with what you've typed so far. This may vary based on your operating system platform and what you have imported into your IPython session:

```
In [1]: import math

In [2]: ma<Tab>
          map           %macro        %%markdown
          math          %magic        %%matplotlib
          max()         %man
```

You can scroll through the identifiers with the up and down arrow keys. As you do, IPython highlights an identifier and shows it to the right of the In [] prompt.

Viewing Identifiers in a Module

To view a list of identifiers defined in a module, type the module's name and a dot (.), then press *Tab*:

```
In [3]: math.<Tab>
        acos()     atan()     copysign()   e       expm1()
        acosh()    atan2()    cos()        erf()   fabs()
        asin()     atanh()    cosh()       erfc()  factorial() >
        asinh()    ceil()     degrees()    exp()   floor()
```

If there are more identifiers to display than are currently shown, IPython displays the > symbol (on some platforms) at the right edge, in this case to the right of factorial(). You can use the up and down arrow keys to scroll through the list. In the list of identifiers:

- Those followed by parentheses are functions (or methods, as you'll see later).

- Single-word identifiers (such as Employee) that begin with an uppercase letter and multiword identifiers in which each word begins with an uppercase letter (such as CommissionEmployee) represent class names (there are none in the preceding list). This naming convention, which the *Style Guide for Python Code* recommends, is known as **CamelCase** because the uppercase letters stand out like a camel's humps.

- Lowercase identifiers without parentheses, such as pi (not shown in the preceding list) and e, are variables. The identifier pi evaluates to 3.141592653589793, and the identifier e evaluates to 2.718281828459045. In the math module, pi and e represent the mathematical constants π and *e*, respectively.

Python does not have *constants*, although many objects in Python are immutable (non-modifiable). So even though pi and e are real-world constants, *you must not assign new values to them*, because that would change their values. To help distinguish constants from other variables, the style guide recommends naming your custom constants with all capital letters.

Using the Currently Highlighted Function

As you navigate through the identifiers, if you wish to use a currently highlighted function, simply start typing its arguments in parentheses. IPython then hides the autocompletion list. If you need more information about the currently highlighted item, you can view its docstring by typing a question mark (?) following the name and pressing *Enter* to view the help documentation. The following shows the fabs function's docstring:

```
In [4]: math.fabs?
Docstring:
fabs(x)

Return the absolute value of the float x.
Type:      builtin_function_or_method
```

The builtin_function_or_method shown above indicates that fabs is part of a Python Standard Library module. Such modules are considered to be built into Python. In this case, fabs is a built-in function from the math module.

4.9 Default Parameter Values

When defining a function, you can specify that a parameter has a **default parameter value**. When calling the function, if you omit the argument for a parameter with a default parameter value, the default value for that parameter is automatically passed. Let's define a function `rectangle_area` with default parameter values:

```
In [1]: def rectangle_area(length=2, width=3):
   ...:         """Return a rectangle's area."""
   ...:         return length * width
   ...:
```

You specify a default parameter value by following a parameter's name with an = and a value—in this case, the default parameter values are 2 and 3 for `length` and `width`, respectively. Any parameters with default parameter values must appear in the parameter list to the *right* of parameters that do not have defaults.

The following call to `rectangle_area` has no arguments, so IPython uses both default parameter values as if you had called `rectangle_area(2, 3)`:

```
In [2]: rectangle_area()
Out[2]: 6
```

The following call to `rectangle_area` has only one argument. Arguments are assigned to parameters from left to right, so 10 is used as the `length`. The interpreter passes the default parameter value 3 for the `width` as if you had called `rectangle_area(10, 3)`:

```
In [3]: rectangle_area(10)
Out[3]: 30
```

The following call to `rectangle_area` has arguments for both `length` and `width`, so IPython ignores the default parameter values:

```
In [4]: rectangle_area(10, 5)
Out[4]: 50
```

4.10 Keyword Arguments

When calling functions, you can use **keyword arguments** to pass arguments in *any* order. To demonstrate keyword arguments, we redefine the `rectangle_area` function—this time without default parameter values:

```
In [1]: def rectangle_area(length, width):
   ...:         """Return a rectangle's area."""
   ...:         return length * width
   ...:
```

Each keyword *argument in a call* has the form *parametername=value*. The following call shows that the order of keyword arguments does not matter—they do not need to match the corresponding parameters' positions in the function definition:

```
In [2]: rectangle_area(width=5, length=10)
Out[3]: 50
```

In each function call, you must place keyword arguments *after* a function's positional arguments—that is, any arguments for which you do not specify the parameter name. Such arguments are assigned to the function's parameters left-to-right, based on the argument's positions in the argument list. Keyword arguments are also helpful for improving the readability of function calls, especially for functions with many arguments.

4.11 Arbitrary Argument Lists

Functions with **arbitrary argument lists**, such as built-in functions min and max, can receive *any* number of arguments. Consider the following min call:

```
min(88, 75, 96, 55, 83)
```

The function's documentation states that min has two *required* parameters (named arg1 and arg2) and an optional third parameter of the form ***args**, indicating that the function can receive any number of additional arguments. The * before the parameter name tells Python to pack any remaining arguments into a tuple that's passed to the args parameter. In the call above, parameter arg1 receives 88, parameter arg2 receives 75 and parameter args receives the tuple (96, 55, 83).

Defining a Function with an Arbitrary Argument List
Let's define an average function that can receive any number of arguments:

```
In [1]: def average(*args):
   ...:     return sum(args) / len(args)
   ...:
```

The parameter name args is used by convention, but you may use any identifier. If the function has multiple parameters, the *args parameter must be the *rightmost* parameter.
Now, let's call average several times with arbitrary argument lists of different lengths:

```
In [2]: average(5, 10)
Out[2]: 7.5

In [3]: average(5, 10, 15)
Out[3]: 10.0

In [4]: average(5, 10, 15, 20)
Out[4]: 12.5
```

To calculate the average, divide the sum of the args tuple's elements (returned by built-in function sum) by the tuple's number of elements (returned by built-in function len). Note in our average definition that if the length of args is 0, a ZeroDivisionError occurs. In the next chapter, you'll see how to access a tuple's elements without unpacking them.

Passing an Iterable's Individual Elements as Function Arguments
You can unpack a tuple's, list's or other iterable's elements to pass them as individual function arguments. The *** operator**, when applied to an iterable argument in a function call, unpacks its elements. The following code creates a five-element grades list, then uses the expression *grades to unpack its elements as average's arguments:

```
In [5]: grades = [88, 75, 96, 55, 83]

In [6]: average(*grades)
Out[6]: 79.4
```

The call shown above is equivalent to average(88, 75, 96, 55, 83).

4.12 Methods: Functions That Belong to Objects

A **method** is simply a function that you call on an object using the form

> *object_name*.*method_name*(*arguments*)

For example, the following session creates the string variable s and assigns it the string object 'Hello'. Then the session calls the object's **lower** and **upper** methods, which produce *new* strings containing all-lowercase and all-uppercase versions of the original string, leaving s unchanged:

```
In [1]: s = 'Hello'

In [2]: s.lower()  # call lower method on string object s
Out[2]: 'hello'

In [3]: s.upper()
Out[3]: 'HELLO'

In [4]: s
Out[4]: 'Hello'
```

The *Python Standard Library* reference at

> https://docs.python.org/3/library/index.html

describes the methods of built-in types and the types in the Python Standard Library. In the "Object-Oriented Programming" chapter, you'll create *custom* types called classes and define custom methods that you can call on objects of those classes.

4.13 Scope Rules

Each identifier has a **scope** that determines where you can use it in your program. For that portion of the program, the identifier is said to be "in scope."

Local Scope
A local variable's identifier has **local scope**. It's "in scope" only from its definition to the end of the function's block. It "goes out of scope" when the function returns to its caller. So, a local variable can be used only inside the function that defines it.

Global Scope
Identifiers defined outside any function (or class) have **global scope**—these may include functions, variables and classes. Variables with global scope are known as **global variables**. Identifiers with global scope can be used in a .py file or interactive session anywhere after they're defined.

Accessing a Global Variable from a Function
You can access a global variable's value inside a function:

```
In [1]: x = 7

In [2]: def access_global():
   ...:         print('x printed from access_global:', x)
   ...:

In [3]: access_global()
x printed from access_global: 7
```

However, by default, you cannot *modify* a global variable in a function—when you first assign a value to a variable in a function's block, Python creates a *new* local variable:

```
In [4]: def try_to_modify_global():
   ...:     x = 3.5
   ...:     print('x printed from try_to_modify_global:', x)
   ...:

In [5]: try_to_modify_global()
x printed from try_to_modify_global: 3.5

In [6]: x
Out[6]: 7
```

In function try_to_modify_global's block, the local x **shadows** the global x, making it inaccessible in the scope of the function's block. Snippet [6] shows that global variable x still exists and has its original value (7) after function try_to_modify_global executes.

To modify a global variable in a function's block, you must use a **global** statement to declare that the variable is defined in the global scope:

```
In [7]: def modify_global():
   ...:     global x
   ...:     x = 'hello'
   ...:     print('x printed from modify_global:', x)
   ...:

In [8]: modify_global()
x printed from modify_global: hello

In [9]: x
Out[9]: 'hello'
```

Blocks vs. Suites

You've now defined function *blocks* and control statement *suites*. When you create a variable in a block, it's *local* to that block. However, when you create a variable in a control statement's suite, the variable's scope depends on where the control statement is defined:

- If the control statement is in the global scope, then any variables defined in the control statement have global scope.

- If the control statement is in a function's block, then any variables defined in the control statement have local scope.

We'll continue our scope discussion in the "Object-Oriented Programming" chapter when we introduce custom classes.

Shadowing Functions

In the preceding chapters, when summing values, we stored the sum in a variable named total. The reason we did this is that sum is a built-in function. If you define a variable named sum, it *shadows* the built-in function, making it inaccessible in your code. When you execute the following assignment, Python binds the identifier sum to the int object containing 15. At this point, the identifier sum no longer references the built-in function. So, when you try to use sum as a function, a TypeError occurs:

```
In [10]: sum = 10 + 5
```

```
In [11]: sum
Out[11]: 15

In [12]: sum([10, 5])
-----------------------------------------------------------------------
TypeError                                Traceback (most recent call last)
<ipython-input-12-1237d97a65fb> in <module>()
----> 1 sum([10, 5])

TypeError: 'int' object is not callable
```

Statements at Global Scope

In the scripts you've seen so far, we've written some statements outside functions at the global scope and some statements inside function blocks. Script statements at global scope execute as soon as they're encountered by the interpreter, whereas statements in a block execute only when the function is called.

4.14 import: A Deeper Look

You've imported modules (such as math and random) with a statement like:

> import *module_name*

then accessed their features via each module's name and a dot (.). Also, you've imported a specific identifier from a module (such as the decimal module's Decimal type) with a statement like:

> from *module_name* import *identifier*

then used that identifier without having to precede it with the module name and a dot (.).

Importing Multiple Identifiers from a Module

Using the from...import statement you can import a comma-separated list of identifiers from a module then use them in your code without having to precede them with the module name and a dot (.):

```
In [1]: from math import ceil, floor

In [2]: ceil(10.3)
Out[2]: 11

In [3]: floor(10.7)
Out[3]: 10
```

Trying to use a function that's not imported causes a NameError, indicating that the name is not defined.

Caution: Avoid Wildcard Imports

You can import *all* identifiers defined in a module with a **wildcard import** of the form

> from *modulename* import *

This makes all of the module's identifiers available for use in your code. Importing a module's identifiers with a wildcard import can lead to subtle errors—it's considered a dangerous practice that you should avoid. Consider the following snippets:

```
In [4]: e = 'hello'

In [5]: from math import *

In [6]: e
Out[6]: 2.718281828459045
```

Initially, we assign the string `'hello'` to a variable named e. After executing snippet [5] though, the variable e is replaced, possibly by accident, with the math module's constant e, representing the mathematical floating-point value *e*.

Binding Names for Modules and Module Identifiers

Sometimes it's helpful to import a module and use an abbreviation for it to simplify your code. The `import` statement's **as** clause allows you to specify the name used to reference the module's identifiers. For example, in Section 3.14 we could have imported the statistics module and accessed its mean function as follows:

```
In [7]: import statistics as stats

In [8]: grades = [85, 93, 45, 87, 93]

In [9]: stats.mean(grades)
Out[9]: 80.6
```

As you'll see in later chapters, import...as is frequently used to import Python libraries with convenient abbreviations, like stats for the `statistics` module. As another example, we'll use the numpy module which typically is imported with

```
import numpy as np
```

Library documentation often mentions popular shorthand names.

Typically, when importing a module, you should use `import` or `import...as` statements, then access the module through the module name or the abbreviation following the as keyword, respectively. This ensures that you do not accidentally import an identifier that conflicts with one in your code.

4.15 Passing Arguments to Functions: A Deeper Look

Let's take a closer look at how arguments are passed to functions. In many programming languages, there are two ways to pass arguments—**pass-by-value** and **pass-by-reference** (sometimes called **call-by-value** and **call-by-reference**, respectively):

- With pass-by-value, the called function receives a *copy* of the argument's *value* and works exclusively with that copy. Changes to the function's copy do *not* affect the original variable's value in the caller.

- With pass-by-reference, the called function can access the argument's value in the caller directly and modify the value if it's mutable.

Python arguments are always passed by reference. Some people call this **pass-by-object-reference**, because "everything in Python is an object."[3] When a function call provides an argument, Python copies the argument object's *reference*—not the object itself—into the

---

3. Even the functions you defined in this chapter and the classes (custom types) you'll define in later chapters are objects in Python.

corresponding parameter. This is important for performance. Functions often manipulate large objects—frequently copying them would consume large amounts of computer memory and significantly slow program performance.

Memory Addresses, References and "Pointers"

You interact with an object via a reference, which behind the scenes is that object's address (or location) in the computer's memory—sometimes called a "pointer" in other languages. After an assignment like

```
x = 7
```

the variable x does not actually contain the value 7. Rather, it contains a reference to an *object* containing 7 stored *elsewhere* in memory. You might say that x "points to" (that is, references) the object containing 7, as in the diagram below:

Built-In Function id and Object Identities

Let's consider how we pass arguments to functions. First, let's create the integer variable x mentioned above—shortly we'll use x as a function argument:

```
In [1]: x = 7
```

Now x refers to (or "points to") the integer object containing 7. No two separate objects can reside at the same address in memory, so every object in memory has a *unique address*. Though we can't see an object's address, we can use the built-in **id function** to obtain a *unique* int value which identifies only that object while it remains in memory (you'll likely get a different value when you run this on your computer):

```
In [2]: id(x)
Out[2]: 4350477840
```

The integer result of calling id is known as the object's **identity**.[4] No two objects in memory can have the same *identity*. We'll use object identities to demonstrate that objects are passed by reference.

Passing an Object to a Function

Let's define a cube function that displays its parameter's identity, then returns the parameter's value cubed:

```
In [3]: def cube(number):
   ...:     print('id(number):', id(number))
   ...:     return number ** 3
   ...:
```

Next, let's call cube with the argument x, which refers to the integer object containing 7:

```
In [4]: cube(x)
id(number): 4350477840
Out[4]: 343
```

---

4. According to the Python documentation, depending on the Python implementation you're using, an object's identity may be the object's actual memory address, but this is not required.

The identity displayed for cube's parameter number—4350477840—is the *same* as that displayed for x previously. Since every object has a unique identity, both the *argument* x and the *parameter* number refer to the *same object* while cube executes. So when function cube uses its parameter number in its calculation, it gets the value of number from the original object in the caller.

Testing Object Identities with the is Operator

You also can prove that the argument and the parameter refer to the same object with Python's **is operator**, which returns True if its two operands have the *same identity*:

```
In [5]: def cube(number):
   ...:     print('number is x:', number is x)   # x is a global variable
   ...:     return number ** 3
   ...:

In [6]: cube(x)
number is x: True
Out[6]: 343
```

Immutable Objects as Arguments

When a function receives as an argument a reference to an *immutable* (unmodifiable) object—such as an int, float, string or tuple—even though you have direct access to the original object in the caller, you cannot modify the original immutable object's value. To prove this, first let's have cube display id(number) before and after assigning a new object to the parameter number via an augmented assignment:

```
In [7]: def cube(number):
   ...:     print('id(number) before modifying number:', id(number))
   ...:     number **= 3
   ...:     print('id(number) after modifying number:', id(number))
   ...:     return number
   ...:

In [8]: cube(x)
id(number) before modifying number: 4350477840
id(number) after modifying number: 4396653744
Out[8]: 343
```

When we call cube(x), the first print statement shows that id(number) initially is the same as id(x) in snippet [2]. Numeric values are immutable, so the statement

```
number **= 3
```

actually creates a *new object* containing the cubed value, then assigns that object's reference to parameter number. Recall that if there are no more references to the *original* object, it will be *garbage collected*. Function cube's second print statement shows the *new* object's identity. Object identities must be unique, so number must refer to a *different* object. To show that x was not modified, we display its value and identity again:

```
In [9]: print(f'x = {x}; id(x) = {id(x)}')
x = 7; id(x) = 4350477840
```

Mutable Objects as Arguments

In the next chapter, we'll show that when a reference to a *mutable* object like a list is passed to a function, the function *can* modify the original object in the caller.

4.16 Recursion

Let's write a program to perform a famous mathematical calculation. Consider the *factorial* of a positive integer n, which is written $n!$ and pronounced "n factorial." This is the product

$$n \cdot (n-1) \cdot (n-2) \cdot \ldots \cdot 1$$

with $1!$ equal to 1 and $0!$ defined to be 1. For example, $5!$ is the product $5 \cdot 4 \cdot 3 \cdot 2 \cdot 1$, which is equal to 120.

Iterative Factorial Approach

You can calculate $5!$ *iteratively* with a for statement, as in:

```
In [1]: factorial = 1

In [2]: for number in range(5, 0, -1):
   ...:     factorial *= number
   ...:

In [3]: factorial
Out[3]: 120
```

Recursive Problem Solving

Recursive problem-solving approaches have several elements in common. When you call a recursive function to solve a problem, it's actually capable of solving only the *simplest case(s)*, or **base case(s)**. If you call the function with a *base case*, it immediately returns a result. If you call the function with a more complex problem, it typically divides the problem into two pieces—one that the function knows how to do and one that it does not know how to do. To make recursion feasible, this latter piece must be a slightly simpler or smaller version of the original problem. Because this new problem resembles the original problem, the function calls a fresh *copy* of itself to work on the smaller problem—this is referred to as a **recursive call** and is also called the **recursion step**. This concept of separating the problem into two smaller portions is a form of the *divide-and-conquer* approach introduced earlier in the book.

The recursion step executes while the original function call is still active (i.e., it has not finished executing). It can result in many more recursive calls as the function divides each new subproblem into two conceptual pieces. For the recursion to eventually terminate, each time the function calls itself with a simpler version of the original problem, the sequence of smaller and smaller problems must *converge on a base case*. When the function recognizes the base case, it returns a result to the previous copy of the function. A sequence of returns ensues until the original function call returns the final result to the caller.

Recursive Factorial Approach

You can arrive at a recursive factorial representation by observing that $n!$ can be written as:

$$n! = n \cdot (n-1)!$$

For example, $5!$ is equal to $5 \cdot 4!$, as in:

$$5! = 5 \cdot 4 \cdot 3 \cdot 2 \cdot 1$$
$$5! = 5 \cdot (4 \cdot 3 \cdot 2 \cdot 1)$$
$$5! = 5 \cdot (4!)$$

Visualizing Recursion

The evaluation of 5! would proceed as shown below. The left column shows how the succession of recursive calls proceeds until 1! (the base case) is evaluated to be 1, which terminates the recursion. The right column shows from bottom to top the values returned from each recursive call to its caller until the final value is calculated and returned.

(a) Sequence of recursive calls   (b) Values returned from each recursive call

Implementing a Recursive Factorial Function

The following session uses recursion to calculate and display the factorials of the integers 0 through 10:

```
In [4]: def factorial(number):
   ...:     """Return factorial of number."""
   ...:     if number <= 1:
   ...:         return 1
   ...:     return number * factorial(number - 1)  # recursive call
   ...:

In [5]: for i in range(11):
   ...:     print(f'{i}! = {factorial(i)}')
   ...:
0! = 1
1! = 1
2! = 2
3! = 6
4! = 24
5! = 120
6! = 720
7! = 5040
8! = 40320
9! = 362880
10! = 3628800
```

Snippet [4]'s recursive function factorial first determines whether the *terminating condition* number <= 1 is True. If this condition *is* True (the base case), factorial returns

1 and no further recursion is necessary. If number is greater than 1, the second return statement expresses the problem as the product of number and a *recursive call* to factorial that evaluates factorial(number - 1). This is a slightly smaller problem than the original calculation, factorial(number). Note that function factorial must receive a *nonnegative* argument. We do not test for this case.

The loop in snippet [5] calls the factorial function for the values from 0 through 10. The output shows that factorial values grow quickly. *Python does not limit the size of an integer*, unlike many other programming languages.

Indirect Recursion

A recursive function may call another function, which may, in turn, make a call back to the recursive function. This is known as an **indirect recursive call** or **indirect recursion**. For example, function A calls function B, which makes a call back to function A. This is still recursion because the second call to function A is made while the first call to function A is active. That is, the first call to function A has not yet finished executing (because it is waiting on function B to return a result to it) and has not returned to function A's original caller.

Stack Overflow and Infinite Recursion

Of course, the amount of memory in a computer is finite, so only a certain amount of memory can be used to store activation records on the function-call stack. If more recursive function calls occur than can have their activation records stored on the stack, a fatal error known as **stack overflow** occurs. This typically is the result of **infinite recursion**, which can be caused by omitting the base case or writing the recursion step incorrectly so that it does not converge on the base case. This error is analogous to the problem of an *infinite loop* in an *iterative* (nonrecursive) solution.

4.17 Functional-Style Programming

Like other popular languages, such as Java and C#, Python is not a purely functional language. Rather, it offers "functional-style" features that help you write code which is less likely to contain errors, more concise and easier to read, debug and modify. Functional-style programs also can be easier to parallelize to get better performance on today's multicore processors. The chart below lists most of Python's key functional-style programming capabilities and shows in parentheses the chapters in which we initially cover many of them.

Functional-style programming topics		
avoiding side effects (4)	generator functions	lazy evaluation (5)
closures	higher-order functions (5)	list comprehensions (5)
declarative programming (4)	immutability (4)	operator module (5, 11, 16)
decorators (10)	internal iteration (4)	pure functions (4)
dictionary comprehensions (6)	iterators (3)	range function (3, 4)
filter/map/reduce (5)	itertools module (16)	reductions (3, 5)
functools module	lambda expressions (5)	set comprehensions (6)
generator expressions (5)		

We cover most of these features throughout the book—many with code examples and others from a literacy perspective. You've already used list, string and built-in function range *iterators* with the for statement, and several *reductions* (functions sum, len, min and max). We discuss declarative programming, immutability and internal iteration below.

What vs. How

As the tasks you perform get more complicated, your code can become harder to read, debug and modify, and more likely to contain errors. Specifying *how* the code works can become complex.

Functional-style programming lets you simply say *what* you want to do. It hides many details of *how* to perform each task. Typically, library code handles the *how* for you. As you'll see, this can eliminate many errors.

Consider the for statement in many other programming languages. Typically, *you* must specify all the details of counter-controlled iteration: a control variable, its initial value, how to increment it and a loop-continuation condition that uses the control variable to determine whether to continue iterating. This style of iteration is known as **external iteration** and is error-prone. For example, you might provide an incorrect initializer, increment or loop-continuation condition. External iteration **mutates** (that is, modifies) the control variable, and the for statement's suite often mutates other variables as well. Every time you modify variables you could introduce errors. Functional-style programming emphasizes **immutability**. That is, it avoids operations that modify variables' values. We'll say more in the next chapter.

Python's for statement and range function *hide* most counter-controlled iteration details. You specify *what* values range should produce and the variable that should receive each value as it's produced. Function range *knows how* to produce those values. Similarly, the for statement *knows how* to get each value from range and *how* to stop iterating when there are no more values. Specifying *what*, but not *how*, is an important aspect of **internal iteration**—a key functional-style programming concept.

The Python built-in functions sum, min and max each use internal iteration. To total the elements of the list grades, you simply declare *what* you want to do—that is, sum(grades). Function sum *knows how* to iterate through the list and add each element to the running total. Stating what you *want* done rather than programming *how* to do it is known as **declarative programming**.

Pure Functions

In pure functional programming language you focus on writing pure functions. A **pure function's** result depends only on the argument(s) you pass to it. Also, given a particular argument (or arguments), a pure function always produces the same result. For example, built-in function sum's return value depends only on the iterable you pass to it. Given a list [1, 2, 3], sum *always* returns 6 no matter how many times you call it. Also, a pure function does not have *side effects*. For example, even if you pass a *mutable* list to a pure function, the list will contain the same values before and after the function call. When you call the pure function sum, it does not modify its argument.

```
In [1]: values = [1, 2, 3]

In [2]: sum(values)
Out[2]: 6
```

```
In [3]: sum(values)  # same call always returns same result
Out[3]: 6

In [4]: values
Out[5]: [1, 2, 3]
```

In the next chapter, we'll continue using functional-style programming concepts. Also, you'll see that *functions are objects* that you can pass to other functions as data.

4.18 Intro to Data Science: Measures of Dispersion

In our discussion of descriptive statistics, we've considered the measures of central tendency—mean, median and mode. These help us categorize typical values in a group—such as the mean height of your classmates or the most frequently purchased car brand (the mode) in a given country.

When we're talking about a group, the entire group is called the **population**. Sometimes a population is quite large, such as the people likely to vote in the next U.S. presidential election, which is a number in excess of 100,000,000 people. For practical reasons, the polling organizations trying to predict who will become the next president work with carefully selected small subsets of the population known as **samples**. Many of the polls in the 2016 election had sample sizes of about 1000 people.

In this section, we continue discussing basic descriptive statistics. We introduce **measures of dispersion** (also called **measures of variability**) that help you understand how spread out the values are. For example, in a class of students, there may be a bunch of students whose height is close to the average, with smaller numbers of students who are considerably shorter or taller.

For our purposes, we'll calculate each measure of dispersion both by hand and with functions from the module `statistics`, using the following population of 10 six-sided die rolls:

    1, 3, 4, 2, 6, 5, 3, 4, 5, 2

Variance

To determine the **variance**,[5] we begin with the mean of these values—3.5. You obtain this result by dividing the sum of the face values, 35, by the number of rolls, 10. Next, we subtract the mean from every die value (this produces some negative results):

    -2.5, -0.5, 0.5, -1.5, 2.5, 1.5, -0.5, 0.5, 1.5, -1.5

Then, we square each of these results (yielding only positives):

    6.25, 0.25, 0.25, 2.25, 6.25, 2.25, 0.25, 0.25, 2.25, 2.25

---

5. For simplicity, we're calculating the *population variance*. There is a subtle difference between the *population variance* and the *sample variance*. Instead of dividing by n (the number of die rolls in our example), sample variance divides by $n - 1$. The difference is pronounced for small samples and becomes insignificant as the sample size increases. The `statistics` module provides the functions `pvariance` and `variance` to calculate the population variance and sample variance, respectively. Similarly, the `statistics` module provides the functions `pstdev` and `stdev` to calculate the population standard deviation and sample standard deviation, respectively.

Finally, we calculate the mean of these squares, which is 2.25 (22.5 / 10)—this is the **population variance**. Squaring the difference between each die value and the mean of all die values emphasizes **outliers**—the values that are farthest from the mean. As we get deeper into data analytics, sometimes we'll want to pay careful attention to outliers, and sometimes we'll want to ignore them. The following code uses the `statistics` module's **pvariance** function to confirm our manual result:

```
In [1]: import statistics

In [2]: statistics.pvariance([1, 3, 4, 2, 6, 5, 3, 4, 5, 2])
Out[2]: 2.25
```

Standard Deviation

The **standard deviation** is the square root of the variance (in this case, 1.5), which tones down the effect of the outliers. The smaller the variance and standard deviation are, the closer the data values are to the mean and the less overall **dispersion** (that is, **spread**) there is between the values and the mean. The following code calculates the **population standard deviation** with the statistics module's **pstdev** function, confirming our manual result:

```
In [3]: statistics.pstdev([1, 3, 4, 2, 6, 5, 3, 4, 5, 2])
Out[3]: 1.5
```

Passing the pvariance function's result to the math module's sqrt function confirms our result of 1.5:

```
In [4]: import math

In [5]: math.sqrt(statistics.pvariance([1, 3, 4, 2, 6, 5, 3, 4, 5, 2]))
Out[5]: 1.5
```

Advantage of Population Standard Deviation vs. Population Variance

Suppose you've recorded the March Fahrenheit temperatures in your area. You might have 31 numbers such as 19, 32, 28 and 35. The units for these numbers are degrees. When you square your temperatures to calculate the population variance, the units of the population variance become "degrees squared." When you take the square root of the population variance to calculate the population standard deviation, the units once again become degrees, which are the *same* units as your temperatures.

4.19 Wrap-Up

In this chapter, we created custom functions. We imported capabilities from the random and math modules. We introduced random-number generation and used it to simulate rolling a six-sided die. We packed multiple values into tuples to return more than one value from a function. We also unpacked a tuple to access its values. We discussed using the Python Standard Library's modules to avoid "reinventing the wheel."

We created functions with default parameter values and called functions with keyword arguments. We also defined functions with arbitrary argument lists. We called methods of objects. We discussed how an identifier's scope determines where in your program you can use it.

We presented more about importing modules. You saw that arguments are passed-by-reference to functions, and how the function-call stack and stack frames support the function-call-and-return mechanism. We also presented a recursive function and began introducing Python's functional-style programming capabilities. We've introduced basic list and tuple capabilities over the last two chapters—in the next chapter, we'll discuss them in detail.

Finally, we continued our discussion of descriptive statistics by introducing measures of dispersion—variance and standard deviation—and calculating them with functions from the Python Standard Library's `statistics` module.

For some types of problems, it's useful to have functions call themselves. A **recursive function** calls itself, either directly or indirectly through another function.

5

Sequences: Lists and Tuples

Objectives

In this chapter, you'll:

- Create and initialize lists and tuples.
- Refer to elements of lists, tuples and strings.
- Sort and search lists, and search tuples.
- Pass lists and tuples to functions and methods.
- Use list methods to perform common manipulations, such as searching for items, sorting a list, inserting items and removing items.
- Use additional Python functional-style programming capabilities, including lambdas and the operations filter, map and reduce.
- Use functional-style list comprehensions to create lists quickly and easily, and use generator expressions to generate values on demand.
- Use two-dimensional lists.
- Enhance your analysis and presentation skills with the Seaborn and Matplotlib visualization libraries.

5.1 Introduction

In the last two chapters, we briefly introduced the list and tuple sequence types for representing ordered collections of items. **Collections** are prepackaged data structures consisting of related data items. Examples of collections include your favorite songs on your smartphone, your contacts list, a library's books, your cards in a card game, your favorite sports team's players, the stocks in an investment portfolio, patients in a cancer study and a shopping list. Python's built-in collections enable you to store and access data conveniently and efficiently. In this chapter, we discuss lists and tuples in more detail.

We'll demonstrate common list and tuple manipulations. You'll see that lists (which are modifiable) and tuples (which are not) have many common capabilities. Each can hold items of the same or different types. Lists can **dynamically resize** as necessary, growing and shrinking at execution time. We discuss one-dimensional and two-dimensional lists.

In the preceding chapter, we demonstrated random-number generation and simulated rolling a six-sided die. We conclude this chapter with our next Intro to Data Science section, which uses the visualization libraries Seaborn and Matplotlib to interactively develop static bar charts containing the die frequencies. In the next chapter's Intro to Data Science section, we'll present an animated visualization in which the bar chart changes *dynamically* as the number of die rolls increases—you'll see the law of large numbers "in action."

5.2 Lists

Here, we discuss lists in more detail and explain how to refer to particular list **elements**. Many of the capabilities shown in this section apply to all sequence types.

Creating a List
Lists typically store **homogeneous data**, that is, values of the *same* data type. Consider the list c, which contains five integer elements:

```
In [1]: c = [-45, 6, 0, 72, 1543]

In [2]: c
Out[2]: [-45, 6, 0, 72, 1543]
```

They also may store **heterogeneous data**, that is, data of many different types. For example, the following list contains a student's first name (a string), last name (a string), grade point average (a float) and graduation year (an int):

```
['Mary', 'Smith', 3.57, 2022]
```

Accessing Elements of a List
You reference a list element by writing the list's name followed by the element's **index** (that is, its **position number**) enclosed in square brackets ([], known as the **subscription operator**). The following diagram shows the list c labeled with its element names:

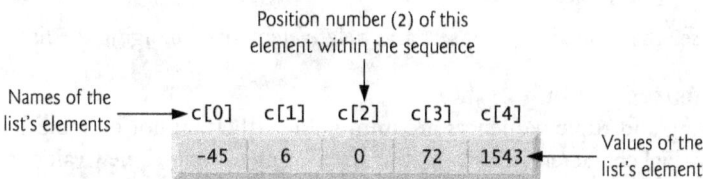

The first element in a list has the index 0. So, in the five-element list c, the first element is named c[0] and the last is c[4]:

```
In [3]: c[0]
Out[3]: -45

In [4]: c[4]
Out[4]: 1543
```

Determining a List's Length
To get a list's length, use the built-in **len function**:

```
In [5]: len(c)
Out[5]: 5
```

Accessing Elements from the End of the List with Negative Indices
Lists also can be accessed from the end by using *negative indices*:

So, list c's last element (c[4]), can be accessed with c[-1] and its first element with c[-5]:

```
In [6]: c[-1]
Out[6]: 1543

In [7]: c[-5]
Out[7]: -45
```

Indices Must Be Integers or Integer Expressions
An index must be an integer or integer expression (or a *slice*, as we'll soon see):

```
In [8]: a = 1

In [9]: b = 2
```

```
In [10]: c[a + b]
Out[10]: 72
```

Using a non-integer index value causes a TypeError.

Lists Are Mutable

Lists are mutable—their elements can be modified:

```
In [11]: c[4] = 17

In [12]: c
Out[12]: [-45, 6, 0, 72, 17]
```

You'll soon see that you also can insert and delete elements, changing the list's length.

Some Sequences Are Immutable

Python's string and tuple sequences are immutable—they cannot be modified. You can get the individual characters in a string, but attempting to assign a new value to one of the characters causes a TypeError:

```
In [13]: s = 'hello'

In [14]: s[0]
Out[14]: 'h'

In [15]: s[0] = 'H'
---------------------------------------------------------------------------
TypeError                                 Traceback (most recent call last)
<ipython-input-15-812ef2514689> in <module>()
----> 1 s[0] = 'H'

TypeError: 'str' object does not support item assignment
```

Attempting to Access a Nonexistent Element

Using an out-of-range list, tuple or string index causes an IndexError:

```
In [16]: c[100]
---------------------------------------------------------------------------
IndexError                                Traceback (most recent call last)
<ipython-input-16-9a31ea1e1a13> in <module>()
----> 1 c[100]

IndexError: list index out of range
```

Using List Elements in Expressions

List elements may be used as variables in expressions:

```
In [17]: c[0] + c[1] + c[2]
Out[17]: -39
```

Appending to a List with +=

Let's start with an *empty* list [], then use a for statement and += to append the values 1 through 5 to the list—the list grows dynamically to accommodate each item:

```
In [18]: a_list = []
```

```
In [19]: for number in range(1, 6):
    ...:     a_list += [number]
    ...:
```

```
In [20]: a_list
Out[20]: [1, 2, 3, 4, 5]
```

When the left operand of += is a list, the right operand must be an *iterable*; otherwise, a TypeError occurs. In snippet [19]'s suite, the square brackets around number create a one-element list, which we append to a_list. If the right operand contains multiple elements, += appends them all. The following appends the characters of 'Python' to the list letters:

```
In [21]: letters = []
```

```
In [22]: letters += 'Python'
```

```
In [23]: letters
Out[23]: ['P', 'y', 't', 'h', 'o', 'n']
```

If the right operand of += is a tuple, its elements also are appended to the list. Later in the chapter, we'll use the list method append to add items to a list.

Concatenating Lists with +

You can **concatenate** two lists, two tuples or two strings using the + operator. The result is a *new* sequence of the same type containing the left operand's elements followed by the right operand's elements. The original sequences are unchanged:

```
In [24]: list1 = [10, 20, 30]
```

```
In [25]: list2 = [40, 50]
```

```
In [26]: concatenated_list = list1 + list2
```

```
In [27]: concatenated_list
Out[27]: [10, 20, 30, 40, 50]
```

A TypeError occurs if the + operator's operands are different sequence types—for example, concatenating a list and a tuple is an error.

Using for and range to Access List Indices and Values

List elements also can be accessed via their indices and the subscription operator ([]):

```
In [28]: for i in range(len(concatenated_list)):
    ...:     print(f'{i}: {concatenated_list[i]}')
    ...:
0: 10
1: 20
2: 30
3: 40
4: 50
```

The function call range(len(concatenated_list)) produces a sequence of integers representing concatenated_list's indices (in this case, 0 through 4). When looping in this manner, you must ensure that indices remain in range. Soon, we'll show a safer way to access element indices and values using built-in function enumerate.

Comparison Operators

You can compare entire lists element-by-element using comparison operators:

```
In [29]: a = [1, 2, 3]

In [30]: b = [1, 2, 3]

In [31]: c = [1, 2, 3, 4]

In [32]: a == b  # True: corresponding elements in both are equal
Out[32]: True

In [33]: a == c  # False: a and c have different elements and lengths
Out[33]: False

In [34]: a < c  # True: a has fewer elements than c
Out[34]: True

In [35]: c >= b  # True: elements 0-2 are equal but c has more elements
Out[35]: True
```

5.3 Tuples

As discussed in the preceding chapter, tuples are immutable and typically store heterogeneous data, but the data can be homogeneous. A tuple's length is its number of elements and cannot change during program execution.

Creating Tuples

To create an empty tuple, use empty parentheses:

```
In [1]: student_tuple = ()

In [2]: student_tuple
Out[2]: ()

In [3]: len(student_tuple)
Out[3]: 0
```

Recall that you can pack a tuple by separating its values with commas:

```
In [4]: student_tuple = 'John', 'Green', 3.3

In [5]: student_tuple
Out[5]: ('John', 'Green', 3.3)

In [6]: len(student_tuple)
Out[6]: 3
```

When you output a tuple, Python always displays its contents in parentheses. You may surround a tuple's comma-separated list of values with optional parentheses:

```
In [7]: another_student_tuple = ('Mary', 'Red', 3.3)

In [8]: another_student_tuple
Out[8]: ('Mary', 'Red', 3.3)
```

The following code creates a one-element tuple:

```
In [9]: a_singleton_tuple = ('red',)  # note the comma

In [10]: a_singleton_tuple
Out[10]: ('red',)
```

The comma (,) that follows the string 'red' identifies a_singleton_tuple as a tuple—the parentheses are optional. If the comma were omitted, the parentheses would be redundant, and a_singleton_tuple would simply refer to the string 'red' rather than a tuple.

Accessing Tuple Elements

A tuple's elements, though related, are often of multiple types. Usually, you do not iterate over them. Rather, you access each individually. Like list indices, tuple indices start at 0. The following code creates time_tuple representing an hour, minute and second, displays the tuple, then uses its elements to calculate the number of seconds since midnight—note that we perform a *different* operation with each value in the tuple:

```
In [11]: time_tuple = (9, 16, 1)

In [12]: time_tuple
Out[12]: (9, 16, 1)

In [13]: time_tuple[0] * 3600 + time_tuple[1] * 60 + time_tuple[2]
Out[13]: 33361
```

Assigning a value to a tuple element causes a TypeError.

Adding Items to a String or Tuple

As with lists, the += augmented assignment statement can be used with strings and tuples, even though they're *immutable*. In the following code, after the two assignments, tuple1 and tuple2 refer to the *same* tuple object:

```
In [14]: tuple1 = (10, 20, 30)

In [15]: tuple2 = tuple1

In [16]: tuple2
Out[16]: (10, 20, 30)
```

Concatenating the tuple (40, 50) to tuple1 creates a *new* tuple, then assigns a reference to it to the variable tuple1—tuple2 still refers to the original tuple:

```
In [17]: tuple1 += (40, 50)

In [18]: tuple1
Out[18]: (10, 20, 30, 40, 50)

In [19]: tuple2
Out[19]: (10, 20, 30)
```

For a string or tuple, the item to the right of += must be a string or tuple, respectively—mixing types causes a TypeError.

Appending Tuples to Lists

You can use += to append a tuple to a list:

```
In [20]: numbers = [1, 2, 3, 4, 5]

In [21]: numbers += (6, 7)

In [22]: numbers
Out[22]: [1, 2, 3, 4, 5, 6, 7]
```

Tuples May Contain Mutable Objects

Let's create a `student_tuple` with a first name, last name and list of grades:

```
In [23]: student_tuple = ('Amanda', 'Blue', [98, 75, 87])
```

Even though the tuple is immutable, its list element is mutable:

```
In [24]: student_tuple[2][1] = 85

In [25]: student_tuple
Out[25]: ('Amanda', 'Blue', [98, 85, 87])
```

In the *double-subscripted name* `student_tuple[2][1]`, Python views `student_tuple[2]` as the element of the tuple containing the list [98, 75, 87], then uses [1] to access the list element containing 75. The assignment in snippet [24] replaces that grade with 85.

5.4 Unpacking Sequences

The previous chapter introduced tuple unpacking. You can unpack any sequence's elements by assigning the sequence to a comma-separated list of variables. A `ValueError` occurs if the number of variables to the left of the assignment symbol is not identical to the number of elements in the sequence on the right:

```
In [1]: student_tuple = ('Amanda', [98, 85, 87])

In [2]: first_name, grades = student_tuple

In [3]: first_name
Out[3]: 'Amanda'

In [4]: grades
Out[4]: [98, 85, 87]
```

The following code unpacks a string, a list and a sequence produced by range:

```
In [5]: first, second = 'hi'

In [6]: print(f'{first}  {second}')
h  i

In [7]: number1, number2, number3 = [2, 3, 5]

In [8]: print(f'{number1}  {number2}  {number3}')
2  3  5

In [9]: number1, number2, number3 = range(10, 40, 10)

In [10]: print(f'{number1}  {number2}  {number3}')
10  20  30
```

Swapping Values Via Packing and Unpacking

You can swap two variables' values using sequence packing and unpacking:

```
In [11]: number1 = 99

In [12]: number2 = 22

In [13]: number1, number2 = (number2, number1)

In [14]: print(f'number1 = {number1}; number2 = {number2}')
number1 = 22; number2 = 99
```

Accessing Indices and Values Safely with Built-in Function enumerate

Earlier, we called range to produce a sequence of index values, then accessed list elements in a for loop using the index values and the subscription operator ([]). This is error-prone because you could pass the wrong arguments to range. If any value produced by range is an out-of-bounds index, using it as an index causes an IndexError.

The preferred mechanism for accessing an element's index *and* value is the built-in function **enumerate**. This function receives an iterable and creates an iterator that, for each element, returns a tuple containing the element's index and value. The following code uses the built-in function **list** to create a list containing enumerate's results:

```
In [15]: colors = ['red', 'orange', 'yellow']

In [16]: list(enumerate(colors))
Out[16]: [(0, 'red'), (1, 'orange'), (2, 'yellow')]
```

Similarly the built-in function **tuple** creates a tuple from a sequence:

```
In [17]: tuple(enumerate(colors))
Out[17]: ((0, 'red'), (1, 'orange'), (2, 'yellow'))
```

The following for loop unpacks each tuple returned by enumerate into the variables index and value and displays them:

```
In [18]: for index, value in enumerate(colors):
    ...:         print(f'{index}: {value}')
    ...:
0: red
1: orange
2: yellow
```

Creating a Primitive Bar Chart

The following script creates a primitive **bar chart** where each bar's length is made of asterisks (*) and is proportional to the list's corresponding element value. We use the function enumerate to access the list's indices and values safely. To run this example, change to this chapter's ch05 examples folder, then enter:

```
ipython fig05_01.py
```

or, if you're in IPython already, use the command:

```
run fig05_01.py
```

```
 1   # fig05_01.py
 2   """Displaying a bar chart"""
 3   numbers = [19, 3, 15, 7, 11]
 4
 5   print('\nCreating a bar chart from numbers:')
 6   print(f'Index{"Value":>8}    Bar')
 7
 8   for index, value in enumerate(numbers):
 9       print(f'{index:>5}{value:>8}    {"*" * value}')
```

```
Creating a bar chart from numbers:
Index    Value    Bar
    0       19    *******************
    1        3    ***
    2       15    ***************
    3        7    *******
    4       11    ***********
```

The for statement uses enumerate to get each element's index and value, then displays a formatted line containing the index, the element value and the corresponding bar of asterisks. The expression

> "*" * value

creates a string consisting of value asterisks. When used with a sequence, the multiplication operator (*) *repeats* the sequence—in this case, the string "*"—value times. Later in this chapter, we'll use the open-source Seaborn and Matplotlib libraries to display a publication-quality bar chart visualization.

5.5 Sequence Slicing

You can **slice** sequences to create new sequences of the same type containing *subsets* of the original elements. Slice operations can modify mutable sequences—those that do *not* modify a sequence work identically for lists, tuples and strings.

Specifying a Slice with Starting and Ending Indices
Let's create a slice consisting of the elements at indices 2 through 5 of a list:

```
In [1]: numbers = [2, 3, 5, 7, 11, 13, 17, 19]

In [2]: numbers[2:6]
Out[2]: [5, 7, 11, 13]
```

The slice *copies* elements from the *starting index* to the left of the colon (2) up to, but not including, the *ending index* to the right of the colon (6). The original list is not modified.

Specifying a Slice with Only an Ending Index
If you omit the starting index, 0 is assumed. So, the slice numbers[:6] is equivalent to the slice numbers[0:6]:

```
In [3]: numbers[:6]
Out[3]: [2, 3, 5, 7, 11, 13]
```

```
In [4]: numbers[0:6]
Out[4]: [2, 3, 5, 7, 11, 13]
```

Specifying a Slice with Only a Starting Index

If you omit the ending index, Python assumes the sequence's length (8 here), so snippet [5]'s slice contains the elements of numbers at indices 6 and 7:

```
In [5]: numbers[6:]
Out[5]: [17, 19]

In [6]: numbers[6:len(numbers)]
Out[6]: [17, 19]
```

Specifying a Slice with No Indices

Omitting both the start and end indices copies the entire sequence:

```
In [7]: numbers[:]
Out[7]: [2, 3, 5, 7, 11, 13, 17, 19]
```

Though slices create new objects, slices make **shallow copies** of the elements—that is, they copy the elements' references but not the objects they point to. So, in the snippet above, the new list's elements refer to the *same objects* as the original list's elements, rather than to separate copies. In the "Array-Oriented Programming with NumPy" chapter, we'll explain *deep* copying, which actually copies the referenced objects themselves, and we'll point out when deep copying is preferred.

Slicing with Steps

The following code uses a *step* of 2 to create a slice with every other element of numbers:

```
In [8]: numbers[::2]
Out[8]: [2, 5, 11, 17]
```

We omitted the start and end indices, so 0 and len(numbers) are assumed, respectively.

Slicing with Negative Indices and Steps

You can use a negative step to select slices in *reverse* order. The following code concisely creates a new list in reverse order:

```
In [9]: numbers[::-1]
Out[9]: [19, 17, 13, 11, 7, 5, 3, 2]
```

This is equivalent to:

```
In [10]: numbers[-1:-9:-1]
Out[10]: [19, 17, 13, 11, 7, 5, 3, 2]
```

Modifying Lists Via Slices

You can modify a list by assigning to a slice of it—the rest of the list is unchanged. The following code replaces numbers' first three elements, leaving the rest unchanged:

```
In [11]: numbers[0:3] = ['two', 'three', 'five']

In [12]: numbers
Out[12]: ['two', 'three', 'five', 7, 11, 13, 17, 19]
```

The following deletes only the first three elements of numbers by assigning an *empty* list to the three-element slice:

```
In [13]: numbers[0:3] = []

In [14]: numbers
Out[14]: [7, 11, 13, 17, 19]
```

The following assigns a list's elements to a slice of every other element of numbers:

```
In [15]: numbers = [2, 3, 5, 7, 11, 13, 17, 19]

In [16]: numbers[::2] = [100, 100, 100, 100]

In [17]: numbers
Out[17]: [100, 3, 100, 7, 100, 13, 100, 19]

In [18]: id(numbers)
Out[18]: 4434456648
```

Let's delete all the elements in numbers, leaving the *existing* list empty:

```
In [19]: numbers[:] = []

In [20]: numbers
Out[20]: []

In [21]: id(numbers)
Out[21]: 4434456648
```

Deleting numbers' contents (snippet [19]) is different from assigning numbers a *new* empty list [] (snippet [22]). To prove this, we display numbers' identity after each operation. The identities are different, so they represent separate objects in memory:

```
In [22]: numbers = []

In [23]: numbers
Out[23]: []

In [24]: id(numbers)
Out[24]: 4406030920
```

When you assign a new object to a variable (as in snippet [21]), the original object will be garbage collected if no other variables refer to it.

5.6 del Statement

The **del statement** also can be used to remove elements from a list and to delete variables from the interactive session. You can remove the element at any valid index or the element(s) from any valid slice.

Deleting the Element at a Specific List Index
Let's create a list, then use del to remove its last element:

```
In [1]: numbers = list(range(0, 10))

In [2]: numbers
Out[2]: [0, 1, 2, 3, 4, 5, 6, 7, 8, 9]
```

```
In [3]: del numbers[-1]

In [4]: numbers
Out[4]: [0, 1, 2, 3, 4, 5, 6, 7, 8]
```

Deleting a Slice from a List
The following deletes the list's first two elements:

```
In [5]: del numbers[0:2]

In [6]: numbers
Out[6]: [2, 3, 4, 5, 6, 7, 8]
```

The following uses a step in the slice to delete every other element from the entire list:

```
In [7]: del numbers[::2]

In [8]: numbers
Out[8]: [3, 5, 7]
```

Deleting a Slice Representing the Entire List
The following code deletes all of the list's elements:

```
In [9]: del numbers[:]

In [10]: numbers
Out[10]: []
```

Deleting a Variable from the Current Session
The del statement can delete any variable. Let's delete numbers from the interactive session, then attempt to display the variable's value, causing a NameError:

```
In [11]: del numbers

In [12]: numbers
-----------------------------------------------------------------------
NameError                                 Traceback (most recent call last)
<ipython-input-12-426f8401232b> in <module>()
----> 1 numbers

NameError: name 'numbers' is not defined
```

5.7 Passing Lists to Functions

In the last chapter, we mentioned that all objects are passed by reference and demonstrated passing an immutable object as a function argument. Here, we discuss references further by examining what happens when a program passes a mutable list object to a function.

Passing an Entire List to a Function
Consider the function modify_elements, which receives a reference to a list and multiplies each of the list's element values by 2:

```
In [1]: def modify_elements(items):
   ...:     """Multiplies all element values in items by 2."""
   ...:     for i in range(len(items)):
   ...:         items[i] *= 2
   ...:

In [2]: numbers = [10, 3, 7, 1, 9]

In [3]: modify_elements(numbers)

In [4]: numbers
Out[4]: [20, 6, 14, 2, 18]
```

Function modify_elements' items parameter receives a reference to the *original* list, so the statement in the loop's suite modifies each element in the original list object.

Passing a Tuple to a Function

When you pass a tuple to a function, attempting to modify the tuple's immutable elements results in a TypeError:

```
In [5]: numbers_tuple = (10, 20, 30)

In [6]: numbers_tuple
Out[6]: (10, 20, 30)

In [7]: modify_elements(numbers_tuple)
-------------------------------------------------------------------
TypeError                                 Traceback (most recent call last)
<ipython-input-7-9339741cd595> in <module>()
----> 1 modify_elements(numbers_tuple)

<ipython-input-1-27acb8f8f44c> in modify_elements(items)
      2     """Multiplies all element values in items by 2."""
      3     for i in range(len(items)):
----> 4         items[i] *= 2
      5
      6

TypeError: 'tuple' object does not support item assignment
```

Recall that tuples may contain mutable objects, such as lists. Those objects still can be modified when a tuple is passed to a function.

A Note Regarding Tracebacks

The previous traceback shows the *two* snippets that led to the TypeError. The first is snippet [7]'s function call. The second is snippet [1]'s function definition. Line numbers precede each snippet's code. We've demonstrated mostly single-line snippets. When an exception occurs in such a snippet, it's always preceded by ----> 1, indicating that line 1 (the snippet's only line) caused the exception. Multiline snippets like the definition of modify_elements show consecutive line numbers starting at 1. The notation ----> 4 above indicates that the exception occurred in line 4 of modify_elements. No matter how long the traceback is, the last line of code with ----> caused the exception.

5.8 Sorting Lists

Sorting enables you to arrange data either in ascending or descending order.

Sorting a List in Ascending Order

List method **sort** *modifies* a list to arrange its elements in ascending order:

```
In [1]: numbers = [10, 3, 7, 1, 9, 4, 2, 8, 5, 6]

In [2]: numbers.sort()

In [3]: numbers
Out[3]: [1, 2, 3, 4, 5, 6, 7, 8, 9, 10]
```

Sorting a List in Descending Order

To sort a list in descending order, call list method sort with the optional keyword argument **reverse** set to True (False is the default):

```
In [4]: numbers.sort(reverse=True)

In [5]: numbers
Out[5]: [10, 9, 8, 7, 6, 5, 4, 3, 2, 1]
```

Built-In Function sorted

Built-in function **sorted** *returns a new list* containing the sorted elements of its argument *sequence*—the original sequence is *unmodified*. The following code demonstrates function sorted for a list, a string and a tuple:

```
In [6]: numbers = [10, 3, 7, 1, 9, 4, 2, 8, 5, 6]

In [7]: ascending_numbers = sorted(numbers)

In [8]: ascending_numbers
Out[8]: [1, 2, 3, 4, 5, 6, 7, 8, 9, 10]

In [9]: numbers
Out[9]: [10, 3, 7, 1, 9, 4, 2, 8, 5, 6]

In [10]: letters = 'fadgchjebi'

In [11]: ascending_letters = sorted(letters)

In [12]: ascending_letters
Out[12]: ['a', 'b', 'c', 'd', 'e', 'f', 'g', 'h', 'i', 'j']

In [13]: letters
Out[13]: 'fadgchjebi'

In [14]: colors = ('red', 'orange', 'yellow', 'green', 'blue')

In [15]: ascending_colors = sorted(colors)

In [16]: ascending_colors
Out[16]: ['blue', 'green', 'orange', 'red', 'yellow']

In [17]: colors
Out[17]: ('red', 'orange', 'yellow', 'green', 'blue')
```

Use the optional keyword argument `reverse` with the value `True` to sort the elements in descending order.

5.9 Searching Sequences

Often, you'll want to determine whether a sequence (such as a list, tuple or string) contains a value that matches a particular **key** value. **Searching** is the process of locating a key.

List Method `index`

List method **index** takes as an argument a search key—the value to locate in the list—then searches through the list from index 0 and returns the index of the *first* element that matches the search key:

```
In [1]: numbers = [3, 7, 1, 4, 2, 8, 5, 6]

In [2]: numbers.index(5)
Out[2]: 6
```

A `ValueError` occurs if the value you're searching for is not in the list.

Specifying the Starting Index of a Search

Using method `index`'s optional arguments, you can search a subset of a list's elements. You can use `*=` to *multiply a sequence*—that is, append a sequence to itself multiple times. After the following snippet, `numbers` contains two copies of the original list's contents:

```
In [3]: numbers *= 2

In [4]: numbers
Out[4]: [3, 7, 1, 4, 2, 8, 5, 6, 3, 7, 1, 4, 2, 8, 5, 6]
```

The following code searches the updated list for the value 5 starting from index 7 and continuing through the end of the list:

```
In [5]: numbers.index(5, 7)
Out[5]: 14
```

Specifying the Starting and Ending Indices of a Search

Specifying the starting and ending indices causes `index` to search from the starting index up to but not including the ending index location. The call to `index` in snippet `[5]`:

```
        numbers.index(5, 7)
```

assumes the length of `numbers` as its optional third argument and is equivalent to:

```
        numbers.index(5, 7, len(numbers))
```

The following looks for the value 7 in the range of elements with indices 0 through 3:

```
In [6]: numbers.index(7, 0, 4)
Out[6]: 1
```

Operators `in` and `not in`

Operator `in` tests whether its right operand's iterable contains the left operand's value:

```
In [7]: 1000 in numbers
Out[7]: False
```

```
In [8]: 5 in numbers
Out[8]: True
```

Similarly, operator not in tests whether its right operand's iterable does *not* contain the left operand's value:

```
In [9]: 1000 not in numbers
Out[9]: True

In [10]: 5 not in numbers
Out[10]: False
```

Using Operator in to Prevent a ValueError

You can use the operator in to ensure that calls to method index do not result in ValueErrors for search keys that are not in the corresponding sequence:

```
In [11]: key = 1000

In [12]: if key in numbers:
    ...:     print(f'found {key} at index {numbers.index(key)}')
    ...: else:
    ...:     print(f'{key} not found')
    ...:
1000 not found
```

Built-In Functions any and all

Sometimes you simply need to know whether *any* item in an iterable is True or whether *all* the items are True. The built-in function **any** returns True if any item in its iterable argument is True. The built-in function **all** returns True if all items in its iterable argument are True. Recall that nonzero values are True and 0 is False. Non-empty iterable objects also evaluate to True, whereas any empty iterable evaluates to False. Functions any and all are additional examples of internal iteration in functional-style programming.

5.10 Other List Methods

Lists also have methods that add and remove elements. Consider the list color_names:

```
In [1]: color_names = ['orange', 'yellow', 'green']
```

Inserting an Element at a Specific List Index

Method **insert** adds a new item at a specified index. The following inserts 'red' at index 0:

```
In [2]: color_names.insert(0, 'red')

In [3]: color_names
Out[3]: ['red', 'orange', 'yellow', 'green']
```

Adding an Element to the End of a List

You can add a new item to the end of a list with method **append**:

```
In [4]: color_names.append('blue')

In [5]: color_names
Out[5]: ['red', 'orange', 'yellow', 'green', 'blue']
```

Adding All the Elements of a Sequence to the End of a List

Use list method **extend** to add all the elements of another sequence to the end of a list:

```
In [6]: color_names.extend(['indigo', 'violet'])

In [7]: color_names
Out[7]: ['red', 'orange', 'yellow', 'green', 'blue', 'indigo', 'violet']
```

This is the equivalent of using +=. The following code adds all the characters of a string then all the elements of a tuple to a list:

```
In [8]: sample_list = []

In [9]: s = 'abc'

In [10]: sample_list.extend(s)

In [11]: sample_list
Out[11]: ['a', 'b', 'c']

In [12]: t = (1, 2, 3)

In [13]: sample_list.extend(t)

In [14]: sample_list
Out[14]: ['a', 'b', 'c', 1, 2, 3]
```

Rather than creating a temporary variable, like t, to store a tuple before appending it to a list, you might want to pass a tuple directly to extend. In this case, the tuple's parentheses are required, because extend expects one iterable argument:

```
In [15]: sample_list.extend((4, 5, 6))   # note the extra parentheses

In [16]: sample_list
Out[16]: ['a', 'b', 'c', 1, 2, 3, 4, 5, 6]
```

A TypeError occurs if you omit the required parentheses.

Removing the First Occurrence of an Element in a List

Method **remove** deletes the first element with a specified value—a ValueError occurs if remove's argument is not in the list:

```
In [17]: color_names.remove('green')

In [18]: color_names
Out[18]: ['red', 'orange', 'yellow', 'blue', 'indigo', 'violet']
```

Emptying a List

To delete all the elements in a list, call method **clear**:

```
In [19]: color_names.clear()

In [20]: color_names
Out[20]: []
```

This is the equivalent of the previously shown slice assignment

```
color_names[:] = []
```

Counting the Number of Occurrences of an Item

List method **count** searches for its argument and returns the number of times it is found:

```
In [21]: responses = [1, 2, 5, 4, 3, 5, 2, 1, 3, 3,
    ...:              1, 4, 3, 3, 3, 2, 3, 3, 2, 2]

In [22]: for i in range(1, 6):
    ...:     print(f'{i} appears {responses.count(i)} times in responses')
    ...:
1 appears 3 times in responses
2 appears 5 times in responses
3 appears 8 times in responses
4 appears 2 times in responses
5 appears 2 times in responses
```

Reversing a List's Elements

List method **reverse** reverses the contents of a list in place, rather than creating a reversed copy, as we did with a slice previously:

```
In [23]: color_names = ['red', 'orange', 'yellow', 'green', 'blue']

In [24]: color_names.reverse()

In [25]: color_names
Out[25]: ['blue', 'green', 'yellow', 'orange', 'red']
```

Copying a List

List method copy returns a *new* list containing a *shallow* copy of the original list:

```
In [26]: copied_list = color_names.copy()

In [27]: copied_list
Out[27]: ['blue', 'green', 'yellow', 'orange', 'red']
```

This is equivalent to the previously demonstrated slice operation:

```
copied_list = color_names[:]
```

5.11 Simulating Stacks with Lists

The preceding chapter introduced the function-call stack. Python does not have a built-in stack type, but you can think of a stack as a constrained list. You *push* using list method append, which adds a new element to the *end* of the list. You *pop* using list method **pop** with no arguments, which removes and returns the item at the *end* of the list.

Let's create an empty list called stack, push (append) two strings onto it, then pop the strings to confirm they're retrieved in last-in, first-out (LIFO) order:

```
In [1]: stack = []

In [2]: stack.append('red')

In [3]: stack
Out[3]: ['red']

In [4]: stack.append('green')
```

```
In [5]: stack
Out[5]: ['red', 'green']

In [6]: stack.pop()
Out[6]: 'green'

In [7]: stack
Out[7]: ['red']

In [8]: stack.pop()
Out[8]: 'red'

In [9]: stack
Out[9]: []

In [10]: stack.pop()
-------------------------------------------------------------------------
IndexError                               Traceback (most recent call last)
<ipython-input-10-50ea7ec13fbe> in <module>()
----> 1 stack.pop()

IndexError: pop from empty list
```

For each pop snippet, the value that pop removes and returns is displayed. Popping from
an empty stack causes an IndexError, just like accessing a nonexistent list element with
[]. To prevent an IndexError, ensure that len(stack) is greater than 0 before calling pop.
You can run out of memory if you keep pushing items faster than you pop them.

   You also can use a list to simulate another popular collection called a **queue** in which
you insert at the back and delete from the front. Items are retrieved from queues in **first-
in, first-out (FIFO) order.**

5.12 List Comprehensions

Here, we continue discussing *functional-style* features with **list comprehensions**—a concise
and convenient notation for creating new lists. List comprehensions can replace many for
statements that iterate over existing sequences and create new lists, such as:

```
In [1]: list1 = []

In [2]: for item in range(1, 6):
   ...:         list1.append(item)
   ...:

In [3]: list1
Out[3]: [1, 2, 3, 4, 5]
```

Using a List Comprehension to Create a List of Integers
We can accomplish the same task in a single line of code with a list comprehension:

```
In [4]: list2 = [item for item in range(1, 6)]

In [5]: list2
Out[5]: [1, 2, 3, 4, 5]
```

Like snippet [2]'s for statement, the list comprehension's **for clause**

```
for item in range(1, 6)
```

iterates over the sequence produced by range(1, 6). For each item, the list comprehension evaluates the expression to the left of the for clause and places the expression's value (in this case, the item itself) in the new list. Snippet [4]'s particular comprehension could have been expressed more concisely using the function list:

```
list2 = list(range(1, 6))
```

Mapping: Performing Operations in a List Comprehension's Expression

A list comprehension's expression can perform tasks, such as calculations, that **map** elements to new values (possibly of different types). Mapping is a common functional-style programming operation that produces a result with the *same* number of elements as the original data being mapped. The following comprehension maps each value to its cube with the expression item ** 3:

```
In [6]: list3 = [item ** 3 for item in range(1, 6)]

In [7]: list3
Out[7]: [1, 8, 27, 64, 125]
```

Filtering: List Comprehensions with if Clauses

Another common functional-style programming operation is **filtering** elements to select only those that match a condition. This typically produces a list with *fewer* elements than the data being filtered. To do this in a list comprehension, use the **if clause**. The following includes in list4 only the even values produced by the for clause:

```
In [8]: list4 = [item for item in range(1, 11) if item % 2 == 0]

In [9]: list4
Out[9]: [2, 4, 6, 8, 10]
```

List Comprehension That Processes Another List's Elements

The for clause can process any iterable. Let's create a list of lowercase strings and use a list comprehension to create a new list containing their uppercase versions:

```
In [10]: colors = ['red', 'orange', 'yellow', 'green', 'blue']

In [11]: colors2 = [item.upper() for item in colors]

In [12]: colors2
Out[12]: ['RED', 'ORANGE', 'YELLOW', 'GREEN', 'BLUE']

In [13]: colors
Out[13]: ['red', 'orange', 'yellow', 'green', 'blue']
```

5.13 Generator Expressions

A **generator expression** is similar to a list comprehension, but creates an iterable **generator object** that produces values *on demand*. This is known as **lazy evaluation**. List comprehensions use **greedy evaluation**—they create lists *immediately* when you execute them. For large numbers of items, creating a list can take substantial memory and time. So generator expressions can reduce your program's memory consumption and improve performance if the whole list is not needed at once.

Generator expressions have the same capabilities as list comprehensions, but you define them in parentheses instead of square brackets. The generator expression in snippet [2] squares and returns only the odd values in numbers:

```
In [1]: numbers = [10, 3, 7, 1, 9, 4, 2, 8, 5, 6]

In [2]: for value in (x ** 2 for x in numbers if x % 2 != 0):
   ...:     print(value, end=' ')
   ...:
9 49 1 81 25
```

To show that a generator expression does not create a list, let's assign the preceding snippet's generator expression to a variable and evaluate the variable:

```
In [3]: squares_of_odds = (x ** 2 for x in numbers if x % 2 != 0)

In [3]: squares_of_odds
Out[3]: <generator object <genexpr> at 0x1085e84c0>
```

The text "generator object <genexpr>" indicates that square_of_odds is a generator object that was created from a generator expression (genexpr).

5.14 Filter, Map and Reduce

The preceding section introduced several functional-style features—list comprehensions, filtering and mapping. Here we demonstrate the built-in filter and map functions for filtering and mapping, respectively. We continue discussing reductions in which you process a collection of elements into a *single* value, such as their count, total, product, average, minimum or maximum.

Filtering a Sequence's Values with the Built-In filter Function
Let's use built-in function **filter** to obtain the odd values in numbers:

```
In [1]: numbers = [10, 3, 7, 1, 9, 4, 2, 8, 5, 6]

In [2]: def is_odd(x):
   ...:     """Returns True only if x is odd."""
   ...:     return x % 2 != 0
   ...:

In [3]: list(filter(is_odd, numbers))
Out[3]: [3, 7, 1, 9, 5]
```

Like data, Python functions are objects that you can assign to variables, pass to other functions and return from functions. Functions that receive other functions as arguments are a functional-style capability called **higher-order functions**. For example, filter's first argument must be a function that receives one argument and returns True if the value should be included in the result. The function is_odd returns True if its argument is odd. The filter function calls is_odd once for each value in its second argument's iterable (numbers). Higher-order functions may also return a function as a result.

Function `filter` returns an iterator, so `filter`'s results are not produced until you iterate through them. This is another example of lazy evaluation. In snippet [3], function `list` iterates through the results and creates a list containing them. We can obtain the same results as above by using a list comprehension with an `if` clause:

```
In [4]: [item for item in numbers if is_odd(item)]
Out[4]: [3, 7, 1, 9, 5]
```

Using a `lambda` Rather than a Function

For simple functions like `is_odd` that `return` only a *single expression's value*, you can use a **lambda expression** (or simply a **lambda**) to define the function inline where it's needed—typically as it's passed to another function:

```
In [5]: list(filter(lambda x: x % 2 != 0, numbers))
Out[5]: [3, 7, 1, 9, 5]
```

We pass `filter`'s return value (an iterator) to function `list` here to convert the results to a list and display them.

A lambda expression is an *anonymous function*—that is, a *function without a name*. In the `filter` call

```
    filter(lambda x: x % 2 != 0, numbers)
```

the first argument is the lambda

```
    lambda x: x % 2 != 0
```

A lambda begins with the **lambda** keyword followed by a comma-separated parameter list, a colon (:) and an expression. In this case, the parameter list has one parameter named x. A `lambda` *implicitly* returns its expression's value. So any simple function of the form

```
    def function_name(parameter_list):
        return expression
```

may be expressed as a more concise `lambda` of the form

```
    lambda parameter_list: expression
```

Mapping a Sequence's Values to New Values

Let's use built-in function **map** with a `lambda` to square each value in `numbers`:

```
In [6]: numbers
Out[6]: [10, 3, 7, 1, 9, 4, 2, 8, 5, 6]

In [7]: list(map(lambda x: x ** 2, numbers))
Out[7]: [100, 9, 49, 1, 81, 16, 4, 64, 25, 36]
```

Function map's first argument is a function that receives one value and returns a new value—in this case, a `lambda` that squares its argument. The second argument is an iterable of values to map. Function map uses lazy evaluation. So, we pass to the `list` function the iterator that map returns. This enables us to iterate through and create a list of the mapped values. Here's an equivalent list comprehension:

```
In [8]: [item ** 2 for item in numbers]
Out[8]: [100, 9, 49, 1, 81, 16, 4, 64, 25, 36]
```

Combining `filter` and `map`

You can combine the preceding `filter` and `map` operations as follows:

```
In [9]: list(map(lambda x: x ** 2,
   ...:          filter(lambda x: x % 2 != 0, numbers)))
   ...:
Out[9]: [9, 49, 1, 81, 25]
```

There is a lot going on in snippet [9], so let's take a closer look at it. First, `filter` returns an iterable representing only the odd values of `numbers`. Then `map` returns an iterable representing the squares of the filtered values. Finally, `list` uses `map`'s iterable to create the list. You might prefer the following list comprehension to the preceding snippet:

```
In [10]: [x ** 2 for x in numbers if x % 2 != 0]
Out[10]: [9, 49, 1, 81, 25]
```

For each value of x in numbers, the expression x ** 2 is performed only if the condition x % 2 != 0 is True.

Reduction: Totaling the Elements of a Sequence with `sum`

As you know reductions process a sequence's elements into a single value. You've performed reductions with the built-in functions `len`, `sum`, `min` and `max`. You also can create custom reductions using the `functools` module's `reduce` function. See `https://docs.python.org/3/library/functools.html` for a code example. When we investigate big data and Hadoop in Chapter 16, we'll demonstrate MapReduce programming, which is based on the filter, map and reduce operations in functional-style programming.

5.15 Other Sequence Processing Functions

Python provides other built-in functions for manipulating sequences.

Finding the Minimum and Maximum Values Using a Key Function

We've previously shown the built-in reduction functions `min` and `max` using arguments, such as `int`s or lists of `int`s. Sometimes you'll need to find the minimum and maximum of more complex objects, such as strings. Consider the following comparison:

```
In [1]: 'Red' < 'orange'
Out[1]: True
```

The letter `'R'` "comes after" `'o'` in the alphabet, so you might expect `'Red'` to be less than `'orange'` and the condition above to be `False`. However, strings are compared by their characters' underlying *numerical values*, and lowercase letters have *higher* numerical values than uppercase letters. You can confirm this with built-in function **ord**, which returns the numerical value of a character:

```
In [2]: ord('R')
Out[2]: 82
```

```
In [3]: ord('o')
Out[3]: 111
```

Consider the list `colors`, which contains strings with uppercase and lowercase letters:

```
In [4]: colors = ['Red', 'orange', 'Yellow', 'green', 'Blue']
```

Let's assume that we'd like to determine the minimum and maximum strings using *alphabetical* order, not *numerical* (lexicographical) order. If we arrange colors alphabetically

```
'Blue', 'green', 'orange', 'Red', 'Yellow'
```

you can see that 'Blue' is the minimum (that is, closest to the beginning of the alphabet), and 'Yellow' is the maximum (that is, closest to the end of the alphabet).

Since Python compares strings using numerical values, you must first convert each string to all lowercase or all uppercase letters. Then their numerical values will also represent *alphabetical* ordering. The following snippets enable min and max to determine the minimum and maximum strings alphabetically:

```
In [5]: min(colors, key=lambda s: s.lower())
Out[5]: 'Blue'

In [6]: max(colors, key=lambda s: s.lower())
Out[6]: 'Yellow'
```

The key keyword argument must be a one-parameter function that returns a value. In this case, it's a lambda that calls string method **lower** to get a string's lowercase version. Functions min and max call the key argument's function for each element and use the results to compare the elements.

Iterating Backward Through a Sequence
Built-in function **reversed** returns an iterator that enables you to iterate over a sequence's values backward. The following list comprehension creates a new list containing the squares of numbers' values in reverse order:

```
In [7]: numbers = [10, 3, 7, 1, 9, 4, 2, 8, 5, 6]

In [8]: reversed_numbers = [item ** 2 for item in reversed(numbers)]

In [9]: reversed_numbers
Out[9]: [36, 25, 64, 4, 16, 81, 1, 49, 9, 100]
```

Combining Iterables into Tuples of Corresponding Elements
Built-in function **zip** enables you to iterate over *multiple* iterables of data at the *same* time. The function receives as arguments any number of iterables and returns an iterator that produces tuples containing the elements at the same index in each. For example, snippet [12]'s call to zip produces the tuples ('Bob', 3.5), ('Sue', 4.0) and ('Amanda', 3.75) consisting of the elements at index 0, 1 and 2 of each list, respectively:

```
In [10]: names = ['Bob', 'Sue', 'Amanda']

In [11]: grade_point_averages = [3.5, 4.0, 3.75]

In [12]: for name, gpa in zip(names, grade_point_averages):
    ...:     print(f'Name={name}; GPA={gpa}')
    ...:
Name=Bob; GPA=3.5
Name=Sue; GPA=4.0
Name=Amanda; GPA=3.75
```

We unpack each tuple into name and gpa and display them. Function zip's shortest argument determines the number of tuples produced. Here both have the same length.

5.16 Two-Dimensional Lists

Lists can contain other lists as elements. A typical use of such nested (or multidimensional) lists is to represent **tables** of values consisting of information arranged in **rows** and **columns**. To identify a particular table element, we specify *two* indices—by convention, the first identifies the element's row, the second the element's column.

Lists that require two indices to identify an element are called **two-dimensional lists** (or **double-indexed lists** or **double-subscripted lists**). Multidimensional lists can have more than two indices. Here, we introduce two-dimensional lists.

Creating a Two-Dimensional List

Consider a two-dimensional list with three rows and four columns (i.e., a 3-by-4 list) that might represent the grades of three students who each took four exams in a course:

```
In [1]: a = [[77, 68, 86, 73], [96, 87, 89, 81], [70, 90, 86, 81]]
```

Writing the list as follows makes its row and column tabular structure clearer:

```
a = [[77, 68, 86, 73],   # first student's grades
     [96, 87, 89, 81],   # second student's grades
     [70, 90, 86, 81]]   # third student's grades
```

Illustrating a Two-Dimensional List

The diagram below shows the list a, with its rows and columns of exam grade values:

	Column 0	Column 1	Column 2	Column 3
Row 0	77	68	86	73
Row 1	96	87	89	81
Row 2	70	90	86	81

Identifying the Elements in a Two-Dimensional List

The following diagram shows the names of list a's elements:

	Column 0	Column 1	Column 2	Column 3
Row 0	a[0][0]	a[0][1]	a[0][2]	a[0][3]
Row 1	a[1][0]	a[1][1]	a[1][2]	a[1][3]
Row 2	a[2][0]	a[2][1]	a[2][2]	a[2][3]

Column index
Row index
List name

Every element is identified by a name of the form a[*i*][*j*]—a is the list's name, and *i* and *j* are the indices that uniquely identify each element's row and column, respectively. The element names in row 0 all have 0 as the first index. The element names in column 3 all have 3 as the second index.

In the two-dimensional list a:

- 77, 68, 86 and 73 initialize a[0][0], a[0][1], a[0][2] and a[0][3], respectively,

- 96, 87, 89 and 81 initialize a[1][0], a[1][1], a[1][2] and a[1][3], respectively, and

- 70, 90, 86 and 81 initialize a[2][0], a[2][1], a[2][2] and a[2][3], respectively.

A list with m rows and n columns is called an **m-by-n list** and has $m \times n$ elements.

The following nested for statement outputs the rows of the preceding two-dimensional list one row at a time:

```
In [2]: for row in a:
   ...:     for item in row:
   ...:         print(item, end=' ')
   ...:     print()
   ...:
77 68 86 73
96 87 89 81
70 90 86 81
```

How the Nested Loops Execute

Let's modify the nested loop to display the list's name and the row and column indices and value of each element:

```
In [3]: for i, row in enumerate(a):
   ...:     for j, item in enumerate(row):
   ...:         print(f'a[{i}][{j}]={item} ', end=' ')
   ...:     print()
   ...:
a[0][0]=77  a[0][1]=68  a[0][2]=86  a[0][3]=73
a[1][0]=96  a[1][1]=87  a[1][2]=89  a[1][3]=81
a[2][0]=70  a[2][1]=90  a[2][2]=86  a[2][3]=81
```

The outer for statement iterates over the two-dimensional list's rows one row at a time. During each iteration of the outer for statement, the inner for statement iterates over *each* column in the current row. So in the first iteration of the outer loop, row 0 is

```
[77, 68, 86, 73]
```

and the nested loop iterates through this list's four elements a[0][0]=77, a[0][1]=68, a[0][2]=86 and a[0][3]=73.

In the second iteration of the outer loop, row 1 is

```
[96, 87, 89, 81]
```

and the nested loop iterates through this list's four elements a[1][0]=96, a[1][1]=87, a[1][2]=89 and a[1][3]=81.

In the third iteration of the outer loop, row 2 is

```
[70, 90, 86, 81]
```

and the nested loop iterates through this list's four elements a[2][0]=70, a[2][1]=90, a[2][2]=86 and a[2][3]=81.

In the "Array-Oriented Programming with NumPy" chapter, we'll cover the NumPy library's ndarray collection and the Pandas library's DataFrame collection. These enable you to manipulate multidimensional collections more concisely and conveniently than the two-dimensional list manipulations you've seen in this section.

5.17 Intro to Data Science: Simulation and Static Visualizations

The last few chapters' Intro to Data Science sections discussed basic descriptive statistics. Here, we focus on visualizations, which help you "get to know" your data. Visualizations give you a powerful way to understand data that goes beyond simply looking at raw data.

We use two open-source visualization libraries—Seaborn and Matplotlib—to display *static* bar charts showing the final results of a six-sided-die-rolling simulation. The **Seaborn visualization library** is built over the **Matplotlib visualization library** and simplifies many Matplotlib operations. We'll use aspects of both libraries, because some of the Seaborn operations return objects from the Matplotlib library. In the next chapter's Intro to Data Science section, we'll make things "come alive" with *dynamic visualizations*.

5.17.1 Sample Graphs for 600, 60,000 and 6,000,000 Die Rolls

The screen capture below shows a vertical bar chart that for 600 die rolls summarizes the frequencies with which each of the six faces appear, and their percentages of the total. Seaborn refers to this type of graph as a **bar plot**:

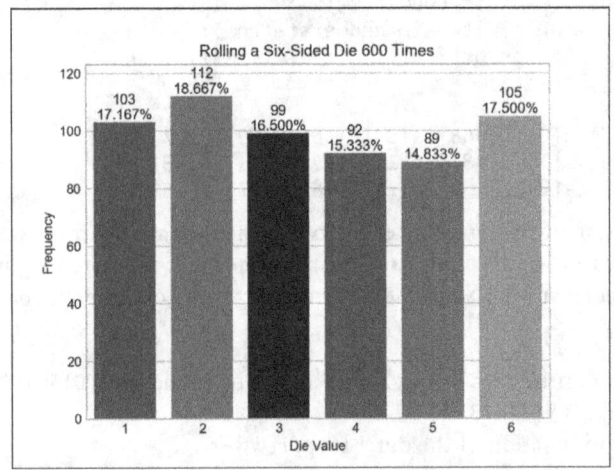

Here we expect about 100 occurrences of each die face. However, with such a small number of rolls, none of the frequencies is exactly 100 (though several are close) and most of the percentages are not close to 16.667% (about 1/6th). As we run the simulation for 60,000 die rolls, the bars will become much closer in size. At 6,000,000 die rolls, they'll appear to be exactly the same size. This is the "law of large numbers" at work. The next chapter will show the lengths of the bars changing dynamically.

We'll discuss how to control the plot's appearance and contents, including:

- the graph title inside the window (**Rolling a Six-Sided Die 600 Times**),
- the descriptive labels **Die Value** for the *x*-axis and **Frequency** for the *y*-axis,

- the text displayed above each bar, representing the *frequency* and *percentage* of the total rolls, and
- the bar colors.

We'll use various Seaborn default options. For example, Seaborn determines the text labels along the *x*-axis from the die face values 1–6 and the text labels along the *y*-axis from the actual die frequencies. Behind the scenes, Matplotlib determines the positions and sizes of the bars, based on the window size and the magnitudes of the values the bars represent. It also positions the **Frequency** axis's numeric labels based on the actual die frequencies that the bars represent. There are many more features you can customize. You should tweak these attributes to your personal preferences.

The first screen capture below shows the results for 60,000 die rolls—imagine trying to do this by hand. In this case, we expect about 10,000 of each face. The second screen capture below shows the results for 6,000,000 rolls—surely something you'd never do by hand! In this case, we expect about 1,000,000 of each face, and the frequency bars appear to be identical in length (they're close but not exactly the same length). Note that with more die rolls, the frequency percentages are much closer to the expected 16.667%.

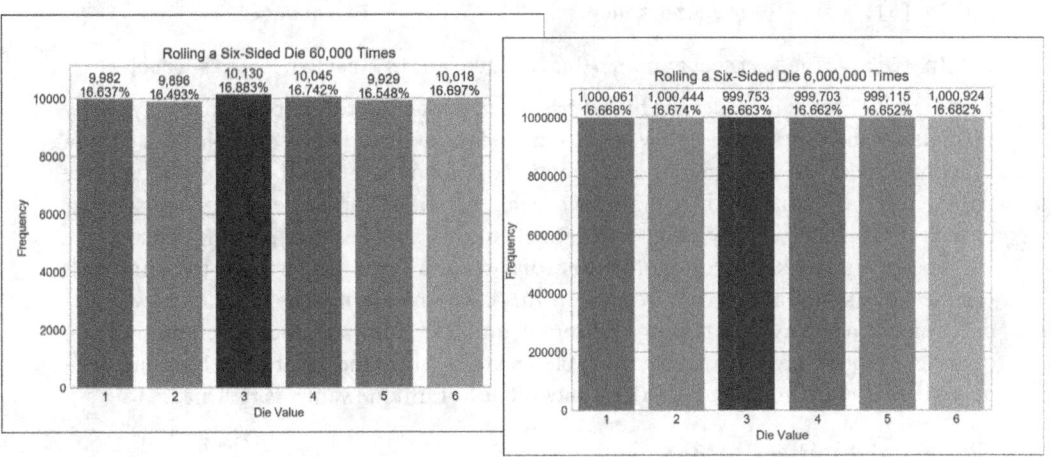

5.17.2 Visualizing Die-Roll Frequencies and Percentages

In this section, you'll interactively develop the bar plots shown in the preceding section.

Launching IPython for Interactive Matplotlib Development

IPython has built-in support for interactively developing Matplotlib graphs, which you also need to develop Seaborn graphs. Simply launch IPython with the command:

```
ipython --matplotlib
```

Importing the Libraries

First, let's import the libraries we'll use:

```
In [1]: import matplotlib.pyplot as plt
```

```
In [2]: import numpy as np
```

```
In [3]: import random
```

```
In [4]: import seaborn as sns
```

1. The **matplotlib.pyplot** module contains the Matplotlib library's graphing capabilities that we use. This module typically is imported with the name plt.

2. The NumPy (Numerical Python) library includes the function unique that we'll use to summarize the die rolls. The **numpy** module typically is imported as np.

3. The random module contains Python's random-number generation functions.

4. The **seaborn** module contains the Seaborn library's graphing capabilities we use. This module typically is imported with the name sns. Search for why this curious abbreviation was chosen.

Rolling the Die and Calculating Die Frequencies

Next, let's use a *list comprehension* to create a list of 600 random die values, then use NumPy's **unique** function to determine the unique roll values (most likely all six possible face values) and their frequencies:

```
In [5]: rolls = [random.randrange(1, 7) for i in range(600)]
```

```
In [6]: values, frequencies = np.unique(rolls, return_counts=True)
```

The NumPy library provides the high-performance **ndarray** collection, which is typically much faster than lists.[1] Though we do not use ndarray directly here, the NumPy unique function expects an ndarray argument and returns an ndarray. If you pass a list (like rolls), NumPy converts it to an ndarray for better performance. The ndarray that unique returns we'll simply assign to a variable for use by a Seaborn plotting function.

Specifying the keyword argument **return_counts**=True tells unique to count each unique value's number of occurrences. In this case, unique returns a tuple of two one-dimensional ndarrays containing the sorted unique values and the corresponding frequencies, respectively. We unpack the tuple's ndarrays into the variables values and frequencies. If return_counts is False, only the list of unique values is returned.

Creating the Initial Bar Plot

Let's create the bar plot's title, set its style, then graph the die faces and frequencies:

```
In [7]: title = f'Rolling a Six-Sided Die {len(rolls):,} Times'
```

```
In [8]: sns.set_style('whitegrid')
```

```
In [9]: axes = sns.barplot(x=values, y=frequencies, palette='bright')
```

Snippet [7]'s f-string includes the number of die rolls in the bar plot's title. The comma (,) format specifier in

```
{len(rolls):,}
```

displays the number with *thousands separators*—so, 60000 would be displayed as 60,000.

By default, Seaborn plots graphs on a plain white background, but it provides several styles to choose from ('darkgrid', 'whitegrid', 'dark', 'white' and 'ticks'). Snippet

---

1. We'll run a performance comparison in Chapter 7 where we discuss ndarray in depth.

[8] specifies the 'whitegrid' style, which displays light-gray horizontal lines in the vertical bar plot. These help you see more easily how each bar's height corresponds to the numeric frequency labels at the bar plot's left side.

Snippet [9] graphs the die frequencies using Seaborn's **barplot function**. When you execute this snippet, the following window appears (because you launched IPython with the --matplotlib option):

Seaborn interacts with Matplotlib to display the bars by creating a Matplotlib **Axes** object, which manages the content that appears in the window. Behind the scenes, Seaborn uses a Matplotlib **Figure** object to manage the window in which the Axes will appear. Function barplot's first two arguments are ndarrays containing the *x*-axis and *y*-axis values, respectively. We used the optional palette keyword argument to choose Seaborn's predefined color palette 'bright'. You can view the palette options at:

> https://seaborn.pydata.org/tutorial/color_palettes.html

Function barplot returns the Axes object that it configured. We assign this to the variable axes so we can use it to configure other aspects of our final plot. Any changes you make to the bar plot after this point will appear *immediately* when you execute the corresponding snippet.

Setting the Window Title and Labeling the x- and y-Axes

The next two snippets add some descriptive text to the bar plot:

```
In [10]: axes.set_title(title)
Out[10]: Text(0.5,1,'Rolling a Six-Sided Die 600 Times')

In [11]: axes.set(xlabel='Die Value', ylabel='Frequency')
Out[11]: [Text(92.6667,0.5,'Frequency'), Text(0.5,58.7667,'Die Value')]
```

Snippet [10] uses the axes object's **set_title** method to display the title string centered above the plot. This method returns a Text object containing the title and its *location* in the window, which IPython simply displays as output for confirmation. You can ignore the Out[]s in the snippets above.

Snippet [11] add labels to each axis. The **set** method receives keyword arguments for the Axes object's properties to set. The method displays the xlabel text along the *x*-axis, and the ylabel text along the *y*-axis, and returns a list of Text objects containing the labels and their locations. The bar plot now appears as follows:

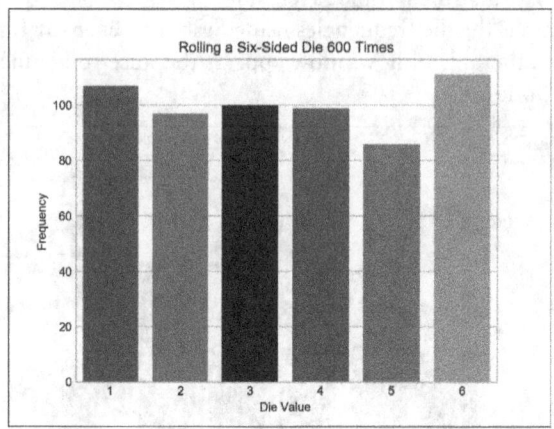

Finalizing the Bar Plot

The next two snippets complete the graph by making room for the text above each bar, then displaying it:

```
In [12]: axes.set_ylim(top=max(frequencies) * 1.10)
Out[12]: (0.0, 122.10000000000001)

In [13]: for bar, frequency in zip(axes.patches, frequencies):
   ...:     text_x = bar.get_x() + bar.get_width() / 2.0
   ...:     text_y = bar.get_height()
   ...:     text = f'{frequency:,}\n{frequency / len(rolls):.3%}'
   ...:     axes.text(text_x, text_y, text,
   ...:               fontsize=11, ha='center', va='bottom')
   ...:
```

To make room for the text above the bars, snippet [12] scales the *y*-axis by 10%. We chose this value via experimentation. The Axes object's **set_ylim** method has many optional keyword arguments. Here, we use only top to change the maximum value represented by the *y*-axis. We multiplied the largest frequency by 1.10 to ensure that the *y*-axis is 10% taller than the tallest bar.

Finally, snippet [13] displays each bar's frequency value and percentage of the total rolls. The axes object's patches collection contains two-dimensional colored shapes that represent the plot's bars. The for statement uses zip to iterate through the patches and their corresponding frequency values. Each iteration unpacks into bar and frequency one of the tuples zip returns. The for statement's suite operates as follows:

- The first statement calculates the center *x*-coordinate where the text will appear. We calculate this as the sum of the bar's left-edge *x*-coordinate (bar.get_x()) and half of the bar's width (bar.get_width() / 2.0).

- The second statement gets the *y*-coordinate where the text will appear—bar.get_y() represents the bar's top.

- The third statement creates a two-line string containing that bar's frequency and the corresponding percentage of the total die rolls.

- The last statement calls the Axes object's **text** method to display the text above the bar. This method's first two arguments specify the text's *x–y* position, and the third argument is the text to display. The keyword argument ha specifies the *horizontal alignment*—we centered text horizontally around the *x*-coordinate. The keyword argument va specifies the *vertical alignment*—we aligned the bottom of the text with at the *y*-coordinate. The final bar plot is shown below:

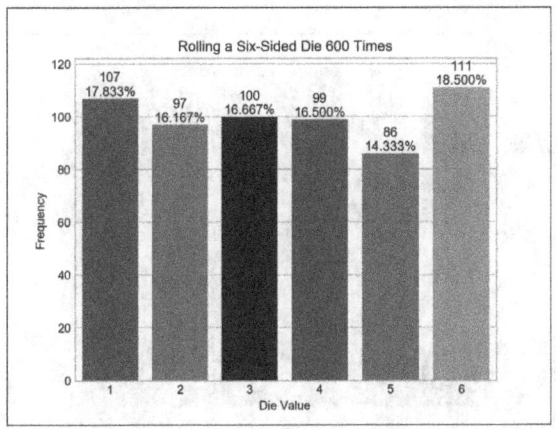

Rolling Again and Updating the Bar Plot—Introducing IPython Magics

Now that you've created a nice bar plot, you probably want to try a different number of die rolls. First, clear the existing graph by calling Matplotlib's **cla** (clear axes) function:

```
In [14]: plt.cla()
```

IPython provides special commands called **magics** for conveniently performing various tasks. Let's use the **%recall magic** to get snippet [5], which created the rolls list, and place the code at the next In [] prompt:

```
In [15]: %recall 5

In [16]: rolls = [random.randrange(1, 7) for i in range(600)]
```

You can now edit the snippet to change the number of rolls to 60000, then press *Enter* to create a new list:

```
In [16]: rolls = [random.randrange(1, 7) for i in range(60000)]
```

Next, recall snippets [6] through [13]. This displays all the snippets in the specified range in the next In [] prompt. Press *Enter* to re-execute these snippets:

```
In [17]: %recall 6-13

In [18]: values, frequencies = np.unique(rolls, return_counts=True)
    ...: title = f'Rolling a Six-Sided Die {len(rolls):,} Times'
    ...: sns.set_style('whitegrid')
    ...: axes = sns.barplot(x=values, y=frequencies, palette='bright')
    ...: axes.set_title(title)
    ...: axes.set(xlabel='Die Value', ylabel='Frequency')
    ...: axes.set_ylim(top=max(frequencies) * 1.10)
```

```
...: for bar, frequency in zip(axes.patches, frequencies):
...:     text_x = bar.get_x() + bar.get_width() / 2.0
...:     text_y = bar.get_height()
...:     text = f'{frequency:,}\n{frequency / len(rolls):.3%}'
...:     axes.text(text_x, text_y, text,
...:               fontsize=11, ha='center', va='bottom')
...:
```

The updated bar plot is shown below:

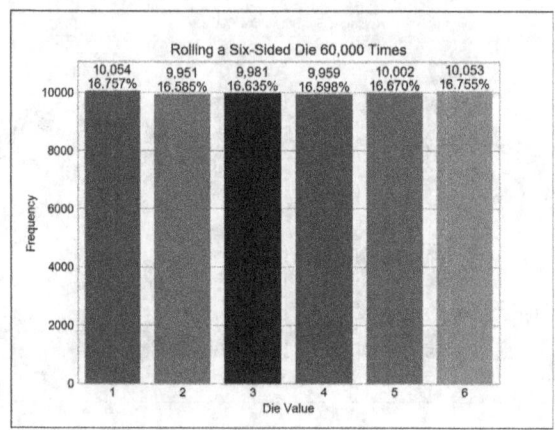

Saving Snippets to a File with the %save Magic

Once you've interactively created a plot, you may want to save the code to a file so you can turn it into a script and run it in the future. Let's use the **%save magic** to save snippets 1 through 13 to a file named RollDie.py. IPython indicates the file to which the lines were written, then displays the lines that it saved:

```
In [19]: %save RollDie.py 1-13
The following commands were written to file `RollDie.py`:
import matplotlib.pyplot as plt
import numpy as np
import random
import seaborn as sns
rolls = [random.randrange(1, 7) for i in range(600)]
values, frequencies = np.unique(rolls, return_counts=True)
title = f'Rolling a Six-Sided Die {len(rolls):,} Times'
sns.set_style("whitegrid")
axes = sns.barplot(values, frequencies, palette='bright')
axes.set_title(title)
axes.set(xlabel='Die Value', ylabel='Frequency')
axes.set_ylim(top=max(frequencies) * 1.10)
for bar, frequency in zip(axes.patches, frequencies):
    text_x = bar.get_x() + bar.get_width() / 2.0
    text_y = bar.get_height()
    text = f'{frequency:,}\n{frequency / len(rolls):.3%}'
    axes.text(text_x, text_y, text,
              fontsize=11, ha='center', va='bottom')
```

Command-Line Arguments; Displaying a Plot from a Script

Provided with this chapter's examples is an edited version of the RollDie.py file you saved above. We added comments and a two modifications so you can run the script with an argument that specifies the number of die rolls, as in:

```
ipython RollDie.py 600
```

The Python Standard Library's **sys module** enables a script to receive *command-line arguments* that are passed into the program. These include the script's name and any values that appear to the right of it when you execute the script. The sys module's **argv** list contains the arguments. In the command above, argv[0] is the *string* 'RollDie.py' and argv[1] is the *string* '600'. To control the number of die rolls with the command-line argument's value, we modified the statement that creates the rolls list as follows:

```
rolls = [random.randrange(1, 7) for i in range(int(sys.argv[1]))]
```

Note that we converted the argv[1] string to an int.

Matplotlib and Seaborn do not automatically display the plot for you when you create it in a script. So at the end of the script we added the following call to Matplotlib's **show** function, which displays the window containing the graph:

```
plt.show()
```

5.18 **Wrap-Up**

This chapter presented more details of the list and tuple sequences. You created lists, accessed their elements and determined their length. You saw that lists are mutable, so you can modify their contents, including growing and shrinking the lists as your programs execute. You saw that accessing a nonexistent element causes an IndexError. You used for statements to iterate through list elements.

We discussed tuples, which like lists are sequences, but are immutable. You unpacked a tuple's elements into separate variables. You used enumerate to create an iterable of tuples, each with a list index and corresponding element value.

You learned that all sequences support slicing, which creates new sequences with subsets of the original elements. You used the del statement to remove elements from lists and delete variables from interactive sessions. We passed lists, list elements and slices of lists to functions. You saw how to search and sort lists, and how to search tuples. We used list methods to insert, append and remove elements, and to reverse a list's elements and copy lists.

We showed how to simulate stacks with lists. We used the concise list-comprehension notation to create new lists. We used additional built-in methods to sum list elements, iterate backward through a list, find the minimum and maximum values, filter values and map values to new values. We showed how nested lists can represent two-dimensional tables in which data is arranged in rows and columns. You saw how nested for loops process two-dimensional lists.

The chapter concluded with an Intro to Data Science section that presented a die-rolling simulation and static visualizations. A detailed code example used the Seaborn and Matplotlib visualization libraries to create a *static* bar plot visualization of the simulation's final results. In the next Intro to Data Science section, we use a die-rolling simulation with a *dynamic* bar plot visualization to make the plot "come alive."

In the next chapter, "Dictionaries and Sets," we'll continue our discussion of Python's built-in collections. We'll use dictionaries to store unordered collections of key–value pairs that map immutable keys to values, just as a conventional dictionary maps words to definitions. We'll use sets to store unordered collections of unique elements.

In the "Array-Oriented Programming with NumPy" chapter, we'll discuss NumPy's ndarray collection in more detail. You'll see that while lists are fine for small amounts of data, they are not efficient for the large amounts of data you'll encounter in big data analytics applications. For such cases, the NumPy library's highly optimized ndarray collection should be used. ndarray (*n*-dimensional array) can be much faster than lists. We'll run Python profiling tests to see just how much faster. As you'll see, NumPy also includes many capabilities for conveniently and efficiently manipulating arrays of *many* dimensions. In big data analytics applications, the processing demands can be humongous, so everything we can do to improve performance significantly matters. In our "Big Data: Hadoop, Spark, NoSQL and IoT" chapter, you'll use one of the most popular high-performance big-data databases—MongoDB.[2]

---

2. The database's name is rooted in the word "humongous."

Dictionaries and Sets

Objectives

In this chapter, you'll:

- Use dictionaries to represent unordered collections of key–value pairs.
- Use sets to represent unordered collections of unique values.
- Create, initialize and refer to elements of dictionaries and sets.
- Iterate through a dictionary's keys, values and key–value pairs.
- Add, remove and update a dictionary's key–value pairs.
- Use dictionary and set comparison operators.
- Combine sets with set operators and methods.
- Use operators in and not in to determine if a dictionary contains a key or a set contains a value.
- Use the mutable set operations to modify a set's contents.
- Use comprehensions to create dictionaries and sets quickly and conveniently.
- Learn how to build dynamic visualizations.
- Enhance your understanding of mutability and immutability.

6.1 Introduction

We've discussed three built-in sequence collections—strings, lists and tuples. Now, we consider the built-in non-sequence collections—dictionaries and sets. A **dictionary** is an *unordered* collection which stores **key–value pairs** that map immutable keys to values, just as a conventional dictionary maps words to definitions. A **set** is an unordered collection of *unique* immutable elements.

6.2 Dictionaries

A dictionary *associates* keys with values. Each key *maps* to a specific value. The following table contains examples of dictionaries with their keys, key types, values and value types:

Keys	Key type	Values	Value type
Country names	`str`	Internet country codes	`str`
Decimal numbers	`int`	Roman numerals	`str`
States	`str`	Agricultural products	list of `str`
Hospital patients	`str`	Vital signs	tuple of `int`s and `float`s
Baseball players	`str`	Batting averages	`float`
Metric measurements	`str`	Abbreviations	`str`
Inventory codes	`str`	Quantity in stock	`int`

Unique Keys

A dictionary's keys must be *immutable* (such as strings, numbers or tuples) and *unique* (that is, no duplicates). Multiple keys can have the same value, such as two different inventory codes that have the same quantity in stock.

6.2.1 Creating a Dictionary

You can create a dictionary by enclosing in curly braces, {}, a comma-separated list of key–value pairs, each of the form *key*: *value*. You can create an empty dictionary with {}.

Let's create a dictionary with the country-name keys `'Finland'`, `'South Africa'` and `'Nepal'` and their corresponding Internet country code values `'fi'`, `'za'` and `'np'`:

```
In [1]: country_codes = {'Finland': 'fi', 'South Africa': 'za',
   ...:                   'Nepal': 'np'}
   ...:

In [2]: country_codes
Out[2]: {'Finland': 'fi', 'South Africa': 'za', 'Nepal': 'np'}
```

When you output a dictionary, its comma-separated list of key–value pairs is always enclosed in curly braces. Because dictionaries are *unordered* collections, the display order can differ from the order in which the key–value pairs were added to the dictionary. In snippet [2]'s output the key–value pairs are displayed in the order they were inserted, but do *not* write code that depends on the order of the key–value pairs.

Determining if a Dictionary Is Empty

The built-in function len returns the number of key–value pairs in a dictionary:

```
In [3]: len(country_codes)
Out[3]: 3
```

You can use a dictionary as a condition to determine if it's empty—a non-empty dictionary evaluates to True:

```
In [4]: if country_codes:
   ...:     print('country_codes is not empty')
   ...: else:
   ...:     print('country_codes is empty')
   ...:
country_codes is not empty
```

An empty dictionary evaluates to False. To demonstrate this, in the following code we call method **clear** to delete the dictionary's key–value pairs, then in snippet [6] we recall and re-execute snippet [4]:

```
In [5]: country_codes.clear()
```

```
In [6]: if country_codes:
   ...:     print('country_codes is not empty')
   ...: else:
   ...:     print('country_codes is empty')
   ...:
country_codes is empty
```

6.2.2 Iterating through a Dictionary

The following dictionary maps month-name strings to int values representing the numbers of days in the corresponding month. Note that *multiple* keys can have the *same* value:

```
In [1]: days_per_month = {'January': 31, 'February': 28, 'March': 31}
```

```
In [2]: days_per_month
Out[2]: {'January': 31, 'February': 28, 'March': 31}
```

Again, the dictionary's string representation shows the key–value pairs in their insertion order, but this is not guaranteed because dictionaries are *unordered*. We'll show how to process keys in *sorted* order later in this chapter.

The following `for` statement iterates through `days_per_month`'s key–value pairs. Dictionary method **items** returns each key–value pair as a tuple, which we unpack into `month` and `days`:

```
In [3]: for month, days in days_per_month.items():
   ...:     print(f'{month} has {days} days')
   ...:
January has 31 days
February has 28 days
March has 31 days
```

6.2.3 Basic Dictionary Operations

For this section, let's begin by creating and displaying the dictionary `roman_numerals`. We intentionally provide the incorrect value 100 for the key `'X'`, which we'll correct shortly:

```
In [1]: roman_numerals = {'I': 1, 'II': 2, 'III': 3, 'V': 5, 'X': 100}

In [2]: roman_numerals
Out[2]: {'I': 1, 'II': 2, 'III': 3, 'V': 5, 'X': 100}
```

Accessing the Value Associated with a Key

Let's get the value associated with the key `'V'`:

```
In [3]: roman_numerals['V']
Out[3]: 5
```

Updating the Value of an Existing Key–Value Pair

You can update a key's associated value in an assignment statement, which we do here to replace the incorrect value associated with the key `'X'`:

```
In [4]: roman_numerals['X'] = 10

In [5]: roman_numerals
Out[5]: {'I': 1, 'II': 2, 'III': 3, 'V': 5, 'X': 10}
```

Adding a New Key–Value Pair

Assigning a value to a nonexistent key inserts the key–value pair in the dictionary:

```
In [6]: roman_numerals['L'] = 50

In [7]: roman_numerals
Out[7]: {'I': 1, 'II': 2, 'III': 3, 'V': 5, 'X': 10, 'L': 50}
```

String keys are case sensitive. Assigning to a nonexistent key inserts a new key–value pair. This may be what you intend, or it could be a logic error.

Removing a Key–Value Pair

You can delete a key–value pair from a dictionary with the `del` statement:

```
In [8]: del roman_numerals['III']

In [9]: roman_numerals
Out[9]: {'I': 1, 'II': 2, 'V': 5, 'X': 10, 'L': 50}
```

You also can remove a key–value pair with the dictionary method **pop**, which returns the value for the removed key:

```
In [10]: roman_numerals.pop('X')
Out[10]: 10

In [11]: roman_numerals
Out[11]: {'I': 1, 'II': 2, 'V': 5, 'L': 50}
```

Attempting to Access a Nonexistent Key
Accessing a nonexistent key results in a KeyError:

```
In [12]: roman_numerals['III']
---------------------------------------------------------------------------
KeyError                                  Traceback (most recent call last)
<ipython-input-12-ccd50c7f0c8b> in <module>()
----> 1 roman_numerals['III']

KeyError: 'III'
```

You can prevent this error by using dictionary method **get**, which normally returns its argument's corresponding value. If that key is not found, get returns None. IPython does not display anything when None is returned in snippet [13]. If you specify a second argument to get, it returns that value if the key is not found:

```
In [13]: roman_numerals.get('III')

In [14]: roman_numerals.get('III', 'III not in dictionary')
Out[14]: 'III not in dictionary'

In [15]: roman_numerals.get('V')
Out[15]: 5
```

Testing Whether a Dictionary Contains a Specified Key
Operators in and not in can determine whether a dictionary contains a specified key:

```
In [16]: 'V' in roman_numerals
Out[16]: True

In [17]: 'III' in roman_numerals
Out[17]: False

In [18]: 'III' not in roman_numerals
Out[18]: True
```

6.2.4 Dictionary Methods keys and values

Earlier, we used dictionary method items to iterate through tuples of a dictionary's key–value pairs. Similarly, methods **keys** and **values** can be used to iterate through only a dictionary's keys or values, respectively:

```
In [1]: months = {'January': 1, 'February': 2, 'March': 3}

In [2]: for month_name in months.keys():
   ...:     print(month_name, end=' ')
   ...:
January February March
```

```
In [3]: for month_number in months.values():
   ...:     print(month_number, end=' ')
   ...:
1  2  3
```

Dictionary Views

Dictionary methods items, keys and values each return a view of a dictionary's data. When you iterate over a **view**, it "sees" the dictionary's current contents—it does *not* have its own copy of the data.

To show that views do *not* maintain their own copies of a dictionary's data, let's first save the view returned by keys into the variable months_view, then iterate through it:

```
In [4]: months_view = months.keys()
```

```
In [5]: for key in months_view:
   ...:     print(key, end=' ')
   ...:
January  February  March
```

Next, let's add a new key–value pair to months and display the updated dictionary:

```
In [6]: months['December'] = 12
```

```
In [7]: months
Out[7]: {'January': 1, 'February': 2, 'March': 3, 'December': 12}
```

Now, let's iterate through months_view again. The key we added above is indeed displayed:

```
In [8]: for key in months_view:
   ...:     print(key, end=' ')
   ...:
January  February  March  December
```

Do not modify a dictionary while iterating through a view. According to Section 4.10.1 of the Python Standard Library documentation,[1] either you'll get a RuntimeError or the loop might not process all of the view's values.

Converting Dictionary Keys, Values and Key–Value Pairs to Lists

You might occasionally need *lists* of a dictionary's keys, values or key–value pairs. To obtain such a list, pass the view returned by keys, values or items to the built-in list function. Modifying these lists does *not* modify the corresponding dictionary:

```
In [9]: list(months.keys())
Out[9]: ['January', 'February', 'March', 'December']
```

```
In [10]: list(months.values())
Out[10]: [1, 2, 3, 12]
```

```
In [11]: list(months.items())
Out[11]: [('January', 1), ('February', 2), ('March', 3), ('December', 12)]
```

---

1. https://docs.python.org/3/library/stdtypes.html#dictionary-view-objects.

Processing Keys in Sorted Order

To process keys in *sorted* order, you can use built-in function sorted as follows:

```
In [12]: for month_name in sorted(months.keys()):
    ...:     print(month_name, end=' ')
    ...:
December  February  January  March
```

6.2.5 Dictionary Comparisons

The comparison operators == and != can be used to determine whether two dictionaries have identical or different contents. An equals (==) comparison evaluates to True if both dictionaries have the same key–value pairs, *regardless* of the order in which those key–value pairs were added to each dictionary:

```
In [1]: country_capitals1 = {'Belgium': 'Brussels',
   ...:                       'Haiti': 'Port-au-Prince'}
   ...:

In [2]: country_capitals2 = {'Nepal': 'Kathmandu',
   ...:                       'Uruguay': 'Montevideo'}
   ...:

In [3]: country_capitals3 = {'Haiti': 'Port-au-Prince',
   ...:                       'Belgium': 'Brussels'}
   ...:

In [4]: country_capitals1 == country_capitals2
Out[4]: False

In [5]: country_capitals1 == country_capitals3
Out[5]: True

In [6]: country_capitals1 != country_capitals2
Out[6]: True
```

6.2.6 Example: Dictionary of Student Grades

The following script represents an instructor's grade book as a dictionary that maps each student's name (a string) to a list of integers containing that student's grades on three exams. In each iteration of the loop that displays the data (lines 13–17), we unpack a key–value pair into the variables name and grades containing one student's name and the corresponding list of three grades. Line 14 uses built-in function sum to total a given student's grades, then line 15 calculates and displays that student's average by dividing total by the number of grades for that student (len(grades)). Lines 16–17 keep track of the total of all four students' grades and the number of grades for all the students, respectively. Line 19 prints the class average of all the students' grades on all the exams.

```
1   # fig06_01.py
2   """Using a dictionary to represent an instructor's grade book."""
3   grade_book = {
4       'Susan': [92, 85, 100],
5       'Eduardo': [83, 95, 79],
6       'Azizi': [91, 89, 82],
7       'Pantipa': [97, 91, 92]
8   }
```

```
 9
10    all_grades_total = 0
11    all_grades_count = 0
12
13    for name, grades in grade_book.items():
14        total = sum(grades)
15        print(f'Average for {name} is {total/len(grades):.2f}')
16        all_grades_total += total
17        all_grades_count += len(grades)
18
19    print(f"Class's average is: {all_grades_total / all_grades_count:.2f}")
```

```
Average for Susan is 92.33
Average for Eduardo is 85.67
Average for Azizi is 87.33
Average for Pantipa is 93.33
Class's average is: 89.67
```

6.2.7 Example: Word Counts[2]

The following script builds a dictionary to count the number of occurrences of each word in a string. Lines 4–5 create a string text that we'll break into words—a process known as **tokenizing a string**. Python automatically concatenates strings separated by whitespace in parentheses. Line 7 creates an empty dictionary. The dictionary's keys will be the unique words, and its values will be integer counts of how many times each word appears in text.

```
 1    # fig06_02.py
 2    """Tokenizing a string and counting unique words."""
 3
 4    text = ('this is sample text with several words '
 5            'this is more sample text with some different words')
 6
 7    word_counts = {}
 8
 9    # count occurrences of each unique word
10    for word in text.split():
11        if word in word_counts:
12            word_counts[word] += 1  # update existing key-value pair
13        else:
14            word_counts[word] = 1  # insert new key-value pair
15
16    print(f'{"WORD":<12}COUNT')
17
18    for word, count in sorted(word_counts.items()):
19        print(f'{word:<12}{count}')
20
21    print('\nNumber of unique words:', len(word_counts))
```

---

2. Techniques like word frequency counting are often used to analyze published works. For example, some people believe that the works of William Shakespeare actually might have been written by Sir Francis Bacon, Christopher Marlowe or others. Comparing the word frequencies of their works with those of Shakespeare can reveal writing-style similarities. We'll look at other document-analysis techniques in the "Natural Language Processing (NLP)" chapter.

```
WORD         COUNT
different    1
is           2
more         1
sample       2
several      1
some         1
text         2
this         2
with         2
words        2
Number of unique words: 10
```

Line 10 tokenizes text by calling string method **split**, which separates the words using the method's delimiter string argument. If you do not provide an argument, split uses a space. The method returns a list of tokens (that is, the words in text). Lines 10–14 iterate through the list of words. For each word, line 11 determines whether that word (the key) is already in the dictionary. If so, line 12 increments that word's count; otherwise, line 14 inserts a new key–value pair for that word with an initial count of 1.

Lines 16–21 summarize the results in a two-column table containing each word and its corresponding count. The for statement in lines 18 and 19 iterates through the dictionary's key–value pairs. It unpacks each key and value into the variables word and count, then displays them in two columns. Line 21 displays the number of unique words.

Python Standard Library Module collections

The Python Standard Library already contains the counting functionality that we implemented using the dictionary and the loop in lines 10–14. The module **collections** contains the type **Counter**, which receives an iterable and summarizes its elements. Let's reimplement the preceding script in fewer lines of code with Counter:

```
In [1]: from collections import Counter

In [2]: text = ('this is sample text with several words '
   ...:         'this is more sample text with some different words')
   ...:

In [3]: counter = Counter(text.split())

In [4]: for word, count in sorted(counter.items()):
   ...:     print(f'{word:<12}{count}')
   ...:
different    1
is           2
more         1
sample       2
several      1
some         1
text         2
this         2
with         2
words        2

In [5]: print('Number of unique keys:', len(counter.keys()))
Number of unique keys: 10
```

Snippet [3] creates the Counter, which summarizes the list of strings returned by text.split(). In snippet [4], Counter method **items** returns each string and its associated count as a tuple. We use built-in function sorted to get a list of these tuples in ascending order. By default sorted orders the tuples by their first elements. If those are identical, then it looks at the second element, and so on. The for statement iterates over the resulting sorted list, displaying each word and count in two columns.

6.2.8 Dictionary Method update

You may insert and update key–value pairs using dictionary method **update**. First, let's create an empty country_codes dictionary:

```
In [1]: country_codes = {}
```

The following update call receives a dictionary of key–value pairs to insert or update:

```
In [2]: country_codes.update({'South Africa': 'za'})

In [3]: country_codes
Out[3]: {'South Africa': 'za'}
```

Method update can convert keyword arguments into key–value pairs to insert. The following call automatically converts the parameter name Australia into the string key 'Australia' and associates the value 'ar' with that key:

```
In [4]: country_codes.update(Australia='ar')

In [5]: country_codes
Out[5]: {'South Africa': 'za', 'Australia': 'ar'}
```

Snippet [4] provided an incorrect country code for Australia. Let's correct this by using another keyword argument to update the value associated with 'Australia':

```
In [6]: country_codes.update(Australia='au')

In [7]: country_codes
Out[7]: {'South Africa': 'za', 'Australia': 'au'}
```

Method update also can receive an iterable object containing key–value pairs, such as a list of two-element tuples.

6.2.9 Dictionary Comprehensions

Dictionary comprehensions provide a convenient notation for quickly generating dictionaries, often by mapping one dictionary to another. For example, in a dictionary with *unique* values, you can reverse the key–value pairs:

```
In [1]: months = {'January': 1, 'February': 2, 'March': 3}

In [2]: months2 = {number: name for name, number in months.items()}

In [3]: months2
Out[3]: {1: 'January', 2: 'February', 3: 'March'}
```

Curly braces delimit a *dictionary comprehension*, and the expression to the left of the for clause specifies a key–value pair of the form *key*: *value*. The comprehension iterates through months.items(), unpacking each key–value pair tuple into the variables name and number. The expression number: name reverses the key and value, so the new dictionary maps the month numbers to the month names.

What if months contained *duplicate* values? As these become the keys in months2, attempting to insert a *duplicate* key simply updates the existing key's value. So if 'February' and 'March' both mapped to 2 originally, the preceding code would have produced

```
{1: 'January', 2: 'March'}
```

A dictionary comprehension also can map a dictionary's values to new values. The following comprehension converts a dictionary of names and lists of grades into a dictionary of names and grade-point averages. The variables k and v commonly mean *key* and *value*:

```
In [4]: grades = {'Sue': [98, 87, 94], 'Bob': [84, 95, 91]}

In [5]: grades2 = {k: sum(v) / len(v) for k, v in grades.items()}

In [6]: grades2
Out[6]: {'Sue': 93.0, 'Bob': 90.0}
```

The comprehension unpacks each tuple returned by grades.items() into k (the name) and v (the list of grades). Then, the comprehension creates a new key–value pair with the key k and the value of sum(v) / len(v), which averages the list's elements.

6.3 Sets

A set is an unordered collection of *unique* values. Sets may contain only immutable objects, like strings, ints, floats and tuples that contain only immutable elements. Though sets are iterable, they are not sequences and do not support indexing and slicing with square brackets, []. Dictionaries also do not support slicing.

Creating a Set with Curly Braces

The following code creates a set of strings named colors:

```
In [1]: colors = {'red', 'orange', 'yellow', 'green', 'red', 'blue'}

In [2]: colors
Out[2]: {'blue', 'green', 'orange', 'red', 'yellow'}
```

Notice that the duplicate string 'red' was ignored (without causing an error). An important use of sets is **duplicate elimination**, which is automatic when creating a set. Also, the resulting set's values are *not* displayed in the same order as they were listed in snippet [1]. Though the color names are displayed in sorted order, sets are *unordered*. You should not write code that depends on the order of their elements.

Determining a Set's Length

You can determine the number of items in a set with the built-in len function:

```
In [3]: len(colors)
Out[3]: 5
```

Checking Whether a Value Is in a Set

You can check whether a set contains a particular value using the in and not in operators:

```
In [4]: 'red' in colors
Out[4]: True
```

```
In [5]: 'purple' in colors
Out[5]: False

In [6]: 'purple' not in colors
Out[6]: True
```

Iterating Through a Set

Sets are iterable, so you can process each set element with a for loop:

```
In [7]: for color in colors:
   ...:         print(color.upper(), end=' ')
   ...:
RED GREEN YELLOW BLUE ORANGE
```

Sets are *unordered*, so there's no significance to the iteration order.

Creating a Set with the Built-In set Function

You can create a set from another collection of values by using the built-in **set** function—
here we create a list that contains several duplicate integer values and use that list as set's
argument:

```
In [8]: numbers = list(range(10)) + list(range(5))

In [9]: numbers
Out[9]: [0, 1, 2, 3, 4, 5, 6, 7, 8, 9, 0, 1, 2, 3, 4]

In [10]: set(numbers)
Out[10]: {0, 1, 2, 3, 4, 5, 6, 7, 8, 9}
```

If you need to create an empty set, you must use the set function with empty parentheses,
rather than empty braces, {}, which represent an empty dictionary:

```
In [11]: set()
Out[11]: set()
```

Python displays an empty set as set() to avoid confusion with Python's string representation of an empty dictionary ({}).

Frozenset: An Immutable Set Type

Sets are *mutable*—you can add and remove elements, but set *elements* must be *immutable*.
Therefore, a set cannot have other sets as elements. A **frozenset** is an *immutable* set—it
cannot be modified after you create it, so a set *can* contain frozensets as elements. The
built-in function **frozenset** creates a frozenset from any iterable.

6.3.1 Comparing Sets

Various operators and methods can be used to compare sets. The following sets contain
the same values, so == returns True and != returns False.

```
In [1]: {1, 3, 5} == {3, 5, 1}
Out[1]: True

In [2]: {1, 3, 5} != {3, 5, 1}
Out[2]: False
```

The < operator tests whether the set to its left is a **proper subset** of the one to its right—that is, all the elements in the left operand are in the right operand, and the sets are not equal:

```
In [3]: {1, 3, 5} < {3, 5, 1}
Out[3]: False

In [4]: {1, 3, 5} < {7, 3, 5, 1}
Out[4]: True
```

The <= operator tests whether the set to its left is an **improper subset** of the one to its right—that is, all the elements in the left operand are in the right operand, and the sets might be equal:

```
In [5]: {1, 3, 5} <= {3, 5, 1}
Out[5]: True

In [6]: {1, 3} <= {3, 5, 1}
Out[6]: True
```

You may also check for an improper subset with the set method **issubset**:

```
In [7]: {1, 3, 5}.issubset({3, 5, 1})
Out[7]: True

In [8]: {1, 2}.issubset({3, 5, 1})
Out[8]: False
```

The > operator tests whether the set to its left is a **proper superset** of the one to its right—that is, all the elements in the right operand are in the left operand, and the left operand has more elements:

```
In [9]: {1, 3, 5} > {3, 5, 1}
Out[9]: False

In [10]: {1, 3, 5, 7} > {3, 5, 1}
Out[10]: True
```

The >= operator tests whether the set to its left is an **improper superset** of the one to its right—that is, all the elements in the right operand are in the left operand, and the sets might be equal:

```
In [11]: {1, 3, 5} >= {3, 5, 1}
Out[11]: True

In [12]: {1, 3, 5} >= {3, 1}
Out[12]: True

In [13]: {1, 3} >= {3, 1, 7}
Out[13]: False
```

You may also check for an improper superset with the set method **issuperset**:

```
In [14]: {1, 3, 5}.issuperset({3, 5, 1})
Out[14]: True

In [15]: {1, 3, 5}.issuperset({3, 2})
Out[15]: False
```

The argument to issubset or issuperset can be *any* iterable. When either of these methods receives a non-set iterable argument, it first converts the iterable to a set, then performs the operation.

6.3.2 Mathematical Set Operations

This section presents the set type's mathematical operators |, &, - and ^ and the corresponding methods.

Union

The **union** of two sets is a set consisting of all the unique elements from both sets. You can calculate the union with the | **operator** or with the set type's **union** method:

```
In [1]: {1, 3, 5} | {2, 3, 4}
Out[1]: {1, 2, 3, 4, 5}

In [2]: {1, 3, 5}.union([20, 20, 3, 40, 40])
Out[2]: {1, 3, 5, 20, 40}
```

The operands of the binary set operators, like |, must both be sets. The corresponding set methods may receive any iterable object as an argument—we passed a list. When a mathematical set method receives a non-set iterable argument, it first converts the iterable to a set, then applies the mathematical operation. Again, though the new sets' string representations show the values in ascending order, you should not write code that depends on this.

Intersection

The **intersection** of two sets is a set consisting of all the unique elements that the two sets have in common. You can calculate the intersection with the **& operator** or with the set type's **intersection** method:

```
In [3]: {1, 3, 5} & {2, 3, 4}
Out[3]: {3}

In [4]: {1, 3, 5}.intersection([1, 2, 2, 3, 3, 4, 4])
Out[4]: {1, 3}
```

Difference

The **difference** between two sets is a set consisting of the elements in the left operand that are not in the right operand. You can calculate the difference with the - **operator** or with the set type's **difference** method:

```
In [5]: {1, 3, 5} - {2, 3, 4}
Out[5]: {1, 5}

In [6]: {1, 3, 5, 7}.difference([2, 2, 3, 3, 4, 4])
Out[6]: {1, 5, 7}
```

Symmetric Difference

The **symmetric difference** between two sets is a set consisting of the elements of both sets that are not in common with one another. You can calculate the symmetric difference with the ^ **operator** or with the set type's **symmetric_difference** method:

```
In [7]: {1, 3, 5} ^ {2, 3, 4}
Out[7]: {1, 2, 4, 5}

In [8]: {1, 3, 5, 7}.symmetric_difference([2, 2, 3, 3, 4, 4])
Out[8]: {1, 2, 4, 5, 7}
```

Disjoint

Two sets are **disjoint** if they do not have any common elements. You can determine this with the set type's **isdisjoint** method:

```
In [9]: {1, 3, 5}.isdisjoint({2, 4, 6})
Out[9]: True

In [10]: {1, 3, 5}.isdisjoint({4, 6, 1})
Out[10]: False
```

6.3.3 Mutable Set Operators and Methods

The operators and methods presented in the preceding section each result in a *new* set. Here we discuss operators and methods that modify an *existing* set.

Mutable Mathematical Set Operations

Like operator |, **union augmented assignment** |= performs a set union operation, but |= modifies its left operand:

```
In [1]: numbers = {1, 3, 5}

In [2]: numbers |= {2, 3, 4}

In [3]: numbers
Out[3]: {1, 2, 3, 4, 5}
```

Similarly, the set type's **update** method performs a union operation modifying the set on which it's called—the argument can be any iterable:

```
In [4]: numbers.update(range(10))

In [5]: numbers
Out[5]: {0, 1, 2, 3, 4, 5, 6, 7, 8, 9}
```

The other mutable set methods are:

- intersection augmented assignment &=
- difference augmented assignment -=
- symmetric difference augmented assignment ^=

and their corresponding methods with iterable arguments are:

- `intersection_update`
- `difference_update`
- `symmetric_difference_update`

Methods for Adding and Removing Elements

Set method **add** inserts its argument if the argument is *not* already in the set; otherwise, the set remains unchanged:

```
In [6]: numbers.add(17)

In [7]: numbers.add(3)

In [8]: numbers
Out[8]: {0, 1, 2, 3, 4, 5, 6, 7, 8, 9, 17}
```

Set method **remove** removes its argument from the set—a KeyError occurs if the value is not in the set:

```
In [9]: numbers.remove(3)

In [10]: numbers
Out[10]: {0, 1, 2, 4, 5, 6, 7, 8, 9, 17}
```

Method **discard** also removes its argument from the set but does not cause an exception if the value is not in the set.

You also can remove an *arbitrary* set element and return it with **pop**, but sets are unordered, so you do not know which element will be returned:

```
In [11]: numbers.pop()
Out[11]: 0

In [12]: numbers
Out[12]: {1, 2, 4, 5, 6, 7, 8, 9, 17}
```

A KeyError occurs if the set is empty when you call pop.

Finally, method **clear** empties the set on which it's called:

```
In [13]: numbers.clear()

In [14]: numbers
Out[14]: set()
```

6.3.4 Set Comprehensions

Like dictionary comprehensions, you define set comprehensions in curly braces. Let's create a new set containing only the unique even values in the list numbers:

```
In [1]: numbers = [1, 2, 2, 3, 4, 5, 6, 6, 7, 8, 9, 10, 10]

In [2]: evens = {item for item in numbers if item % 2 == 0}

In [3]: evens
Out[3]: {2, 4, 6, 8, 10}
```

6.4 Intro to Data Science: Dynamic Visualizations

The preceding chapter's Intro to Data Science section introduced visualization. We simulated rolling a six-sided die and used the Seaborn and Matplotlib visualization libraries to create a publication-quality *static* bar plot showing the frequencies and percentages of each roll value. In this section, we make things "come alive" with *dynamic visualizations*.

The Law of Large Numbers

When we introduced random-number generation, we mentioned that if the `random` module's `randrange` function indeed produces integers at random, then every number in the specified range has an equal probability (or likelihood) of being chosen each time the function is called. For a six-sided die, each value 1 through 6 should occur one-sixth of the time, so the probability of any one of these values occurring is $1/6^{th}$ or about 16.667%.

In the next section, we create and execute a *dynamic* (that is, *animated*) die-rolling simulation script. In general, you'll see that the more rolls we attempt, the closer each die value's percentage of the total rolls gets to 16.667% and the heights of the bars gradually become about the same. This is a manifestation of the *law of large numbers*.

6.4.1 How Dynamic Visualization Works

The plots produced with Seaborn and Matplotlib in the previous chapter's Intro to Data Science section help you analyze the results for a fixed number of die rolls *after* the simulation completes. This section's enhances that code with the Matplotlib **animation** module's **FuncAnimation** function, which updates the bar plot *dynamically*. You'll see the bars, die frequencies and percentages "come alive," updating *continuously* as the rolls occur.

Animation Frames

FuncAnimation drives a **frame-by-frame animation**. Each **animation frame** specifies everything that should change during one plot update. Stringing together many of these updates over time creates the animation effect. You decide what each frame displays with a function you define and pass to FuncAnimation.

Each animation frame will:

- roll the dice a specified number of times (from 1 to as many as you'd like), updating die frequencies with each roll,

- clear the current plot,

- create a new set of bars representing the updated frequencies, and

- create new frequency and percentage text for each bar.

Generally, displaying more frames-per-second yields smoother animation. For example, video games with fast-moving elements try to display *at least* 30 frames-per-second and often more. Though you'll specify the number of milliseconds between animation frames, the actual number of frames-per-second can be affected by the amount of work you perform in each frame and the speed of your computer's processor. This example displays an animation frame every 33 milliseconds—yielding approximately 30 (1000 / 33) frames-per-second. Try larger and smaller values to see how they affect the animation. Experimentation is important in developing the best visualizations.

Running RollDieDynamic.py

In the previous chapter's Intro to Data Science section, we developed the static visualization *interactively* so you could see how the code updates the bar plot as you execute each statement. The actual bar plot with the final frequencies and percentages was drawn only once.

For this dynamic visualization, the screen results update frequently so that you can see the animation. Many things change continuously—the lengths of the bars, the frequencies and percentages above the bars, the spacing and labels on the axes and the total number of die rolls shown in the plot's title. For this reason, we present this visualization as a script, rather than interactively developing it.

The script takes two command-line arguments:

- `number_of_frames`—The number of animation frames to display. This value determines the total number of times that FuncAnimation updates the graph. For each animation frame, FuncAnimation calls a function that you define (in this example, update) to specify how to change the plot.

- `rolls_per_frame`—The number of times to roll the die in each animation frame. We'll use a loop to roll the die this number of times, summarize the results, then update the graph with bars and text representing the new frequencies.

To understand how we use these two values, consider the following command:

```
ipython RollDieDynamic.py 6000 1
```

In this case, FuncAnimation calls our update function 6000 times, rolling one die per frame for a total of 6000 rolls. This enables you to see the bars, frequencies and percentages update one roll at a time. On our system, this animation took about 3.33 minutes (6000 frames / 30 frames-per-second / 60 seconds-per-minute) to show you only 6000 die rolls.

Displaying animation frames to the screen is a relatively slow *input–output-bound* operation compared to the die rolls, which occur at the computer's super fast CPU speeds. If we roll only one die per animation frame, we won't be able to run a large number of rolls in a reasonable amount of time. Also, for small numbers of rolls, you're unlikely to see the die percentages converge on their expected 16.667% of the total rolls.

To see the law of large numbers in action, you can increase the execution speed by rolling the die more times per animation frame. Consider the following command:

```
ipython RollDieDynamic.py 10000 600
```

In this case, FuncAnimation will call our update function 10,000 times, performing 600 rolls-per-frame for a total of 6,000,000 rolls. On our system, this took about 5.55 minutes (10,000 frames / 30 frames-per-second / 60 seconds-per-minute), but displayed approximately 18,000 rolls-per-second (30 frames-per-second * 600 rolls-per-frame), so we could quickly see the frequencies and percentages converge on their expected values of about 1,000,000 rolls per face and 16.667% per face.

Experiment with the numbers of rolls and frames until you feel that the program is helping you visualize the results most effectively. It's fun and informative to watch it run and to tweak it until you're satisfied with the animation quality.

Sample Executions

We took the following four screen captures during each of two sample executions. In the first, the screens show the graph after just 64 die rolls, then again after 604 of the 6000 total die rolls. Run this script live to see over time how the bars update dynamically. In the second execution, the screen captures show the graph after 7200 die rolls and again after 166,200 out of the 6,000,000 rolls. With more rolls, you can see the percentages closing in on their expected values of 16.667% as predicted by the law of large numbers.

Execute 6000 animation frames rolling the die once per frame:
`ipython RollDieDynamic.py 6000 1`

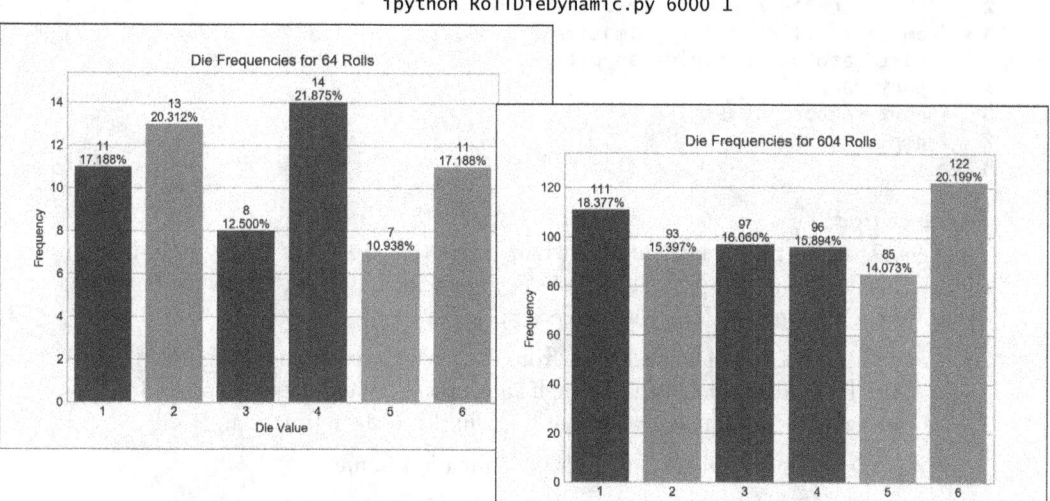

Execute 10,000 animation frames rolling the die 600 times per frame:
`ipython RollDieDynamic.py 10000 600`

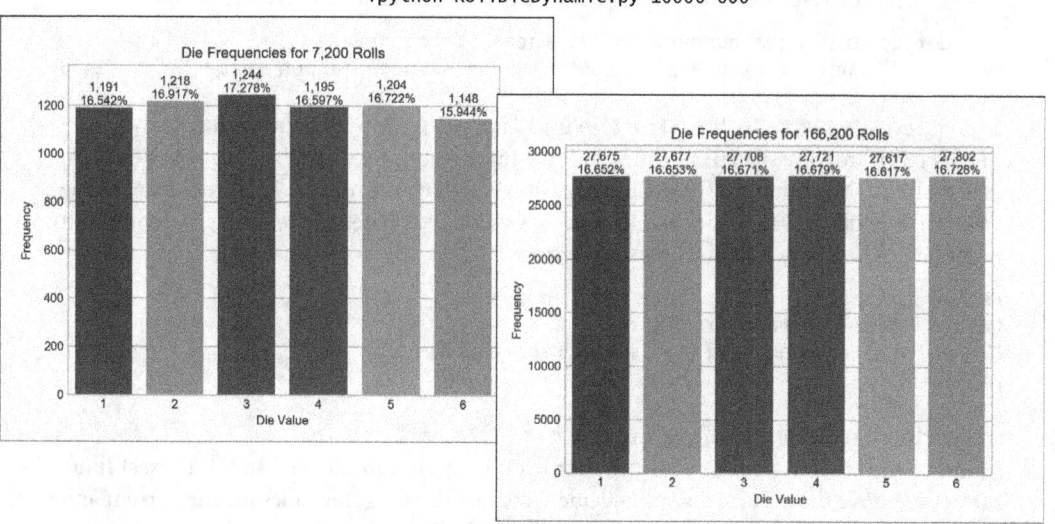

6.4.2 Implementing a Dynamic Visualization

The script we present in this section uses the same Seaborn and Matplotlib features shown in the previous chapter's Intro to Data Science section. We reorganized the code for use with Matplotlib's *animation* capabilities.

Importing the Matplotlib animation Module
We focus primarily on the new features used in this example. Line 3 imports the Matplotlib animation module.

```
1   # RollDieDynamic.py
2   """Dynamically graphing frequencies of die rolls."""
3   from matplotlib import animation
4   import matplotlib.pyplot as plt
5   import random
6   import seaborn as sns
7   import sys
8
```

Function update
Lines 9–27 define the update function that FuncAnimation calls once per animation frame. This function must provide at least one argument. Lines 9–10 show the beginning of the function definition. The parameters are:

- frame_number—The next value from FuncAnimation's frames argument, which we'll discuss momentarily. Though FuncAnimation requires the update function to have this parameter, we do not use it in this update function.
- rolls—The number of die rolls per animation frame.
- faces—The die face values used as labels along the graph's x-axis.
- frequencies—The list in which we summarize the die frequencies.

We discuss the rest of the function's body in the next several subsections.

```
9   def update(frame_number, rolls, faces, frequencies):
10      """Configures bar plot contents for each animation frame."""
```

Function update: Rolling the Die and Updating the frequencies List
Lines 12–13 roll the die rolls times and increment the appropriate frequencies element for each roll. Note that we subtract 1 from the die value (1 through 6) before incrementing the corresponding frequencies element—as you'll see, frequencies is a six-element list (defined in line 36), so its indices are 0 through 5.

```
11      # roll die and update frequencies
12      for i in range(rolls):
13          frequencies[random.randrange(1, 7) - 1] += 1
14
```

Function update: Configuring the Bar Plot and Text
Line 16 in function update calls the matplotlib.pyplot module's **cla** (clear axes) function to remove the existing bar plot elements before drawing new ones for the current animation frame. We discussed the code in lines 17–27 in the previous chapter's Intro to Data Science section. Lines 17–20 create the bars, set the bar plot's title, set the x- and y-axis labels and scale the plot to make room for the frequency and percentage text above each bar. Lines 23–27 display the frequency and percentage text.

```
15      # reconfigure plot for updated die frequencies
16      plt.cla()  # clear old contents contents of current Figure
17      axes = sns.barplot(faces, frequencies, palette='bright')  # new bars
18      axes.set_title(f'Die Frequencies for {sum(frequencies):,} Rolls')
19      axes.set(xlabel='Die Value', ylabel='Frequency')
20      axes.set_ylim(top=max(frequencies) * 1.10)  # scale y-axis by 10%
21
```

```
22    # display frequency & percentage above each patch (bar)
23    for bar, frequency in zip(axes.patches, frequencies):
24        text_x = bar.get_x() + bar.get_width() / 2.0
25        text_y = bar.get_height()
26        text = f'{frequency:,}\n{frequency / sum(frequencies):.3%}'
27        axes.text(text_x, text_y, text, ha='center', va='bottom')
28
```

Variables Used to Configure the Graph and Maintain State

Lines 30 and 31 use the sys module's argv list to get the script's command-line arguments. Line 33 specifies the Seaborn 'whitegrid' style. Line 34 calls the matplotlib.pyplot module's **figure** function to get the Figure object in which FuncAnimation displays the animation. The function's argument is the window's title. As you'll soon see, this is one of FuncAnimation's required arguments. Line 35 creates a list containing the die face values 1–6 to display on the plot's *x*-axis. Line 36 creates the six-element frequencies list with each element initialized to 0—we update this list's counts with each die roll.

```
29    # read command-line arguments for number of frames and rolls per frame
30    number_of_frames = int(sys.argv[1])
31    rolls_per_frame = int(sys.argv[2])
32
33    sns.set_style('whitegrid')  # white background with gray grid lines
34    figure = plt.figure('Rolling a Six-Sided Die')  # Figure for animation
35    values = list(range(1, 7))  # die faces for display on x-axis
36    frequencies = [0] * 6  # six-element list of die frequencies
37
```

Calling the animation Module's FuncAnimation Function

Lines 39–41 call the Matplotlib animation module's FuncAnimation function to update the bar chart dynamically. The function returns an object representing the animation. Though this is not used explicitly, you *must* store the reference to the animation; otherwise, Python immediately terminates the animation and returns its memory to the system.

```
38    # configure and start animation that calls function update
39    die_animation = animation.FuncAnimation(
40        figure, update, repeat=False, frames=number_of_frames, interval=33,
41        fargs=(rolls_per_frame, values, frequencies))
42
43    plt.show()  # display window
```

FuncAnimation has two required arguments:

- figure—the Figure object in which to display the animation, and
- update—the function to call once per animation frame.

In this case, we also pass the following optional keyword arguments:

- **repeat**—False terminates the animation after the specified number of frames. If True (the default), when the animation completes it restarts from the beginning.
- **frames**—The total number of animation frames, which controls how many times FunctAnimation calls update. Passing an integer is equivalent to passing a range—for example, 600 means range(600). FuncAnimation passes one value from this range as the first argument in each call to update.

- **interval**—The number of milliseconds (33, in this case) between animation frames (the default is 200). After each call to update, FuncAnimation waits 33 milliseconds before making the next call.

- **fargs** (short for "function arguments")—A tuple of other arguments to pass to the function you specified in FuncAnimation's second argument. The arguments you specify in the fargs tuple correspond to update's parameters rolls, faces and frequencies (line 9).

For a list of FuncAnimation's other optional arguments, see

```
https://matplotlib.org/api/_as_gen/
matplotlib.animation.FuncAnimation.html
```

Finally, line 43 displays the window.

6.5 Wrap-Up

In this chapter, we discussed Python's dictionary and set collections. We said what a dictionary is and presented several examples. We showed the syntax of key–value pairs and showed how to use them to create dictionaries with comma-separated lists of key–value pairs in curly braces, {}. You also created dictionaries with dictionary comprehensions.

You used square brackets, [], to retrieve the value corresponding to a key, and to insert and update key–value pairs. You also used the dictionary method update to change a key's associated value. You iterated through a dictionary's keys, values and items.

You created sets of unique immutable values. You compared sets with the comparison operators, combined sets with set operators and methods, changed sets' values with the mutable set operations and created sets with set comprehensions. You saw that sets are mutable. Frozensets are immutable, so they can be used as set and frozenset elements.

In the Intro to Data Science section, we continued our visualization introduction by presenting the die-rolling simulation with a *dynamic* bar plot to make the law of large numbers "come alive." In addition, to the Seaborn and Matplotlib features shown in the previous chapter's Intro to Data Science section, we used Matplotlib's FuncAnimation function to control a frame-by-frame animation. FuncAnimation called a function we defined that specified what to display in each animation frame.

In the next chapter, we discuss array-oriented programming with the popular NumPy library. As you'll see, NumPy's ndarray collection can be up to two orders of magnitude faster than performing many of the same operations with Python's built-in lists. This power will come in handy for today's big data applications.

7

Array-Oriented Programming with NumPy

Objectives

In this chapter you'll:

- Learn how arrays differ from lists.
- Use the numpy module's high-performance ndarrays.
- Compare list and ndarray performance with the IPython %timeit magic.
- Use ndarrays to store and retrieve data efficiently.
- Create and initialize ndarrays.
- Refer to individual ndarray elements.
- Iterate through ndarrays.
- Create and manipulate multidimensional ndarrays.
- Perform common ndarray manipulations.
- Create and manipulate pandas one-dimensional Series and two-dimensional DataFrames.
- Customize Series and DataFrame indices.
- Calculate basic descriptive statistics for data in a Series and a DataFrame.
- Customize floating-point number precision in pandas output formatting.

7.1 Introduction

The **NumPy (Numerical Python)** library first appeared in 2006 and is the preferred Python array implementation. It offers a high-performance, richly functional *n*-dimensional array type called **ndarray**, which from this point forward we'll refer to by its synonym, `array`. NumPy is one of the many open-source libraries that the Anaconda Python distribution installs. Operations on `arrays` are up to two orders of magnitude faster than those on lists. In a big-data world in which applications may do massive amounts of processing on vast amounts of array-based data, this performance advantage can be critical. According to `libraries.io`, over 450 Python libraries depend on NumPy. Many popular data science libraries such as Pandas, SciPy (Scientific Python) and Keras (for deep learning) are built on or depend on NumPy.

In this chapter, we explore `array`'s basic capabilities. Lists can have multiple dimensions. You generally process multi-dimensional lists with nested loops or list comprehensions with multiple `for` clauses. A strength of NumPy is "array-oriented programming," which uses functional-style programming with *internal* iteration to make array manipulations concise and straightforward, eliminating the kinds of bugs that can occur with the *external* iteration of explicitly programmed loops.

In this chapter's Intro to Data Science section, we begin our multi-section introduction to the *pandas* library that you'll use in many of the data science case study chapters. Big data applications often need more flexible collections than NumPy's `arrays`—collections that support mixed data types, custom indexing, missing data, data that's not structured consistently and data that needs to be manipulated into forms appropriate for the databases and data analysis packages you use. We'll introduce pandas array-like one-dimensional `Series` and two-dimensional `DataFrames` and begin demonstrating their powerful capabilities. After reading this chapter, you'll be familiar with four array-like collections—lists, arrays, `Series` and `DataFrames`. We'll add a fifth—tensors—in the "Deep Learning" chapter.

7.2 Creating `arrays` from Existing Data

The NumPy documentation recommends importing the **numpy module** as np so that you can access its members with "np.":

```
In [1]: import numpy as np
```

The numpy module provides various functions for creating arrays. Here we use the **array** function, which receives as an argument an array or other collection of elements and returns a new array containing the argument's elements. Let's pass a list:

```
In [2]: numbers = np.array([2, 3, 5, 7, 11])
```

The array function copies its argument's contents into the array. Let's look at the type of object that function array returns and display its contents:

```
In [3]: type(numbers)
Out[3]: numpy.ndarray

In [4]: numbers
Out[4]: array([ 2,  3,  5,  7, 11])
```

Note that the *type* is numpy.ndarray, but all arrays are output as "array." When outputting an array, NumPy separates each value from the next with a comma and a space and *right-aligns* all the values using the same field width. It determines the field width based on the value that occupies the *largest* number of character positions. In this case, the value 11 occupies the two character positions, so all the values are formatted in two-character fields. That's why there's a leading space between the [and 2.

Multidimensional Arguments

The array function copies its argument's dimensions. Let's create an array from a two-row-by-three-column list:

```
In [5]: np.array([[1, 2, 3], [4, 5, 6]])
Out[5]:
array([[1, 2, 3],
       [4, 5, 6]])
```

NumPy auto-formats arrays, based on their number of dimensions, aligning the columns within each row.

7.3 array Attributes

An array object provides **attributes** that enable you to discover information about its structure and contents. In this section we'll use the following arrays:

```
In [1]: import numpy as np

In [2]: integers = np.array([[1, 2, 3], [4, 5, 6]])

In [3]: integers
Out[3]:
array([[1, 2, 3],
       [4, 5, 6]])

In [4]: floats = np.array([0.0, 0.1, 0.2, 0.3, 0.4])

In [5]: floats
Out[5]: array([ 0. ,  0.1,  0.2,  0.3,  0.4])
```

NumPy does not display trailing 0s to the right of the decimal point in floating-point values.

Determining an array's Element Type

The array function determines an array's element type from its argument's elements. You can check the element type with an array's **dtype** attribute:

```
In [6]: integers.dtype
Out[6]: dtype('int64')  # int32 on some platforms

In [7]: floats.dtype
Out[7]: dtype('float64')
```

As you'll see in the next section, various array-creation functions receive a dtype keyword argument so you can specify an array's element type.

For performance reasons, NumPy is written in the C programming language and uses C's data types. By default, NumPy stores integers as the NumPy type int64 values—which correspond to 64-bit (8-byte) integers in C—and stores floating-point numbers as the NumPy type float64 values—which correspond to 64-bit (8-byte) floating-point values in C. In our examples, most commonly you'll see the types int64, float64, bool (for Boolean) and object for non-numeric data (such as strings). The complete list of supported types is at https://docs.scipy.org/doc/numpy/user/basics.types.html.

Determining an array's Dimensions

The attribute **ndim** contains an array's number of dimensions and the attribute **shape** contains a *tuple* specifying an array's dimensions:

```
In [8]: integers.ndim
Out[8]: 2

In [9]: floats.ndim
Out[9]: 1

In [10]: integers.shape
Out[10]: (2, 3)

In [11]: floats.shape
Out[11]: (5,)
```

Here, integers has 2 rows and 3 columns (6 elements) and floats is one-dimensional, so snippet [11] shows a one-element tuple (indicated by the comma) containing floats' number of elements (5).

Determining an array's Number of Elements and Element Size

You can view an array's total number of elements with the attribute **size** and the number of bytes required to store each element with **itemsize**:

```
In [12]: integers.size
Out[12]: 6

In [13]: integers.itemsize  # 4 if C compiler uses 32-bit ints
Out[13]: 8

In [14]: floats.size
Out[14]: 5

In [15]: floats.itemsize
Out[15]: 8
```

Note that integers' size is the product of the shape tuple's values—two rows of three elements each for a total of six elements. In each case, itemsize is 8 because integers contains int64 values and floats contains float64 values, which each occupy 8 bytes.

Iterating Through a Multidimensional array's Elements

You'll generally manipulate arrays using concise functional-style programming techniques. However, because arrays are *iterable*, you can use external iteration if you'd like:

```
In [16]: for row in integers:
    ...:     for column in row:
    ...:         print(column, end=' ')
    ...:     print()
    ...:
1 2 3
4 5 6
```

You can iterate through a multidimensional array as if it were one-dimensional by using its **flat** attribute:

```
In [17]: for i in integers.flat:
    ...:     print(i, end=' ')
    ...:
1 2 3 4 5 6
```

7.4 Filling arrays with Specific Values

NumPy provides functions **zeros**, **ones** and **full** for creating arrays containing 0s, 1s or a specified value, respectively. By default, zeros and ones create arrays containing float64 values. We'll show how to customize the element type momentarily. The first argument to these functions must be an integer or a tuple of integers specifying the desired dimensions. For an integer, each function returns a one-dimensional array with the specified number of elements:

```
In [1]: import numpy as np

In [2]: np.zeros(5)
Out[2]: array([ 0.,  0.,  0.,  0.,  0.])
```

For a tuple of integers, these functions return a multidimensional array with the specified dimensions. You can specify the array's element type with the zeros and ones function's dtype keyword argument:

```
In [3]: np.ones((2, 4), dtype=int)
Out[3]:
array([[1, 1, 1, 1],
       [1, 1, 1, 1]])
```

The array returned by full contains elements with the second argument's value and type:

```
In [4]: np.full((3, 5), 13)
Out[4]:
array([[13, 13, 13, 13, 13],
       [13, 13, 13, 13, 13],
       [13, 13, 13, 13, 13]])
```

7.5 **Creating arrays from Ranges**

NumPy provides optimized functions for creating arrays from ranges. We focus on simple evenly spaced integer and floating-point ranges, but NumPy also supports nonlinear ranges.[1]

Creating Integer Ranges with arange

Let's use NumPy's **arange** function to create integer ranges—similar to using built-in function range. In each case, arange first determines the resulting array's number of elements, allocates the memory, then stores the specified range of values in the array:

```
In [1]: import numpy as np

In [2]: np.arange(5)
Out[2]: array([0, 1, 2, 3, 4])

In [3]: np.arange(5, 10)
Out[3]: array([5, 6, 7, 8, 9])

In [4]: np.arange(10, 1, -2)
Out[4]: array([10,  8,  6,  4,  2])
```

Though you can create arrays by passing ranges as arguments, always use arange as it's optimized for arrays. Soon we'll show how to determine the execution time of various operations so you can compare their performance.

Creating Floating-Point Ranges with linspace

You can produce evenly spaced floating-point ranges with NumPy's **linspace** function. The function's first two arguments specify the starting and ending values in the range, and the ending value *is included* in the array. The optional keyword argument num specifies the number of evenly spaced values to produce—this argument's default value is 50:

```
In [5]: np.linspace(0.0, 1.0, num=5)
Out[5]: array([ 0. ,  0.25,  0.5 ,  0.75,  1. ])
```

Reshaping an array

You also can create an array from a range of elements, then use array method **reshape** to transform the one-dimensional array into a multidimensional array. Let's create an array containing the values from 1 through 20, then reshape it into four rows by five columns:

```
In [6]: np.arange(1, 21).reshape(4, 5)
Out[6]:
array([[ 1,  2,  3,  4,  5],
       [ 6,  7,  8,  9, 10],
       [11, 12, 13, 14, 15],
       [16, 17, 18, 19, 20]])
```

Note the *chained method calls* in the preceding snippet. First, arange produces an array containing the values 1–20. Then we call reshape on that array to get the 4-by-5 array that was displayed.

---

1. https://docs.scipy.org/doc/numpy/reference/routines.array-creation.html

You can reshape any `array`, provided that the new shape has the *same* number of elements as the original. So a six-element one-dimensional `array` can become a 3-by-2 or 2-by-3 `array`, and vice versa, but attempting to reshape a 15-element array into a 4-by-4 array (16 elements) causes a `ValueError`.

Displaying Large `arrays`

When displaying an `array`, if there are 1000 items or more, NumPy drops the middle rows, columns or both from the output. The following snippets generate 100,000 elements. The first case shows all four rows but only the first and last three of the 25,000 columns. The notation ... represents the missing data. The second case shows the first and last three of the 100 rows, and the first and last three of the 1000 columns:

```
In [7]: np.arange(1, 100001).reshape(4, 25000)
Out[7]:
array([[     1,     2,     3, ...,  24998,  24999,  25000],
       [ 25001, 25002, 25003, ...,  49998,  49999,  50000],
       [ 50001, 50002, 50003, ...,  74998,  74999,  75000],
       [ 75001, 75002, 75003, ...,  99998,  99999, 100000]])

In [8]: np.arange(1, 100001).reshape(100, 1000)
Out[8]:
array([[     1,     2,     3, ...,    998,    999,   1000],
       [  1001,  1002,  1003, ...,   1998,   1999,   2000],
       [  2001,  2002,  2003, ...,   2998,   2999,   3000],
       ...,
       [ 97001, 97002, 97003, ...,  97998,  97999,  98000],
       [ 98001, 98002, 98003, ...,  98998,  98999,  99000],
       [ 99001, 99002, 99003, ...,  99998,  99999, 100000]])
```

7.6 List vs. array Performance: Introducing `%timeit`

Most array operations execute *significantly* faster than corresponding list operations. To demonstrate, we'll use the IPython **%timeit magic** command, which times the *average* duration of operations. Note that the times displayed on your system may vary from what we show here.

Timing the Creation of a List Containing Results of 6,000,000 Die Rolls

We've demonstrated rolling a six-sided die 6,000,000 times. Here, let's use the `random` module's `randrange` function with a list comprehension to create a list of six million die rolls and time the operation using `%timeit`. Note that we used the line-continuation character (\) to split the statement in snippet [2] over two lines:

```
In [1]: import random

In [2]: %timeit rolls_list = \
   ...:     [random.randrange(1, 7) for i in range(0, 6_000_000)]
6.29 s ± 119 ms per loop (mean ± std. dev. of 7 runs, 1 loop each)
```

By default, `%timeit` executes a statement in a loop, and it runs the loop *seven* times. If you do not indicate the number of loops, `%timeit` chooses an appropriate value. In our testing, operations that on average took more than 500 milliseconds iterated only once, and operations that took fewer than 500 milliseconds iterated 10 times or more.

After executing the statement, %timeit displays the statement's *average* execution time, as well as the standard deviation of all the executions. On average, %timeit indicates that it took 6.29 seconds (s) to create the list with a standard deviation of 119 milliseconds (ms). In total, the preceding snippet took about 44 seconds to run the snippet seven times.

Timing the Creation of an array Containing Results of 6,000,000 Die Rolls
Now, let's use the **randint** function from the **numpy.random** module to create an array of 6,000,000 die rolls

```
In [3]: import numpy as np

In [4]: %timeit rolls_array = np.random.randint(1, 7, 6_000_000)
72.4 ms ± 635 µs per loop (mean ± std. dev. of 7 runs, 10 loops each)
```

On average, %timeit indicates that it took only 72.4 *milliseconds* with a standard deviation of 635 microseconds (µs) to create the array. In total, the preceding snippet took just under half a second to execute on our computer—about 1/100th of the time snippet [2] took to execute. The operation is *two orders of magnitude faster* with array!

60,000,000 and 600,000,000 Die Rolls
Now, let's create an array of 60,000,000 die rolls:

```
In [5]: %timeit rolls_array = np.random.randint(1, 7, 60_000_000)
873 ms ± 29.4 ms per loop (mean ± std. dev. of 7 runs, 1 loop each)
```

On average, it took only 873 milliseconds to create the array.
Finally, let's do 600,000,000 million die rolls:

```
In [6]: %timeit rolls_array = np.random.randint(1, 7, 600_000_000)
10.1 s ± 232 ms per loop (mean ± std. dev. of 7 runs, 1 loop each)
```

It took about 10 seconds to create 600,000,000 elements with NumPy vs. about 6 seconds to create only 6,000,000 elements with a list comprehension.

Based on these timing studies, you can see clearly why arrays are preferred over lists for compute-intensive operations. In the data science case studies, we'll enter the performance-intensive worlds of big data and AI. We'll see how clever hardware, software, communications and algorithm designs combine to meet the often enormous computing challenges of today's applications.

Customizing the %timeit Iterations
The number of iterations within each %timeit loop and the number of loops are customizable with the -n and -r options. The following executes snippet [4]'s statement three times per loop and runs the loop twice:[2]

```
In [7]: %timeit -n3 -r2 rolls_array = np.random.randint(1, 7, 6_000_000)
85.5 ms ± 5.32 ms per loop (mean ± std. dev. of 2 runs, 3 loops each)
```

Other IPython Magics
IPython provides dozens of magics for a variety of tasks—for a complete list, see the IPython magics documentation.[3] Here are a few helpful ones:

---

2. For most readers, using %timeit's default settings should be fine.
3. http://ipython.readthedocs.io/en/stable/interactive/magics.html

- **%load** to read code into IPython from a local file or URL.

- **%save** to save snippets to a file.

- **%run** to execute a .py file from IPython.

- **%precision** to change the default floating-point precision for IPython outputs.

- **%cd** to change directories without having to exit IPython first.

- **%edit** to launch an external editor—handy if you need to modify more complex snippets.

- **%history** to view a list of all snippets and commands you've executed in the current IPython session.

7.7 array Operators

NumPy provides many operators which enable you to write simple expressions that perform operations on entire arrays. Here, we demonstrate arithmetic between arrays and numeric values and between arrays of the same shape.

Arithmetic Operations with arrays and Individual Numeric Values

First, let's perform *element-wise arithmetic* with arrays and numeric values by using arithmetic operators and augmented assignments. Element-wise operations are applied to every element, so snippet [4] multiplies every element by 2 and snippet [5] cubes every element. Each returns a *new* array containing the result:

```
In [1]: import numpy as np

In [2]: numbers = np.arange(1, 6)

In [3]: numbers
Out[3]: array([1, 2, 3, 4, 5])

In [4]: numbers * 2
Out[4]: array([ 2,  4,  6,  8, 10])

In [5]: numbers ** 3
Out[5]: array([  1,   8,  27,  64, 125])

In [6]: numbers  # numbers is unchanged by the arithmetic operators
Out[6]: array([1, 2, 3, 4, 5])
```

Snippet [6] shows that the arithmetic operators did not modify numbers. Operators + and * are *commutative*, so snippet [4] could also be written as 2 * numbers.

Augmented assignments *modify* every element in the left operand.

```
In [7]: numbers += 10

In [8]: numbers
Out[8]: array([11, 12, 13, 14, 15])
```

Broadcasting

Normally, the arithmetic operations require as operands two arrays of the *same size and shape*. When one operand is a single value, called a **scalar**, NumPy performs the element-wise calculations as if the scalar were an `array` of the same shape as the other operand, but with the scalar value in all its elements. This is called **broadcasting**. Snippets [4], [5] and [7] each use this capability. For example, snippet [4] is equivalent to:

```
numbers * [2, 2, 2, 2, 2]
```

Broadcasting also can be applied between arrays of different sizes and shapes, enabling some concise and powerful manipulations. We'll show more examples of broadcasting later in the chapter when we introduce NumPy's universal functions.

Arithmetic Operations Between arrays

You may perform arithmetic operations and augmented assignments between `arrays` of the *same* shape. Let's multiply the one-dimensional `arrays` numbers and numbers2 (created below) that each contain five elements:

```
In [9]: numbers2 = np.linspace(1.1, 5.5, 5)

In [10]: numbers2
Out[10]: array([ 1.1,  2.2,  3.3,  4.4,  5.5])

In [11]: numbers * numbers2
Out[11]: array([ 12.1,  26.4,  42.9,  61.6,  82.5])
```

The result is a new array formed by multiplying the `arrays` *element-wise* in each operand— 11 * 1.1, 12 * 2.2, 13 * 3.3, etc. Arithmetic between `arrays` of integers and floating-point numbers results in an `array` of floating-point numbers.

Comparing arrays

You can compare `arrays` with individual values and with other `arrays`. Comparisons are performed *element-wise*. Such comparisons produce `arrays` of Boolean values in which each element's `True` or `False` value indicates the comparison result:

```
In [12]: numbers
Out[12]: array([11, 12, 13, 14, 15])

In [13]: numbers >= 13
Out[13]: array([False, False,  True,  True,  True])

In [14]: numbers2
Out[14]: array([ 1.1,  2.2,  3.3,  4.4,  5.5])

In [15]: numbers2 < numbers
Out[15]: array([ True,  True,  True,  True,  True])

In [16]: numbers == numbers2
Out[16]: array([False, False, False, False, False])

In [17]: numbers == numbers
Out[17]: array([ True,  True,  True,  True,  True])
```

Snippet [13] uses broadcasting to determine whether each element of numbers is greater than or equal to 13. The remaining snippets compare the corresponding elements of each `array` operand.

7.8 NumPy Calculation Methods

An array has various methods that perform calculations using its contents. By default, these methods ignore the array's shape and use *all* the elements in the calculations. For example, calculating the mean of an array totals all of its elements regardless of its shape, then divides by the total number of elements. You can perform these calculations on each dimension as well. For example, in a two-dimensional array, you can calculate each row's mean and each column's mean.

Consider an array representing four students' grades on three exams:

```
In [1]: import numpy as np

In [2]: grades = np.array([[87, 96, 70], [100, 87, 90],
   ...:                    [94, 77, 90], [100, 81, 82]])
   ...:

In [3]: grades
Out[3]:
array([[ 87,  96,  70],
       [100,  87,  90],
       [ 94,  77,  90],
       [100,  81,  82]])
```

We can use methods to calculate **sum**, **min**, **max**, **mean**, **std** (standard deviation) and **var** (variance)—each is a functional-style programming *reduction*:

```
In [4]: grades.sum()
Out[4]: 1054

In [5]: grades.min()
Out[5]: 70

In [6]: grades.max()
Out[6]: 100

In [7]: grades.mean()
Out[7]: 87.83333333333333

In [8]: grades.std()
Out[8]: 8.792357792739987

In [9]: grades.var()
Out[9]: 77.30555555555556
```

Calculations by Row or Column

Many calculation methods can be performed on specific array dimensions, known as the array's *axes*. These methods receive an axis keyword argument that specifies which dimension to use in the calculation, giving you a quick way to perform calculations by row or column in a two-dimensional array.

Assume that you want to calculate the average grade on each *exam*, represented by the columns of grades. Specifying axis=0 performs the calculation on all the *row* values within each column:

```
In [10]: grades.mean(axis=0)
Out[10]: array([95.25, 85.25, 83.  ])
```

So 95.25 above is the average of the first column's grades (87, 100, 94 and 100), 85.25 is the average of the second column's grades (96, 87, 77 and 81) and 83 is the average of the third column's grades (70, 90, 90 and 82). Again, NumPy does *not* display trailing 0s to the right of the decimal point in '83.'. Also note that it *does* display all element values in the same field width, which is why '83.' is followed by two spaces.

Similarly, specifying axis=1 performs the calculation on all the *column* values within each individual row. To calculate each student's average grade for all exams, we can use:

```
In [11]: grades.mean(axis=1)
Out[11]: array([84.33333333, 92.33333333, 87.       , 87.66666667])
```

This produces four averages—one each for the values in each row. So 84.33333333 is the average of row 0's grades (87, 96 and 70), and the other averages are for the remaining rows.

NumPy arrays have many more calculation methods. For the complete list, see

> https://docs.scipy.org/doc/numpy/reference/arrays.ndarray.html

7.9 Universal Functions

NumPy offers dozens of standalone **universal functions** (or **ufuncs**) that perform various element-wise operations. Each performs its task using one or two array or array-like (such as lists) arguments. Some of these functions are called when you use operators like + and * on arrays. Each returns a new array containing the results.

Let's create an array and calculate the square root of its values, using the **sqrt** universal function:

```
In [1]: import numpy as np

In [2]: numbers = np.array([1, 4, 9, 16, 25, 36])

In [3]: np.sqrt(numbers)
Out[3]: array([1., 2., 3., 4., 5., 6.])
```

Let's add two arrays with the same shape, using the **add universal function**:

```
In [4]: numbers2 = np.arange(1, 7) * 10

In [5]: numbers2
Out[5]: array([10, 20, 30, 40, 50, 60])

In [6]: np.add(numbers, numbers2)
Out[6]: array([11, 24, 39, 56, 75, 96])
```

The expression np.add(numbers, numbers2) is equivalent to:

```
numbers + numbers2
```

Broadcasting with Universal Functions

Let's use the **multiply** universal function to multiply every element of numbers2 by the scalar value 5:

```
In [7]: np.multiply(numbers2, 5)
Out[7]: array([ 50, 100, 150, 200, 250, 300])
```

The expression np.multiply(numbers2, 5) is equivalent to:

```
numbers2 * 5
```

Let's reshape numbers2 into a 2-by-3 array, then multiply its values by a one-dimensional array of three elements:

```
In [8]: numbers3 = numbers2.reshape(2, 3)

In [9]: numbers3
Out[9]:
array([[10, 20, 30],
       [40, 50, 60]])

In [10]: numbers4 = np.array([2, 4, 6])

In [11]: np.multiply(numbers3, numbers4)
Out[11]:
array([[ 20,  80, 180],
       [ 80, 200, 360]])
```

This works because numbers4 has the same length as each row of numbers3, so NumPy can apply the multiply operation by treating numbers4 as if it were the following array:

```
array([[2, 4, 6],
       [2, 4, 6]])
```

If a universal function receives two arrays of different shapes that do not support broadcasting, a ValueError occurs. You can view the broadcasting rules at:

```
https://docs.scipy.org/doc/numpy/user/basics.broadcasting.html
```

Other Universal Functions

The NumPy documentation lists universal functions in five categories—math, trigonometry, bit manipulation, comparison and floating point. The following table lists some functions from each category. You can view the complete list, their descriptions and more information about universal functions at:

```
https://docs.scipy.org/doc/numpy/reference/ufuncs.html
```

NumPy universal functions
Math—add, subtract, multiply, divide, remainder, exp, log, sqrt, power, and more.
Trigonometry—sin, cos, tan, hypot, arcsin, arccos, arctan, and more.
Bit manipulation—bitwise_and, bitwise_or, bitwise_xor, invert, left_shift and right_shift.
Comparison—greater, greater_equal, less, less_equal, equal, not_equal, logical_and, logical_or, logical_xor, logical_not, minimum, maximum, and more.
Floating point—floor, ceil, isinf, isnan, fabs, trunc, and more.

7.10 Indexing and Slicing

One-dimensional arrays can be indexed and sliced using the same syntax and techniques we demonstrated in the "Sequences: Lists and Tuples" chapter. Here, we focus on array-specific indexing and slicing capabilities.

Indexing with Two-Dimensional arrays

To select an element in a two-dimensional array, specify a tuple containing the element's row and column indices in square brackets (as in snippet [4]):

```
In [1]: import numpy as np

In [2]: grades = np.array([[87, 96, 70], [100, 87, 90],
   ...:                    [94, 77, 90], [100, 81, 82]])
   ...:

In [3]: grades
Out[3]:
array([[ 87,  96,  70],
       [100,  87,  90],
       [ 94,  77,  90],
       [100,  81,  82]])

In [4]: grades[0, 1]  # row 0, column 1
Out[4]: 96
```

Selecting a Subset of a Two-Dimensional array's Rows

To select a single row, specify only one index in square brackets:

```
In [5]: grades[1]
Out[5]: array([100, 87,  90])
```

To select multiple sequential rows, use slice notation:

```
In [6]: grades[0:2]
Out[6]:
array([[ 87,  96,  70],
       [100,  87,  90]])
```

To select multiple non-sequential rows, use a list of row indices:

```
In [7]: grades[[1, 3]]
Out[7]:
array([[100,  87,  90],
       [100,  81,  82]])
```

Selecting a Subset of a Two-Dimensional array's Columns

You can select subsets of the columns by providing a tuple specifying the row(s) and column(s) to select. Each can be a specific index, a slice or a list. Let's select only the elements in the first column:

```
In [8]: grades[:, 0]
Out[8]: array([ 87, 100,  94, 100])
```

The 0 after the comma indicates that we're selecting only column 0. The : before the comma indicates which rows within that column to select. In this case, : is a *slice* representing *all* rows. This also could be a specific row number, a slice representing a subset of the rows or a list of specific row indices to select, as in snippets [5]–[7].

You can select consecutive columns using a slice:

```
In [9]: grades[:, 1:3]
Out[9]:
array([[96, 70],
       [87, 90],
       [77, 90],
       [81, 82]])
```

or specific columns using a *list* of column indices:

```
In [10]: grades[:, [0, 2]]
Out[10]:
array([[ 87,  70],
       [100,  90],
       [ 94,  90],
       [100,  82]])
```

7.11 Views: Shallow Copies

The previous chapter introduced *view objects*—that is, objects that "see" the data in other objects, rather than having their own copies of the data. Views are shallow copies. Various array methods and slicing operations produce views of an array's data.

The array method **view** returns a *new* array object with a *view* of the original array object's data. First, let's create an array and a view of that array:

```
In [1]: import numpy as np

In [2]: numbers = np.arange(1, 6)

In [3]: numbers
Out[3]: array([1, 2, 3, 4, 5])

In [4]: numbers2 = numbers.view()

In [5]: numbers2
Out[5]: array([1, 2, 3, 4, 5])
```

We can use the built-in id function to see that numbers and numbers2 are *different* objects:

```
In [6]: id(numbers)
Out[6]: 4462958592

In [7]: id(numbers2)
Out[7]: 4590846240
```

To prove that numbers2 views the *same* data as numbers, let's modify an element in numbers, then display both arrays:

```
In [8]: numbers[1] *= 10

In [9]: numbers2
Out[9]: array([ 1, 20,  3,  4,  5])

In [10]: numbers
Out[10]: array([ 1, 20,  3,  4,  5])
```

Similarly, changing a value in the view also changes that value in the original array:

```
In [11]: numbers2[1] /= 10

In [12]: numbers
Out[12]: array([1, 2, 3, 4, 5])

In [13]: numbers2
Out[13]: array([1, 2, 3, 4, 5])
```

Slice Views

Slices also create views. Let's make `numbers2` a slice that views only the first three elements of `numbers`:

```
In [14]: numbers2 = numbers[0:3]

In [15]: numbers2
Out[15]: array([1, 2, 3])
```

Again, we can confirm that `numbers` and `numbers2` are different objects with `id`:

```
In [16]: id(numbers)
Out[16]: 4462958592

In [17]: id(numbers2)
Out[17]: 4590848000
```

We can confirm that `numbers2` is a view of *only* the first *three* `numbers` elements by attempting to access `numbers2[3]`, which produces an `IndexError`:

```
In [18]: numbers2[3]
-------------------------------------------------------------------------
IndexError                                Traceback (most recent call last)
<ipython-input-18-582053f52daa> in <module>()
----> 1 numbers2[3]

IndexError: index 3 is out of bounds for axis 0 with size 3
```

Now, let's modify an element both arrays share, then display them. Again, we see that `numbers2` is a view of `numbers`:

```
In [19]: numbers[1] *= 20

In [20]: numbers
Out[20]: array([1, 2, 3, 4, 5])

In [21]: numbers2
Out[21]: array([ 1, 40,  3])
```

7.12 Deep Copies

Though views are *separate* array objects, they save memory by sharing element data from other arrays. However, when sharing *mutable* values, sometimes it's necessary to create a **deep copy** with *independent* copies of the original data. This is especially important in multi-core programming, where separate parts of your program could attempt to modify your data at the same time, possibly corrupting it.

The **array method copy** returns a new array object with a *deep copy* of the original array object's data. First, let's create an array and a deep copy of that array:

```
In [1]: import numpy as np

In [2]: numbers = np.arange(1, 6)

In [3]: numbers
Out[3]: array([1, 2, 3, 4, 5])

In [4]: numbers2 = numbers.copy()
```

```
In [5]: numbers2
Out[5]: array([1, 2, 3, 4, 5])
```

To prove that numbers2 has a separate copy of the data in numbers, let's modify an element in numbers, then display both arrays:

```
In [6]: numbers[1] *= 10

In [7]: numbers
Out[7]: array([ 1, 20,  3,  4,  5])

In [8]: numbers2
Out[8]: array([ 1,  2,  3,  4,  5])
```

As you can see, the change appears only in numbers.

Module copy—Shallow vs. Deep Copies for Other Types of Python Objects
In previous chapters, we covered *shallow copying*. In this chapter, we've covered how to *deep copy* array objects using their copy method. If you need deep copies of other types of Python objects, pass them to the **copy** module's **deepcopy** function.

7.13 Reshaping and Transposing

We've used array method reshape to produce two-dimensional arrays from one-dimensional ranges. NumPy provides various other ways to reshape arrays.

reshape vs. resize
The array methods reshape and resize both enable you to change an array's dimensions. Method reshape returns a *view* (shallow copy) of the original array with the new dimensions. It does *not* modify the original array:

```
In [1]: import numpy as np

In [2]: grades = np.array([[87, 96, 70], [100, 87, 90]])

In [3]: grades
Out[3]:
array([[ 87,  96,  70],
       [100,  87,  90]])

In [4]: grades.reshape(1, 6)
Out[4]: array([[ 87,  96,  70, 100,  87,  90]])

In [5]: grades
Out[5]:
array([[ 87,  96,  70],
       [100,  87,  90]])
```

Method **resize** *modifies the original array's shape*:

```
In [6]: grades.resize(1, 6)

In [7]: grades
Out[7]: array([[ 87,  96,  70, 100,  87,  90]])
```

flatten vs. ravel

You can take a multidimensional array and flatten it into a single dimension with the methods **flatten** and **ravel**. Method flatten *deep copies* the original array's data:

```
In [8]: grades = np.array([[87, 96, 70], [100, 87, 90]])

In [9]: grades
Out[9]:
array([[ 87,  96,  70],
       [100,  87,  90]])

In [10]: flattened = grades.flatten()

In [11]: flattened
Out[11]: array([ 87,  96,  70, 100,  87,  90])

In [12]: grades
Out[12]:
array([[ 87,  96,  70],
       [100,  87,  90]])
```

To confirm that grades and flattened do *not* share the data, let's modify an element of flattened, then display both arrays:

```
In [13]: flattened[0] = 100

In [14]: flattened
Out[14]: array([100,  96,  70, 100,  87,  90])

In [15]: grades
Out[15]:
array([[ 87,  96,  70],
       [100,  87,  90]])
```

Method ravel produces a *view* of the original array, which *shares* the grades array's data:

```
In [16]: raveled = grades.ravel()

In [17]: raveled
Out[17]: array([ 87,  96,  70, 100,  87,  90])

In [18]: grades
Out[18]:
array([[ 87,  96,  70],
       [100,  87,  90]])
```

To confirm that grades and raveled *share* the same data, let's modify an element of raveled, then display both arrays:

```
In [19]: raveled[0] = 100

In [20]: raveled
Out[20]: array([100,  96,  70, 100,  87,  90])

In [21]: grades
Out[21]:
array([[100,  96,  70],
       [100,  87,  90]])
```

Transposing Rows and Columns

You can quickly **transpose** an array's rows and columns—that is "flip" the array, so the rows become the columns and the columns become the rows. The **T attribute** returns a transposed *view* (shallow copy) of the array. The original grades array represents two students' grades (the rows) on three exams (the columns). Let's transpose the rows and columns to view the data as the grades on three exams (the rows) for two students (the columns):

```
In [22]: grades.T
Out[22]:
array([[100, 100],
       [ 96,  87],
       [ 70,  90]])
```

Transposing does *not* modify the original array:

```
In [23]: grades
Out[23]:
array([[100, 96, 70],
       [100, 87, 90]])
```

Horizontal and Vertical Stacking

You can combine arrays by adding more columns or more rows—known as *horizontal stacking* and *vertical stacking*. Let's create another 2-by-3 array of grades:

```
In [24]: grades2 = np.array([[94, 77, 90], [100, 81, 82]])
```

Let's assume grades2 represents three additional exam grades for the two students in the grades array. We can combine grades and grades2 with NumPy's **hstack (horizontal stack) function** by passing a tuple containing the arrays to combine. The extra parentheses are required because hstack expects one argument:

```
In [25]: np.hstack((grades, grades2))
Out[25]:
array([[100, 96, 70, 94, 77, 90],
       [100, 87, 90, 100, 81, 82]])
```

Next, let's assume that grades2 represents two more students' grades on three exams. In this case, we can combine grades and grades2 with NumPy's **vstack (vertical stack) function**:

```
In [26]: np.vstack((grades, grades2))
Out[26]:
array([[100, 96, 70],
       [100, 87, 90],
       [ 94, 77, 90],
       [100, 81, 82]])
```

7.14 Intro to Data Science: pandas Series and DataFrames

NumPy's array is optimized for homogeneous numeric data that's accessed via integer indices. Data science presents unique demands for which more customized data structures are required. Big data applications must support mixed data types, customized indexing, missing data, data that's not structured consistently and data that needs to be manipulated into forms appropriate for the databases and data analysis packages you use.

Pandas is the most popular library for dealing with such data. It provides two key collections that you'll use in several of our Intro to Data Science sections and throughout the data science case studies—**Series** for one-dimensional collections and **DataFrames** for two-dimensional collections. You can use pandas' **MultiIndex** to manipulate multi-dimensional data in the context of Series and DataFrames.

Wes McKinney created pandas in 2008 while working in industry. The name pandas is derived from the term "panel data," which is data for measurements over time, such as stock prices or historical temperature readings. McKinney needed a library in which the same data structures could handle both time- and non-time-based data with support for data alignment, missing data, common database-style data manipulations, and more.[4]

NumPy and pandas are intimately related. Series and DataFrames use arrays "under the hood." Series and DataFrames are valid arguments to many NumPy operations. Similarly, arrays are valid arguments to many Series and DataFrame operations.

Pandas is a massive topic—the PDF of its documentation[5] is over 2000 pages. In this and the next chapters' Intro to Data Science sections, we present an introduction to pandas. We discuss its Series and DataFrames collections, and use them in support of data preparation. You'll see that Series and DataFrames make it easy for you to perform common tasks like selecting elements a variety of ways, filter/map/reduce operations (central to functional-style programming and big data), mathematical operations, visualization and more.

7.14.1 pandas Series

A **Series** is an enhanced one-dimensional array. Whereas arrays use only zero-based integer indices, Series support custom indexing, including even non-integer indices like strings. Series also offer additional capabilities that make them more convenient for many data-science oriented tasks. For example, Series may have missing data, and many Series operations ignore missing data by default.

Creating a Series with Default Indices

By default, a Series has integer indices numbered sequentially from 0. The following creates a Series of student grades from a list of integers:

```
In [1]: import pandas as pd

In [2]: grades = pd.Series([87, 100, 94])
```

The initializer also may be a tuple, a dictionary, an array, another Series or a single value. We'll show a single value momentarily.

Displaying a Series

Pandas displays a Series in two-column format with the indices *left aligned* in the left column and the values *right aligned* in the right column. After listing the Series elements, pandas shows the data type (dtype) of the underlying array's elements:

4. McKinney, Wes. *Python for Data Analysis: Data Wrangling with Pandas, NumPy, and IPython*, pp. 123–165. Sebastopol, CA: OReilly Media, 2018.
5. For the latest pandas documentation, see http://pandas.pydata.org/pandas-docs/stable/.

```
In [3]: grades
Out[3]:
0     87
1    100
2     94
dtype: int64
```

Note how easy it is to display a Series in this format, compared to the corresponding code for displaying a list in the same two-column format.

Creating a Series with All Elements Having the Same Value

You can create a Series of elements that all have the same value:

```
In [4]: pd.Series(98.6, range(3))
Out[4]:
0    98.6
1    98.6
2    98.6
dtype: float64
```

The second argument is a one-dimensional iterable object (such as a list, an array or a range) containing the Series' indices. The number of indices determines the number of elements.

Accessing a Series' Elements

You can access a Series's elements via square brackets containing an index:

```
In [5]: grades[0]
Out[5]: 87
```

Producing Descriptive Statistics for a Series

Series provides many methods for common tasks including producing various descriptive statistics. Here we show count, mean, min, max and std (standard deviation):

```
In [6]: grades.count()
Out[6]: 3

In [7]: grades.mean()
Out[7]: 93.66666666666667

In [8]: grades.min()
Out[8]: 87

In [9]: grades.max()
Out[9]: 100

In [10]: grades.std()
Out[10]: 6.506407098647712
```

Each of these is a functional-style reduction. Calling Series method **describe** produces all these stats and more:

```
In [11]: grades.describe()
Out[11]:
count       3.000000
mean       93.666667
std         6.506407
```

```
min         87.000000
25%         90.500000
50%         94.000000
75%         97.000000
max        100.000000
dtype: float64
```

The 25%, 50% and 75% are **quartiles**:

- 50% represents the median of the sorted values.

- 25% represents the median of the first half of the sorted values.

- 75% represents the median of the second half of the sorted values.

For the quartiles, if there are two middle elements, then their average is that quartile's median. We have only three values in our `Series`, so the 25% quartile is the average of 87 and 94, and the 75% quartile is the average of 94 and 100. Together, the **interquartile range** is the 75% quartile minus the 25% quartile, which is another measure of dispersion, like standard deviation and variance. Of course, quartiles and interquartile range are more useful in larger datasets.

Creating a Series with Custom Indices
You can specify *custom* indices with the `index` keyword argument:

```
In [12]: grades = pd.Series([87, 100, 94], index=['Wally', 'Eva', 'Sam'])

In [13]: grades
Out[13]:
Wally       87
Eva        100
Sam         94
dtype: int64
```

In this case, we used string indices, but you can use other immutable types, including integers not beginning at 0 and nonconsecutive integers. Again, notice how nicely and concisely pandas formats a `Series` for display.

Dictionary Initializers
If you initialize a `Series` with a dictionary, its keys become the `Series`' indices, and its values become the `Series`' element values:

```
In [14]: grades = pd.Series({'Wally': 87, 'Eva': 100, 'Sam': 94})

In [15]: grades
Out[15]:
Wally       87
Eva        100
Sam         94
dtype: int64
```

Accessing Elements of a Series Via Custom Indices
In a `Series` with custom indices, you can access individual elements via square brackets containing a custom index value:

```
In [16]: grades['Eva']
Out[16]: 100
```

If the custom indices are strings that could represent valid Python identifiers, pandas automatically adds them to the Series as attributes that you can access via a dot (.), as in:

```
In [17]: grades.Wally
Out[17]: 87
```

Series also has *built-in* attributes. For example, the **dtype attribute** returns the underlying array's element type:

```
In [18]: grades.dtype
Out[18]: dtype('int64')
```

and the **values attribute** returns the underlying array:

```
In [19]: grades.values
Out[19]: array([ 87, 100,  94])
```

Creating a Series of Strings

If a Series contains strings, you can use its **str attribute** to call string methods on the elements. First, let's create a Series of hardware-related strings:

```
In [20]: hardware = pd.Series(['Hammer', 'Saw', 'Wrench'])

In [21]: hardware
Out[21]:
0    Hammer
1       Saw
2    Wrench
dtype: object
```

Note that pandas also *right-aligns* string element values and that the dtype for strings is object.

Let's call string method contains on each element to determine whether the value of each element contains a lowercase 'a':

```
In [22]: hardware.str.contains('a')
Out[22]:
0     True
1     True
2    False
dtype: bool
```

Pandas returns a Series containing bool values indicating the contains method's result for each element—the element at index 2 ('Wrench') does not contain an 'a', so its element in the resulting Series is False. Note that pandas handles the iteration internally for you—another example of functional-style programming. The str attribute provides many string-processing methods that are similar to those in Python's string type. For a list, see: https://pandas.pydata.org/pandas-docs/stable/api.html#string-handling.

The following uses string method upper to produce a *new* Series containing the uppercase versions of each element in hardware:

```
In [23]: hardware.str.upper()
Out[23]:
0    HAMMER
1       SAW
2    WRENCH
dtype: object
```

7.14.2 DataFrames

A **DataFrame** is an enhanced two-dimensional array. Like Series, DataFrames can have custom row and column indices, and offer additional operations and capabilities that make them more convenient for many data-science oriented tasks. DataFrames also support missing data. Each column in a DataFrame is a Series. The Series representing each column may contain different element types, as you'll soon see when we discuss loading datasets into DataFrames.

Creating a DataFrame from a Dictionary

Let's create a DataFrame from a dictionary that represents student grades on three exams:

```
In [1]: import pandas as pd

In [2]: grades_dict = {'Wally': [87, 96, 70], 'Eva': [100, 87, 90],
   ...:                'Sam': [94, 77, 90], 'Katie': [100, 81, 82],
   ...:                'Bob': [83, 65, 85]}
   ...:

In [3]: grades = pd.DataFrame(grades_dict)

In [4]: grades
Out[4]:
   Wally  Eva  Sam  Katie  Bob
0     87  100   94    100   83
1     96   87   77     81   65
2     70   90   90     82   85
```

Pandas displays DataFrames in tabular format with the indices *left aligned* in the index column and the remaining columns' values *right aligned*. The dictionary's *keys* become the column names and the *values* associated with each key become the element values in the corresponding column. Shortly, we'll show how to "flip" the rows and columns. By default, the row indices are auto-generated integers starting from 0.

Customizing a DataFrame's Indices with the index Attribute

We could have specified custom indices with the index keyword argument when we created the DataFrame, as in:

```
pd.DataFrame(grades_dict, index=['Test1', 'Test2', 'Test3'])
```

Let's use the **index attribute** to change the DataFrame's indices from sequential integers to labels:

```
In [5]: grades.index = ['Test1', 'Test2', 'Test3']

In [6]: grades
Out[6]:
       Wally  Eva  Sam  Katie  Bob
Test1     87  100   94    100   83
Test2     96   87   77     81   65
Test3     70   90   90     82   85
```

When specifying the indices, you must provide a one-dimensional collection that has the same number of elements as there are *rows* in the DataFrame; otherwise, a ValueError occurs. Series also provides an **index attribute** for changing an existing Series' indices.

Accessing a DataFrame's Columns
One benefit of pandas is that you can quickly and conveniently look at your data in many different ways, including selecting portions of the data. Let's start by getting Eva's grades by name, which displays her column as a Series:

```
In [7]: grades['Eva']
Out[7]:
Test1    100
Test2     87
Test3     90
Name: Eva, dtype: int64
```

If a DataFrame's column-name strings are valid Python identifiers, you can use them as attributes. Let's get Sam's grades with the Sam *attribute*:

```
In [8]: grades.Sam
Out[8]:
Test1    94
Test2    77
Test3    90
Name: Sam, dtype: int64
```

Selecting Rows via the loc and iloc Attributes
Though DataFrames support indexing capabilities with [], the pandas documentation recommends using the attributes loc, iloc, at and iat, which are optimized to access Data-Frames and also provide additional capabilities beyond what you can do only with []. Also, the documentation states that indexing with [] *often* produces a copy of the data, which is a logic error if you attempt to assign new values to the DataFrame by assigning to the result of the [] operation.

You can access a row by its label via the DataFrame's **loc attribute**. The following lists all the grades in the row 'Test1':

```
In [9]: grades.loc['Test1']
Out[9]:
Wally     87
Eva      100
Sam       94
Katie    100
Bob       83
Name: Test1, dtype: int64
```

You also can access rows by integer zero-based indices using the **iloc attribute** (the i in iloc means that it's used with integer indices). The following lists all the grades in the second row:

```
In [10]: grades.iloc[1]
Out[10]:
Wally    96
Eva      87
Sam      77
Katie    81
Bob      65
Name: Test2, dtype: int64
```

Selecting Rows via Slices and Lists with the `loc` and `iloc` Attributes

The index can be a *slice*. When using slices containing labels with `loc`, the range specified *includes* the high index ('Test3'):

```
In [11]: grades.loc['Test1':'Test3']
Out[11]:
       Wally  Eva  Sam  Katie  Bob
Test1     87  100   94    100   83
Test2     96   87   77     81   65
Test3     70   90   90     82   85
```

When using slices containing integer indices with `iloc`, the range you specify *excludes* the high index (2):

```
In [12]: grades.iloc[0:2]
Out[12]:
       Wally  Eva  Sam  Katie  Bob
Test1     87  100   94    100   83
Test2     96   87   77     81   65
```

To select *specific rows*, use a *list* rather than slice notation with `loc` or `iloc`:

```
In [13]: grades.loc[['Test1', 'Test3']]
Out[13]:
       Wally  Eva  Sam  Katie  Bob
Test1     87  100   94    100   83
Test3     70   90   90     82   85
```

```
In [14]: grades.iloc[[0, 2]]
Out[14]:
       Wally  Eva  Sam  Katie  Bob
Test1     87  100   94    100   83
Test3     70   90   90     82   85
```

Selecting Subsets of the Rows and Columns

So far, we've selected only *entire* rows. You can focus on small subsets of a DataFrame by selecting rows *and* columns using two slices, two lists or a combination of slices and lists.

Suppose you want to view only Eva's and Katie's grades on Test1 and Test2. We can do that by using `loc` with a slice for the two consecutive rows and a list for the two non-consecutive columns:

```
In [15]: grades.loc['Test1':'Test2', ['Eva', 'Katie']]
Out[15]:
       Eva  Katie
Test1  100    100
Test2   87     81
```

The slice 'Test1':'Test2' selects the rows for Test1 and Test2. The list ['Eva', 'Katie'] selects only the corresponding grades from those two columns.

Let's use `iloc` with a list and a slice to select the first and third tests and the first three columns for those tests:

```
In [16]: grades.iloc[[0, 2], 0:3]
Out[16]:
       Wally  Eva  Sam
Test1     87  100   94
Test3     70   90   90
```

Boolean Indexing

One of pandas' more powerful selection capabilities is **Boolean indexing**. For example, let's select all the A grades—that is, those that are greater than or equal to 90:

```
In [17]: grades[grades >= 90]
Out[17]:
       Wally    Eva    Sam  Katie  Bob
Test1    NaN  100.0   94.0  100.0  NaN
Test2   96.0    NaN    NaN    NaN  NaN
Test3    NaN   90.0   90.0    NaN  NaN
```

Pandas checks every grade to determine whether its value is greater than or equal to 90 and, if so, includes it in the new `DataFrame`. Grades for which the condition is `False` are represented as **NaN** (**not a number**) in the new `DataFrame`. NaN is pandas' notation for missing values.

Let's select all the B grades in the range 80–89:

```
In [18]: grades[(grades >= 80) & (grades < 90)]
Out[18]:
       Wally   Eva  Sam  Katie   Bob
Test1   87.0   NaN  NaN    NaN  83.0
Test2    NaN  87.0  NaN   81.0   NaN
Test3    NaN   NaN  NaN   82.0  85.0
```

Pandas Boolean indices combine multiple conditions with the Python operator & (bitwise AND), *not* the and Boolean operator. For or conditions, use | (bitwise OR). NumPy also supports Boolean indexing for `arrays`, but always returns a one-dimensional array containing only the values that satisfy the condition.

Accessing a Specific `DataFrame` Cell by Row and Column

You can use a `DataFrame`'s **at** and **iat** attributes to get a single value from a `DataFrame`. Like `loc` and `iloc`, at uses labels and iat uses integer indices. In each case, the row and column indices must be separated by a comma. Let's select Eva's `Test2` grade (87) and `Wally`'s `Test3` grade (70)

```
In [19]: grades.at['Test2', 'Eva']
Out[19]: 87

In [20]: grades.iat[2, 0]
Out[20]: 70
```

You also can assign new values to specific elements. Let's change Eva's `Test2` grade to 100 using at, then change it back to 87 using `iat`:

```
In [21]: grades.at['Test2', 'Eva'] = 100

In [22]: grades.at['Test2', 'Eva']
Out[22]: 100

In [23]: grades.iat[1, 1] = 87

In [24]: grades.iat[1, 1]
Out[24]: 87.0
```

Descriptive Statistics

Both Series and DataFrames have a **describe method** that calculates basic descriptive statistics for the data and returns them as a DataFrame. In a DataFrame, the statistics are calculated by column (again, soon you'll see how to flip rows and columns):

```
In [25]: grades.describe()
Out[25]:
             Wally         Eva         Sam       Katie         Bob
count     3.000000    3.000000    3.000000    3.000000    3.000000
mean     84.333333   92.333333   87.000000   87.666667   77.666667
std      13.203535    6.806859    8.888194   10.692677   11.015141
min      70.000000   87.000000   77.000000   81.000000   65.000000
25%      78.500000   88.500000   83.500000   81.500000   74.000000
50%      87.000000   90.000000   90.000000   82.000000   83.000000
75%      91.500000   95.000000   92.000000   91.000000   84.000000
max      96.000000  100.000000   94.000000  100.000000   85.000000
```

As you can see, describe gives you a quick way to summarize your data. It nicely demonstrates the power of array-oriented programming with a clean, concise functional-style call. Pandas handles internally all the details of calculating these statistics for each column. You might be interested in seeing similar statistics on test-by-test basis so you can see how all the students performs on Tests 1, 2 and 3—we'll show how to do that shortly.

By default, pandas calculates the descriptive statistics with floating-point values and displays them with six digits of precision. You can control the precision and other default settings with pandas' **set_option** function:

```
In [26]: pd.set_option('precision', 2)

In [27]: grades.describe()
Out[27]:
         Wally     Eva     Sam   Katie     Bob
count     3.00    3.00    3.00    3.00    3.00
mean     84.33   92.33   87.00   87.67   77.67
std      13.20    6.81    8.89   10.69   11.02
min      70.00   87.00   77.00   81.00   65.00
25%      78.50   88.50   83.50   81.50   74.00
50%      87.00   90.00   90.00   82.00   83.00
75%      91.50   95.00   92.00   91.00   84.00
max      96.00  100.00   94.00  100.00   85.00
```

For student grades, the most important of these statistics is probably the mean. You can calculate that for each student simply by calling mean on the DataFrame:

```
In [28]: grades.mean()
Out[28]:
Wally     84.33
Eva       92.33
Sam       87.00
Katie     87.67
Bob       77.67
dtype: float64
```

In a moment, we'll show how to get the average of all the students' grades on each test in one line of additional code.

Transposing the `DataFrame` with the `T` Attribute

You can quickly **transpose** the rows and columns—so the rows become the columns, and the columns become the rows—by using the **T attribute**:

```
In [29]: grades.T
Out[29]:
        Test1  Test2  Test3
Wally      87     96     70
Eva       100     87     90
Sam        94     77     90
Katie     100     81     82
Bob        83     65     85
```

`T` returns a transposed *view* (not a copy) of the `DataFrame`.

Let's assume that rather than getting the summary statistics by student, you want to get them by test. Simply call `describe` on `grades.T`, as in:

```
In [30]: grades.T.describe()
Out[30]:
         Test1  Test2  Test3
count     5.00   5.00   5.00
mean     92.80  81.20  83.40
std       7.66  11.54   8.23
min      83.00  65.00  70.00
25%      87.00  77.00  82.00
50%      94.00  81.00  85.00
75%     100.00  87.00  90.00
max     100.00  96.00  90.00
```

To see the average of all the students' grades on each test, just call `mean` on the `T` attribute:

```
In [31]: grades.T.mean()
Out[31]:
Test1    92.8
Test2    81.2
Test3    83.4
dtype: float64
```

Sorting by Rows by Their Indices

You'll often sort data for easier readability. You can sort a `DataFrame` by its rows or columns, based on their indices or values. Let's sort the rows by their *indices* in *descending* order using **sort_index** and its keyword argument `ascending=False` (the default is to sort in *ascending* order). This returns a new `DataFrame` containing the sorted data:

```
In [32]: grades.sort_index(ascending=False)
Out[32]:
       Wally  Eva  Sam  Katie  Bob
Test3     70   90   90     82   85
Test2     96   87   77     81   65
Test1     87  100   94    100   83
```

Sorting by Column Indices

Now let's sort the columns into ascending order (left-to-right) by their column names. Passing the **axis=1 keyword argument** indicates that we wish to sort the *column* indices, rather than the row indices—`axis=0` (the default) sorts the *row* indices:

```
In [33]: grades.sort_index(axis=1)
Out[33]:
        Bob  Eva  Katie  Sam  Wally
Test1    83  100    100   94     87
Test2    65   87     81   77     96
Test3    85   90     82   90     70
```

Sorting by Column Values

Let's assume we want to see Test1's grades in descending order so we can see the students' names in highest-to-lowest grade order. We can call the method **sort_values** as follows:

```
In [34]: grades.sort_values(by='Test1', axis=1, ascending=False)
Out[34]:
        Eva  Katie  Sam  Wally  Bob
Test1   100    100   94     87   83
Test2    87     81   77     96   65
Test3    90     82   90     70   85
```

The by and axis keyword arguments work together to determine which values will be sorted. In this case, we sort based on the column values (axis=1) for Test1.

Of course, it might be easier to read the grades and names if they were in a column, so we can sort the transposed DataFrame instead. Here, we did not need to specify the axis keyword argument, because sort_values sorts data in a specified column by default:

```
In [35]: grades.T.sort_values(by='Test1', ascending=False)
Out[35]:
       Test1  Test2  Test3
Eva      100     87     90
Katie    100     81     82
Sam       94     77     90
Wally     87     96     70
Bob       83     65     85
```

Finally, since you're sorting only Test1's grades, you might not want to see the other tests at all. So, let's combine selection with sorting:

```
In [36]: grades.loc['Test1'].sort_values(ascending=False)
Out[36]:
Katie    100
Eva      100
Sam       94
Wally     87
Bob       83
Name: Test1, dtype: int64
```

Copy vs. In-Place Sorting

By default the sort_index and sort_values return a *copy* of the original DataFrame, which could require substantial memory in a big data application. You can sort the Data-Frame *in place*, rather than *copying* the data. To do so, pass the keyword argument inplace=True to either sort_index or sort_values.

We've shown many pandas Series and DataFrame features. In the next chapter's Intro to Data Science section, we'll use Series and DataFrames for *data munging*—cleaning and preparing data for use in your database or analytics software.

7.15 Wrap-Up

This chapter explored the use of NumPy's high-performance ndarrays for storing and retrieving data, and for performing common data manipulations concisely and with reduced chance of errors with functional-style programming. We refer to ndarrays simply by their synonym, arrays.

The chapter examples demonstrated how to create, initialize and refer to individual elements of one- and two-dimensional arrays. We used attributes to determine an array's size, shape and element type. We showed functions that create arrays of 0s, 1s, specific values or ranges values. We compared list and array performance with the IPython %timeit magic and saw that arrays are up to two orders of magnitude faster.

We used array operators and NumPy universal functions to perform element-wise calculations on every element of arrays that have the same shape. You also saw that NumPy uses broadcasting to perform element-wise operations between arrays and scalar values, and between arrays of different shapes. We introduced various built-in array methods for performing calculations using all elements of an array, and we showed how to perform those calculations row-by-row or column-by-column. We demonstrated various array slicing and indexing capabilities that are more powerful than those provided by Python's built-in collections. We demonstrated various ways to reshape arrays. We discussed how to shallow copy and deep copy arrays and other Python objects.

In the Intro to Data Science section, we began our multisection introduction to the popular pandas library that you'll use in many of the data science case study chapters. You saw that many big data applications need more flexible collections than NumPy's arrays, collections that support mixed data types, custom indexing, missing data, data that's not structured consistently and data that needs to be manipulated into forms appropriate for the databases and data analysis packages you use.

We showed how to create and manipulate pandas array-like one-dimensional Series and two-dimensional DataFrames. We customized Series and DataFrame indices. You saw pandas' nicely formatted outputs and customized the precision of floating-point values. We showed various ways to access and select data in Series and DataFrames. We used method describe to calculate basic descriptive statistics for Series and DataFrames. We showed how to transpose DataFrame rows and columns via the T attribute. You saw several ways to sort DataFrames using their index values, their column names, the data in their rows and the data in their columns. You're now familiar with four powerful array-like collections—lists, arrays, Series and DataFrames—and the contexts in which to use them. We'll add a fifth—tensors—in the "Deep Learning" chapter.

In the next chapter, we take a deeper look at strings, string formatting and string methods. We also introduce regular expressions, which we'll use to match patterns in text. The capabilities you'll see will help you prepare for the "Natural Language Processing (NLP)" chapter and other key data science chapters. In the next chapter's Intro to Data Science section, we'll introduce pandas *data munging*—preparing data for use in your database or analytics software. In subsequent chapters, we'll use pandas for basic time-series analysis and introduce pandas visualization capabilities.

8

Strings: A Deeper Look

Objectives

In this chapter, you'll:

- Understand text processing.
- Use string methods.
- Format string content.
- Concatenate and repeat strings.
- Strip whitespace from the ends of strings.
- Change characters from lowercase to uppercase and vice versa.
- Compare strings with the comparison operators.
- Search strings for substrings and replace substrings.
- Split strings into tokens.
- Concatenate strings into a single string with a specified separator between items.
- Create and use regular expressions to match patterns in strings, replace substrings and validate data.
- Use regular expression metacharacters, quantifiers, character classes and grouping.
- Understand how critical string manipulations are to natural language processing.
- Understand the data science terms data munging, data wrangling and data cleaning, and use regular expressions to munge data into preferred formats.

8.1 Introduction

We've introduced strings, basic string formatting and several string operators and methods. You saw that strings support many of the same sequence operations as lists and tuples, and that strings, like tuples, are immutable. Now, we take a deeper look at strings and introduce regular expressions and the re module, which we'll use to match patterns[1] in text. Regular expressions are particularly important in today's data rich applications. The capabilities presented here will help you prepare for the "Natural Language Processing (NLP)" chapter and other key data science chapters. In the NLP chapter, we'll look at other ways to have computers manipulate and even "understand" text. The table below shows many string-processing and NLP-related applications. In the Intro to Data Science section, we briefly introduce data cleaning/munging/wrangling with Pandas Series and DataFrames.

String and NLP applications		
Anagrams	Inter-language translation	Spam classification
Automated grading of written homework	Legal document preparation	Speech-to-text engines
	Monitoring social media posts	Spell checkers
Automated teaching systems	Natural language understanding	Steganography
Categorizing articles		Text editors
Chatbots	Opinion analysis	Text-to-speech engines
Compilers and interpreters	Page-composition software	Web scraping
Creative writing	Palindromes	Who authored Shakespeare's works?
Cryptography	Parts-of-speech tagging	
Document classification	Project Gutenberg free books	Word clouds
Document similarity	Reading books, articles, documentation and absorbing knowledge	Word games
Document summarization		Writing medical diagnoses from x-rays, scans, blood tests
Electronic book readers		
Fraud detection	Search engines	
Grammar checkers	Sentiment analysis	and many more...

---

1. We'll see in the data science case study chapters that searching for patterns in text is a crucial part of machine learning.

8.2 Formatting Strings

Proper text formatting makes data easier to read and understand. Here, we present many text-formatting capabilities.

8.2.1 Presentation Types

You've seen basic string formatting with f-strings. When you specify a placeholder for a value in an f-string, Python assumes the value should be displayed as a string unless you specify another type. In some cases, the type is required. For example, let's format the float value 17.489 rounded to the hundredths position:

```
In [1]: f'{17.489:.2f}'
Out[1]: '17.49'
```

Python supports precision *only* for floating-point and Decimal values. Formatting is *type dependent*—if you try to use .2f to format a string like 'hello', a ValueError occurs. So the **presentation type** f in the *format specifier* .2f is required. It indicates what type is being formatted so Python can determine whether the other formatting information is allowed for that type. Here, we show some common presentation types. You can view the complete list at

> https://docs.python.org/3/library/string.html#formatspec

Integers
The **d presentation type** formats integer values as strings:

```
In [2]: f'{10:d}'
Out[2]: '10'
```

There also are integer presentation types (b, o and x or X) that format integers using the binary, octal or hexadecimal number systems.[2]

Characters
The **c presentation type** formats an integer character code as the corresponding character:

```
In [3]: f'{65:c} {97:c}'
Out[3]: 'A a'
```

Strings
The **s presentation type** is the default. If you specify s explicitly, the value to format must be a variable that references a string, an expression that produces a string or a string literal, as in the first placeholder below. If you do not specify a presentation type, as in the second placeholder below, non-string values like the integer 7 are converted to strings:

```
In [4]: f'{"hello":s} {7}'
Out[4]: 'hello 7'
```

In this snippet, "hello" is enclosed in double quotes. Recall that you cannot place single quotes inside a single-quoted string.

---

2. See the online appendix "Number Systems" for information about the binary, octal and hexadecimal number systems.

Floating-Point and Decimal Values

You've used the f presentation type to format floating-point and Decimal values. For extremely large and small values of these types, **Exponential (scientific) notation** can be used to format the values more compactly. Let's show the difference between f and e for a large value, each with three digits of precision to the right of the decimal point:

```
In [5]: from decimal import Decimal

In [6]: f'{Decimal("10000000000000000000000000.0"):.3f}'
Out[6]: '10000000000000000000000000.000'

In [7]: f'{Decimal("10000000000000000000000000.0"):.3e}'
Out[7]: '1.000e+25'
```

For the **e presentation type** in snippet [5], the formatted value 1.000e+25 is equivalent to

$$1.000 \times 10^{25}$$

If you prefer a capital E for the exponent, use the **E presentation type** rather than e.

8.2.2 Field Widths and Alignment

Previously you used *field widths* to format text in a specified number of character positions. By default, Python *right-aligns* numbers and *left-aligns* other values such as strings—we enclose the results below in brackets ([]) so you can see how the values align in the field:

```
In [1]: f'[{27:10d}]'
Out[1]: '[        27]'

In [2]: f'[{3.5:10f}]'
Out[2]: '[  3.500000]'

In [3]: f'[{"hello":10}]'
Out[3]: '[hello     ]'
```

Snippet [2] shows that Python formats float values with six digits of precision to the right of the decimal point by default. For values that have fewer characters than the field width, the remaining character positions are filled with spaces. Values with more characters than the field width use as many character positions as they need.

Explicitly Specifying Left and Right Alignment in a Field

Recall that you can specify left and right alignment with < and >:

```
In [4]: f'[{27:<15d}]'
Out[4]: '[27             ]'

In [5]: f'[{3.5:<15f}]'
Out[5]: '[3.500000       ]'

In [6]: f'[{"hello":>15}]'
Out[6]: '[          hello]'
```

Centering a Value in a Field

In addition, you can *center* values:

```
In [7]: f'[{27:^7d}]'
Out[7]: '[  27   ]'
```

```
In [8]: f'[{3.5:^7.1f}]'
Out[8]: '[  3.5  ]'

In [9]: f'[{"hello":^7}]'
Out[9]: '[ hello ]'
```

Centering attempts to spread the remaining unoccupied character positions equally to the left and right of the formatted value. Python places the extra space to the right if an odd number of character positions remain.

8.2.3 Numeric Formatting

There are a variety of numeric formatting capabilities.

Formatting Positive Numbers with Signs

Sometimes it's desirable to force the sign on a positive number:

```
In [1]: f'[{27:+10d}]'
Out[1]: '[       +27]'
```

The + before the field width specifies that a positive number should be preceded by a +. A negative number always starts with a -. To fill the remaining characters of the field with 0s rather than spaces, place a 0 before the field width (and *after* the + if there is one):

```
In [2]: f'[{27:+010d}]'
Out[2]: '[+000000027]'
```

Using a Space Where a + Sign Would Appear in a Positive Value

A space indicates that positive numbers should show a space character in the sign position. This is useful for aligning positive and negative values for display purposes:

```
In [3]: print(f'{27:d}\n{27: d}\n{-27: d}')
27
 27
-27
```

Note that the two numbers with a space in their format specifiers align. If a field width is specified, the space should appear *before* the field width.

Grouping Digits

You can format numbers with **thousands separators** by using a **comma (,)**, as follows:

```
In [4]: f'{12345678:,d}'
Out[4]: '12,345,678'

In [5]: f'{123456.78:,.2f}'
Out[5]: '123,456.78'
```

8.2.4 String's format Method

Python's f-strings were added to the language in version 3.6. Before that, formatting was performed with the string method **format**. In fact, f-string formatting is based on the format method's capabilities. We show you the format method here because you'll encounter it in code written prior to Python 3.6. You'll often see the format method in the Python documentation and in the many Python books and articles written before f-strings were introduced. However, we recommend using the newer f-string formatting that we've presented to this point.

You call method `format` on a *format string* containing curly brace (`{}`) *placeholders*, possibly with format specifiers. You pass to the method the values to be formatted. Let's format the `float` value `17.489` rounded to the hundredths position:

```
In [1]: '{:.2f}'.format(17.489)
Out[1]: '17.49'
```

In a placeholder, if there's a format specifier, you precede it by a colon (`:`), as in f-strings. The result of the `format` call is a new string containing the formatted results.

Multiple Placeholders

A format string may contain multiple placeholders, in which case the `format` method's arguments correspond to the placeholders from left to right:

```
In [2]: '{} {}'.format('Amanda', 'Cyan')
Out[2]: 'Amanda Cyan'
```

Referencing Arguments By Position Number

The format string can reference specific arguments by their position in the `format` method's argument list, starting with position 0:

```
In [3]: '{0} {0} {1}'.format('Happy', 'Birthday')
Out[3]: 'Happy Happy Birthday'
```

Note that we used the position number 0 (`'Happy'`) twice—you can reference each argument as often as you like and in any order.

Referencing Keyword Arguments

You can reference keyword arguments by their keys in the placeholders:

```
In [4]: '{first} {last}'.format(first='Amanda', last='Gray')
Out[4]: 'Amanda Gray'

In [5]: '{last} {first}'.format(first='Amanda', last='Gray')
Out[5]: 'Gray Amanda'
```

8.3 Concatenating and Repeating Strings

In earlier chapters, we used the + operator to concatenate strings and the * operator to repeat strings. You also can perform these operations with augmented assignments. Strings are immutable, so each operation assigns a new string object to the variable:

```
In [1]: s1 = 'happy'

In [2]: s2 = 'birthday'

In [3]: s1 += ' ' + s2

In [4]: s1
Out[4]: 'happy birthday'

In [5]: symbol = '>'

In [6]: symbol *= 5
```

```
In [7]: symbol
Out[7]: '>>>>>'
```

8.4 Stripping Whitespace from Strings

There are several string methods for removing whitespace from the ends of a string. Each returns a new string leaving the original unmodified. Strings are immutable, so each method that appears to modify a string returns a new one.

Removing Leading and Trailing Whitespace
Let's use string method **strip** to remove the leading and trailing whitespace from a string:

```
In [1]: sentence = '\t \n This is a test string. \t\t \n'

In [2]: sentence.strip()
Out[2]: 'This is a test string.'
```

Removing Leading Whitespace
Method **lstrip** removes only leading whitespace:

```
In [3]: sentence.lstrip()
Out[3]: 'This is a test string. \t\t \n'
```

Removing Trailing Whitespace
Method **rstrip** removes only trailing whitespace:

```
In [4]: sentence.rstrip()
Out[4]: '\t \n This is a test string.'
```

As the outputs demonstrate, these methods remove all kinds of whitespace, including spaces, newlines and tabs.

8.5 Changing Character Case

In earlier chapters, you used string methods lower and upper to convert strings to all lowercase or all uppercase letters. You also can change a string's capitalization with methods capitalize and title.

Capitalizing Only a String's First Character
Method **capitalize** copies the original string and returns a new string with only the first letter capitalized (this is sometimes called *sentence capitalization*):

```
In [1]: 'happy birthday'.capitalize()
Out[1]: 'Happy birthday'
```

Capitalizing the First Character of Every Word in a String
Method **title** copies the original string and returns a new string with only the first character of each word capitalized (this is sometimes called *book-title capitalization*):

```
In [2]: 'strings: a deeper look'.title()
Out[2]: 'Strings: A Deeper Look'
```

8.6 Comparison Operators for Strings

Strings may be compared with the comparison operators. Recall that strings are compared based on their underlying integer numeric values. So uppercase letters compare as less than lowercase letters because uppercase letters have lower integer values. For example, `'A'` is 65 and `'a'` is 97. You've seen that you can check character codes with ord:

```
In [1]: print(f'A: {ord("A")}; a: {ord("a")}')
A: 65; a: 97
```

Let's compare the strings `'Orange'` and `'orange'` using the comparison operators:

```
In [2]: 'Orange' == 'orange'
Out[2]: False

In [3]: 'Orange' != 'orange'
Out[3]: True

In [4]: 'Orange' < 'orange'
Out[4]: True

In [5]: 'Orange' <= 'orange'
Out[5]: True

In [6]: 'Orange' > 'orange'
Out[6]: False

In [7]: 'Orange' >= 'orange'
Out[7]: False
```

8.7 Searching for Substrings

You can search in a string for one or more adjacent characters—known as a *substring*—to count the number of occurrences, determine whether a string contains a substring, or determine the index at which a substring resides in a string. Each method shown in this section compares characters lexicographically using their underlying numeric values.

Counting Occurrences

String method **count** returns the number of times its argument occurs in the string on which the method is called:

```
In [1]: sentence = 'to be or not to be that is the question'

In [2]: sentence.count('to')
Out[2]: 2
```

If you specify as the second argument a *start_index*, count searches only the slice *string[start_index:]*—that is, from *start_index* through end of the string:

```
In [3]: sentence.count('to', 12)
Out[3]: 1
```

If you specify as the second and third arguments the *start_index* and *end_index*, count searches only the slice *string[start_index:end_index]*—that is, from *start_index* up to, but not including, *end_index*:

```
In [4]: sentence.count('that', 12, 25)
Out[4]: 1
```

Like count, each of the other string methods presented in this section has *start_index* and *end_index* arguments for searching only a slice of the original string.

Locating a Substring in a String
String method **index** searches for a substring within a string and returns the first index at which the substring is found; otherwise, a ValueError occurs:

```
In [5]: sentence.index('be')
Out[5]: 3
```

String method **rindex** performs the same operation as index, but searches from the end of the string and returns the *last* index at which the substring is found; otherwise, a Value-Error occurs:

```
In [6]: sentence.rindex('be')
Out[6]: 16
```

String methods **find** and **rfind** perform the same tasks as index and rindex but, if the substring is not found, return -1 rather than causing a ValueError.

Determining Whether a String Contains a Substring
If you need to know only whether a string contains a substring, use operator in or not in:

```
In [7]: 'that' in sentence
Out[7]: True

In [8]: 'THAT' in sentence
Out[8]: False

In [9]: 'THAT' not in sentence
Out[9]: True
```

Locating a Substring at the Beginning or End of a String
String methods **startswith** and **endswith** return True if the string starts with or ends with a specified substring:

```
In [10]: sentence.startswith('to')
Out[10]: True

In [11]: sentence.startswith('be')
Out[11]: False

In [12]: sentence.endswith('question')
Out[12]: True

In [13]: sentence.endswith('quest')
Out[13]: False
```

8.8 Replacing Substrings

A common text manipulation is to locate a substring and replace its value. Method **replace** takes two substrings. It searches a string for the substring in its first argument and replaces *each* occurrence with the substring in its second argument. The method returns a new string containing the results. Let's replace tab characters with commas:

```
In [1]: values = '1\t2\t3\t4\t5'

In [2]: values.replace('\t', ',')
Out[2]: '1,2,3,4,5'
```

Method `replace` can receive an optional third argument specifying the maximum number of replacements to perform.

8.9 Splitting and Joining Strings

When you read a sentence, your brain breaks it into individual words, or **tokens,** each of which conveys meaning. Interpreters like IPython tokenize statements, breaking them into individual components such as keywords, identifiers, operators and other elements of a programming language. Tokens typically are separated by whitespace characters such as blank, tab and newline, though other characters may be used—the separators are known as **delimiters.**

Splitting Strings

We showed previously that string method `split` with *no* arguments tokenizes a string by breaking it into substrings at each whitespace character, then returns a list of tokens. To tokenize a string at a custom delimiter (such as each comma-and-space pair), specify the delimiter string (such as, `', '`) that `split` uses to tokenize the string:

```
In [1]: letters = 'A, B, C, D'

In [2]: letters.split(', ')
Out[2]: ['A', 'B', 'C', 'D']
```

If you provide an integer as the second argument, it specifies the maximum number of splits. The last token is the remainder of the string after the maximum number of splits:

```
In [3]: letters.split(', ', 2)
Out[3]: ['A', 'B', 'C, D']
```

There is also an **rsplit** method that performs the same task as `split` but processes the maximum number of splits from the end of the string toward the beginning.

Joining Strings

String method **join** concatenates the strings in its argument, which must be an iterable containing only string values; otherwise, a `TypeError` occurs. The separator between the concatenated items is the string on which you call `join`. The following code creates strings containing comma-separated lists of values:

```
In [4]: letters_list = ['A', 'B', 'C', 'D']

In [5]: ','.join(letters_list)
Out[5]: 'A,B,C,D'
```

The next snippet joins the results of a list comprehension that creates a list of strings:

```
In [6]: ','.join([str(i) for i in range(10)])
Out[6]: '0,1,2,3,4,5,6,7,8,9'
```

In the "Files and Exceptions" chapter, you'll see how to work with files that contain comma-separated values. These are known as **CSV files** and are a common format for storing data that can be loaded by spreadsheet applications like Microsoft Excel or Google Sheets. In the data science case study chapters, you'll see that many key libraries, such as NumPy, Pandas and Seaborn, provide built-in capabilities for working with CSV data.

String Methods `partition` and `rpartition`

String method **partition** splits a string into a tuple of three strings based on the method's *separator* argument. The three strings are

- the part of the original string before the separator,
- the separator itself, and
- the part of the string after the separator.

This might be useful for splitting more complex strings. Consider a string representing a student's name and grades:

```
'Amanda: 89, 97, 92'
```

Let's split the original string into the student's name, the separator `': '` and a string representing the list of grades:

```
In [7]: 'Amanda: 89, 97, 92'.partition(': ')
Out[7]: ('Amanda', ': ', '89, 97, 92')
```

To search for the separator from the end of the string instead, use method **rpartition** to split. For example, consider the following URL string:

```
'http://www.deitel.com/books/PyCDS/table_of_contents.html'
```

Let's use `rpartition` split `'table_of_contents.html'` from the rest of the URL:

```
In [8]: url = 'http://www.deitel.com/books/PyCDS/table_of_contents.html'

In [9]: rest_of_url, separator, document = url.rpartition('/')

In [10]: document
Out[10]: 'table_of_contents.html'

In [11]: rest_of_url
Out[11]: 'http://www.deitel.com/books/PyCDS'
```

String Method `splitlines`

In the "Files and Exceptions" chapter, you'll read text from a file. If you read large amounts of text into a string, you might want to split the string into a list of lines based on newline characters. Method **splitlines** returns a list of new strings representing the lines of text split at each newline character in the original string. Recall that Python stores multiline strings with embedded \n characters to represent the line breaks, as shown in snippet `[13]`:

```
In [12]: lines = """This is line 1
    ...: This is line2
    ...: This is line3"""

In [13]: lines
Out[13]: 'This is line 1\nThis is line2\nThis is line3'

In [14]: lines.splitlines()
Out[14]: ['This is line 1', 'This is line2', 'This is line3']
```

Passing True to splitlines keeps the newlines at the end of each string:

```
In [15]: lines.splitlines(True)
Out[15]: ['This is line 1\n', 'This is line2\n', 'This is line3']
```

8.10 Characters and Character-Testing Methods

Many programming languages have separate string and character types. In Python, a character is simply a one-character string.

Python provides string methods for testing whether a string matches certain characteristics. For example, string method **isdigit** returns True if the string on which you call the method contains only the digit characters (0–9). You might use this when validating user input that must contain only digits:

```
In [1]: '-27'.isdigit()
Out[1]: False

In [2]: '27'.isdigit()
Out[2]: True
```

and the string method isalnum returns True if the string on which you call the method is alphanumeric—that is, it contains only digits and letters:

```
In [3]: 'A9876'.isalnum()
Out[3]: True

In [4]: '123 Main Street'.isalnum()
Out[4]: False
```

The table below shows many of the character-testing methods. Each method returns False if the condition described is not satisfied:

String Method	Description
isalnum()	Returns True if the string contains only *alphanumeric* characters (i.e., digits and letters).
isalpha()	Returns True if the string contains only *alphabetic* characters (i.e., letters).
isdecimal()	Returns True if the string contains only *decimal integer* characters (that is, base 10 integers) and does not contain a + or - sign.
isdigit()	Returns True if the string contains only digits (e.g., '0', '1', '2').
isidentifier()	Returns True if the string represents a valid *identifier*.
islower()	Returns True if all alphabetic characters in the string are *lowercase* characters (e.g., 'a', 'b', 'c').
isnumeric()	Returns True if the characters in the string represent a *numeric value* without a + or - sign and without a decimal point.
isspace()	Returns True if the string contains only *whitespace* characters.
istitle()	Returns True if the first character of each word in the string is the only *uppercase* character in the word.
isupper()	Returns True if all alphabetic characters in the string are *uppercase* characters (e.g., 'A', 'B', 'C').

8.11 Raw Strings

Recall that backslash characters in strings introduce *escape sequences*—like \n for newline and \t for tab. So, if you wish to include a backslash in a string, you must use two back-slash characters \\. This makes some strings difficult to read. For example, Microsoft Windows uses backslashes to separate folder names when specifying a file's location. To represent a file's location on Windows, you might write:

```
In [1]: file_path = 'C:\\MyFolder\\MySubFolder\\MyFile.txt'

In [2]: file_path
Out[2]: 'C:\\MyFolder\\MySubFolder\\MyFile.txt'
```

For such cases, **raw strings**—preceded by the character r—are more convenient. They treat each backslash as a regular character, rather than the beginning of an escape sequence:

```
In [3]: file_path = r'C:\MyFolder\MySubFolder\MyFile.txt'

In [4]: file_path
Out[4]: 'C:\\MyFolder\\MySubFolder\\MyFile.txt'
```

Python converts the raw string to a regular string that still uses the two backslash characters in its internal representation, as shown in the last snippet. Raw strings can make your code more readable, particularly when using the regular expressions that we discuss in the next section. Regular expressions often contain many backslash characters.

8.12 Introduction to Regular Expressions

Sometimes you'll need to recognize *patterns* in text, like phone numbers, e-mail addresses, ZIP Codes, web page addresses, Social Security numbers and more. A **regular expression** string describes a *search pattern* for *matching* characters in other strings.

Regular expressions can help you extract data from unstructured text, such as social media posts. They're also important for ensuring that data is in the correct format before you attempt to process it.[3]

Validating Data

Before working with text data, you'll often use regular expressions to *validate the data*. For example, you can check that:

- A U.S. ZIP Code consists of five digits (such as 02215) or five digits followed by a hyphen and four more digits (such as 02215-4775).
- A string last name contains only letters, spaces, apostrophes and hyphens.
- An e-mail address contains only the allowed characters in the allowed order.
- A U.S. Social Security number contains three digits, a hyphen, two digits, a hyphen and four digits, and adheres to other rules about the specific numbers that can be used in each group of digits.

---

3. The topic of regular expressions might feel more challenging than most other Python features you've used. After mastering this subject, you'll often write more concise code than with conventional string-processing techniques, speeding the code-development process. You'll also deal with "fringe" cases you might not ordinarily think about, possibly avoiding subtle bugs.

You'll rarely need to create your own regular expressions for common items like these. Websites like

- `https://regex101.com`
- `http://www.regexlib.com`
- `https://www.regular-expressions.info`

and others offer repositories of existing regular expressions that you can copy and use. Many sites like these also provide interfaces in which you can test regular expressions to determine whether they'll meet your needs.

Other Uses of Regular Expressions
In addition to validating data, regular expressions often are used to:

- Extract data from text (sometimes known as *scraping*)—For example, locating all URLs in a web page. [You might prefer tools like BeautifulSoup, XPath and lxml.]

- Clean data—For example, removing data that's not required, removing duplicate data, handling incomplete data, fixing typos, ensuring consistent data formats, dealing with outliers and more.

- Transform data into other formats—For example, reformatting data that was collected as tab-separated or space-separated values into comma-separated values (CSV) for an application that requires data to be in CSV format.

8.12.1 re Module and Function `fullmatch`
To use regular expressions, import the Python Standard Library's **re** module:

```
In [1]: import re
```

One of the simplest regular expression functions is **fullmatch**, which checks whether the *entire* string in its second argument matches the pattern in its first argument.

Matching Literal Characters
Let's begin by matching *literal characters*—that is, characters that match themselves:

```
In [2]: pattern = '02215'

In [3]: 'Match' if re.fullmatch(pattern, '02215') else 'No match'
Out[3]: 'Match'

In [4]: 'Match' if re.fullmatch(pattern, '51220') else 'No match'
Out[4]: 'No match'
```

The function's first argument is the regular expression pattern to match. Any string can be a regular expression. The variable pattern's value, `'02215'`, contains only *literal digits* that match *themselves* in the specified order. The second argument is the string that should entirely match the pattern.

If the second argument matches the pattern in the first argument, `fullmatch` returns an object containing the matching text, which evaluates to `True`. We'll say more about this object later. In snippet [4], even though the second argument contains the *same digits* as the regular expression, they're in a *different* order. So there's no match, and `fullmatch` returns `None`, which evaluates to `False`.

Metacharacters, Character Classes and Quantifiers

Regular expressions typically contain various special symbols called **metacharacters**, which are shown in the table below:

Regular expression metacharacters
[] {} () \ * + ^ $? .	

The **\ metacharacter** begins each of the predefined **character classes**, each matching a specific set of characters. Let's validate a five-digit ZIP Code:

```
In [5]: 'Valid' if re.fullmatch(r'\d{5}', '02215') else 'Invalid'
Out[5]: 'Valid'

In [6]: 'Valid' if re.fullmatch(r'\d{5}', '9876') else 'Invalid'
Out[6]: 'Invalid'
```

In the regular expression \d{5}, \d is a character class representing a digit (0–9). A character class is a *regular expression escape sequence* that matches *one* character. To match more than one, follow the character class with a **quantifier**. The quantifier {5} repeats \d five times, as if we had written \d\d\d\d\d, to match five consecutive digits. In snippet [6], fullmatch returns None because '9876' contains only four consecutive digit characters.

Other Predefined Character Classes

The table below shows some common predefined character classes and the groups of characters they match. To match any metacharacter as its *literal* value, precede it by a backslash (\). For example, \\ matches a backslash (\) and \$ matches a dollar sign ($).

Character class	Matches
\d	Any digit (0–9).
\D	Any character that is *not* a digit.
\s	Any whitespace character (such as spaces, tabs and newlines).
\S	Any character that is *not* a whitespace character.
\w	Any **word character** (also called an **alphanumeric character**)—that is, any uppercase or lowercase letter, any digit or an underscore
\W	Any character that is *not* a word character.

Custom Character Classes

Square brackets, [], define a **custom character class** that matches a *single* character. For example, [aeiou] matches a lowercase vowel, [A-Z] matches an uppercase letter, [a-z] matches a lowercase letter and [a-zA-Z] matches any lowercase or uppercase letter.

Let's validate a simple first name with no spaces or punctuation. We'll ensure that it begins with an uppercase letter (A–Z) followed by any number of lowercase letters (a–z):

```
In [7]: 'Valid' if re.fullmatch('[A-Z][a-z]*', 'Wally') else 'Invalid'
Out[7]: 'Valid'

In [8]: 'Valid' if re.fullmatch('[A-Z][a-z]*', 'eva') else 'Invalid'
Out[8]: 'Invalid'
```

A first name might contain many letters. The * **quantifier** matches *zero or more occurrences* of the subexpression to its left (in this case, [a-z]). So [A-Z][a-z]* matches an uppercase letter followed by *zero or more* lowercase letters, such as 'Amanda', 'Bo' or even 'E'.

When a custom character class starts with a **caret** (∧), the class matches any character that's *not* specified. So [∧a-z] matches any character that's *not* a lowercase letter:

```
In [9]: 'Match' if re.fullmatch('[∧a-z]', 'A') else 'No match'
Out[9]: 'Match'

In [10]: 'Match' if re.fullmatch('[∧a-z]', 'a') else 'No match'
Out[10]: 'No match'
```

Metacharacters in a custom character class are treated as literal characters—that is, the characters themselves. So [*+$] matches a *single* *, + or $ character:

```
In [11]: 'Match' if re.fullmatch('[*+$]', '*') else 'No match'
Out[11]: 'Match'

In [12]: 'Match' if re.fullmatch('[*+$]', '!') else 'No match'
Out[12]: 'No match'
```

* vs. + Quantifier
If you want to require *at least one* lowercase letter in a first name, you can replace the * quantifier in snippet [7] with +, which matches *at least one occurrence* of a subexpression:

```
In [13]: 'Valid' if re.fullmatch('[A-Z][a-z]+', 'Wally') else 'Invalid'
Out[13]: 'Valid'

In [14]: 'Valid' if re.fullmatch('[A-Z][a-z]+', 'E') else 'Invalid'
Out[14]: 'Invalid'
```

Both * and + are **greedy**—they match as many characters as possible. So the regular expression [A-Z][a-z]+ matches 'Al', 'Eva', 'Samantha', 'Benjamin' and any other words that begin with a capital letter followed at least one lowercase letter.

Other Quantifiers
The **? quantifier** matches *zero or one occurrences* of a subexpression:

```
In [15]: 'Match' if re.fullmatch('labell?ed', 'labelled') else 'No match'
Out[15]: 'Match'

In [16]: 'Match' if re.fullmatch('labell?ed', 'labeled') else 'No match'
Out[16]: 'Match'

In [17]: 'Match' if re.fullmatch('labell?ed', 'labellled') else 'No match'
Out[17]: 'No match'
```

The regular expression labell?ed matches labelled (the U.K. English spelling) and labeled (the U.S. English spelling), but not the misspelled word labellled. In each snippet above, the first five literal characters in the regular expression (label) match the first five characters of the second arguments. Then l? indicates that there can be *zero or one more* l characters before the remaining literal ed characters.

You can match *at least n occurrences* of a subexpression with the **{n,} quantifier**. The following regular expression matches strings containing *at least* three digits:

```
In [18]: 'Match' if re.fullmatch(r'\d{3,}', '123') else 'No match'
Out[18]: 'Match'

In [19]: 'Match' if re.fullmatch(r'\d{3,}', '1234567890') else 'No match'
Out[19]: 'Match'

In [20]: 'Match' if re.fullmatch(r'\d{3,}', '12') else 'No match'
Out[20]: 'No match'
```

You can match *between n and m (inclusive) occurrences* of a subexpression with the **{n, m} quantifier**. The following regular expression matches strings containing 3 to 6 digits:

```
In [21]: 'Match' if re.fullmatch(r'\d{3,6}', '123') else 'No match'
Out[21]: 'Match'

In [22]: 'Match' if re.fullmatch(r'\d{3,6}', '123456') else 'No match'
Out[22]: 'Match'

In [23]: 'Match' if re.fullmatch(r'\d{3,6}', '1234567') else 'No match'
Out[23]: 'No match'

In [24]: 'Match' if re.fullmatch(r'\d{3,6}', '12') else 'No match'
Out[24]: 'No match'
```

8.12.2 Replacing Substrings and Splitting Strings

The re module provides function sub for replacing patterns in a string, and function split for breaking a string into pieces, based on patterns.

Function sub—Replacing Patterns

By default, the re module's **sub function** replaces *all* occurrences of a pattern with the replacement text you specify. Let's convert a tab-delimited string to comma-delimited:

```
In [1]: import re

In [2]: re.sub(r'\t', ', ', '1\t2\t3\t4')
Out[2]: '1, 2, 3, 4'
```

The sub function receives three required arguments:

- the *pattern to match* (the tab character '\t')
- the *replacement text* (', ') and
- the *string to be searched* ('1\t2\t3\t4')

and returns a new string. The keyword argument count can be used to specify the maximum number of replacements:

```
In [3]: re.sub(r'\t', ', ', '1\t2\t3\t4', count=2)
Out[3]: '1, 2, 3\t4'
```

Function split

The **split function** *tokenizes* a string, using a regular expression to specify the *delimiter*, and returns a list of strings. Let's tokenize a string by splitting it at any comma that's followed by 0 or more whitespace characters—\s is the whitespace character class and * indicates *zero or more* occurrences of the preceding subexpression:

```
In [4]: re.split(r',\s*', '1,   2,   3,4,     5,6,7,8')
Out[4]: ['1', '2', '3', '4', '5', '6', '7', '8']
```

Use the keyword argument `maxsplit` to specify the maximum number of splits:

```
In [5]: re.split(r',\s*', '1,   2,   3,4,     5,6,7,8', maxsplit=3)
Out[5]: ['1', '2', '3', '4,     5,6,7,8']
```

In this case, after the 3 splits, the fourth string contains the rest of the original string.

8.12.3 Other Search Functions; Accessing Matches

Earlier we used the `fullmatch` function to determine whether an *entire* string matched a regular expression. There are several other searching functions. Here, we discuss the `search`, `match`, `findall` and `finditer` functions, and show how to access the matching substrings.

Function `search`—Finding the First Match Anywhere in a String

Function **search** looks in a string for the *first* occurrence of a substring that matches a regular expression and returns a **match object** (of type **SRE_Match**) that contains the matching substring. The match object's **group** method returns that substring:

```
In [1]: import re

In [2]: result = re.search('Python', 'Python is fun')

In [3]: result.group() if result else 'not found'
Out[3]: 'Python'
```

Function search returns None if the string does *not* contain the pattern:

```
In [4]: result2 = re.search('fun!', 'Python is fun')

In [5]: result2.group() if result2 else 'not found'
Out[5]: 'not found'
```

You can search for a match only at the *beginning* of a string with function **match**.

Ignoring Case with the Optional `flags` Keyword Argument

Many re module functions receive an optional `flags` keyword argument that changes how regular expressions are matched. For example, matches are *case sensitive* by default, but by using the re module's IGNORECASE constant, you can perform a *case-insensitive* search:

```
In [6]: result3 = re.search('Sam', 'SAM WHITE', flags=re.IGNORECASE)

In [7]: result3.group() if result3 else 'not found'
Out[7]: 'SAM'
```

Here, 'SAM' matches the pattern 'Sam' because both have the same letters, even though 'SAM' contains only uppercase letters.

Metacharacters That Restrict Matches to the Beginning or End of a String

The ∧ **metacharacter** at the beginning of a regular expression (and not inside square brackets) is an anchor indicating that the expression matches only the *beginning* of a string:

```
In [8]: result = re.search('∧Python', 'Python is fun')
```

```
In [9]: result.group() if result else 'not found'
Out[9]: 'Python'

In [10]: result = re.search('^fun', 'Python is fun')

In [11]: result.group() if result else 'not found'
Out[11]: 'not found'
```

Similarly, the **$ metacharacter** at the end of a regular expression is an anchor indicating that the expression matches only the *end* of a string:

```
In [12]: result = re.search('Python$', 'Python is fun')

In [13]: result.group() if result else 'not found'
Out[13]: 'not found'

In [14]: result = re.search('fun$', 'Python is fun')

In [15]: result.group() if result else 'not found'
Out[15]: 'fun'
```

Function `findall` and `finditer`—Finding All Matches in a String

Function **findall** finds *every* matching substring in a string and returns a list of the matching substrings. Let's extract all the U.S. phone numbers from a string. For simplicity we'll assume that U.S. phone numbers have the form ###-###-####:

```
In [16]: contact = 'Wally White, Home: 555-555-1234, Work: 555-555-4321'

In [17]: re.findall(r'\d{3}-\d{3}-\d{4}', contact)
Out[17]: ['555-555-1234', '555-555-4321']
```

Function **finditer** works like findall, but returns a lazy *iterable* of match objects. For large numbers of matches, using finditer can save memory because it returns one match at a time, whereas findall returns all the matches at once:

```
In [18]: for phone in re.finditer(r'\d{3}-\d{3}-\d{4}', contact):
    ...:     print(phone.group())
    ...:
555-555-1234
555-555-4321
```

Capturing Substrings in a Match

You can use **parentheses metacharacters**—**(** and **)**—to capture substrings in a match. For example, let's capture as separate substrings the name and e-mail address in the string text:

```
In [19]: text = 'Charlie Cyan, e-mail: demo1@deitel.com'

In [20]: pattern = r'([A-Z][a-z]+ [A-Z][a-z]+), e-mail: (\w+@\w+\.\w{3})'

In [21]: result = re.search(pattern, text)
```

The regular expression specifies two substrings to capture, each denoted by the metacharacters (and). These metacharacters do *not* affect whether the pattern is found in the string text—the match function returns a match object *only* if the *entire* pattern is found in the string text.

Let's consider the regular expression:

- `'([A-Z][a-z]+ [A-Z][a-z]+)'` matches two words separated by a space. Each word must have an initial capital letter.

- `', e-mail: '` contains literal characters that match themselves.

- `(\w+@\w+\.\w{3})` matches a *simple* e-mail address consisting of one or more alphanumeric characters (`\w+`), the @ character, one or more alphanumeric characters (`\w+`), a dot (`\.`) and three alphanumeric characters (`\w{3}`). We preceded the dot with \ because a dot (.) is a regular expression metacharacter that matches one character.

The match object's **groups** method returns a tuple of the captured substrings:

```
In [22]: result.groups()
Out[22]: ('Charlie Cyan', 'demo1@deitel.com')
```

The match object's **group** method returns the *entire* match as a single string:

```
In [23]: result.group()
Out[23]: 'Charlie Cyan, e-mail: demo1@deitel.com'
```

You can access each captured substring by passing an integer to the group method. The captured substrings are *numbered from 1* (unlike list indices, which start at 0):

```
In [24]: result.group(1)
Out[24]: 'Charlie Cyan'

In [25]: result.group(2)
Out[25]: 'demo1@deitel.com'
```

8.13 Intro to Data Science: Pandas, Regular Expressions and Data Munging

Data does not always come in forms ready for analysis. It could, for example, be in the wrong format, incorrect or even missing. Industry experience has shown that data scientists can spend as much as 75% of their time preparing data before they begin their studies. Preparing data for analysis is called **data munging** or **data wrangling**. These are synonyms—from this point forward, we'll say data munging.

Two of the most important steps in data munging are *data cleaning* and *transforming data* into the optimal formats for your database systems and analytics software. Some common data cleaning examples are:

- deleting observations with missing values,
- substituting reasonable values for missing values,
- deleting observations with bad values,
- substituting reasonable values for bad values,
- tossing outliers (although sometimes you'll want to keep them),
- duplicate elimination (although sometimes duplicates are valid),
- dealing with inconsistent data,
- and more.

You're probably already thinking that data cleaning is a difficult and messy process where you could easily make bad decisions that would negatively impact your results. This is correct. When you get to the data science case studies in the later chapters, you'll see that data science is more of an **empirical science**, like medicine, and less of a theoretical science, like theoretical physics. Empirical sciences base their conclusions on observations and experience. For example, many medicines that effectively solve medical problems today were developed by observing the effects that early versions of these medicines had on lab animals and eventually humans, and gradually refining ingredients and dosages. The actions data scientists take can vary per project, be based on the quality and nature of the data and be affected by evolving organization and professional standards.

Some common data transformations include:

- removing unnecessary data and *features* (we'll say more about features in the data science case studies),

- combining related features,

- sampling data to obtain a representative subset (we'll see in the data science case studies that *random sampling* is particularly effective for this and we'll say why),

- standardizing data formats,

- grouping data,

- and more.

It's always wise to hold onto your original data. We'll show simple examples of cleaning and transforming data in the context of Pandas `Series` and `DataFrames`.

Cleaning Your Data

Bad data values and missing values can significantly impact data analysis. Some data scientists advise against any attempts to insert "reasonable values." Instead, they advocate clearly marking missing data and leaving it up to the data analytics package to handle the issue. Others offer strong cautions.[4]

Let's consider a hospital that records patients' temperatures (and probably other vital signs) four times per day. Assume that the data consists of a name and four `float` values, such as

```
['Brown, Sue', 98.6, 98.4, 98.7, 0.0]
```

The preceding patient's first three recorded temperatures are 99.7, 98.4 and 98.7. The last temperature was missing and recorded as 0.0, perhaps because the sensor malfunctioned. The average of the first three values is 98.57, which is close to normal. However, if you calculate the average temperature *including* the missing value for which 0.0 was substituted, the average is only 73.93, clearly a questionable result. Certainly, doctors would not want to take drastic remedial action on this patient—it's crucial to "get the data right."

---

4.   This footnote was abstracted from a comment sent to us July 20, 2018 by one of the book's reviewers, Dr. Alison Sanchez of the University of San Diego School of Business. She commented: "Be cautious when mentioning 'substituting reasonable values' for missing or bad values. A stern warning: 'Substituting' values that increase statistical significance or give more 'reasonable' or 'better' results is not permitted. 'Substituting' data should not turn into 'fudging' data. The first rule readers should learn is not to eliminate or change values that contradict their hypotheses. 'Substituting reasonable values' does not mean readers should feel free to change values to get the results they want."

One common way to clean the data is to substitute a *reasonable* value for the missing temperature, such as the average of the patient's other readings. Had we done that above, then the patient's average temperature would remain 98.57—a much more likely average temperature, based on the other readings.

Data Validation

Let's begin by creating a `Series` of five-digit ZIP Codes from a dictionary of city-name/five-digit-ZIP-Code key–value pairs. We intentionally entered an invalid ZIP Code for Miami:

```
In [1]: import pandas as pd

In [2]: zips = pd.Series({'Boston': '02215', 'Miami': '3310'})

In [3]: zips
Out[3]:
Boston      02215
Miami        3310
dtype: object
```

Though `zips` looks like a two-dimensional array, it's actually one-dimensional. The "second column" represents the `Series`' ZIP Code *values* (from the dictionary's values), and the "first column" represents their *indices* (from the dictionary's keys).

We can use regular expressions with Pandas to validate data. The **str attribute** of a `Series` provides string-processing and various regular expression methods. Let's use the `str` attribute's **match method** to check whether each ZIP Code is valid:

```
In [4]: zips.str.match(r'\d{5}')
Out[4]:
Boston       True
Miami       False
dtype: bool
```

Method `match` applies the regular expression `\d{5}` to *each* `Series` element, attempting to ensure that the element is comprised of exactly five digits. You do not need to loop explicitly through all the ZIP Codes—`match` does this for you. This is another example of functional-style programming with internal rather than external iteration. The method returns a new `Series` containing `True` for each valid element. In this case, the ZIP Code for Miami did *not* match, so its element is `False`.

There are several ways to deal with invalid data. One is to catch it at its source and interact with the source to correct the value. That's not always possible. For example, the data could be coming from high-speed sensors in the Internet of Things. In that case, we would not be able to correct it at the source, so we could apply data cleaning techniques. In the case of the bad Miami ZIP Code of 3310, we might look for Miami ZIP Codes beginning with 3310. There are two—33101 and 33109—and we could pick one of those.

Sometimes, rather than matching an *entire* value to a pattern, you'll want to know whether a value contains a *substring* that matches the pattern. In this case, use method **contains** instead of `match`. Let's create a `Series` of strings, each containing a U.S. city, state and ZIP Code, then determine whether each string contains a substring matching the pattern `' [A-Z]{2} '` (a space, followed by two uppercase letters, followed by a space):

```
In [5]: cities = pd.Series(['Boston, MA 02215', 'Miami, FL 33101'])
```

```
In [6]: cities
Out[6]:
0    Boston, MA 02215
1     Miami, FL 33101
dtype: object

In [7]: cities.str.contains(r' [A-Z]{2} ')
Out[7]:
0    True
1    True
dtype: bool

In [8]: cities.str.match(r' [A-Z]{2} ')
Out[8]:
0    False
1    False
dtype: bool
```

We did not specify the index values, so the Series uses zero-based indexes by default (snippet [6]). Snippet [7] uses contains to show that both Series elements contain substrings that match ' [A-Z]{2} '. Snippet [8] uses match to show that neither element's value matches that pattern in its entirety, because each has other characters in its complete value.

Reformatting Your Data

We've discussed data cleaning. Now let's consider munging data into a different format. As a simple example, assume that an application requires U.S. phone numbers in the format ###-###-####, with hyphens separating each group of digits. The phone numbers have been provided to us as 10-digit strings without hyphens. Let's create the DataFrame:

```
In [9]: contacts = [['Mike Green', 'demo1@deitel.com', '5555555555'],
   ...:             ['Sue Brown', 'demo2@deitel.com', '5555551234']]

In [10]: contactsdf = pd.DataFrame(contacts,
   ...:                  columns=['Name', 'Email', 'Phone'])

In [11]: contactsdf
Out[11]:
          Name             Email       Phone
0   Mike Green   demo1@deitel.com  5555555555
1    Sue Brown   demo2@deitel.com  5555551234
```

In this DataFrame, we specified column indices via the columns keyword argument but did *not* specify row indices, so the rows are indexed from 0. Also, the output shows the column values right aligned by default. This differs from Python formatting in which numbers in a field are *right aligned* by default but non-numeric values are *left aligned* by default.

Now, let's munge the data with a little more functional-style programming. We can *map* the phone numbers to the proper format by calling the Series method **map** on the DataFrame's 'Phone' column. Method map's argument is a *function* that receives a value and returns the *mapped* value. The function get_formatted_phone maps 10 consecutive digits into the format ###-###-####:

```
In [12]: import re

In [13]: def get_formatted_phone(value):
   ...:     result = re.fullmatch(r'(\d{3})(\d{3})(\d{4})', value)
   ...:     return '-'.join(result.groups()) if result else value
   ...:
   ...:
```

The regular expression in the block's first statement matches *only* 10 consecutive digits. It captures substrings containing the first three digits, the next three digits and the last four digits. The return statement operates as follows:

- If result is None, we simply return value unmodified.

- Otherwise, we call result.groups() to get a tuple containing the captured substrings and pass that tuple to string method join to concatenate the elements, separating each from the next with '-' to form the mapped phone number.

Series method map returns a new Series containing the results of calling its function argument for each value in the column. Snippet [15] displays the result, including the column's name and type:

```
In [14]: formatted_phone = contactsdf['Phone'].map(get_formatted_phone)

In [15]: formatted_phone
0    555-555-5555
1    555-555-1234
Name: Phone, dtype: object
```

Once you've confirmed that the data is in the correct format, you can update it in the original DataFrame by assigning the new Series to the 'Phone' column:

```
In [16]: contactsdf['Phone'] = formatted_phone

In [17]: contactsdf
Out[17]:
        Name              Email         Phone
0  Mike Green    demo1@deitel.com  555-555-5555
1   Sue Brown    demo2@deitel.com  555-555-1234
```

We'll continue our pandas discussion in the next chapter's Intro to Data Science section, and we'll use pandas in several later chapters.

8.14 Wrap-Up

In this chapter, we presented various string formatting and processing capabilities. You formatted data in f-strings and with the string method format. We showed the augmented assignments for concatenating and repeating strings. You used string methods to remove whitespace from the beginning and end of strings and to change their case. We discussed additional methods for splitting strings and for joining iterables of strings. We introduced various character-testing methods.

We showed raw strings that treat backslashes (\) as literal characters rather than the beginning of escape sequences. These were particularly useful for defining regular expressions, which often contain many backslashes.

Next, we introduced the powerful pattern-matching capabilities of regular expressions with functions from the re module. We used the fullmatch function to ensure that an entire string matched a pattern, which is useful for validating data. We showed how to use the replace function to search for and replace substrings. We used the split function to tokenize strings based on delimiters that match a regular expression pattern. Then we showed various ways to search for patterns in strings and to access the resulting matches.

In the Intro to Data Science section, we introduced the synonyms data munging and data wrangling and showed a sample data munging operation, namely transforming data. We continued our discussion of Panda's Series and DataFrames by using regular expressions to validate and munge data.

In the next chapter, we'll continue using various string-processing capabilities as we introduce reading text from files and writing text to files. We'll use the csv module for manipulating comma-separated value (CSV) files. We'll also introduce exception handling so we can process exceptions as they occur, rather than displaying a traceback.

9

Files and Exceptions

Objectives

In this chapter, you'll:

- Understand the notions of files and persistent data.
- Read, write and update files.
- Read and write CSV files, a common format for machine-learning datasets.
- Serialize objects into the JSON data-interchange format—commonly used to transmit over the Internet—and deserialize JSON into objects.
- Use the `with` statement to ensure that resources are properly released, avoiding "resource leaks."
- Use the `try` statement to delimit code in which exceptions may occur and handle those exceptions with associated `except` clauses.
- Use the `try` statement's `else` clause to execute code when no exceptions occur in the `try` suite.
- Use the `try` statement's `finally` clause to execute code regardless of whether an exception occurs in the `try`.
- `raise` exceptions to indicate runtime problems.
- Understand the traceback of functions and methods that led to an exception.
- Use pandas to load into a `DataFrame` and process the Titanic Disaster CSV dataset.

9.1 Introduction

Variables, lists, tuples, dictionaries, sets, arrays, pandas Series and pandas DataFrames offer only *temporary* data storage. The data is lost when a local variable "goes out of scope" or when the program terminates. **Files** provide long-term retention of typically large amounts of data, even after the program that created the data terminates, so data maintained in files is persistent. Computers store files on secondary storage devices, including solid-state drives, hard disks and more. In this chapter, we explain how Python programs create, update and process data files.

We consider text files in several popular formats—plain text, JSON (JavaScript Object Notation) and CSV (comma-separated values). We'll use JSON to serialize and deserialize objects to facilitate saving those objects to secondary storage and transmitting them over the Internet. Be sure to read this chapter's Intro to Data Science section in which we'll use both the Python Standard Library's csv module and pandas to load and manipulate CSV data. In particular, we'll look at the CSV version of the Titanic disaster dataset. We'll use many popular datasets in upcoming data-science case-study chapters on natural language processing, data mining Twitter, IBM Watson, machine learning, deep learning and big data.

As part of our continuing emphasis on Python security, we'll discuss the security vulnerabilities of serializing and deserializing data with the Python Standard Library's pickle module. We recommend JSON serialization in preference to pickle.

We also introduce **exception handling**. An exception indicates an execution-time problem. You've seen exceptions of types ZeroDivisionError, NameError, ValueError, StatisticsError, TypeError, IndexError, KeyError and RuntimeError. We'll show how to deal with exceptions as they occur by using try statements and associated except clauses to *handle* exceptions. We'll also discuss the try statement's else and finally clauses. The features presented here help you write *robust, fault-tolerant* programs that can deal with problems and continue executing or *terminate gracefully.*

Programs typically request and release resources (such as files) during program execution. Often, these are in limited supply or can be used only by one program at a time. We show how to guarantee that after a program uses a resource, it's released for use by other programs, even if an exception has occurred. You'll use the with statement for this purpose.

9.2 Files

Python views a **text file** as a sequence of characters and a **binary file** (for images, videos and more) as a sequence of bytes. As in lists and arrays, the first character in a text file and byte in a binary file is located at position 0, so in a file of n characters or bytes, the highest position number is $n - 1$. The diagram below shows a conceptual view of a file:

For each file you **open**, Python creates a **file object** that you'll use to interact with the file.

End of File

Every operating system provides a mechanism to denote the end of a file. Some represent it with an **end-of-file marker** (as in the preceding figure), while others might maintain a count of the total characters or bytes in the file. Programming languages generally hide these operating-system details from you.

Standard File Objects

When a Python program begins execution, it creates three **standard file objects**:

- **sys.stdin**—the **standard input file object**
- **sys.stdout**—the **standard output file object**, and
- **sys.stderr**—the **standard error file object**.

Though these are considered file objects, they do not read from or write to files by default. The input function implicitly uses sys.stdin to get user input from the keyboard. Function print implicitly outputs to sys.stdout, which appears in the command line. Python implicitly outputs program errors and tracebacks to sys.stderr, which also appears in the command line. You must import the sys module if you need to refer to these objects explicitly in your code, but this is rare.

9.3 Text-File Processing

In this section, we'll write a simple text file that might be used by an accounts-receivable system to track the money owed by a company's clients. We'll then read that text file to confirm that it contains the data. For each client, we'll store the client's account number, last name and account balance owed to the company. Together, these data fields represent a client **record**. Python imposes no structure on a file, so notions such as records do not exist natively in Python. Programmers must structure files to meet their applications' requirements. We'll create and maintain this file in order by account number. In this sense, the account number may be thought of as a **record key**. For this chapter, we assume that you launch IPython from the ch09 examples folder.

9.3.1 Writing to a Text File: Introducing the `with` Statement

Let's create an `accounts.txt` file and write five client records to the file. Generally, records in text files are stored one per line, so we end each record with a newline character:

```
In [1]: with open('accounts.txt', mode='w') as accounts:
   ...:         accounts.write('100 Jones 24.98\n')
   ...:         accounts.write('200 Doe 345.67\n')
   ...:         accounts.write('300 White 0.00\n')
   ...:         accounts.write('400 Stone -42.16\n')
   ...:         accounts.write('500 Rich 224.62\n')
   ...:
```

You can also write to a file with `print` (which automatically outputs a \n), as in

```
print('100 Jones 24.98', file=accounts)
```

The `with` Statement

Many applications *acquire* resources, such as files, network connections, database connections and more. You should *release* resources as soon as they're no longer needed. This practice ensures that other applications can use the resources. Python's **with statement**:

- acquires a resource (in this case, the file object for `accounts.txt`) and assigns its corresponding object to a variable (`accounts` in this example),
- allows the application to use the resource via that variable, and
- calls the resource object's `close` method to release the resource when program control reaches the end of the `with` statement's suite.

Built-In Function open

The built-in **open function** opens the file `accounts.txt` and associates it with a file object. The `mode` argument specifies the **file-open mode**, indicating whether to open a file for reading from the file, for writing to the file or both. The mode `'w'` opens the file for *writing*, creating the file if it does not exist. If you do not specify a path to the file, Python creates it in the current folder (ch09). Be careful—opening a file for writing *deletes* all the existing data in the file. By convention, the **.txt file extension** indicates a plain text file.

Writing to the File

The `with` statement assigns the object returned by open to the variable accounts in the **as clause**. In the `with` statement's suite, we use the variable `accounts` to interact with the file. In this case, we call the file object's **write method** five times to write five records to the file, each as a separate line of text ending in a newline. At the end of the `with` statement's suite, the `with` statement *implicitly* calls the file object's **close** method to close the file.

Contents of `accounts.txt` File

After executing the previous snippet, your ch09 directory contains the file `accounts.txt` with the following contents, which you can view by opening the file in a text editor:

```
100 Jones 24.98
200 Doe 345.67
300 White 0.00
400 Stone -42.16
500 Rich 224.62
```

In the next section, you'll read the file and display its contents.

9.3.2 Reading Data from a Text File

We just created the text file accounts.txt and wrote data to it. Now let's read that data from the file sequentially from beginning to end. The following session reads records from the file accounts.txt and displays the contents of each record in columns with the Account and Name columns *left aligned* and the Balance column *right aligned*, so the decimal points align vertically:

```
In [1]: with open('accounts.txt', mode='r') as accounts:
   ...:     print(f'{"Account":<10}{"Name":<10}{"Balance":>10}')
   ...:     for record in accounts:
   ...:         account, name, balance = record.split()
   ...:         print(f'{account:<10}{name:<10}{balance:>10}')
   ...:
Account   Name          Balance
100       Jones           24.98
200       Doe            345.67
300       White            0.00
400       Stone          -42.16
500       Rich           224.62
```

If the contents of a file should not be modified, open the file for reading only. This prevents the program from accidentally modifying the file. You open a file for reading by passing the 'r' file-open mode as function open's second argument. If you do not specify the folder in which to store the file, open assumes the file is in the current folder.

Iterating through a file object, as shown in the preceding for statement, reads one line at a time from the file and returns it as a string. For each record (that is, line) in the file, string method split returns tokens in the line as a list, which we unpack into the variables account, name and balance.[1] The last statement in the for statement's suite displays these variables in columns using field widths.

File Method readlines

The file object's **readlines** method also can be used to read an *entire* text file. The method returns each line as a string in a list of strings. For small files, this works well, but iterating over the lines in a file object, as shown above, can be more efficient.[2] Calling readlines for a large file can be a time-consuming operation, which must complete before you can begin using the list of strings. Using the file object in a for statement enables your program to process each text line as it's read.

Seeking to a Specific File Position

While reading through a file, the system maintains a **file-position pointer** representing the location of the next character to read. Sometimes it's necessary to process a file sequentially from the beginning *several times* during a program's execution. Each time, you must reposition the file-position pointer to the beginning of the file, which you can do either by closing and reopening the file, or by calling the file object's **seek** method, as in

file_object.seek(0)

The latter approach is faster.

---

1. When splitting strings on spaces (the default), split automatically discards the newline character.
2. https://docs.python.org/3/tutorial/inputoutput.html#methods-of-file-objects.

9.4 **Updating Text Files**

Formatted data written to a text file cannot be modified without the risk of destroying other data. If the name 'White' needs to be changed to 'Williams' in accounts.txt, the old name cannot simply be overwritten. The original record for White is stored as

```
300 White 0.00
```

If you overwrite the name 'White' with the name 'Williams', the record becomes

```
300 Williams00
```

The new last name contains three more characters than the original one, so the characters beyond the second "i" in 'Williams' overwrite other characters in the line. The problem is that in the formatted input–output model, records and their fields can vary in size. For example, 7, 14, –117, 2074 and 27383 are all integers and are stored in the same number of "raw data" bytes internally (typically 4 or 8 bytes in today's systems). However, when these integers are output as formatted text, they become different-sized fields. For example, 7 is one character, 14 is two characters and 27383 is five characters.

To make the preceding name change, we can:

- copy the records before 300 White 0.00 into a temporary file,

- write the updated and correctly formatted record for account 300 to this file,

- copy the records after 300 White 0.00 to the temporary file,

- delete the old file and

- rename the temporary file to use the original file's name.

This can be cumbersome because it requires processing *every* record in the file, even if you need to update only one record. Updating a file as described above is more efficient when an application needs to update many records in one pass of the file.[3]

Updating accounts.txt

Let's use a with statement to update the accounts.txt file to change account 300's name from 'White' to 'Williams' as described above:

```
In [1]: accounts = open('accounts.txt', 'r')

In [2]: temp_file = open('temp_file.txt', 'w')

In [3]: with accounts, temp_file:
   ...:     for record in accounts:
   ...:         account, name, balance = record.split()
   ...:         if account != '300':
   ...:             temp_file.write(record)
   ...:         else:
   ...:             new_record = ' '.join([account, 'Williams', balance])
   ...:             temp_file.write(new_record + '\n')
   ...:
```

For readability, we opened the file objects (snippets [1] and [2]), then specified their variable names in the first line of snippet [3]. This with statement manages two resource objects,

---

3. In the chapter, "Big Data: Hadoop, Spark, NoSQL and IoT," you'll see that database systems solve this "update in place" problem efficiently.

specified in a comma-separated list after with. The for statement unpacks each record into account, name and balance. If the account is not '300', we write record (which contains a newline) to temp_file. Otherwise, we assemble the new record containing 'Williams' in place of 'White' and write it to the file. After snippet [3], temp_file.txt contains:

```
100 Jones 24.98
200 Doe 345.67
300 Williams 0.00
400 Stone -42.16
500 Rich 224.62
```

os Module File-Processing Functions

At this point, we have the old accounts.txt file and the new temp_file.txt. To complete the update, let's delete the old accounts.txt file, then rename temp_file.txt as accounts.txt. The **os module**[4] provides functions for interacting with the operating system, including several that manipulate your system's files and directories. Now that we've created the temporary file, let's use the **remove function**[5] to delete the original file:

```
In [4]: import os

In [5]: os.remove('accounts.txt')
```

Next, let's use the **rename function** to rename the temporary file as 'accounts.txt':

```
In [6]: os.rename('temp_file.txt', 'accounts.txt')
```

9.5 Serialization with JSON

Many libraries we'll use to interact with cloud-based services, such as Twitter, IBM Watson and others, communicate with your applications via JSON objects. **JSON (JavaScript Object Notation)** is a text-based, human-and-computer-readable, data-interchange format used to represent objects as collections of name–value pairs. JSON can even represent objects of custom classes like those you'll build in the next chapter.

JSON has become the preferred data format for transmitting objects across platforms. This is especially true for invoking cloud-based web services, which are functions and methods that you call over the Internet. You'll become proficient at working with JSON data. In the "Data Mining Twitter" chapter, you'll access JSON objects containing tweets and their metadata. In the "IBM Watson and Cognitive Computing" chapter, you'll access data in the JSON responses returned by Watson services. In the "Big Data: Hadoop, Spark, NoSQL and IoT" chapter, we'll store JSON tweet objects that we obtain from Twitter in MongoDB, a popular NoSQL database. In that chapter, we'll also work with other web services that send and receive data as JSON objects.

JSON Data Format

JSON objects are similar to Python dictionaries. Each JSON object contains a comma-separated list of *property names* and *values*, in curly braces. For example, the following key–value pairs might represent a client record:

```
{"account": 100, "name": "Jones", "balance": 24.98}
```

---

4. https://docs.python.org/3/library/os.html.
5. Use remove with caution—it does not warn you that you're *permanently* deleting the file.

JSON also supports arrays which, like Python lists, are comma-separated values in square brackets. For example, the following is an acceptable JSON array of numbers:

```
[100, 200, 300]
```

Values in JSON objects and arrays can be:

- strings in *double quotes* (like `"Jones"`),
- numbers (like `100` or `24.98`),
- JSON Boolean values (represented as `true` or `false` in JSON),
- `null` (to represent no value, like `None` in Python),
- arrays (like `[100, 200, 300]`), and
- other JSON objects.

Python Standard Library Module `json`

The **json module** enables you to convert objects to JSON (JavaScript Object Notation) text format. This is known as **serializing** the data. Consider the following dictionary, which contains one key–value pair consisting of the key `'accounts'` with its associated value being a list of dictionaries representing two accounts. Each account dictionary contains three key–value pairs for the account number, name and balance:

```
In [1]: accounts_dict = {'accounts': [
   ...:     {'account': 100, 'name': 'Jones', 'balance': 24.98},
   ...:     {'account': 200, 'name': 'Doe', 'balance': 345.67}]}
```

Serializing an Object to JSON

Let's write that object in JSON format to a file:

```
In [2]: import json

In [3]: with open('accounts.json', 'w') as accounts:
   ...:     json.dump(accounts_dict, accounts)
   ...:
```

Snippet [3] opens the file `accounts.json` and uses the `json` module's **dump function** to serialize the dictionary `accounts_dict` into the file. The resulting file contains the following text, which we reformatted slightly for readability:

```
{"accounts":
  [{"account": 100, "name": "Jones", "balance": 24.98},
   {"account": 200, "name": "Doe", "balance": 345.67}]}
```

Note that JSON delimits strings with *double-quote characters*.

Deserializing the JSON Text

The `json` module's **load function** reads the entire JSON contents of its file object argument and converts the JSON into a Python object. This is known as **deserializing** the data. Let's reconstruct the original Python object from this JSON text:

```
In [4]: with open('accounts.json', 'r') as accounts:
   ...:     accounts_json = json.load(accounts)
   ...:
   ...:
```

We can now interact with the loaded object. For example, we can display the dictionary:

```
In [5]: accounts_json
Out[5]:
{'accounts': [{'account': 100, 'name': 'Jones', 'balance': 24.98},
  {'account': 200, 'name': 'Doe', 'balance': 345.67}]}
```

As you'd expect, you can access the dictionary's contents. Let's get the list of dictionaries associated with the 'accounts' key:

```
In [6]: accounts_json['accounts']
Out[6]:
[{'account': 100, 'name': 'Jones', 'balance': 24.98},
  {'account': 200, 'name': 'Doe', 'balance': 345.67}]
```

Now, let's get the individual account dictionaries:

```
In [7]: accounts_json['accounts'][0]
Out[7]: {'account': 100, 'name': 'Jones', 'balance': 24.98}

In [8]: accounts_json['accounts'][1]
Out[8]: {'account': 200, 'name': 'Doe', 'balance': 345.67}
```

Though we did not do so here, you can modify the dictionary as well. For example, you could add accounts to or remove accounts from the list, then write the dictionary back into the JSON file.

Displaying the JSON Text

The json module's **dumps function** (dumps is short for "dump string") returns a Python string representation of an object in JSON format. Using dumps with load, you can read the JSON from the file and display it in a nicely indented format—sometimes called "pretty printing" the JSON. When the dumps function call includes the indent keyword argument, the string contains newline characters and indentation for pretty printing—you also can use indent with the dump function when writing to a file:

```
In [9]: with open('accounts.json', 'r') as accounts:
   ...:     print(json.dumps(json.load(accounts), indent=4))
   ...:
{
    "accounts": [
        {
            "account": 100,
            "name": "Jones",
            "balance": 24.98
        },
        {
            "account": 200,
            "name": "Doe",
            "balance": 345.67
        }
    ]
}
```

9.6 Focus on Security: `pickle` Serialization and Deserialization

The Python Standard Library's **pickle module** can serialize objects into in a Python-specific data format. **Caution: The Python documentation provides the following warnings about `pickle`:**

- "Pickle files can be hacked. If you receive a raw pickle file over the network, don't trust it! It could have malicious code in it, that would run arbitrary Python when you try to de-pickle it. However, if you are doing your own pickle writing and reading, you're safe (provided no one else has access to the pickle file, of course.)"[6]

- "Pickle is a protocol which allows the serialization of arbitrarily complex Python objects. As such, it is specific to Python and cannot be used to communicate with applications written in other languages. It is also insecure by default: deserializing pickle data coming from an untrusted source can execute arbitrary code, if the data was crafted by a skilled attacker."[7]

We do not recommend using `pickle`, but it's been used for many years, so you're likely to encounter it in **legacy code**—old code that's often no longer supported.

9.7 Additional Notes Regarding Files

The following table summarizes the various file-open modes for text files, including the modes for reading and writing we've introduced. The *writing* and *appending* modes create the file if it does not exist. The *reading* modes raise a `FileNotFoundError` if the file does not exist. Each text-file mode has a corresponding binary-file mode specified with b, as in `'rb'` or `'wb+'`. You'd use these modes, for example, if you were reading or writing binary files, such as images, audio, video, compressed ZIP files and many other popular custom file formats.

Mode	Description
`'r'`	Open a text file for reading. This is the default if you do not specify the file-open mode when you call open.
`'w'`	Open a text file for writing. Existing file contents are *deleted*.
`'a'`	Open a text file for appending at the end, creating the file if it does not exist. New data is written at the end of the file.
`'r+'`	Open a text file reading and writing.
`'w+'`	Open a text file reading and writing. Existing file contents are *deleted*.
`'a+'`	Open a text file reading and appending at the end. New data is written at the end of the file. If the file does not exist, it is created.

---

6. `https://wiki.python.org/moin/UsingPickle`.
7. `https://docs.python.org/3/tutorial/inputoutput.html#reading-and-writing-files`.

Other File Object Methods

Here are a few more useful file-object methods.

- For a text file, the **read** method returns a string containing the number of characters specified by the method's integer argument. For a binary file, the method returns the specified number of bytes. If no argument is specified, the method returns the entire contents of the file.

- The **readline** method returns one line of text as a string, including the newline character if there is one. This method returns an empty string when it encounters the end of the file.

- The **writelines** method receives a list of strings and writes its contents to a file.

The classes that Python uses to create file objects are defined in the Python Standard Library's **io module** (https://docs.python.org/3/library/io.html).

9.8 Handling Exceptions

Various types of exceptions can occur when you work with files, including:

- A **FileNotFoundError** occurs if you attempt to open a non-existent file for reading with the 'r' or 'r+' modes.

- A **PermissionsError** occurs if you attempt an operation for which you do not have permission. This might occur if you try to open a file that your account is not allowed to access or create a file in a folder where your account does not have permission to write, such as where your computer's operating system is stored.

- A **ValueError** (with the error message 'I/O operation on closed file.') occurs when you attempt to write to a file that has already been closed.

9.8.1 Division by Zero and Invalid Input

Let's revisit two exceptions that you saw earlier in the book.

Division By Zero

Recall that attempting to divide by 0 results in a ZeroDivisionError:

```
In [1]: 10 / 0
-------------------------------------------------------------------------
ZeroDivisionError                         Traceback (most recent call last)
<ipython-input-1-a243dfbf119d> in <module>()
----> 1 10 / 0

ZeroDivisionError: division by zero

In [2]:
```

In this case, the interpreter is said to **raise an exception** of type ZeroDivisionError. When an exception is raised in IPython, it:

- terminates the snippet,

- displays the exception's traceback, then

- shows the next In [] prompt so you can input the next snippet.

If an exception occurs in a script, it terminates and IPython displays the traceback.

Invalid Input

Recall that the int function raises a ValueError if you attempt to convert to an integer a string (like 'hello') that does not represent a number:

```
In [2]: value = int(input('Enter an integer: '))
Enter an integer: hello
-------------------------------------------------------------------
ValueError                                Traceback (most recent call last)
<ipython-input-2-b521605464d6> in <module>()
----> 1 value = int(input('Enter an integer: '))

ValueError: invalid literal for int() with base 10: 'hello'

In [3]:
```

9.8.2 try Statements

Now let's see how to *handle* these exceptions so that you can enable code to continue processing. Consider the following script and sample execution. Its loop attempts to read two integers from the user, then display the first number divided by the second. The script uses exception handling to catch and handle (i.e., deal with) any ZeroDivisionErrors and ValueErrors that arise—in this case, allowing the user to re-enter the input.

```
 1   # dividebyzero.py
 2   """Simple exception handling example."""
 3
 4   while True:
 5       # attempt to convert and divide values
 6       try:
 7           number1 = int(input('Enter numerator: '))
 8           number2 = int(input('Enter denominator: '))
 9           result = number1 / number2
10       except ValueError:  # tried to convert non-numeric value to int
11           print('You must enter two integers\n')
12       except ZeroDivisionError:  # denominator was 0
13           print('Attempted to divide by zero\n')
14       else:  # executes only if no exceptions occur
15           print(f'{number1:.3f} / {number2:.3f} = {result:.3f}')
16           break  # terminate the loop
```

```
Enter numerator: 100
Enter denominator: 0
Attempted to divide by zero

Enter numerator: 100
Enter denominator: hello
You must enter two integers

Enter numerator: 100
Enter denominator: 7
100.000 / 7.000 = 14.286
```

try Clause

Python uses **try statements** (like lines 6–16) to enable exception handling. The try statement's **try clause** (lines 6–9) begins with keyword try, followed by a colon (:) and a suite of statements that *might* raise exceptions.

except Clause
A try clause may be followed by one or more **except clauses** (lines 10–11 and 12–13) that immediately follow the try clause's suite. These also are known as *exception handlers*. Each except clause specifies the type of exception it handles. In this example, each exception handler just displays a message indicating the problem that occurred.

else Clause
After the last except clause, an optional **else clause** (lines 14–16) specifies code that should execute only if the code in the try suite did not raise exceptions. If no exceptions occur in this example's try suite, line 15 displays the division result and line 16 terminates the loop.

Flow of Control for a ZeroDivisionError
Now let's consider this example's flow of control, based on the first three lines of the sample output:

- First, the user enters 100 for the numerator in response to line 7 in the try suite.
- Next, the user enters 0 for the denominator in response to line 8 in the try suite.
- At this point, we have two integer values, so line 9 attempts to divide 100 by 0, causing Python to raise a ZeroDivisionError. The point in the program at which an exception occurs is often referred to as the **raise point**.

When an exception occurs in a try suite, it terminates immediately. If there are any except handlers following the try suite, program control transfers to the first one. If there are no except handlers, a process called *stack unwinding* occurs, which we discuss later in the chapter.

In this example, there *are* except handlers, so the interpreter searches for the *first one* that matches the type of the raised exception:

- The except clause at lines 10–11 handles ValueErrors. This does not match the type ZeroDivisionError, so that except clause's suite does not execute and program control transfers to the next except handler.
- The except clause at lines 12–13 handles ZeroDivisionErrors. This *is* a match, so that except clause's suite executes, displaying "Attempted to divide by zero".

When an except clause successfully handles the exception, program execution resumes with the finally clause (if there is one), then with the next statement after the try statement. In this example, we reach the end of the loop, so execution resumes with the next loop iteration. Note that after an exception is handled, program control does *not* return to the raise point. Rather, control resumes after the try statement. We'll discuss the finally clause shortly.

Flow of Control for a ValueError
Now let's consider the flow of control, based on the next three lines of the sample output:

- First, the user enters 100 for the numerator in response to line 7 in the try suite.
- Next, the user enters hello for the denominator in response to line 8 in the try suite. The input is not a valid integer, so the int function raises a ValueError.

The exception terminates the try suite and program control transfers to the first except handler. In this case, the except clause at lines 10–11 is a match, so its suite executes, displaying "You must enter two integers". Then, program execution resumes with the next statement after the try statement. Again, that's the end of the loop, so execution resumes with the next loop iteration.

Flow of Control for a Successful Division

Now let's consider the flow of control, based on the last three lines of the sample output:

- First, the user enters 100 for the numerator in response to line 7 in the try suite.

- Next, the user enters 7 for the denominator in response to line 8 in the try suite.

- At this point, we have two valid integer values and the denominator is not 0, so line 9 successfully divides 100 by 7.

When no exceptions occur in the try suite, program execution resumes with the else clause (if there is one); otherwise, program execution resumes with the next statement after the try statement. In this example's else clause, we display the division result, then terminate the loop, and the program terminates.

9.8.3 Catching Multiple Exceptions in One except Clause

It's relatively common for a try clause to be followed by several except clauses to handle various types of exceptions. If several except suites are identical, you can catch those exception types by specifying them as a tuple in a *single* except handler, as in:

```
except (type1, type2, ...) as variable_name:
```

The as clause is optional. Typically, programs do not need to reference the caught exception object directly. If you do, you can use the variable in the as clause to reference the exception object in the except suite.

9.8.4 What Exceptions Does a Function or Method Raise?

Exceptions may surface via statements in a try suite, via functions or methods called directly or indirectly from a try suite, or via the Python interpreter as it executes the code (for example, ZeroDivisionErrors).

Before using any function or method, read its online API documentation, which specifies what exceptions are thrown (if any) by the function or method and indicates reasons why such exceptions may occur. Next, read the online API documentation for each exception type to see potential reasons why such an exception occurs.

9.8.5 What Code Should Be Placed in a try Suite?

Place in a try suite a significant logical section of a program in which several statements can raise exceptions, rather than wrapping a separate try statement around every statement that raises an exception. However, for proper exception-handling granularity, each try statement should enclose a section of code small enough that, when an exception occurs, the specific context is known and the except handlers can process the exception properly. If many statements in a try suite raise the same exception types, multiple try statements may be required to determine each exception's context.

9.9 finally Clause

Operating systems typically can prevent more than one program from manipulating a file at once. When a program finishes processing a file, the program should close it to release the resource so other programs can access it. Closing the file helps prevent a **resource leak**.

The finally Clause of the try Statement

A try statement may have a finally clause after any except clauses or the else clause. The **finally** clause is guaranteed to execute.[8] In other languages that have finally, this makes the finally suite an ideal location to place resource-deallocation code for resources acquired in the corresponding try suite. In Python, we prefer the with statement for this purpose and place other kinds of "clean up" code in the finally suite.

Example

The following IPython session demonstrates that the finally clause always executes, regardless of whether an exception occurs in the corresponding try suite. First, let's consider a try statement in which no exceptions occur in the try suite:

```
In [1]: try:
   ...:     print('try suite with no exceptions raised')
   ...: except:
   ...:     print('this will not execute')
   ...: else:
   ...:     print('else executes because no exceptions in the try suite')
   ...: finally:
   ...:     print('finally always executes')
   ...:
try suite with no exceptions raised
else executes because no exceptions in the try suite
finally always executes

In [2]:
```

The preceding try suite displays a message but does not raise any exceptions. When program control successfully reaches the end of the try suite, the except clause is skipped, the else clause executes and the finally clause displays a message showing that it always executes. When the finally clause terminates, program control continues with the next statement after the try statement. In an IPython session, the next In [] prompt appears.

Now let's consider a try statement in which an exception occurs in the try suite:

```
In [2]: try:
   ...:     print('try suite that raises an exception')
   ...:     int('hello')
   ...:     print('this will not execute')
   ...: except ValueError:
   ...:     print('a ValueError occurred')
   ...: else:
   ...:     print('else will not execute because an exception occurred')
   ...: finally:
   ...:     print('finally always executes')
   ...:
```

---

8. The only reason a finally suite will not execute if program control enters the corresponding try suite is if the application terminates first, for example by calling the sys module's exit function.

```
        try suite that raises an exception
        a ValueError occurred
        finally always executes

In [3]:
```

This `try` suite begins by displaying a message. The second statement attempts to convert the string `'hello'` to an integer, which causes the `int` function to raise a `ValueError`. The `try` suite immediately terminates, skipping its last `print` statement. The `except` clause catches the `ValueError` exception and displays a message. The `else` clause does not execute because an exception occurred. Then, the `finally` clause displays a message showing that it always executes. When the `finally` clause terminates, program control continues with the next statement after the try statement. In an IPython session, the next `In []` prompt appears.

Combining `with` Statements and `try...except` Statements

Most resources that require explicit release, such as files, network connections and database connections, have potential exceptions associated with processing those resources. For example, a program that processes a file might raise `IOError`s. For this reason, *robust* file-processing code normally appears in a `try` suite containing a `with` statement to guarantee that the resource gets released. The code is in a `try` suite, so you can catch in `except` handlers any exceptions that occur and you do not need a `finally` clause because the `with` statement handles resource deallocation.

To demonstrate this, first let's assume you're asking the user to supply the name of a file and they provide that name incorrectly, such as gradez.txt rather than the file we created earlier grades.txt. In this case, the open call raises a `FileNotFoundError` by attempting to open a non-existent file:

```
In [3]: open('gradez.txt')
------------------------------------------------------------------------------
FileNotFoundError                         Traceback (most recent call last)
<ipython-input-3-b7f41b2d5969> in <module>()
----> 1 open('gradez.txt')

FileNotFoundError: [Errno 2] No such file or directory: 'gradez.txt'
```

To catch exceptions like `FileNotFoundError` that occur when you try to open a file for reading, wrap the `with` statement in a `try` suite, as in:

```
In [4]: try:
   ...:     with open('gradez.txt', 'r') as accounts:
   ...:         print(f'{"ID":<3}{"Name":<7}{"Grade"}')
   ...:         for record in accounts:
   ...:             student_id, name, grade = record.split()
   ...:             print(f'{student_id:<3}{name:<7}{grade}')
   ...: except FileNotFoundError:
   ...:     print('The file name you specified does not exist')
   ...:
The file name you specified does not exist
```

9.10 **Explicitly Raising an Exception**

You've seen various exceptions raised by your Python code. Sometimes you might need to write functions that raise exceptions to inform callers of errors that occur. The **raise** statement explicitly raises an exception. The simplest form of the raise statement is

> raise *ExceptionClassName*

The raise statement creates an object of the specified exception class. Optionally, the exception class name may be followed by parentheses containing arguments to initialize the exception object—typically to provide a custom error message string. Code that raises an exception first should release any resources acquired before the exception occurred. In the next section, we'll show an example of raising an exception.

In most cases, when you need to raise an exception, it's recommended that you use one of Python's many built-in exception types[9] listed at:

> https://docs.python.org/3/library/exceptions.html

9.11 **(Optional) Stack Unwinding and Tracebacks**

Each exception object stores information indicating the precise series of function calls that led to the exception. This is helpful when debugging your code. Consider the following function definitions—function1 calls function2 and function2 raises an Exception:

```
In [1]: def function1():
   ...:     function2()
   ...:

In [2]: def function2():
   ...:     raise Exception('An exception occurred')
   ...:
```

Calling function1 results in the following traceback. For emphasis, we placed in bold the parts of the traceback indicating the lines of code that led to the exception:

```
In [3]: function1()
---------------------------------------------------------------------
Exception                                 Traceback (most recent call last)
<ipython-input-3-c0b3cafe2087> in <module>()
----> 1 function1()

<ipython-input-1-a9f4faeeeb0c> in function1()
      1 def function1():
----> 2     function2()
      3

<ipython-input-2-c65e19d6b45b> in function2()
      1 def function2():
----> 2     raise Exception('An exception occurred')

Exception: An exception occurred
```

---

9. You may be tempted to create custom exception classes that are specific to your application. We'll say more about custom exceptions in the next chapter.

Traceback Details

The traceback shows the type of exception that occurred (Exception) followed by the complete function call stack that led to the raise point. The stack's bottom function call is listed *first* and the top is *last*, so the interpreter displays the following text as a reminder:

```
Traceback (most recent call last)
```

In this traceback, the following text indicates the bottom of the function-call stack—the function1 call in snippet [3] (indicated by ipython-input-3):

```
<ipython-input-3-c0b3cafe2087> in <module>()
----> 1 function1()
```

Next, we see that function1 called function2 from line 2 in snippet [1]:

```
<ipython-input-1-a9f4faeeeb0c> in function1()
      1 def function1():
----> 2     function2()
      3
```

Finally, we see the *raise point*—in this case, line 2 in snippet [2] raised the exception:

```
<ipython-input-2-c65e19d6b45b> in function2()
      1 def function2():
----> 2     raise Exception('An exception occurred')
```

Stack Unwinding

In our previous exception-handling examples, the raise point occurred in a try suite, and the exception was handled in one of the try statement's corresponding except handlers. When an exception is *not* caught in a given function, **stack unwinding** occurs. Let's consider stack unwinding in the context of this example:

- In function2, the raise statement raises an exception. This is not in a try suite, so function2 terminates, its stack frame is removed from the function-call stack, and control returns to the statement in function1 that called function2.

- In function1, the statement that called function2 is not in a try suite, so function1 terminates, its stack frame is removed from the function-call stack, and control returns to the statement that called function1—snippet [3] in the IPython session.

- The call in snippet [3] call is not in a try suite, so that function call terminates. Because the exception was not caught (known as an **uncaught exception**), IPython displays the traceback, then awaits your next input. If this occurred in a typical script, the script would terminate.[10]

Tip for Reading Tracebacks

You'll often call functions and methods that belong to libraries of code you did not write. Sometimes those functions and methods raise exceptions. When reading a traceback, start from the end of the traceback and read the error message first. Then, read upward through the traceback, looking for the first line that indicates code you wrote in your program. Typically, this is the location in your code that led to the exception.

---

10. In more advanced applications that use threads, an uncaught exception terminates only the thread in which the exception occurs, not necessarily the entire application.

Exceptions in `finally` Suites

Raising an exception in a `finally` suite can lead to subtle, hard-to-find problems. If an exception occurs and is not processed by the time the `finally` suite executes, stack unwinding occurs. If the `finally` suite raises a *new* exception that the suite does not catch, the first exception is *lost*, and the *new* exception is passed to the next enclosing `try` statement. For this reason, a `finally` suite should always enclose in a `try` statement any code that may raise an exception, so that the exceptions will be processed within that suite.

9.12 Intro to Data Science: Working with CSV Files

Throughout this book, you'll work with many datasets as we present data-science concepts. CSV (**comma-separated values**) is a particularly popular file format. In this section, we'll demonstrate CSV file processing with a Python Standard Library module and pandas.

9.12.1 Python Standard Library Module `csv`

The **csv module**[11] provides functions for working with CSV files. Many other Python libraries also have built-in CSV support.

Writing to a CSV File

Let's create an `accounts.csv` file using CSV format. The `csv` module's documentation recommends opening CSV files with the additional keyword argument `newline=''` to ensure that newlines are processed properly:

```
In [1]: import csv

In [2]: with open('accounts.csv', mode='w', newline='') as accounts:
   ...:     writer = csv.writer(accounts)
   ...:     writer.writerow([100, 'Jones', 24.98])
   ...:     writer.writerow([200, 'Doe', 345.67])
   ...:     writer.writerow([300, 'White', 0.00])
   ...:     writer.writerow([400, 'Stone', -42.16])
   ...:     writer.writerow([500, 'Rich', 224.62])
   ...:
```

The **.csv file extension** indicates a CSV-format file. The `csv` module's **writer function** returns an object that writes CSV data to the specified file object. Each call to the `writer`'s **writerow method** receives an iterable to store in the file. Here we're using lists. By default, `writerow` delimits values with commas, but you can specify custom delimiters.[12] After the preceding snippet, `accounts.csv` contains:

```
100,Jones,24.98
200,Doe,345.67
300,White,0.00
400,Stone,-42.16
500,Rich,224.62
```

CSV files generally do not contain spaces after commas, but some people use them to enhance readability. The `writerow` calls above can be replaced with one **writerows** call that outputs a comma-separated list of iterables representing the records.

---

11. https://docs.python.org/3/library/csv.html.
12. https://docs.python.org/3/library/csv.html#csv-fmt-params.

If you write data that contains commas within a given string, writerow encloses that string in double quotes. For example, consider the following Python list:

```
[100, 'Jones, Sue', 24.98]
```

The single-quoted string 'Jones, Sue' contains a comma separating the last name and first name. In this case, writerow would output the record as

```
100,"Jones, Sue",24.98
```

The quotes around "Jones, Sue" indicate that this is a *single* value. Programs reading this from a CSV file would break the record into *three* pieces—100, 'Jones, Sue' and 24.98.

Reading from a CSV File

Now let's read the CSV data from the file. The following snippet reads records from the file accounts.csv and displays the contents of each record, producing the same output we showed earlier:

```
In [3]: with open('accounts.csv', 'r', newline='') as accounts:
   ...:     print(f'{"Account":<10}{"Name":<10}{"Balance":>10}')
   ...:     reader = csv.reader(accounts)
   ...:     for record in reader:
   ...:         account, name, balance = record
   ...:         print(f'{account:<10}{name:<10}{balance:>10}')
   ...:
Account   Name         Balance
100       Jones          24.98
200       Doe           345.67
300       White            0.0
400       Stone         -42.16
500       Rich          224.62
```

The csv module's **reader function** returns an object that reads CSV-format data from the specified file object. Just as you can iterate through a file object, you can iterate through the reader object one record of comma-delimited values at a time. The preceding for statement returns each record as a list of values, which we unpack into the variables account, name and balance, then display.

Caution: Commas in CSV Data Fields

Be careful when working with strings containing embedded commas, such as the name 'Jones, Sue'. If you accidentally enter this as the two strings 'Jones' and 'Sue', then writerow would, of course, create a CSV record with *four* fields, not *three*. Programs that read CSV files typically expect every record to have the *same* number of fields; otherwise, problems occur. For example, consider the following two lists:

```
[100, 'Jones', 'Sue', 24.98]
[200, 'Doe'  , 345.67]
```

The first list contains *four* values and the second contains only *three*. If these two records were written into the CSV file, then read into a program using the previous snippet, the following statement would fail when we attempt to unpack the four-field record into only three variables:

```
account, name, balance = record
```

Caution: Missing Commas and Extra Commas in CSV Files

Be careful when preparing and processing CSV files. For example, suppose your file is composed of records, each with *four* comma-separated `int` values, such as:

```
100,85,77,9
```

If you accidentally omit one of these commas, as in:

```
100,8577,9
```

then the record has only *three* fields, one with the invalid value `8577`.

If you put two adjacent commas where only one is expected, as in:

```
100,85,,77,9
```

then you have *five* fields rather than *four*, and one of the fields erroneously would be *empty*. Each of these comma-related errors could confuse programs trying to process the record.

9.12.2 Reading CSV Files into Pandas DataFrames

In the Intro to Data Science sections in the previous two chapters, we introduced many pandas fundamentals. Here, we demonstrate pandas' ability to load files in CSV format, then perform some basic data-analysis tasks.

Datasets

In the data-science case studies, we'll use various free and open datasets to demonstrate machine learning and natural language processing concepts. There's an enormous variety of free datasets available online. The popular **Rdatasets repository** provides links to over 1100 free datasets in comma-separated values (CSV) format. These were originally provided with the R programming language for people learning about and developing statistical software, though they are not specific to R. They are now available on GitHub at:

> https://vincentarelbundock.github.io/Rdatasets/datasets.html

This repository is so popular that there's a **pydataset module** specifically for accessing Rdatasets. For instructions on installing `pydataset` and accessing datasets with it, see:

> https://github.com/iamaziz/PyDataset

Another large source of datasets is:

> https://github.com/awesomedata/awesome-public-datasets

A commonly used machine-learning dataset for beginners is the **Titanic disaster dataset**, which lists all the passengers and whether they survived when the ship *Titanic* struck an iceberg and sank April 14–15, 1912. We'll use it here to show how to load a dataset, view some of its data and display some descriptive statistics. We'll dig deeper into a variety of popular datasets in the data-science chapters later in the book.

Working with Locally Stored CSV Files

You can load a CSV dataset into a `DataFrame` with the pandas function **read_csv**. The following loads and displays the CSV file `accounts.csv` that you created earlier in this chapter:

```
In [1]: import pandas as pd
```

```
In [2]: df = pd.read_csv('accounts.csv',
   ...:                   names=['account', 'name', 'balance'])
   ...:

In [3]: df
Out[3]:
   account   name   balance
0      100  Jones     24.98
1      200    Doe    345.67
2      300  White      0.00
3      400  Stone    -42.16
4      500   Rich    224.62
```

The names argument specifies the DataFrame's column names. Without this argument, read_csv assumes that the CSV file's first row is a comma-delimited list of column names.

To save a DataFrame to a file using CSV format, call DataFrame method **to_csv**:

```
In [4]: df.to_csv('accounts_from_dataframe.csv', index=False)
```

The index=False keyword argument indicates that the row names (0–4 at the left of the DataFrame's output in snippet [3]) are not written to the file. The resulting file contains the column names as the first row:

```
account,name,balance
100,Jones,24.98
200,Doe,345.67
300,White,0.0
400,Stone,-42.16
500,Rich,224.62
```

9.12.3 Reading the Titanic Disaster Dataset

The Titanic disaster dataset is one of the most popular machine-learning datasets. The dataset is available in many formats, including CSV.

Loading the Titanic Dataset via a URL
If you have a URL representing a CSV dataset, you can load it into a DataFrame with read_csv. Let's load the Titanic Disaster dataset directly from GitHub:

```
In [1]: import pandas as pd

In [2]: titanic = pd.read_csv('https://vincentarelbundock.github.io/' +
   ...:        'Rdatasets/csv/carData/TitanicSurvival.csv')
   ...:
```

Viewing Some of the Rows in the Titanic Dataset
This dataset contains over 1300 rows, each representing one passenger. According to Wikipedia, there were approximately 1317 passengers and 815 of them died.[13] For large datasets, displaying the DataFrame shows only the first 30 rows, followed by "…" and the last 30 rows. To save space, let's view the first five and last five rows with DataFrame methods **head** and **tail**. Both methods return five rows by default, but you can specify the number of rows to display as an argument:

```
In [3]: pd.set_option('precision', 2)   # format for floating-point values
```

---

13. https://en.wikipedia.org/wiki/Passengers_of_the_RMS_Titanic.

```
In [4]: titanic.head()
Out[4]:
                     Unnamed: 0 survived     sex    age passengerClass
0     Allen, Miss. Elisabeth Walton    yes  female  29.00            1st
1     Allison, Master. Hudson Trevor   yes    male   0.92            1st
2      Allison, Miss. Helen Loraine    no  female   2.00            1st
3   Allison, Mr. Hudson Joshua Crei    no    male  30.00            1st
4   Allison, Mrs. Hudson J C (Bessi    no  female  25.00            1st

In [5]: titanic.tail()
Out[5]:
                     Unnamed: 0 survived     sex    age passengerClass
1304         Zabour, Miss. Hileni    no  female  14.50            3rd
1305        Zabour, Miss. Thamine    no  female    NaN            3rd
1306    Zakarian, Mr. Mapriededer    no    male  26.50            3rd
1307          Zakarian, Mr. Ortin    no    male  27.00            3rd
1308          Zimmerman, Mr. Leo    no    male  29.00            3rd
```

Note that pandas adjusts each column's width, based on the widest value in the column or based on the column name, whichever is wider. Also, note the value in the age column of row 1305 is NaN (not a number), indicating a missing value in the dataset.

Customizing the Column Names

The first column in this dataset has a strange name ('Unnamed: 0'). We can clean that up by setting the column names. Let's change 'Unnamed: 0' to 'name' and let's shorten 'passengerClass' to 'class':

```
In [6]: titanic.columns = ['name', 'survived', 'sex', 'age', 'class']

In [7]: titanic.head()
Out[7]:
                              name survived     sex    age class
0     Allen, Miss. Elisabeth Walton    yes  female  29.00   1st
1     Allison, Master. Hudson Trevor   yes    male   0.92   1st
2      Allison, Miss. Helen Loraine    no  female   2.00   1st
3   Allison, Mr. Hudson Joshua Crei    no    male  30.00   1st
4   Allison, Mrs. Hudson J C (Bessi    no  female  25.00   1st
```

9.12.4 Simple Data Analysis with the Titanic Disaster Dataset

Now, you can use pandas to perform some simple analysis. For example, let's look at some descriptive statistics. When you call describe on a DataFrame containing both numeric and non-numeric columns, describe calculates these statistics *only for the numeric columns*—in this case, just the age column:

```
In [8]: titanic.describe()
Out[8]:
                age
count     1046.00
mean        29.88
std         14.41
min          0.17
25%         21.00
50%         28.00
75%         39.00
max         80.00
```

Note the discrepancy in the count (1046) vs. the dataset's number of rows (1309—the last row's index was 1308 when we called tail). Only 1046 (the count above) of the records contained an age value. The rest were *missing* and marked as NaN, as in row 1305. When performing calculations, Pandas *ignores missing data (NaN) by default*. For the 1046 people with valid ages, the average (mean) age was 29.88 years old. The youngest passenger (min) was just over two months old (0.17 * 12 is 2.04), and the oldest (max) was 80. The median age was 28 (indicated by the 50% quartile). The 25% quartile is the median age in the first half of the passengers (sorted by age), and the 75% quartile is the median of the second half of passengers.

Let's say you want to determine some statistics about people who survived. We can compare the survived column to 'yes' to get a new Series containing True/False values, then use describe to summarize the results:

```
In [9]: (titanic.survived == 'yes').describe()
Out[9]:
count      1309
unique        2
top       False
freq        809
Name: survived, dtype: object
```

For non-numeric data, describe displays different descriptive statistics:

- count is the total number of items in the result.

- unique is the number of unique values (2) in the result—True (survived) and False (died).

- top is the most frequently occurring value in the result.

- freq is the number of occurrences of the top value.

9.12.5 Passenger Age Histogram

Visualization is a nice way to get to know your data. Pandas has many built-in visualization capabilities that are implemented with Matplotlib. To use them, first enable Matplotlib support in IPython:

```
In [10]: %matplotlib
```

A histogram visualizes the distribution of numerical data over a range of values. A DataFrame's **hist** method automatically analyzes each numerical column's data and produces a corresponding histogram. To view histograms of each numerical data column, call hist on your DataFrame:

```
In [11]: histogram = titanic.hist()
```

The Titanic dataset contains only one numerical data column, so the diagram shows one histogram for the age distribution. For datasets with multiple numerical columns, hist creates a separate histogram for each numerical column.

9.13 Wrap-Up

In this chapter, we introduced text-file processing and exception handling. Files are used to store data persistently. We discussed file objects and mentioned that Python views a file as a sequence of characters or bytes. We also mentioned the standard file objects that are automatically created for you when a Python program begins executing.

We showed how to create, read, write and update text files. We considered several popular file formats—plain text, JSON (JavaScript Object Notation) and CSV (comma-separated values). We used the built-in open function and the with statement to open a file, write to or read from the file and automatically close the file to prevent resource leaks when the with statement terminates. We used the Python Standard Library's json module to serialize objects into JSON format and store them in a file, load JSON objects from a file, deserialize them into Python objects and pretty-print a JSON object for readability.

We discussed how exceptions indicate execution-time problems and listed the various exceptions you've already seen. We showed how to deal with exceptions by wrapping code in try statements that provide except clauses to handle specific types of exceptions that may occur in the try suite, making your programs more robust and fault-tolerant.

We discussed the try statement's finally clause for executing code if program flow entered the corresponding try suite. You can use either the with statement or a try statement's finally clause for this purpose—we prefer the with statement.

In the Intro to Data Science section, we used both the Python Standard Library's csv module and capabilities of the pandas library to load, manipulate and store CSV data. Finally, we loaded the Titanic disaster dataset into a pandas DataFrame, changed some column names for readability, displayed the head and tail of the dataset, and performed simple analysis of the data. In the next chapter, we'll discuss Python's object-oriented programming capabilities.

10

Object-Oriented Programming

Objectives

In this chapter, you'll:

- Create custom classes and objects of those classes.
- Understand the benefits of crafting valuable classes.
- Control access to attributes.
- Appreciate the value of object orientation.
- Use Python special methods __repr__, __str__ and __format__ to get an object's string representations.
- Use Python special methods to overload (redefine) operators to use them with objects of new classes.
- Inherit methods, properties and attributes from existing classes into new classes, then customize those classes.
- Understand the inheritance notions of base classes (superclasses) and derived classes (subclasses).
- Understand duck typing and polymorphism that enable "programming in the general."
- Understand class object from which all classes inherit fundamental capabilities.
- Compare composition and inheritance.
- Build test cases into docstrings and run these tests with doctest.
- Understand namespaces and how they affect scope.

10.1 Introduction

Section 1.2 introduced the basic terminology and concepts of object-oriented programming. Everything in Python is an object, so you've been using objects constantly throughout this book. Just as houses are built from blueprints, objects are built from classes—one of the core technologies of object-oriented programming. Building a new object from even a large class is simple—you typically write one statement.

Crafting Valuable Classes

You've already used lots of classes created by other people. In this chapter you'll create your own *custom* classes. You'll focus on "crafting valuable classes" that help you meet the requirements of the applications you'll build. You'll use object-oriented programming with its core technologies of classes, objects, inheritance and polymorphism. Software applications are becoming larger and more richly functional. Object-oriented programming makes it easier for you to design, implement, test, debug and update such edge-of-the-practice applications. Read Sections 10.1 through 10.9 for a code-intensive introduction to these technologies. Most people can skip Sections 10.10 through 10.15, which provide additional perspectives on these technologies and present additional related features.

Class Libraries and Object-Based Programming

The vast majority of object-oriented programming you'll do in Python is **object-based programming** in which you primarily create and use objects of *existing* classes. You've been doing this throughout the book with built-in types like int, float, str, list, tuple, dict and set, with Python Standard Library types like Decimal, and with NumPy arrays, Matplotlib Figures and Axes, and pandas Series and DataFrames.

To take maximum advantage of Python you must familiarize yourself with lots of pre-existing classes. Over the years, the Python open-source community has crafted an enormous number of valuable classes and packaged them into class libraries. This makes it easy for you to reuse existing classes rather than "reinventing the wheel." Widely used open-source library classes are more likely to be thoroughly tested, bug free, performance tuned and portable across a wide range of devices, operating systems and Python versions. You'll find abundant Python libraries on the Internet at sites like GitHub, BitBucket, Source-Forge and more—most easily installed with conda or pip. This is a key reason for Python's popularity. The vast majority of the classes you'll need are likely to be freely available in open-source libraries.

Creating Your Own Custom Classes

Classes are new data types. Each Python Standard Library class and third-party library class is a custom type built by someone else. In this chapter, you'll develop application-specific classes, like CommissionEmployee, Time, Card, DeckOfCards and more.

Most applications you'll build for your own use will commonly use either no custom classes or just a few. If you become part of a development team in industry, you may work on applications that contain hundreds, or even thousands, of classes. You can contribute your custom classes to the Python open-source community, but you are not obligated to do so. Organizations often have policies and procedures related to open-sourcing code.

Inheritance

Perhaps most exciting is the notion that new classes can be formed through inheritance and composition from classes in abundant class libraries. Eventually, software will be constructed predominantly from **standardized, reusable components** just as hardware is constructed from interchangeable parts today. This will help meet the challenges of developing ever more powerful software.

When creating a new class, instead of writing all new code, you can designate that the new class is to be formed initially by **inheriting** the attributes (variables) and methods (the class version of functions) of a previously defined **base class** (also called a **superclass**). The new class is called a **derived class** (or **subclass**). After inheriting, you then customize the derived class to meet the specific needs of your application. To minimize the customization effort, you should always try to inherit from the base class that's closest to your needs. To do that effectively, you should familiarize yourself with the class libraries that are geared to the kinds of applications you'll be building.

Polymorphism

We explain and demonstrate **polymorphism**, which enables you to conveniently program "in the general" rather than "in the specific." You simply send the *same* method call to objects possibly of many *different* types. Each object responds by "doing the right thing." So the same method call takes on "many forms," hence the term "poly-morphism." We'll explain how to implement polymorphism through inheritance and a Python feature called duck typing. We'll explain both and show examples of each.

An Entertaining Case Study: Card-Shuffling-and-Dealing Simulation
You've already used a random-numbers-based die-rolling simulation and used those techniques to implement the popular dice game craps. Here, we present a card-shuffling-and-dealing simulation, which you can use to implement your favorite card games. You'll use Matplotlib with attractive public-domain card images to display the full deck of cards both before and after the deck is shuffled.

Data Classes
Python 3.7's new *data classes* help you build classes faster by using a more concise notation and by autogenerating portions of the classes. The Python community's early reaction to data classes has been positive. As with any major new feature, it may take time before it's widely used. We present class development with both the older and newer technologies.

Other Concepts Introduced in This Chapter
Other concepts we present include:

- How to specify that certain identifiers should be used only inside a class and not be accessible to clients of the class.

- Special methods for creating string representations of your classes' objects and specifying how objects of your classes work with Python's built-in operators (a process called *operator overloading*).

- An introduction to the Python exception class hierarchy and creating custom exception classes.

- Testing code with the Python Standard Library's doctest module.

- How Python uses namespaces to determine the scopes of identifiers.

10.2 **Custom Class Account**

Let's begin with a bank Account class that holds an account holder's name and balance. An actual bank account class would likely include lots of other information, such as address, birth date, telephone number, account number and more. The Account class accepts deposits that increase the balance and withdrawals that decrease the balance.

10.2.1 Test-Driving Class Account

Each new class you create becomes a new *data type* that can be used to create objects. This is one reason why Python is said to be an **extensible language**. Before we look at class Account's definition, let's demonstrate its capabilities.

Importing Classes Account and Decimal
To use the new Account class, launch your IPython session from the ch10 examples folder, then import class Account:

```
In [1]: from account import Account
```

Class Account maintains and manipulates the account balance as a Decimal, so we also import class Decimal:

```
In [2]: from decimal import Decimal
```

Create an Account Object with a Constructor Expression

To create a Decimal object, we can write:

```
value = Decimal('12.34')
```

This is known as a **constructor expression** because it builds and initializes an object of the class, similar to the way a house is constructed from a blueprint then painted with the buyer's preferred colors. Constructor expressions create new objects and initialize their data using argument(s) specified in parentheses. The parentheses following the class name are required, even if there are no arguments.

Let's use a constructor expression to create an Account object and initialize it with an account holder's name (a string) and balance (a Decimal):

```
In [3]: account1 = Account('John Green', Decimal('50.00'))
```

Getting an Account's Name and Balance

Let's access the Account object's name and balance attributes:

```
In [4]: account1.name
Out[4]: 'John Green'

In [5]: account1.balance
Out[5]: Decimal('50.00')
```

Depositing Money into an Account

An Account's deposit method receives a positive dollar amount and adds it to the balance:

```
In [6]: account1.deposit(Decimal('25.53'))

In [7]: account1.balance
Out[7]: Decimal('75.53')
```

Account Methods Perform Validation

Class Account's methods validate their arguments. For example, if a deposit amount is negative, deposit raises a ValueError:

```
In [8]: account1.deposit(Decimal('-123.45'))
---------------------------------------------------------------------------
ValueError                                Traceback (most recent call last)
<ipython-input-8-27dc468365a7> in <module>()
----> 1 account1.deposit(Decimal('-123.45'))

~/Documents/examples/ch10/account.py in deposit(self, amount)
     21         # if amount is less than 0.00, raise an exception
     22         if amount < Decimal('0.00'):
---> 23             raise ValueError('Deposit amount must be positive.')
     24
     25         self.balance += amount

ValueError: Deposit amount must be positive.
```

10.2.2 Account Class Definition

Now, let's look at Account's class definition, which is located in the file account.py.

Defining a Class

A class definition begins with the keyword **class** (line 5) followed by the class's name and a colon (:). This line is called the **class header**. The *Style Guide for Python Code* recommends that you begin each word in a multi-word class name with an uppercase letter (for example, CommissionEmployee). Every statement in a class's suite is indented.

```
1   # account.py
2   """Account class definition."""
3   from decimal import Decimal
4
5   class Account:
6       """Account class for maintaining a bank account balance."""
7
```

Each class typically provides a descriptive docstring (line 6). When provided, it must appear in the line or lines immediately following the class header. To view any class's docstring in IPython, type the class name and a question mark, then press *Enter*:

```
In [9]: Account?
Init signature: Account(name, balance)
Docstring:      Account class for maintaining a bank account balance.
Init docstring: Initialize an Account object.
File:           ~/Documents/examples/ch10/account.py
Type:           type
```

The identifier Account is both the class name and the name used in a constructor expression to create an Account object and invoke the class's __init__ method. For this reason, IPython's help mechanism shows both the class's docstring ("Docstring:") and the __init__ method's docstring ("Init docstring:").

Initializing Account Objects: Method __init__

The constructor expression in snippet [3] from the preceding section:

```
account1 = Account('John Green', Decimal('50.00'))
```

creates a new object, then initializes its data by calling the class's **__init__** method. Each new class you create can provide an __init__ method that specifies how to initialize an object's data attributes. Returning a value other than None from __init__ results in a TypeError. Recall that None is returned by any function or method that does not contain a return statement. Class Account's __init__ method (lines 8–16) initializes an Account object's name and balance attributes if the balance is valid:

```
8        def __init__(self, name, balance):
9            """Initialize an Account object."""
10
11           # if balance is less than 0.00, raise an exception
12           if balance < Decimal('0.00'):
13               raise ValueError('Initial balance must be >= to 0.00.')
14
15           self.name = name
16           self.balance = balance
17
```

When you call a method for a specific object, Python implicitly passes a reference to that object as the method's first argument. For this reason, all methods of a class must specify at least one parameter. By convention most Python programmers call a method's first parameter `self`. A class's methods must use that reference (`self`) to access the object's attributes and other methods. Class Account's `__init__` method also specifies parameters for the `name` and `balance`.

The `if` statement *validates* the balance parameter. If `balance` is less than `0.00`, `__init__` raises a `ValueError`, which terminates the `__init__` method. Otherwise, the method creates and initializes the new `Account` object's `name` and `balance` attributes.

When an object of class `Account` is created, it does not yet have any attributes. They're added *dynamically* via assignments of the form:

> `self.`*attribute_name* `=` *value*

Python classes may define many **special methods**, like `__init__`, each identified by leading and trailing double-underscores (`__`) in the method name. Python class **object**, which we'll discuss later in this chapter, defines the special methods that are available for *all* Python objects.

Method `deposit`

The `Account` class's `deposit` method adds a positive `amount` to the account's `balance` attribute. If the `amount` argument is less than `0.00`, the method raises a `ValueError`, indicating that only positive deposit amounts are allowed. If the `amount` is valid, line 25 adds it to the object's `balance` attribute.

```
18      def deposit(self, amount):
19          """Deposit money to the account."""
20
21          # if amount is less than 0.00, raise an exception
22          if amount < Decimal('0.00'):
23              raise ValueError('amount must be positive.')
24
25          self.balance += amount
```

10.2.3 Composition: Object References as Members of Classes

An `Account` *has a* name, and an `Account` *has a* `balance`. Recall that "everything in Python is an object." This means that an object's attributes are references to objects of other classes. For example, an `Account` object's `name` attribute is a reference to a string object and an `Account` object's `balance` attribute is a reference to a `Decimal` object. Embedding references to objects of other types is a form of software reusability known as **composition** and is sometimes referred to as the **"has a" relationship**. Later in this chapter, we'll discuss *inheritance*, which establishes *"is a"* relationships.

10.3 Controlling Access to Attributes

Class Account's methods validate their arguments to ensure that the `balance` is *always* valid—that is, always greater than or equal to `0.00`. In the previous example, we used the attributes `name` and `balance` only to *get* the values of those attributes. It turns out that we also can use those attributes to *modify* their values. Consider the `Account` object in the following IPython session:

```
In [1]: from account import Account

In [2]: from decimal import Decimal

In [3]: account1 = Account('John Green', Decimal('50.00'))

In [4]: account1.balance
Out[4]: Decimal('50.00')
```

Initially, `account1` contains a valid balance. Now, let's set the `balance` attribute to an *invalid* negative value, then display the `balance`:

```
In [5]: account1.balance = Decimal('-1000.00')

In [6]: account1.balance
Out[6]: Decimal('-1000.00')
```

Snippet [6]'s output shows that `account1`'s `balance` is now negative. As you can see, unlike methods, data attributes cannot validate the values you assign to them.

Encapsulation

A class's **client code** is any code that uses objects of the class. Most object-oriented programming languages enable you to **encapsulate** (or *hide*) an object's data from the client code. Such data in these languages is said to be *private data*.

Leading Underscore (_) Naming Convention

Python does *not* have private data. Instead, you use *naming conventions* to design classes that encourage correct use. By convention, Python programmers know that any attribute name beginning with an underscore (_) is for a class's *internal use only*. Client code should use the class's methods and—as you'll see in the next section—the class's properties to interact with each object's internal-use data attributes. Attributes whose identifiers do *not* begin with an underscore (_) are considered *publicly accessible* for use in client code. In the next section, we'll define a `Time` class and use these naming conventions. However, even when we use these conventions, attributes are always accessible.

10.4 Properties for Data Access

Let's develop a `Time` class that stores the time in 24-hour clock format with hours in the range 0–23, and minutes and seconds each in the range 0–59. For this class, we'll provide *properties*, which look like data attributes to client-code programmers, but control the manner in which they get and modify an object's data. This assumes that other programmers follow Python conventions to correctly use objects of your class.

10.4.1 Test-Driving Class Time

Before we look at class `Time`'s definition, let's demonstrate its capabilities. First, ensure that you're in the ch10 folder, then import class `Time` from `timewithproperties.py`:

```
In [1]: from timewithproperties import Time
```

Creating a Time Object

Next, let's create a Time object. Class Time's __init__ method has hour, minute and second parameters, each with a default argument value of 0. Here, we specify the hour and minute—second defaults to 0:

```
In [2]: wake_up = Time(hour=6, minute=30)
```

Displaying a Time Object

Class Time defines two methods that produce string representations of Time object. When you evaluate a variable in IPython as in snippet [3], IPython calls the object's __repr__ special method to produce a string representation of the object. Our __repr__ implementation creates a string in the following format:

```
In [3]: wake_up
Out[3]: Time(hour=6, minute=30, second=0)
```

We'll also provide the __str__ special method, which is called when an object is converted to a string, such as when you output the object with print.[1] Our __str__ implementation creates a string in 12-hour clock format:

```
In [4]: print(wake_up)
6:30:00 AM
```

Getting an Attribute Via a Property

Class time provides hour, minute and second **properties**, which provide the convenience of data attributes for getting and modifying an object's data. However, as you'll see, properties are implemented as methods, so they may contain additional logic, such as specifying the format in which to return a data attribute's value or validating a new value before using it to modify a data attribute. Here, we get the wake_up object's hour value:

```
In [5]: wake_up.hour
Out[5]: 6
```

Though this snippet appears to simply get an hour data attribute's value, it's actually a call to an hour *method* that returns the value of a data attribute (which we named _hour, as you'll see in the next section).

Setting the Time

You can set a new time with the Time object's set_time method. Like method __init__, method set_time provides hour, minute and second parameters, each with a default of 0:

```
In [6]: wake_up.set_time(hour=7, minute=45)

In [7]: wake_up
Out[7]: Time(hour=7, minute=45, second=0)
```

Setting an Attribute via a Property

Class Time also supports setting the hour, minute and second values individually via its properties. Let's change the hour value to 6:

---

1. If a class does not provide __str__ and an object of the class is converted to a string, the class's __repr__ method is called instead.

```
In [8]: wake_up.hour = 6

In [9]: wake_up
Out[9]: Time(hour=6, minute=45, second=0)
```

Though snippet [8] appears to simply assign a value to a data attribute, it's actually a call to an hour method that takes 6 as an argument. The method validates the value, then assigns it to a corresponding data attribute (which we named _hour, as you'll see in the next section).

Attempting to Set an Invalid Value

To prove that class Time's properties *validate* the values you assign to them, let's try to assign an invalid value to the hour property, which results in a ValueError:

```
In [10]: wake_up.hour = 100
-------------------------------------------------------------------------
ValueError                                Traceback (most recent call last)
<ipython-input-10-1fce0716ef14> in <module>()
----> 1 wake_up.hour = 100

~/Documents/examples/ch10/timewithproperties.py in hour(self, hour)
    20            """Set the hour."""
    21            if not (0 <= hour < 24):
---> 22                raise ValueError(f'Hour ({hour}) must be 0-23')
    23
    24            self._hour = hour

ValueError: Hour (100) must be 0-23
```

10.4.2 Class Time Definition

Now that we've seen class Time in action, let's look at its definition.

Class Time: __init__ Method with Default Parameter Values

Class Time's __init__ method specifies hour, minute and second parameters, each with a default argument of 0. Similar to class Account's __init__ method, recall that the self parameter is a reference to the Time object being initialized. The statements containing self.hour, self.minute and self.second *appear* to create hour, minute and second attributes for the new Time object (self). However, these statements actually call methods that implement the class's hour, minute and second *properties* (lines 13–50). Those methods then create attributes named _hour, _minute and _second that are meant for use only inside the class:

```
 1  # timewithproperties.py
 2  """Class Time with read-write properties."""
 3
 4  class Time:
 5      """Class Time with read-write properties."""
 6
 7      def __init__(self, hour=0, minute=0, second=0):
 8          """Initialize each attribute."""
 9          self.hour = hour      # 0-23
10          self.minute = minute  # 0-59
11          self.second = second  # 0-59
12
```

Class Time: hour Read-Write Property

Lines 13–24 define a *publicly accessible* **read-write property** named hour that manipulates a data attribute named _hour. The single-leading-underscore (_) naming convention indicates that client code should not access _hour directly. As you saw in the previous section's snippets [5] and [8], properties look like data attributes to programmers working with Time objects. However, notice that properties are implemented as *methods*. Each property defines a *getter* method which *gets* (that is, returns) a data attribute's value and can *optionally* define a *setter* method which *sets* a data attribute's value:

```
13      @property
14      def hour(self):
15          """Return the hour."""
16          return self._hour
17
18      @hour.setter
19      def hour(self, hour):
20          """Set the hour."""
21          if not (0 <= hour < 24):
22              raise ValueError(f'Hour ({hour}) must be 0-23')
23
24          self._hour = hour
25
```

The **@property decorator** precedes the property's *getter* method, which receives only a self parameter. Behind the scenes, a decorator adds code to the decorated function—in this case to make the hour function work with attribute syntax. The *getter* method's name is the property name. This *getter* method returns the _hour data attribute's value. The following client-code expression invokes the *getter* method:

```
wake_up.hour
```

You also can use the *getter* method inside the class, as you'll see shortly.

A decorator of the form **@*property_name*.setter** (in this case, @hour.setter) precedes the property's *setter* method. The method receives two parameters—self and a parameter (hour) representing the value being assigned to the property. If the hour parameter's value is *valid,* this method assigns it to the self object's _hour attribute; otherwise, the method raises a ValueError. The following client-code expression invokes the *setter* by assigning a value to the property:

```
wake_up.hour = 8
```

We also invoked this setter inside the class at line 9 of __init__:

```
self.hour = hour
```

Using the *setter* enabled us to *validate* __init__'s hour argument *before* creating and initializing the object's _hour attribute, which occurs the *first* time the hour property's *setter* executes as a result of line 9. A **read-write property** has both a *getter* and a *setter*. A **read-only property** has only a *getter*.

Class Time: minute and second Read-Write Properties

Lines 26–37 and 39–50 define read-write minute and second properties. Each property's setter ensures that its second argument is in the range 0–59 (the valid range of values for minutes and seconds):

```
26        @property
27        def minute(self):
28            """Return the minute."""
29            return self._minute
30
31        @minute.setter
32        def minute(self, minute):
33            """Set the minute."""
34            if not (0 <= minute < 60):
35                raise ValueError(f'Minute ({minute}) must be 0-59')
36
37            self._minute = minute
38
39        @property
40        def second(self):
41            """Return the second."""
42            return self._second
43
44        @second.setter
45        def second(self, second):
46            """Set the second."""
47            if not (0 <= second < 60):
48                raise ValueError(f'Second ({second}) must be 0-59')
49
50            self._second = second
51
```

Class Time: Method `set_time`

We provide method set_time as a convenient way to change *all three* attributes with a *single* method call. Lines 54–56 invoke the *setters* for the hour, minute and second properties:

```
52        def set_time(self, hour=0, minute=0, second=0):
53            """Set values of hour, minute, and second."""
54            self.hour = hour
55            self.minute = minute
56            self.second = second
57
```

Class Time: Special Method `__repr__`

When you pass an object to built-in function repr—which happens implicitly when you evaluate a variable in an IPython session—the corresponding class's **__repr__** special method is called to get a string representation of the object:

```
58        def __repr__(self):
59            """Return Time string for repr()."""
60            return (f'Time(hour={self.hour}, minute={self.minute}, ' +
61                    f'second={self.second})')
62
```

The Python documentation indicates that __repr__ returns the "official" string representation of the object. Typically this string looks like a constructor expression that creates and initializes the object,[2] as in:

---

2. https://docs.python.org/3/reference/datamodel.html.

```
'Time(hour=6, minute=30, second=0)'
```

which is similar to the constructor expression in the previous section's snippet [2]. Python has a built-in function **eval** that could receive the preceding string as an argument and use it to create and initialize a Time object containing values specified in the string.

Class Time: Special Method __str__

For our class Time we also define the **__str__** special method. This method is called implicitly when you convert an object to a string with the built-in function str, such as when you print an object or call str explicitly. Our implementation of __str__ creates a string in 12-hour clock format, such as '7:59:59 AM' or '12:30:45 PM':

```
63      def __str__(self):
64          """Print Time in 12-hour clock format."""
65          return (('12' if self.hour in (0, 12) else str(self.hour % 12)) +
66                  f':{self.minute:0>2}:{self.second:0>2}' +
67                  (' AM' if self.hour < 12 else ' PM'))
```

10.4.3 Class Time Definition Design Notes

Let's consider some class-design issues in the context of our Time class.

Interface of a Class

Class Time's properties and methods define the class's **public interface**—that is, the set of properties and methods programmers should use to interact with objects of the class.

Attributes Are Always Accessible

Though we provided a well-defined interface, Python does *not* prevent you from directly manipulating the data attributes _hour, _minute and _second, as in:

```
In [1]: from timewithproperties import Time

In [2]: wake_up = Time(hour=7, minute=45, second=30)

In [3]: wake_up._hour
Out[3]: 7

In [4]: wake_up._hour = 100

In [5]: wake_up
Out[5]: Time(hour=100, minute=45, second=30)
```

After snippet [4], the wake_up object contains *invalid* data. Unlike many other object-oriented programming languages, such as C++, Java and C#, data attributes in Python cannot be hidden from client code. The Python tutorial says, "**nothing in Python makes it possible to enforce data hiding—it is all based upon convention.**"[3]

Internal Data Representation

We chose to represent the time as three integer values for hours, minutes and seconds. It would be perfectly reasonable to represent the time internally as the number of seconds since midnight. Though we'd have to reimplement the properties hour, minute and sec-

---

3. https://docs.python.org/3/tutorial/classes.html#random-remarks.

ond, programmers could use the *same* interface and get the *same* results without being aware of these changes. We leave it to you to make this change and show that client code using Time objects does not need to change.

Evolving a Class's Implementation Details
When you design a class, carefully consider the class's interface before making that class available to other programmers. Ideally, you'll design the interface such that existing code will not break if you update the class's implementation details—that is, the internal data representation or how its method bodies are implemented.

If Python programmers follow convention and do not access attributes that begin with leading underscores, then class designers can evolve class implementation details without breaking client code.

Properties
It may seem that providing properties with both *setters* and *getters* has no benefit over accessing the data attributes directly, but there are subtle differences. A *getter* seems to allow clients to read the data at will, but the *getter* can control the formatting of the data. A *setter* can scrutinize attempts to modify the value of a data attribute to prevent the data from being set to an invalid value.

Utility Methods
Not all methods need to serve as part of a class's interface. Some serve as **utility methods** used only *inside* the class and are not intended to be part of the class's public interface used by client code. Such methods should be named with a single leading underscore. In other object-oriented languages like C++, Java and C#, such methods typically are implemented as private methods.

Module datetime
In professional Python development, rather than building your own classes to represent times and dates, you'll typically use the Python Standard Library's datetime module capabilities. For more details about the datetime module, see:

```
https://docs.python.org/3/library/datetime.html
```

10.5 Simulating "Private" Attributes
In programming languages such as C++, Java and C#, classes state explicitly which class members are *publicly accessible*. Class members that may not be accessed outside a class definition are **private** and visible only within the class that defines them. Python programmers often use "private" attributes for data or utility methods that are essential to a class's inner workings but are not part of the class's public interface.

As you've seen, Python objects' attributes are *always* accessible. However, Python has a naming convention for "private" attributes. Suppose we want to create an object of class Time and to *prevent* the following assignment statement:

```
wake_up._hour = 100
```

that would set the hour to an invalid value. Rather than _hour, we can name the attribute __hour with *two* leading underscores. This convention indicates that __hour is "private" and should not be accessible to the class's clients. To help prevent clients from accessing "private" attributes, Python *renames* them by preceding the attribute name with _*ClassName*, as in _Time__hour. This is called **name mangling**. If you try assign to __hour, as in

> wake_up.__hour = 100

Python raises an AttributeError, indicating that the class does not have an __hour attribute. We'll show this momentarily.

IPython Auto-Completion Shows Only "Public" Attributes

In addition, IPython does not show attributes with one or two leading underscores when you try to auto-complete an expression like

> wake_up.

by pressing *Tab*. Only attributes that are part of the wake_up object's "public" interface are displayed in the IPython auto-completion list.

Demonstrating "Private" Attributes

To demonstrate name mangling, consider class PrivateClass with one "public" data attribute public_data and one "private" data attribute __private_data:

```
 1  # private.py
 2  """Class with public and private attributes."""
 3
 4  class PrivateClass:
 5      """Class with public and private attributes."""
 6
 7      def __init__(self):
 8          """Initialize the public and private attributes."""
 9          self.public_data = "public"  # public attribute
10          self.__private_data = "private"  # private attribute
```

Let's create an object of class PrivateData to demonstrate these data attributes:

```
In [1]: from private import PrivateClass

In [2]: my_object = PrivateClass()
```

Snippet [3] shows that we can access the public_data attribute directly:

```
In [3]: my_object.public_data
Out[3]: 'public'
```

However, when we attempt to access __private_data directly in snippet [4], we get an AttributeError indicating that the class does not have an attribute by that name:

```
In [4]: my_object.__private_data
---------------------------------------------------------------
AttributeError                            Traceback (most recent call last)
<ipython-input-4-d896bfdf2053> in <module>()
----> 1 my_object.__private_data

AttributeError: 'PrivateClass' object has no attribute '__private_data'
```

This occurs because python changed the attribute's name. Unfortunately, the attribute __private_data is still indirectly accessible.

10.6 Case Study: Card Shuffling and Dealing Simulation

Our next example presents two custom classes that you can use to shuffle and deal a deck of cards. Class Card represents a playing card that has a face ('Ace', '2', '3', ..., 'Jack', 'Queen', 'King') and a suit ('Hearts', 'Diamonds', 'Clubs', 'Spades'). Class DeckOf-Cards represents a deck of 52 playing cards as a list of Card objects. First, we'll test-drive these classes in an IPython session to demonstrate card shuffling and dealing capabilities and displaying the cards as text. Then we'll look at the class definitions. Finally, we'll use another IPython session to display the 52 cards as images using Matplotlib. We'll show you where to get nice-looking public-domain card images.

10.6.1 Test-Driving Classes Card and DeckOfCards

Before we look at classes Card and DeckOfCards, let's use an IPython session to demonstrate their capabilities.

Creating, Shuffling and Dealing the Cards

First, import class DeckOfCards from deck.py and create an object of the class:

```
In [1]: from deck import DeckOfCards

In [2]: deck_of_cards = DeckOfCards()
```

DeckOfCards method __init__ creates the 52 Card objects in order by suit and by face within each suit. You can see this by printing the deck_of_cards object, which calls the DeckOfCards class's __str__ method to get the deck's string representation. Read each row left-to-right to confirm that all the cards are displayed in order from each suit (Hearts, Diamonds, Clubs and Spades):

```
In [3]: print(deck_of_cards)
Ace of Hearts      2 of Hearts        3 of Hearts        4 of Hearts
5 of Hearts        6 of Hearts        7 of Hearts        8 of Hearts
9 of Hearts        10 of Hearts       Jack of Hearts     Queen of Hearts
King of Hearts     Ace of Diamonds    2 of Diamonds      3 of Diamonds
4 of Diamonds      5 of Diamonds      6 of Diamonds      7 of Diamonds
8 of Diamonds      9 of Diamonds      10 of Diamonds     Jack of Diamonds
Queen of Diamonds  King of Diamonds   Ace of Clubs       2 of Clubs
3 of Clubs         4 of Clubs         5 of Clubs         6 of Clubs
7 of Clubs         8 of Clubs         9 of Clubs         10 of Clubs
Jack of Clubs      Queen of Clubs     King of Clubs      Ace of Spades
2 of Spades        3 of Spades        4 of Spades        5 of Spades
6 of Spades        7 of Spades        8 of Spades        9 of Spades
10 of Spades       Jack of Spades     Queen of Spades    King of Spades
```

Next, let's shuffle the deck and print the deck_of_cards object again. We did not specify a seed for reproducibility, so each time you shuffle, you'll get different results:

```
In [4]: deck_of_cards.shuffle()

In [5]: print(deck_of_cards)
King of Hearts     Queen of Clubs     Queen of Diamonds  10 of Clubs
5 of Hearts        7 of Hearts        4 of Hearts        2 of Hearts
```

5 of Clubs	8 of Diamonds	3 of Hearts	10 of Hearts
8 of Spades	5 of Spades	Queen of Spades	Ace of Clubs
8 of Clubs	7 of Spades	Jack of Diamonds	10 of Spades
4 of Diamonds	8 of Hearts	6 of Spades	King of Spades
9 of Hearts	4 of Spades	6 of Clubs	King of Clubs
3 of Spades	9 of Diamonds	3 of Clubs	Ace of Spades
Ace of Hearts	3 of Diamonds	2 of Diamonds	6 of Hearts
King of Diamonds	Jack of Spades	Jack of Clubs	2 of Spades
5 of Diamonds	4 of Clubs	Queen of Hearts	9 of Clubs
10 of Diamonds	2 of Clubs	Ace of Diamonds	7 of Diamonds
9 of Spades	Jack of Hearts	6 of Diamonds	7 of Clubs

Dealing Cards

We can deal one Card at a time by calling method deal_card. IPython calls the returned Card object's __repr__ method to produce the string output shown in the Out[] prompt:

```
In [6]: deck_of_cards.deal_card()
Out[6]: Card(face='King', suit='Hearts')
```

Class Card's Other Features

To demonstrate class Card's __str__ method, let's deal another card and pass it to the built-in str function:

```
In [7]: card = deck_of_cards.deal_card()

In [8]: str(card)
Out[8]: 'Queen of Clubs'
```

Each Card has a corresponding image file name, which you can get via the image_name read-only property. We'll use this soon when we display the Cards as images:

```
In [9]: card.image_name
Out[9]: 'Queen_of_Clubs.png'
```

10.6.2 Class Card—Introducing Class Attributes

Each Card object contains three string properties representing that Card's face, suit and image_name (a file name containing a corresponding image). As you saw in the preceding section's IPython session, class Card also provides methods for initializing a Card and for getting various string representations.

Class Attributes FACES and SUITS

Each object of a class has its own copies of the class's data attributes. For example, each Account object has its own name and balance. Sometimes, an attribute should be shared by *all* objects of a class. A **class attribute** (also called a **class variable**) represents *class-wide* information. It belongs to the *class*, not to a specific object of that class. Class Card defines two class attributes (lines 5–7):

- FACES is a list of the card face names.
- SUITS is a list of the card suit names.

```
 1   # card.py
 2   """Card class that represents a playing card and its image file name."""
 3
 4   class Card:
 5       FACES = ['Ace', '2', '3', '4', '5', '6',
 6                '7', '8', '9', '10', 'Jack', 'Queen', 'King']
 7       SUITS = ['Hearts', 'Diamonds', 'Clubs', 'Spades']
 8
```

You define a class attribute by assigning a value to it inside the class's definition, but not inside any of the class's methods or properties (in which case, they'd be local variables). FACES and SUITS are *constants* that are not meant to be modified. Recall that the *Style Guide for Python Code* recommends naming your constants with all capital letters.[4]

We'll use elements of these lists to initialize each Card we create. However, we do not need a separate copy of each list in every Card object. Class attributes can be accessed through any object of the class, but are typically accessed through the class's name (as in, Card.FACES or Card.SUITS). Class attributes exist as soon as you import their class's definition.

Card Method __init__

When you create a Card object, method __init__ defines the object's _face and _suit data attributes:

```
 9       def __init__(self, face, suit):
10           """Initialize a Card with a face and suit."""
11           self._face = face
12           self._suit = suit
13
```

Read-Only Properties face, suit and image_name

Once a Card is created, its face, suit and image_name do not change, so we implement these as read-only properties (lines 14–17, 19–22 and 24–27). Properties face and suit return the corresponding data attributes _face and _suit. A property is not required to have a corresponding data attribute. To demonstrate this, the Card property image_name's value is *created dynamically* by getting the Card object's string representation with str(self), replacing any spaces with underscores and appending the '.png' filename extension. So, 'Ace of Spades' becomes 'Ace_of_Spades.png'. We'll use this file name to load a PNG-format image representing the Card. PNG (Portable Network Graphics) is a popular image format for web-based images.

```
14       @property
15       def face(self):
16           """Return the Card's self._face value."""
17           return self._face
18
19       @property
20       def suit(self):
21           """Return the Card's self._suit value."""
22           return self._suit
```

---

4. Recall that Python does not have true constants, so FACES and SUITS are still modifiable.

```
23
24      @property
25      def image_name(self):
26          """Return the Card's image file name."""
27          return str(self).replace(' ', '_') + '.png'
28
```

Methods That Return String Representations of a Card

Class Card provides three special methods that return string representations. As in class Time, method __repr__ returns a string representation that looks like a constructor expression for creating and initializing a Card object:

```
29      def __repr__(self):
30          """Return string representation for repr()."""
31          return f"Card(face='{self.face}', suit='{self.suit}')"
32
```

Method __str__ returns a string of the format '*face* of *suit*', such as 'Ace of Hearts':

```
33      def __str__(self):
34          """Return string representation for str()."""
35          return f'{self.face} of {self.suit}'
36
```

When the preceding section's IPython session printed the entire deck, you saw that the Cards were displayed in four left-aligned columns. As you'll see in the __str__ method of class DeckOfCards, we use f-strings to format the Cards in fields of 19 characters each. Class Card's special method **__format__** is called when a Card object is *formatted* as a string, such as in an f-string:

```
37      def __format__(self, format):
38          """Return formatted string representation for str()."""
39          return f'{str(self):{format}}'
```

This method's second argument is the format string used to format the object. To use the format parameter's value as the format specifier, enclose the parameter name in braces to the *right* of the colon. In this case, we're formatting the Card object's string representation returned by str(self). We'll discuss __format__ again when we present the __str__ method in class DeckOfCards.

10.6.3 Class DeckOfCards

Class DeckOfCards has a class attribute NUMBER_OF_CARDS, representing the number of Cards in a deck, and creates two data attributes:

- _current_card keeps track of which Card will be dealt next (0–51) and
- _deck (line 12) is a list of 52 Card objects.

Method __init__

DeckOfCards method __init__ initializes a _deck of Cards. The for statement fills the list _deck by appending new Card objects, each initialized with two strings—one from the list

Card.FACES and one from Card.SUITS. The calculation count % 13 *always* results in a value from 0 to 12 (the 13 indices of Card.FACES), and the calculation count // 13 *always* results in a value from 0 to 3 (the four indices of Card.SUITS). When the _deck list is initialized, it contains the Cards with faces 'Ace' through 'King' in order for all the Hearts, then the Diamonds, then the Clubs, then the Spades.

```
1    # deck.py
2    """Deck class represents a deck of Cards."""
3    import random
4    from card import Card
5
6    class DeckOfCards:
7        NUMBER_OF_CARDS = 52  # constant number of Cards
8
9        def __init__(self):
10           """Initialize the deck."""
11           self._current_card = 0
12           self._deck = []
13
14           for count in range(DeckOfCards.NUMBER_OF_CARDS):
15               self._deck.append(Card(Card.FACES[count % 13],
16                   Card.SUITS[count // 13]))
17
```

Method shuffle

Method shuffle resets _current_card to 0, then shuffles the Cards in _deck using the random module's shuffle function:

```
18       def shuffle(self):
19           """Shuffle deck."""
20           self._current_card = 0
21           random.shuffle(self._deck)
22
```

Method deal_card

Method deal_card deals one Card from _deck. Recall that _current_card indicates the index (0–51) of the next Card to be dealt (that is, the Card at the top of the deck). Line 26 tries to get the _deck element at index _current_card. If successful, the method increments _current_card by 1, then returns the Card being dealt; otherwise, the method returns None to indicate there are no more Cards to deal.

```
23       def deal_card(self):
24           """Return one Card."""
25           try:
26               card = self._deck[self._current_card]
27               self._current_card += 1
28               return card
29           except:
30               return None
31
```

Method __str__

Class DeckOfCards also defines special method __str__ to get a string representation of the deck in four columns with each Card left aligned in a field of 19 characters. When line 37 formats a given Card, its __format__ special method is called with format specifier '<19' as the method's format argument. Method __format__ then uses '<19' to create the Card's formatted string representation.

```
32      def __str__(self):
33          """Return a string representation of the current _deck."""
34          s = ''
35
36          for index, card in enumerate(self._deck):
37              s += f'{self._deck[index]:<19}'
38              if (index + 1) % 4 == 0:
39                  s += '\n'
40
41          return s
```

10.6.4 Displaying Card Images with Matplotlib

So far, we've displayed Cards as text. Now, let's display Card images. For this demonstration, we downloaded public-domain[5] card images from Wikimedia Commons:

> https://commons.wikimedia.org/wiki/
>   Category:SVG_English_pattern_playing_cards

These are located in the ch10 examples folder's card_images subfolder. First, let's create a DeckOfCards:

```
In [1]: from deck import DeckOfCards

In [2]: deck_of_cards = DeckOfCards()
```

Enable Matplotlib in IPython

Next, enable Matplotlib support in IPython by using the %matplotlib magic:

```
In [3]: %matplotlib
Using matplotlib backend: Qt5Agg
```

Create the Base Path for Each Image

Before displaying each image, we must load it from the card_images folder. We'll use the pathlib module's **Path class** to construct the full path to each image on our system. Snippet [5] creates a Path object for the current folder (the ch10 examples folder), which is represented by '.', then uses Path method **joinpath** to append the subfolder containing the card images:

```
In [4]: from pathlib import Path

In [5]: path = Path('.').joinpath('card_images')
```

---

5. https://creativecommons.org/publicdomain/zero/1.0/deed.en.

Import the Matplotlib Features
Next, let's import the Matplotlib modules we'll need to display the images. We'll use a function from **matplotlib.image** to load the images:

```
In [6]: import matplotlib.pyplot as plt

In [7]: import matplotlib.image as mpimg
```

Create the Figure and Axes Objects
The following snippet uses Matplotlib function **subplots** to create a Figure object in which we'll display the images as 52 *subplots* with four rows (nrows) and 13 columns (ncols). The function returns a tuple containing the Figure and an array of the subplots' Axes objects. We unpack these into variables figure and axes_list:

```
In [8]: figure, axes_list = plt.subplots(nrows=4, ncols=13)
```

When you execute this statement in IPython, the Matplotlib window appears immediately with 52 empty subplots.

Configure the Axes Objects and Display the Images
Next, we iterate through all the Axes objects in axes_list. Recall that ravel provides a one-dimensional view of a multidimensional array. For each Axes object, we perform the following tasks:

- We're not plotting data, so we do not need axis lines and labels for each image. The first two statements in the loop hide the *x*- and *y*-axes.

- The third statement deals a Card and gets its image_name.

- The fourth statement uses Path method joinpath to append the image_name to the Path, then calls Path method **resolve** to determine the full path to the image on our system. We pass the resulting Path object to the built-in str function to get the string representation of the image's location. Then, we pass that string to the matplotlib.image module's **imread function**, which loads the image.

- The last statement calls Axes method **imshow** to display the current image in the current subplot.

```
In [9]: for axes in axes_list.ravel():
   ...:     axes.get_xaxis().set_visible(False)
   ...:     axes.get_yaxis().set_visible(False)
   ...:     image_name = deck_of_cards.deal_card().image_name
   ...:     img = mpimg.imread(str(path.joinpath(image_name).resolve()))
   ...:     axes.imshow(img)
   ...:
```

Maximize the Image Sizes
At this point, all the images are displayed. To make the cards as large as possible, you can maximize the window, then call the Matplotlib Figure object's **tight_layout method**. This removes most of the extra white space in the window:

```
In [10]: figure.tight_layout()
```

The following image shows the contents of the resulting window:

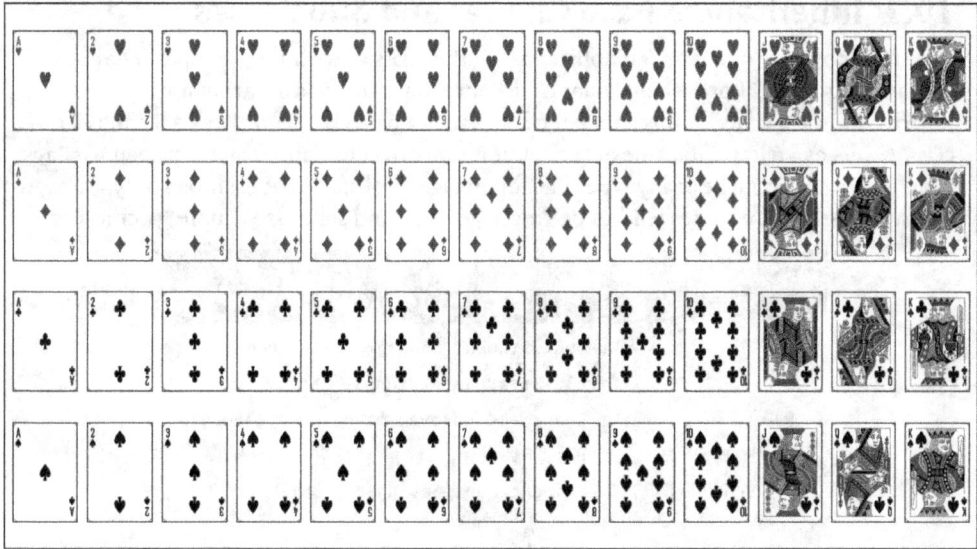

Shuffle and Re-Deal the Deck

To see the images shuffled, call method `shuffle`, then re-execute snippet [9]'s code:

```
In [11]: deck_of_cards.shuffle()

In [12]: for axes in axes_list.ravel():
    ...:     axes.get_xaxis().set_visible(False)
    ...:     axes.get_yaxis().set_visible(False)
    ...:     image_name = deck_of_cards.deal_card().image_name
    ...:     img = mpimg.imread(str(path.joinpath(image_name).resolve()))
    ...:     axes.imshow(img)
    ...:
```

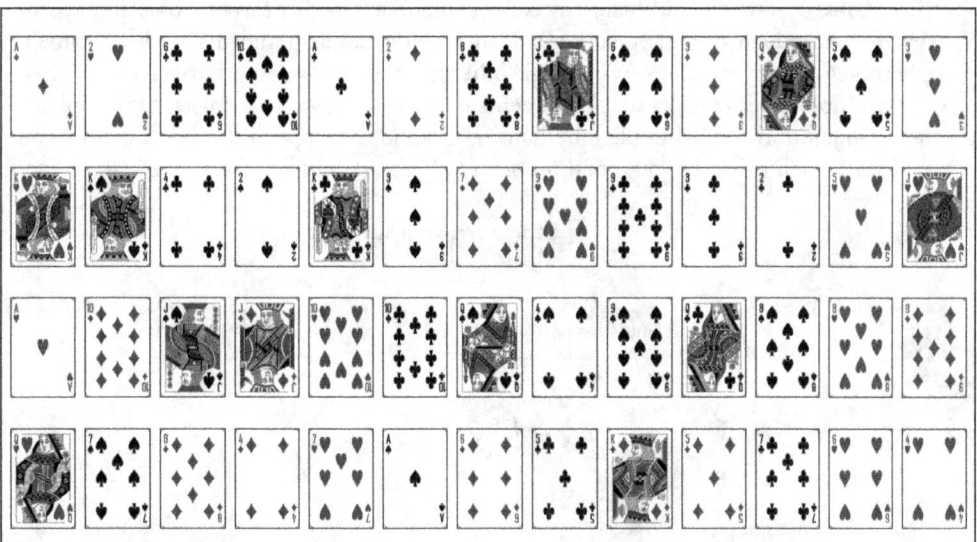

10.7 Inheritance: Base Classes and Subclasses

Often, an object of one class *is an* object of another class as well. For example, a CarLoan *is a* Loan as are HomeImprovementLoans and MortgageLoans. Class CarLoan can be said to inherit from class Loan. In this context, class Loan is a base class, and class CarLoan is a subclass. A CarLoan *is a* specific type of Loan, but it's incorrect to claim that every Loan *is a* CarLoan—the Loan could be of any type. The following table lists simple examples of base classes and subclasses—base classes tend to be "more general" and subclasses "more specific":

Base class	Subclasses
Student	GraduateStudent, UndergraduateStudent
Shape	Circle, Triangle, Rectangle, Sphere, Cube
Loan	CarLoan, HomeImprovementLoan, MortgageLoan
Employee	Faculty, Staff
BankAccount	CheckingAccount, SavingsAccount

Because every subclass object *is an* object of its base class, and one base class can have many subclasses, the set of objects represented by a base class is often larger than the set of objects represented by any of its subclasses. For example, the base class Vehicle represents *all* vehicles, including cars, trucks, boats, bicycles and so on. By contrast, subclass Car represents a smaller, more specific subset of vehicles.

CommunityMember Inheritance Hierarchy

Inheritance relationships form tree-like *hierarchical* structures. A base class exists in a hierarchical relationship with its subclasses. Let's develop a sample class hierarchy (shown in the following diagram), also called an **inheritance hierarchy**. A university community has thousands of members, including employees, students and alumni. Employees are either faculty or staff members. Faculty members are either administrators (e.g., deans and department chairpersons) or teachers. The hierarchy could contain many other classes. For example, students can be graduate or undergraduate students. Undergraduate students can be freshmen, sophomores, juniors or seniors. With **single inheritance**, a class is derived from *one* base class. With **multiple inheritance**, a subclass inherits from *two or more* base classes. Single inheritance is straightforward. Multiple inheritance is beyond the scope of this book. Before you use it, search online for the "diamond problem in Python multiple inheritance."

Each arrow in the hierarchy represents an *is-a* relationship. As we follow the arrows upward in this class hierarchy, we can state, for example, that "an Employee *is a* CommunityMember" and "a Teacher *is a* Faculty member." CommunityMember is the direct base class of Employee, Student and Alum and is an indirect base class of all the other classes in the diagram. Starting from the bottom, you can follow the arrows and apply the *is-a* relationship up to the topmost superclass. For example, Administrator *is a* Faculty member, *is an* Employee, *is a* CommunityMember and, of course, ultimately *is an* object.

Shape Inheritance Hierarchy

Now consider the Shape inheritance hierarchy in the following class diagram, which begins with base class Shape, followed by subclasses TwoDimensionalShape and ThreeDimensionalShape. Each Shape is either a TwoDimensionalShape or a ThreeDimensionalShape. The third level of this hierarchy contains *specific* types of TwoDimensionalShapes and ThreeDimensionalShapes. Again, we can follow the arrows from the bottom of the diagram to the topmost base class in this class hierarchy to identify several *is-a* relationships. For example, a Triangle *is a* TwoDimensionalShape and *is a* Shape, while a Sphere *is a* ThreeDimensionalShape and *is a* Shape. This hierarchy could contain many other classes. For example, ellipses and trapezoids also are TwoDimensionalShapes, and cones and cylinders also are ThreeDimensionalShapes.

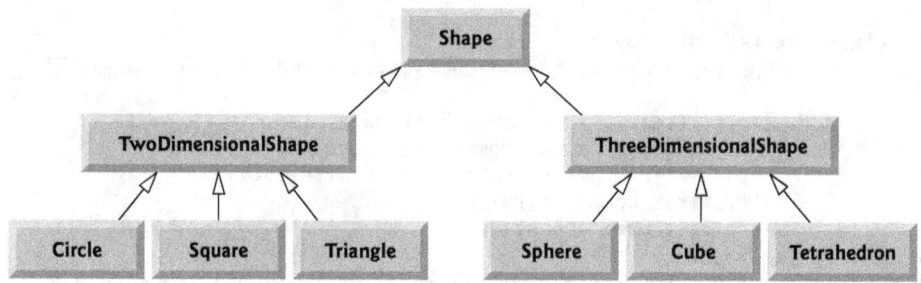

"is a" vs. "has a"

Inheritance produces **"is-a" relationships** in which an object of a subclass type may also be treated as an object of the base-class type. You've also seen **"has-a"** (composition) relationships in which a class has references to one or more objects of other classes as members.

10.8 Building an Inheritance Hierarchy; Introducing Polymorphism

Let's use a hierarchy containing types of employees in a company's payroll app to discuss the relationship between a base class and its subclass. All employees of the company have a lot in common, but *commission employees* (who will be represented as objects of a base class) are paid a percentage of their sales, while *salaried commission employees* (who will be represented as objects of a subclass) receive a percentage of their sales *plus* a base salary.

First, we present *base class* CommissionEmployee. Next, we create a *subclass* SalariedCommissionEmployee that inherits from class CommissionEmployee. Then, we use an IPython session to create a SalariedCommissionEmployee object and demonstrate that it has all the capabilities of the base class *and* the subclass, but calculates its earnings differently.

10.8.1 Base Class CommissionEmployee

Consider class `CommissionEmployee`, which provides the following features:

- Method `__init__` (lines 8–15), which creates the data attributes `_first_name`, `_last_name` and `_ssn` (Social Security number), and uses the setters of properties `gross_sales` and `commission_rate` to create their corresponding data attributes.

- Read-only properties `first_name` (lines 17–19), `last_name` (lines 21–23) and `ssn` (line 25–27), which return the corresponding data attributes.

- Read-write properties `gross_sales` (lines 29–39) and `commission_rate` (lines 41–52), in which the setters perform data validation.

- Method `earnings` (lines 54–56), which calculates and returns a `CommissionEmployee`'s earnings.

- Method `__repr__` (lines 58–64), which returns a string representation of a `CommissionEmployee`.

```python
1   # commmissionemployee.py
2   """CommissionEmployee base class."""
3   from decimal import Decimal
4
5   class CommissionEmployee:
6       """An employee who gets paid commission based on gross sales."""
7
8       def __init__(self, first_name, last_name, ssn,
9                    gross_sales, commission_rate):
10          """Initialize CommissionEmployee's attributes."""
11          self._first_name = first_name
12          self._last_name = last_name
13          self._ssn = ssn
14          self.gross_sales = gross_sales  # validate via property
15          self.commission_rate = commission_rate  # validate via property
16
17      @property
18      def first_name(self):
19          return self._first_name
20
21      @property
22      def last_name(self):
23          return self._last_name
24
25      @property
26      def ssn(self):
27          return self._ssn
28
29      @property
30      def gross_sales(self):
31          return self._gross_sales
32
```

```
33        @gross_sales.setter
34        def gross_sales(self, sales):
35            """Set gross sales or raise ValueError if invalid."""
36            if sales < Decimal('0.00'):
37                raise ValueError('Gross sales must be >= to 0')
38
39            self._gross_sales = sales
40
41        @property
42        def commission_rate(self):
43            return self._commission_rate
44
45        @commission_rate.setter
46        def commission_rate(self, rate):
47            """Set commission rate or raise ValueError if invalid."""
48            if not (Decimal('0.0') < rate < Decimal('1.0')):
49                raise ValueError(
50                    'Interest rate must be greater than 0 and less than 1')
51
52            self._commission_rate = rate
53
54    def earnings(self):
55        """Calculate earnings."""
56        return self.gross_sales * self.commission_rate
57
58    def __repr__(self):
59        """Return string representation for repr()."""
60        return ('CommissionEmployee: ' +
61            f'{self.first_name} {self.last_name}\n' +
62            f'social security number: {self.ssn}\n' +
63            f'gross sales: {self.gross_sales:.2f}\n' +
64            f'commission rate: {self.commission_rate:.2f}')
```

Properties `first_name`, `last_name` and `ssn` are read-only. We chose not to validate them, though we could have. For example, we could validate the first and last names—perhaps by ensuring that they're of a reasonable length. We could validate the Social Security number to ensure that it contains nine digits, with or without dashes (for example, to ensure that it's in the format ###-##-#### or #########, where each # is a digit).

All Classes Inherit Directly or Indirectly from Class `object`

You use inheritance to create new classes from existing ones. In fact, *every* Python class inherits from an existing class. When you do not explicitly specify the base class for a new class, Python assumes that the class inherits directly from class `object`. The Python class hierarchy begins with class `object`, the direct or indirect base class of *every* class. So, class `CommissionEmployee`'s header could have been written as

```
class CommissionEmployee(object):
```

The parentheses after `CommissionEmployee` indicate inheritance and may contain a single class for single inheritance or a comma-separated list of base classes for multiple inheritance. Once again, multiple inheritance is beyond the scope of this book.

Class `CommissionEmployee` inherits all the methods of class `object`. Class `object` does not have any data attributes. Two of the many methods inherited from `object` are `_repr_` and `_str_`. So *every* class has these methods that return string representations of the objects on which they're called. When a base-class method implementation is inappropriate for a derived class, that method can be **overridden** (i.e., redefined) in the derived class with an appropriate implementation. Method `_repr_` (lines 58–64) overrides the default implementation inherited into class `CommissionEmployee` from class `object`.[6]

Testing Class `CommissionEmployee`
Let's quickly test some of `CommissionEmployee`'s features. First, create and display a CommissionEmployee:

```
In [1]: from commissionemployee import CommissionEmployee

In [2]: from decimal import Decimal

In [3]: c = CommissionEmployee('Sue', 'Jones', '333-33-3333',
   ...:     Decimal('10000.00'), Decimal('0.06'))
   ...:

In [4]: c
Out[4]:
CommissionEmployee: Sue Jones
social security number: 333-33-3333
gross sales: 10000.00
commission rate: 0.06
```

Next, let's calculate and display the `CommissionEmployee`'s earnings:

```
In [5]: print(f'{c.earnings():,.2f}')
600.00
```

Finally, let's change the `CommissionEmployee`'s gross sales and commission rate, then recalculate the earnings:

```
In [6]: c.gross_sales = Decimal('20000.00')

In [7]: c.commission_rate = Decimal('0.1')

In [8]: print(f'{c.earnings():,.2f}')
2,000.00
```

10.8.2 Subclass `SalariedCommissionEmployee`

With single inheritance, the subclass starts essentially the same as the base class. The real strength of inheritance comes from the ability to define in the subclass additions, replacements or refinements for the features inherited from the base class.

Many of a `SalariedCommissionEmployee`'s capabilities are similar, if not identical, to those of class `CommissionEmployee`. Both types of employees have first name, last name, Social Security number, gross sales and commission rate data attributes, and properties and methods to manipulate that data. To create class `SalariedCommissionEmployee` *without* using inheritance, we could have *copied* class `CommissionEmployee`'s code and *pasted* it into class `SalariedCommissionEmployee`. Then we could have modified the new class to

---

6. See https://docs.python.org/3/reference/datamodel.html for object's overridable methods.

include a base salary data attribute, and the properties and methods that manipulate the base salary, including a new earnings method. This *copy-and-paste approach* is often error-prone. Worse yet, it can spread many physical copies of the same code (including errors) throughout a system, making your code less maintainable. Inheritance enables us to "absorb" the features of a class *without* duplicating code. Let's see how.

Declaring Class SalariedCommissionEmployee

We now declare the subclass SalariedCommissionEmployee, which *inherits* most of its capabilities from class CommissionEmployee (line 6). A SalariedCommissionEmployee *is a* CommissionEmployee (because inheritance passes on the capabilities of class CommissionEmployee), but class SalariedCommissionEmployee also has the following features:

- Method __init__ (lines 10–15), which initializes all the data inherited from class CommissionEmployee (we'll say more about this momentarily), then uses the base_salary property's setter to create a _base_salary data attribute.

- Read-write property base_salary (lines 17–27), in which the setter performs data validation.

- A customized version of method earnings (lines 29–31).

- A customized version of method __repr__ (lines 33–36).

```python
1   # salariedcommissionemployee.py
2   """SalariedCommissionEmployee derived from CommissionEmployee."""
3   from commissionemployee import CommissionEmployee
4   from decimal import Decimal
5
6   class SalariedCommissionEmployee(CommissionEmployee):
7       """An employee who gets paid a salary plus
8       commission based on gross sales."""
9
10      def __init__(self, first_name, last_name, ssn,
11                   gross_sales, commission_rate, base_salary):
12          """Initialize SalariedCommissionEmployee's attributes."""
13          super().__init__(first_name, last_name, ssn,
14                           gross_sales, commission_rate)
15          self.base_salary = base_salary  # validate via property
16
17      @property
18      def base_salary(self):
19          return self._base_salary
20
21      @base_salary.setter
22      def base_salary(self, salary):
23          """Set base salary or raise ValueError if invalid."""
24          if salary < Decimal('0.00'):
25              raise ValueError('Base salary must be >= to 0')
26
27          self._base_salary = salary
28
29      def earnings(self):
30          """Calculate earnings."""
31          return super().earnings() + self.base_salary
32
```

```
33        def __repr__(self):
34            """Return string representation for repr()."""
35            return ('Salaried' + super().__repr__() +
36                f'\nbase salary: {self.base_salary:.2f}')
```

Inheriting from Class CommissionEmployee

To inherit from a class, you must first import its definition (line 3). Line 6

```
class SalariedCommissionEmployee(CommissionEmployee):
```

specifies that class SalariedCommissionEmployee *inherits* from CommissionEmployee. Though you do not see class CommissionEmployee's data attributes, properties and methods in class SalariedCommissionEmployee, they're nevertheless part of the new class, as you'll soon see.

Method __init__ and Built-In Function super

Each subclass __init__ must explicitly call its base class's __init__ to initialize the data attributes inherited from the base class. This call should be the first statement in the subclass's __init__ method. SalariedCommissionEmployee's __init__ method explicitly calls class CommissionEmployee's __init__ method (lines 13–14) to initialize the base-class portion of a SalariedCommissionEmployee object (that is, the five inherited data attributes from class CommissionEmployee). The notation super().__init__ uses the built-in function **super** to locate and call the base class's __init__ method, passing the five arguments that initialize the inherited data attributes.

Overriding Method earnings

Class SalariedCommissionEmployee's earnings method (lines 29–31) overrides class CommissionEmployee's earnings method (Section 10.8.1, lines 54–56) to calculate the earnings of a SalariedCommissionEmployee. The new version obtains the portion of the earnings based on *commission alone* by calling CommissionEmployee's earnings method with the expression super().earnings() (line 31). SalariedCommissionEmployee's earnings method then adds the base_salary to this value to calculate the total earnings. By having SalariedCommissionEmployee's earnings method invoke CommissionEmployee's earnings method to calculate part of a SalariedCommissionEmployee's earnings, we avoid duplicating the code and reduce code-maintenance problems.

Overriding Method __repr__

SalariedCommissionEmployee's __repr__ method (lines 33–36) overrides class CommissionEmployee's __repr__ method (Section 10.8.1, lines 58–64) to return a String representation that's appropriate for a SalariedCommissionEmployee. The subclass creates part of the string representation by concatenating 'Salaried' and the string returned by super().__repr__(), which calls CommissionEmployee's __repr__ method. The overridden method then concatenates the base salary information and returns the resulting string.

Testing Class SalariedCommissionEmployee

Let's test class SalariedCommissionEmployee to show that it indeed inherited capabilities from class CommissionEmployee. First, let's create a SalariedCommissionEmployee and print all of its properties:

```
In [9]: from salariedcommissionemployee import SalariedCommissionEmployee

In [10]: s = SalariedCommissionEmployee('Bob', 'Lewis', '444-44-4444',
    ...:          Decimal('5000.00'), Decimal('0.04'), Decimal('300.00'))
    ...:

In [11]: print(s.first_name, s.last_name, s.ssn, s.gross_sales,
    ...:          s.commission_rate, s.base_salary)
Bob Lewis 444-44-4444 5000.00 0.04 300.00
```

Notice that the SalariedCommissionEmployee object has *all* of the properties of classes
CommissionEmployee *and* SalariedCommissionEmployee.

Next, let's calculate and display the SalariedCommissionEmployee's earnings.
Because we call method earnings on a SalariedCommissionEmployee object, the *subclass
version* of the method executes:

```
In [12]: print(f'{s.earnings():,.2f}')
500.00
```

Now, let's modify the gross_sales, commission_rate and base_salary properties,
then display the updated data via the SalariedCommissionEmployee's __repr__ method:

```
In [13]: s.gross_sales = Decimal('10000.00')

In [14]: s.commission_rate = Decimal('0.05')

In [15]: s.base_salary = Decimal('1000.00')

In [16]: print(s)
SalariedCommissionEmployee: Bob Lewis
social security number: 444-44-4444
gross sales: 10000.00
commission rate: 0.05
base salary: 1000.00
```

Again, because this method is called on a SalariedCommissionEmployee object, the *subclass version* of the method executes. Finally, let's calculate and display the Salaried-
CommissionEmployee's updated earnings:

```
In [17]: print(f'{s.earnings():,.2f}')
1,500.00
```

Testing the "is a" Relationship
Python provides two built-in functions—**issubclass** and **isinstance**—for testing "is a"
relationships. Function issubclass determines whether one class is derived from another:

```
In [18]: issubclass(SalariedCommissionEmployee, CommissionEmployee)
Out[18]: True
```

Function isinstance determines whether an object has an "is a" relationship with a
specific type. Because SalariedCommissionEmployee inherits from CommissionEmployee,
both of the following snippets return True, confirming the "is a" relationship

```
In [19]: isinstance(s, CommissionEmployee)
Out[19]: True

In [20]: isinstance(s, SalariedCommissionEmployee)
Out[20]: True
```

10.8.3 Processing CommissionEmployees and SalariedCommissionEmployees Polymorphically

With inheritance, every object of a subclass also may be treated as an object of that subclass's base class. We can take advantage of this "subclass-object-is-a-base-class-object" relationship to perform some interesting manipulations. For example, we can place objects related through inheritance into a list, then iterate through the list and treat each element as a base-class object. This allows a variety of objects to be processed in a *general* way. Let's demonstrate this by placing the CommissionEmployee and SalariedCommissionEmployee objects in a list, then for each element displaying its string representation and earnings:

```
In [21]: employees = [c, s]

In [22]: for employee in employees:
   ...:     print(employee)
   ...:     print(f'{employee.earnings():,.2f}\n')
   ...:
CommissionEmployee: Sue Jones
social security number: 333-33-3333
gross sales: 20000.00
commission rate: 0.10
2,000.00

SalariedCommissionEmployee: Bob Lewis
social security number: 444-44-4444
gross sales: 10000.00
commission rate: 0.05
base salary: 1000.00
1,500.00
```

As you can see, the correct string representation and earnings are displayed for each employee. This is called *polymorphism*—a key capability of object-oriented programming (OOP).

10.8.4 A Note About Object-Based and Object-Oriented Programming

Inheritance with method overriding is a powerful way to build software components that are *like* existing components but need to be customized to your application's unique needs. In the Python open-source world, there are a huge number of well-developed class libraries for which your programming style is:

- know what libraries are available,
- know what classes are available,
- make objects of existing classes, and
- send them messages (that is, call their methods).

This style of programming is called *object-based programming (OBP)*. When you do composition with objects of known classes, you're still doing object-based programming. Adding inheritance with overriding to customize methods to the unique needs of your applications and possibly process objects polymorphically is called *object-oriented programming (OOP)*. If you do composition with objects of inherited classes, that's also object-oriented programming.

10.9 Duck Typing and Polymorphism

Most other object-oriented programming languages require inheritance-based "is a" relationships to achieve polymorphic behavior. Python is more flexible. It uses a concept called **duck typing**, which the Python documentation describes as:

> *A programming style which does not look at an object's type to determine if it has the right interface; instead, the method or attribute is simply called or used ("If it looks like a duck and quacks like a duck, it must be a duck.").*[7]

So, when processing an object at execution time, its type does not matter. As long as the object has the data attribute, property or method (with the appropriate parameters) you wish to access, the code will work.

Let's reconsider the loop at the end of Section 10.8.3, which processes a list of employees:

```
for employee in employees:
    print(employee)
    print(f'{employee.earnings():,.2f}\n')
```

In Python, this loop works properly as long as `employees` contains only objects that:

- can be displayed with `print` (that is, they have a string representation) and

- have an `earnings` method which can be called with no arguments.

All classes inherit from `object` directly or indirectly, so they *all* inherit the default methods for obtaining string representations that `print` can display. If a class has an `earnings` method that can be called with no arguments, we can include objects of that class in the list `employees`, even if the object's class does not have an "is a" relationship with class `CommissionEmployee`. To demonstrate this, consider class `WellPaidDuck`:

```
In [1]: class WellPaidDuck:
   ...:     def __repr__(self):
   ...:         return 'I am a well-paid duck'
   ...:     def earnings(self):
   ...:         return Decimal('1_000_000.00')
   ...:
```

`WellPaidDuck` objects, which clearly are not meant to be employees, will work with the preceding loop. To prove this, let's create objects of our classes `CommissionEmployee`, `SalariedCommissionEmployee` and `WellPaidDuck` and place them in a list:

```
In [2]: from decimal import Decimal

In [3]: from commissionemployee import CommissionEmployee

In [4]: from salariedcommissionemployee import SalariedCommissionEmployee

In [5]: c = CommissionEmployee('Sue', 'Jones', '333-33-3333',
   ...:                 Decimal('10000.00'), Decimal('0.06'))
   ...:

In [6]: s = SalariedCommissionEmployee('Bob', 'Lewis', '444-44-4444',
   ...:         Decimal('5000.00'), Decimal('0.04'), Decimal('300.00'))
   ...:
```

---

7. https://docs.python.org/3/glossary.html#term-duck-typing.

```
In [7]: d = WellPaidDuck()

In [8]: employees = [c, s, d]
```

Now, let's process the list using the loop from Section 10.8.3. As you can see in the output, Python is able to use duck typing to *polymorphically* process all three objects in the list:

```
In [9]: for employee in employees:
   ...:     print(employee)
   ...:     print(f'{employee.earnings():,.2f}\n')
   ...:
CommissionEmployee: Sue Jones
social security number: 333-33-3333
gross sales: 10000.00
commission rate: 0.06
600.00

SalariedCommissionEmployee: Bob Lewis
social security number: 444-44-4444
gross sales: 5000.00
commission rate: 0.04
base salary: 300.00
500.00

I am a well-paid duck
1,000,000.00
```

10.10 Operator Overloading

You've seen that you can interact with objects by accessing their attributes and properties and by calling their methods. Method-call notation can be cumbersome for certain kinds of operations, such as arithmetic. In these cases, it would be more convenient to use Python's rich set of built-in operators.

This section shows how to use **operator overloading** to define how Python's operators should handle objects of your own types. You've already used operator overloading frequently across wide ranges of types. For example, you've used:

- the + operator for adding numeric values, concatenating lists, concatenating strings and adding a value to every element in a NumPy array.
- the [] operator for accessing elements in lists, tuples, strings and arrays and for accessing the value for a specific key in a dictionary.
- the * operator for multiplying numeric values, repeating a sequence and multiplying every element in a NumPy array by a specific value.

You can overload most operators. For every overloadable operator, class object defines a special method, such as __add__ for the addition (+) operator or __mul__ for the multiplication (*) operator. Overriding these methods enables you to define how a given operator works for objects of your custom class. For a complete list of special methods, see

https://docs.python.org/3/reference/datamodel.html#special-method-names

Operator Overloading Restrictions

There are some restrictions on operator overloading:

- The precedence of an operator cannot be changed by overloading. However, parentheses can be used to force evaluation order in an expression.

- The left-to-right or right-to-left grouping of an operator cannot be changed by overloading.

- The "arity" of an operator—that is, whether it's a unary or binary operator—cannot be changed.

- You cannot create new operators—only existing operators can be overloaded.

- The meaning of how an operator works on objects of built-in types cannot be changed. You cannot, for example, change + so that it subtracts two integers.

- Operator overloading works only with objects of custom classes or with a mixture of an object of a custom class and an object of a built-in type.

Complex Numbers

To demonstrate operator overloading, we'll define a class named `Complex` that represents complex numbers.[8] Complex numbers, like −3 + 4i and 6.2 − 11.73i, have the form

> *realPart* + *imaginaryPart* * i

where i is $\sqrt{-1}$. Like `int`s, `float`s and `Decimal`s, complex numbers are arithmetic types. In this section, we'll create a class `Complex` that overloads just the + addition operator and the += augmented assignment, so we can add `Complex` objects using Python's mathematical notations.

10.10.1 Test-Driving Class `Complex`

First, let's use class `Complex` to demonstrate its capabilities. We'll discuss the class's details in the next section. Import class `Complex` from `complexnumber.py`:

```
In [1]: from complexnumber import Complex
```

Next, create and display a couple of `Complex` objects. Snippets [3] and [5] implicitly call the `Complex` class's __repr__ method to get a string representation of each object:

```
In [2]: x = Complex(real=2, imaginary=4)

In [3]: x
Out[3]: (2 + 4i)

In [4]: y = Complex(real=5, imaginary=-1)

In [5]: y
Out[5]: (5 - 1i)
```

We chose the __repr__ string format shown in snippets [3] and [5] to mimic the __repr__ strings produced by Python's built-in `complex` type.[9]

---

8. Python has built-in support for complex values, so this class is simply for demonstration purposes.

Now, let's use the + operator to add the Complex objects x and y. This expression adds the real parts of the two operands (2 and 5) and the imaginary parts of the two operands (4i and -1i), then returns a new Complex object containing the result:

```
In [6]: x + y
Out[6]: (7 + 3i)
```

The + operator does not modify either of its operands:

```
In [7]: x
Out[7]: (2 + 4i)

In [8]: y
Out[8]: (5 - 1i)
```

Finally, let's use the += operator to add y to x and store the result in x. The += operator *modifies* its left operand but not its right operand:

```
In [9]: x += y

In [10]: x
Out[10]: (7 + 3i)

In [11]: y
Out[11]: (5 - 1i)
```

10.10.2 Class Complex Definition

Now that we've seen class Complex in action, let's look at its definition to see how those capabilities were implemented.

Method __init__

The class's __init__ method receives parameters to initialize the real and imaginary data attributes:

```
1   # complexnumber.py
2   """Complex class with overloaded operators."""
3
4   class Complex:
5       """Complex class that represents a complex number
6       with real and imaginary parts."""
7
8       def __init__(self, real, imaginary):
9           """Initialize Complex class's attributes."""
10          self.real = real
11          self.imaginary = imaginary
12
```

Overloaded + Operator

The following overridden special method __add__ defines how to overload the + operator for use with two Complex objects:

---

9. Python uses j rather than i for $\sqrt{-1}$. For example, 3+4j (with no spaces around the operator) creates a complex object with real and imag attributes. The __repr__ string for this complex value is '(3+4j)'.

```
13        def __add__(self, right):
14            """Overrides the + operator."""
15            return Complex(self.real + right.real,
16                           self.imaginary + right.imaginary)
17
```

Methods that overload binary operators must provide two parameters—the *first* (self) is the *left* operand and the *second* (right) is the *right* operand. Class Complex's __add__ method takes two Complex objects as arguments and returns a new Complex object containing the sum of the operands' real parts and the sum of the operands' imaginary parts.

   We do *not* modify the contents of either of the original operands. This matches our intuitive sense of how this operator should behave. Adding two numbers does not modify either of the original values.

Overloaded += Augmented Assignment

Lines 18–22 overload special method **__iadd__** to define how the += operator adds two Complex objects:

```
18        def __iadd__(self, right):
19            """Overrides the += operator."""
20            self.real += right.real
21            self.imaginary += right.imaginary
22            return self
23
```

Augmented assignments modify their left operands, so method __iadd__ modifies the self object, which represents the left operand, then returns self.

Method __repr__

Lines 24–28 return the string representation of a Complex number.

```
24        def __repr__(self):
25            """Return string representation for repr()."""
26            return (f'({self.real} ' +
27                    ('+' if self.imaginary >= 0 else '-') +
28                    f' {abs(self.imaginary)}i)')
```

10.11 Exception Class Hierarchy and Custom Exceptions

In the previous chapter, we introduced exception handling. Every exception is an object of a class in Python's exception class hierarchy[10] or an object of a class that inherits from one of those classes. Exception classes inherit directly or indirectly from base class Base-Exception and are defined in module **exceptions**.

   Python defines four primary BaseException subclasses—**SystemExit, KeyboardInterrupt, GeneratorExit** and **Exception**:

- SystemExit terminates program execution (or terminates an interactive session) and when uncaught does not produce a traceback like other exception types.

- KeyboardInterrupt exceptions occur when the user types the interrupt command—*Ctrl* + *C* (or *control* + *C*) on most systems.

---

10. https://docs.python.org/3/library/exceptions.html.

- GeneratorExit exceptions occur when a generator closes—normally when a generator finishes producing values or when its close method is called explicitly.

- Exception is the base class for most common exceptions you'll encounter. You've seen exceptions of the Exception subclasses ZeroDivisionError, NameError, ValueError, StatisticsError, TypeError, IndexError, KeyError, RuntimeError and AttributeError. Often, Exceptions can be caught and handled, so the program can continue running.

Catching Base-Class Exceptions

One of the benefits of the exception class hierarchy is that an except handler can catch exceptions of a particular type or can use a base-class type to catch those base-class exceptions and all related subclass exceptions. For example, an except handler that specifies the base class Exception can catch objects of *any* subclass of Exception. Placing an except handler that catches type Exception before other except handlers is a logic error, because all exceptions would be caught before other exception handlers could be reached. Thus, subsequent exception handlers are unreachable.

Custom Exception Classes

When you raise an exception from your code, you should generally use one of the existing exception classes from the Python Standard Library. However, using the inheritance techniques presented earlier in this chapter, you can create your own custom exception classes that derive directly or indirectly from class Exception. Generally, that's discouraged, especially among novice programmers. Before creating custom exception classes, look for an appropriate existing exception class in the Python exception hierarchy. Define new exception classes only if you need to catch and handle the exceptions differently from other existing exception types. That should be rare.

10.12 Named Tuples

You've used tuples to aggregate several data attributes into a single object. The Python Standard Library's **collections module** also provides **named tuples** that enable you to reference a tuple's members by name rather than by index number.

Let's create a simple named tuple that might be used to represent a card in a deck of cards. First, import function namedtuple:

```
In [1]: from collections import namedtuple
```

Function **namedtuple** creates a subclass of the built-in tuple type. The function's first argument is your new type's name and the second is a list of strings representing the identifiers you'll use to reference the new type's members:

```
In [2]: Card = namedtuple('Card', ['face', 'suit'])
```

We now have a new tuple type named Card that we can use anywhere a tuple can be used. Let's create a Card object, access its members by name and display its string representation:

```
In [3]: card = Card(face='Ace', suit='Spades')

In [4]: card.face
Out[4]: 'Ace'
```

```
In [5]: card.suit
Out[5]: 'Spades'

In [6]: card
Out[6]: Card(face='Ace', suit='Spades')
```

Other Named Tuple Features
Each named tuple type has additional methods. The type's **_make class method** (that is, a method called on the *class*) receives an iterable of values and returns an object of the named tuple type:

```
In [7]: values = ['Queen', 'Hearts']

In [8]: card = Card._make(values)

In [9]: card
Out[9]: Card(face='Queen', suit='Hearts')
```

This could be useful, for example, if you have a named tuple type representing records in a CSV file. As you read and tokenize CSV records, you could convert them into named tuple objects.

For a given object of a named tuple type, you can get an **OrderedDict** dictionary representation of the object's member names and values. An OrderedDict remembers the order in which its key–value pairs were inserted in the dictionary:

```
In [10]: card._asdict()
Out[10]: OrderedDict([('face', 'Queen'), ('suit', 'Hearts')])
```

For additional named tuple features see:

> https://docs.python.org/3/library/
>   collections.html#collections.namedtuple

10.13 A Brief Intro to Python 3.7's New Data Classes

Though named tuples allow you to reference their members by name, they're still just tuples, not classes. For some of the benefits of named tuples, plus the capabilities that traditional Python classes provide, you can use Python 3.7's new **data classes**[11] from the Python Standard Library's **dataclasses module**.

Data classes are among Python 3.7's most important new features. They help you build classes *faster* by using more *concise* notation and by *autogenerating* "boilerplate" code that's common in most classes. They could become the preferred way to define many Python classes. In this section, we'll present data-class fundamentals. At the end of the section, we'll provide links to more information.

Data Classes Autogenerate Code
Most classes you'll define provide an __init__ method to create and initialize an object's attributes and a __repr__ method to specify an object's custom string representation. If a class has many data attributes, creating these methods can be tedious.

Data classes *autogenerate* the data attributes and the __init__ and __repr__ methods for you. This can be particularly useful for classes that primarily aggregate related data

---

11. https://www.python.org/dev/peps/pep-0557/.

items. For example, in an application that processes CSV records, you might want a class that represents each record's fields as data attributes in an object. Data classes also can be generated *dynamically* from a list of field names.

Data classes also autogenerate method **__eq__**, which overloads the == operator. Any class that has an __eq__ method also implicitly supports !=. *All* classes inherit class object's default **__ne__** (not equals) method implementation, which returns the opposite of __eq__ (or NotImplemented if the class does not define __eq__). Data classes do *not* automatically generate methods for the <, <=, > and >= comparison operators, but they can.

10.13.1 Creating a Card Data Class

Let's reimplement class Card from Section 10.6.2 as a data class. The new class is defined in carddataclass.py. As you'll see, defining a data class requires some new syntax. In the subsequent subsections, we'll use our new Card data class in class DeckOfCards to show that it's interchangeable with the original Card class, then discuss some of the benefits of data classes over named tuples and traditional Python classes.

Importing from the dataclasses and typing Modules

The Python Standard Library's dataclasses module defines decorators and functions for implementing data classes. We'll use the **@dataclass decorator** (imported at line 4) to specify that a new class is a data class and causes various code to be written for you. Recall that our original Card class defined *class variables* FACES and SUITS, which are lists of the strings used to initialize Cards. We use **ClassVar** and **List** from the Python Standard Library's **typing module** (imported at line 5) to indicate that FACES and SUITS are *class variables* that refer to *lists*. We'll say more about these momentarily:

```
1   # carddataclass.py
2   """Card data class with class attributes, data attributes,
3   autogenerated methods and explicitly defined methods."""
4   from dataclasses import dataclass
5   from typing import ClassVar, List
6
```

Using the @dataclass Decorator

To specify that a class is a *data class*, precede its definition with the @dataclass decorator:[12]

```
7   @dataclass
8   class Card:
```

Optionally, the @dataclass decorator may specify parentheses containing arguments that help the data class determine what autogenerated methods to include. For example, the decorator @dataclass(order=True) would cause the data class to autogenerate overloaded comparison operator methods for <, <=, > and >=. This might be useful, for example, if you need to sort your data-class objects.

Variable Annotations: Class Attributes

Unlike regular classes, data classes declare both class attributes and data attributes *inside* the class, but *outside* the class's methods. In a regular class, only *class attributes* are declared

---

12. https://docs.python.org/3/library/dataclasses.html#module-level-decorators-classes-and-functions.

this way, and data attributes typically are created in __init__. Data classes require additional information, or *hints*, to distinguish class attributes from data attributes, which also affects the autogenerated methods' implementation details.

Lines 9–11 define and initialize the *class attributes* FACES and SUITS:

```
 9    FACES: ClassVar[List[str]] = ['Ace', '2', '3', '4', '5', '6', '7',
10                                  '8', '9', '10', 'Jack', 'Queen', 'King']
11    SUITS: ClassVar[List[str]] = ['Hearts', 'Diamonds', 'Clubs', 'Spades']
12
```

In lines 9 and 11, The notation

```
   : ClassVar[List[str]]
```

is a **variable annotation**[13,14] (sometimes called a *type hint*) specifying that FACES is a class attribute (ClassVar) which refers to a *list* of strings (List[str]). SUITS also is a class attribute which refers to a list of strings.

Class variables are initialized in their definitions and are specific to the *class*, not individual *objects* of the class. Methods __init__, __repr__ and __eq__, however, are for use with *objects* of the class. When a data class generates these methods, it inspects all the variable annotations and includes only the *data attributes* in the method implementations.

Variable Annotations: Data Attributes

Normally, we create an object's data attributes in the class's __init__ method (or methods called by __init__) via assignments of the form self.*attribute_name* = *value*. Because a data class *autogenerates* its __init__ method, we need another way to specify data attributes in a data class's definition. We cannot simply place their names inside the class, which generates a NameError, as in:

```
In [1]: from dataclasses import dataclass

In [2]: @dataclass
   ...: class Demo:
   ...:     x  # attempting to create a data attribute x
   ...:
---------------------------------------------------------------------------
NameError                                 Traceback (most recent call last)
<ipython-input-2-79ffe37b1ba2> in <module>()
----> 1 @dataclass
      2 class Demo:
      3     x  # attempting to create a data attribute x
      4

<ipython-input-2-79ffe37b1ba2> in Demo()
      1 @dataclass
      2 class Demo:
----> 3     x  # attempting to create a data attribute x
      4

NameError: name 'x' is not defined
```

---

13. https://www.python.org/dev/peps/pep-0526/.
14. Variable annotations are a recent language feature and are optional for regular classes. You will not see them in most legacy Python code.

Like class attributes, each data attribute must be declared with a variable annotation. Lines 13–14 define the data attributes `face` and `suit`. The variable annotation ": str" indicates that each should refer to string objects:

```
13      face: str
14      suit: str
```

Defining a Property and Other Methods

Data classes are classes, so they may contain properties and methods and participate in class hierarchies. For this `Card` data class, we defined the same read-only `image_name` property and custom special methods `__str__` and `__format__` as in our original `Card` class earlier in the chapter:

```
15      @property
16      def image_name(self):
17          """Return the Card's image file name."""
18          return str(self).replace(' ', '_') + '.png'
19
20      def __str__(self):
21          """Return string representation for str()."""
22          return f'{self.face} of {self.suit}'
23
24      def __format__(self, format):
25          """Return formatted string representation."""
26          return f'{str(self):{format}}'
```

Variable Annotation Notes

You can specify variable annotations using built-in type names (like `str`, `int` and `float`), class types or types defined by the `typing` module (such as `ClassVar` and `List` shown earlier). Even with type annotations, Python is still a *dynamically typed language*. So, type annotations are *not* enforced at execution time. So, even though a `Card`'s `face` is meant to be a string, you can assign any type of object to `face`.

10.13.2 Using the Card Data Class

Let's demonstrate the new `Card` data class. First, create a `Card`:

```
In [1]: from carddataclass import Card

In [2]: c1 = Card(Card.FACES[0], Card.SUITS[3])
```

Next, let's use `Card`'s autogenerated `__repr__` method to display the `Card`:

```
In [3]: c1
Out[3]: Card(face='Ace', suit='Spades')
```

Our custom `__str__` method, which `print` calls when passing it a `Card` object, returns a string of the form '*face* of *suit*':

```
In [4]: print(c1)
Ace of Spades
```

Let's access our data class's attributes and read-only property:

```
In [5]: c1.face
Out[5]: 'Ace'
```

```
In [6]: c1.suit
Out[6]: 'Spades'

In [7]: c1.image_name
Out[7]: 'Ace_of_Spades.png'
```

Next, let's demonstrate that Card objects can be compared via the *autogenerated* == operator and inherited != operator. First, create two additional Card objects—one identical to the first and one different:

```
In [8]: c2 = Card(Card.FACES[0], Card.SUITS[3])

In [9]: c2
Out[9]: Card(face='Ace', suit='Spades')

In [10]: c3 = Card(Card.FACES[0], Card.SUITS[0])

In [11]: c3
Out[11]: Card(face='Ace', suit='Hearts')
```

Now, compare the objects using == and !=:

```
In [12]: c1 == c2
Out[12]: True

In [13]: c1 == c3
Out[13]: False

In [14]: c1 != c3
Out[14]: True
```

Our Card data class is interchangeable with the Card class developed earlier in this chapter. To demonstrate this, we created the deck2.py file containing a copy of class DeckOfCards from earlier in the chapter and imported the Card data class into the file. The following snippets import class DeckOfCards, create an object of the class and print it. Recall that print implicitly calls the DeckOfCards __str__ method, which formats each Card in a field of 19 characters, resulting in a call to each Card's __format__ method. Read each row left-to-right to confirm that all the Cards are displayed in order from each suit (Hearts, Diamonds, Clubs and Spades):

```
In [15]: from deck2 import DeckOfCards  # uses Card data class

In [16]: deck_of_cards = DeckOfCards()

In [17]: print(deck_of_cards)
Ace of Hearts      2 of Hearts        3 of Hearts        4 of Hearts
5 of Hearts        6 of Hearts        7 of Hearts        8 of Hearts
9 of Hearts        10 of Hearts       Jack of Hearts     Queen of Hearts
King of Hearts     Ace of Diamonds    2 of Diamonds      3 of Diamonds
4 of Diamonds      5 of Diamonds      6 of Diamonds      7 of Diamonds
8 of Diamonds      9 of Diamonds      10 of Diamonds     Jack of Diamonds
Queen of Diamonds  King of Diamonds   Ace of Clubs       2 of Clubs
3 of Clubs         4 of Clubs         5 of Clubs         6 of Clubs
7 of Clubs         8 of Clubs         9 of Clubs         10 of Clubs
Jack of Clubs      Queen of Clubs     King of Clubs      Ace of Spades
2 of Spades        3 of Spades        4 of Spades        5 of Spades
6 of Spades        7 of Spades        8 of Spades        9 of Spades
10 of Spades       Jack of Spades     Queen of Spades    King of Spades
```

10.13.3 Data Class Advantages over Named Tuples

Data classes offer several advantages over named tuples[15]:

- Although each named tuple technically represents a different type, a named tuple *is a* tuple and *all* tuples can be compared to one another. So, objects of *different* named tuple types could compare as equal if they have the same number of members and the same values for those members. Comparing objects of different data classes *always* returns False, as does comparing a data class object to a tuple object.

- If you have code that unpacks a tuple, adding more members to that tuple breaks the unpacking code. Data class objects cannot be unpacked. So you can add more data attributes to a data class without breaking existing code.

- A data class can be a base class or a subclass in an inheritance hierarchy.

10.13.4 Data Class Advantages over Traditional Classes

Data classes also offer various advantages over the traditional Python classes you saw earlier in this chapter:

- A data class autogenerates __init__, __repr__ and __eq__, saving you time.

- A data class can autogenerate the special methods that overload the <, <=, > and >= comparison operators.

- When you change data attributes defined in a data class, then use it in a script or interactive session, the autogenerated code updates automatically. So, you have less code to maintain and debug.

- The required variable annotations for class attributes and data attributes enable you to take advantage of static code analysis tools. So, you might be able to eliminate additional errors before they can occur at execution time.

- Some static code analysis tools and IDEs can inspect variable annotations and issue warnings if your code uses the wrong type. This can help you locate logic errors in your code *before* you execute it.

More Information

Data classes have additional capabilities, such as creating "frozen" instances which do not allow you to assign values to a data class object's attributes after the object is created. For a complete list of data class benefits and capabilities, see

```
https://www.python.org/dev/peps/pep-0557/
```

and

```
https://docs.python.org/3/library/dataclasses.html
```

---

15. https://www.python.org/dev/peps/pep-0526/.

10.14 **Unit Testing with Docstrings and doctest**

A key aspect of software development is testing your code to ensure that it works correctly. Even with extensive testing, however, your code may still contain bugs. According to the famous Dutch computer scientist Edsger Dijkstra, "Testing shows the presence, not the absence of bugs."[16]

Module doctest and the testmod Function
The Python Standard Library provides the **doctest module** to help you test your code and conveniently retest it after you make modifications. When you execute the doctest module's **testmod function**, it inspects your functions', methods' and classes' docstrings looking for sample Python statements preceded by >>>, each followed on the next line by the given statement's expected output (if any).[17] The testmod function then executes those statements and confirms that they produce the expected output. If they do not, testmod reports errors indicating which tests failed so you can locate and fix the problems in your code. Each test you define in a docstring typically tests a specific *unit of code*, such as a function, a method or a class. Such tests are called **unit tests**.

Modified Account Class
The file accountdoctest.py contains the class Account from this chapter's first example. We modified the __init__ method's docstring to include four tests which can be used to ensure that the method works correctly:

- The test in line 11 creates a sample Account object named account1. This statement does not produce any output.

- The test in line 12 shows what the value of account1's name attribute should be if line 11 executed successfully. The sample output is shown in line 13.

- The test in line 14 shows what the value of account1's balance attribute should be if line 11 executed successfully. The sample output is shown in line 15.

- The test in line 18 creates an Account object with an invalid initial balance. The sample output shows that a ValueError exception should occur in this case. For exceptions, the doctest module's documentation recommends showing just the first and last lines of the traceback.[18]

You can intersperse your tests with descriptive text, such as line 17.

```
1  # accountdoctest.py
2  """Account class definition."""
3  from decimal import Decimal
4
5  class Account:
6      """Account class for demonstrating doctest."""
7
```

---

16. J. N. Buxton and B. Randell, eds, *Software Engineering Techniques*, April 1970, p. 16. Report on a conference sponsored by the NATO Science Committee, Rome, Italy, 27–31 October 1969
17. The notation >>> mimics the standard python interpreter's input prompts.
18. https://docs.python.org/3/library/doctest.html?highlight=doctest#module-doctest.

```
 8      def __init__(self, name, balance):
 9          """Initialize an Account object.
10
11          >>> account1 = Account('John Green', Decimal('50.00'))
12          >>> account1.name
13          'John Green'
14          >>> account1.balance
15          Decimal('50.00')
16
17          The balance argument must be greater than or equal to 0.
18          >>> account2 = Account('John Green', Decimal('-50.00'))
19          Traceback (most recent call last):
20              ...
21          ValueError: Initial balance must be >= to 0.00.
22          """
23
24          # if balance is less than 0.00, raise an exception
25          if balance < Decimal('0.00'):
26              raise ValueError('Initial balance must be >= to 0.00.')
27
28          self.name = name
29          self.balance = balance
30
31      def deposit(self, amount):
32          """Deposit money to the account."""
33
34          # if amount is less than 0.00, raise an exception
35          if amount < Decimal('0.00'):
36              raise ValueError('amount must be positive.')
37
38          self.balance += amount
39
40  if __name__ == '__main__':
41      import doctest
42      doctest.testmod(verbose=True)
```

Module __main__

When you load any module, Python assigns a string containing the module's name to a global attribute of the module called __name__. When you execute a Python source file (such as accountdoctest.py) as a *script*, Python uses the string '__main__' as the module's name. You can use __name__ in an if statement like lines 40–42 to specify code that should execute only if the source file is executed as a *script*. In this example, line 41 imports the doctest module and line 42 calls the module's testmod function to execute the docstring unit tests.

Running Tests

Run the file accountdoctest.py as a script to execute the tests. By default, if you call testmod with no arguments, it does not show test results for *successful* tests. In that case, if you get no output, all the tests executed successfully. In this example, line 42 calls testmod with the keyword argument verbose=True. This tells testmod to produce verbose output showing *every* test's results:

```
Trying:
    account1 = Account('John Green', Decimal('50.00'))
Expecting nothing
ok
Trying:
    account1.name
Expecting:
    'John Green'
ok
Trying:
    account1.balance
Expecting:
    Decimal('50.00')
ok
Trying:
    account2 = Account('John Green', Decimal('-50.00'))
Expecting:
    Traceback (most recent call last):
        ...
    ValueError: Initial balance must be >= to 0.00.
ok
3 items had no tests:
    __main__
    __main__.Account
    __main__.Account.deposit
1 items passed all tests:
    4 tests in __main__.Account.__init__
4 tests in 4 items.
4 passed and 0 failed.
Test passed.
```

In verbose mode, testmod shows for each test what it's "Trying" to do and what it's "Expecting" as a result, followed by "ok" if the test is successful. After completing the tests in verbose mode, testmod shows a summary of the results.

To demonstrate a *failed* test, "comment out" lines 25–26 in accountdoctest.py by preceding each with a #, then run accountdoctest.py as a script. To save space, we show just the portions of the doctest output indicating the failed test:

```
...
*********************************************************************
File "accountdoctest.py", line 18, in __main__.Account.__init__
Failed example:
    account2 = Account('John Green', Decimal('-50.00'))
Expected:
    Traceback (most recent call last):
        ...
    ValueError: Initial balance must be >= to 0.00.
Got nothing
*********************************************************************
1 items had failures:
    1 of   4 in __main__.Account.__init__
4 tests in 4 items.
3 passed and 1 failed.
***Test Failed*** 1 failures.
```

In this case, we see that line 18's test failed. The `testmod` function was *expecting* a traceback indicating that a `ValueError` was raised due to the invalid initial balance. That exception did *not* occur, so the test failed. As the programmer responsible for defining this class, this failing test would be an indication that something is wrong with the validation code in your `__init__` method.

IPython %doctest_mode Magic

A convenient way to create doctests for existing code is to use an IPython interactive session to test your code, then copy and paste that session into a docstring. IPython's In [] and Out[] prompts are not compatible with doctest, so IPython provides the magic **%doctest_mode** to display prompts in the correct doctest format. The magic toggles between the two prompt styles. The first time you execute %doctest_mode, IPython switches to >>> prompts for input and no output prompts. The second time you execute %doctest_mode, IPython switches back to In [] and Out[] prompts.

10.15 Namespaces and Scopes

In the "Functions" chapter, we showed that each identifier has a scope that determines where you can use it in your program, and we introduced the local and global scopes. Here we continue our discussion of scopes with an introduction to namespaces.

Scopes are determined by **namespaces**, which associate identifiers with objects and are implemented "under the hood" as dictionaries. All namespaces are independent of one another. So, the same identifier may appear in multiple namespaces. There are three primary namespaces—local, global and built-in.

Local Namespace

Each function and method has a **local namespace** that associates local identifiers (such as, parameters and local variables) with objects. The local namespace exists from the moment the function or method is called until it terminates and is accessible *only* to that function or method. In a function's or method's suite, *assigning* to a variable that does not exist creates a local variable and adds it to the local namespace. Identifiers in the local namespace are *in scope* from the point at which you define them until the function or method terminates.

Global Namespace

Each module has a **global namespace** that associates a module's global identifiers (such as global variables, function names and class names) with objects. Python creates a module's global namespace when it loads the module. A module's global namespace exists and its identifiers are *in scope* to the code within that module until the program (or interactive session) terminates. An IPython session has its own global namespace for all the identifiers you create in that session.

Each module's global namespace also has an identifier called **__name__** containing the module's name, such as 'math' for the math module or 'random' for the random module. As you saw in the previous section's doctest example, __name__ contains '__main__' for a .py file that you run as a script.

Built-In Namespace

The **built-in namespace** associates identifiers for Python's built-in functions (such as, input and range) and types (such as, int, float and str) with objects that define those functions and types. Python creates the built-in namespace when the interpreter starts executing. The built-in namespace's identifiers remain *in scope* for all code until the program (or interactive session) terminates.[19]

Finding Identifiers in Namespaces

When you use an identifier, Python searches for that identifier in the currently accessible namespaces, proceeding from *local* to *global* to *built-in*. To help you understand the namespace search order, consider the following IPython session:

```
In [1]: z = 'global z'

In [2]: def print_variables():
   ...:     y = 'local y in print_variables'
   ...:     print(y)
   ...:     print(z)
   ...:

In [3]: print_variables()
local y in print_variables
global z
```

The identifiers you define in an IPython session are placed in the session's *global* namespace. When snippet [3] calls print_variables, Python searches the *local*, *global* and *built-in* namespaces as follows:

- Snippet [3] is not in a function or method, so the session's *global* namespace and the *built-in* namespace are currently accessible. Python first searches the session's *global* namespace, which contains print_variables. So print_variables is *in scope* and Python uses the corresponding object to call print_variables.

- As print_variables begins executing, Python creates the function's *local* namespace. When function print_variables defines the local variable y, Python adds y to the function's *local* namespace. The variable y is now *in scope* until the function finishes executing.

- Next, print_variables calls the *built-in* function print, passing y as the argument. To execute this call, Python must resolve the identifiers y and print. The identifier y is defined in the *local* namespace, so it's *in scope* and Python will use the corresponding object (the string 'local y in print_variables') as print's argument. To call the function, Python must find print's corresponding object. First, it looks in the *local* namespace, which does *not* define print. Next, it looks in the session's *global* namespace, which does *not* define print. Finally, it looks in the *built-in* namespace, which *does* define print. So, print is *in scope* and Python uses the corresponding object to call print.

- Next, print_variables calls the *built-in* function print again with the argument z, which is *not* defined in the *local* namespace. So, Python looks in the

---

19. This assumes you do not shadow the built-in functions or types by redefining their identifiers in a local or global namespace. We discussed shadowing in the "Functions" chapter.

global namespace. The argument z *is* defined in the *global* namespace, so z is *in scope* and Python will use the corresponding object (the string 'global z') as print's argument. Again, Python finds the identifier print in the *built-in* namespace and uses the corresponding object to call print.

- At this point, we reach the end of the print_variables function's suite, so the function terminates and its *local* namespace no longer exists, meaning the local variable y is now undefined.

To prove that y is undefined, let's try to display y:

```
In [4]: y
--------------------------------------------------------------------------
NameError                                 Traceback (most recent call last)
<ipython-input-4-9063a9f0e032> in <module>()
----> 1 y

NameError: name 'y' is not defined
```

In this case, there's no *local* namespace, so Python searches for y in the session's *global* namespace. The identifier y is *not* defined there, so Python searches for y in the *built-in* namespace. Again, Python does not find y. There are no more namespaces to search, so Python raises a NameError, indicating that y is not defined.

The identifiers print_variables and z still exist in the session's *global* namespace, so we can continue using them. For example, let's evaluate z to see its value:

```
In [5]: z
Out[5]: 'global z'
```

Nested Functions

One namespace we did not cover in the preceding discussion is the **enclosing namespace**. Python allows you to define **nested functions** inside other functions or methods. For example, if a function or method performs the same task several times, you might define a nested function to avoid repeating code in the enclosing function. When you access an identifier inside a nested function, Python searches the nested function's *local* namespace first, then the *enclosing* function's namespace, then the *global* namespace and finally the *built-in* namespace. This is sometimes referred to as the **LEGB (local, enclosing, global, built-in) rule**.

Class Namespace

A class has a namespace in which its class attributes are stored. When you access a class attribute, Python looks for that attribute first in the class's namespace, then in the base class's namespace, and so on, until either it finds the attribute or it reaches class object. If the attribute is not found, a NameError occurs.

Object Namespace

Each object has its own namespace containing the object's methods and data attributes. The class's __init__ method starts with an empty object (self) and adds each attribute to the object's namespace. Once you define an attribute in an object's namespace, clients using the object may access the attribute's value.

10.16 Intro to Data Science: Time Series and Simple Linear Regression

We've looked at sequences, such as lists, tuples and arrays. In this section, we'll discuss **time series**, which are sequences of values (called **observations**) associated with points in time. Some examples are daily closing stock prices, hourly temperature readings, the changing positions of a plane in flight, annual crop yields and quarterly company profits. Perhaps the ultimate time series is the stream of time-stamped tweets coming from Twitter users worldwide. In the "Data Mining Twitter" chapter, we'll study Twitter data in depth.

In this section, we'll use a technique called simple linear regression to make predictions from time series data. We'll use the 1895 through 2018 January average high temperatures in New York City to predict future average January high temperatures and to estimate the average January high temperatures for years preceding 1895.

In the "Machine Learning" chapter, we'll revisit this example using the scikit-learn library. In the "Deep Learning" chapter, we'll use *recurrent neural networks (RNNs)* to analyze time series.

In later chapters, we'll see that time series are popular in financial applications and with the Internet of Things (IoT), which we'll discuss in the "Big Data: Hadoop, Spark, NoSQL and IoT" chapter.

In this section, we'll display graphs with Seaborn and pandas, which both use Matplotlib, so launch IPython with Matplotlib support:

```
ipython --matplotlib
```

Time Series

The data we'll use is a time series in which the observations are *ordered* by year. **Univariate time series** have *one* observation per time, such as the average of the January high temperatures in New York City for a particular year. **Multivariate time series** have *two or more* observations per time, such as temperature, humidity and barometric pressure readings in a weather application. Here, we'll analyze a univariate time series.

Two tasks often performed with time series are:

- **Time series analysis,** which looks at existing time series data for patterns, helping data analysts understand the data. A common analysis task is to look for **seasonality** in the data. For example, in New York City, the monthly average high temperature varies significantly based on the seasons (winter, spring, summer or fall).

- **Time series forecasting,** which uses past data to predict the future.

We'll perform time series forecasting in this section.

Simple Linear Regression

Using a technique called **simple linear regression,** we'll make predictions by finding a linear relationship between the months (January of each year) and New York City's average January high temperatures. Given a collection of values representing an **independent variable** (the month/year combination) and a **dependent variable** (the average high temperature for that month/year), simple linear regression describes the relationship between these variables with a straight line, known as the **regression line.**

Linear Relationships

To understand the general concept of a linear relationship, consider Fahrenheit and Celsius temperatures. Given a Fahrenheit temperature, we can calculate the corresponding Celsius temperature using the following formula:

```
c = 5 / 9 * (f - 32)
```

In this formula, f (the Fahrenheit temperature) is the *independent variable*, and c (the Celsius temperature) is the *dependent variable*—each value of c *depends on* the value of f used in the calculation.

Plotting Fahrenheit temperatures and their corresponding Celsius temperatures produces a straight line. To show this, let's first create a lambda for the preceding formula and use it to calculate the Celsius equivalents of the Fahrenheit temperatures 0–100 in 10-degree increments. We store each Fahrenheit/Celsius pair as a tuple in temps:

```
In [1]: c = lambda f: 5 / 9 * (f - 32)

In [2]: temps = [(f, c(f)) for f in range(0, 101, 10)]
```

Next, let's place the data in a DataFrame, then use its **plot method** to display the linear relationship between the Fahrenheit and Celsius temperatures. The plot method's style keyword argument controls the data's appearance. The period in the string '.-' indicates that each point should appear as a dot, and the dash indicates that lines should connect the dots. We manually set the *y*-axis label to 'Celsius' because the plot method shows 'Celsius' only in the graph's upper-left corner legend, by default.

```
In [3]: import pandas as pd

In [4]: temps_df = pd.DataFrame(temps, columns=['Fahrenheit', 'Celsius'])

In [5]: axes = temps_df.plot(x='Fahrenheit', y='Celsius', style='.-')

In [6]: y_label = axes.set_ylabel('Celsius')
```

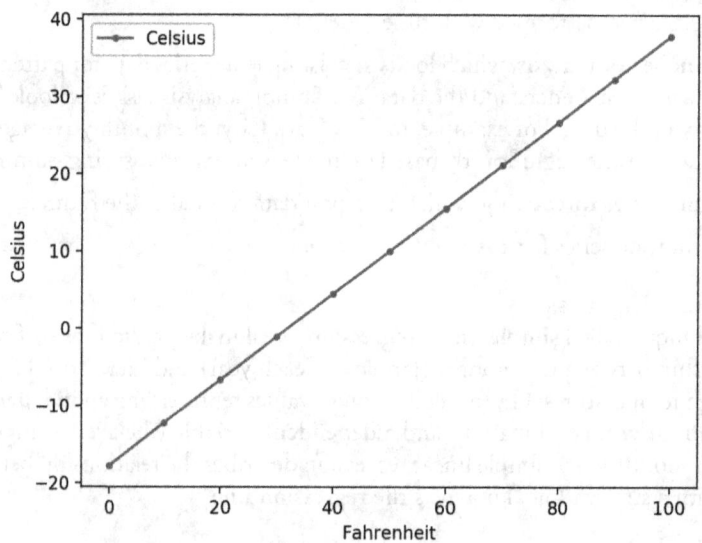

Components of the Simple Linear Regression Equation
The points along any straight line (in two dimensions) like those shown in the preceding graph can be calculated with the equation:

$$y = mx + b$$

where

- m is the line's **slope**,
- b is the line's **intercept** with the y-axis (at $x = 0$),
- x is the independent variable (the date in this example), and
- y is the dependent variable (the temperature in this example).

In simple linear regression, y is the *predicted value* for a given x.

Function `linregress` from the SciPy's `stats` Module
Simple linear regression determines the slope (m) and intercept (b) of a straight line that best fits your data. Consider the following diagram, which shows a few of the time-series data points we'll process in this section and a corresponding regression line. We added vertical lines to indicate each data point's distance from the regression line:

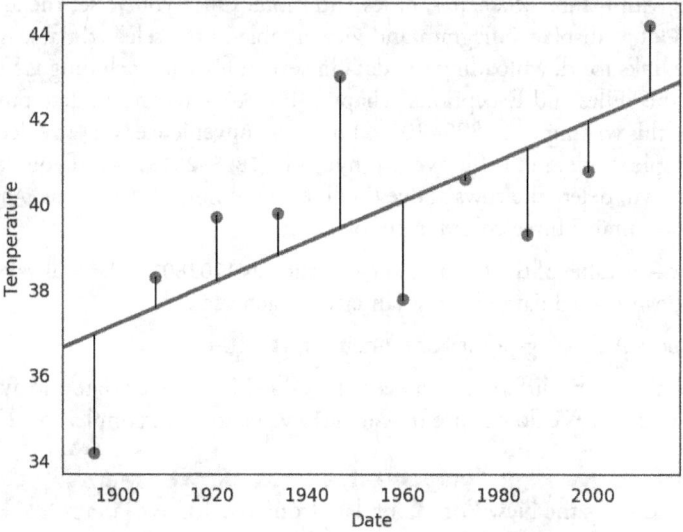

The simple linear regression algorithm iteratively adjusts the slope and intercept and, for each adjustment, calculates the square of each point's distance from the line. The "best fit" occurs when the slope and intercept values minimize the sum of those squared distances. This is known as an **ordinary least squares** calculation.[20]

The **SciPy (Scientific Python) library** is widely used for engineering, science and math in Python. This library's `linregress` function (from the `scipy.stats` module) performs simple linear regression for you. After calling `linregress`, you'll plug the resulting slope and intercept into the $y = mx + b$ equation to make predictions.

---

20. https://en.wikipedia.org/wiki/Ordinary_least_squares.

Pandas

In the three previous Intro to Data Science sections, you used pandas to work with data. You'll continue using pandas throughout the rest of the book. In this example, we'll load the data for New York City's 1895–2018 average January high temperatures from a CSV file into a DataFrame. We'll then format the data for use in this example.

Seaborn Visualization

We'll use Seaborn to plot the DataFrame's data with a regression line that shows the average high-temperature trend over the period 1895–2018.

Getting Weather Data from NOAA

Let's get the data for our study. The National Oceanic and Atmospheric Administration (NOAA)[21] offers lots of public historical data including time series for average high temperatures in specific cities over various time intervals.

We obtained the January average high temperatures for New York City from 1895 through 2018 from NOAA's "Climate at a Glance" time series at:

> https://www.ncdc.noaa.gov/cag/

On that web page, you can select temperature, precipitation and other data for the entire U.S., regions within the U.S., states, cities and more. Once you've set the area and time frame, click **Plot** to display a diagram and view a table of the selected data. At the top of that table are links for downloading the data in several formats including CSV, which we discussed in the "Files and Exceptions" chapter. NOAA's maximum date range available at the time of this writing was 1895–2018. For your convenience, we provided the data in the ch10 examples folder in the file ave_hi_nyc_jan_1895-2018.csv. If you download the data on your own, delete the rows above the line containing "Date,Value,Anomaly".

This data contains three columns per observation:

- Date—A value of the form 'YYYYMM' (such as '201801'). MM is always 01 because we downloaded data for only January of each year.

- Value—A floating-point Fahrenheit temperature.

- Anomaly—The difference between the value for the given date and average values for all dates. We do not use the Anomaly value in this example, so we'll ignore it.

Loading the Average High Temperatures into a DataFrame

Let's load and display the New York City data from ave_hi_nyc_jan_1895-2018.csv:

```
In [7]: nyc = pd.read_csv('ave_hi_nyc_jan_1895-2018.csv')
```

We can look at the DataFrame's head and tail to get a sense of the data:

```
In [8]: nyc.head()
Out[8]:
     Date  Value  Anomaly
0  189501   34.2     -3.2
1  189601   34.7     -2.7
2  189701   35.5     -1.9
3  189801   39.6      2.2
4  189901   36.4     -1.0
```

---

21. http://www.noaa.gov.

```
In [9]: nyc.tail()
Out[9]:
         Date  Value  Anomaly
119    201401   35.5     -1.9
120    201501   36.1     -1.3
121    201601   40.8      3.4
122    201701   42.8      5.4
123    201801   38.7      1.3
```

Cleaning the Data

We'll soon use Seaborn to graph the Date-Value pairs and a regression line. When plotting data from a DataFrame, Seaborn labels a graph's axes using the DataFrame's column names. For readability, let's rename the 'Value' column as 'Temperature':

```
In [10]: nyc.columns = ['Date', 'Temperature', 'Anomaly']

In [11]: nyc.head(3)
Out[11]:
     Date  Temperature  Anomaly
0  189501         34.2     -3.2
1  189601         34.7     -2.7
2  189701         35.5     -1.9
```

Seaborn labels the tick marks on the x-axis with Date values. Since this example processes only January temperatures, the x-axis labels will be more readable if they do not contain 01 (for January), we'll remove it from each Date. First, let's check the column's type:

```
In [12]: nyc.Date.dtype
Out[12]: dtype('int64')
```

The values are integers, so we can divide by 100 to truncate the last two digits. Recall that each column in a DataFrame is a Series. Calling Series method floordiv performs *integer division* on every element of the Series:

```
In [13]: nyc.Date = nyc.Date.floordiv(100)

In [14]: nyc.head(3)
Out[14]:
   Date  Temperature  Anomaly
0  1895         34.2     -3.2
1  1896         34.7     -2.7
2  1897         35.5     -1.9
```

Calculating Basic Descriptive Statistics for the Dataset

For some quick statistics on the dataset's temperatures, call describe on the Temperature column. We can see that there are 124 observations, the mean value of the observations is 37.60, and the lowest and highest observations are 26.10 and 47.60 degrees, respectively:

```
In [15]: pd.set_option('precision', 2)

In [16]: nyc.Temperature.describe()
Out[16]:
count    124.00
mean      37.60
std        4.54
```

```
min        26.10
25%        34.58
50%        37.60
75%        40.60
max        47.60
Name: Temperature, dtype: float64
```

Forecasting Future January Average High Temperatures

The **SciPy (Scientific Python) library** is widely used for engineering, science and math in
Python. Its **stats module** provides function **linregress**, which calculates a regression
line's *slope* and *intercept* for a given set of data points:

```
In [17]: from scipy import stats

In [18]: linear_regression = stats.linregress(x=nyc.Date,
    ...:                                       y=nyc.Temperature)
    ...:
```

Function linregress receives two one-dimensional arrays[22] of the same length representing the data points' *x*- and *y*-coordinates. The keyword arguments x and y represent the
independent and dependent variables, respectively. The object returned by linregress
contains the regression line's slope and intercept:

```
In [19]: linear_regression.slope
Out[19]: 0.00014771361132966167

In [20]: linear_regression.intercept
Out[20]: 8.694845520062952
```

We can use these values with the simple linear regression equation for a straight line,
$y = mx + b$, to predict the average January temperature in New York City for a given year.
Let's predict the average Fahrenheit temperature for January of 2019. In the following calculation, linear_regression.slope is *m*, 2019 is *x* (the date value for which you'd like to
predict the temperature), and linear_regression.intercept is *b*:

```
In [21]: linear_regression.slope * 2019 + linear_regression.intercept
Out[21]: 38.51837136113298
```

We also can approximate what the average temperature might have been in the years
before 1895. For example, let's approximate the average temperature for January of 1890:

```
In [22]: linear_regression.slope * 1890 + linear_regression.intercept
Out[22]: 36.612865774980335
```

For this example, we had data for 1895–2018. You should expect that the further you go
outside this range, the less reliable the predictions will be.

Plotting the Average High Temperatures and a Regression Line

Next, let's use Seaborn's **regplot function** to plot each data point with the dates on the
x-axis and the temperatures on the *y*-axis. The regplot function creates the following **scatter plot** or **scattergram** in which the scattered dots represent the Temperatures for the
given Dates, and the straight line displayed through the points is the regression line:

---

22. These arguments also can be one-dimensional array-like objects, such as lists or pandas Series.

First, close the prior Matplotlib window if you have not done so already—otherwise, `regplot` will use the existing window that already contains a graph. Function `regplot`'s x and y keyword arguments are one-dimensional arrays[23] of the same length representing the *x-y* coordinate pairs to plot. Recall that pandas automatically creates attributes for each column name if the name can be a valid Python identifier:[24]

```
In [23]: import seaborn as sns

In [24]: sns.set_style('whitegrid')

In [25]: axes = sns.regplot(x=nyc.Date, y=nyc.Temperature)
```

The regression line's slope (lower at the left and higher at the right) indicates a warming trend over the last 124 years. In this graph, the *y*-axis represents a 21.5-degree temperature range between the minimum of 26.1 and the maximum of 47.6, so the data appears to be spread significantly above and below the regression line, making it difficult to see the linear relationship. This is a common issue in data analytics visualizations. When you have axes that reflect different kinds of data (dates and temperatures in this case), how do you reasonably determine their respective scales? In the preceding graph, this is purely an issue of the graph's height—Seaborn and Matplotlib *auto-scale* the axes, based on the data's range of values. We can scale the *y*-axis range of values to emphasize the linear relationship. Here, we scaled the *y*-axis from a 21.5-degree range to a 60-degree range (from 10 to 70 degrees):

```
In [26]: axes.set_ylim(10, 70)
Out[26]: (10, 70)
```

---

23. These arguments also can be one-dimensional array-like objects, such as lists or pandas `Series`.
24. For readers with more statistics background, the shaded area surrounding the regression line is the 95% *confidence interval* for the regression line (`https://en.wikipedia.org/wiki/Simple_lin-ear_regression#Confidence_intervals`). To draw the diagram without a confidence interval, add the keyword argument `ci=None` to the `regplot` function's argument list.

Getting Time Series Datasets

Here are some popular sites where you can find time series to use in your studies:

Time-series dataset sources
`https://data.gov/` This is the U.S. government's open data portal. Searching for "time series" yields over 7200 time-series datasets.
`https://www.ncdc.noaa.gov/cag/` The National Oceanic and Atmospheric Administration (NOAA) Climate at a Glance portal provides both global and U.S. weather-related time series.
`https://www.esrl.noaa.gov/psd/data/timeseries/` NOAA's Earth System Research Laboratory (ESRL) portal provides monthly and seasonal climate-related time series.
`https://www.quandl.com/search` Quandl provides hundreds of free financial-related time series, as well as fee-based time series.
`https://datamarket.com/data/list/?q=provider:tsdl` The Time Series Data Library (TSDL) provides links to hundreds of time series datasets across many industries.
`http://archive.ics.uci.edu/ml/datasets.html` The University of California Irvine (UCI) Machine Learning Repository contains dozens of time-series datasets for a variety of topics.
`http://inforumweb.umd.edu/econdata/econdata.html` The University of Maryland's EconData service provides links to thousands of economic time series from various U.S. government agencies.

10.17 Wrap-Up

In this chapter, we discussed the details of crafting valuable classes. You saw how to define a class, create objects of the class, access an object's attributes and call its methods. You defined the special method __init__ to create and initialize a new object's data attributes.

We discussed controlling access to attributes and using properties. We showed that all object attributes may be accessed directly by a client. We discussed identifiers with single leading underscores (_), which indicate attributes that are not meant to be accessed by client code. We showed how to implement "private" attributes via the double-leading-underscore (__) naming convention, which tells Python to mangle an attribute's name.

We implemented a card shuffling and dealing simulation consisting of a Card class and a DeckOfCards class that maintained a list of Cards, and displayed the deck both as strings and as card images using Matplotlib. We introduced special methods __repr__, __str__ and __format__ for creating string representations of objects.

Next, we looked at Python's capabilities for creating base classes and subclasses. We showed how to create a subclass that inherits many of its capabilities from its superclass, then adds more capabilities, possibly by overriding the base class's methods. We created a list containing both base class and subclass objects to demonstrate Python's polymorphic programming capabilities.

We introduced operator overloading for defining how Python's built-in operators work with objects of custom class types. You saw that overloaded operator methods are implemented by overriding various special methods that all classes inherit from class object. We discussed the Python exception class hierarchy and creating custom exception classes.

We showed how to create a named tuple that enables you to access tuple elements via attribute names rather than index numbers. Next, we introduced Python 3.7's new data classes, which can autogenerate various boilerplate code commonly provided in class definitions, such as the __init__, __repr__ and __eq__ special methods.

You saw how to write unit tests for your code in docstrings, then execute those tests conveniently via the doctest module's testmod function. Finally, we discussed the various namespaces that Python uses to determine the scopes of identifiers.

In the next part of the book, we present a series of implementation case studies that use a mix of AI and big-data technologies. We explore natural language processing, data mining Twitter, IBM Watson and cognitive computing, supervised and unsupervised machine learning, and deep learning with convolutional neural networks and recurrent neural networks. We discuss big-data software and hardware infrastructure, including NoSQL databases, Hadoop and Spark with a major emphasis on performance. You're about to see some really cool stuff!

Natural Language Processing (NLP)

Objectives

In this chapter you'll:

- Perform natural language processing (NLP) tasks, which are fundamental to many of the forthcoming data science case study chapters.
- Run lots of NLP demos.
- Use the TextBlob, NLTK, Textatistic and spaCy NLP libraries and their pretrained models to perform various NLP tasks.
- Tokenize text into words and sentences.
- Use parts-of-speech tagging.
- Use sentiment analysis to determine whether text is positive, negative or neutral.
- Detect the language of text and translate between languages using TextBlob's Google Translate support.
- Get word roots via stemming and lemmatization.
- Use TextBlob's spell checking and correction capabilities.
- Get word definitions, synonyms and antonyms.
- Remove stop words from text.
- Create word clouds.
- Determine text readability with Textatistic.
- Use the spaCy library for named entity recognition and similarity detection.

11.1 **Introduction**

Your alarm wakes you, and you hit the "Alarm Off" button. You reach for your smart-phone and read your text messages and check the latest news clips. You listen to TV hosts interviewing celebrities. You speak to family, friends and colleagues and listen to their responses. You have a hearing-impaired friend with whom you communicate via sign language and who enjoys close-captioned video programs. You have a blind colleague who reads braille, listens to books being read by a computerized book reader and listens to a screen reader speak about what's on his computer screen. You read emails, distinguishing junk from important communications and send email. You read novels or works of non-fiction. You drive, observing road signs like "Stop," "Speed Limit 35" and "Road Under Construction." You give your car verbal commands, like "call home," "play classical music" or ask questions like, "Where's the nearest gas station?" You teach a child how to speak and read. You send a sympathy card to a friend. You read books. You read newspapers and magazines. You take notes during a class or meeting. You learn a foreign language to prepare for travel abroad. You receive a client email in Spanish and run it through a free translation program. You respond in English knowing that your client can easily translate your email back to Spanish. You are uncertain about the language of an email, but language detection software instantly figures that out for you and translates the email to English.

These are examples of **natural language** communications in text, voice, video, sign language, braille and other forms with languages like English, Spanish, French, Russian, Chinese, Japanese and hundreds more. In this chapter, you'll master many natural language processing (NLP) capabilities through a series of hands-on demos and IPython sessions. You'll use many of these NLP capabilities in the upcoming data science case study chapters.

Natural language processing is performed on text collections, composed of Tweets, Facebook posts, conversations, movie reviews, Shakespeare's plays, historic documents, news items, meeting logs, and so much more. A text collection is known as a **corpus**, the plural of which is **corpora**.

Natural language lacks mathematical precision. Nuances of meaning make natural language understanding difficult. A text's meaning can be influenced by its context and the reader's "world view." Search engines, for example, can get to "know you" through your prior searches. The upside is better search results. The downside could be invasion of privacy.

11.2 TextBlob[1]

TextBlob is an object-oriented NLP text-processing library that is built on the **NLTK** and **pattern** NLP libraries and simplifies many of their capabilities. Some of the NLP tasks TextBlob can perform include:

- **Tokenization**—splitting text into pieces called **tokens**, which are meaningful units, such as words and numbers.

- **Parts-of-speech (POS) tagging**—identifying each word's part of speech, such as noun, verb, adjective, etc.

- **Noun phrase extraction**—locating groups of words that represent nouns, such as "red brick factory."[2]

- **Sentiment analysis**—determining whether text has positive, neutral or negative sentiment.

- **Inter-language translation** and **language detection** powered by Google Translate.

- **Inflection**[3]—pluralizing and singularizing words. There are other aspects of inflection that are not part of TextBlob.

- **Spell checking** and **spelling correction**.

- **Stemming**—reducing words to their stems by removing prefixes or suffixes. For example, the stem of "varieties" is "varieti."

- **Lemmatization**—like stemming, but produces real words based on the original words' context. For example, the lemmatized form of "varieties" is "variety."

- **Word frequencies**—determining how often each word appears in a corpus.

- **WordNet integration** for finding word definitions, synonyms and antonyms.

- **Stop word elimination**—removing common words, such as a, an, the, I, we, you and more to analyze the important words in a corpus.

- **n-grams**—producing sets of consecutive words in a corpus for use in identifying words that frequently appear adjacent to one another.

---

1. `https://textblob.readthedocs.io/en/latest/`.
2. The phrase "red brick factory" illustrates why natural language is such a difficult subject. Is a "red brick factory" a factory that makes red bricks? Is it a red factory that makes bricks of any color? Is it a factory built of red bricks that makes products of any type? In today's music world, it could even be the name of a rock band or the name of a game on your smartphone.
3. `https://en.wikipedia.org/wiki/Inflection`.

Many of these capabilities are used as part of more complex NLP tasks. In this section, we'll perform these NLP tasks using TextBlob and NLTK.

Installing the TextBlob Module

To install TextBlob, open your Anaconda Prompt (Windows), Terminal (macOS/Linux) or shell (Linux), then execute the following command:

```
conda install -c conda-forge textblob
```

Windows users might need to run the Anaconda Prompt as an Administrator for proper software installation privileges. To do so, right-click Anaconda Prompt in the start menu and select **More > Run as administrator.**

Once installation completes, execute the following command to download the NLTK corpora used by TextBlob:

```
ipython -m textblob.download_corpora
```

These include:

- The Brown Corpus (created at Brown University[4]) for parts-of-speech tagging.
- Punkt for English sentence tokenization.
- WordNet for word definitions, synonyms and antonyms.
- Averaged Perceptron Tagger for parts-of-speech tagging.
- conll2000 for breaking text into components, like nouns, verbs, noun phrases and more—known as **chunking** the text. The name conll2000 is from the conference that created the chunking data—Conference on Computational Natural Language Learning.
- Movie Reviews for sentiment analysis.

Project Gutenberg

A great source of text for analysis is the free e-books at Project Gutenberg:

```
https://www.gutenberg.org
```

The site contains over 57,000 e-books in various formats, including plain text files. These are out of copyright in the United States. For information about Project Gutenberg's Terms of Use and copyright in other countries, see:

```
https://www.gutenberg.org/wiki/Gutenberg:Terms_of_Use
```

In some of this section's examples, we use the plain-text e-book file for Shakespeare's *Romeo and Juliet*, which you can find at:

```
https://www.gutenberg.org/ebooks/1513
```

Project Gutenberg does not allow programmatic access to its e-books. You're required to copy the books for that purpose.[5] To download *Romeo and Juliet* as a plain-text e-book, right click the **Plain Text UTF-8** link on the book's web page, then select **Save Link As...** (Chrome/FireFox), **Download Linked File As...** (Safari) or **Save target as** (Microsoft Edge) option to save the book to your system. Save it as RomeoAndJuliet.txt in the ch11 exam-

---

4. https://en.wikipedia.org/wiki/Brown_Corpus.
5. https://www.gutenberg.org/wiki/Gutenberg:Information_About_Robot_Access_to_our_Pages.

ples folder to ensure that our code examples will work correctly. For analysis purposes, we removed the Project Gutenberg text before "THE TRAGEDY OF ROMEO AND JULIET", as well as the Project Guttenberg information at the end of the file starting with:

```
End of the Project Gutenberg EBook of Romeo and Juliet,
by William Shakespeare
```

11.2.1 Create a TextBlob

TextBlob[6] is the fundamental class for NLP with the **textblob module**. Let's create a TextBlob containing two sentences:

```
In [1]: from textblob import TextBlob

In [2]: text = 'Today is a beautiful day. Tomorrow looks like bad weather.'

In [3]: blob = TextBlob(text)

In [4]: blob
Out[4]: TextBlob("Today is a beautiful day. Tomorrow looks like bad
weather.")
```

TextBlobs—and, as you'll see shortly, Sentences and Words—support string methods and can be compared with strings. They also provide methods for various NLP tasks. Sentences, Words and TextBlobs inherit from **BaseBlob**, so they have many common methods and properties.

11.2.2 Tokenizing Text into Sentences and Words

Natural language processing often requires tokenizing text before performing other NLP tasks. TextBlob provides convenient properties for accessing the sentences and words in TextBlobs. Let's use the **sentence property** to get a list of **Sentence** objects:

```
In [5]: blob.sentences
Out[5]:
[Sentence("Today is a beautiful day."),
 Sentence("Tomorrow looks like bad weather.")]
```

The **words property** returns a **WordList** object containing a list of **Word** objects, representing each word in the TextBlob with the punctuation removed:

```
In [6]: blob.words
Out[6]: WordList(['Today', 'is', 'a', 'beautiful', 'day', 'Tomorrow',
'looks', 'like', 'bad', 'weather'])
```

11.2.3 Parts-of-Speech Tagging

Parts-of-speech (POS) tagging is the process of evaluating words based on their context to determine each word's part of speech. There are eight primary English parts of speech—nouns, pronouns, verbs, adjectives, adverbs, prepositions, conjunctions and interjections (words that express emotion and that are typically followed by punctuation, like "Yes!" or "Ha!"). Within each category there are many subcategories.

---

6. `http://textblob.readthedocs.io/en/latest/api_reference.html#textblob.blob.TextBlob`.

Some words have multiple meanings. For example, the words "set" and "run" have hundreds of meanings each! If you look at the dictionary.com definitions of the word "run," you'll see that it can be a verb, a noun, an adjective or a part of a verb phrase. An important use of POS tagging is determining a word's meaning among its possibly many meanings. This is important for helping computers "understand" natural language.

The **tags property** returns a list of tuples, each containing a word and a string representing its part-of-speech tag:

```
In [7]: blob
Out[7]: TextBlob("Today is a beautiful day. Tomorrow looks like bad
weather.")

In [8]: blob.tags
Out[8]:
[('Today', 'NN'),
 ('is', 'VBZ'),
 ('a', 'DT'),
 ('beautiful', 'JJ'),
 ('day', 'NN'),
 ('Tomorrow', 'NNP'),
 ('looks', 'VBZ'),
 ('like', 'IN'),
 ('bad', 'JJ'),
 ('weather', 'NN')]
```

By default, TextBlob uses a PatternTagger to determine parts-of-speech. This class uses the parts-of-speech tagging capabilities of the *pattern library*:

> https://www.clips.uantwerpen.be/pattern

You can view the library's 63 parts-of-speech tags at

> https://www.clips.uantwerpen.be/pages/MBSP-tags

In the preceding snippet's output:

- Today, day and weather are tagged as NN—a singular noun or mass noun.
- is and looks are tagged as VBZ—a third person singular present verb.
- a is tagged as DT—a determiner.[7]
- beautiful and bad are tagged as JJ—an adjective.
- Tomorrow is tagged as NNP—a proper singular noun.
- like is tagged as IN—a subordinating conjunction or preposition.

11.2.4 Extracting Noun Phrases

Let's say you're preparing to purchase a water ski so you're researching them online. You might search for "best water ski." In this case, "water ski" is a noun phrase. If the search engine does not parse the noun phrase properly, you probably will not get the best search results. Go online and try searching for "best water," "best ski" and "best water ski" and see what you get.

---

7. https://en.wikipedia.org/wiki/Determiner.

A TextBlob's **noun_phrases property** returns a WordList object containing a list of Word objects—one for each noun phrase in the text:

```
In [9]: blob
Out[9]: TextBlob("Today is a beautiful day. Tomorrow looks like bad
weather.")

In [10]: blob.noun_phrases
Out[10]: WordList(['beautiful day', 'tomorrow', 'bad weather'])
```

Note that a Word representing a noun phrase can contain multiple words. A WordList is an extension of Python's built-in list type. WordLists provide additional methods for stemming, lemmatizing, singularizing and pluralizing.

11.2.5 Sentiment Analysis with TextBlob's Default Sentiment Analyzer

One of the most common and valuable NLP tasks is **sentiment analysis**, which determines whether text is positive, neutral or negative. For instance, companies might use this to determine whether people are speaking positively or negatively online about their products. Consider the positive word "good" and the negative word "bad." Just because a sentence contains "good" or "bad" does not mean the sentence's sentiment necessarily is positive or negative. For example, the sentence

> The food is not good.

clearly has negative sentiment. Similarly, the sentence

> The movie was not bad.

clearly has positive sentiment, though perhaps not as positive as something like

> The movie was excellent!

Sentiment analysis is a complex machine-learning problem. However, libraries like TextBlob have pretrained machine learning models for performing sentiment analysis.

Getting the Sentiment of a TextBlob

A TextBlob's **sentiment property** returns a **Sentiment** object indicating whether the text is positive or negative and whether it's objective or subjective:

```
In [11]: blob
Out[11]: TextBlob("Today is a beautiful day. Tomorrow looks like bad
weather.")

In [12]: blob.sentiment
Out[12]: Sentiment(polarity=0.07500000000000007,
subjectivity=0.8333333333333333)
```

In the preceding output, the polarity indicates sentiment with a value from -1.0 (negative) to 1.0 (positive) with 0.0 being neutral. The subjectivity is a value from 0.0 (objective) to 1.0 (subjective). Based on the values for our TextBlob, the overall sentiment is close to neutral, and the text is mostly subjective.

Getting the polarity and subjectivity from the Sentiment Object

The values displayed above probably provide more precision that you need in most cases. This can detract from numeric output's readability. The IPython magic **%precision** allows you to specify the default precision for *standalone* float objects and float objects in *built-in types* like lists, dictionaries and tuples. Let's use the magic to *round* the polarity and subjectivity values to three digits to the right of the decimal point:

```
In [13]: %precision 3
Out[13]: '%.3f'

In [14]: blob.sentiment.polarity
Out[14]: 0.075

In [15]: blob.sentiment.subjectivity
Out[15]: 0.833
```

Getting the Sentiment of a Sentence
You also can get the sentiment at the individual sentence level. Let's use the sentence property to get a list of **Sentence**[8] objects, then iterate through them and display each Sentence's sentiment property:

```
In [16]: for sentence in blob.sentences:
    ...:     print(sentence.sentiment)
    ...:
Sentiment(polarity=0.85, subjectivity=1.0)
Sentiment(polarity=-0.6999999999999998, subjectivity=0.6666666666666666)
```

This might explain why the entire TextBlob's sentiment is close to 0.0 (neutral)—one sentence is positive (0.85) and the other negative (-0.6999999999999998).

11.2.6 Sentiment Analysis with the NaiveBayesAnalyzer

By default, a TextBlob and the Sentences and Words you get from it determine sentiment using a PatternAnalyzer, which uses the same sentiment analysis techniques as in the Pattern library. The TextBlob library also comes with a **NaiveBayesAnalyzer**[9] (module **textblob.sentiments**), which was trained on a database of movie reviews. Naive Bayes[10] is a commonly used machine learning text-classification algorithm. The following uses the analyzer keyword argument to specify a TextBlob's sentiment analyzer. Recall from earlier in this ongoing IPython session that text contains 'Today is a beautiful day. Tomorrow looks like bad weather.':

```
In [17]: from textblob.sentiments import NaiveBayesAnalyzer

In [18]: blob = TextBlob(text, analyzer=NaiveBayesAnalyzer())

In [19]: blob
Out[19]: TextBlob("Today is a beautiful day. Tomorrow looks like bad
weather.")
```

Let's use the TextBlob's sentiment property to display the text's sentiment using the NaiveBayesAnalyzer:

```
In [20]: blob.sentiment
Out[20]: Sentiment(classification='neg', p_pos=0.47662917962091056,
p_neg=0.5233708203790892)
```

8. http://textblob.readthedocs.io/en/latest/api_reference.html#textblob.blob.Sentence.
9. https://textblob.readthedocs.io/en/latest/api_reference.html#module-textblob.en.sentiments.
10. https://en.wikipedia.org/wiki/Naive_Bayes_classifier.

In this case, the overall sentiment is classified as negative (classification='neg'). The Sentiment object's p_pos indicates that the TextBlob is 47.66% positive, and its p_neg indicates that the TextBlob is 52.34% negative. Since the overall sentiment is just slightly more negative we'd probably view this TextBlob's sentiment as neutral overall.

Now, let's get the sentiment of each Sentence:

```
In [21]: for sentence in blob.sentences:
    ...:     print(sentence.sentiment)
    ...:
Sentiment(classification='pos', p_pos=0.8117563121751951,
p_neg=0.18824368782480477)
Sentiment(classification='neg', p_pos=0.174363226578349,
p_neg=0.8256367734216521)
```

Notice that rather than polarity and subjectivity, the Sentiment objects we get from the NaiveBayesAnalyzer contain a *classification*—'pos' (positive) or 'neg' (negative)— and p_pos (percentage positive) and p_neg (percentage negative) values from 0.0 to 1.0. Once again, we see that the first sentence is positive and the second is negative.

11.2.7 Language Detection and Translation

Inter-language translation is a challenging problem in natural language processing and artificial intelligence. With advances in machine learning, artificial intelligence and natural language processing, services like Google Translate (100+ languages) and Microsoft Bing Translator (60+ languages) can translate between languages instantly.

Inter-language translation also is great for people traveling to foreign countries. They can use translation apps to translate menus, road signs and more. There are even efforts at live speech translation so that you'll be able to converse in real time with people who do not know your natural language.[11,12] Some smartphones, can now work together with in-ear headphones to provide near-live translation of many languages.[13,14,15] In the "IBM Watson and Cognitive Computing" chapter, we develop a script that does near real-time inter-language translation among languages supported by Watson.

The TextBlob library uses Google Translate to detect a text's language and translate TextBlobs, Sentences and Words into other languages.[16] Let's use **detect_language method** to detect the language of the text we're manipulating ('en' is English):

```
In [22]: blob
Out[22]: TextBlob("Today is a beautiful day. Tomorrow looks like bad
weather.")

In [23]: blob.detect_language()
Out[23]: 'en'
```

---

11. https://www.skype.com/en/features/skype-translator/.
12. https://www.microsoft.com/en-us/translator/business/live/.
13. https://www.telegraph.co.uk/technology/2017/10/04/googles-new-headphones-can-translate-foreign-languages-real/.
14. https://store.google.com/us/product/google_pixel_buds?hl=en-US.
15. http://www.chicagotribune.com/bluesky/originals/ct-bsi-google-pixel-buds-review-20171115-story.html.
16. These features require an Internet connection.

Next, let's use the **translate method** to translate the text to Spanish (`'es'`) then detect the language on the result. The to keyword argument specifies the target language.

```
In [24]: spanish = blob.translate(to='es')

In [25]: spanish
Out[25]: TextBlob("Hoy es un hermoso dia. Mañana parece mal tiempo.")

In [26]: spanish.detect_language()
Out[26]: 'es'
```

Next, let's translate our TextBlob to simplified Chinese (specified as `'zh'` or `'zh-CN'`) then detect the language on the result:

```
In [27]: chinese = blob.translate(to='zh')

In [28]: chinese
Out[28]: TextBlob("今天是美好的一天。明天看起来像恶劣的天气。")

In [29]: chinese.detect_language()
Out[29]: 'zh-CN'
```

Method detect_language's output always shows simplified Chinese as `'zh-CN'`, even though the translate function can receive simplified Chinese as `'zh'` or `'zh-CN'`.

In each of the preceding cases, Google Translate automatically detects the source language. You can specify a source language explicitly by passing the from_lang keyword argument to the translate method, as in

```
chinese = blob.translate(from_lang='en', to='zh')
```

Google Translate uses iso-639-1[17] language codes listed at

```
https://en.wikipedia.org/wiki/List_of_ISO_639-1_codes
```

For the supported languages, you'd use these codes as the values of the from_lang and to keyword arguments. Google Translate's list of supported languages is at:

```
https://cloud.google.com/translate/docs/languages
```

Calling translate without arguments translates from the detected source language to English:

```
In [30]: spanish.translate()
Out[30]: TextBlob("Today is a beautiful day. Tomorrow seems like bad
weather.")

In [31]: chinese.translate()
Out[31]: TextBlob("Today is a beautiful day. Tomorrow looks like bad
weather.")
```

Note the slight difference in the English results.

11.2.8 Inflection: Pluralization and Singularization

Inflections are different forms of the same words, such as singular and plural (like "person" and "people") and different verb tenses (like "run" and "ran"). When you're calculating word frequencies, you might first want to convert all inflected words to the same form for

---

17. ISO is the International Organization for Standardization (`https://www.iso.org/`).

more accurate word frequencies. Words and WordLists each support converting words to their singular or plural forms. Let's pluralize and singularize a couple of Word objects:

```
In [1]: from textblob import Word

In [2]: index = Word('index')

In [3]: index.pluralize()
Out[3]: 'indices'

In [4]: cacti = Word('cacti')

In [5]: cacti.singularize()
Out[5]: 'cactus'
```

Pluralizing and singularizing are sophisticated tasks which, as you can see above, are not as simple as adding or removing an "s" or "es" at the end of a word.

You can do the same with a WordList:

```
In [6]: from textblob import TextBlob

In [7]: animals = TextBlob('dog cat fish bird').words

In [8]: animals.pluralize()
Out[8]: WordList(['dogs', 'cats', 'fish', 'birds'])
```

Note that the word "fish" is the same in both its singular and plural forms.

11.2.9 Spell Checking and Correction

For natural language processing tasks, it's important that the text be free of spelling errors. Software packages for writing and editing text, like Microsoft Word, Google Docs and others automatically check your spelling as you type and typically display a red line under misspelled words. Other tools enable you to manually invoke a spelling checker.

You can check a Word's spelling with its **spellcheck method**, which returns a list of tuples containing possible correct spellings and a confidence value. Let's assume we meant to type the word "they" but we misspelled it as "theyr." The spell checking results show two possible corrections with the word 'they' having the highest confidence value:

```
In [1]: from textblob import Word

In [2]: word = Word('theyr')

In [3]: %precision 2
Out[3]: '%.2f'

In [4]: word.spellcheck()
Out[4]: [('they', 0.57), ('their', 0.43)]
```

Note that the word with the highest confidence value might *not* be the correct word for the given context.

TextBlobs, Sentences and Words all have a **correct method** that you can call to correct spelling. Calling correct on a Word returns the correctly spelled word that has the highest confidence value (as returned by spellcheck):

```
In [5]: word.correct()  # chooses word with the highest confidence value
Out[5]: 'they'
```

Calling correct on a TextBlob or Sentence checks the spelling of each word. For each incorrect word, correct replaces it with the correctly spelled one that has the highest confidence value:

```
In [6]: from textblob import Word

In [7]: sentence = TextBlob('Ths sentense has missplled wrds.')

In [8]: sentence.correct()
Out[8]: TextBlob("The sentence has misspelled words.")
```

11.2.10 Normalization: Stemming and Lemmatization

Stemming removes a prefix or suffix from a word leaving only a stem, which may or may not be a real word. **Lemmatization** is similar, but factors in the word's part of speech and meaning and results in a real word.

Stemming and lemmatization are **normalization** operations, in which you prepare words for analysis. For example, before calculating statistics on words in a body of text, you might convert all words to lowercase so that capitalized and lowercase words are not treated differently. Sometimes, you might want to use a word's root to represent the word's many forms. For example, in a given application, you might want to treat all of the following words as "program": program, programs, programmer, programming and programmed (and perhaps U.K. English spellings, like programmes as well).

Words and WordLists each support stemming and lemmatization via the methods **stem** and **lemmatize**. Let's use both on a Word:

```
In [1]: from textblob import Word

In [2]: word = Word('varieties')

In [3]: word.stem()
Out[3]: 'varieti'

In [4]: word.lemmatize()
Out[4]: 'variety'
```

11.2.11 Word Frequencies

Various techniques for detecting similarity between documents rely on word frequencies. As you'll see here, TextBlob automatically counts word frequencies. First, let's load the e-book for Shakespeare's *Romeo and Juliet* into a TextBlob. To do so, we'll use the **Path class** from the Python Standard Library's **pathlib module**:

```
In [1]: from pathlib import Path

In [2]: from textblob import TextBlob

In [3]: blob = TextBlob(Path('RomeoAndJuliet.txt').read_text())
```

Use the file RomeoAndJuliet.txt[18] that you downloaded earlier. We assume here that you started your IPython session from that folder. When you read a file with Path's **read_text method**, it closes the file immediately after it finishes reading the file.

---

18. Each Project Gutenberg e-book includes additional text, such as their licensing information, that's not part of the e-book itself. For this example, we used a text editor to remove that text from our copy of the e-book.

You can access the word frequencies through the TextBlob's **word_counts dictionary**. Let's get the counts of several words in the play:

```
In [4]: blob.word_counts['juliet']
Out[4]: 190

In [5]: blob.word_counts['romeo']
Out[5]: 315

In [6]: blob.word_counts['thou']
Out[6]: 278
```

If you already have tokenized a TextBlob into a WordList, you can count specific words in the list via the **count method**:

```
In [7]: blob.words.count('joy')
Out[7]: 14

In [8]: blob.noun_phrases.count('lady capulet')
Out[8]: 46
```

11.2.12 Getting Definitions, Synonyms and Antonyms from WordNet

WordNet[19] is a word database created by Princeton University. The TextBlob library uses the NLTK library's WordNet interface, enabling you to look up word definitions, and get synonyms and antonyms. For more information, check out the NLTK WordNet interface documentation at:

```
https://www.nltk.org/api/nltk.corpus.reader.html#module-
    nltk.corpus.reader.wordnet
```

Getting Definitions

First, let's create a Word:

```
In [1]: from textblob import Word

In [2]: happy = Word('happy')
```

The Word class's **definitions property** returns a list of all the word's definitions in the WordNet database:

```
In [3]: happy.definitions
Out[3]:
['enjoying or showing or marked by joy or pleasure',
 'marked by good fortune',
 'eagerly disposed to act or to be of service',
 'well expressed and to the point']
```

The database does not necessarily contain every dictionary definition of a given word. There's also a **define** method that enables you to pass a part of speech as an argument so you can get definitions matching only that part of speech.

Getting Synonyms

You can get a Word's **synsets**—that is, its sets of synonyms—via the **synsets property**. The result is a list of Synset objects:

---

19. https://wordnet.princeton.edu/.

```
In [4]: happy.synsets
Out[4]:
[Synset('happy.a.01'),
 Synset('felicitous.s.02'),
 Synset('glad.s.02'),
 Synset('happy.s.04')]
```

Each Synset represents a group of synonyms. In the notation happy.a.01:

- happy is the original Word's lemmatized form (in this case, it's the same).

- a is the part of speech, which can be a for adjective, n for noun, v for verb, r for adverb or s for adjective satellite. Many adjective synsets in WordNet have satellite synsets that represent similar adjectives.

- 01 is a 0-based index number. Many words have multiple meanings, and this is the index number of the corresponding meaning in the WordNet database.

There's also a **get_synsets method** that enables you to pass a part of speech as an argument so you can get Synsets matching only that part of speech.

You can iterate through the synsets list to find the original word's synonyms. Each Synset has a **lemmas method** that returns a list of Lemma objects representing the synonyms. A Lemma's name method returns the synonymous word as a string. In the following code, for each Synset in the synsets list, the nested for loop iterates through that Synset's Lemmas (if any). Then we add the synonym to the set named synonyms. We used a set collection because it automatically eliminates any duplicates we add to it:

```
In [5]: synonyms = set()

In [6]: for synset in happy.synsets:
   ...:     for lemma in synset.lemmas():
   ...:         synonyms.add(lemma.name())
   ...:

In [7]: synonyms
Out[7]: {'felicitous', 'glad', 'happy', 'well-chosen'}
```

Getting Antonyms

If the word represented by a Lemma has antonyms in the WordNet database, invoking the Lemma's antonyms method returns a list of Lemmas representing the antonyms (or an empty list if there are no antonyms in the database). In snippet [4] you saw there were four Synsets for 'happy'. First, let's get the Lemmas for the Synset at index 0 of the synsets list:

```
In [8]: lemmas = happy.synsets[0].lemmas()

In [9]: lemmas
Out[9]: [Lemma('happy.a.01.happy')]
```

In this case, lemmas returned a list of one Lemma element. We can now check whether the database has any corresponding antonyms for that Lemma:

```
In [10]: lemmas[0].antonyms()
Out[10]: [Lemma('unhappy.a.01.unhappy')]
```

The result is list of Lemmas representing the antonym(s). Here, we see that the one antonym for 'happy' in the database is 'unhappy'.

11.2.13 Deleting Stop Words

Stop words are common words in text that are often removed from text before analyzing it because they typically do not provide useful information. The following table shows NLTK's list of English stop words, which is returned by the NLTK `stopwords` module's words function[20] (which we'll use momentarily):

NLTK's English stop words list
['a', 'about', 'above', 'after', 'again', 'against', 'ain', 'all', 'am', 'an', 'and', 'any', 'are', 'aren', "aren't", 'as', 'at', 'be', 'because', 'been', 'before', 'being', 'below', 'between', 'both', 'but', 'by', 'can', 'couldn', "couldn't", 'd', 'did', 'didn', "didn't", 'do', 'does', 'doesn', "doesn't", 'doing', 'don', "don't", 'down', 'during', 'each', 'few', 'for', 'from', 'further', 'had', 'hadn', "hadn't", 'has', 'hasn', "hasn't", 'have', 'haven', "haven't", 'having', 'he', 'her', 'here', 'hers', 'herself', 'him', 'himself', 'his', 'how', 'i', 'if', 'in', 'into', 'is', 'isn', "isn't", 'it', "it's", 'its', 'itself', 'just', 'll', 'm', 'ma', 'me', 'mightn', "mightn't", 'more', 'most', 'mustn', "mustn't", 'my', 'myself', 'needn', "needn't", 'no', 'nor', 'not', 'now', 'o', 'of', 'off', 'on', 'once', 'only', 'or', 'other', 'our', 'ours', 'ourselves', 'out', 'over', 'own', 're', 's', 'same', 'shan', "shan't", 'she', "she's", 'should', "should've", 'shouldn', "shouldn't", 'so', 'some', 'such', 't', 'than', 'that', "that'll", 'the', 'their', 'theirs', 'them', 'themselves', 'then', 'there', 'these', 'they', 'this', 'those', 'through', 'to', 'too', 'under', 'until', 'up', 've', 'very', 'was', 'wasn', "wasn't", 'we', 'were', 'weren', "weren't", 'what', 'when', 'where', 'which', 'while', 'who', 'whom', 'why', 'will', 'with', 'won', "won't", 'wouldn', "wouldn't", 'y', 'you', "you'd", "you'll", "you're", "you've", 'your', 'yours', 'yourself', 'yourselves']

The NLTK library has lists of stop words for several other natural languages as well. Before using NLTK's stop-words lists, you must download them, which you do with the `nltk` module's **download function:**

```
In [1]: import nltk

In [2]: nltk.download('stopwords')
[nltk_data] Downloading package stopwords to
[nltk_data]     C:\Users\PaulDeitel\AppData\Roaming\nltk_data...
[nltk_data]   Unzipping corpora\stopwords.zip.
Out[2]: True
```

For this example, we'll load the `'english'` stop words list. First import `stopwords` from the `nltk.corpus` module, then use `stopwords` method words to load the `'english'` stop words list:

```
In [3]: from nltk.corpus import stopwords

In [4]: stops = stopwords.words('english')
```

Next, let's create a `TextBlob` from which we'll remove stop words:

```
In [5]: from textblob import TextBlob

In [6]: blob = TextBlob('Today is a beautiful day.')
```

---

20. https://www.nltk.org/book/ch02.html.

Finally, to remove the stop words, let's use the `TextBlob`'s words in a list comprehension that adds each word to the resulting list only if the word is not in `stops`:

```
In [7]: [word for word in blob.words if word not in stops]
Out[7]: ['Today', 'beautiful', 'day']
```

11.2.14 n-grams

An **n-gram**[21] is a sequence of *n* text items, such as letters in words or words in a sentence. In natural language processing, *n*-grams can be used to identify letters or words that frequently appear adjacent to one another. For text-based user input, this can help predict the next letter or word a user will type—such as when completing items in IPython with tab-completion or when entering a message to a friend in your favorite smartphone messaging app. For speech-to-text, *n*-grams might be used to improve the quality of the transcription. N-grams are a form of **co-occurrence** in which words or letters appear near each other in a body of text.

`TextBlob`'s **ngrams method** produces a list of `WordList` *n*-grams of length three by default—known as *trigrams*. You can pass the keyword argument n to produce *n*-grams of any desired length. The output shows that the first trigram contains the first three words in the sentence (`'Today'`, `'is'` and `'a'`). Then, `ngrams` creates a trigram starting with the second word (`'is'`, `'a'` and `'beautiful'`) and so on until it creates a trigram containing the last three words in the `TextBlob`:

```
In [1]: from textblob import TextBlob

In [2]: text = 'Today is a beautiful day. Tomorrow looks like bad weather.'

In [3]: blob = TextBlob(text)

In [4]: blob.ngrams()
Out[4]:
[WordList(['Today', 'is', 'a']),
 WordList(['is', 'a', 'beautiful']),
 WordList(['a', 'beautiful', 'day']),
 WordList(['beautiful', 'day', 'Tomorrow']),
 WordList(['day', 'Tomorrow', 'looks']),
 WordList(['Tomorrow', 'looks', 'like']),
 WordList(['looks', 'like', 'bad']),
 WordList(['like', 'bad', 'weather'])]
```

The following produces *n*-grams consisting of five words:

```
In [5]: blob.ngrams(n=5)
Out[5]:
[WordList(['Today', 'is', 'a', 'beautiful', 'day']),
 WordList(['is', 'a', 'beautiful', 'day', 'Tomorrow']),
 WordList(['a', 'beautiful', 'day', 'Tomorrow', 'looks']),
 WordList(['beautiful', 'day', 'Tomorrow', 'looks', 'like']),
 WordList(['day', 'Tomorrow', 'looks', 'like', 'bad']),
 WordList(['Tomorrow', 'looks', 'like', 'bad', 'weather'])]
```

---

21. https://en.wikipedia.org/wiki/N-gram.

11.3 Visualizing Word Frequencies with Bar Charts and Word Clouds

Earlier, we obtained frequencies for a few words in *Romeo and Juliet*. Sometimes frequency visualizations enhance your corpus analyses. There's often more than one way to visualize data, and sometimes one is superior to others. For example, you might be interested in word frequencies relative to one another, or you may just be interested in relative uses of words in a corpus. In this section, we'll look at two ways to visualize word frequencies:

- A bar chart that *quantitatively* visualizes the top 20 words in *Romeo and Juliet* as bars representing each word and its frequency.

- A **word cloud** that *qualitatively* visualizes more frequently occurring words in bigger fonts and less frequently occurring words in smaller fonts.

11.3.1 Visualizing Word Frequencies with Pandas

Let's visualize *Romeo and Juliet*'s top 20 words that are *not* stop words. To do this, we'll use features from TextBlob, NLTK and pandas. Pandas visualization capabilities are based on Matplotlib, so launch IPython with the following command for this session:

```
ipython --matplotlib
```

Loading the Data
First, let's load *Romeo and Juliet*. Launch IPython from the ch11 examples folder before executing the following code so you can access the e-book file RomeoAndJuliet.txt that you downloaded earlier in the chapter:

```
In [1]: from pathlib import Path

In [2]: from textblob import TextBlob

In [3]: blob = TextBlob(Path('RomeoAndJuliet.txt').read_text())
```

Next, load the NLTK stopwords:

```
In [4]: from nltk.corpus import stopwords

In [5]: stop_words = stopwords.words('english')
```

Getting the Word Frequencies
To visualize the top 20 words, we need each word and its frequency. Let's call the blob.word_counts dictionary's items method to get a list of word-frequency tuples:

```
In [6]: items = blob.word_counts.items()
```

Eliminating the Stop Words
Next, let's use a list comprehension to eliminate any tuples containing stop words:

```
In [7]: items = [item for item in items if item[0] not in stop_words]
```

The expression item[0] gets the word from each tuple so we can check whether it's in stop_words.

Sorting the Words by Frequency
To determine the top 20 words, let's sort the tuples in items in descending order by frequency. We can use built-in function sorted with a key argument to sort the tuples by

the frequency element in each tuple. To specify the tuple element to sort by, use the **itemgetter** function from the Python Standard Library's **operator** module:

```
In [8]: from operator import itemgetter
```

```
In [9]: sorted_items = sorted(items, key=itemgetter(1), reverse=True)
```

As sorted orders items' elements, it accesses the element at index 1 in each tuple via the expression itemgetter(1). The reverse=True keyword argument indicates that the tuples should be sorted in *descending* order.

Getting the Top 20 Words

Next, we use a slice to get the top 20 words from sorted_items. When TextBlob tokenizes a corpus, it splits all contractions at their apostrophes and counts the total number of apostrophes as one of the "words." *Romeo and Juliet* has many contractions. If you display sorted_items[0], you'll see that they are the most frequently occurring "word" with 867 of them.[22] We want to display only words, so we ignore element 0 and get a slice containing elements 1 through 20 of sorted_items:

```
In [10]: top20 = sorted_items[1:21]
```

Convert top20 to a DataFrame

Next, let's convert the top20 list of tuples to a pandas DataFrame so we can visualize it conveniently:

```
In [11]: import pandas as pd
```

```
In [12]: df = pd.DataFrame(top20, columns=['word', 'count'])
```

```
In [13]: df
Out[13]:
         word  count
0       romeo    315
1        thou    278
2      juliet    190
3         thy    170
4     capulet    163
5       nurse    149
6        love    148
7        thee    138
8        lady    117
9       shall    110
10      friar    105
11       come     94
12    mercutio     88
13    lawrence     82
14       good     80
15    benvolio     79
16     tybalt     79
17      enter     75
18         go     75
19      night     73
```

---

22. In some locales this does not happen and element 0 is indeed 'romeo'.

Visualizing the `DataFrame`

To visualize the data, we'll use the **bar method** of the `DataFrame`'s **plot property**. The arguments indicate which column's data should be displayed along the *x*- and *y*-axes, and that we do not want to display a legend on the graph:

```
In [14]: axes = df.plot.bar(x='word', y='count', legend=False)
```

The bar method creates and displays a Matplotlib bar chart.

When you look at the initial bar chart that appears, you'll notice that some of the words are truncated. To fix that, use Matplotlib's `gcf` (get current figure) function to get the Matplotlib figure that pandas displayed, then call the figure's `tight_layout` method. This compresses the bar chart to ensure all its components fit:

```
In [15]: import matplotlib.pyplot as plt
```

```
In [16]: plt.gcf().tight_layout()
```

The final graph is shown below:

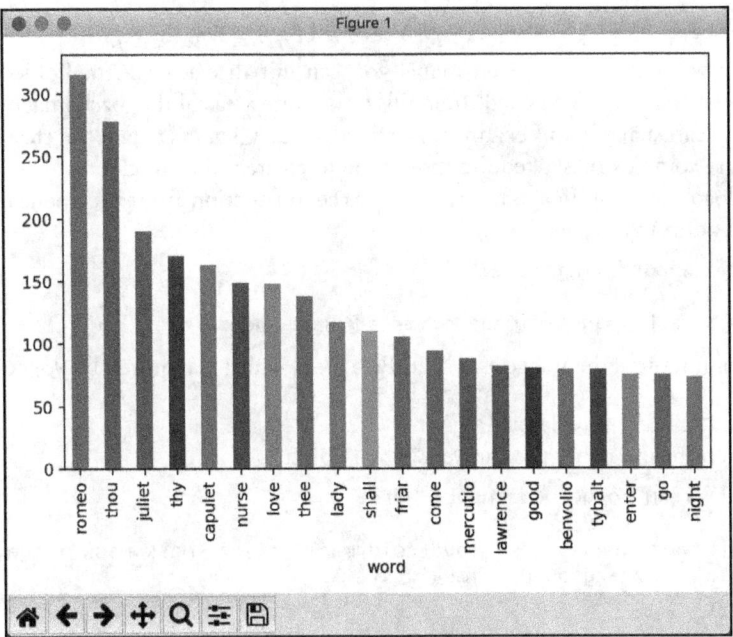

11.3.2 Visualizing Word Frequencies with Word Clouds

Next, we'll build a word cloud that visualizes the top 200 words in *Romeo and Juliet*. You can use the open source **wordcloud module's**[23] **WordCloud class** to generate word clouds with just a few lines of code. By default, `wordcloud` creates rectangular word clouds, but as you'll see the library can create word clouds with arbitrary shapes.

---

23. `https://github.com/amueller/word_cloud`.

Installing the `wordcloud` Module

To install `wordcloud`, open your Anaconda Prompt (Windows), Terminal (macOS/Linux) or shell (Linux) and enter the command:

```
conda install -c conda-forge wordcloud
```

Windows users might need to run the Anaconda Prompt as an Administrator for proper software installation privileges. To do so, right-click Anaconda Prompt in the start menu and select **More > Run as administrator**.

Loading the Text

First, let's load *Romeo and Juliet*. Launch IPython from the `ch11` examples folder before executing the following code so you can access the e-book file `RomeoAndJuliet.txt` you downloaded earlier:

```
In [1]: from pathlib import Path

In [2]: text = Path('RomeoAndJuliet.txt').read_text()
```

Loading the Mask Image that Specifies the Word Cloud's Shape

To create a word cloud of a given shape, you can initialize a `WordCloud` object with an image known as a *mask*. The `WordCloud` fills non-white areas of the mask image with text. We'll use a heart shape in this example, provided as `mask_heart.png` in the `ch11` examples folder. More complex masks require more time to create the word cloud.

Let's load the mask image by using the **imread function** from the `imageio` module that comes with Anaconda:

```
In [3]: import imageio

In [4]: mask_image = imageio.imread('mask_heart.png')
```

This function returns the image as a NumPy `array`, which is required by `WordCloud`.

Configuring the WordCloud Object

Next, let's create and configure the `WordCloud` object:

```
In [5]: from wordcloud import WordCloud

In [6]: wordcloud = WordCloud(colormap='prism', mask=mask_image,
   ...:     background_color='white')
   ...:
```

The default `WordCloud` width and height in pixels is 400x200, unless you specify `width` and `height` keyword arguments or a mask image. For a mask image, the `WordCloud` size is the image's size. `WordCloud` uses Matplotlib under the hood. `WordCloud` assigns random colors from a color map. You can supply the `colormap` keyword argument and use one of Matplotlib's named color maps. For a list of color map names and their colors, see:

```
https://matplotlib.org/examples/color/colormaps_reference.html
```

The mask keyword argument specifies the `mask_image` we loaded previously. By default, the word is drawn on a black background, but we customized this with the `background_-color` keyword argument by specifying a `'white'` background. For a complete list of `WordCloud`'s keyword arguments, see

```
http://amueller.github.io/word_cloud/generated/
    wordcloud.WordCloud.html
```

Generating the Word Cloud
WordCloud's **generate method** receives the text to use in the word cloud as an argument and creates the word cloud, which it returns as a WordCloud object:

```
In [7]: wordcloud = wordcloud.generate(text)
```

Before creating the word cloud, generate first removes stop words from the text argument using the wordcloud module's built-in stop-words list. Then generate calculates the word frequencies for the remaining words. The method uses a maximum of 200 words in the word cloud by default, but you can customize this with the max_words keyword argument.

Saving the Word Cloud as an Image File
Finally, we use WordCloud's **to_file method** to save the word cloud image into the specified file:

```
In [8]: wordcloud = wordcloud.to_file('RomeoAndJulietHeart.png')
```

You can now go to the ch11 examples folder and double-click the RomeoAndJuliet.png image file on your system to view it—your version might have the words in different positions and different colors:

Generating a Word Cloud from a Dictionary
If you already have a dictionary of key–value pairs representing word counts, you can pass it to WordCloud's **fit_words method**. This method assumes you've already removed the stop words.

Displaying the Image with Matplotlib

If you'd like to display the image on the screen, you can use the IPython magic

```
%matplotlib
```

to enable interactive Matplotlib support in IPython, then execute the following state-ments:

```
import matplotlib.pyplot as plt
plt.imshow(wordcloud)
```

11.4 Readability Assessment with Textatistic

An interesting use of natural language processing is assessing text **readability**, which is affected by the vocabulary used, sentence structure, sentence length, topic and more. While writing this book, we used the paid tool Grammarly to help tune the writing and ensure the text's readability for a wide audience.

In this section, we'll use the **Textatistic library**[24] to assess readability.[25] There are many formulas used in natural language processing to calculate readability. Textatistic uses five popular readability formulas—Flesch Reading Ease, Flesch-Kincaid, Gunning Fog, Simple Measure of Gobbledygook (SMOG) and Dale-Chall.

Install Textatistic

To install Textatistic, open your Anaconda Prompt (Windows), Terminal (macOS/Linux) or shell (Linux), then execute the following command:

```
pip install textatistic
```

Windows users might need to run the Anaconda Prompt as an Administrator for proper software installation privileges. To do so, right-click Anaconda Prompt in the start menu and select **More > Run as administrator**.

Calculating Statistics and Readability Scores

First, let's load *Romeo and Juliet* into the text variable:

```
In [1]: from pathlib import Path

In [2]: text = Path('RomeoAndJuliet.txt').read_text()
```

Calculating statistics and readability scores requires a **Textatistic** object that's ini-tialized with the text you want to assess:

```
In [3]: from textatistic import Textatistic

In [4]: readability = Textatistic(text)
```

Textatistic method **dict** returns a dictionary containing various statistics and the readability scores[26]:

```
In [5]: %precision 3
Out[5]: '%.3f'
```

24. https://github.com/erinhengel/Textatistic.
25. Some other Python readability assessment libraries include readability-score, textstat, readability and pylinguistics.

```
In [6]: readability.dict()
Out[6]:
{'char_count': 115141,
 'word_count': 26120,
 'sent_count': 3218,
 'sybl_count': 30166,
 'notdalechall_count': 5823,
 'polysyblword_count': 549,
 'flesch_score': 100.892,
 'fleschkincaid_score': 1.203,
 'gunningfog_score': 4.087,
 'smog_score': 5.489,
 'dalechall_score': 7.559}
```

Each of the values in the dictionary is also accessible via a Textatistic property of the same name as the keys shown in the preceding output. The statistics produced include:

- char_count—The number of characters in the text.

- word_count—The number of words in the text.

- sent_count—The number of sentences in the text.

- sybl_count—The number of syllables in the text.

- notdalechall_count—A count of the words that are not on the Dale-Chall list, which is a list of words understood by 80% of 5th graders.[27] The higher this number is compared to the total word count, the less readable the text is considered to be.

- polysyblword_count—The number of words with three or more syllables.

- flesch_score—The Flesch Reading Ease score, which can be mapped to a grade level. Scores over 90 are considered readable by 5th graders. Scores under 30 require a college degree. Ranges in between correspond to the other grade levels.

- fleschkincaid_score—The Flesch-Kincaid score, which corresponds to a specific grade level.

- gunningfog_score—The Gunning Fog index value, which corresponds to a specific grade level.

- smog_score—The Simple Measure of Gobbledygook (SMOG), which corresponds to the years of education required to understand text. This measure is considered particularly effective for healthcare materials.[28]

- dalechall_score—The Dale-Chall score, which can be mapped to grade levels from 4 and below to college graduate (grade 16) and above. This score considered to be most reliable for a broad range of text types.[29,30]

26. Each Project Gutenberg e-book includes additional text, such as their licensing information, that's not part of the e-book itself. For this example, we used a text editor to remove that text from our copy of the e-book.
27. http://www.readabilityformulas.com/articles/dale-chall-readability-word-list.php.
28. https://en.wikipedia.org/wiki/SMOG.
29. https://en.wikipedia.org/wiki/Readability#The_Dale%E2%80%93Chall_formula.
30. http://www.readabilityformulas.com/articles/how-do-i-decide-which-readability-formula-to-use.php.

For more details on each of the readability scores produced here and several others, see

```
https://en.wikipedia.org/wiki/Readability
```

The Textatistic documentation also shows the readability formulas used:

```
http://www.erinhengel.com/software/textatistic/
```

11.5 Named Entity Recognition with spaCy

NLP can determine what a text is about. A key aspect of this is **named entity recognition**, which attempts to locate and categorize items like dates, times, quantities, places, people, things, organizations and more. In this section, we'll use the named entity recognition capabilities in the **spaCy NLP library**[31],[32] to analyze text.

Install spaCy
To install spaCy, open your Anaconda Prompt (Windows), Terminal (macOS/Linux) or shell (Linux), then execute the following command:

```
conda install -c conda-forge spacy
```

Windows users might need to run the Anaconda Prompt as an Administrator for proper software installation privileges. To do so, right-click Anaconda Prompt in the start menu and select **More > Run as administrator**.

Once the install completes, you also need to execute the following command, so spaCy can download additional components it needs for processing English (en) text:

```
python -m spacy download en
```

Loading the Language Model
The first step in using spaCy is to load the language model representing the natural language of the text you're analyzing. To do this, you'll call the spacy module's **load function**. Let's load the English model that we downloaded above:

```
In [1]: import spacy

In [2]: nlp = spacy.load('en')
```

The spaCy documentation recommends the variable name nlp.

Creating a spaCy Doc
Next, you use the nlp object to create a spaCy **Doc** object[33] representing the document to process. Here we used a sentence from the introduction to the World Wide Web in many of our books:

```
In [3]: document = nlp('In 1994, Tim Berners-Lee founded the ' +
   ...:     'World Wide Web Consortium (W3C), devoted to ' +
   ...:     'developing web technologies')
   ...:
```

---

31. https://spacy.io/.
32. You may also want to check out Textacy (https://github.com/chartbeat-labs/textacy)—an NLP library built on spaCy that supports additional NLP tasks.
33. https://spacy.io/api/doc.

Getting the Named Entities

The Doc object's **ents property** returns a tuple of **Span** objects representing the named entities found in the Doc. Each Span has many properties.[34] Let's iterate through the Spans and display the text and label_ properties:

```
In [4]: for entity in document.ents:
   ...:     print(f'{entity.text}: {entity.label_}')
   ...:
1994: DATE
Tim Berners-Lee: PERSON
the World Wide Web Consortium: ORG
```

Each Span's **text property** returns the entity as a string, and the **label_ property** returns a string indicating the entity's kind. Here, spaCy found three entities representing a DATE (1994), a PERSON (Tim Berners-Lee) and an ORG (organization; the World Wide Web Consortium). For more spaCy information and to take a look at its Quickstart guide, see

```
https://spacy.io/usage/models#section-quickstart
```

11.6 Similarity Detection with spaCy

Similarity detection is the process of analyzing documents to determine how alike they are. One possible similarity detection technique is word frequency counting. For example, some people believe that the works of William Shakespeare actually might have been written by Sir Francis Bacon, Christopher Marlowe or others.[35] Comparing the word frequencies of their works with those of Shakespeare can reveal writing-style similarities.

Various machine-learning techniques we'll discuss in later chapters can be used to study document similarity. However, as is often the case in Python, there are libraries such as spaCy and Gensim that can do this for you. Here, we'll use spaCy's similarity detection features to compare Doc objects representing Shakespeare's *Romeo and Juliet* with Christopher Marlowe's *Edward the Second*. You can download *Edward the Second* from Project Gutenberg as we did for *Romeo and Juliet* earlier in the chapter.[36]

Loading the Language Model and Creating a spaCy Doc

As in the preceding section, we first load the English model:

```
In [1]: import spacy

In [2]: nlp = spacy.load('en')
```

Creating the spaCy Docs

Next, we create two Doc objects—one for *Romeo and Juliet* and one for *Edward the Second*:

```
In [3]: from pathlib import Path

In [4]: document1 = nlp(Path('RomeoAndJuliet.txt').read_text())

In [5]: document2 = nlp(Path('EdwardTheSecond.txt').read_text())
```

34. https://spacy.io/api/span.
35. https://en.wikipedia.org/wiki/Shakespeare_authorship_question.
36. Each Project Gutenberg e-book includes additional text, such as their licensing information, that's not part of the e-book itself. For this example, we used a text editor to remove that text from our copies of the e-books.

Comparing the Books' Similarity

Finally, we use the Doc class's **similarity method** to get a value from 0.0 (not similar) to 1.0 (identical) indicating how similar the documents are:

```
In [6]: document1.similarity(document2)
Out[6]: 0.9349950179100041
```

spaCy believes these two documents have significant similarities. For comparison purposes, we created a Doc representing a current news story and compared it with *Romeo and Juliet*. As expected, spaCy returned a low value indicating little similarity between them. Try copying a current news article into a text file, then performing the similarity comparison yourself.

11.7 Other NLP Libraries and Tools

We've shown you various NLP libraries, but it's always a good idea to investigate the range of options available to you so you can leverage the best tools for your tasks. Below are some additional mostly free and open source NLP libraries and APIs:

- Gensim—Similarity detection and topic modeling.
- Google Cloud Natural Language API—Cloud-based API for NLP tasks such as named entity recognition, sentiment analysis, parts-of-speech analysis and visualization, determining content categories and more.
- Microsoft Linguistic Analysis API.
- Bing sentiment analysis—Microsoft's Bing search engine now uses sentiment in its search results. At the time of this writing, sentiment analysis in search results is available only in the United States.
- PyTorch NLP—Deep learning library for NLP.
- Stanford CoreNLP—A Java NLP library, which also provides a Python wrapper. Includes corefererence resolution, which finds all references to the same thing.
- Apache OpenNLP—Another Java-based NLP library for common tasks, including coreference resolution. Python wrappers are available.
- PyNLPl (pineapple)—Python NLP library, includes basic and more sophisticated NLP capabilities.
- SnowNLP—Python library that simplifies Chinese text processing.
- KoNLPy—Korean language NLP.
- stop-words—Python library with stop words for many languages. We used NLTK's stop words lists in this chapter.
- TextRazor—A paid cloud-based NLP API that provides a free tier.

11.8 Machine Learning and Deep Learning Natural Language Applications

There are many natural language applications that require machine learning and deep learning techniques. We'll discuss some of the following in our machine learning and deep learning chapters:

- Answering natural language questions—For example, our publisher Pearson Education, has a partnership with IBM Watson that uses Watson as a virtual tutor. Students ask Watson natural language questions and get answers.

- Summarizing documents—analyzing documents and producing short summaries (also called abstracts) that can, for example, be included with search results and can help you decide what to read.

- Speech synthesis (speech-to-text) and speech recognition (text-to-speech)—We use these in our "IBM Watson" chapter, along with inter-language text-to-text translation, to develop a near real-time inter-language voice-to-voice translator.

- Collaborative filtering—used to implement recommender systems ("if you liked this movie, you might also like…").

- Text classification—for example, classifying news articles by categories, such as world news, national news, local news, sports, business, entertainment, etc.

- Topic modeling—finding the topics discussed in documents.

- Sarcasm detection—often used with sentiment analysis.

- Text simplification—making text more concise and easier to read.

- Speech to sign language and vice versa—to enable a conversation with a hearing-impaired person.

- Lip reader technology—for people who can't speak, convert lip movement to text or speech to enable conversation.

- Closed captioning—adding text captions to video.

11.9 Natural Language Datasets

There's a tremendous number of text data sources available to you for working with natural language processing:

- Wikipedia—some or all of Wikipedia (`https://meta.wikimedia.org/wiki/Datasets`).

- IMDB (Internet Movie Database)—various movie and TV datasets are available.

- UCI's text datasets—many datasets, including the Spambase dataset.

- Project Gutenberg—50,000+ free e-books that are out-of-copyright in the U.S.

- Jeopardy! dataset—200,000+ questions from the Jeopardy! TV show. A milestone in AI occurred in 2011 when IBM Watson famously beat two of the world's best Jeopardy! players.

- Natural language processing datasets: `https://machinelearningmastery.com/datasets-natural-language-processing/`.

- NLTK data: `https://www.nltk.org/data.html`.

- Sentiment labeled sentences data set (from sources including IMDB.com, amazon.com, yelp.com.)

- Registry of Open Data on AWS—a searchable directory of datasets hosted on Amazon Web Services (`https://registry.opendata.aws`).

- Amazon Customer Reviews Dataset—130+ million product reviews (`https://registry.opendata.aws/amazon-reviews/`).

- Pitt.edu corpora (`http://mpqa.cs.pitt.edu/corpora/`).

11.10 Wrap-Up

In this chapter, you performed a broad range of natural language processing (NLP) tasks using several NLP libraries. You saw that NLP is performed on text collections known as corpora. We discussed nuances of meaning that make natural language understanding difficult.

We focused on the TextBlob NLP library, which is built on the NLTK and pattern libraries, but easier to use. You created `TextBlob`s and tokenized them into `Sentences` and `Words`. You determined the part of speech for each word in a `TextBlob`, and you extracted noun phrases.

We demonstrated how to evaluate the positive or negative sentiment of `TextBlobs` and `Sentences` with the TextBlob library's default sentiment analyzer and with the `NaiveBayesAnalyzer`. You used the TextBlob library's integration with Google Translate to detect the language of text and perform inter-language translation.

We showed various other NLP tasks, including singularization and pluralization, spell checking and correction, normalization with stemming and lemmatization, and getting word frequencies. You obtained word definitions, synonyms and antonyms from WordNet. You also used NLTK's stop words list to eliminate stop words from text, and you created n-grams containing groups of consecutive words.

We showed how to visualize word frequencies quantitatively as a bar chart using pandas' built-in plotting capabilities. Then, we used the `wordcloud` library to visualize word frequencies qualitatively as word clouds. You performed readability assessments using the Textatistic library. Finally, you used spaCy to locate named entities and to perform similarity detection among documents. In the next chapter, you'll continue using natural language processing as we introduce data mining tweets using the Twitter APIs.

Data Mining Twitter

Objectives

In this chapter, you'll:

- Understand Twitter's impact on businesses, brands, reputation, sentiment analysis, predictions and more.
- Use Tweepy, one of the most popular Python Twitter API clients for data mining Twitter.
- Use the Twitter Search API to download past tweets that meet your criteria.
- Use the Twitter Streaming API to sample the stream of live tweets as they're happening.
- See that the tweet objects returned by Twitter contain valuable information beyond the tweet text.
- Use the natural language processing techniques from the last chapter to clean and preprocess tweets to prepare them for analysis.
- Perform sentiment analysis on tweets.
- Spot trends with Twitter's Trends API.
- Map tweets using folium and OpenStreetMap.
- Understand various ways to store tweets using techniques discussed throughout this book.

12.1 Introduction

We're always trying to predict the future. Will it rain on our upcoming picnic? Will the stock market or individual securities go up or down, and when and by how much? How will people vote in the next election? What's the chance that a new oil exploration venture will strike oil and if so how much would it likely produce? Will a baseball team win more games if it changes its batting philosophy to "swing for the fences?" How much customer traffic does an airline anticipate over the next many months? And hence how should the company buy oil commodity futures to guarantee that it will have the supply it needs and hopefully at a minimal cost? What track is a hurricane likely to take and how powerful will it likely become (category 1, 2, 3, 4 or 5)? That kind of information is crucial to emergency preparedness efforts. Is a financial transaction likely to be fraudulent? Will a mortgage default? Is a disease likely to spread rapidly and, if so, to what geographic area?

Prediction is a challenging and often costly process, but the potential rewards are great. With the technologies in this and the upcoming chapters, we'll see how AI, often in concert with big data, is rapidly improving prediction capabilities.

In this chapter we concentrate on data mining Twitter, looking for the sentiment in tweets. **Data mining** is the process of searching through large collections of data, often big data, to find insights that can be valuable to individuals and organizations. The sentiment that you data mine from tweets could help predict the results of an election, the revenues a new movie is likely to generate and the success of a company's marketing campaign. It could also help companies spot weaknesses in competitors' product offerings.

You'll connect to Twitter via web services. You'll use Twitter's Search API to tap into the enormous base of past tweets. You'll use Twitter's Streaming API to sample the flood of new tweets as they happen. With the Twitter Trends API, you'll see what topics are trending. You'll find that much of what we presented in the "Natural Language Processing (NLP)" chapter will be useful in building Twitter applications.

As you've seen throughout this book, because of powerful libraries, you'll often perform significant tasks with just a few lines of code. This is why Python and its robust open-source community are appealing.

Twitter has displaced the major news organizations as the first source for newsworthy events. Most Twitter posts are public and happen in real-time as events unfold globally. People speak frankly about any subject and tweet about their personal and business lives. They comment on the social, entertainment and political scenes and whatever else comes to mind. With their mobile phones, they take and post photos and videos of events as they happen. You'll commonly hear the terms **Twitterverse** and **Twittersphere** to mean the hundreds of millions of users who have anything to do with sending, receiving and analyzing tweets.

What Is Twitter?

Twitter was founded in 2006 as a microblogging company and today is one of the most popular sites on the Internet. Its concept is simple. People write short messages called *tweets*, initially limited to 140 characters but recently increased for most languages to 280 characters. Anyone can generally choose to follow anyone else. This is different from the closed, tight communities on other social media platforms such as Facebook, LinkedIn and many others, where the "following relationships" must be reciprocal.

Twitter Statistics

Twitter has hundreds of millions of users and hundreds of millions of tweets are sent every day with many thousands sent per second.[1] Searching online for "Internet statistics" and "Twitter statistics" will help you put these numbers in perspective. Some "tweeters" have more than 100 million followers. Dedicated tweeters generally post several per day to keep their followers engaged. Tweeters with the largest followings are typically entertainers and politicians. Developers can tap into the live stream of tweets as they're happening. This has been likened to "drinking from a fire hose," because the tweets come at you so quickly.

Twitter and Big Data

Twitter has become a favorite big data source for researchers and business people worldwide. Twitter allows regular users free access to a small portion of the more recent tweets. Through special arrangements with Twitter, some third-party businesses (and Twitter itself) offer paid access to much larger portions of the all-time tweets database.

Cautions

You can't always trust everything you read on the Internet, and tweets are no exception. For example, people might use false information to try to manipulate financial markets or influence political elections. Hedge funds often trade securities based in part on the tweet streams they follow, but they're cautious. That's one of the challenges of building *business-critical* or *mission-critical* systems based on social media content.

Going forward, we use web services extensively. Internet connections can be lost, services can change and some services are not available in all countries. This is the real world

---

1. `http://www.internetlivestats.com/twitter-statistics/`.

of cloud-based programming. We cannot program with the same reliability as desktop apps when using web services.

12.2 Overview of the Twitter APIs

Twitter's APIs are cloud-based web services, so an Internet connection is required to execute the code in this chapter. **Web services** are methods that you call in the cloud, as you'll do with the Twitter APIs in this chapter, the IBM Watson APIs in the next chapter and other APIs you'll use as computing becomes more cloud-based. Each API method has a web service **endpoint**, which is represented by a URL that's used to invoke that method over the Internet.

Twitter's APIs include many categories of functionality, some free and some paid. Most have **rate limits** that restrict the number of times you can use them in 15-minute intervals. In this chapter, you'll use the **Tweepy library** to invoke methods from the following Twitter APIs:

- **Authentication API**—Pass your Twitter credentials (discussed shortly) to Twitter so you can use the other APIs.

- **Accounts and Users API**—Access information about an account.

- **Tweets API**—Search through past tweets, access tweet streams to tap into tweets happening now and more.

- **Trends API**—Find locations of trending topics and get lists of trending topics by location.

See the extensive list of Twitter API categories, subcategories and individual methods at:

> https://developer.twitter.com/en/docs/api-reference-index.html

Rate Limits: A Word of Caution

Twitter expects developers to use its services responsibly. Each Twitter API method has a **rate limit**, which is the maximum number of requests (that is, calls) you can make during a 15-minute window. Twitter may block you from using its APIs if you continue to call a given API method after that method's rate limit has been reached.

Before using any API method, read its documentation and understand its rate limits.[2] We'll configure Tweepy to wait when it encounters rate limits. This helps prevent you from exceeding the rate-limit restrictions. Some methods list both user rate limits and app rate limits. All of this chapter's examples use *app rate limits*. User rate limits are for apps that enable individual users to log into Twitter, like third-party apps that interact with Twitter on your behalf, such as smartphone apps from other vendors.

For details on rate limiting, see

> https://developer.twitter.com/en/docs/basics/rate-limiting

For specific rate limits on individual API methods, see

> https://developer.twitter.com/en/docs/basics/rate-limits

and each API method's documentation.

---

2. Keep in mind that Twitter could change these limits in the future.

Other Restrictions

Twitter is a goldmine for data mining and they allow you to do a lot with their free services. You'll be amazed at the valuable applications you can build and how these will help you improve your personal and career endeavors. **However, if you do not follow Twitter's rules and regulations, your developer account could be terminated. You should carefully read the following and the documents they link to:**

- Terms of Service: `https://twitter.com/tos`

- Developer   Agreement: `https://developer.twitter.com/en/developer-terms/agreement-and-policy.html`

- Developer   Policy: `https://developer.twitter.com/en/developer-terms/policy.html`

- Other   restrictions: `https://developer.twitter.com/en/developer-terms/more-on-restricted-use-cases`

You'll see later in this chapter that you can search tweets only for the last seven days and get only a limited number of tweets using the free Twitter APIs. Some books and articles say you can get around those limits by scraping tweets directly from `twitter.com`. However, the Terms of Service explicitly say that "**scraping the Services without the prior consent of Twitter is expressly prohibited.**"

12.3 Creating a Twitter Account

Twitter requires you to apply for a developer account to be able to use their APIs. Go to

> `https://developer.twitter.com/en/apply-for-access`

and submit your application. You'll have to register for one as part of this process if you do not already have one. You'll be asked questions about the purpose of your account. You must *carefully* read and agree to Twitter's terms to complete the application, then confirm your email address.

Twitter reviews every application. Approval is not guaranteed. At the time of this writing, *personal-use accounts* were approved immediately. For company accounts, the process was taking from a few days to several weeks, according to the Twitter developer forums.

12.4 Getting Twitter Credentials—Creating an App

Once you have a Twitter developer account, you must obtain **credentials** for interacting with the Twitter APIs. To do so, you'll create an **app**. Each app has separate credentials. To create an app, log into

> `https://developer.twitter.com`

and perform the following steps:

1. At the top-right of the page, click the drop-down menu for your account and select **Apps**.

2. Click **Create an app**.

3. In the **App name** field, specify your app's name. If you *send* tweets via the API, this app name will be the tweets' sender. It also will be shown to users if you create

applications that require a user to log in via Twitter. We will not do either in this chapter, so a name like "*YourName* Test App" is fine for use with this chapter.

4. In the **Application description field**, enter a description for your app. When creating Twitter-based apps that will be used by other people, this would describe what your app does. For this chapter, you can use "Learning to use the Twitter API."

5. In the **Website URL** field, enter your website. When creating Twitter-based apps, this is supposed to be the website where you host your app. You can use your Twitter URL: https://twitter.com/*YourUserName*, where *YourUserName* is your Twitter account screen name. For example, https://twitter.com/nasa corresponds to the NASA screen name @nasa.

6. The **Tell us how this app will be used** field is a description of at least 100 characters that helps Twitter employees understand what your app does. We entered "I am new to Twitter app development and am simply learning how to use the Twitter APIs for educational purposes."

7. Leave the remaining fields empty and click **Create**, then carefully review the (lengthy) developer terms and click **Create** again.

Getting Your Credentials

After you complete *Step 7* above, Twitter displays a web page for managing your app. At the top of the page are **App details**, **Keys and tokens** and **Permissions** tabs. Click the **Keys and tokens** tab to view your app's credentials. Initially, the page shows the **Consumer API keys**—the **API key** and the **API secret key**. Click **Create** to get an **access token** and **access token secret**. All four of these will be used to authenticate with Twitter so that you may invoke its APIs.

Storing Your Credentials

As a good practice, do not include your API keys and access tokens (or any other credentials, like usernames and passwords) directly in your source code, as that would expose them to anyone reading the code. You should store your keys in a separate file and never share that file with anyone.[3]

The code you'll execute in subsequent sections assumes that you place your consumer key, consumer secret, access token and access token secret values into the file keys.py shown below. You can find this file in the ch12 examples folder:

```
consumer_key='YourConsumerKey'
consumer_secret='YourConsumerSecret'
access_token='YourAccessToken'
access_token_secret='YourAccessTokenSecret'
```

Edit this file, replacing YourConsumerKey, YourConsumerSecret, YourAccessToken and YourAccessTokenSecret with your consumer key, consumer secret, access token and access token secret values. Then, save the file.

---

3. Good practice would be to use an encryption library such as bcrypt (https://github.com/pyca/bcrypt/) to encrypt your keys, access tokens or any other credentials you use in your code, then read them in and decrypt them only as you pass them to Twitter.

OAuth 2.0
The consumer key, consumer secret, access token and access token secret are each part of the **OAuth 2.0** authentication process[4,5]—sometimes called the *OAuth dance*—that Twitter uses to enable access to its APIs. The Tweepy library enables you to provide the consumer key, consumer secret, access token and access token secret and handles the OAuth 2.0 authentication details for you.

12.5 What's in a Tweet?
The Twitter API methods return JSON objects. **JSON (JavaScript Object Notation)** is a text-based data-interchange format used to represent objects as collections of name–value pairs. It's commonly used when invoking web services. JSON is both a human-readable and computer-readable format that makes data easy to send and receive across the Internet.

JSON objects are similar to Python dictionaries. Each JSON object contains a list of *property names* and *values*, in the following curly braced format:

> {*propertyName1*: *value1*, *propertyName2*: *value2*}

As in Python, JSON lists are comma-separated values in square brackets:

> [*value1*, *value2*, *value3*]

For your convenience, Tweepy handles the JSON for you behind the scenes, converting JSON to Python objects using classes defined in the Tweepy library.

Key Properties of a Tweet Object
A tweet (also called a *status update*) may contain a maximum of 280 characters, but the tweet objects returned by the Twitter APIs contain many **metadata** attributes that describe aspects of the tweet, such as:

- when it was created,
- who created it,
- lists of the hashtags, urls, @-mentions and media (such as images and videos, which are specified via their URLs) included in the tweet,
- and more.

The following table lists a few key attributes of a tweet object:

Attribute	Description
created_at	The creation date and time in UTC (Coordinated Universal Time) format.
entities	Twitter extracts hashtags, urls, user_mentions (that is, @*username* mentions), media (such as images and videos), symbols and polls from tweets and places them into the entities dictionary as lists that you can access with these keys.
extended_tweet	For tweets over 140 characters, contains details such as the tweet's full_text and entities

---

4. https://developer.twitter.com/en/docs/basics/authentication/overview.
5. https://oauth.net/.

Attribute (Cont.)	Description
favorite_count	Number of times other users favorited the tweet.
coordinates	The coordinates (latitude and longitude) from which the tweet was sent. This is often null (None in Python) because many users disable sending location data.
place	Users can associate a place with a tweet. If they do, this will be a place object: https://developer.twitter.com/en/docs/tweets/data-dictionary/overview/geo-objects#place-dictionary; otherwise, it'll be null (None in Python).
id	The integer ID of the tweet. Twitter recommends using id_str for portability.
id_str	The string representation of the tweet's integer ID.
lang	Language of the tweet, such as 'en' for English or 'fr' for French.
retweet_count	Number of times other users retweeted the tweet.
text	The text of the tweet. If the tweet uses the new 280-character limit and contains more than 140 characters, this property will be truncated and the truncated property will be set to *true*. This might also occur if a 140-character tweet was retweeted and became more than 140 characters as a result.
user	The User object representing the user that posted the tweet. For the User object JSON properties, see: https://developer.twitter.com/en/docs/tweets/data-dictionary/overview/user-object.

Sample Tweet JSON

Let's look at sample JSON for the following tweet from the @nasa account:

> @NoFear1075 Great question, Anthony! Throughout its seven-year mission, our Parker #SolarProbe spacecraft... https://t.co/xKd6ym8waT'

We added line numbers and reformatted some of the JSON due to wrapping. Note that some fields in Tweet JSON are not supported in every Twitter API method; such differences are explained in the online documentation for each method.

```
1   {'created_at': 'Wed Sep 05 18:19:34 +0000 2018',
2    'id': 1037404890354606082,
3    'id_str': '1037404890354606082',
4    'text': '@NoFear1075 Great question, Anthony! Throughout its seven-year
         mission, our Parker #SolarProbe spacecraft… https://t.co/xKd6ym8waT',
5    'truncated': True,
6    'entities': {'hashtags': [{'text': 'SolarProbe', 'indices': [84, 95]}],
7       'symbols': [],
8       'user_mentions': [{'screen_name': 'NoFear1075',
9          'name': 'Anthony Perrone',
10         'id': 284339791,
11         'id_str': '284339791',
12         'indices': [0, 11]}],
13      'urls': [{'url': 'https://t.co/xKd6ym8waT',
14          'expanded_url': 'https://twitter.com/i/web/status/
         1037404890354606082',
15          'display_url': 'twitter.com/i/web/status/1…',
16          'indices': [117, 140]}]},
17   'source': '<a href="http://twitter.com" rel="nofollow">Twitter Web
         Client</a>',
```

```
18    'in_reply_to_status_id': 1037390542424956928,
19    'in_reply_to_status_id_str': '1037390542424956928',
20    'in_reply_to_user_id': 284339791,
21    'in_reply_to_user_id_str': '284339791',
22    'in_reply_to_screen_name': 'NoFear1075',
23    'user': {'id': 11348282,
24      'id_str': '11348282',
25      'name': 'NASA',
26      'screen_name': 'NASA',
27      'location': '',
28      'description': 'Explore the universe and discover our home planet with
             @NASA. We usually post in EST (UTC-5)',
29      'url': 'https://t.co/TcEE6NS8nD',
30      'entities': {'url': {'urls': [{'url': 'https://t.co/TcEE6NS8nD',
31              'expanded_url': 'http://www.nasa.gov',
32              'display_url': 'nasa.gov',
33              'indices': [0, 23]}]},
34        'description': {'urls': []}},
35      'protected': False,
36      'followers_count': 29486081,
37      'friends_count': 287,
38      'listed_count': 91928,
39      'created_at': 'Wed Dec 19 20:20:32 +0000 2007',
40      'favourites_count': 3963,
41      'time_zone': None,
42      'geo_enabled': False,
43      'verified': True,
44      'statuses_count': 53147,
45      'lang': 'en',
46      'contributors_enabled': False,
47      'is_translator': False,
48      'is_translation_enabled': False,
49      'profile_background_color': '000000',
50      'profile_background_image_url': 'http://abs.twimg.com/images/themes/
             theme1/bg.png',
51      'profile_background_image_url_https': 'https://abs.twimg.com/images/
             themes/theme1/bg.png',
52      'profile_image_url': 'http://pbs.twimg.com/profile_images/188302352/
             nasalogo_twitter_normal.jpg',
53      'profile_image_url_https': 'https://pbs.twimg.com/profile_images/
             188302352/nasalogo_twitter_normal.jpg',
54      'profile_banner_url': 'https://pbs.twimg.com/profile_banners/11348282/
             1535145490',
55      'profile_link_color': '205BA7',
56      'profile_sidebar_border_color': '000000',
57      'profile_sidebar_fill_color': 'F3F2F2',
58      'profile_text_color': '000000',
59      'profile_use_background_image': True,
60      'has_extended_profile': True,
61      'default_profile': False,
62      'default_profile_image': False,
63      'following': True,
64      'follow_request_sent': False,
65      'notifications': False,
66      'translator_type': 'regular'},
```

```
67    'geo': None,
68    'coordinates': None,
69    'place': None,
70    'contributors': None,
71    'is_quote_status': False,
72    'retweet_count': 7,
73    'favorite_count': 19,
74    'favorited': False,
75    'retweeted': False,
76    'possibly_sensitive': False,
77    'lang': 'en'}
```

Twitter JSON Object Resources

For a complete, more readable list of the tweet object attributes, see:

```
https://developer.twitter.com/en/docs/tweets/data-dictionary/over-
    view/tweet-object.html
```

For additional details that were added when Twitter moved from a limit of 140 to 280 characters per tweet, see

```
https://developer.twitter.com/en/docs/tweets/data-dictionary/over-
    view/intro-to-tweet-json.html#extendedtweet
```

For a general overview of all the JSON objects that Twitter APIs return, and links to the specific object details, see

```
https://developer.twitter.com/en/docs/tweets/data-dictionary/over-
    view/intro-to-tweet-json
```

12.6 Tweepy

We'll use the Tweepy library[6] (http://www.tweepy.org/)—one of the most popular Python libraries for interacting with the Twitter APIs. Tweepy makes it easy to access Twitter's capabilities and hides from you the details of processing the JSON objects returned by the Twitter APIs. You can view Tweepy's documentation[7] at

```
http://docs.tweepy.org/en/latest/
```

For additional information and the Tweepy source code, visit

```
https://github.com/tweepy/tweepy
```

Installing Tweepy

To install Tweepy, open your Anaconda Prompt (Windows), Terminal (macOS/Linux) or shell (Linux), then execute the following command:

```
pip install tweepy==3.7
```

---

6. Other Python libraries recommended by Twitter include Birdy, python-twitter, Python Twitter Tools, TweetPony, TwitterAPI, twitter-gobject, TwitterSearch and twython. See https://develop-er.twitter.com/en/docs/developer-utilities/twitter-libraries.html for details.

7. The Tweepy documentation is a work in progress. At the time of this writing, Tweepy does not have documentation for their classes corresponding to the JSON objects the Twitter APIs return. Tweepy's classes use the same attribute names and structure as the JSON objects. You can determine the correct attribute names to access by looking at Twitter's JSON documentation. We'll explain any attributes we use in our code and provide footnotes with links to the Twitter JSON descriptions.

Windows users might need to run the Anaconda Prompt as an Administrator for proper software installation privileges. To do so, right-click Anaconda Prompt in the start menu and select **More > Run as administrator**.

Installing geopy
As you work with Tweepy, you'll also use functions from our `tweetutilities.py` file (provided with this chapter's example code). One of the utility functions in that file depends on the **geopy library** (`https://github.com/geopy/geopy`), which we'll discuss in Section 12.15. To install geopy, execute:

```
conda install -c conda-forge geopy
```

12.7 Authenticating with Twitter Via Tweepy

In the next several sections, you'll invoke various cloud-based Twitter APIs via Tweepy. Here you'll begin by using Tweepy to authenticate with Twitter and create a **Tweepy API object**, which is your gateway to using the Twitter APIs over the Internet. In subsequent sections, you'll work with various Twitter APIs by invoking methods on your API object.

Before you can invoke any Twitter API, you must use your API key, API secret key, access token and access token secret to authenticate with Twitter.[8] Launch IPython from the ch12 examples folder, then import the **tweepy module** and the `keys.py` file that you modified earlier in this chapter. You can import any `.py` file as a module by using the file's name *without* the `.py` extension in an `import` statement:

```
In [1]: import tweepy
```

```
In [2]: import keys
```

When you import `keys.py` as a module, you can individually access each of the four variables defined in that file as `keys.variable_name`.

Creating and Configuring an OAuthHandler to Authenticate with Twitter
Authenticating with Twitter via Tweepy involves two steps. First, create an object of the tweepy module's **OAuthHandler class**, passing your API key and API secret key to its constructor. A **constructor** is a function that has the same name as the class (in this case, OAuthHandler) and receives the arguments used to configure the new object:

```
In [3]: auth = tweepy.OAuthHandler(keys.consumer_key,
   ...:                            keys.consumer_secret)
   ...:
```

Specify your access token and access token secret by calling the OAuthHandler object's **set_access_token** method:

```
In [4]: auth.set_access_token(keys.access_token,
   ...:                       keys.access_token_secret)
   ...:
```

---

8. You may wish to create apps that enable users to log into their Twitter accounts, manage them, post tweets, read tweets from other users, search for tweets, etc. For details on user authentication see the Tweepy Authentication tutorial at `http://docs.tweepy.org/en/latest/auth_tutorial.html`.

Creating an API Object

Now, create the API object that you'll use to interact with Twitter:

```
In [5]: api = tweepy.API(auth, wait_on_rate_limit=True,
   ...:                       wait_on_rate_limit_notify=True)
   ...:
```

We specified three arguments in this call to the API constructor:

- auth is the OAuthHandler object containing your credentials.

- The keyword argument wait_on_rate_limit=True tells Tweepy to wait 15 minutes each time it reaches a given API method's rate limit. This ensures that you do not violate Twitter's rate-limit restrictions.

- The keyword argument wait_on_rate_limit_notify=True tells Tweepy that, if it needs to wait due to rate limits, it should notify you by displaying a message at the command line.

You're now ready to interact with Twitter via Tweepy. Note that the code examples in the next several sections are presented as a continuing IPython session, so the authorization process you went through here need not be repeated.

12.8 Getting Information About a Twitter Account

After authenticating with Twitter, you can use the Tweepy API object's **get_user method** to get a **tweepy.models.User object** containing information about a user's Twitter account. Let's get a User object for NASA's @nasa Twitter account:

```
In [6]: nasa = api.get_user('nasa')
```

The get_user method calls the Twitter API's users/show method.[9] Each Twitter method you call through Tweepy has a rate limit. You can call Twitter's users/show method up to 900 times every 15 minutes to get information on specific user accounts. As we mention other Twitter API methods, we'll provide a footnote with a link to each method's documentation in which you can view its rate limits.

The tweepy.models classes each correspond to the JSON that Twitter returns. For example, the User class corresponds to a Twitter **user object**:

```
https://developer.twitter.com/en/docs/tweets/data-dictionary/over-
   view/user-object
```

Each tweepy.models class has a method that reads the JSON and turns it into an object of the corresponding Tweepy class.

Getting Basic Account Information

Let's access some User object properties to display information about the @nasa account:

- The **id property** is the account ID number created by Twitter when the user joined Twitter.

- The **name property** is the name associated with the user's account.

---

9. https://developer.twitter.com/en/docs/accounts-and-users/follow-search-get-users/
    api-reference/get-users-show.

- The **screen_name property** is the user's Twitter handle (@nasa). Both the name and screen_name could be created names to protect a user's privacy.

- The **description property** is the description from the user's profile.

```
In [7]: nasa.id
Out[7]: 11348282

In [8]: nasa.name
Out[8]: 'NASA'

In [9]: nasa.screen_name
Out[9]: 'NASA'

In [10]: nasa.description
Out[10]: 'Explore the universe and discover our home planet with @NASA.
We usually post in EST (UTC-5)'
```

Getting the Most Recent Status Update

The User object's **status property** returns a **tweepy.models.Status** object, which corresponds to a Twitter **tweet object**:

> https://developer.twitter.com/en/docs/tweets/data-dictionary/overview/tweet-object

The Status object's **text property** contains the text of the account's most recent tweet:

```
In [11]: nasa.status.text
Out[11]: 'The interaction of a high-velocity young star with the cloud of
gas and dust may have created this unusually sharp-... https://t.co/
J6uUf7MYMI'
```

The text property was originally for tweets up to 140 characters. The ... above indicates that the tweet text was *truncated*. When Twitter increased the limit to 280 characters, they added an **extended_tweet property** (demonstrated later) for accessing the text and other information from tweets between 141 and 280 characters. In this case, Twitter sets text to a truncated version of the extended_tweet's text. Also, retweeting often results in truncation because a retweet adds characters that could exceed the character limit.

Getting the Number of Followers

You can view an account's number of followers with the **followers_count** property:

```
In [12]: nasa.followers_count
Out[12]: 29453541
```

Though this number is large, there are accounts with over 100 million followers.[10]

Getting the Number of Friends

Similarly, you can view an account's number of friends (that is, the number of accounts an account follows) with the **friends_count** property:

```
In [13]: nasa.friends_count
Out[13]: 287
```

---

10. https://friendorfollow.com/twitter/most-followers/.

Getting Your Own Account's Information

You can use the properties in this section on your own account as well. To do so, call the Tweepy `API` object's **me method**, as in:

```
me = api.me()
```

This returns a `User` object for the account you used to authenticate with Twitter in the preceding section.

12.9 Introduction to Tweepy Cursors: Getting an Account's Followers and Friends

When invoking Twitter API methods, you often receive as results collections of objects, such as tweets in your Twitter timeline, tweets in another account's timeline or lists of tweets that match specified search criteria. A **timeline** consists of tweets sent by that user and by that user's friends—that is, other accounts that the user follows.

Each Twitter API method's documentation discusses the maximum number of items the method can return in one call—this is known as a **page** of results. When you request more results than a given method can return, Twitter's JSON responses indicate that there are more pages to get. Tweepy's `Cursor` class handles these details for you. A **Cursor** invokes a specified method and checks whether Twitter indicated that there is another page of results. If so, the Cursor automatically calls the method again to get those results. This continues, subject to the method's rate limits, until there are no more results to process. If you configure the API object to wait when rate limits are reached (as we did), the Cursor will adhere to the rate limits and wait as needed between calls. The following subsections discuss Cursor fundamentals. For more details, see the Cursor tutorial at:

```
http://docs.tweepy.org/en/latest/cursor_tutorial.html
```

12.9.1 Determining an Account's Followers

Let's use a Tweepy Cursor to invoke the `API` object's **followers method**, which calls the Twitter API's `followers/list` method[11] to obtain an account's followers. Twitter returns these in groups of 20 by default, but you can request up to 200 at a time. For demonstration purposes, we'll grab 10 of NASA's followers.

Method `followers` returns `tweepy.models.User` objects containing information about each follower. Let's begin by creating a list in which we'll store the `User` objects:

```
In [14]: followers = []
```

Creating a Cursor

Next, let's create a `Cursor` object that will call the `followers` method for NASA's account, which is specified with the `screen_name` keyword argument:

```
In [15]: cursor = tweepy.Cursor(api.followers, screen_name='nasa')
```

The Cursor's constructor receives as its argument the name of the method to call—`api.followers` indicates that the Cursor will call the `api` object's `followers` method. If the Cursor constructor receives any additional keyword arguments, like `screen_name`,

---

11. https://developer.twitter.com/en/docs/accounts-and-users/follow-search-get-users/
    api-reference/get-followers-list.

these will be passed to the method specified in the constructor's first argument. So, this Cursor specifically gets followers for the @nasa Twitter account.

Getting Results

Now, we can use the Cursor to get some followers. The following for statement iterates through the results of the expression cursor.items(10). The Cursor's **items method** initiates the call to api.followers and returns the followers method's results. In this case, we pass 10 to the items method to request only 10 results:

```
In [16]: for account in cursor.items(10):
    ...:         followers.append(account.screen_name)
    ...:

In [17]: print('Followers:',
    ...:         ' '.join(sorted(followers, key=lambda s: s.lower())))
    ...:
Followers: abhinavborra BHood1976 Eshwar12341 Harish90469614 heshamkisha
Highyaan2407 JiraaJaarra KimYooJ91459029 Lindsey06771483 Wendy_UAE_NL
```

The preceding snippet displays the followers in ascending order by calling the built-in sorted function. The function's second argument is the function used to determine how the elements of followers are sorted. In this case, we used a lambda that converts every follower name to lowercase letters so we can perform a case-insensitive sort.

Automatic Paging

If the number of results requested is more than can be returned by one call to followers, the items method automatically "pages" through the results by making multiple calls to api.followers. Recall that followers returns up to 20 followers at a time by default, so the preceding code needs to call followers only once. To get up to 200 followers at a time, we can create the Cursor with the count keyword argument, as in:

```
cursor = tweepy.Cursor(api.followers, screen_name='nasa', count=200)
```

If you do not specify an argument to the items method, The Cursor attempts to get *all* of the account's followers. For large numbers of followers, this could take a significant amount of time due to Twitter's rate limits. The Twitter API's followers/list method can return a maximum of 200 followers at a time and Twitter allows a maximum of 15 calls every 15 minutes. Thus, you can only get 3000 followers every 15 minutes using Twitter's free APIs. Recall that we configured the API object to automatically wait when it hits a rate limit, so if you try to get all followers and an account has more than 3000, Tweepy will automatically pause for 15 minutes after every 3000 followers and display a message. At the time of this writing, NASA has over 29.5 million followers. At 12,000 followers per hour, it would take over 100 days to get all of NASA's followers.

Note that for this example, we could have called the followers method directly, rather than using a Cursor, since we're getting only a small number of followers. We used a Cursor here to show how you'll typically call followers. In some later examples, we'll call API methods directly to get just a few results, rather than using Cursors.

Getting Follower IDs Rather Than Followers

Though you can get complete User objects for a maximum of 200 followers at a time, you can get many more Twitter ID numbers by calling the API object's **followers_ids**

method. This calls the Twitter API's followers/ids method, which returns up to 5000 ID numbers at a time (again, these rate limits could change).[12] You can invoke this method up to 15 times every 15 minutes, so you can get 75,000 account ID numbers per rate-limit interval. This is particularly useful when combined with the API object's **lookup_users method**. This calls the Twitter API's users/lookup method[13] which can return up to 100 User objects at a time and can be called up to 300 times every 15 minutes. So using this combination, you could get up to 30,000 User objects per rate-limit interval.

12.9.2 Determining Whom an Account Follows

The API object's **friends method** calls the Twitter API's friends/list method[14] to get a list of User objects representing an account's friends. Twitter returns these in groups of 20 by default, but you can request up to 200 at a time, just as we discussed for method followers. Twitter allows you to call the friends/list method up to 15 times every 15 minutes. Let's get 10 of NASA's friend accounts:

```
In [18]: friends = []

In [19]: cursor = tweepy.Cursor(api.friends, screen_name='nasa')

In [20]: for friend in cursor.items(10):
    ...:     friends.append(friend.screen_name)
    ...:

In [21]: print('Friends:',
    ...:     ' '.join(sorted(friends, key=lambda s: s.lower())))
    ...:
Friends: AFSpace Astro2fish Astro_Kimiya AstroAnnimal AstroDuke NA-
SA3DPrinter NASASMAP Outpost_42 POTUS44 VicGlover
```

12.9.3 Getting a User's Recent Tweets

The API method **user_timeline** returns tweets from the timeline of a specific account. A timeline includes that account's tweets and tweets from that account's friends. The method calls the Twitter API's statuses/user_timeline method[15], which returns the most recent 20 tweets, but can return up to 200 at a time. This method can return only an account's 3200 most recent tweets. Applications using this method may call it up to 1500 times every 15 minutes.

Method user_timeline returns Status objects with each one representing a tweet. Each Status's user property refers to a tweepy.models.User object containing information about the user who sent that tweet, such as that user's screen_name. A Status's text

---

12. https://developer.twitter.com/en/docs/accounts-and-users/follow-search-get-users/ api-reference/get-followers-ids.
13. https://developer.twitter.com/en/docs/accounts-and-users/follow-search-get-users/ api-reference/get-users-lookup.
14. https://developer.twitter.com/en/docs/accounts-and-users/follow-search-get-users/ api-reference/get-friends-list.
15. https://developer.twitter.com/en/docs/tweets/timelines/api-reference/get-status- es-user_timeline.

property contains the tweet's text. Let's display the screen_name and text for three tweets from @nasa:

```
In [22]: nasa_tweets = api.user_timeline(screen_name='nasa', count=3)

In [23]: for tweet in nasa_tweets:
    ...:         print(f'{tweet.user.screen_name}: {tweet.text}\n')
    ...:
NASA: Your Gut in Space: Microorganisms in the intestinal tract play an
especially important role in human health. But wh… https://t.co/uLO-
sUhwn5p

NASA: We need your help! Want to see panels at @SXSW related to space ex-
ploration? There are a number of exciting panels… https://t.co/ycqMMdGKUB

NASA: "You are as good as anyone in this town, but you are no better than
any of them," says retired @NASA_Langley mathem… https://t.co/nhMD4n84Nf
```

These tweets were truncated (as indicated by …), meaning that they probably use the newer 280-character tweet limit. We'll use the extended_tweet property shortly to access full text for such tweets.

In the preceding snippets, we chose to call the user_timeline method directly and use the count keyword argument to specify the number of tweets to retrieve. If you wish to get more than the maximum number of tweets per call (200), then you should use a Cursor to call user_timeline as demonstrated previously. Recall that a Cursor automatically pages through the results by calling the method multiple times, if necessary.

Grabbing Recent Tweets from Your Own Timeline
You can call the API method **home_timeline**, as in:

```
api.home_timeline()
```

to get tweets from *your* home timeline[16]—that is, your tweets and tweets from the people *you* follow. This method calls Twitter's statuses/home_timeline method.[17] By default, home_timeline returns the most recent 20 tweets, but can get up to 200 at a time. Again, for more than 200 tweets from your home timeline, you should use a Tweepy Cursor to call home_timeline.

12.10 Searching Recent Tweets

The Tweepy API method **search** returns tweets that match a query string. According to the method's documentation, Twitter maintains its search index only for the previous seven days' tweets, and a search is not guaranteed to return all matching tweets. Method search calls Twitter's search/tweets method[18], which returns 15 tweets at a time by default, but can return up to 100.

---

16. Specifically for the account you used to authenticate with Twitter.
17. https://developer.twitter.com/en/docs/tweets/timelines/api-reference/get-statuses-home_timeline.
18. https://developer.twitter.com/en/docs/tweets/search/api-reference/get-search-tweets.

Utility Function `print_tweets` from `tweetutilities.py`

For this section, we created a utility function `print_tweets` that receives the results of a call to API method `search` and for each tweet displays the user's `screen_name` and the tweet's `text`. If the tweet is not in English and the `tweet.lang` is not `'und'` (undefined), we'll also translate the tweet to English using `TextBlob`, as you did in the "Natural Language Processing (NLP)" chapter. To use this function, import it from `tweetutilities.py`:

```
In [24]: from tweetutilities import print_tweets
```

Just the `print_tweets` function's definition from that file is shown below:

```
def print_tweets(tweets):
    """For each Tweepy Status object in tweets, display the
    user's screen_name and tweet text. If the language is not
    English, translate the text with TextBlob."""
    for tweet in tweets:
        print(f'{tweet.screen_name}:', end=' ')

        if 'en' in tweet.lang:
            print(f'{tweet.text}\n')
        elif 'und' not in tweet.lang:  # translate to English first
            print(f'\n  ORIGINAL: {tweet.text}')
            print(f'TRANSLATED: {TextBlob(tweet.text).translate()}\n')
```

Searching for Specific Words

Let's search for three recent tweets about NASA's Mars Opportunity Rover. The `search` method's q keyword argument specifies the query string, which indicates what to search for and the count keyword argument specifies the number of tweets to return:

```
In [25]: tweets = api.search(q='Mars Opportunity Rover', count=3)

In [26]: print_tweets(tweets)
Jacker760: NASA set a deadline on the Mars Rover opportunity! As the dust
on Mars settles the Rover will start to regain power… https://t.co/
KQ7xaFgrzr

Shivak32637174: RT @Gadgets360: NASA 'Cautiously Optimistic' of Hearing
Back From Opportunity Rover as Mars Dust Storm Settles
https://t.co/O1iTTwRvFq

ladyanakina: NASA's Opportunity Rover Still Silent on #Mars. https://
t.co/njcyP6zCm3
```

As with other methods, if you plan to request more results than can be returned by one call to `search`, you should use a `Cursor` object.

Searching with Twitter Search Operators

You can use various Twitter search operators in your query strings to refine your search results. The following table shows several Twitter search operators. Multiple operators can be combined to construct more complex queries. To see all the operators, visit

```
https://twitter.com/search-home
```

and click the **operators** link.

Example	Finds tweets containing
`python twitter`	Implicit *logical and* operator—Finds tweets containing `python` *and* `twitter`.
`python OR twitter`	Logical `OR` operator—Finds tweets containing `python` *or* `twitter` *or both*.
`python ?`	`?` (question mark)—Finds tweets asking questions about `python`.
`planets -mars`	`-` (minus sign)—Finds tweets containing `planets` but not `mars`.
`python :)`	`:)` (happy face)—Finds *positive sentiment* tweets containing `python`.
`python :(`	`:(` (sad face)—Finds *negative sentiment* tweets containing `python`.
`since:2018-09-01`	Finds tweets *on or after* the specified date, which must be in the form `YYYY-MM-DD`.
`near:"New York City"`	Finds tweets that were sent near `"New York City"`.
`from:nasa`	Finds tweets from the account @nasa.
`to:nasa`	Finds tweets to the account @nasa.

Let's use the `from` and `since` operators to get three tweets from NASA since September 1, 2018—you should use a date within seven days before you execute this code:

```
In [27]: tweets = api.search(q='from:nasa since:2018-09-01', count=3)

In [28]: print_tweets(tweets)
NASA: @WYSIW Our missions detect active burning fires, track the trans-
port of fire smoke, provide info for fire managemen… https://t.co/jx2iUoM-
lIy

NASA: Scarring of the landscape is evident in the wake of the Mendocino
Complex fire, the largest #wildfire in California… https://t.co/Nboo5GD9Om

NASA: RT @NASAglenn: To celebrate the #NASA60th anniversary, we're explor-
ing our history. In this image, Research Pilot Bill Swann prepares for a…
```

Searching for a Hashtag
Tweets often contain **hashtags** that begin with # to indicate something of importance, like a trending topic. Let's get two tweets containing the hashtag #collegefootball:

```
In [29]: tweets = api.search(q='#collegefootball', count=2)

In [30]: print_tweets(tweets)
dmcreek: So much for #FAU giving #OU a game. #Oklahoma #FloridaAtlantic
#CollegeFootball #LWOS

theangrychef: It's game day folks! And our BBQ game is strong. #bbq #at-
lanta #collegefootball #gameday @ Smoke Ring https://t.co/J4lkKhCQE7
```

12.11 Spotting Trends: Twitter Trends API

If a topic "goes viral," you could have thousands or even millions of people tweeting about it at once. Twitter refers to these as **trending topics** and maintains lists of the trending topics worldwide. Via the Twitter Trends API, you can get lists of locations with trending topics and lists of the top 50 trending topics for each location.

12.11.1 Places with Trending Topics

The Tweepy API's **trends_available method** calls the Twitter API's trends/avail-
able[19] method to get a list of all locations for which Twitter has trending topics. Method
trends_available returns a *list of dictionaries* representing these locations. When we executed this code, there were 467 locations with trending topics:

```
In [31]: trends_available = api.trends_available()

In [32]: len(trends_available)
Out[32]: 467
```

The dictionary in each list element returned by trends_available has various information, including the location's name and woeid (discussed below):

```
In [33]: trends_available[0]
Out[33]:
{'name': 'Worldwide',
 'placeType': {'code': 19, 'name': 'Supername'},
 'url': 'http://where.yahooapis.com/v1/place/1',
 'parentid': 0,
 'country': '',
 'woeid': 1,
 'countryCode': None}

In [34]: trends_available[1]
Out[34]:
{'name': 'Winnipeg',
 'placeType': {'code': 7, 'name': 'Town'},
 'url': 'http://where.yahooapis.com/v1/place/2972',
 'parentid': 23424775,
 'country': 'Canada',
 'woeid': 2972,
 'countryCode': 'CA'}
```

The Twitter Trends API's trends/place method (discussed momentarily) uses
Yahoo! Where on Earth IDs (WOEIDs) to look up trending topics. The WOEID 1 represents *worldwide*. Other locations have unique WOEID values greater than 1. We'll use
WOEID values in the next two subsections to get worldwide trending topics and trending
topics for a specific city. The following table shows WOEID values for several landmarks,
cities, states and continents. Note that although these are all valid WOEIDs, Twitter does
not necessarily have trending topics for all these locations.

Place	WOEID	Place	WOEID
Statue of Liberty	23617050	Iguazu Falls	468785
Los Angeles, CA	2442047	United States	23424977
Washington, D.C.	2514815	North America	24865672
Paris, France	615702	Europe	24865675

---

19. https://developer.twitter.com/en/docs/trends/locations-with-trending-topics/api-
    reference/get-trends-available.

You also can search for locations close to a location that you specify with latitude and longitude values. To do so, call the Tweepy API's **trends_closest method**, which invokes the Twitter API's trends/closest method.[20]

12.11.2 Getting a List of Trending Topics

The Tweepy API's **trends_place method** calls the Twitter Trends API's trends/place method[21] to get the top 50 trending topics for the location with the specified WOEID. You can get the WOEIDs from the woeid attribute in each dictionary returned by the trends_available or trends_closest methods discussed in the previous section, or you can find a location's Yahoo! Where on Earth ID (WOEID) by searching for a city/town, state, country, address, zip code or landmark at

> http://www.woeidlookup.com

You also can look up WOEID's programmatically using Yahoo!'s web services via Python libraries like woeid[22]:

> https://github.com/Ray-SunR/woeid

Worldwide Trending Topics

Let's get today's worldwide trending topics (your results will differ):

```
In [35]: world_trends = api.trends_place(id=1)
```

Method trends_place returns a one-element list containing a dictionary. The dictionary's 'trends' key refers to a list of dictionaries representing each trend:

```
In [36]: trends_list = world_trends[0]['trends']
```

Each trend dictionary has name, url, promoted_content (indicating the tweet is an advertisement), query and tweet_volume keys (shown below). The following trend is in Spanish—#BienvenidoSeptiembre means "Welcome September":

```
In [37]: trends_list[0]
Out[37]:
{'name': '#BienvenidoSeptiembre',
 'url': 'http://twitter.com/search?q=%23BienvenidoSeptiembre',
 'promoted_content': None,
 'query': '%23BienvenidoSeptiembre',
 'tweet_volume': 15186}
```

For trends with more than 10,000 tweets, the tweet_volume is the number of tweets; otherwise, it's None. Let's use a list comprehension to filter the list so that it contains only trends with more than 10,000 tweets:

```
In [38]: trends_list = [t for t in trends_list if t['tweet_volume']]
```

Next, let's sort the trends in *descending* order by tweet_volume:

```
In [39]: from operator import itemgetter

In [40]: trends_list.sort(key=itemgetter('tweet_volume'), reverse=True)
```

---

20. https://developer.twitter.com/en/docs/trends/locations-with-trending-topics/api-reference/get-trends-closest.
21. https://developer.twitter.com/en/docs/trends/trends-for-location/api-reference/get-trends-place.
22. You'll need a Yahoo! API key as described in the woeid module's documentation.

Now, let's display the names of the top five trending topics:

```
In [41]: for trend in trends_list[:5]:
    ...:         print(trend['name'])
    ...:
#HBDJanaSenaniPawanKalyan
#BackToHogwarts
Khalil Mack
#ItalianGP
Alisson
```

New York City Trending Topics
Now, let's get the top five trending topics for New York City (WOEID 2459115). The following code performs the same tasks as above, but for the different WOEID:

```
In [42]: nyc_trends = api.trends_place(id=2459115)  # New York City WOEID

In [43]: nyc_list = nyc_trends[0]['trends']

In [44]: nyc_list = [t for t in nyc_list if t['tweet_volume']]

In [45]: nyc_list.sort(key=itemgetter('tweet_volume'), reverse=True)

In [46]: for trend in nyc_list[:5]:
    ...:         print(trend['name'])
    ...:
#IDOL100M
#TuesdayThoughts
#HappyBirthdayLiam
NAFTA
#USOpen
```

12.11.3 Create a Word Cloud from Trending Topics

In the "Natural Language Processing" chapter, we used the WordCloud library to create word clouds. Let's use it again here, to visualize New York City's trending topics that have more than 10,000 tweets each. First, let's create a dictionary of key–value pairs consisting of the trending topic names and tweet_volumes:

```
In [47]: topics = {}

In [48]: for trend in nyc_list:
    ...:         topics[trend['name']] = trend['tweet_volume']
    ...:
```

Next, let's create a WordCloud from the topics dictionary's key–value pairs, then output the word cloud to the image file TrendingTwitter.png (shown after the code). The argument prefer_horizontal=0.5 *suggests* that 50% of the words should be horizontal, though the software may ignore that to fit the content:

```
In [49]: from wordcloud import WordCloud

In [50]: wordcloud = WordCloud(width=1600, height=900,
    ...:         prefer_horizontal=0.5, min_font_size=10, colormap='prism',
    ...:         background_color='white')
    ...:

In [51]: wordcloud = wordcloud.fit_words(topics)
```

```
In [52]: wordcloud = wordcloud.to_file('TrendingTwitter.png')
```

The resulting word cloud is shown below—yours will differ based on the trending topics the day you run the code:

12.12 **Cleaning/Preprocessing Tweets for Analysis**

Data cleaning is one of the most common tasks that data scientists perform. Depending on how you intend to process tweets, you'll need to use natural language processing to normalize them by performing some or all of the data cleaning tasks in the following table. Many of these can be performed using the libraries introduced in the "Natural Language Processing (NLP)" chapter:

Tweet cleaning tasks	
Converting all text to the same case	Removing stop words
Removing # symbol from hashtags	Removing RT (retweet) and FAV (favorite)
Removing @-mentions	Removing URLs
Removing duplicates	Stemming
Removing excess whitespace	Lemmatization
Removing hashtags	Tokenization
Removing punctuation	

tweet-preprocessor Library and TextBlob Utility Functions
In this section, we'll use the **tweet-preprocessor library**

```
https://github.com/s/preprocessor
```

to perform some basic tweet cleaning. It can automatically remove any combination of:

- URLs,
- @-mentions (like @nasa),
- hashtags (like #mars),
- Twitter reserved words (like, RT for retweet and FAV for favorite, which is similar to a "like" on other social networks),
- emojis (all or just smileys) and
- numbers

The following table shows the module's constants representing each option:

Option	Option constant
@-Mentions (e.g., @nasa)	OPT.MENTION
Emoji	OPT.EMOJI
Hashtag (e.g., #mars)	OPT.HASHTAG
Number	OPT.NUMBER
Reserved Words (RT and FAV)	OPT.RESERVED
Smiley	OPT.SMILEY
URL	OPT.URL

Installing tweet-preprocessor

To install tweet-preprocessor, open your Anaconda Prompt (Windows), Terminal (macOS/Linux) or shell (Linux), then issue the following command:

```
pip install tweet-preprocessor
```

Windows users might need to run the Anaconda Prompt as an administrator for proper software installation privileges. To do so, right-click Anaconda Prompt in the start menu and select **More > Run as administrator**.

Cleaning a Tweet

Let's do some basic tweet cleaning that we'll use in a later example in this chapter. The tweet-preprocessor library's module name is preprocessor. Its documentation recommends that you import the module as follows:

```
In [1]: import preprocessor as p
```

To set the cleaning options you'd like to use call the module's **set_options** function. In this case, we'd like to remove URLs and Twitter reserved words:

```
In [2]: p.set_options(p.OPT.URL, p.OPT.RESERVED)
```

Now let's clean a sample tweet containing a reserved word (RT) and a URL:

```
In [3]: tweet_text = 'RT A sample retweet with a URL https://nasa.gov'
```

```
In [4]: p.clean(tweet_text)
Out[4]: 'A sample retweet with a URL'
```

12.13 Twitter Streaming API

Twitter's free Streaming API sends to your app *randomly selected* tweets dynamically as they occur—up to a maximum of one percent of the tweets per day. According to InternetLiveStats.com, there are approximately 6000 tweets per second, which is over 500 million tweets per day.[23] So the Streaming API gives you access to approximately five million tweets per day. Twitter used to allow free access to 10% of streaming tweets, but this service—called the *fire hose*—is now available only as a paid service. In this section, we'll use a class definition and an IPython session to walk through the steps for processing

---

23. http://www.internetlivestats.com/twitter-statistics/.

streaming tweets. Note that the code for receiving a tweet stream requires creating a *custom class* that *inherits* from another class. These topics are covered in Chapter 10.

12.13.1 Creating a Subclass of StreamListener

The Streaming API returns tweets as they happen that match your search criteria. Rather than connecting to Twitter on each method call, a stream uses a *persistent* connection to **push** (that is, send) tweets to your app. The rate at which those tweets arrive varies tremendously, based on your search criteria. The more popular a topic is, the more likely it is that the tweets will arrive quickly.

You create a subclass of Tweepy's **StreamListener class** to process the tweet stream. An object of this class is the *listener* that's notified when each new tweet (or other message sent by Twitter[24]) arrives. Each message Twitter sends results in a call to a StreamListener method. The following table summarizes several such methods. StreamListener already defines each method, so you redefine only the methods you need—this is known as *overriding*. For additional StreamListener methods, see:

> https://github.com/tweepy/tweepy/blob/master/tweepy/streaming.py

Method	Description
on_connect(self)	Called when you successfully connect to the Twitter stream. This is for statements that should execute only if your app is connected to the stream.
on_status(self, status)	Called when a tweet arrives—status is an object of Tweepy's Status.
on_limit(self, track)	Called when a limit notice arrives. This occurs if your search matches more tweets than Twitter can deliver based on its current streaming rate limits. In this case, the limit notice contains the number of matching tweets that could not be delivered.
on_error(self, status_code)	Called in response to error codes sent by Twitter.
on_timeout(self)	Called if the connection times out—that is, the Twitter server is not responding.
on_warning(self, notice)	Called if Twitter sends a disconnect warning to indicate that the connection might be closed. For example, Twitter maintains a queue of the tweets it's pushing to your app. If the app does not read the tweets fast enough, on_warning's notice argument will contain a warning message indicating that the connection will terminate if the queue becomes full.

Class TweetListener
Our StreamListener subclass TweetListener is defined in tweetlistener.py. We discuss the TweetListener's components here. Line 6 indicates that class TweetListener is a subclass of tweepy.StreamListener. This ensures that our new class has class StreamListener's default method implementations.

---

24. For details on the messages, see https://developer.twitter.com/en/docs/tweets/filter-realtime/guides/streaming-message-types.html.

```
 1   # tweetlistener.py
 2   """tweepy.StreamListener subclass that processes tweets as they arrive."""
 3   import tweepy
 4   from textblob import TextBlob
 5
 6   class TweetListener(tweepy.StreamListener):
 7       """Handles incoming Tweet stream."""
 8
```

Class TweetListener: __init__ Method

The following lines define the TweetListener class's __init__ method, which is called when you create a new TweetListener object. The api parameter is the Tweepy API object that TweetListener will use to interact with Twitter. The limit parameter is the total number of tweets to process—10 by default. We added this parameter to enable you to control the number of tweets to receive. As you'll soon see, we terminate the stream when that limit is reached. If you set limit to None, the stream will not terminate automatically. Line 11 creates an instance variable to keep track of the number of tweets processed so far, and line 12 creates a constant to store the limit. If you're not familiar with __init__ and super() from previous chapters, line 13 ensures that the api object is stored properly for use by your listener object.

```
 9       def __init__(self, api, limit=10):
10           """Create instance variables for tracking number of tweets."""
11           self.tweet_count = 0
12           self.TWEET_LIMIT = limit
13           super().__init__(api)  # call superclass's init
14
```

Class TweetListener: on_connect Method

Method **on_connect** is called when your app successfully connects to the Twitter stream. We override the default implementation to display a "Connection successful" message.

```
15       def on_connect(self):
16           """Called when your connection attempt is successful, enabling
17           you to perform appropriate application tasks at that point."""
18           print('Connection successful\n')
19
```

Class TweetListener: on_status Method

Method **on_status** is called by Tweepy when each tweet arrives. This method's second parameter receives a Tweepy Status object representing the tweet. Lines 23–26 get the tweet's text. First, we assume the tweet uses the new 280-character limit, so we attempt to access the tweet's extended_tweet property and get its full_text. An exception will occur if the tweet does not have an extended_tweet property. In this case, we get the text property instead. Lines 28–30 then display the screen_name of the user who sent the tweet, the lang (that is language) of the tweet and the tweet_text. If the language is not English ('en'), lines 32–33 use a TextBlob to translate the tweet and display it in English. We increment self.tweet_count (line 36), then compare it to self.TWEET_LIMIT in the return statement. If on_status returns True, the stream remains open. When on_status returns False, Tweepy disconnects from the stream.

```
20      def on_status(self, status):
21          """Called when Twitter pushes a new tweet to you."""
22          # get the tweet text
23          try:
24              tweet_text = status.extended_tweet.full_text
25          except:
26              tweet_text = status.text
27
28          print(f'Screen name: {status.user.screen_name}:')
29          print(f'   Language: {status.lang}')
30          print(f'      Status: {tweet_text}')
31
32          if status.lang != 'en':
33              print(f' Translated: {TextBlob(tweet_text).translate()}')
34
35          print()
36          self.tweet_count += 1  # track number of tweets processed
37
38          # if TWEET_LIMIT is reached, return False to terminate streaming
39          return self.tweet_count != self.TWEET_LIMIT
```

12.13.2 Initiating Stream Processing

Let's use an IPython session to test our new TweetListener.

Authenticating

First, you must authenticate with Twitter and create a Tweepy API object:

```
In [1]: import tweepy

In [2]: import keys

In [3]: auth = tweepy.OAuthHandler(keys.consumer_key,
   ...:                            keys.consumer_secret)
   ...:

In [4]: auth.set_access_token(keys.access_token,
   ...:                       keys.access_token_secret)
   ...:

In [5]: api = tweepy.API(auth, wait_on_rate_limit=True,
   ...:                  wait_on_rate_limit_notify=True)
   ...:
```

Creating a TweetListener

Next, create an object of the TweetListener class and initialize it with the api object:

```
In [6]: from tweetlistener import TweetListener

In [7]: tweet_listener = TweetListener(api)
```

We did not specify the limit argument, so this TweetListener terminates after 10 tweets.

Creating a Stream

A Tweepy **Stream** object manages the connection to the Twitter stream and passes the messages to your TweetListener. The Stream constructor's auth keyword argument receives the api object's auth property, which contains the previously configured OAuth-Handler object. The listener keyword argument receives your listener object:

```
In [8]: tweet_stream = tweepy.Stream(auth=api.auth,
   ...:                              listener=tweet_listener)
   ...:
```

Starting the Tweet Stream

The Stream object's **filter method** begins the streaming process. Let's track tweets about the NASA Mars rovers. Here, we use the track parameter to pass a list of search terms:

```
In [9]: tweet_stream.filter(track=['Mars Rover'], is_async=True)
```

The Streaming API will return full tweet JSON objects for tweets that match any of the terms, not just in the tweet's text, but also in @-mentions, hashtags, expanded URLs and other information that Twitter maintains in a tweet object's JSON. So, you might not see the search terms you're tracking if you look only at the tweet's text.

Asynchronous vs. Synchronous Streams

The is_async=True argument indicates that filter should initiate an **asynchronous tweet stream**. This allows your code to continue executing while your listener waits to receive tweets and is useful if you decide to terminate the stream early. When you execute an asynchronous tweet stream in IPython, you'll see the next In [] prompt and can terminate the tweet stream by setting the Stream object's **running property** to False, as in:

```
tweet_stream.running=False
```

Without the is_async=True argument, filter initiates a **synchronous tweet stream**. In this case, IPython would display the next In [] prompt *after* the stream terminates. Asynchronous streams are particularly handy in GUI applications so your users can continue to interact with other parts of the application while tweets arrive. The following shows a portion of the output consisting of two tweets:

```
Connection successful

Screen name: bevjoy:
    Language: en
       Status: RT @SPACEdotcom: With Mars Dust Storm Clearing, Opportunity
Rover Could Finally Wake Up https://t.co/OIRP9UyB8C https://t.co/gTf-
FR3RUkG

Screen name: tourmaline1973:
    Language: en
       Status: RT @BennuBirdy: Our beloved Mars rover isn't done yet, but
she urgently needs our support! Spread the word that you want to keep
calling ou…

...
```

Other filter Method Parameters

Method filter also has parameters for refining your tweet searches by Twitter user ID numbers (to follow tweets from specific users) and by location. For details, see:

```
https://developer.twitter.com/en/docs/tweets/filter-realtime/guides/
    basic-stream-parameters
```

Twitter Restrictions Note

Marketers, researchers and others frequently store tweets they receive from the Streaming API. If you're storing tweets, Twitter requires you to delete any message or location data for which you receive a deletion message. This will occur if a user deletes a tweet or the tweets location data after Twitter pushes that tweet to you. In each case, your listener's **on_delete** method will be called. For deletion rules and message details, see

> https://developer.twitter.com/en/docs/tweets/filter-realtime/guides/
> streaming-message-types

12.14 Tweet Sentiment Analysis

In the "Natural Language Processing (NLP)" chapter, we demonstrated sentiment analysis on sentences. Many researchers and companies perform sentiment analysis on tweets. For example, political researchers might check tweet sentiment during elections season to understand how people feel about specific politicians and issues. Companies might check tweet sentiment to see what people are saying about their products and competitors' products.

In this section, we'll use the techniques introduced in the preceding section to create a script (sentimentlistener.py) that enables you to check the sentiment on a specific topic. The script will keep totals of all the positive, neutral and negative tweets it processes and display the results.

The script receives two command-line arguments representing the topic of the tweets you wish to receive and the number of tweets for which to check the sentiment—only those tweets that are not eliminated are counted. For viral topics, there are large numbers of retweets, which we are not counting, so it could take some time get the number of tweets you specify. You can run the script from the ch12 folder as follows:

```
ipython sentimentlistener.py football 10
```

which produces output like the following. Positive tweets are preceded by a +, negative tweets by a - and neutral tweets by a space:

```
- ftblNeutral: Awful game of football. So boring slow hoofball complete
waste of another 90 minutes of my life that I'll never get back #BURMUN

+ TBulmer28: I've seen 2 successful onside kicks within a 40 minute span.
I love college football

+ CMayADay12: The last normal Sunday for the next couple months. Don't
text me don't call me. I am busy. Football season is finally here?

  rpimusic: My heart legitimately hurts for Kansas football fans

+ DSCunningham30: @LeahShieldsWPSD It's awsome that u like college foot-
ball, but my favorite team is ND - GO IRISH!!!

  damanr: I'm bummed I don't know enough about football to roast @sames-
fandiari properly about the Raiders

+ jamesianosborne: @TheRochaSays @WatfordFC @JackHind Haha.... just when
you think an American understands Football.... so close. Wat…
```

```
    + Tshanerbeer: @PennStateFball @PennStateOnBTN Ah yes, welcome back col-
    lege football. You've been missed.

    - cougarhokie: @hokiehack @skiptyler I can verify the badness of that
    football

    + Unite_Reddevils: @Pablo_di_Don Well make yourself clear it's football
    not soccer we follow European football not MLS soccer

    Tweet sentiment for "football"
    Positive: 6
     Neutral: 2
    Negative: 2
```

The script (`sentimentlistener.py`) is presented below. We focus only on the new capabilities in this example.

Imports

Lines 4–8 import the `keys.py` file and the libraries used throughout the script:

```
1   # sentimentlisener.py
2   """Script that searches for tweets that match a search string
3   and tallies the number of positive, neutral and negative tweets."""
4   import keys
5   import preprocessor as p
6   import sys
7   from textblob import TextBlob
8   import tweepy
9
```

Class SentimentListener: __init__ Method

In addition to the API object that interacts with Twitter, the `__init__` method receives
three additional parameters:

- `sentiment_dict`—a dictionary in which we'll keep track of the tweet sentiments,

- `topic`—the topic we're searching for so we can ensure that it appears in the tweet
  text and

- `limit`—the number of tweets to process (not including the ones we eliminate).

Each of these is stored in the current `SentimentListener` object (`self`).

```
10   class SentimentListener(tweepy.StreamListener):
11       """Handles incoming Tweet stream."""
12
13       def __init__(self, api, sentiment_dict, topic, limit=10):
14           """Configure the SentimentListener."""
15           self.sentiment_dict = sentiment_dict
16           self.tweet_count = 0
17           self.topic = topic
18           self.TWEET_LIMIT = limit
19
20           # set tweet-preprocessor to remove URLs/reserved words
21           p.set_options(p.OPT.URL, p.OPT.RESERVED)
22           super().__init__(api)  # call superclass's init
23
```

Method `on_status`

When a tweet is received, method `on_status`:

- gets the tweet's text (lines 27–30)

- skips the tweet if it's a retweet (lines 33–34)

- cleans the tweet to remove URLs and reserved words like RT and FAV (line 36)

- skips the tweet if it does not have the topic in the tweet text (lines 39–40)

- uses a `TextBlob` to check the tweet's sentiment and updates the `sentiment_dict` accordingly (lines 43–52)

- prints the tweet text (line 55) preceded by + for positive sentiment, space for neutral sentiment or - for negative sentiment and

- checks whether we've processed the specified number of tweets yet (lines 57–60).

```
24    def on_status(self, status):
25        """Called when Twitter pushes a new tweet to you."""
26        # get the tweet's text
27        try:
28            tweet_text = status.extended_tweet.full_text
29        except:
30            tweet_text = status.text
31
32        # ignore retweets
33        if tweet_text.startswith('RT'):
34            return
35
36        tweet_text = p.clean(tweet_text)  # clean the tweet
37
38        # ignore tweet if the topic is not in the tweet text
39        if self.topic.lower() not in tweet_text.lower():
40            return
41
42        # update self.sentiment_dict with the polarity
43        blob = TextBlob(tweet_text)
44        if blob.sentiment.polarity > 0:
45            sentiment = '+'
46            self.sentiment_dict['positive'] += 1
47        elif blob.sentiment.polarity == 0:
48            sentiment = ' '
49            self.sentiment_dict['neutral'] += 1
50        else:
51            sentiment = '-'
52            self.sentiment_dict['negative'] += 1
53
54        # display the tweet
55        print(f'{sentiment} {status.user.screen_name}: {tweet_text}\n')
56
57        self.tweet_count += 1  # track number of tweets processed
58
59        # if TWEET_LIMIT is reached, return False to terminate streaming
60        return self.tweet_count != self.TWEET_LIMIT
61
```

Main Application

The main application is defined in the function main (lines 62–87; discussed after the following code), which is called by lines 90–91 when you execute the file as a script. So sentimentlistener.py can be imported into IPython or other modules to use class SentimentListener as we did with TweetListener in the previous section:

```
62  def main():
63      # configure the OAuthHandler
64      auth = tweepy.OAuthHandler(keys.consumer_key, keys.consumer_secret)
65      auth.set_access_token(keys.access_token, keys.access_token_secret)
66
67      # get the API object
68      api = tweepy.API(auth, wait_on_rate_limit=True,
69                       wait_on_rate_limit_notify=True)
70
71      # create the StreamListener subclass object
72      search_key = sys.argv[1]
73      limit = int(sys.argv[2])   # number of tweets to tally
74      sentiment_dict = {'positive': 0, 'neutral': 0, 'negative': 0}
75      sentiment_listener = SentimentListener(api,
76          sentiment_dict, search_key, limit)
77
78      # set up Stream
79      stream = tweepy.Stream(auth=api.auth, listener=sentiment_listener)
80
81      # start filtering English tweets containing search_key
82      stream.filter(track=[search_key], languages=['en'], is_async=False)
83
84      print(f'Tweet sentiment for "{search_key}"')
85      print('Positive:', sentiment_dict['positive'])
86      print(' Neutral:', sentiment_dict['neutral'])
87      print('Negative:', sentiment_dict['negative'])
88
89  # call main if this file is executed as a script
90  if __name__ == '__main__':
91      main()
```

Lines 72–73 get the command-line arguments. Line 74 creates the sentiment_dict dictionary that keeps track of the tweet sentiments. Lines 75–76 create the SentimentListener. Line 79 creates the Stream object. We once again initiate the stream by calling Stream method filter (line 82). However, this example uses a synchronous stream so that lines 84–87 display the sentiment report only after the specified number of tweets (limit) are processed. In this call to filter, we also provided the keyword argument languages, which specifies a list of language codes. The one language code 'en' indicates Twitter should return only English language tweets.

12.15 Geocoding and Mapping

In this section, we'll collect streaming tweets, then plot the locations of those tweets. Most tweets do not include latitude and longitude coordinates, because Twitter disables this by default for all users. Those who wish to include their precise location in tweets must opt into that feature. Though most tweets do not include precise location information, a large percentage include the user's home location information; however, even that is sometimes invalid, such as "Far Away" or a fictitious location from a user's favorite movie.

In this section, for simplicity, we'll use the `location` property of the tweet's `User` object to plot that user's location on an interactive map. The map will let you zoom in and out and drag to move the map around so you can look at different areas (known as *panning*). For each tweet, we'll display a map marker that you can click to see a popup containing the user's screen name and tweet text.

We'll ignore retweets and tweets that do not contain the search topic. For other tweets, we'll track the percentage of tweets with location information. When we get the latitude and longitude information for those locations, we'll also track the percentage of those tweets that had invalid location data.

geopy Library

We'll use the **geopy library** (`https://github.com/geopy/geopy`) to translate locations into latitude and longitude coordinates—known as **geocoding**—so we can place markers on a map. The library supports dozens of geocoding web services, many of which have free or lite tiers. For this example, we'll use the **OpenMapQuest geocoding service** (discussed shortly). You installed geopy in Section 12.6.

OpenMapQuest Geocoding API

We'll use the OpenMapQuest Geocoding API to convert locations, such as Boston, MA into their latitudes and longitudes, such as 42.3602534 and -71.0582912, for plotting on maps. OpenMapQuest currently allows 15,000 transactions per month on their free tier. To use the service, first sign up at

```
https://developer.mapquest.com/
```

Once logged in, go to

```
https://developer.mapquest.com/user/me/apps
```

and click **Create a New Key**, fill in the **App Name** field with a name of your choosing, leave the **Callback URL** empty and click **Create App** to create an API key. Next, click your app's name in the web page to see your consumer key. In the `keys.py` file you used earlier in the chapter, store the consumer key by replacing *YourKeyHere* in the line

```
mapquest_key = 'YourKeyHere'
```

As we did earlier in the chapter, we'll import `keys.py` to access this key.

Folium Library and Leaflet.js JavaScript Mapping Library

For the maps in this example, we'll use the **folium library**

```
https://github.com/python-visualization/folium
```

which uses the popular Leaflet.js JavaScript mapping library to display maps. The maps that folium produces are saved as HTML files that you can view in your web browser. To install folium, execute the following command:

```
pip install folium
```

Maps from OpenStreetMap.org

By default, Leaflet.js uses open source maps from `OpenStreetMap.org`. These maps are copyrighted by the OpenStreetMap.org contributors. To use these maps[25], they require the following copyright notice:

```
Map data © OpenStreetMap contributors
```

and they state:

> *You must make it clear that the data is available under the Open Database License. This can be achieved by providing a "License" or "Terms" link which links to* www.openstreetmap.org/copyright *or* www.opendatacommons.org/licenses/odbl.

12.15.1 Getting and Mapping the Tweets

Let's interactively develop the code that plots tweet locations. We'll use utility functions from our `tweetutilities.py` file and class `LocationListener` in `locationlistener.py`. We'll explain the details of the utility functions and class in the subsequent sections.

Get the API Object

As in the other streaming examples, let's authenticate with Twitter and get the Tweepy `API` object. In this case, we do this via the `get_API` utility function in `tweetutilities.py`:

```
In [1]: from tweetutilities import get_API

In [2]: api = get_API()
```

Collections Required By `LocationListener`

Our `LocationListener` class requires two collections: A list (`tweets`) to store the tweets we collect and a dictionary (`counts`) to track the total number of tweets we collect and the number that have location data:

```
In [3]: tweets = []

In [4]: counts = {'total_tweets': 0, 'locations': 0}
```

Creating the `LocationListener`

For this example, the `LocationListener` will collect 50 tweets about `'football'`:

```
In [5]: from locationlistener import LocationListener

In [6]: location_listener = LocationListener(api, counts_dict=counts,
   ...:     tweets_list=tweets, topic='football', limit=50)
   ...:
```

The `LocationListener` will use our utility function `get_tweet_content` to extract the screen name, tweet text and location from each tweet, place that data in a dictionary.

Configure and Start the Stream of Tweets

Next, let's set up our `Stream` to look for English language `'football'` tweets:

```
In [7]: import tweepy
```

---

25. https://wiki.osmfoundation.org/wiki/Licence/Licence_and_Legal_FAQ.

```
In [8]: stream = tweepy.Stream(auth=api.auth, listener=location_listener)

In [9]: stream.filter(track=['football'], languages=['en'], is_async=False)
```

Now wait to receive the tweets. Though we do not show them here (to save space), the
LocationListener displays each tweet's screen name and text so you can see the live
stream. If you're not receiving any (perhaps because it is not football season), you might
want to type *Ctrl + C* to terminate the previous snippet then try again with a different
search term.

Displaying the Location Statistics
When the next In [] prompt displays, we can check how many tweets we processed, how
many had locations and the percentage that had locations:

```
In [10]: counts['total_tweets']
Out[10]: 63

In [11]: counts['locations']
Out[11]: 50

In [12]: print(f'{counts["locations"] / counts["total_tweets"]:.1%}')
79.4%
```

In this particular execution, 79.4% of the tweets contained location data.

Geocoding the Locations
Now, let's use our get_geocodes utility function from tweetutilities.py to geocode the
location of each tweet stored in the list tweets:

```
In [13]: from tweetutilities import get_geocodes

In [14]: bad_locations = get_geocodes(tweets)
Getting coordinates for tweet locations...
OpenMapQuest service timed out. Waiting.
OpenMapQuest service timed out. Waiting.
Done geocoding
```

Sometimes the OpenMapQuest geocoding service times out, meaning that it cannot
handle your request immediately and you need to try again. In that case, our function get_-
geocodes displays a message, waits for a short time, then retries the geocoding request.

As you'll soon see, for each tweet with a *valid* location, the get_geocodes function
adds to the tweet's dictionary in the tweets list two new keys—'latitude' and 'longitude'. For the corresponding values, the function uses the tweet's coordinates that Open-
MapQuest returns.

Displaying the Bad Location Statistics
When the next In [] prompt displays, we can check the percentage of tweets that had
invalid location data:

```
In [15]: bad_locations
Out[15]: 7

In [16]: print(f'{bad_locations / counts["locations"]:.1%}')
14.0%
```

In this case, of the 50 tweets with location data, 7 (14%) had invalid locations.

Cleaning the Data

Before we plot the tweet locations on a map, let's use a pandas DataFrame to clean the data. When you create a DataFrame from the tweets list, it will contain the value NaN for the 'latitude' and 'longitude' of any tweet that did not have a valid location. We can remove any such rows by calling the DataFrame's **dropna method**:

```
In [17]: import pandas as pd

In [18]: df = pd.DataFrame(tweets)

In [19]: df = df.dropna()
```

Creating a Map with Folium

Now, let's create a folium **Map** on which we'll plot the tweet locations:

```
In [20]: import folium

In [21]: usmap = folium.Map(location=[39.8283, -98.5795],
    ...:                     tiles='Stamen Terrain',
    ...:                     zoom_start=5, detect_retina=True)
    ...:
```

The location keyword argument specifies a sequence containing latitude and longitude coordinates for the map's center point. The values above are the geographic center of the continental United States (http://bit.ly/CenterOfTheUS). It's possible that some of the tweets we plot will be outside the U.S. In this case, you will not see them initially when you open the map. You can zoom in and out using the + and - buttons at the top-left of the map, or you can pan the map by dragging it with the mouse to see anywhere in the world.

The zoom_start keyword argument specifies the map's initial zoom level, lower values show more of the world and higher values show less. On our system, 5 displays the entire continental United States. The detect_retina keyword argument enables folium to detect high-resolution screens. When it does, it requests higher-resolution maps from OpenStreetMap.org and changes the zoom level accordingly.

Creating Popup Markers for the Tweet Locations

Next, let's iterate through the DataFrame and add to the Map folium Popup objects containing each tweet's text. In this case, we'll use method **itertuples** to create tuples from each row of the DataFrame. Each tuple will contain a property for each DataFrame column:

```
In [22]: for t in df.itertuples():
    ...:     text = ': '.join([t.screen_name, t.text])
    ...:     popup = folium.Popup(text, parse_html=True)
    ...:     marker = folium.Marker((t.latitude, t.longitude),
    ...:                            popup=popup)
    ...:     marker.add_to(usmap)
    ...:
```

First, we create a string (text) containing the user's screen_name and tweet text separated by a colon. This will be displayed on the map if you click the corresponding marker. The second statement creates a folium **Popup** to display the text. The third statement creates a folium **Marker** object using a tuple to specify the Marker's latitude and longitude. The popup keyword argument associates the tweet's Popup object with the new Marker. Finally, the last statement calls the Marker's **add_to method** to specify the Map that will display the Marker.

Saving the Map

The last step is to call the Map's **save** method to store the map in an HTML file, which you can then double click to open in your web browser:

```
In [23]: usmap.save('tweet_map.html')
```

The resulting map follows. The Markers on your map will differ:

Map data © OpenStreetMap contributors.
The data is available under the Open Database License www.openstreetmap.org/copyright.

12.15.2 Utility Functions in tweetutilities.py

Here we present the utility functions get_tweet_content and get_geo_codes used in the preceding section's IPython session. In each case, the line numbers start from 1 for discussion purposes. These are both defined in tweetutilities.py, which is included in the ch12 examples folder.

get_tweet_content Utility Function

Function get_tweet_content receives a Status object (tweet) and creates a dictionary containing the tweet's screen_name (line 4), text (lines 7–10) and location (lines 12–13). The location is included only if the location keyword argument is True. For the tweet's text, we try to use the full_text property of an extended_tweet. If it's not available, we use the text property:

```
1  def get_tweet_content(tweet, location=False):
2      """Return dictionary with data from tweet (a Status object)."""
3      fields = {}
4      fields['screen_name'] = tweet.user.screen_name
5
6      # get the tweet's text
7      try:
8          fields['text'] = tweet.extended_tweet.full_text
9      except:
10         fields['text'] = tweet.text
11
```

```
12        if location:
13            fields['location'] = tweet.user.location
14
15        return fields
```

get_geocodes Utility Function

Function `get_geocodes` receives a list of dictionaries containing tweets and geocodes their locations. If geocoding is successful for a tweet, the function adds the latitude and longitude to the tweet's dictionary in `tweet_list`. This code requires class **OpenMapQuest** from the geopy module, which we import into the file tweetutilities.py as follows:

```python
from geopy import OpenMapQuest
```

```python
1   def get_geocodes(tweet_list):
2       """Get the latitude and longitude for each tweet's location.
3       Returns the number of tweets with invalid location data."""
4       print('Getting coordinates for tweet locations...')
5       geo = OpenMapQuest(api_key=keys.mapquest_key)  # geocoder
6       bad_locations = 0
7
8       for tweet in tweet_list:
9           processed = False
10          delay = .1  # used if OpenMapQuest times out to delay next call
11          while not processed:
12              try:  # get coordinates for tweet['location']
13                  geo_location = geo.geocode(tweet['location'])
14                  processed = True
15              except:  # timed out, so wait before trying again
16                  print('OpenMapQuest service timed out. Waiting.')
17                  time.sleep(delay)
18                  delay += .1
19
20          if geo_location:
21              tweet['latitude'] = geo_location.latitude
22              tweet['longitude'] = geo_location.longitude
23          else:
24              bad_locations += 1  # tweet['location'] was invalid
25
26      print('Done geocoding')
27      return bad_locations
```

The function operates as follows:

- Line 5 creates the OpenMapQuest object we'll use to geocode locations. The api_key keyword argument is loaded from the keys.py file you edited earlier.

- Line 6 initializes bad_locations which we use to keep track of the number of invalid locations in the tweet objects we collected.

- In the loop, lines 9–18 attempt to geocode the current tweet's location. Sometimes the OpenMapQuest geocoding service will time out, meaning that it's temporarily unavailable. This can happen if you make too many requests too quickly. So, the while loop continues executing as long as processed is False. In each iteration, this loop calls the OpenMapQuest object's **geocode method** with the tweet's location string as an argument. If successful, processed is set to True and the loop terminates.

Otherwise, lines 16–18 display a time-out message, wait for delay seconds and increase the delay in case we get another time out. Line 17 calls the Python Standard Library time module's sleep method to pause the code execution.

• After the while loop terminates, lines 20–24 check whether location data was returned and, if so, add it to the tweet's dictionary. Otherwise, line 24 increments the bad_locations counter.

• Finally, the function prints a message that it's done geocoding and returns the bad_locations value.

12.15.3 Class LocationListener

Class LocationListener performs many of the same tasks we demonstrated in the prior streaming examples, so we'll focus on just a few lines in this class:

```
1   # locationlistener.py
2   """Receives tweets matching a search string and stores a list of
3   dictionaries containing each tweet's screen_name/text/location."""
4   import tweepy
5   from tweetutilities import get_tweet_content
6
7   class LocationListener(tweepy.StreamListener):
8       """Handles incoming Tweet stream to get location data."""
9
10      def __init__(self, api, counts_dict, tweets_list, topic, limit=10):
11          """Configure the LocationListener."""
12          self.tweets_list = tweets_list
13          self.counts_dict = counts_dict
14          self.topic = topic
15          self.TWEET_LIMIT = limit
16          super().__init__(api)  # call superclass's init
17
18      def on_status(self, status):
19          """Called when Twitter pushes a new tweet to you."""
20          # get each tweet's screen_name, text and location
21          tweet_data = get_tweet_content(status, location=True)
22
23          # ignore retweets and tweets that do not contain the topic
24          if (tweet_data['text'].startswith('RT') or
25              self.topic.lower() not in tweet_data['text'].lower()):
26              return
27
28          self.counts_dict['total_tweets'] += 1  # original tweet
29
30          # ignore tweets with no location
31          if not status.user.location:
32              return
33
34          self.counts_dict['locations'] += 1  # tweet with location
35          self.tweets_list.append(tweet_data)  # store the tweet
36          print(f'{status.user.screen_name}: {tweet_data["text"]}\n')
37
38          # if TWEET_LIMIT is reached, return False to terminate streaming
39          return self.counts_dict['locations'] != self.TWEET_LIMIT
```

In this case, the __init__ method receives a counts dictionary that we use to keep track of the total number of tweets processed and a tweet_list in which we store the dictionaries returned by the get_tweet_content utility function.

Method on_status:

- Calls get_tweet_content to get the screen name, text and location of each tweet.

- Ignores the tweet if it is a retweet or if the text does not include the topic we're searching for—we'll use only original tweets containing the search string.

- Adds 1 to the value of the 'total_tweets' key in the counts dictionary to track the number of original tweets we process.

- Ignores tweets that have no location data.

- Adds 1 to the value of the 'locations' key in the counts dictionary to indicate that we found a tweet with a location.

- Appends to the tweets_list the tweet_data dictionary that get_tweet_content returned.

- Displays the tweet's screen name and tweet text so you can see that the app is making progress.

- Checks whether the TWEET_LIMIT has been reached and, if so, returns False to terminate the stream.

12.16 Ways to Store Tweets

For analysis, you'll commonly store tweets in:

- CSV files—A file format that we introduced in the "Files and Exceptions" chapter.

- pandas DataFrames in memory—CSV files can be loaded easily into DataFrames for cleaning and manipulation.

- SQL databases—Such as MySQL, a free and open source relational database management system (RDBMS).

- NoSQL databases—Twitter returns tweets as JSON documents, so the natural way to store them is in a NoSQL JSON document database, such as MongoDB. Tweepy generally hides the JSON from the developer. If you'd like to manipulate the JSON directly, use the techniques we present in the "Big Data: Hadoop, Spark, NoSQL and IoT" chapter, where we'll look at the PyMongo library.

12.17 Twitter and Time Series

A time series is a sequence of values with timestamps. Some examples are daily closing stock prices, daily high temperatures at a given location, monthly U.S. job-creation numbers, quarterly earnings for a given company and more. Tweets are natural for time-series analysis because they're time stamped. In the "Machine Learning" chapter, we'll use a technique called simple linear regression to make predictions with time series. We'll take another look at time series in the "Deep Learning" chapter when we discuss recurrent neural networks.

12.18 **Wrap-Up**

In this chapter, we explored data mining Twitter, perhaps the most open and accessible of all the social media sites, and one of the most commonly used big-data sources. You created a Twitter developer account and connected to Twitter using your account credentials. We discussed Twitter's rate limits and some additional rules, and the importance of conforming to them.

We looked at the JSON representation of a tweet. We used Tweepy—one of the most widely used Twitter API clients—to authenticate with Twitter and access its APIs. We saw that tweets returned by the Twitter APIs contain much metadata in addition to a tweet's text. We determined an account's followers and whom an account follows, and looked at a user's recent tweets.

We used Tweepy Cursors to conveniently request successive pages of results from various Twitter APIs. We used Twitter's Search API to download past tweets that met specified criteria. We used Twitter's Streaming API to tap into the flow of live tweets as they happened. We used the Twitter Trends API to determine trending topics for various locations and created a word cloud from trending topics.

We used the tweet-preprocessor library to clean and preprocess tweets to prepare them for analysis, and performed sentiment analysis on tweets. We used the folium library to create a map of tweet locations and interacted with it to see the tweets at particular locations. We enumerated common ways to store tweets and noted that tweets are a natural form of time series data. In the next chapter, we'll present IBM's Watson and its cognitive computing capabilities.

13

IBM Watson and Cognitive Computing

Objectives

In this chapter, you'll:

- See Watson's range of services and use their Lite tier to become familiar with them at no charge.
- Try lots of demos of Watson services.
- Understand what cognitive computing is and how you can incorporate it into your applications.
- Register for an IBM Cloud account and get credentials to use various services.
- Install the Watson Developer Cloud Python SDK to interact with Watson services.
- Develop a traveler's companion language translator app by using Python to weave together a mashup of the Watson Speech to Text, Language Translator and Text to Speech services.
- Check out additional resources, such as IBM Watson Redbooks that will help you jump start your custom Watson application development.

13.1 Introduction: IBM Watson and Cognitive Computing

In Chapter 1, we discussed some key IBM artificial-intelligence accomplishments, including beating the two best human Jeopardy! players in a $1 million match. Watson won the competition and IBM donated the prize money to charity. Watson simultaneously executed hundreds of language-analysis algorithms to locate correct answers in 200 million pages of content (including all of Wikipedia) requiring four terabytes of storage.[1,2] IBM researchers trained Watson using machine-learning and reinforcement-learning techniques (which we discuss in upcoming chapters).[3]

Early in our research for this book, we recognized the rapidly growing importance of Watson, so we placed Google Alerts on Watson and related topics. Through those alerts and the newsletters and blogs we follow, we accumulated 900+ current Watson-related articles, documentation pieces and videos. We investigated many competitive services and found Watson's "no credit card required" policy and free *Lite tier* services[4] to be among friendliest to people who'd like to experiment with Watson's services at no charge.

IBM Watson is a cloud-based cognitive-computing platform being employed across a wide range of real-world scenarios. Cognitive-computing systems simulate the pattern-recognition and decision-making capabilities of the human brain to "learn" as they consume more data.[5,6,7] We overview Watson's broad range of web services and provide a hands-on Watson treatment, demonstrating many Watson capabilities. The table on the next page shows just a few of the ways in which organizations are using Watson.

Watson offers an intriguing set of capabilities that you can incorporate into your applications. In this chapter, you'll set up an IBM Cloud account[8] and use the *Lite tier* and IBM's Watson demos to experiment with various web services, such as natural language translation, speech-to-text, text-to-speech, natural language understanding, chatbots, analyzing text for tone and visual object recognition in images and video. We'll briefly overview some additional Watson services and tools.

---

1. `https://www.techrepublic.com/article/ibm-watson-the-inside-story-of-how-the-jeopardy-winning-supercomputer-was-born-and-what-it-wants-to-do-next/`.
2. `https://en.wikipedia.org/wiki/Watson_(computer)`.
3. `https://www.aaai.org/Magazine/Watson/watson.php`, *AI Magazine*, Fall 2010.
4. Always check the latest terms on IBM's website as the terms and services may change.
5. `http://whatis.techtarget.com/definition/cognitive-computing`.
6. `https://en.wikipedia.org/wiki/Cognitive_computing`.
7. `https://www.forbes.com/sites/bernardmarr/2016/03/23/what-everyone-should-know-about-cognitive-computing`.
8. IBM Cloud previously was called Bluemix. You'll still see "`bluemix`" in many of this chapter's URLs.

Watson use cases		
ad targeting	fraud prevention	personal assistants
artificial intelligence	game playing	predictive maintenance
augmented intelligence	genetics	product recommendations
augmented reality	healthcare	robots and drones
chatbots	image processing	self-driving cars
closed captioning	IoT (Internet of Things)	sentiment and mood analysis
cognitive computing	language translation	smart homes
conversational interfaces	machine learning	sports
crime prevention	malware detection	supply-chain management
customer support	medical diagnosis and treatment	threat detection
detecting cyberbullying	medical imaging	virtual reality
drug development	music	voice analysis
education	natural language processing	weather forecasting
facial recognition	natural language understanding	workplace safety
finance	object recognition	

You'll install the Watson Developer Cloud Python Software Development Kit (SDK) for programmatic access to Watson services from your Python code. Then, in our hands-on implementation case study, you'll develop a traveler's companion translation app by quickly and conveniently *mashing up* several Watson services. The app enables English-only and Spanish-only speakers to communicate with one another verbally, despite the language barrier. You'll transcribe English and Spanish audio recordings to text, translate the text to the other language, then synthesize and play English and Spanish audio from the translated text.

Watson is a dynamic and evolving set of capabilities. During the time we worked on this book, new services were added and existing services were updated and/or removed multiple times. The descriptions of the Watson services and the steps we present were accurate as of the time of this writing. We'll post updates as necessary on the book's web page at www.deitel.com.

13.2 IBM Cloud Account and Cloud Console

You'll need a free IBM Cloud account to access Watson's Lite tier services. Each service's description web page lists the service's tiered offerings and what you get with each tier. Though the Lite tier services limit your use, they typically offer what you'll need to familiarize yourself with Watson features and begin using them to develop apps. The limits are subject to change, so rather than list them here, we point you to each service's web page. IBM increased the limits significantly on some services while we were writing this book. Paid tiers are available for use in commercial-grade applications.

To get a free IBM Cloud account, follow the instructions at:

```
https://console.bluemix.net/docs/services/watson/index.html#about
```

You'll receive an e-mail. Follow its instructions to confirm your account. Then you can log in to the IBM Cloud console. Once there, you can go to the **Watson dashboard** at:

```
https://console.bluemix.net/developer/watson/dashboard
```

where you can:

- Browse the Watson services.

- Link to the services you've already registered to use.

- Look at the developer resources, including the Watson documentation, SDKs and various resources for learning Watson.

- View the apps you've created with Watson.

Later, you'll register for and get your credentials to use various Watson services. You can view and manage your list of services and your credentials in the **IBM Cloud dashboard** at:

```
https://console.bluemix.net/dashboard/apps
```

You can also click **Existing Services** in the Watson dashboard to get to this list.

13.3 Watson Services

This section overviews many of Watson's services and provides links to the details for each. Be sure to run the demos to see the services in action. For links to each Watson service's documentation and API reference, visit:

```
https://console.bluemix.net/developer/watson/documentation
```

We provide footnotes with links to each service's details. When you're ready to use a particular service, click the **Create** button on its details page to set up your credentials.

Watson Assistant

The **Watson Assistant service**[9] helps you build chatbots and virtual assistants that enable users to interact via natural language text. IBM provides a web interface that you can use to *train* the Watson Assistant service for specific scenarios associated with your app. For example, a weather chatbot could be trained to respond to questions like, "What is the weather forecast for New York City?" In a customer service scenario, you could create chatbots that answer customer questions and route customers to the correct department, if necessary. Try the demo at the following site to see some sample interactions:

```
https://www.ibm.com/watson/services/conversation/demo/
    index.html#demo
```

Visual Recognition

The **Visual Recognition service**[10] enables apps to locate and understand information in images and video, including colors, objects, faces, text, food and inappropriate content. IBM provides predefined models (used in the service's demo), or you can train and use your own (as you'll do in the "Deep Learning" chapter). Try the following demo with the images provided and upload some of your own:

```
https://watson-visual-recognition-duo-dev.ng.bluemix.net/
```

---

9. `https://console.bluemix.net/catalog/services/watson-assistant-formerly-conversation`.

10. `https://console.bluemix.net/catalog/services/visual-recognition`.

Speech to Text

The **Speech to Text service**,[11] which we'll use in building this chapter's app, converts speech audio files to text transcriptions of the audio. You can give the service keywords to "listen" for, and it tells you whether it found them, what the likelihood of a match was and where the match occurred in the audio. The service can distinguish among multiple speakers. You could use this service to help implement voice-controlled apps, transcribe live audio and more. Try the following demo with its sample audio clips or upload your own:

```
https://speech-to-text-demo.ng.bluemix.net/
```

Text to Speech

The **Text to Speech service**,[12] which we'll also use in building this chapter's app, enables you to synthesize speech from text. You can use **Speech Synthesis Markup Language** (**SSML**) to embed instructions in the text for control over voice inflection, cadence, pitch and more. Currently, this service supports English (U.S. and U.K.), French, German, Italian, Spanish, Portuguese and Japanese. Try the following demo with its plain sample text, its sample text that includes SSML and text that you provide:

```
https://text-to-speech-demo.ng.bluemix.net/
```

Language Translator

The **Language Translator service**,[13] which we'll also use in building in this chapter's app, has two key components:

- translating text between languages and
- identifying text as being written in one of over 60 languages.

Translation is supported to and from English and many languages, as well as between other languages. Try translating text into various languages with the following demo:

```
https://language-translator-demo.ng.bluemix.net/
```

Natural Language Understanding

The **Natural Language Understanding service**[14] analyzes text and produces information including the text's overall sentiment and emotion and keywords ranked by their relevance. Among other things, the service can identify

- people, places, job titles, organizations, companies and quantities.
- categories and concepts like sports, government and politics.
- parts of speech like subjects and verbs.

You also can train the service for industry- and application-specific domains with Watson Knowledge Studio (discussed shortly). Try the following demo with its sample text, with text that you paste in or by providing a link to an article or document online:

```
https://natural-language-understanding-demo.ng.bluemix.net/
```

---

11. `https://console.bluemix.net/catalog/services/speech-to-text`.
12. `https://console.bluemix.net/catalog/services/text-to-speech`.
13. `https://console.bluemix.net/catalog/services/language-translator`.
14. `https://console.bluemix.net/catalog/services/natural-language-understanding`.

Discovery

The **Watson Discovery service**[15] shares many features with the Natural Language Under-standing service but also enables enterprises to store and manage documents. So, for example, organizations can use Watson Discovery to store all their text documents and be able to use natural language understanding across the entire collection. Try this service's demo, which enables you to search recent news articles for companies:

> https://discovery-news-demo.ng.bluemix.net/

Personality Insights

The **Personality Insights service**[16] analyzes text for personality traits. According to the service description, it can help you "gain insight into how and why people think, act, and feel the way they do. This service applies linguistic analytics and personality theory to infer attributes from a person's unstructured text." This information could be used to target product advertising at the people most likely to purchase those products. Try the following demo with tweets from various Twitter accounts or documents built into the demo, with text documents that you paste into the demo or with your own Twitter account:

> https://personality-insights-livedemo.ng.bluemix.net/

Tone Analyzer

The **Tone Analyzer service**[17] analyzes text for its tone in three categories:

- emotions—anger, disgust, fear, joy, sadness.
- social propensities—openness, conscientiousness, extroversion, agreeableness and emotional range.
- language style—analytical, confident, tentative.

Try the following demo with sample tweets, a sample product review, a sample e-mail or text you provide. You'll see the tone analyses at both the document and sentence levels:

> https://tone-analyzer-demo.ng.bluemix.net/

Natural Language Classifier

You *train* the **Natural Language Classifier service**[18] with sentences and phrases that are specific to your application and classify each sentence or phrase. For example, you might classify "I need help with your product" as "tech support" and "My bill is incorrect" as "billing." Once you've trained your classifier, the service can receive sentences and phrases, then use Watson's cognitive computing capabilities and your classifier to return the best matching classifications and their match probabilities. You might then use the returned classifications and probabilities to determine the next steps in your app. For example, in a customer service app where someone is calling in with a question about a particular product, you might use Speech to Text to convert a question into text, use the Natural Language Classifier service to classify the text, then route the call to the appropriate person or department. This service *does not offer a Lite tier*. In the following demo, enter a question

---

15. https://console.bluemix.net/catalog/services/discovery.
16. https://console.bluemix.net/catalog/services/personality-insights.
17. https://console.bluemix.net/catalog/services/tone-analyzer.
18. https://console.bluemix.net/catalog/services/natural-language-classifier.

about the weather—the service will respond by indicating whether your question was about the temperature or the weather conditions:

```
https://natural-language-classifier-demo.ng.bluemix.net/
```

Synchronous and Asynchronous Capabilities
Many of the APIs we discuss throughout the book are **synchronous**—when you call a function or method, the program *waits* for the function or method to return before moving on to the next task. **Asynchronous** programs can start a task, continue doing other things, then be *notified* when the original task completes and returns its results. Many Watson services offer both synchronous and asynchronous APIs.

The Speech to Text demo is a good example of asynchronous APIs. The demo processes sample audio of two people speaking. As the service transcribes the audio, it returns intermediate transcription results, even if it has not yet been able to distinguish among the speakers. The demo displays these intermediate results in parallel with the service's continued work. Sometimes the demo displays "Detecting speakers" while the service figures out who is speaking. Eventually, the service sends updated transcription results for distinguishing among the speakers, and the demo then replaces the prior transcription results.

With today's multi-core computers and multi-computer clusters, the asynchronous APIs can help you improve program performance. However, programming with them can be more complicated than programming with synchronous APIs. When we discuss installing the Watson Developer Cloud Python SDK, we provide a link to the SDK's code examples on GitHub, where you can see examples that use synchronous and asynchronous versions of several services. Each service's API reference provides the complete details.

13.4 Additional Services and Tools

In this section, we overview several Watson advanced services and tools.

Watson Studio
Watson Studio[19] is the new Watson interface for creating and managing your Watson projects and for collaborating with your team members on those projects. You can add data, prepare your data for analysis, create Jupyter Notebooks for interacting with your data, create and train models and work with Watson's deep-learning capabilities. Watson Studio offers a single-user Lite tier. Once you've set up your Watson Studio Lite access by clicking **Create** on the service's details web page

```
https://console.bluemix.net/catalog/services/data-science-experience
```

you can access Watson Studio at

```
https://dataplatform.cloud.ibm.com/
```

Watson Studio contains preconfigured projects.[20] Click **Create a project** to view them:

- Standard—"Work with any type of asset. Add services for analytical assets as you need them."

---

19. https://console.bluemix.net/catalog/services/data-science-experience.
20. https://dataplatform.cloud.ibm.com/.

- Data Science—"Analyze data to discover insights and share your findings with others."

- Visual Recognition—"Tag and classify visual content using the Watson Visual Recognition service."

- Deep Learning—"Build neural networks and deploy deep learning models."

- Modeler—"Build modeler flows to train SPSS models or design deep neural networks."

- Business Analytics—"Create visual dashboards from your data to gain insights faster."

- Data Engineering—"Combine, cleanse, analyze, and shape data using Data Refinery."

- Streams Flow—"Ingest and analyze streaming data using the Streaming Analytics service."

Knowledge Studio

Various Watson services work with *predefined* models, but also allow you to provide custom models that are trained for specific industries or applications. Watson's **Knowledge Studio**[21] helps you build custom models. It allows enterprise teams to work together to create and train new models, which can then be deployed for use by Watson services.

Machine Learning

The **Watson Machine Learning service**[22] enables you to add predictive capabilities to your apps via popular machine-learning frameworks, including Tensorflow, Keras, scikit-learn and others. You'll use scikit-learn and Keras in the next two chapters.

Knowledge Catalog

The **Watson Knowledge Catalog**[23,24] is an advanced enterprise-level tool for securely managing, finding and sharing your organization's data. The tool offers:

- Central access to an enterprise's local and cloud-based data and machine learning models.

- Watson Studio support so users can find and access data, then easily use it in machine-learning projects.

- Security policies that ensure only the people who should have access to specific data actually do.

- Support for over 100 data cleaning and wrangling operations.

- And more.

---

21. https://console.bluemix.net/catalog/services/knowledge-studio.
22. https://console.bluemix.net/catalog/services/machine-learning.
23. https://medium.com/ibm-watson/introducing-ibm-watson-knowledge-catalog-cf42c13032c1.
24. https://dataplatform.cloud.ibm.com/docs/content/catalog/overview-wkc.html.

Cognos Analytics

The IBM **Cognos Analytics**[25] service, which has a 30-day free trial, uses AI and machine learning to discover and visualize information in your data, without any programming on your part. It also provides a natural-language interface that enables you to ask questions which Cognos Analytics answers based on the knowledge it gathers from your data.

13.5 Watson Developer Cloud Python SDK

In this section, you'll install the modules required for the next section's full-implementation Watson case study. For your coding convenience, IBM provides the **Watson Developer Cloud Python SDK** (software development kit). Its `watson_developer_cloud` **module** contains classes that you'll use to interact with Watson services. You'll create objects for each service you need, then interact with the service by calling the object's methods.

To install the SDK[26] open an Anaconda Prompt (Windows; open as Administrator), Terminal (macOS/Linux) or shell (Linux), then execute the following command[27]:

```
pip install --upgrade watson-developer-cloud
```

Modules We'll Need for Audio Recording and Playback

You'll also need two additional modules for audio recording (PyAudio) and playback (PyDub). To install these, use the following commands[28]:

```
pip install pyaudio
pip install pydub
```

SDK Examples

On GitHub, IBM provides sample code demonstrating how to access Watson services using the Watson Developer Cloud Python SDK's classes. You can find the examples at:

```
https://github.com/watson-developer-cloud/python-sdk/tree/master/
    examples
```

13.6 Case Study: Traveler's Companion Translation App

Suppose you're traveling in a Spanish-speaking country, but you do not speak Spanish, and you need to communicate with someone who does not speak English. You could use a translation app to speak in English, and the app could translate that, then speak it in Spanish. The Spanish-speaking person could then respond, and the app could translate that and speak it to you in English.

Here, you'll use three powerful IBM Watson services to implement such a traveler's companion translation app,[29] enabling people who speak different languages to converse

---

25. `https://www.ibm.com/products/cognos-analytics`.
26. For detailed installation instructions and troubleshooting tips, see `https://github.com/watson-developer-cloud/python-sdk/blob/develop/README.md`.
27. Windows users might need to install Microsoft's C++ build tools from `https://visualstudio.microsoft.com/visual-cpp-build-tools/`, then install the `watson-developer-cloud` module.
28. Mac users might need to first execute `conda install -c conda-forge portaudio`.
29. These services could change in the future. If they do, we'll post updates on the book's web page at `http://www.deitel.com/books/IntroToPython`.

in near real time. Combining services like this is known as creating a **mashup**. This app also uses simple file-processing capabilities that we introduced in the "Files and Exceptions" chapter.

13.6.1 Before You Run the App

You'll build this app using the Lite (free) tiers of several IBM Watson services. Before executing the app, make sure that you've registered for an IBM Cloud account, as we discussed earlier in the chapter, so you can get credentials for each of the three services the app uses. Once you have your credentials (described below), you'll insert them in our keys.py file (located in the ch13 examples folder) that we import into the example. Never share your credentials.

As you configure the services below, each service's credentials page also shows you the service's URL. These are the default URLs used by the Watson Developer Cloud Python SDK, so you do not need to copy them. In Section 13.6.3, we present the SimpleLanguageTranslator.py script and a detailed walkthrough of the code.

Registering for the Speech to Text Service

This app uses the Watson Speech to Text service to transcribe English and Spanish audio files to English and Spanish text, respectively. To interact with the service, you must get a username and password. To do so:

1. *Create a Service Instance:* Go to https://console.bluemix.net/catalog/services/speech-to-text and click the **Create** button on the bottom of the page. This auto-generates an API key for you and takes you to a tutorial for working with the Speech to Text service.

2. *Get Your Service Credentials:* To see your API key, click **Manage** at the top-left of the page. To the right of **Credentials**, click **Show credentials**, then copy the **API Key**, and paste it into the variable speech_to_text_key's string in the keys.py file provided in this chapter's ch13 examples folder.

Registering for the Text to Speech Service

In this app, you'll use the Watson Text to Speech service to synthesize speech from text. This service also requires you to get a username and password. To do so:

1. *Create a Service Instance:* Go to https://console.bluemix.net/catalog/services/text-to-speech and click the **Create** button on the bottom of the page. This auto-generates an API key for you and takes you to a tutorial for working with the Text to Speech service.

2. *Get Your Service Credentials:* To see your API key, click **Manage** at the top-left of the page. To the right of **Credentials**, click **Show credentials**, then copy the **API Key** and paste it into the variable text_to_speech_key's string in the keys.py file provided in this chapter's ch13 examples folder.

Registering for the Language Translator Service

In this app, you'll use the Watson Language Translator service to pass text to Watson and receive back the text translated into another language. This service requires you to get an API key. To do so:

1. *Create a Service Instance:* Go to `https://console.bluemix.net/catalog/services/language-translator` and click the **Create** button on the bottom of the page. This auto-generates an API key for you and takes you to a page to manage your instance of the service.

2. *Get Your Service Credentials:* To the right of **Credentials**, click **Show credentials**, then copy the **API Key** and paste it into the variable `translate_key`'s string in the `keys.py` file provided in this chapter's `ch13` examples folder.

Retrieving Your Credentials

To view your credentials at any time, click the appropriate service instance at:

```
https://console.bluemix.net/dashboard/apps
```

13.6.2 Test-Driving the App

Once you've added your credentials to the script, open an Anaconda Prompt (Windows), a Terminal (macOS/Linux) or a shell (Linux). Run the script[30] by executing the following command from the `ch13` examples folder:

```
ipython SimpleLanguageTranslator.py
```

Processing the Question

The app performs 10 steps, which we point out via comments in the code. When the app begins executing:

Step 1 prompts for and records a question. First, the app displays:

```
Press Enter then ask your question in English
```

and waits for you to press *Enter*. When you do, the app displays:

```
Recording 5 seconds of audio
```

Speak your question. We said, "Where is the closest bathroom?" After five seconds, the app displays:

```
Recording complete
```

Step 2 interacts with Watson's Speech to Text service to transcribe your audio to text and displays the result:

```
English: where is the closest bathroom
```

Step 3 then uses Watson's Language Translator service to translate the English text to Spanish and displays the translated text returned by Watson:

```
Spanish: ¿Dónde está el baño más cercano?
```

Step 4 passes this Spanish text to Watson's Text to Speech service to convert the text to an audio file.

Step 5 plays the resulting Spanish audio file.

---

30. The `pydub.playback` module we use in this app issues a warning when you run our script. The warning has to do with module features we don't use and can be ignored. To eliminate this warning, you can install `ffmpeg` for Windows, macOS or Linux from `https://www.ffmpeg.org`.

Processing the Response

At this point, we're ready to process the Spanish speaker's response.

Step 6 displays:

```
Press Enter then speak the Spanish answer
```

and waits for you to press *Enter*. When you do, the app displays:

```
Recording 5 seconds of audio
```

and the Spanish speaker records a response. We do not speak Spanish, so we used Watson's Text to Speech service to *prerecord* Watson saying the Spanish response "El baño más cercano está en el restaurante," then played that audio loud enough for our computer's microphone to record it. We provided this prerecorded audio for you as SpokenResponse.wav in the ch13 folder. If you use this file, play it quickly after pressing *Enter* above as the app records for only 5 seconds.[31] To ensure that the audio loads and plays quickly, you might want to play it once before you press *Enter* to begin recording. After five seconds, the app displays:

```
Recording complete
```

Step 7 interacts with Watson's Speech to Text service to transcribe the Spanish audio to text and displays the result:

```
Spanish response: el baño más cercano está en el restaurante
```

Step 8 then uses Watson's Language Translator service to translate the Spanish text to English and displays the result:

```
English response: The nearest bathroom is in the restaurant
```

Step 9 passes the English text to Watson's Text to Speech service to convert the text to an audio file.

Step 10 then plays the resulting English audio.

13.6.3 SimpleLanguageTranslator.py Script Walkthrough

In this section, we present the SimpleLanguageTranslator.py script's source code, which we've divided into small consecutively numbered pieces. Let's use a top-down approach as we did in the "Control Statements" chapter. Here's the top:

Create a translator app that enables English and Spanish speakers to communicate.

The first refinement is:

Translate a question spoken in English into Spanish speech.
Translate the answer spoken in Spanish into English speech.

We can break the first line of the second refinement into five steps:

Step 1: Prompt for then record English speech into an audio file.
Step 2: Transcribe the English speech to English text.
Step 3: Translate the English text into Spanish text.
Step 4: Synthesize the Spanish text into Spanish speech and save it into an audio file.
Step 5: Play the Spanish audio file.

---

31. For simplicity, we set the app to record five seconds of audio. You can control the duration with the variable SECONDS in function record_audio. It's possible to create a recorder that begins recording once it detects sound and stops recording after a period of silence, but the code is more complicated.

We can break the second line of the second refinement into five steps:

Step 6: Prompt for then record Spanish speech into an audio file.
Step 7: Transcribe the Spanish speech to Spanish text.
Step 8: Translate the Spanish text into English text.
Step 9: Synthesize the English text into English speech and save it into an audio file.
Step 10: Play the English audio.

This top-down development makes the benefits of the divide-and-conquer approach clear, focusing our attention on small pieces of a more significant problem.

In this section's script, we implement the 10 steps specified in the second refinement. **Steps 2** and **7** use the Watson Speech to Text service, **Steps 3** and **8** use the Watson Language Translator service, and **Steps 4** and **9** use the Watson Text to Speech service.

Importing Watson SDK Classes

Lines 4–6 import classes from the watson_developer_cloud module that was installed with the Watson Developer Cloud Python SDK. Each of these classes uses the Watson credentials you obtained earlier to interact with a corresponding Watson service:

- Class **SpeechToTextV1**[32] enables you to pass an audio file to the Watson Speech to Text service and receive a JSON[33] document containing the text transcription.

- Class **LanguageTranslatorV3** enables you to pass text to the Watson Language Translator service and receive a JSON document containing the translated text.

- Class **TextToSpeechV1** enables you to pass text to the Watson Text to Speech service and receive audio of the text spoken in a specified language.

```
1  # SimpleLanguageTranslator.py
2  """Use IBM Watson Speech to Text, Language Translator and Text to Speech
3     APIs to enable English and Spanish speakers to communicate."""
4  from watson_developer_cloud import SpeechToTextV1
5  from watson_developer_cloud import LanguageTranslatorV3
6  from watson_developer_cloud import TextToSpeechV1
```

Other Imported Modules

Line 7 imports the keys.py file containing your Watson credentials. Lines 8–11 import modules that support this app's audio-processing capabilities:

- The pyaudio module enables us to record audio from the microphone.

- pydub and pydub.playback modules enable us to load and play audio files.

- The Python Standard Library's wave module enables us to save WAV (Waveform Audio File Format) files. WAV is a popular audio format originally developed by Microsoft and IBM. This app uses the wave module to save the recorded audio to a .wav file that we send to Watson's Speech to Text service for transcription.

---

32. The V1 in the class name indicates the service's version number. As IBM revises its services, it adds new classes to the watson_developer_cloud module, rather than modifying the existing classes. This ensures that existing apps do not break when the services are updated. The Speech to Text and Text to Speech services are each Version 1 (V1) and the Language Translator service is Version 3 (V3) at the time of this writing.
33. We introduced JSON in the previous chapter, "Data Mining Twitter."

```
 7    import keys  # contains your API keys for accessing Watson services
 8    import pyaudio  # used to record from mic
 9    import pydub  # used to load a WAV file
10    import pydub.playback  # used to play a WAV file
11    import wave  # used to save a WAV file
12
```

Main Program: Function run_translator

Let's look at the main part of the program defined in function run_translator (lines 13–54), which calls the functions defined later in the script. For discussion purposes, we broke run_translator into the 10 steps it performs. In **Step 1** (lines 15–17), we prompt in English for the user to press *Enter*, then speak a question. Function record_audio then records audio for five seconds and stores it in the file english.wav:

```
13    def run_translator():
14        """Calls the functions that interact with Watson services."""
15        # Step 1: Prompt for then record English speech into an audio file
16        input('Press Enter then ask your question in English')
17        record_audio('english.wav')
18
```

In **Step 2**, we call function speech_to_text, passing the file english.wav for transcription and telling the Speech to Text service to transcribe the text using its *predefined* model 'en-US_BroadbandModel'.[34] We then display the transcribed text:

```
19        # Step 2: Transcribe the English speech to English text
20        english = speech_to_text(
21            file_name='english.wav', model_id='en-US_BroadbandModel')
22        print('English:', english)
23
```

In **Step 3**, we call function translate, passing the transcribed text from **Step 2** as the text to translate. Here we tell the Language Translator service to translate the text using its *predefined* model 'en-es' to translate from English (en) to Spanish (es). We then display the Spanish translation:

```
24        # Step 3: Translate the English text into Spanish text
25        spanish = translate(text_to_translate=english, model='en-es')
26        print('Spanish:', spanish)
27
```

In **Step 4**, we call function text_to_speech, passing the Spanish text from **Step 3** for the Text to Speech service to speak using its voice 'es-US_SofiaVoice'. We also specify the file in which the audio should be saved:

```
28        # Step 4: Synthesize the Spanish text into Spanish speech
29        text_to_speech(text_to_speak=spanish, voice_to_use='es-US_SofiaVoice',
30            file_name='spanish.wav')
31
```

---

34. For most languages, the Watson Speech to Text service supports *broadband* and *narrowband* models. Each has to do with the audio quality. For audio captured at 16 kHZ and higher, IBM recommends using the broadband models. In this app, we capture the audio at 44.1 kHZ.

In **Step 5**, we call function play_audio to play the file 'spanish.wav', which contains the Spanish audio for the text we translated in **Step 3**.

```
32          # Step 5: Play the Spanish audio file
33          play_audio(file_name='spanish.wav')
34
```

Finally, **Steps 6–10** repeat what we did in **Steps 1–5**, but for Spanish speech to English speech:

- **Step 6** records the *Spanish* audio.

- **Step 7** transcribes the Spanish audio to Spanish text using the Speech to Text service's predefined model 'es-ES_BroadbandModel'.

- **Step 8** translates the Spanish text to English text using the Language Translator Service's 'es-en' (Spanish-to-English) model.

- **Step 9** creates the English audio using the Text to Speech Service's voice 'en-US_AllisonVoice'.

- **Step 10** plays the English audio.

```
35          # Step 6: Prompt for then record Spanish speech into an audio file
36          input('Press Enter then speak the Spanish answer')
37          record_audio('spanishresponse.wav')
38
39          # Step 7: Transcribe the Spanish speech to Spanish text
40          spanish = speech_to_text(
41              file_name='spanishresponse.wav', model_id='es-ES_BroadbandModel')
42          print('Spanish response:', spanish)
43
44          # Step 8: Translate the Spanish text into English text
45          english = translate(text_to_translate=spanish, model='es-en')
46          print('English response:', english)
47
48          # Step 9: Synthesize the English text into English speech
49          text_to_speech(text_to_speak=english,
50              voice_to_use='en-US_AllisonVoice',
51              file_name='englishresponse.wav')
52
53          # Step 10: Play the English audio
54          play_audio(file_name='englishresponse.wav')
55
```

Now let's implement the functions we call from *Steps 1* through *10*.

Function speech_to_text

To access Watson's Speech to Text service, function speech_to_text (lines 56–87) creates a SpeechToTextV1 object named stt (short for speech-to-text), passing as the argument the API key you set up earlier. The with statement (lines 62–65) opens the audio file specified by the file_name parameter and assigns the resulting file object to audio_file. The open mode 'rb' indicates that we'll read (r) binary data (b)—audio files are stored as bytes in binary format. Next, lines 64–65 use the SpeechToTextV1 object's **recognize method** to invoke the Speech to Text service. The method receives three keyword arguments:

- audio is the file (audio_file) to pass to the Speech to Text service.

- content_type is the media type of the file's contents—'audio/wav' indicates that this is an audio file stored in WAV format.[35]

- model indicates which spoken language model the service will use to recognize the speech and transcribe it to text. This app uses predefined models—either 'en-US_BroadbandModel' (for English) or 'es-ES_BroadbandModel' (for Spanish).

```
56  def speech_to_text(file_name, model_id):
57      """Use Watson Speech to Text to convert audio file to text."""
58      # create Watson Speech to Text client
59      stt = SpeechToTextV1(iam_apikey=keys.speech_to_text_key)
60
61      # open the audio file
62      with open(file_name, 'rb') as audio_file:
63          # pass the file to Watson for transcription
64          result = stt.recognize(audio=audio_file,
65              content_type='audio/wav', model=model_id).get_result()
66
67      # Get the 'results' list. This may contain intermediate and final
68      # results, depending on method recognize's arguments. We asked
69      # for only final results, so this list contains one element.
70      results_list = result['results']
71
72      # Get the final speech recognition result--the list's only element.
73      speech_recognition_result  = results_list[0]
74
75      # Get the 'alternatives' list. This may contain multiple alternative
76      # transcriptions, depending on method recognize's arguments. We did
77      # not ask for alternatives, so this list contains one element.
78      alternatives_list = speech_recognition_result['alternatives']
79
80      # Get the only alternative transcription from alternatives_list.
81      first_alternative = alternatives_list[0]
82
83      # Get the 'transcript' key's value, which contains the audio's
84      # text transcription.
85      transcript = first_alternative['transcript']
86
87      return transcript  # return the audio's text transcription
88
```

The recognize method returns a DetailedResponse object. Its getResult method returns a JSON document containing the transcribed text, which we store in result. The JSON will look similar to the following but depends on the question you ask:

---

35. Media types were formerly known as **MIME (Multipurpose Internet Mail Extensions) types**—a standard that specifies data formats, which programs can use to interpret data correctly.

```
{
    "results": [                                                    Line 70
        {                                                           Line 73
            "alternatives": [                                       Line 78
                {                                                   Line 81
                    "confidence": 0.983,
                    "transcript": "where is the closest bathroom "  Line 85
                }
            ],
            "final": true
        }
    ],
    "result_index": 0
}
```

The JSON contains *nested* dictionaries and lists. To simplify navigating this data structure, lines 70–85 use separate small statements to "pick off" one piece at a time until we get the transcribed text—"where is the closest bathroom ", which we then return. The boxes around portions of the JSON and the line numbers in each box correspond to the statements in lines 70–85. The statements operate as follows:

- Line 70 assigns to `results_list` the list associated with the key `'results'`:

  ```
  results_list = result['results']
  ```

  Depending on the arguments you pass to method `recognize`, this list may contain intermediate and final results. Intermediate results might be useful, for example, if you were transcribing live audio, such as a newscast. We asked for only final results, so this list contains one element.[36]

- Line 73 assigns to `speech_recognition_result` the final speech-recognition result—the only element in `results_list`:

  ```
  speech_recognition_result = results_list[0]
  ```

- Line 78

  ```
  alternatives_list = speech_recognition_result['alternatives']
  ```

  assigns to `alternatives_list` the list associated with the key `'alternatives'`. This list may contain multiple alternative transcriptions, depending on method `recognize`'s arguments. The arguments we passed result in a one-element list.

- Line 81 assigns to `first_alternative` the only element in `alternatives_list`:

  ```
  first_alternative = alternatives_list[0]
  ```

- Line 85 assigns to `transcript` the `'transcript'` key's value, which contains the audio's text transcription:

  ```
  transcript = first_alternative['transcript']
  ```

- Finally, line 87 returns the audio's text transcription.

36. For method `recognize`'s arguments and JSON response details, see https://www.ibm.com/watson/developercloud/speech-to-text/api/v1/python.html?python#recognize-sessionless.

Lines 70–85 could be replaced with the denser statement

```
return result['results'][0]['alternatives'][0]['transcript']
```

but we prefer the separate simpler statements.

Function translate

To access the Watson Language Translator service, function translate (lines 89–111) first creates a LanguageTranslatorV3 object named language_translator, passing as arguments the service version ('2018-05-31'[37]), the API Key you set up earlier and the service's URL. Lines 93–94 use the LanguageTranslatorV3 object's **translate method** to invoke the Language Translator service, passing two keyword arguments:

- text is the string to translate to another language.

- model_id is the predefined model that the Language Translator service will use to understand the original text and translate it into the appropriate language. In this app, model will be one of IBM's *predefined* translation models—'en-es' (for English to Spanish) or 'es-en' (for Spanish to English).

```
89  def translate(text_to_translate, model):
90      """Use Watson Language Translator to translate English to Spanish
91         (en-es) or Spanish to English (es-en) as specified by model."""
92      # create Watson Translator client
93      language_translator = LanguageTranslatorV3(version='2018-05-31',
94          iam_apikey=keys.translate_key)
95
96      # perform the translation
97      translated_text = language_translator.translate(
98          text=text_to_translate, model_id=model).get_result()
99
100     # Get 'translations' list. If method translate's text argument has
101     # multiple strings, the list will have multiple entries. We passed
102     # one string, so the list contains only one element.
103     translations_list = translated_text['translations']
104
105     # get translations_list's only element
106     first_translation = translations_list[0]
107
108     # get 'translation' key's value, which is the translated text
109     translation = first_translation['translation']
110
111     return translation  # return the translated string
112
```

The method returns a DetailedResponse. That object's getResult method returns a JSON document, like:

---

37. According to the Language Translator service's API reference, '2018-05-31' is the current version string at the time of this writing. IBM changes the version string only if they make API changes that are not backward compatible. Even when they do, the service will respond to your calls using the API version you specify in the version string. For more details, see https://www.ibm.com/watson/developercloud/language-translator/api/v3/python.html?python#versioning.

```
{
    "translations": [                                              Line 103
    {                                                              Line 106
      "translation": "¿Dónde está el baño más cercano? "          Line 109
    }
    ],
    "word_count": 5,
    "character_count": 30
}
```

The JSON you get as a response depends on the question you asked and, again, contains nested dictionaries and lists. Lines 103–109 use small statements to pick off the translated text "¿Dónde está el baño más cercano? ". The boxes around portions of the JSON and the line numbers in each box correspond to the statements in lines 103–109. The statements operate as follows:

- Line 103 gets the 'translations' list:

    ```
    translations_list = translated_text['translations']
    ```

    If method translate's text argument has multiple strings, the list will have multiple entries. We passed only one string, so the list contains only one element.

- Line 106 gets translations_list's only element:

    ```
    first_translation = translations_list[0]
    ```

- Line 109 gets the 'translation' key's value, which is the translated text:

    ```
    translation = first_translation['translation']
    ```

- Line 111 returns the translated string.

Lines 103–109 could be replaced with the more concise statement

```
return translated_text['translations'][0]['translation']
```

but again, we prefer the separate simpler statements.

Function text_to_speech

To access the Watson Text to Speech service, function text_to_speech (lines 113–122) creates a TextToSpeechV1 object named tts (short for text-to-speech), passing as the argument the API key you set up earlier. The with statement opens the file specified by file_name and associates the file with the name audio_file. The mode 'wb' opens the file for writing (w) in binary (b) format. We'll write into that file the contents of the audio returned by the Speech to Text service.

```
113  def text_to_speech(text_to_speak, voice_to_use, file_name):
114      """Use Watson Text to Speech to convert text to specified voice
115         and save to a WAV file."""
116      # create Text to Speech client
117      tts = TextToSpeechV1(iam_apikey=keys.text_to_speech_key)
118
119      # open file and write the synthesized audio content into the file
120      with open(file_name, 'wb') as audio_file:
121          audio_file.write(tts.synthesize(text_to_speak,
122              accept='audio/wav', voice=voice_to_use).get_result().content)
123
```

Lines 121–122 call two methods. First, we invoke the Speech to Text service by calling the TextToSpeechV1 object's **synthesize method**, passing three arguments:

- text_to_speak is the string to speak.

- the keyword argument accept is the media type indicating the audio format the Speech to Text service should return—again, 'audio/wav' indicates an audio file in WAV format.

- the keyword argument voice is one of the Speech to Text service's predefined voices. In this app, we'll use 'en-US_AllisonVoice' to speak English text and 'es-US_SofiaVoice' to speak Spanish text. Watson provides many male and female voices across various languages.[38]

Watson's DetailedResponse contains the spoken text audio file, accessible via get_result. We access the returned file's content attribute to get the bytes of the audio and pass them to the audio_file object's write method to output the bytes to a .wav file.

Function record_audio

The pyaudio module enables you to record audio from the microphone. The function record_audio (lines 124–154) defines several constants (lines 126–130) used to configure the stream of audio information coming from your computer's microphone. We used the settings from the pyaudio module's online documentation:

- FRAME_RATE—44100 frames-per-second represents 44.1 kHz, which is common for CD-quality audio.

- CHUNK—1024 is the number of frames streamed into the program at a time.

- FORMAT—pyaudio.paInt16 is the size of each frame (in this case, 16-bit or 2-byte integers).

- CHANNELS—2 is the number of samples per frame.

- SECONDS—5 is the number of seconds for which we'll record audio in this app.

```
124  def record_audio(file_name):
125      """Use pyaudio to record 5 seconds of audio to a WAV file."""
126      FRAME_RATE = 44100  # number of frames per second
127      CHUNK = 1024  # number of frames read at a time
128      FORMAT = pyaudio.paInt16  # each frame is a 16-bit (2-byte) integer
129      CHANNELS = 2  # 2 samples per frame
130      SECONDS = 5  # total recording time
131
132      recorder = pyaudio.PyAudio()  # opens/closes audio streams
133
134      # configure and open audio stream for recording (input=True)
135      audio_stream = recorder.open(format=FORMAT, channels=CHANNELS,
136          rate=FRAME_RATE, input=True, frames_per_buffer=CHUNK)
137      audio_frames = []  # stores raw bytes of mic input
138      print('Recording 5 seconds of audio')
139
```

38. For a complete list, see https://www.ibm.com/watson/developercloud/text-to-speech/api/v1/python.html?python#get-voice. Try experimenting with other voices.

```
140         # read 5 seconds of audio in CHUNK-sized pieces
141         for i in range(0, int(FRAME_RATE * SECONDS / CHUNK)):
142             audio_frames.append(audio_stream.read(CHUNK))
143
144         print('Recording complete')
145         audio_stream.stop_stream()  # stop recording
146         audio_stream.close()
147         recorder.terminate()  # release underlying resources used by PyAudio
148
149         # save audio_frames to a WAV file
150         with wave.open(file_name, 'wb') as output_file:
151             output_file.setnchannels(CHANNELS)
152             output_file.setsampwidth(recorder.get_sample_size(FORMAT))
153             output_file.setframerate(FRAME_RATE)
154             output_file.writeframes(b''.join(audio_frames))
155
```

Line 132 creates the **PyAudio** object from which we'll obtain the input stream to record audio from the microphone. Lines 135–136 use the PyAudio object's **open method** to open the input stream, using the constants FORMAT, CHANNELS, FRAME_RATE and CHUNK to configure the stream. Setting the input keyword argument to True indicates that the stream will be used to *receive* audio input. The open method returns a pyaudio **Stream** object for interacting with the stream.

Lines 141–142 use the Stream object's **read method** to get 1024 (that is, CHUNK) frames at a time from the input stream, which we then append to the audio_frames list. To determine the total number of loop iterations required to produce 5 seconds of audio using CHUNK frames at a time, we multiply the FRAME_RATE by SECONDS, then divide the result by CHUNK. Once reading is complete, line 145 calls the Stream object's **stop_stream method** to terminate recording, line 146 calls the Stream object's **close method** to close the Stream, and line 147 calls the PyAudio object's **terminate method** to release the underlying audio resources that were being used to manage the audio stream.

The with statement in lines 150–154 uses the wave module's open function to open the WAV file specified by file_name for writing in binary format ('wb'). Lines 151–153 configure the WAV file's number of channels, sample width (obtained from the PyAudio object's **get_sample_size method**) and frame rate. Then line 154 writes the audio content to the file. The expression b''.join(audio_frames) concatenates all the frames' bytes into a **byte string**. Prepending a string with b indicates that it's a string of bytes rather than a string of characters.

Function play_audio

To play the audio files returned by Watson's Text to Speech service, we use features of the pydub and pydub.playback modules. First, from the pydub module, line 158 uses the **AudioSegment** class's **from_wav method** to load a WAV file. The method returns a new AudioSegment object representing the audio file. To play the AudioSegment, line 159 calls the pydub.playback module's **play function**, passing the AudioSegment as an argument.

```
156 def play_audio(file_name):
157     """Use the pydub module (pip install pydub) to play a WAV file."""
158     sound = pydub.AudioSegment.from_wav(file_name)
159     pydub.playback.play(sound)
160
```

Executing the run_translator Function

We call the `run_translator` function when you execute `SimpleLanguageTranslator.py` as a script:

```
161  if __name__ == '__main__':
162      run_translator()
```

Hopefully, the fact that we took a divide-and-conquer approach on this substantial case study script made it manageable. Many of the steps matched up nicely with some key Watson services, enabling us to quickly create a powerful mashup application.

13.7 Watson Resources

IBM provides a wide range of developer resources to help you familiarize yourself with their services and begin using them to build applications.

Watson Services Documentation

The Watson Services documentation is at:

> https://console.bluemix.net/developer/watson/documentation

For each service, there are documentation and API reference links. Each service's documentation typically includes some or all of the following:

- a getting started tutorial.
- a video overview of the service.
- a link to a service demo.
- links to more specific how-to and tutorial documents.
- sample apps.
- additional resources, such as more advanced tutorials, videos, blog posts and more.

Each service's API reference shows all the details of interacting with the service using any of several languages, including Python. Click the **Python** tab to see the Python-specific documentation and corresponding code samples for the Watson Developer Cloud Python SDK. The API reference explains all the options for invoking a given service, the kinds of responses it can return, sample responses, and more.

Watson SDKs

We used the Watson Developer Cloud Python SDK to develop this chapter's script. There are SDKs for many other languages and platforms. The complete list is located at:

> https://console.bluemix.net/developer/watson/sdks-and-tools

Learning Resources

On the Learning Resources page

> https://console.bluemix.net/developer/watson/learning-resources

you'll find links to:

- Blog posts on Watson features and how Watson and AI are being used in industry.
- Watson's GitHub repository (developer tools, SDKs and sample code).

- The Watson YouTube channel (discussed below).
- Code patterns, which IBM refers to as "roadmaps for solving complex programming challenges." Some are implemented in Python, but you may still find the other code patterns helpful in designing and implementing your Python apps.

Watson Videos

The Watson YouTube channel

```
https://www.youtube.com/user/IBMWatsonSolutions/
```

contains hundreds of videos showing you how to use all aspects of Watson. There are also spotlight videos showing how Watson is being used.

IBM Redbooks

The following IBM Redbooks publications cover IBM Cloud and Watson services in detail, helping you develop your Watson skills.

- Essentials of Application Development on IBM Cloud:
  http://www.redbooks.ibm.com/abstracts/sg248374.html
- Building Cognitive Applications with IBM Watson Services: Volume 1 **Getting Started**: http://www.redbooks.ibm.com/abstracts/sg248387.html
- Building Cognitive Applications with IBM Watson Services: Volume 2 **Conversation** (now called Watson Assistant): http://www.redbooks.ibm.com/abstracts/sg248394.html
- Building Cognitive Applications with IBM Watson Services: Volume 3 **Visual Recognition**: http://www.redbooks.ibm.com/abstracts/sg248393.html
- Building Cognitive Applications with IBM Watson Services: Volume 4 **Natural Language Classifier**: http://www.redbooks.ibm.com/abstracts/sg248391.html
- Building Cognitive Applications with IBM Watson Services: Volume 5 **Language Translator**: http://www.redbooks.ibm.com/abstracts/sg248392.html
- Building Cognitive Applications with IBM Watson Services: Volume 6 **Speech to Text and Text to Speech**:
  http://www.redbooks.ibm.com/abstracts/sg248388.html
- Building Cognitive Applications with IBM Watson Services: Volume 7 **Natural Language Understanding**:
  http://www.redbooks.ibm.com/abstracts/sg248398.html

13.8 Wrap-Up

In this chapter, we introduced IBM's Watson cognitive-computing platform and overviewed its broad range of services. You saw that Watson offers intriguing capabilities that you can integrate into your applications. IBM encourages learning and experimentation via its free Lite tiers. To take advantage of that, you set up an IBM Cloud account. You tried Watson demos to experiment with various services, such as natural language translation, speech-to-text, text-to-speech, natural language understanding, chatbots, analyzing text for tone and visual object recognition in images and video.

You installed the Watson Developer Cloud Python SDK for programmatic access to Watson services from your Python code. In the traveler's companion translation app, we mashed up several Watson services to enable English-only and Spanish-only speakers to communicate easily with one another verbally. We transcribed English and Spanish audio recordings to text, translated the text to the other language, then synthesized English and Spanish audio from the translated text. Finally, we discussed various Watson resources, including documentation, blogs, the Watson GitHub repository, the Watson YouTube channel, code patterns implemented in Python (and other languages) and IBM Redbooks.

14

Machine Learning: Classification, Regression and Clustering

Objectives

In this chapter you'll:

- Use scikit-learn with popular datasets to perform machine learning studies.
- Use Seaborn and Matplotlib to visualize and explore data.
- Perform supervised machine learning with k-nearest neighbors classification and linear regression.
- Perform multi-classification with Digits dataset.
- Divide a dataset into training, test and validation sets.
- Tune model hyperparameters with k-fold cross-validation.
- Measure model performance.
- Display a confusion matrix showing classification prediction hits and misses.
- Perform multiple linear regression with the California Housing dataset.
- Perform dimensionality reduction with PCA and t-SNE on the Iris and Digits datasets to prepare them for two-dimensional visualizations.
- Perform unsupervised machine learning with k-means clustering and the Iris dataset.

14.1 Introduction to Machine Learning

In this chapter and the next, we'll present machine learning—one of the most exciting and promising subfields of artificial intelligence. You'll see how to quickly solve challenging and intriguing problems that novices and most experienced programmers probably would not have attempted just a few years ago. Machine learning is a big, complex topic that raises lots of subtle issues. Our goal here is to give you a friendly, hands-on introduction to a few of the simpler machine-learning techniques.

What Is Machine Learning?

Can we really make our machines (that is, our computers) learn? In this and the next chapter, we'll show exactly how that magic happens. What's the "secret sauce" of this new application-development style? It's data and lots of it. Rather than programming expertise into our applications, we program them to learn from data. We'll present many Python-based code examples that build working machine-learning models then use them to make remarkably accurate predictions.

Prediction

Wouldn't it be fantastic if you could improve weather forecasting to save lives, minimize injuries and property damage? What if we could improve cancer diagnoses and treatment regimens to save lives, or improve business forecasts to maximize profits and secure people's jobs? What about detecting fraudulent credit-card purchases and insurance claims? How about predicting customer "churn," what prices houses are likely to sell for, ticket sales of new movies, and anticipated revenue of new products and services? How about predicting the best strategies for coaches and players to use to win more games and championships? All of these kinds of predictions are happening today with machine learning.

Machine Learning Applications

Here's a table of some popular machine-learning applications:

Machine learning applications		
Anomaly detection	Detecting objects in scenes	Recommender systems ("people who bought this product also bought…")
Chatbots	Detecting patterns in data	
Classifying emails as spam or not spam	Diagnostic medicine	
	Facial recognition	Self-Driving cars (more generally, autonomous vehicles)
Classifying news articles as sports, financial, politics, etc.	Insurance fraud detection	
	Intrusion detection in computer networks	Sentiment analysis (like classifying movie reviews as positive, negative or neutral)
Computer vision and image classification	Handwriting recognition	
Credit-card fraud detection	Marketing: Divide customers into clusters	Spam filtering
Customer churn prediction		Time series predictions like stock-price forecasting and weather forecasting
Data compression	Natural language translation (English to Spanish, French to Japanese, etc.)	
Data exploration		Voice recognition
Data mining social media (like Facebook, Twitter, LinkedIn)	Predict mortgage loan defaults	

14.1.1 Scikit-Learn

We'll use the popular *scikit-learn machine learning library*. Scikit-learn, also called sklearn, conveniently packages the most effective machine-learning algorithms as *estimators*. Each is encapsulated, so you don't see the intricate details and heavy mathematics of how these algorithms work. You should feel comfortable with this—you drive your car without knowing the intricate details of how engines, transmissions, braking systems and steering systems work. Think about this the next time you step into an elevator and select your destination floor, or turn on your television and select the program you'd like to watch. Do you really understand the internal workings of your smart phone's hardware and software?

With scikit-learn and a small amount of Python code, you'll create powerful models quickly for analyzing data, extracting insights from the data and most importantly making predictions. You'll use scikit-learn to *train* each model on a subset of your data, then *test* each model on the rest to see how well your model works. Once your models are trained, you'll put them to work making predictions based on data they have not seen. You'll often be amazed at the results. All of a sudden your computer that you've used mostly on rote chores will take on characteristics of intelligence.

Scikit-learn has tools that automate training and testing your models. Although you can specify parameters to customize the models and possibly improve their performance, in this chapter, we'll typically use the models' *default parameters*, yet still obtain impressive results.

There also are tools like auto-sklearn (https://automl.github.io/auto-sklearn), which automates many of the tasks you perform with scikit-learn.

Which Scikit-Learn Estimator Should You Choose for Your Project

It's difficult to know in advance which model(s) will perform best on your data, so you typically try many models and pick the one that performs best. As you'll see, scikit-learn makes this convenient for you. A popular approach is to run many models and pick the best one(s). How do we evaluate which model performed best?

You'll want to experiment with lots of different models on different kinds of datasets. You'll rarely get to know the details of the complex mathematical algorithms in the sklearn estimators, but with experience, you'll become familiar with which algorithms may be best for particular types of datasets and problems. Even with that experience, it's unlikely that you'll be able to intuit the best model for each new dataset. So scikit-learn makes it easy for you to "try 'em all." It takes at most a few lines of code for you to create and use each model. The models report their performance so you can compare the results and pick the model(s) with the best performance.

14.1.2 Types of Machine Learning

We'll present the two main types of machine learning—*supervised machine learning*, which works with *labeled data*, and *unsupervised machine learning*, which works with *unlabeled data*.

If, for example, you're developing a computer vision application to recognize dogs and cats, you'll train your model on lots of dog photos labeled "dog" and cat photos labeled "cat." If your model is effective, when you put it to work processing unlabeled photos it will recognize dogs and cats it has never seen before. The more photos you train with, the greater the chance that your model will accurately predict which new photos are dogs and which are cats. In this era of big data and massive, economical computer power, you should be able to build some pretty accurate models with the techniques you're about to see.

How can looking at unlabeled data be useful? Online booksellers sell lots of books. They record enormous amounts of (unlabeled) book purchase transaction data. They noticed early on that people who bought certain books were likely to purchase other books on the same or similar topics. That led to their *recommendation systems*. Now, when you browse a bookseller site for a particular book, you're likely to see recommendations like, "people who bought this book also bought these other books." Recommendation systems are big business today, helping to maximize product sales of all kinds.

Supervised Machine Learning

Supervised machine learning falls into two categories—*classification* and *regression*. You train machine-learning models on datasets that consist of rows and columns. Each row represents a data *sample*. Each column represents a *feature* of that sample. In supervised machine learning, each sample has an associated label called a *target* (like "dog" or "cat"). This is the value you're trying to predict for new data that you present to your models.

Datasets

You'll work with some "toy" datasets, each with a small number of samples with a limited number of features. You'll also work with several richly featured real-world datasets, one containing a few thousand samples and one containing tens of thousands of samples. In the world of big data, datasets commonly have, millions and billions of samples, or even more.

There's an enormous number of free and open datasets available for data science studies. Libraries like scikit-learn package up popular datasets for you to experiment with and provide mechanisms for loading datasets from various repositories (such as openml.org). Governments, businesses and other organizations worldwide offer datasets on a vast range of subjects. You'll work with several popular free datasets, using a variety of machine learning techniques.

Classification

We'll use one of the simplest classification algorithms, *k-nearest neighbors*, to analyze the Digits dataset bundled with scikit-learn. Classification algorithms predict the discrete classes (categories) to which samples belong. Binary classification uses two classes, such as "spam" or "not spam" in an email classification application. Multi-classification uses more than two classes, such as the 10 classes, 0 through 9, in the Digits dataset. A classification scheme looking at movie descriptions might try to classify them as "action," "adventure," "fantasy," "romance," "history" and the like.

Regression

Regression models predict a *continuous output*, such as the predicted temperature output in the weather *time series* analysis from Chapter 10's Intro to Data Science section. In this chapter, we'll revisit that *simple linear regression* example, this time implementing it using scikit-learn's LinearRegression estimator. Next, we use a LinearRegression estimator to perform *multiple linear regression* with the California Housing dataset that's bundled with scikit-learn. We'll predict the median house value of a U. S. census block of homes, considering eight features per block, such as the average number of rooms, median house age, average number of bedrooms and median income. The LinearRegression estimator, by default, uses *all* the numerical features in a dataset to make more sophisticated predictions than you can with a single-feature simple linear regression.

Unsupervised Machine Learning

Next, we'll introduce unsupervised machine learning with *clustering* algorithms. We'll use *dimensionality reduction* (with scikit-learn's TSNE estimator) to *compress* the Digits dataset's 64 features down to two for visualization purposes. This will enable us to see how nicely the Digits data "cluster up." This dataset contains handwritten digits like those the post office's computers must recognize to route each letter to its designated zip code. This is a challenging computer-vision problem, given that each person's handwriting is unique. Yet, we'll build this clustering model with just a few lines of code and achieve impressive results. And we'll do this without having to understand the inner workings of the clustering algorithm. This is the beauty of object-based programming. We'll see this kind of convenient object-based programming again in the next chapter, where we'll build powerful deep learning models using the open source Keras library.

K-Means Clustering and the Iris Dataset

We'll present the simplest unsupervised machine-learning algorithm, *k-means clustering*, and use it on the Iris dataset that's also bundled with scikit-learn. We'll use dimensionality reduction (with scikit-learn's PCA estimator) to compress the Iris dataset's four features to two for visualization purposes. We'll show the clustering of the three *Iris* species in the dataset and graph each cluster's *centroid,* which is the cluster's center point. Finally, we'll run multiple clustering estimators to compare their ability to divide the Iris dataset's samples effectively into three clusters.

You normally specify the desired number of clusters, *k*. K-means works through the data trying to divide it into that many clusters. As with many machine learning algorithms, k-means is *iterative* and gradually zeros in on the clusters to match the number you specify.

K-means clustering can find similarities in unlabeled data. This can ultimately help with assigning labels to that data so that supervised learning estimators can then process it. Given that it's tedious and error-prone for humans to have to assign labels to unlabeled data, and given that the vast majority of the world's data is unlabeled, unsupervised machine learning is an important tool.

Big Data and Big Computer Processing Power

The amount of data that's available today is already enormous and continues to grow exponentially. The data produced in the world in the last few years equals the amount produced up to that point since the dawn of civilization. We commonly talk about big data, but "big" may not be a strong enough term to describe truly how huge data is getting.

People used to say "I'm drowning in data and I don't know what to do with it." With machine learning, we now say, "Flood me with big data so I can use machine-learning technology to extract insights and make predictions from it."

This is occurring at a time when computing power is *exploding* and computer memory and secondary storage are *exploding* in capacity while costs dramatically decline. All of this enables us to think differently about the solution approaches. We now can program computers to *learn* from data, and lots of it. It's now all about predicting from data.

14.1.3 Datasets Bundled with Scikit-Learn

The following table lists scikit-learn's bundled datasets.[1] It also provides capabilities for loading datasets from other sources, such as the 20,000+ datasets available at openml.org.

Datasets bundled with scikit-learn	
"Toy" datasets	*Real-world datasets*
Boston house prices	Olivetti faces
Iris plants	20 newsgroups text
Diabetes	Labeled Faces in the Wild face recognition
Optical recognition of handwritten digits	Forest cover types
Linnerrud	RCV1
Wine recognition	Kddcup 99
Breast cancer Wisconsin (diagnostic)	California Housing

---

1. http://scikit-learn.org/stable/datasets/index.html.

14.1.4 Steps in a Typical Data Science Study

We'll perform the steps of a typical machine-learning case study, including:

- loading the dataset

- exploring the data with pandas and visualizations

- transforming your data (converting non-numeric data to numeric data because scikit-learn requires numeric data; in the chapter, we use datasets that are "ready to go," but we'll discuss the issue again in the "Deep Learning" chapter)

- splitting the data for training and testing

- creating the model

- training and testing the model

- tuning the model and evaluating its accuracy

- making predictions on live data that the model hasn't seen before.

In the "Array-Oriented Programming with NumPy" and "Strings: A Deeper Look" chapters' Intro to Data Science sections, we discussed using pandas to deal with missing and erroneous values. These are important steps in cleaning your data before using it for machine learning.

14.2 Case Study: Classification with k-Nearest Neighbors and the Digits Dataset, Part I

To process mail efficiently and route each letter to the correct destination, postal service computers must be able to scan handwritten names, addresses and zip codes and recognize the letters and digits. As you'll see in this chapter, powerful libraries like scikit-learn enable even novice programmers to make such machine-learning problems manageable. In the next chapter, we'll use even more powerful computer-vision capabilities when we present the deep learning technology of convolutional neural networks.

Classification Problems

In this section, we'll look at **classification** in supervised machine learning, which attempts to predict the distinct class[2] to which a sample belongs. For example, if you have images of dogs and images of cats, you can classify each image as a "dog" or a "cat." This is a **binary classification problem** because there are *two* classes.

We'll use the **Digits dataset**[3] bundled with scikit-learn, which consists of 8-by-8 pixel images representing 1797 hand-written digits (0 through 9). Our goal is to predict which digit an image represents. Since there are 10 possible digits (the classes), this is a **multi-classification problem**. You train a classification model using **labeled data**—we know in advance each digit's class. In this case study, we'll use one of the simplest machine-learning classification algorithms, *k-nearest neighbors (k-NN)*, to recognize handwritten digits.

---

2. Note that the term "class" in this case means "category," not the Python concept of a class.
3. `http://scikit-learn.org/stable/datasets/index.html#optical-recognition-of-handwritten-digits-dataset.`

The following low-resolution digit visualization of a 5 was produced with Matplotlib from one digit's 8-by-8 pixel raw data. We'll show how to display images like this with Matplotlib momentarily:

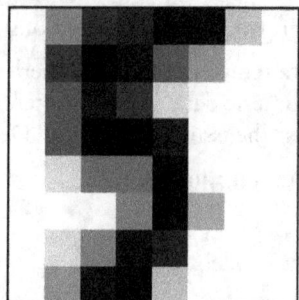

Researchers created the images in this dataset from the MNIST database's tens of thousands of 32-by-32 pixel images that were produced in the early 1990s. At today's high-definition camera and scanner resolutions, such images can be captured with much higher resolutions.

Our Approach

We'll cover this case study over two sections. In this section, we'll begin with the basic steps of a machine learning case study:

- Decide the data from which to train a model.
- Load and explore the data.
- Split the data for training and testing.
- Select and build the model.
- Train the model.
- Make predictions.

As you'll see, in scikit-learn each of these steps requires at most a few lines of code. In the next section, we'll

- Evaluate the results.
- Tune the model.
- Run several classification models to choose the best one(s).

We'll visualize the data using Matplotlib and Seaborn, so launch IPython with Matplotlib support:

```
ipython --matplotlib
```

14.2.1 k-Nearest Neighbors Algorithm

Scikit-learn supports many **classification algorithms**, including the simplest—**k-nearest neighbors (k-NN)**. This algorithm attempts to predict a test sample's class by looking at the k training samples that are nearest (in distance) to the test sample. For example, consider the following diagram in which the filled dots represent four sample classes—A, B, C and D. For this discussion, we'll use these letters as the class names:

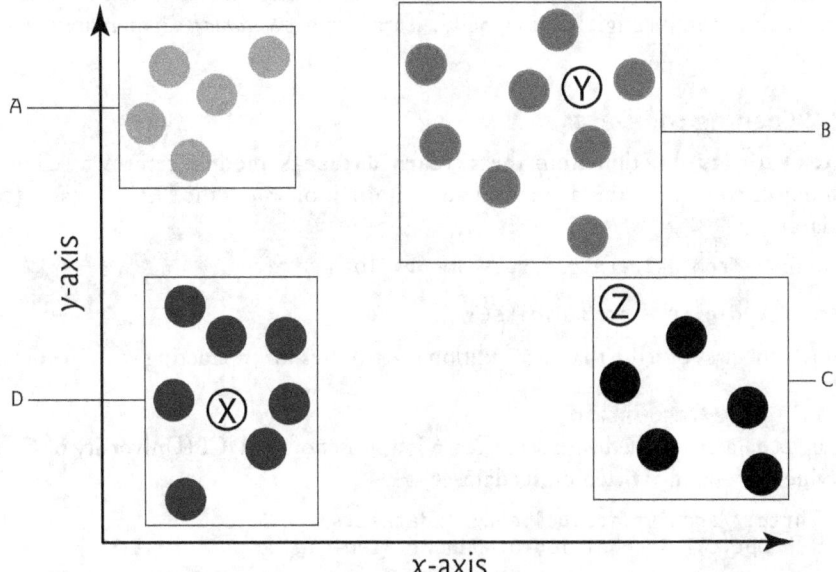

We want to predict the classes to which the new samples **X**, **Y** and **Z** belong. Let's assume we'd like to make these predictions using each sample's *three* nearest neighbors— *three* is *k* in the k-nearest neighbors algorithm:

- Sample **X**'s three nearest neighbors are all class D dots, so we'd predict that **X**'s class is D.

- Sample **Y**'s three nearest neighbors are all class B dots, so we'd predict that **Y**'s class is B.

- For **Z**, the choice is not as clear, because it appears *between* the B *and* C dots. Of the three nearest neighbors, one is class B and two are class C. In the k-nearest neighbors algorithm, the class with the most "votes" wins. So, based on two C votes to one B vote, we'd predict that **Z**'s class is C. Picking an odd *k* value in the kNN algorithm avoids ties by ensuring there's never an equal number of votes.

Hyperparameters and Hyperparameter Tuning

In machine learning, a **model** implements a machine-learning algorithm. In scikit-learn, models are called **estimators**. There are two parameter types in machine learning:

- those the estimator calculates as it learns from the data you provide and

- those you specify in advance when you create the scikit-learn estimator object that represents the model.

The parameters specified in advance are called **hyperparameters**.

In the k-nearest neighbors algorithm, *k* is a hyperparameter. For simplicity, we'll use scikit-learn's *default* hyperparameter values. In real-world machine-learning studies, you'll want to experiment with different values of k to produce the best possible models for your studies. This process is called **hyperparameter tuning**. Later we'll use hyperparameter tuning to choose the value of k that enables the k-nearest neighbors algorithm to make the best predictions for the Digits dataset. Scikit-learn also has *automated* hyperparameter tuning capabilities.

14.2.2 Loading the Dataset

The `load_digits` function from the **sklearn.datasets** module returns a scikit-learn **Bunch** object containing the digits data and information *about* the Digits dataset (called **metadata**):

```
In [1]: from sklearn.datasets import load_digits

In [2]: digits = load_digits()
```

Bunch is a subclass of dict that has additional attributes for interacting with the dataset.

Displaying the Description

The Digits dataset bundled with scikit-learn is a subset of the **UCI (University of California Irvine) ML hand-written digits dataset** at:

```
http://archive.ics.uci.edu/ml/datasets/
     Optical+Recognition+of+Handwritten+Digits
```

The original UCI dataset contains 5620 samples—3823 for training and 1797 for testing. The version of the dataset bundled with scikit-learn contains only the *1797 testing samples*. A Bunch's **DESCR attribute** contains a description of the dataset. According to the Digits dataset's description[4], each sample has 64 features (as specified by Number of Attributes) that represent an 8-by-8 image with pixel values in the range 0–16 (specified by Attribute Information). This dataset has *no missing values* (as specified by Missing Attribute Values). The 64 features may seem like a lot, but real-world datasets can sometimes have hundreds, thousands or even millions of features.

```
In [3]: print(digits.DESCR)
.. _digits_dataset:

Optical recognition of handwritten digits dataset
-------------------------------------------------

**Data Set Characteristics:**

    :Number of Instances: 5620
    :Number of Attributes: 64
    :Attribute Information: 8x8 image of integer pixels in the range
     0..16.
    :Missing Attribute Values: None
    :Creator: E. Alpaydin (alpaydin '@' boun.edu.tr)
    :Date: July; 1998

This is a copy of the test set of the UCI ML hand-written digits datasets
http://archive.ics.uci.edu/ml/datasets/
     Optical+Recognition+of+Handwritten+Digits
```

---

4. We highlighted some key information in bold.

The data set contains images of hand-written digits: 10 classes where each class refers to a digit.

Preprocessing programs made available by NIST were used to extract normalized bitmaps of handwritten digits from a preprinted form. From a total of 43 people, 30 contributed to the training set and different 13 to the test set. 32x32 bitmaps are divided into nonoverlapping blocks of 4x4 and the number of on pixels are counted in each block. This generates an input matrix of 8x8 where each element is an integer in the range 0..16. This reduces dimensionality and gives invariance to small distortions.

For info on NIST preprocessing routines, see M. D. Garris, J. L. Blue, G. T. Candela, D. L. Dimmick, J. Geist, P. J. Grother, S. A. Janet, and C. L. Wilson, NIST Form-Based Handprint Recognition System, NISTIR 5469, 1994.

.. topic:: References

  - C. Kaynak (1995) Methods of Combining Multiple Classifiers and Their Applications to Handwritten Digit Recognition, MSc Thesis, Institute of Graduate Studies in Science and Engineering, Bogazici University.
  - E. Alpaydin, C. Kaynak (1998) Cascading Classifiers, Kybernetika.
  - Ken Tang and Ponnuthurai N. Suganthan and Xi Yao and A. Kai Qin. Linear dimensionality reduction using relevance weighted LDA. School of Electrical and Electronic Engineering Nanyang Technological University. 2005.
  - Claudio Gentile. A New Approximate Maximal Margin Classification Algorithm. NIPS. 2000.

Checking the Sample and Target Sizes
The Bunch object's **data** and **target attributes** are NumPy arrays:

- The data array contains the 1797 samples (the digit images), each with 64 features, having values in the range 0–16, representing *pixel intensities*. With Matplotlib, we'll visualize these intensities in grayscale shades from white (0) to black (16):

- The target array contains the images' labels—that is, the classes indicating which digit each image represents. The array is called target because, when you make predictions, you're aiming to "hit the target" values. To see labels of samples throughout the dataset, let's display the target values of every 100th sample:

```
In [4]: digits.target[::100]
Out[4]: array([0, 4, 1, 7, 4, 8, 2, 2, 4, 4, 1, 9, 7, 3, 2, 1, 2, 5])
```

We can confirm the number of samples and features (per sample) by looking at the data array's shape attribute, which shows that there are 1797 rows (samples) and 64 columns (features):

```
In [5]: digits.data.shape
Out[5]: (1797, 64)
```

You can confirm that the number of target values matches the number of samples by look-ing at the target array's shape:

```
In [6]: digits.target.shape
Out[6]: (1797,)
```

A Sample Digit Image

Each image is two-dimensional—it has a width and a height in pixels. The Bunch object returned by load_digits contains an images attribute—an array in which each element is a two-dimensional 8-by-8 array representing a digit image's pixel intensities. Though the original dataset represents each pixel as an integer value from 0–16, scikit-learn stores these values as *floating-point* values (NumPy type float64). For example, here's the two-dimensional array representing the sample image at index 13:

```
In [7]: digits.images[13]
Out[7]:
array([[ 0.,  2.,  9., 15., 14.,  9.,  3.,  0.],
       [ 0.,  4., 13.,  8.,  9., 16.,  8.,  0.],
       [ 0.,  0.,  0.,  6., 14., 15.,  3.,  0.],
       [ 0.,  0.,  0., 11., 14.,  2.,  0.,  0.],
       [ 0.,  0.,  0.,  2., 15., 11.,  0.,  0.],
       [ 0.,  0.,  0.,  0.,  2., 15.,  4.,  0.],
       [ 0.,  1.,  5.,  6., 13., 16.,  6.,  0.],
       [ 0.,  2., 12., 12., 13., 11.,  0.,  0.]]])
```

and here's the image represented by this two-dimensional array—we'll soon show the code for displaying this image:

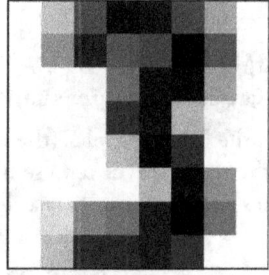

Preparing the Data for Use with Scikit-Learn

Scikit-learn's machine-learning algorithms require samples to be stored in a *two-dimen-sional array* of *floating-point values* (or two-dimensional *array-like* collection, such as a list of lists or a pandas DataFrame):

- Each row represents one *sample*.
- Each column in a given row represents one *feature* for that sample.

To represent every sample as one row, multi-dimensional data like the two-dimensional image array shown in snippet [7] must be *flattened* into a one-dimensional array.

If you were working with a data containing **categorical features** (typically represented as strings, such as 'spam' or 'not-spam'), you'd also have to *preprocess* those features into numerical values—known as one-hot encoding, which we cover in the next chapter. Scikit-learn's **sklearn.preprocessing** module provides capabilities for converting cate-gorical data to numeric data. The Digits dataset has no categorical features.

For your convenience, the `load_digits` function returns the preprocessed data ready for machine learning. The Digits dataset is numerical, so `load_digits` simply flattens each image's two-dimensional array into a one-dimensional array. For example, the 8-by-8 array `digits.images[13]` shown in snippet [7] corresponds to the 1-by-64 array `digits.data[13]` shown below:

```
In [8]: digits.data[13]
Out[8]:
array([ 0.,  2.,  9., 15., 14.,  9.,  3.,  0.,  0.,  4., 13.,  8.,  9.,
       16.,  8.,  0.,  0.,  0.,  0.,  6., 14., 15.,  3.,  0.,  0.,  0.,
        0., 11., 14.,  2.,  0.,  0.,  0.,  0.,  0.,  2., 15., 11.,  0.,
        0.,  0.,  0.,  0.,  0.,  2., 15.,  4.,  0.,  0.,  1.,  5.,  6.,
       13., 16.,  6.,  0.,  0.,  2., 12., 12., 13., 11.,  0.,  0.])
```

In this one-dimensional array, the first eight elements are the two-dimensional array's row 0, the next eight elements are the two-dimensional array's row 1, and so on.

14.2.3 Visualizing the Data

You should always familiarize yourself with your data. This process is called **data exploration**. For the digit images, you can get a sense of what they look like by displaying them with the Matplotlib `implot` function. The following image shows the dataset's first 24 images. To see how difficult a problem handwritten digit recognition is, consider the *variations* among the images of the 3s in the first, third and fourth rows, and look at the images of the 2s in the first, third and fourth rows.

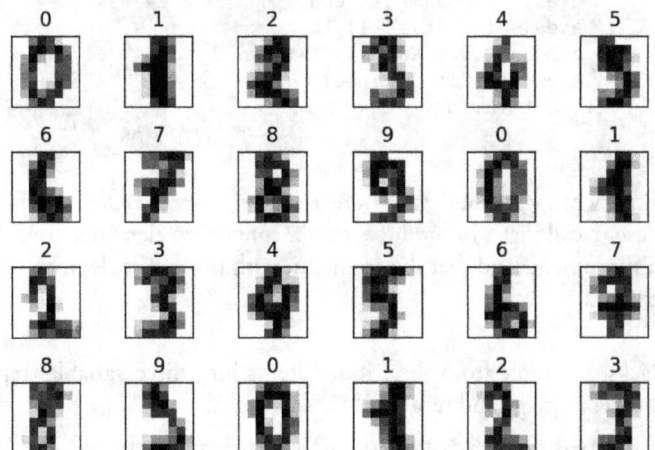

Creating the Diagram

Let's look at the code that displayed these 24 digits. The following call to function `subplots` creates a 6-by-4 inch `Figure` (specified by the `figsize(6, 4)` keyword argument) containing 24 subplots arranged in 4 rows (`nrows=4`) and 6 columns (`ncols=6`). Each subplot has its own `Axes` object, which we'll use to display one digit image:

```
In [9]: import matplotlib.pyplot as plt

In [10]: figure, axes = plt.subplots(nrows=4, ncols=6, figsize=(6, 4))
```

Function subplots returns the Axes objects in a two-dimensional NumPy array. Initially, the Figure appears as shown below with labels (which we'll remove) on every subplot's *x*- and *y*-axes:

Displaying Each Image and Removing the Axes Labels

Next, use a for statement with the built-in zip function to iterate in parallel through the 24 Axes objects, the first 24 images in digits.images and the first 24 values in dig-its.target:

```
In [11]: for item in zip(axes.ravel(), digits.images, digits.target):
    ...:     axes, image, target = item
    ...:     axes.imshow(image, cmap=plt.cm.gray_r)
    ...:     axes.set_xticks([])  # remove x-axis tick marks
    ...:     axes.set_yticks([])  # remove y-axis tick marks
    ...:     axes.set_title(target)
    ...: plt.tight_layout()
    ...:
    ...:
```

Recall that NumPy array method ravel creates a *one-dimensional view* of a multidimensional array. Also, recall that zip produces tuples containing elements from the same index in each of zip's arguments and that the argument with the fewest elements determines how many tuples zip returns.

Each iteration of the loop:

- Unpacks one tuple from the zipped items into three variables representing the Axes object, image and target value.

- Calls the Axes object's imshow method to display one image. The keyword argument cmap=plt.cm.gray_r determines the colors displayed in the image. The value plt.cm.gray_r is a **color map**—a group of colors that are typically chosen to work well together. This particular color map enables us to display the image's pixels in grayscale, with 0 as white, 16 as black and the values in between as gradually darkening shades of gray. For Matplotlib's color map names see https://matplotlib.org/examples/color/colormaps_reference.html. Each can be accessed through the plt.cm object or via a string, like 'gray_r'.

- Calls the Axes object's set_xticks and set_yticks methods with empty lists to indicate that the *x*- and *y*-axes should not have tick marks.

- Calls the Axes object's set_title method to display the target value above the image—this shows the actual value that the image represents.

After the loop, we call tight_layout to remove the extra whitespace at the Figure's top, right, bottom and left, so the rows and columns of digit images can fill more of the Figure.

14.2.4 Splitting the Data for Training and Testing

You typically train a machine-learning model with a subset of a dataset. Typically, the more data you have for training, the better you can train the model. It's important to set aside a portion of your data for testing, so you can evaluate a model's performance using data that the model has not yet seen. Once you're confident that the model is performing well, you can use it to make predictions using new data it hasn't seen.

We first break the data into a **training set** and a **testing set** to prepare to train and test the model. The function **train_test_split** from the **sklearn.model_selection** module *shuffles* the data to randomize it, then splits the samples in the data array and the target values in the target array into training and testing sets. This helps ensure that the training and testing sets have similar characteristics. The shuffling and splitting is performed conveniently for you by a **ShuffleSplit** object from the sklearn.model_selection module. Function train_test_split returns a tuple of four elements in which the first two are the *samples* split into training and testing sets, and the last two are the corresponding *target values* split into training and testing sets. By convention, uppercase X is used to represent the samples, and lowercase y is used to represent the target values:

```
In [12]: from sklearn.model_selection import train_test_split

In [13]: X_train, X_test, y_train, y_test = train_test_split(
    ...:     digits.data, digits.target, random_state=11)
    ...:
```

We assume the data has **balanced classes**—that is, the samples are divided evenly among the classes. This is the case for each of scikit-learn's bundled classification datasets. Unbalanced classes could lead to incorrect results.

In the "Functions" chapter, you saw how to *seed* a random-number generator for *reproducibility*. In machine-learning studies, this helps others confirm your results by working with the *same* randomly selected data. Function train_test_split provides the keyword argument random_state for *reproducibility*. When you run the code in the future with the *same* seed value, train_test_split will select the *same* data for the training set and the *same* data for the testing set. We chose the seed value (11) arbitrarily.

Training and Testing Set Sizes

Looking at X_train's and X_test's shapes, you can see that, *by default*, train_test_split reserves 75% of the data for training and 25% for testing:

```
In [14]: X_train.shape
Out[14]: (1347, 64)

In [15]: X_test.shape
Out[15]: (450, 64)
```

To specify *different* splits, you can set the sizes of the testing and training sets with the `train_test_split` function's keyword arguments `test_size` and `train_size`. Use floating-point values from 0.0 through 1.0 to specify the percentages of the data to use for each. You can use integer values to set the precise numbers of samples. If you specify one of these keyword arguments, the other is inferred. For example, the statement

```
X_train, X_test, y_train, y_test = train_test_split(
    digits.data, digits.target, random_state=11, test_size=0.20)
```

specifies that 20% of the data is for testing, so `train_size` is inferred to be 0.80.

14.2.5 Creating the Model

The **KNeighborsClassifier** estimator (module **sklearn.neighbors**) implements the k-nearest neighbors algorithm. First, we create the KNeighborsClassifier estimator object:

```
In [16]: from sklearn.neighbors import KNeighborsClassifier

In [17]: knn = KNeighborsClassifier()
```

To create an estimator, you simply create an object. The internal details of how this object implements the k-nearest neighbors algorithm are hidden in the object. You'll simply call its methods. This is the essence of Python *object-based programming*.

14.2.6 Training the Model

Next, we invoke the KNeighborsClassifier object's **fit method**, which loads the sample training set (X_train) and target training set (y_train) into the estimator:

```
In [18]: knn.fit(X=X_train, y=y_train)
Out[18]:
KNeighborsClassifier(algorithm='auto', leaf_size=30, metric='minkowski',
          metric_params=None, n_jobs=None, n_neighbors=5, p=2,
          weights='uniform')
```

For most, scikit-learn estimators, the `fit` method loads the data into the estimator then uses that data to perform complex calculations behind the scenes that learn from the data and train the model. The KNeighborsClassifier's `fit` method just loads the data into the estimator, because k-NN actually has no initial learning process. The estimator is said to be **lazy** because its work is performed only when you use it to make predictions. In this and the next chapter, you'll use lots of models that have significant training phases. In the real-world machine-learning applications, it can sometimes take minutes, hours, days or even months to train your models. We'll see in the next chapter, "Deep Learning," that special-purpose, high-performance hardware called GPUs and TPUs can significantly reduce model training time.

As shown in snippet [18]'s output, the `fit` method returns the estimator, so IPython displays its string representation, which includes the estimator's *default* settings. The n_neighbors value corresponds to k in the k-nearest neighbors algorithm. By default, a KNeighborsClassifier looks at the five nearest neighbors to make its predictions. For simplicity, we generally use the default estimator settings. For KNeighborsClassifier, these are described at:

```
http://scikit-learn.org/stable/modules/generated/
    sklearn.neighbors.KNeighborsClassifier.html
```

Many of these settings are beyond the scope of this book. In Part 2 of this case study, we'll discuss how to choose the best value for n_neighbors.

14.2.7 Predicting Digit Classes

Now that we've loaded the data into the KNeighborsClassifier, we can use it with the test samples to make predictions. Calling the estimator's **predict method** with X_test as an argument returns an array containing the predicted class of each test image:

```
In [19]: predicted = knn.predict(X=X_test)

In [20]: expected = y_test
```

Let's look at the predicted digits vs. expected digits for the first 20 test samples:

```
In [21]: predicted[:20]
Out[21]: array([0, 4, 9, 9, 3, 1, 4, 1, 5, 0, 4, 9, 4, 1, 5, 3, 3, 8, 5, 6])

In [22]: expected[:20]
Out[22]: array([0, 4, 9, 9, 3, 1, 4, 1, 5, 0, 4, 9, 4, 1, 5, 3, 3, 8, 3, 6])
```

As you can see, in the first 20 elements, only the predicted and expected arrays' values at index 18 do not match. We expected a 3, but the model predicted a 5.

Let's use a list comprehension to locate *all* the incorrect predictions for the *entire* test set—that is, the cases in which the predicted and expected values do *not* match:

```
In [23]: wrong = [(p, e) for (p, e) in zip(predicted, expected) if p != e]

In [24]: wrong
Out[24]:
[(5, 3),
 (8, 9),
 (4, 9),
 (7, 3),
 (7, 4),
 (2, 8),
 (9, 8),
 (3, 8),
 (3, 8),
 (1, 8)]
```

The list comprehension uses zip to create tuples containing the corresponding elements in predicted and expected. We include a tuple in the result only if its p (the predicted value) and e (the expected value) differ—that is, the predicted value was incorrect. In this example, the estimator incorrectly predicted only 10 of the 450 test samples. So the prediction accuracy of this estimator is an impressive 97.78%, even though we used only the estimator's default parameters.

14.3 Case Study: Classification with k-Nearest Neighbors and the Digits Dataset, Part 2

In this section, we continue the digit classification case study. We'll:

• evaluate the k-NN classification estimator's accuracy,

- execute multiple estimators and can compare their results so you can choose the best one(s), and

- show how to tune k-NN's hyperparameter *k* to get the best performance out of a KNeighborsClassifier.

14.3.1 Metrics for Model Accuracy

Once you've trained and tested a model, you'll want to measure its accuracy. Here, we'll look at two ways of doing this—a classification estimator's score method and a *confusion matrix*.

Estimator Method score

Each estimator has a **score** method that returns an indication of how well the estimator performs for the test data you pass as arguments. For classification estimators, this method returns the *prediction accuracy* for the test data:

```
In [25]: print(f'{knn.score(X_test, y_test):.2%}')
97.78%
```

The kNeighborsClassifier's with its default *k* (that is, n_neighbors=5) achieved 97.78% prediction accuracy. Shortly, we'll perform hyperparameter tuning to try to determine the optimal value for *k*, hoping that we get even better accuracy.

Confusion Matrix

Another way to check a classification estimator's accuracy is via a **confusion matrix**, which shows the correct and incorrect predicted values (also known as the *hits* and *misses*) for a given class. Simply call the function **confusion_matrix** from the **sklearn.metrics** module, passing the expected classes and the predicted classes as arguments, as in:

```
In [26]: from sklearn.metrics import confusion_matrix
```

```
In [27]: confusion = confusion_matrix(y_true=expected, y_pred=predicted)
```

The y_true keyword argument specifies the test samples' actual classes. People looked at the dataset's images and labeled them with specific classes (the digit values). The y_pred keyword argument specifies the predicted digits for those test images.

Below is the confusion matrix produced by the preceding call. The correct predictions are shown on the diagonal from top-left to bottom-right. This is called the **principal diagonal**. The nonzero values that are not on the principal diagonal indicate incorrect predictions:

```
In [28]: confusion
Out[28]:
array([[45,  0,  0,  0,  0,  0,  0,  0,  0,  0],
       [ 0, 45,  0,  0,  0,  0,  0,  0,  0,  0],
       [ 0,  0, 54,  0,  0,  0,  0,  0,  0,  0],
       [ 0,  0,  0, 42,  0,  1,  0,  1,  0,  0],
       [ 0,  0,  0,  0, 49,  0,  0,  1,  0,  0],
       [ 0,  0,  0,  0,  0, 38,  0,  0,  0,  0],
       [ 0,  0,  0,  0,  0,  0, 42,  0,  0,  0],
       [ 0,  0,  0,  0,  0,  0,  0, 45,  0,  0],
       [ 0,  1,  1,  2,  0,  0,  0,  0, 39,  1],
       [ 0,  0,  0,  0,  1,  0,  0,  0,  1, 41]]])
```

Each row represents one distinct class—that is, one of the digits 0–9. The columns within a row specify how many of the test samples were classified into each distinct class. For example, row 0:

```
[45,  0,  0,  0,  0,  0,  0,  0,  0,  0]
```

represents the digit 0 class. The columns represent the ten possible target classes 0 through 9. Because we're working with digits, the classes (0–9) and the row and column index numbers (0–9) happen to match. According to row 0, 45 test samples were classified as the digit 0, and *none* of the test samples were misclassified as any of the digits 1 through 9. So 100% of the 0s were correctly predicted.

On the other hand, consider row 8 which represents the results for the digit 8:

```
[ 0,  1,  1,  2,  0,  0,  0,  0, 39,  1]
```

- The 1 at column index 1 indicates that one 8 was *incorrectly* classified as a 1.
- The 1 at column index 2 indicates that one 8 was *incorrectly* classified as a 2.
- The 2 at column index 3 indicates that two 8s were *incorrectly* classified as 3s.
- The 39 at column index 8 indicates that 39 8s were *correctly* classified as 8s.
- The 1 at column index 9 indicates that one 8 was *incorrectly* classified as a 9.

So the algorithm correctly predicted 88.63% (39 of 44) of the 8s. Earlier we saw that the overall prediction accuracy of this estimator was 97.78%. The lower prediction accuracy for 8s indicates that they're apparently harder to recognize than the other digits.

Classification Report

The `sklearn.metrics` module also provides function **classification_report**, which produces a table of **classification metrics**[5] based on the expected and predicted values:

```
In [29]: from sklearn.metrics import classification_report

In [30]: names = [str(digit) for digit in digits.target_names]

In [31]: print(classification_report(expected, predicted,
    ...:     target_names=names))
    ...:
              precision    recall  f1-score   support

           0       1.00      1.00      1.00        45
           1       0.98      1.00      0.99        45
           2       0.98      1.00      0.99        54
           3       0.95      0.95      0.95        44
           4       0.98      0.98      0.98        50
           5       0.97      1.00      0.99        38
           6       1.00      1.00      1.00        42
           7       0.96      1.00      0.98        45
           8       0.97      0.89      0.93        44
           9       0.98      0.95      0.96        43
```

---

5. http://scikit-learn.org/stable/modules/model_evaluation.html#precision-recall-and-f-measures.

micro avg	0.98	0.98	0.98	450
macro avg	0.98	0.98	0.98	450
weighted avg	0.98	0.98	0.98	450

In the report:

- **precision** is the total number of correct predictions for a given digit divided by the total number of predictions for that digit. You can confirm the precision by looking at each column in the confusion matrix. For example, if you look at column index 7, you'll see 1s in rows 3 and 4, indicating that one 3 and one 4 were incorrectly classified as 7s and a 45 in row 7 indicating the 45 images were correctly classified as 7s. So the *precision* for the digit 7 is 45/47 or 0.96.

- **recall** is the total number of correct predictions for a given digit divided by the total number of samples that should have been predicted as that digit. You can confirm the recall by looking at each row in the confusion matrix. For example, if you look at row index 8, you'll see three 1s and a 2 indicating that some 8s were incorrectly classified as other digits and a 39 indicating that 39 images were correctly classified. So the *recall* for the digit 8 is 39/44 or 0.89.

- **f1-score**—This is the average of the *precision* and the *recall*.

- **support**—The number of samples with a given expected value. For example, 50 samples were labeled as 4s, and 38 samples were labeled as 5s.

For details on the averages displayed at the bottom of the report, see:

```
http://scikit-learn.org/stable/modules/generated/
    sklearn.metrics.classification_report.html
```

Visualizing the Confusion Matrix

A **heat map** displays values as colors, often with values of higher magnitude displayed as more intense colors. Seaborn's graphing functions work with two-dimensional data. When using a pandas DataFrame as the data source, Seaborn automatically labels its visualizations using the column names and row indices. Let's convert the confusion matrix into a DataFrame, then graph it:

```
In [32]: import pandas as pd

In [33]: confusion_df = pd.DataFrame(confusion, index=range(10),
    ...:         columns=range(10))
    ...:

In [34]: import seaborn as sns

In [35]: axes = sns.heatmap(confusion_df, annot=True,
    ...:                    cmap='nipy_spectral_r')
    ...:
```

The Seaborn function **heatmap** creates a heat map from the specified DataFrame. The keyword argument annot=True (short for "annotation") displays a color bar to the right of the diagram, showing how the values correspond to the heat map's colors. The cmap='nipy_spectral_r' keyword argument specifies which color map to use. We used the nipy_spectral_r color map with the colors shown in the heat map's color bar. When you display a confusion matrix as a heat map, the principal diagonal and the incorrect predictions stand out nicely.

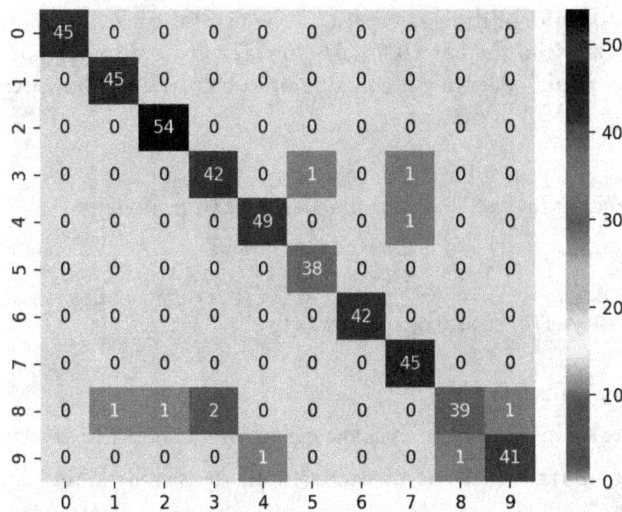

14.3.2 K-Fold Cross-Validation

K-fold cross-validation enables you to use all of your data for *both* training *and* testing, to get a better sense of how well your model will make predictions for new data by repeatedly training and testing the model with different portions of the dataset. K-fold cross-validation splits the dataset into *k* equal-size **folds** (this *k* is unrelated to *k* in the k-nearest neighbors algorithm). You then repeatedly train your model with *k* − 1 folds and test the model with the remaining fold. For example, consider using *k* = 10 with folds numbered 1 through 10. With 10 folds, we'd do 10 successive training and testing cycles:

- First, we'd train with folds 1–9, then test with fold 10.

- Next, we'd train with folds 1–8 and 10, then test with fold 9.

- Next, we'd train with folds 1–7 and 9–10, then test with fold 8.

This training and testing cycle continues until each fold has been used to test the model.

KFold Class

Scikit-learn provides the **KFold** class and the **cross_val_score function** (both in the module sklearn.model_selection) to help you perform the training and testing cycles described above. Let's perform k-fold cross-validation with the Digits dataset and the KNeighborsClassifier created earlier. First, create a KFold object:

```
In [36]: from sklearn.model_selection import KFold
```

```
In [37]: kfold = KFold(n_splits=10, random_state=11, shuffle=True)
```

The keyword arguments are:

- n_splits=10, which specifies the number of folds.

- random_state=11, which seeds the random number generator for *reproducibility*.

- shuffle=True, which causes the KFold object to randomize the data by shuffling it before splitting it into folds. This is particularly important if the samples might be ordered or grouped. For example, the Iris dataset we'll use later in this chapter has 150 samples of three *Iris* species—the first 50 are *Iris setosa*, the next 50 are *Iris versicolor* and the last 50 are *Iris virginica*. If we do not shuffle the samples, then the training data might contain none of a particular *Iris* species and the test data might be all of one species.

Using the `KFold` Object with Function `cross_val_score`

Next, use function `cross_val_score` to train and test your model:

```
In [38]: from sklearn.model_selection import cross_val_score

In [39]: scores = cross_val_score(estimator=knn, X=digits.data,
    ...:     y=digits.target, cv=kfold)
    ...:
```

The keyword arguments are:

- `estimator=knn`, which specifies the estimator you'd like to validate.

- `X=digits.data`, which specifies the samples to use for training and testing.

- `y=digits.target`, which specifies the target predictions for the samples.

- `cv=kfold`, which specifies the cross-validation generator that defines how to split the samples and targets for training and testing.

Function `cross_val_score` returns an array of accuracy scores—one for each fold. As you can see below, the model was quite accurate. Its *lowest* accuracy score was `0.97777778` (97.78%) and in one case it was 100% accurate in predicting an entire fold:

```
In [40]: scores
Out[40]:
array([0.97777778, 0.99444444, 0.98888889, 0.97777778, 0.98888889,
       0.99444444, 0.97777778, 0.98882682, 1.        , 0.98324022])
```

Once you have the accuracy scores, you can get an overall sense of the model's accuracy by calculating the mean accuracy score and the standard deviation among the 10 accuracy scores (or whatever number of folds you choose):

```
In [41]: print(f'Mean accuracy: {scores.mean():.2%}')
Mean accuracy: 98.72%

In [42]: print(f'Accuracy standard deviation: {scores.std():.2%}')
Accuracy standard deviation: 0.75%
```

On average, the model was 98.72% accurate—even better than the 97.78% we achieved when we trained the model with 75% of the data and tested the model with 25% earlier.

14.3.3 Running Multiple Models to Find the Best One

It's difficult to know in advance which machine learning model(s) will perform best for a given dataset, especially when they hide the details of how they operate from their users. Even though the `KNeighborsClassifier` predicts digit images with a high degree of accuracy, it's possible that other scikit-learn estimators are even more accurate. Scikit-learn provides many models with which you can quickly train and test your data. This encourages you to run *multiple models* to determine which is the best for a particular machine learning study.

Let's use the techniques from the preceding section to compare several classification estimators—KNeighborsClassifier, SVC and GaussianNB (there are more). Though we have not studied the SVC and GaussianNB estimators, scikit-learn nevertheless makes it easy for you to test-drive them by using their default settings.[6] First, let's import the other two estimators:

```
In [43]: from sklearn.svm import SVC

In [44]: from sklearn.naive_bayes import GaussianNB
```

Next, let's create the estimators. The following dictionary contains key–value pairs for the existing KNeighborsClassifier we created earlier, plus new SVC and GaussianNB estimators:

```
In [45]: estimators = {
    ...:     'KNeighborsClassifier': knn,
    ...:     'SVC': SVC(gamma='scale'),
    ...:     'GaussianNB': GaussianNB()}
    ...:
```

Now, we can execute the models:

```
In [46]: for estimator_name, estimator_object in estimators.items():
    ...:     kfold = KFold(n_splits=10, random_state=11, shuffle=True)
    ...:     scores = cross_val_score(estimator=estimator_object,
    ...:         X=digits.data, y=digits.target, cv=kfold)
    ...:     print(f'{estimator_name:>20}: ' +
    ...:         f'mean accuracy={scores.mean():.2%}; ' +
    ...:         f'standard deviation={scores.std():.2%}')
    ...:
KNeighborsClassifier: mean accuracy=98.72%; standard deviation=0.75%
                 SVC: mean accuracy=99.00%; standard deviation=0.85%
          GaussianNB: mean accuracy=84.48%; standard deviation=3.47%
```

This loop iterates through items in the estimators dictionary and for each key-value pair performs the following tasks:

- Unpacks the key into estimator_name and value into estimator_object.

- Creates a KFold object that shuffles the data and produces 10 folds. The keyword argument random_state is particularly important here because it ensures that each estimator works with identical folds, so we're comparing "apples to apples."

- Evaluates the current estimator_object using cross_val_score.

- Prints the estimator's name, followed by the mean and standard deviation of the accuracy scores' computed for each of the 10 folds.

Based on the results, it appears that we can get slightly better accuracy from the SVC estimator—at least when using the estimator's default settings. It's possible that by tuning some of the estimators' settings, we could get even better results. The KNeighborsClassifier and SVC estimators' accuracies are nearly identical so we might want to perform hyperparameter tuning on each to determine the best.

---

6. To avoid a warning in the current scikit-learn version at the time of this writing (version 0.20), we supplied one keyword argument when creating the SVC estimator. This argument's value will become the default in scikit-learn version 0.22.

Scikit-Learn Estimator Diagram

The scikit-learn documentation provides a helpful diagram for choosing the right estimator, based on the kind and size of your data and the machine learning task you wish to perform:

```
https://scikit-learn.org/stable/tutorial/machine_learning_map/
    index.html
```

14.3.4 Hyperparameter Tuning

Earlier in this section, we mentioned that k in the k-nearest neighbors algorithm is a hyperparameter of the algorithm. Hyperparameters are set *before* using the algorithm to train your model. In real-world machine learning studies, you'll want to use hyperparameter tuning to choose hyperparameter values that produce the best possible predictions.

To determine the best value for k in the kNN algorithm, try different values of k then compare the estimator's performance with each. We can do this using techniques similar to comparing estimators. The following loop creates `KNeighborsClassifiers` with odd k values from 1 through 19 (again, we use odd k values in kNN to avoid ties) and performs k-fold cross-validation on each. As you can see from the accuracy scores and standard deviations, the k value 1 in kNN produces the most accurate predictions for the Digits dataset. You can also see that accuracy tends to decrease for higher k values:

```
In [47]: for k in range(1, 20, 2):
    ...:     kfold = KFold(n_splits=10, random_state=11, shuffle=True)
    ...:     knn = KNeighborsClassifier(n_neighbors=k)
    ...:     scores = cross_val_score(estimator=knn,
    ...:         X=digits.data, y=digits.target, cv=kfold)
    ...:     print(f'k={k:<2}; mean accuracy={scores.mean():.2%}; ' +
    ...:         f'standard deviation={scores.std():.2%}')
    ...:
k=1 ; mean accuracy=98.83%; standard deviation=0.58%
k=3 ; mean accuracy=98.78%; standard deviation=0.78%
k=5 ; mean accuracy=98.72%; standard deviation=0.75%
k=7 ; mean accuracy=98.44%; standard deviation=0.96%
k=9 ; mean accuracy=98.39%; standard deviation=0.80%
k=11; mean accuracy=98.39%; standard deviation=0.80%
k=13; mean accuracy=97.89%; standard deviation=0.89%
k=15; mean accuracy=97.89%; standard deviation=1.02%
k=17; mean accuracy=97.50%; standard deviation=1.00%
k=19; mean accuracy=97.66%; standard deviation=0.96%
```

Machine learning is not without its costs, especially as we head toward big data and deep learning. You must "know your data" and "know your tools." For example, compute time grows rapidly with k, because k-NN needs to perform more calculations to find the nearest neighbors. There is also function `cross_validate`, which does cross-validation *and* times the results.

14.4 Case Study: Time Series and Simple Linear Regression

In the previous section, we demonstrated classification in which each sample was associated with a *distinct* class. Here, we continue our discussion of simple linear regression—

the simplest of the regression algorithms—that began in Chapter 10's Intro to Data Science section. Recall that given a collection of numeric values representing an independent variable and a dependent variable, simple linear regression describes the relationship between these variables with a straight line, known as the regression line.

Previously, we performed simple linear regression on a time series of average New York City January high-temperature data for 1895 through 2018. In that example, we used Seaborn's regplot function to create a scatter plot of the data with a corresponding regression line. We also used the scipy.stats module's linregress function to calculate the regression line's slope and intercept. We then used those values to predict future temperatures and estimate past temperatures.

In this section, we'll

- use a *scikit-learn estimator* to reimplement the simple linear regression we showed in Chapter 10,

- use Seaborn's scatterplot function to plot the data and Matplotlib's plot function to display the regression line, then

- use the coefficient and intercept values calculated by the scikit-learn estimator to make predictions.

Later, we'll look at *multiple linear regression* (also simply called *linear regression*).

For your convenience, we provide the temperature data in the ch14 examples folder in a CSV file named ave_hi_nyc_jan_1895-2018.csv. Once again, launch IPython with the --matplotlib option:

```
ipython --matplotlib
```

Loading the Average High Temperatures into a DataFrame
As we did in Chapter 10, let's load the data from ave_hi_nyc_jan_1895-2018.csv, rename the 'Value' column to 'Temperature', remove 01 from the end of each date value and display a few data samples:

```
In [1]: import pandas as pd

In [2]: nyc = pd.read_csv('ave_hi_nyc_jan_1895-2018.csv')

In [3]: nyc.columns = ['Date', 'Temperature', 'Anomaly']

In [4]: nyc.Date = nyc.Date.floordiv(100)

In [5]: nyc.head(3)
Out[5]:
   Date  Temperature  Anomaly
0  1895         34.2     -3.2
1  1896         34.7     -2.7
2  1897         35.5     -1.9
```

Splitting the Data for Training and Testing
In this example, we'll use the **LinearRegression** estimator from **sklearn.linear_model**. By default, this estimator uses *all* the numeric features in a dataset, performing a **multiple linear regression** (which we'll discuss in the next section). Here, we perform *simple linear*

regression using *one* feature as the independent variable. So, we'll need to select one feature (the Date) from the dataset.

When you select one column from a two-dimensional DataFrame, the result is a *one-dimensional* Series. However, scikit-learn estimators require their training and testing data to be *two-dimensional arrays* (or two-dimensional *array-like* data, such as lists of lists or pandas DataFrames). To use one-dimensional data with an estimator, you must transform it from one dimension containing *n* elements, into two dimensions containing *n rows* and one *column* as you'll see below.

As we did in the previous case study, let's split the data into training and testing sets. Once again, we used the keyword argument random_state for reproducibility:

```
In [6]: from sklearn.model_selection import train_test_split

In [7]: X_train, X_test, y_train, y_test = train_test_split(
   ...:     nyc.Date.values.reshape(-1, 1), nyc.Temperature.values,
   ...:     random_state=11)
   ...:
```

The expression nyc.Date returns the Date column's Series, and the Series' values attribute returns the NumPy array containing that Series' values. To transform this one-dimensional array into two dimensions, we call the array's **reshape method**. Normally, two arguments are the precise number of rows and columns. However, the first argument -1 tells reshape to *infer* the number of rows, based on the number of columns (1) and the number of elements (124) in the array. The transformed array will have only one column, so reshape infers the number of rows to be 124, because the only way to fit 124 elements into an array with one column is by distributing them over 124 rows.

We can confirm the 75%–25% train-test split by checking the shapes of X_train and X_test:

```
In [8]: X_train.shape
Out[8]: (93, 1)

In [9]: X_test.shape
Out[9]: (31, 1)
```

Training the Model
Scikit-learn does not have a separate class for simple linear regression because it's just a special case of multiple linear regression, so let's train a LinearRegression estimator:

```
In [10]: from sklearn.linear_model import LinearRegression

In [11]: linear_regression = LinearRegression()

In [12]: linear_regression.fit(X=X_train, y=y_train)
Out[12]:
LinearRegression(copy_X=True, fit_intercept=True, n_jobs=None,
         normalize=False)
```

After training the estimator, fit returns the estimator, and IPython displays its string representation. For descriptions of the default settings, see:

```
http://scikit-learn.org/stable/modules/generated/
    sklearn.linear_model.LinearRegression.html
```

To find the best fitting regression line for the data, the LinearRegression estimator iteratively adjusts the slope and intercept values to minimize the sum of the squares of the data points' distances from the line. In Chapter 10's Intro to Data Science section, we gave some insight into how the slope and intercept values are discovered.

Now, we can get the slope and intercept used in the $y = mx + b$ calculation to make predictions. The slope is stored in the estimator's **coeff_** attribute (m in the equation) and the intercept is stored in the estimator's *intercept_* attribute (b in the equation):

```
In [13]: linear_regression.coef_
Out[13]: array([0.01939167])

In [14]: linear_regression.intercept_
Out[14]: -0.30779820252656265
```

We'll use these later to plot the regression line and make predictions for specific dates.

Testing the Model

Let's test the model using the data in X_test and check some of the predictions throughout the dataset by displaying the predicted and expected values for every fifth element—we discuss how to assess the regression model's accuracy in Section 14.5.8:

```
In [15]: predicted = linear_regression.predict(X_test)

In [16]: expected = y_test

In [17]: for p, e in zip(predicted[::5], expected[::5]):
    ...:     print(f'predicted: {p:.2f}, expected: {e:.2f}')
    ...:
predicted: 37.86, expected: 31.70
predicted: 38.69, expected: 34.80
predicted: 37.00, expected: 39.40
predicted: 37.25, expected: 45.70
predicted: 38.05, expected: 32.30
predicted: 37.64, expected: 33.80
predicted: 36.94, expected: 39.70
```

Predicting Future Temperatures and Estimating Past Temperatures

Let's use the coefficient and intercept values to predict the January 2019 average high temperature and to estimate what the average high temperature was in January of 1890. The lambda in the following snippet implements the equation for a line

$$y = mx + b$$

using the coef_ as m and the intercept_ as b.

```
In [18]: predict = (lambda x: linear_regression.coef_ * x +
    ...:                       linear_regression.intercept_)
    ...:

In [19]: predict(2019)
Out[19]: array([38.84399018])

In [20]: predict(1890)
Out[20]: array([36.34246432])
```

Visualizing the Dataset with the Regression Line

Next, let's create a scatter plot of the dataset using Seaborn's **scatterplot** function and Matplotlib's **plot** function. First, use scatterplot with the nyc DataFrame to display the data points:

```
In [21]: import seaborn as sns

In [22]: axes = sns.scatterplot(data=nyc, x='Date', y='Temperature',
    ...:     hue='Temperature', palette='winter', legend=False)
    ...:
```

The keyword arguments are:

- data, which specifies the DataFrame (nyc) containing the data to display.

- x and y, which specify the names of nyc's columns that are the source of the data along the x- and y-axes, respectively. In this case, x is the 'Date' and y is the 'Temperature'. The corresponding values from each column form x-y coordinate pairs used to plot the dots.

- hue, which specifies which column's data should be used to determine the dot colors. In this case, we use the 'Temperature' column. Color is not particularly important in this example, but we wanted to add some visual interest to the graph.

- palette, which specifies a Matplotlib color map from which to choose the dots' colors.

- legend=False, which specifies that scatterplot should not show a legend for the graph—the default is True, but we do not need a legend for this example.

As we did in Chapter 10, let's scale the y-axis range of values so you'll be able to see the linear relationship better once we display the regression line:

```
In [23]: axes.set_ylim(10, 70)
Out[23]: (10, 70)
```

Next, let's display the regression line. First, create an array containing the minimum and maximum date values in nyc.Date. These are the x-coordinates of the regression line's start and end points:

```
In [24]: import numpy as np

In [25]: x = np.array([min(nyc.Date.values), max(nyc.Date.values)])
```

Passing the array x to the predict lambda from snippet [16] produces an array containing the corresponding predicted values, which we'll use as the y-coordinates:

```
In [26]: y = predict(x)
```

Finally, we can use Matplotlib's plot function to plot a line based on the x and y arrays, which represent the x- and y-coordinates of the points, respectively:

```
In [27]: import matplotlib.pyplot as plt

In [28]: line = plt.plot(x, y)
```

The resulting scatterplot and regression line are shown below. This graph is nearly identical to the one you saw in Chapter 10's Intro to Data Science section.

Overfitting/Underfitting

When creating a model, a key goal is to ensure that it is capable of making accurate predictions for data it has not yet seen. Two common problems that prevent accurate predictions are overfitting and underfitting:

- **Underfitting** occurs when a model is too simple to make predictions, based on its training data. For example, you may use a linear model, such as simple linear regression, when in fact, the problem really requires a non-linear model. For example, temperatures vary significantly throughout the four seasons. If you're trying to create a general model that can predict temperatures year-round, a simple linear regression model will underfit the data.

- **Overfitting** occurs when your model is too complex. The most extreme case, would be a model that memorizes its training data. That may be acceptable if your new data looks *exactly* like your training data, but ordinarily that's not the case. When you make predictions with an overfit model, new data that matches the training data will produce perfect predictions, but the model will not know what to do with data it has never seen.

For additional information on underfitting and overfitting, see

- `https://en.wikipedia.org/wiki/Overfitting`
- `https://machinelearningmastery.com/overfitting-and-underfitting-with-machine-learning-algorithms/`

14.5 Case Study: Multiple Linear Regression with the California Housing Dataset

In Chapter 10's Intro to Data Science section, we performed simple linear regression on a small weather data time series using pandas, Seaborn's `regplot` function and the SciPy's `stats` module's `linregress` function. In the previous section, we reimplemented that same example using scikit-learn's `LinearRegression` estimator, Seaborn's `scatterplot` function and Matplotlib's `plot` function. Now, we'll perform linear regression with a much larger real-world dataset.

The **California Housing dataset**[7] bundled with scikit-learn has 20,640 samples, each with eight numerical features. We'll perform a *multiple linear regression* that uses all eight numerical features to make more sophisticated housing price predictions than if we were to use only a single feature or a subset of the features. Once again, scikit-learn will do most of the work for you—`LinearRegression` performs multiple linear regression by default.

We'll visualize some of the data using Matplotlib and Seaborn, so launch IPython with Matplotlib support:

```
ipython --matplotlib
```

14.5.1 Loading the Dataset

According to the California Housing Prices dataset's description in scikit-learn, "This dataset was derived from the 1990 U.S. census, using one row per census block group. A block group is the smallest geographical unit for which the U.S. Census Bureau publishes sample data (a block group typically has a population of 600 to 3,000 people)." The dataset has 20,640 samples—one per block group—with eight features each:

- median income—in tens of thousands, so 8.37 would represent $83,700
- median house age—in the dataset, the maximum value for this feature is 52
- average number of rooms
- average number of bedrooms
- block population
- average house occupancy
- house block latitude
- house block longitude

Each sample also has as its *target* a corresponding median house value in hundreds of thousands, so 3.55 would represent $355,000. In the dataset, the maximum value for this feature is 5, which represents $500,000.

It's reasonable to expect that more bedrooms or more rooms or higher income would mean higher house value. By combining these features to make predictions, we're more likely to get more accurate predictions.

Loading the Data

Let's load the dataset and familiarize ourselves with it. The **fetch_california_housing** function from the `sklearn.datasets` module returns a `Bunch` object containing the data and other information about the dataset:

```
In [1]: from sklearn.datasets import fetch_california_housing

In [2]: california = fetch_california_housing()
```

---

7. http://lib.stat.cmu.edu/datasets. Pace, R. Kelley and Ronald Barry, Sparse Spatial Autoregressions, Statistics and Probability Letters, 33 (1997) 291-297. Submitted to the StatLib Datasets Archive by Kelley Pace (kpace@unix1.sncc.lsu.edu). [9/Nov/99].

Displaying the Dataset's Description

Let's look at the dataset's description. The DESCR information includes:

- Number of Instances—this dataset contains 20,640 samples.

- Number of Attributes—there are 8 features (attributes) per sample.

- Attribute Information—feature descriptions.

- Missing Attribute Values—none are missing in this dataset.

According to the description, the target variable in this dataset is the *median house value*—this is the value we'll be trying to predict via multiple linear regression.

```
In [3]: print(california.DESCR)
.. _california_housing_dataset:

California Housing dataset
--------------------------

**Data Set Characteristics:**

    :Number of Instances: 20640

    :Number of Attributes: 8 numeric, predictive attributes and
        the target

    :Attribute Information:
        - MedInc        median income in block
        - HouseAge      median house age in block
        - AveRooms      average number of rooms
        - AveBedrms     average number of bedrooms
        - Population    block population
        - AveOccup      average house occupancy
        - Latitude      house block latitude
        - Longitude     house block longitude

    :Missing Attribute Values: None

This dataset was obtained from the StatLib repository.
http://lib.stat.cmu.edu/datasets/

The target variable is the median house value for California districts.

This dataset was derived from the 1990 U.S. census, using one row per
census block group. A block group is the smallest geographical unit for
which the U.S. Census Bureau publishes sample data (a block group typi-
cally has a population of 600 to 3,000 people).

It can be downloaded/loaded using the
:func:`sklearn.datasets.fetch_california_housing` function.

.. topic:: References

    - Pace, R. Kelley and Ronald Barry, Sparse Spatial Autoregressions,
      Statistics and Probability Letters, 33 (1997) 291-297
```

Again, the Bunch object's data and target attributes are NumPy arrays containing the 20,640 samples and their target values respectively. We can confirm the number of samples (rows) and features (columns) by looking at the data array's shape attribute, which shows that there are 20,640 rows and 8 columns:

```
In [4]: california.data.shape
Out[4]: (20640, 8)
```

Similarly, you can see that the number of target values—that is, the median house values—matches the number of samples by looking at the target array's shape:

```
In [5]: california.target.shape
Out[5]: (20640,)
```

The Bunch's **feature_names attribute** contains the names that correspond to each column in the data array:

```
In [6]: california.feature_names
Out[6]:
['MedInc',
 'HouseAge',
 'AveRooms',
 'AveBedrms',
 'Population',
 'AveOccup',
 'Latitude',
 'Longitude']
```

14.5.2 Exploring the Data with Pandas

Let's use a pandas DataFrame to explore the data further. We'll also use the DataFrame with Seaborn in the next section to visualize some of the data. First, let's import pandas and set some options:

```
In [7]: import pandas as pd

In [8]: pd.set_option('precision', 4)

In [9]: pd.set_option('max_columns', 9)

In [10]: pd.set_option('display.width', None)
```

In the preceding set_option calls:

- 'precision' is the maximum number of digits to display to the right of each decimal point.

- 'max_columns' is the maximum number of columns to display when you output the DataFrame's string representation. By default, if pandas cannot fit all of the columns left-to-right, it cuts out columns in the middle and displays an ellipsis (…) instead. The 'max_columns' setting enables pandas to show all the columns using multiple rows of output. As you'll see momentarily, we'll have nine columns in the DataFrame—the eight dataset features in california.data and an additional column for the target median house values (california.target).

- 'display.width' specifies the width in characters of your Command Prompt (Windows), Terminal (macOS/Linux) or shell (Linux). The value None tells pandas to auto-detect the display width when formatting string representations of Series and DataFrames.

Next, let's create a DataFrame from the Bunch's data, target and feature_names arrays. The first snippet below creates the initial DataFrame using the data in california.data and with the column names specified by california.feature_names. The second statement adds a column for the median house values stored in california.target:

```
In [11]: california_df = pd.DataFrame(california.data,
    ...:                             columns=california.feature_names)
    ...:

In [12]: california_df['MedHouseValue'] = pd.Series(california.target)
```

We can peek at some of the data using the head function. Notice that pandas displays the DataFrame's first six columns, then skips a line of output and displays the remaining columns. The \ to the right of the column head "AveOccup" indicates that there are more columns displayed below. You'll see the \ only if the window in which IPython is running is too narrow to display all the columns left-to-right:

```
In [13]: california_df.head()
Out[13]:
   MedInc  HouseAge  AveRooms  AveBedrms  Population  AveOccup  \
0  8.3252      41.0    6.9841     1.0238       322.0    2.5556
1  8.3014      21.0    6.2381     0.9719      2401.0    2.1098
2  7.2574      52.0    8.2881     1.0734       496.0    2.8023
3  5.6431      52.0    5.8174     1.0731       558.0    2.5479
4  3.8462      52.0    6.2819     1.0811       565.0    2.1815

   Latitude  Longitude  MedHouseValue
0     37.88    -122.23          4.526
1     37.86    -122.22          3.585
2     37.85    -122.24          3.521
3     37.85    -122.25          3.413
4     37.85    -122.25          3.422
```

Let's get a sense of the data in each column by calculating the DataFrame's summary statistics. Note that the median income and house values (again, measured in hundreds of thousands) are from 1990 and are significantly higher today:

```
In [14]: california_df.describe()
Out[14]:
              MedInc    HouseAge     AveRooms    AveBedrms   Population  \
count   20640.0000  20640.0000   20640.0000   20640.0000   20640.0000
mean        3.8707     28.6395       5.4290       1.0967    1425.4767
std         1.8998     12.5856       2.4742       0.4739    1132.4621
min         0.4999      1.0000       0.8462       0.3333       3.0000
25%         2.5634     18.0000       4.4407       1.0061     787.0000
50%         3.5348     29.0000       5.2291       1.0488    1166.0000
75%         4.7432     37.0000       6.0524       1.0995    1725.0000
max        15.0001     52.0000     141.9091      34.0667   35682.0000
```

	AveOccup	Latitude	Longitude	MedHouseValue
count	20640.0000	20640.0000	20640.0000	20640.0000
mean	3.0707	35.6319	-119.5697	2.0686
std	10.3860	2.1360	2.0035	1.1540
min	0.6923	32.5400	-124.3500	0.1500
25%	2.4297	33.9300	-121.8000	1.1960
50%	2.8181	34.2600	-118.4900	1.7970
75%	3.2823	37.7100	-118.0100	2.6472
max	1243.3333	41.9500	-114.3100	5.0000

14.5.3 Visualizing the Features

It's helpful to visualize your data by plotting the target value against *each* feature—in this case, to see how the median home value relates to each feature. To make our visualizations clearer, let's use DataFrame method **sample** to randomly select 10% of the 20,640 samples for graphing purposes:

```
In [15]: sample_df = california_df.sample(frac=0.1, random_state=17)
```

The keyword argument frac specifies the fraction of the data to select (0.1 for 10%), and the keyword argument random_state enables you to seed the random number generator. The integer seed value (17), which we chose arbitrarily, is crucial for *reproducibility*. Each time you use the *same* seed value, method sample selects the *same* random subset of the DataFrame's rows. Then, when we graph the data, you should get the *same* results.

Next, we'll use Matplotlib and Seaborn to display scatter plots of each of the eight features. Both libraries can display scatter plots. Seaborn's are more attractive and require less code, so we'll use Seaborn to create the following scatter plots. First, we import both libraries and use Seaborn function set to scale each diagram's fonts to two times their default size:

```
In [16]: import matplotlib.pyplot as plt

In [17]: import seaborn as sns

In [18]: sns.set(font_scale=2)

In [19]: sns.set_style('whitegrid')
```

The following snippet displays the scatter plots.[8] Each shows one feature along the *x*-axis and the median home value (california.target) along the *y*-axis, so we can see how each feature and the median house values relate to one another. We display each scatter plot in a separate window. The windows are displayed in the order the features were listed in snippet [6] with the most recently displayed window in the foreground:

```
In [20]: for feature in california.feature_names:
    ...:     plt.figure(figsize=(16, 9))
    ...:     sns.scatterplot(data=sample_df, x=feature,
    ...:                     y='MedHouseValue', hue='MedHouseValue',
    ...:                     palette='cool', legend=False)
    ...:
```

---

8. When you execute this code in IPython, each window will be displayed in front of the previous one. As you close each, you'll see the one behind it.

For each feature name, the snippet first creates a 16-inch-by-9-inch Matplotlib Fig-ure—we're plotting many data points, so we chose to use a larger window. If this window is larger than your screen, Matplotlib fits the Figure to the screen. Seaborn uses the cur-rent Figure to display the scatter plot. If you do not create a Figure first, Seaborn will create one. We created the Figure first here so we could display a large window for a scat-ter plot containing over 2000 points.

Next, the snippet creates a Seaborn scatterplot in which the x-axis shows the cur-rent feature, the y-axis shows the 'MedHouseValue' (*median house values*), and the 'Med-HouseValue' determines the dot colors (hue). Some interesting things to notice in these graphs:

- The graphs showing the latitude and longitude each have two areas of especially significant density. If you search online for the latitude and longitude values where those dense areas appear, you'll see that these represent the greater Los Angeles and greater San Francisco areas where house prices tend to be higher.

- In each graph, there is a horizontal line of dots at the y-axis value 5, which rep-resents the median house value $500,000. The highest home value that could be chosen on the 1990 census form was "$500,000 or more."[9] So any block group with a median house value over $500,000 is listed in the dataset as 5. Being able to spot characteristics like this is a compelling reason to do data exploration and visualization.

- In the HouseAge graph, there is a vertical line of dots at the x-axis value 52. The highest home age that could be chosen on the 1990 census form was 52, so any block group with a median house age over 52 is listed in the dataset as 52.

---

9. https://www.census.gov/prod/1/90dec/cph4/appdxe.pdf.

14.5.4 Splitting the Data for Training and Testing

Once again, to prepare for training and testing the model, let's break the data into training and testing sets using the `train_test_split` function then check their sizes:

```
In [21]: from sklearn.model_selection import train_test_split

In [22]: X_train, X_test, y_train, y_test = train_test_split(
    ...:     california.data, california.target, random_state=11)
    ...:

In [23]: X_train.shape
Out[23]: (15480, 8)

In [24]: X_test.shape
Out[24]: (5160, 8)
```

We used `train_test_split`'s keyword argument `random_state` to seed the random number generator for reproducibility.

14.5.5 Training the Model

Next, we'll train the model. By default, a `LinearRegression` estimator uses *all* the features in the dataset's data array to perform a multiple linear regression. An error occurs if any of the features are *categorical* rather than numeric. If a dataset contains categorical data, you either must preprocess the categorical features into numerical ones (which you'll do in the next chapter) or must exclude the categorical features from the training process. A benefit of working with scikit-learn's bundled datasets is that they're already in the correct format for machine learning using scikit-learn's models.

As you saw in the previous two snippets, X_train and X_test each contain 8 columns—one per feature. Let's create a `LinearRegression` estimator and invoke its `fit` method to train the estimator using X_train and y_train:

```
In [25]: from sklearn.linear_model import LinearRegression

In [26]: linear_regression = LinearRegression()
```

```
In [27]: linear_regression.fit(X=X_train, y=y_train)
Out[27]:
LinearRegression(copy_X=True, fit_intercept=True, n_jobs=None,
        normalize=False)
```

Multiple linear regression produces separate coefficients for each feature (stored in coeff_) in the dataset and one intercept (stored in intercept_):

```
In [28]: for i, name in enumerate(california.feature_names):
   ...:       print(f'{name:>10}: {linear_regression.coef_[i]}')
   ...:
    MedInc: 0.4377030215382206
  HouseAge: 0.009216834565797713
  AveRooms: -0.10732526637360985
 AveBedrms: 0.611713307391811
Population: -5.756822009298454e-06
  AveOccup: -0.0033845664657163703
  Latitude: -0.419481860964907
 Longitude: -0.4337713349874016

In [29]: linear_regression.intercept_
Out[29]: -36.88295065605547
```

For positive coefficients, the median house value *increases* as the feature value *increases*. For negative coefficients, the median house value *decreases* as the feature value *increases*. Note that the population coefficient has a *negative exponent* (e-06), so the coefficient's value is actually -0.000005756822009298454. This is close to zero, so a block group's population apparently has little effect the median house value.

You can use these values with the following equation to make predictions:

$$y = m_1 x_1 + m_2 x_2 + \ldots m_n x_n + b$$

where

- $m_1, m_2, \ldots, m_n$ are the feature coefficients,
- b is the intercept,
- $x_1, x_2, \ldots, x_n$ are the feature values (that is, the values of the independent variables), and
- y is the predicted value (that is, the dependent variable).

14.5.6 Testing the Model

Now, let's test the model by calling the estimator's predict method with the test samples as an argument. As we've done in each of the previous examples, we store the array of predictions in predicted and the array of expected values in expected:

```
In [30]: predicted = linear_regression.predict(X_test)

In [31]: expected = y_test
```

Let's look at the first five predictions and their corresponding expected values:

```
In [32]: predicted[:5]
Out[32]: array([1.25396876, 2.34693107, 2.03794745, 1.8701254 ,
2.53608339])
```

```
In [33]: expected[:5]
Out[33]: array([0.762, 1.732, 1.125, 1.37 , 1.856])
```

With classification, we saw that the predictions were distinct classes that matched existing classes in the dataset. With regression, it's tough to get exact predictions, because you have continuous outputs. Every possible value of $x_1, x_2 \ldots x_n$ in the calculation

$$y = m_1 x_1 + m_2 x_2 + \ldots m_n x_n + b$$

predicts a value.

14.5.7 Visualizing the Expected vs. Predicted Prices

Let's look at the expected vs. predicted median house values for the test data. First, let's create a DataFrame containing columns for the expected and predicted values:

```
In [34]: df = pd.DataFrame()

In [35]: df['Expected'] = pd.Series(expected)

In [36]: df['Predicted'] = pd.Series(predicted)
```

Now let's plot the data as a scatter plot with the expected (target) prices along the x-axis and the predicted prices along the y-axis:

```
In [37]: figure = plt.figure(figsize=(9, 9))

In [38]: axes = sns.scatterplot(data=df, x='Expected', y='Predicted',
    ...:     hue='Predicted', palette='cool', legend=False)
    ...:
```

Next, let's set the x- and y-axes' limits to use the same scale along both axes:

```
In [39]: start = min(expected.min(), predicted.min())

In [40]: end = max(expected.max(), predicted.max())

In [41]: axes.set_xlim(start, end)
Out[41]: (-0.6830978604144491, 7.155719818496834)

In [42]: axes.set_ylim(start, end)
Out[42]: (-0.6830978604144491, 7.155719818496834)
```

Now, let's plot a line that represents *perfect predictions* (note that this is *not* a regression line). The following snippet displays a line between the points representing the lower-left corner of the graph (start, start) and the upper-right corner of the graph (end, end). The third argument ('k--') indicates the line's style. The letter k represents the color black, and the -- indicates that plot should draw a dashed line:

```
In [43]: line = plt.plot([start, end], [start, end], 'k--')
```

If every predicted value were to match the expected value, then all the dots would be plotted along the dashed line. In the following diagram, it appears that as the expected median house value increases, more of the predicted values fall below the line. So the model seems to *predict* lower median house values as the *expected* median house value increases.

14.5.8 Regression Model Metrics

Scikit-learn provides many metrics functions for evaluating how well estimators predict results and for comparing estimators to choose the best one(s) for your particular study. These metrics vary by estimator type. For example, the sklearn.metrics functions confusion_matrix and classification_report used in the Digits dataset classification case study are two of many metrics functions specifically for evaluating *classification* estimators.

Among the many metrics for regression estimators is the model's **coefficient of determination**, which is also called the R^2 **score**. To calculate an estimator's R^2 score, call the sklearn.metrics module's **r2_score** function with the arrays representing the expected and predicted results:

```
In [44]: from sklearn import metrics

In [45]: metrics.r2_score(expected, predicted)
Out[45]: 0.6008983115964333
```

R^2 scores range from 0.0 to 1.0 with 1.0 being the best. An R^2 score of 1.0 indicates that the estimator perfectly predicts the dependent variable's value, given the independent variable(s) value(s). An R^2 score of 0.0 indicates the model cannot make predictions with any accuracy, based on the independent variables' values.

Another common metric for regression models is the **mean squared error**, which

- calculates the difference between each expected and predicted value—this is called the *error*,

- squares each difference and

- calculates the average of the squared values.

To calculate an estimator's mean squared error, call function **mean_squared_error** (from module sklearn.metrics) with the arrays representing the expected and predicted results:

```
In [46]: metrics.mean_squared_error(expected, predicted)
Out[46]: 0.5350149774449119
```

When comparing estimators with the mean squared error metric, the one with the value closest to 0 best fits your data. In the next section, we'll run several regression estimators using the California Housing dataset. For the list of scikit-learn's metrics functions by estimator category, see

```
https://scikit-learn.org/stable/modules/model_evaluation.html
```

14.5.9 Choosing the Best Model

As we did in the classification case study, let's try several estimators to determine whether any produces better results than the `LinearRegression` estimator. In this example, we'll use the `linear_regression` estimator we already created as well as `ElasticNet`, `Lasso` and `Ridge` regression estimators (all from the `sklearn.linear_model` module). For information about these estimators, see

```
https://scikit-learn.org/stable/modules/linear_model.html
```

```
In [47]: from sklearn.linear_model import ElasticNet, Lasso, Ridge

In [48]: estimators = {
    ...:     'LinearRegression': linear_regression,
    ...:     'ElasticNet': ElasticNet(),
    ...:     'Lasso': Lasso(),
    ...:     'Ridge': Ridge()
    ...: }
```

Once again, we'll run the estimators using k-fold cross-validation with a `KFold` object and the `cross_val_score` function. Here, we pass to `cross_val_score` the additional keyword argument `scoring='r2'`, which indicates that the function should report the R^2 scores for each fold—again, 1.0 is the best, so it appears that `LinearRegression` and `Ridge` are the best models for this dataset:

```
In [49]: from sklearn.model_selection import KFold, cross_val_score

In [50]: for estimator_name, estimator_object in estimators.items():
    ...:     kfold = KFold(n_splits=10, random_state=11, shuffle=True)
    ...:     scores = cross_val_score(estimator=estimator_object,
    ...:         X=california.data, y=california.target, cv=kfold,
    ...:         scoring='r2')
    ...:     print(f'{estimator_name:>16}: ' +
    ...:         f'mean of r2 scores={scores.mean():.3f}')
    ...:
LinearRegression: mean of r2 scores=0.599
      ElasticNet: mean of r2 scores=0.423
           Lasso: mean of r2 scores=0.285
           Ridge: mean of r2 scores=0.599
```

14.6 Case Study: Unsupervised Machine Learning, Part 1—Dimensionality Reduction

In our data science presentations, we've focused on getting to know your data. **Unsupervised machine learning** and visualization can help you do this by finding patterns and relationships among unlabeled samples.

For datasets like the univariate time series we used earlier in this chapter, visualizing the data is easy. In that case, we had two variables—date and temperature—so we plotted the data in two dimensions with one variable along each axis. Using Matplotlib, Seaborn and other visualization libraries, you also can plot datasets with three variables using 3D visualizations. But how do you visualize data with more than three dimensions? For example, in the Digits dataset, every sample has 64 features and a target value. In big data, samples can have hundreds, thousands or even millions of features.

To visualize a dataset with many features (that is, many dimensions), we'll first *reduce* the data to two or three dimensions. This requires an unsupervised machine learning technique called **dimensionality reduction**. When you graph the resulting information, you might see patterns in the data that will help you choose the most appropriate machine learning algorithms to use. For example, if the visualization contains *clusters* of points, it might indicate that there are distinct classes of information within the dataset. So a classification algorithm might be appropriate. Of course, you'd first need to determine the class of the samples in each cluster. This might require studying the samples in a cluster to see what they have in common.

Dimensionality reduction also serves other purposes. Training estimators on big data with significant numbers of dimensions can take hours, days, weeks or longer. It's also difficult for humans to think about data with large numbers of dimensions. This is called the **curse of dimensionality**. If the data has closely correlated features, some could be eliminated via dimensionality reduction to improve the training performance. This, however, might reduce the accuracy of the model.

Recall that the Digits dataset is already labeled with 10 classes representing the digits 0–9. Let's ignore those labels and use dimensionality reduction to reduce the dataset's features to two dimensions, so we can visualize the resulting data.

Loading the Digits Dataset
Launch IPython with:

```
ipython --matplotlib
```

then load the dataset:

```
In [1]: from sklearn.datasets import load_digits

In [2]: digits = load_digits()
```

Creating a TSNE Estimator for Dimensionality Reduction
Next, we'll use the **TSNE estimator** (from the `sklearn.manifold` module) to perform dimensionality reduction. This estimator uses an algorithm called t-distributed Stochastic Neighbor Embedding (t-SNE)[10] to analyze a dataset's features and reduce them to the specified number of dimensions. We first tried the popular PCA (principal components analysis) estimator but did not like the results we were getting, so we switched to TSNE. We'll show PCA later in this case study.

---

10. The algorithm's details are beyond this book's scope. For more information, see https://scikit-learn.org/stable/modules/manifold.html#t-sne.

Let's create a TSNE object for reducing a dataset's features to two dimensions, as specified by the keyword argument n_components. As with the other estimators we've presented, we used the random_state keyword argument to ensure the reproducibility of the "render sequence" when we display the digit clusters:

```
In [3]: from sklearn.manifold import TSNE
```

```
In [4]: tsne = TSNE(n_components=2, random_state=11)
```

Transforming the Digits Dataset's Features into Two Dimensions

Dimensionality reduction in scikit-learn typically involves two steps—training the estimator with the dataset, then using the estimator to transform the data into the specified number of dimensions. These steps can be performed separately with the TSNE methods **fit** and **transform**, or they can be performed in one statement using the **fit_transform** method:[11]

```
In [5]: reduced_data = tsne.fit_transform(digits.data)
```

TSNE's fit_transform method takes some time to train the estimator then perform the reduction. On our system, this took about 20 seconds. When the method completes its task, it returns an array with the same number of rows as digits.data, but only two columns. You can confirm this by checking reduced_data's shape:

```
In [6]: reduced_data.shape
Out[6]: (1797, 2)
```

Visualizing the Reduced Data

Now that we've reduced the original dataset to only two dimensions, let's use a scatter plot to display the data. In this case, rather than Seaborn's scatterplot function, we'll use Matplotlib's **scatter function**, because it returns a collection of the plotted items. We'll use that feature in a second scatter plot momentarily:

```
In [7]: import matplotlib.pyplot as plt
```

```
In [8]: dots = plt.scatter(reduced_data[:, 0], reduced_data[:, 1],
   ...:                     c='black')
   ...:
```

Function scatter's first two arguments are reduced_data's columns (0 and 1) containing the data for the *x*- and *y*-axes. The keyword argument c='black' specifies the color of the dots. We did not label the axes, because they do not correspond to specific features of the original dataset. The new features produced by the TSNE estimator could be quite different from the dataset's original features.

---

11. Every call to fit_transform trains the estimator. If you intend to reuse the estimator to reduce the dimensions of samples multiple times, use fit to once train the estimator, then use transform to perform the reductions. We'll use this technique with PCA later in this case study.

The following diagram shows the resulting scatter plot. There are clearly *clusters* of related data points, though there appear to be 11 main clusters, rather than 10. There also are "loose" data points that do not appear to be part of specific clusters. Based on our earlier study of the Digits dataset this makes sense because some digits were difficult to classify.

Visualizing the Reduced Data with Different Colors for Each Digit

Though the preceding diagram shows clusters, we do not know whether all the items in each cluster represent the same digit. If they do not, then the clusters are not helpful. Let's use the known `targets` in the Digits dataset to color all the dots so we can see whether these clusters indeed represent specific digits:

```
In [9]: dots = plt.scatter(reduced_data[:, 0], reduced_data[:, 1],
   ...:     c=digits.target, cmap=plt.cm.get_cmap('nipy_spectral_r', 10))
   ...:
   ...:
```

In this case, `scatter`'s keyword argument `c=digits.target` specifies that the `target` values determine the dot colors. We also added the keyword argument

```
cmap=plt.cm.get_cmap('nipy_spectral_r', 10)
```

which specifies a color map to use when coloring the dots. In this case, we know we're coloring 10 digits, so we use `get_cmap` method of Matplotlib's `cm` object (from module `matplotlib.pyplot`) to load a color map (`'nipy_spectral_r'`) and select 10 distinct colors from the color map.

The following statement adds a color bar key to the right of the diagram so you can see which digit each color represents:

```
In [10]: colorbar = plt.colorbar(dots)
```

Voila! We see 10 clusters corresponding to the digits 0–9. Again, there are a few smaller groups of dots standing alone. Based on this, we might decide that a supervised-learning approach like k-nearest neighbors would work well with this data. As an experiment, you might want to investigate Matplotlib's **Axes3D**, which provides *x-*, *y-* and *z-*axes for plotting in three-dimensional graphs.

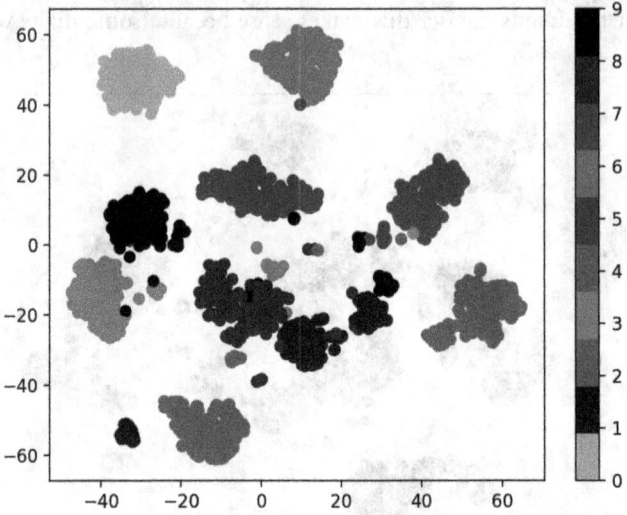

14.7 Case Study: Unsupervised Machine Learning, Part 2—k-Means Clustering

In this section, we introduce perhaps the simplest unsupervised machine learning algorithms—**k-means clustering**. This algorithm analyzes *unlabeled* samples and attempts to place them in clusters that appear to be related. The *k* in "k-means" represents the number of clusters you'd like to see imposed on your data.

The algorithm organizes samples into the number of clusters you specify in advance, using distance calculations similar to the k-nearest neighbors clustering algorithm. Each cluster of samples is grouped around a **centroid**—the cluster's center point. Initially, the algorithm chooses *k* centroids at random from the dataset's samples. Then the remaining samples are placed in the cluster whose centroid is the closest. The centroids are iteratively recalculated and the samples re-assigned to clusters until, for all clusters, the distances from a given centroid to the samples in its cluster are minimized. The algorithm's results are:

- a one-dimensional array of labels indicating the cluster to which each sample belongs and
- a two-dimensional array of centroids representing the center of each cluster.

Iris Dataset

We'll work with the popular **Iris dataset**[12] bundled with scikit-learn, which is commonly analyzed with both classification and clustering. Although this dataset is labeled, we'll ignore those labels here to demonstrate clustering. Then, we'll use the labels to determine how well the k-means algorithm clustered the samples.

---

12. Fisher, R.A., "The use of multiple measurements in taxonomic problems," Annual Eugenics, 7, Part II, 179-188 (1936); also in "Contributions to Mathematical Statistics" (John Wiley, NY, 1950).

The Iris dataset is referred to as a "toy dataset" because it has only 150 samples and four features. The dataset describes 50 samples for each of three *Iris* flower species—*Iris setosa*, *Iris versicolor* and *Iris virginica*. Photos of these are shown below. Each sample's features are the sepal length, sepal width, petal length and petal width, all measured in centimeters. The *sepals* are the larger outer parts of each flower that protect the smaller inside *petals* before the flower buds bloom.

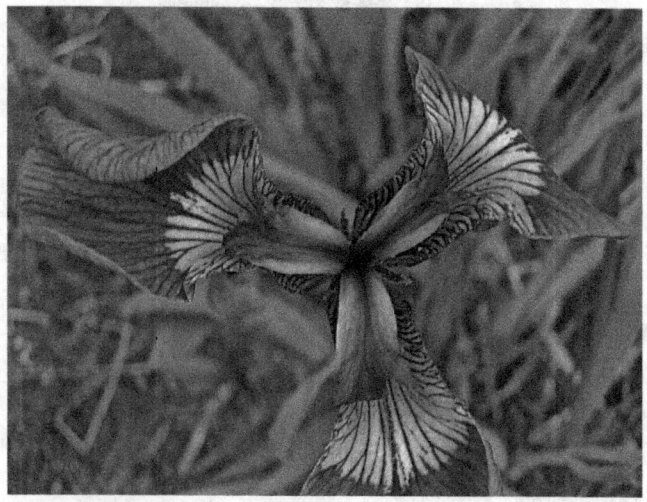

Iris setosa: https://commons.wikimedia.org/wiki/File:Wild_iris_KEFJ_(9025144383).jpg.
Credit: Courtesy of Nation Park services.

Iris versicolor: https://commons.wikimedia.org/wiki/Iris_versicolor#/media/
File:IrisVersicolor-FoxRoost-Newfoundland.jpg.
Credit: Courtesy of Jefficus,
https://commons.wikimedia.org/w/index.php?title=User:Jefficus&action=edit&redlink=1

Iris virginica: `https://commons.wikimedia.org/wiki/File:IMG_7911-Iris_virginica.jpg`.
Credit: Christer T Johansson.

14.7.1 Loading the Iris Dataset

Launch IPython with `ipython --matplotlib`, then use the `sklearn.datasets` module's **`load_iris` function** to get a Bunch containing the dataset:

```
In [1]: from sklearn.datasets import load_iris
```

```
In [2]: iris = load_iris()
```

The `Bunch`'s `DESCR` attribute indicates that there are 150 samples (`Number of Instances`), each with four features (`Number of Attributes`). There are no missing values in this dataset. The dataset classifies the samples by labeling them with the integers 0, 1 and 2, representing *Iris setosa*, *Iris versicolor* and *Iris virginica*, respectively. We'll *ignore* the labels and let the k-means clustering algorithm try to determine the samples' classes. We show some key `DESCR` information in bold.:

```
In [3]: print(iris.DESCR)
.. _iris_dataset:

Iris plants dataset
--------------------

**Data Set Characteristics:**

    :Number of Instances: 150 (50 in each of three classes)
    :Number of Attributes: 4 numeric, predictive attributes and the class
    :Attribute Information:
        - sepal length in cm
        - sepal width in cm
        - petal length in cm
        - petal width in cm
```

```
      - class:
              - Iris-Setosa
              - Iris-Versicolour
              - Iris-Virginica

  :Summary Statistics:

  =============== ==== ==== ======= ===== ====================
                  Min  Max  Mean    SD    Class Correlation
  =============== ==== ==== ======= ===== ====================
  sepal length:   4.3  7.9  5.84    0.83    0.7826
  sepal width:    2.0  4.4  3.05    0.43   -0.4194
  petal length:   1.0  6.9  3.76    1.76    0.9490  (high!)
  petal width:    0.1  2.5  1.20    0.76    0.9565  (high!)
  =============== ==== ==== ======= ===== ====================

  :Missing Attribute Values: None
  :Class Distribution: 33.3% for each of 3 classes.
  :Creator: R.A. Fisher
  :Donor: Michael Marshall (MARSHALL%PLU@io.arc.nasa.gov)
  :Date: July, 1988
```

The famous Iris database, first used by Sir R.A. Fisher. The dataset is taken from Fisher's paper. Note that it's the same as in R, but not as in the UCI Machine Learning Repository, which has two wrong data points.

This is perhaps the **best known database to be found in the pattern recognition literature.** Fisher's paper is a classic in the field and is referenced frequently to this day. (See Duda & Hart, for example.) The data set contains 3 classes of 50 instances each, where each class refers to a type of iris plant. One class is linearly separable from the other 2; the latter are NOT linearly separable from each other.

.. topic:: References

  - Fisher, R.A. "The use of multiple measurements in taxonomic problems"
    Annual Eugenics, 7, Part II, 179-188 (1936); also in "Contributions to Mathematical Statistics" (John Wiley, NY, 1950).
  - Duda, R.O., & Hart, P.E. (1973) Pattern Classification and Scene Analysis.
    (Q327.D83) John Wiley & Sons. ISBN 0-471-22361-1. See page 218.
  - Dasarathy, B.V. (1980) "Nosing Around the Neighborhood: A New System Structure and Classification Rule for Recognition in Partially Exposed Environments". IEEE Transactions on Pattern Analysis and Machine Intelligence, Vol. PAMI-2, No. 1, 67-71.
  - Gates, G.W. (1972) "The Reduced Nearest Neighbor Rule". IEEE Transactions on Information Theory, May 1972, 431-433.
  - See also: 1988 MLC Proceedings, 54-64. Cheeseman et al"s AUTOCLASS II conceptual clustering system finds 3 classes in the data.
  - Many, many more ...

Checking the Numbers of Samples, Features and Targets

You can confirm the number of samples and features per sample via the data array's shape, and you can confirm the number of targets via the target array's shape:

```
In [4]: iris.data.shape
Out[4]: (150, 4)

In [5]: iris.target.shape
Out[5]: (150,)
```

The array target_names contains the names for the target array's numeric labels—dtype='<U10' indicates that the elements are strings with a maximum of 10 characters:

```
In [6]: iris.target_names
Out[6]: array(['setosa', 'versicolor', 'virginica'], dtype='<U10')
```

The array feature_names contains a list of string names for each column in the data array:

```
In [7]: iris.feature_names
Out[7]:
['sepal length (cm)',
 'sepal width (cm)',
 'petal length (cm)',
 'petal width (cm)']
```

14.7.2 Exploring the Iris Dataset: Descriptive Statistics with Pandas

Let's use a DataFrame to explore the Iris dataset. As we did in the California Housing case study, let's set the pandas options for formatting the column-based outputs:

```
In [8]: import pandas as pd

In [9]: pd.set_option('max_columns', 5)

In [10]: pd.set_option('display.width', None)
```

Create a DataFrame containing the data array's contents, using the contents of the feature_names array as the column names:

```
In [11]: iris_df = pd.DataFrame(iris.data, columns=iris.feature_names)
```

Next, add a column containing each sample's species name. The list comprehension in the following snippet uses each value in the target array to look up the corresponding species name in the target_names array:

```
In [12]: iris_df['species'] = [iris.target_names[i] for i in iris.target]
```

Let's use pandas' to look at a few samples. Once again notice that pandas displays a \ to the right of the column heads to indicate that there are more columns displayed below:

```
In [13]: iris_df.head()
Out[13]:
   sepal length (cm)  sepal width (cm)  petal length (cm)  \
0                5.1               3.5                1.4
1                4.9               3.0                1.4
2                4.7               3.2                1.3
3                4.6               3.1                1.5
4                5.0               3.6                1.4
```

```
     petal width (cm) species
0                 0.2  setosa
1                 0.2  setosa
2                 0.2  setosa
3                 0.2  setosa
4                 0.2  setosa
```

Let's calculate some descriptive statistics for the numerical columns:

```
In [14]: pd.set_option('precision', 2)

In [15]: iris_df.describe()
Out[15]:
       sepal length (cm)  sepal width (cm)  petal length (cm)  \
count             150.00            150.00             150.00
mean                5.84              3.06               3.76
std                 0.83              0.44               1.77
min                 4.30              2.00               1.00
25%                 5.10              2.80               1.60
50%                 5.80              3.00               4.35
75%                 6.40              3.30               5.10
max                 7.90              4.40               6.90

       petal width (cm)
count            150.00
mean               1.20
std                0.76
min                0.10
25%                0.30
50%                1.30
75%                1.80
max                2.50
```

Calling the describe method on the 'species' column confirms that it contains three unique values. Here, we know in advance of working with this data that there are three classes to which the samples belong, though this is not always the case in unsupervised machine learning.

```
In [16]: iris_df['species'].describe()
Out[16]:
count         150
unique          3
top        setosa
freq           50
Name: species, dtype: object
```

14.7.3 Visualizing the Dataset with a Seaborn pairplot

Let's visualize the features in this dataset. One way to learn more about your data is to see how the features relate to one another. The dataset has four features. We cannot graph one against the other three in a single graph. However, we can plot pairs of features against one another. Snippet [20] uses Seaborn function **pairplot** to create a grid of graphs plotting each feature against itself and the other specified features:

```
In [17]: import seaborn as sns
```

```
In [18]: sns.set(font_scale=1.1)

In [19]: sns.set_style('whitegrid')

In [20]: grid = sns.pairplot(data=iris_df, vars=iris_df.columns[0:4],
    ...:     hue='species')
    ...:
```

The keyword arguments are:

- data—The DataFrame[13] containing the data to plot.

- vars—A sequence containing the names of the variables to plot. For a Data-Frame, these are the names of the columns to plot. Here, we use the first four DataFrame columns, representing the sepal length, sepal width, petal length and petal width, respectively.

- hue—The DataFrame column that's used to determine colors of the plotted data. In this case, we'll color the data by *Iris* species.

The preceding call to pairplot produces the following 4-by-4 grid of graphs—be sure to run this example live so you can see the pairplot's three different dot colors:

The graphs along the top-left-to-bottom-right diagonal, show the **distribution** of just the feature plotted in that column, with the range of values (left-to-right) and the number of samples with those values (top-to-bottom). Consider the sepal-length distributions:

---

13. This also may be a two-dimensional array or list.

sepal length (cm)

The tallest shaded area indicates that the range of sepal length values (shown along the *x*-axis) for *Iris setosa* is approximately 4–6 centimeters and that most *Iris setosa* samples are in the middle of that range (approximately 5 centimeters). Similarly, the rightmost shaded area indicates that the range of sepal length values for *Iris virginica* is approximately 4–8.5 centimeters and that the majority of *Iris virginica* samples have sepal length values between 6 and 7 centimeters.

The other graphs in a column show scatter plots of the other features against the feature on the *x*-axis. In the first column, the other three graphs plot the sepal width, petal length and petal width, respectively, along the *y*-axis and the sepal length along the *x*-axis.

When you run this code, you'll see in the full color output that using separate colors for each *Iris* species shows how the species relate to one another on a feature-by-feature basis. Interestingly, all the scatter plots clearly separate the Iris *setosa* blue dots from the other species' orange and green dots, indicating that *Iris setosa* is indeed in a "class by itself." We also can see that the other two species can sometimes be confused with one another, as indicated by the overlapping orange and green dots. For example, if you look at the scatter plot for sepal width vs. sepal length, you'll see the *Iris versicolor* and *Iris virginica* dots are intermixed. This indicates that it would be difficult to distinguish between these two species if we had only the sepal measurements available to us.

Displaying the `pairplot` in One Color

If you remove the hue keyword argument, `pairplot` function uses only one color to plot all the data because it does not know how to distinguish the species:

```
In [21]: grid = sns.pairplot(data=iris_df, vars=iris_df.columns[0:4])
```

As you can see in the resulting pair plot on the next page, in this case, the graphs along the diagonal are histograms showing the distributions of all the values for that feature, regardless of the species. As you study each scatter plot, it appears that there may be only *two* distinct clusters, even though for this dataset we know there are *three* species. If you do not know the number of clusters in advance, you might ask a **domain expert** who is thoroughly familiar with the data. Such a person might know that there are three species in the dataset, which would be valuable information as we try to perform machine learning on the data.

The `pairplot` diagrams work well for a *small number of features* or a subset of features so that you have a small number of rows and columns, and for a relatively small number of samples so you can see the data points. As the number of features and samples increases, each scatter plot quickly becomes too small to read. For larger datasets, you may choose to plot a subset of the features and potentially a randomly selected subset of the samples to get a feel for your data.

14.7.4 Using a KMeans Estimator

In this section, we'll use k-means clustering via scikit-learn's **KMeans estimator** (from the `sklearn.cluster` module) to place each sample in the Iris dataset into a cluster. As with the other estimators you've used, the KMeans estimator hides from you the algorithm's complex mathematical details, making it straightforward to use.

Creating the Estimator

Let's create the KMeans object:

```
In [22]: from sklearn.cluster import KMeans

In [23]: kmeans = KMeans(n_clusters=3, random_state=11)
```

The keyword argument `n_clusters` specifies the k-means clustering algorithm's hyperparameter k, which KMeans requires to calculate the clusters and label each sample. When you train a KMeans estimator, the algorithm calculates for each cluster a centroid representing the cluster's center data point.

The default value for the `n_clusters` parameter is 8. Often, you'll rely on domain experts knowledgeable about the data to help choose an appropriate k value. However, with hyperparameter tuning, you can estimate the appropriate k, as we'll do later. In this case, we know there are three species, so we'll use `n_clusters=3` to see how well KMeans does in labeling the Iris samples. Once again, we used the `random_state` keyword argument for reproducibility.

Fitting the Model

Next, we'll train the estimator by calling the KMeans object's fit method. This step performs the k-means algorithm discussed earlier:

```
In [24]: kmeans.fit(iris.data)
Out[24]:
KMeans(algorithm='auto', copy_x=True, init='k-means++', max_iter=300,
       n_clusters=3, n_init=10, n_jobs=None, precompute_distances='auto',
       random_state=11, tol=0.0001, verbose=0)
```

As with the other estimator's, the fit method returns the estimator object and IPython displays its string representation. You can see the KMeans default arguments at:

> https://scikit-learn.org/stable/modules/generated/sklearn.cluster.KMeans.html

When the training completes, the KMeans object contains:

- A labels_ array with values from 0 to n_clusters - 1 (in this example, 0–2), indicating the clusters to which the samples belong.

- A cluster_centers_ array in which each row represents a centroid.

Comparing the Computer Cluster Labels to the Iris Dataset's Target Values

Because the Iris dataset is labeled, we can look at its target array values to get a sense of how well the k-means algorithm clustered the samples for the three *Iris* species. With unlabeled data, we'd need to depend on a domain expert to help evaluate whether the predicted classes make sense.

In this dataset, the first 50 samples are *Iris setosa*, the next 50 are *Iris versicolor*, and the last 50 are *Iris virginica*. The Iris dataset's target array represents these with the values 0–2. If the KMeans estimator chose the clusters perfectly, then each group of 50 elements in the estimator's labels_ array should have a distinct label. As you study the results below, note that the KMeans estimator uses the values 0 through $k - 1$ to label clusters, but these are not related to the Iris dataset's target array.

Let's use slicing to see how each group of 50 Iris samples was clustered. The following snippet shows that the first 50 samples were all placed in cluster 1:

```
In [25]: print(kmeans.labels_[0:50])
[1 1 1 1 1 1 1 1 1 1 1 1 1 1 1 1 1 1 1 1 1 1 1 1 1 1 1 1 1 1 1 1 1 1 1 1 1 1
 1 1 1 1 1 1 1 1 1 1 1 1]
```

The next 50 samples should be placed into a second cluster. The following snippet shows that most were placed in cluster 0, but two samples were placed in cluster 2:

```
In [26]: print(kmeans.labels_[50:100])
[0 0 2 0 0 0 0 0 0 0 0 0 0 0 0 0 0 0 0 0 0 0 0 0 0 0 0 2 0 0 0 0 0 0 0 0 0 0
 0 0 0 0 0 0 0 0 0 0 0 0]
```

Similarly, the last 50 samples should be placed into a third cluster. The following snippet shows that many of these samples were placed in cluster 2, but 14 of the samples were placed in cluster 0, indicating that the algorithm thought they belonged to a different cluster:

```
In [27]: print(kmeans.labels_[100:150])
[2 0 2 2 2 2 0 2 2 2 2 2 2 0 0 2 2 2 2 0 2 0 2 0 2 2 0 0 2 2 2 2 2 0 2 2 2 2
 2 2 0 2 2 2 0 2 2 0 2 2 0]
```

The results of these three snippets confirm what we saw in the pairplot diagrams earlier in this section—that *Iris setosa* is "in a class by itself" and that there is some confusion between *Iris versicolor* and *Iris virginica*.

14.7.5 Dimensionality Reduction with Principal Component Analysis

Next, we'll use the **PCA estimator** (from the **sklearn.decomposition** module) to perform dimensionality reduction. This estimator uses an algorithm called principal component analysis[14] to analyze a dataset's features and reduce them to the specified number of dimensions. For the Iris dataset, we first tried the TSNE estimator shown earlier but did not like the results we were getting. So we switched to PCA for the following demonstration.

Creating the PCA Object
Like the TSNE estimator, a PCA estimator uses the keyword argument n_components to specify the number of dimensions:

```
In [28]: from sklearn.decomposition import PCA

In [29]: pca = PCA(n_components=2, random_state=11)
```

Transforming the Iris Dataset's Features into Two Dimensions
Let's train the estimator and produce the reduced data by calling the PCA estimator's methods **fit** and **transform** methods:

```
In [30]: pca.fit(iris.data)
Out[30]:
PCA(copy=True, iterated_power='auto', n_components=2, random_state=11,
    svd_solver='auto', tol=0.0, whiten=False)

In [31]: iris_pca = pca.transform(iris.data)
```

When the method completes its task, it returns an array with the same number of rows as iris.data, but only two columns. Let's confirm this by checking iris_pca's shape:

```
In [32]: iris_pca.shape
Out[32]: (150, 2)
```

Note that we *separately* called the PCA estimator's fit and transform methods, rather than fit_transform, which we used with the TSNE estimator. In this example, we're going to *reuse* the trained estimator (produced with fit) to perform a second transform to reduce the cluster centroids from four dimensions to two. This will enable us to plot the centroid locations on each cluster.

Visualizing the Reduced Data
Now that we've reduced the original dataset to only two dimensions, let's use a scatter plot to display the data. In this case, we'll use Seaborn's scatterplot function. First, let's transform the reduced data into a DataFrame and add a species column that we'll use to determine the dot colors:

```
In [33]: iris_pca_df = pd.DataFrame(iris_pca,
    ...:                            columns=['Component1', 'Component2'])
    ...:
```

---

14. The algorithm's details are beyond this book's scope. For more information, see https://scikit-learn.org/stable/modules/decomposition.html#pca.

```
In [34]: iris_pca_df['species'] = iris_df.species
```

Next, let's scatterplot the data in Seaborn:

```
In [35]: axes = sns.scatterplot(data=iris_pca_df, x='Component1',
    ...:     y='Component2', hue='species', legend='brief',
    ...:     palette='cool')
    ...:
```

Each centroid in the KMeans object's cluster_centers_ array has the *same* number of features as the original dataset (four in this case). To plot the centroids, we must reduce their dimensions. You can think of a centroid as the "average" sample in its cluster. So each centroid should be transformed using the same PCA estimator we used to reduce the other samples in that cluster:

```
In [36]: iris_centers = pca.transform(kmeans.cluster_centers_)
```

Now, we'll plot the centroids of the three clusters as larger black dots. Rather than transform the iris_centers array into a DataFrame first, let's use Matplotlib's scatter function to plot the three centroids:

```
In [37]: import matplotlib.pyplot as plt

In [38]: dots = plt.scatter(iris_centers[:,0], iris_centers[:,1],
    ...:                     s=100, c='k')
    ...:
```

The keyword argument s=100 specifies the size of the plotted points, and the keyword argument c='k' specifies that the points should be displayed in black. Be sure to run this example so you can see the three different colors in the following scatter plot.

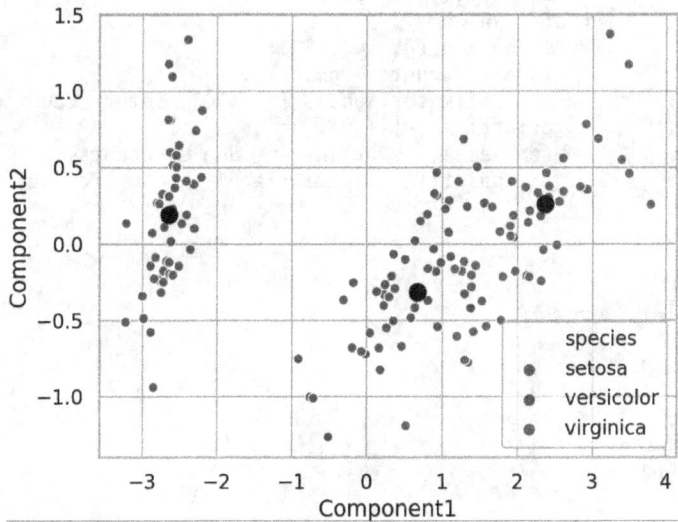

14.7.6 Choosing the Best Clustering Estimator

As we did in the classification and regression case studies, let's run multiple clustering algorithms and see how well they cluster the three species of Iris flowers. Here we'll attempt to cluster the Iris dataset's samples using the kmeans object we created earlier[15] and objects of scikit-learn's DBSCAN, MeanShift, SpectralClustering and AgglomerativeClustering estimators. Like KMeans, you specify the number of clusters in advance for the SpectralClustering and AgglomerativeClustering estimators:

```
In [39]: from sklearn.cluster import DBSCAN, MeanShift,\
    ...:     SpectralClustering, AgglomerativeClustering

In [40]: estimators = {
    ...:     'KMeans': kmeans,
    ...:     'DBSCAN': DBSCAN(),
    ...:     'MeanShift': MeanShift(),
    ...:     'SpectralClustering': SpectralClustering(n_clusters=3),
    ...:     'AgglomerativeClustering':
    ...:         AgglomerativeClustering(n_clusters=3)
    ...: }
```

Each iteration of the following loop calls one estimator's fit method with iris.data as an argument, then uses NumPy's unique function to get the cluster labels and counts for the three groups of 50 samples and displays the results. Recall that for the DBSCAN and MeanShift estimators, we did *not* specify the number of clusters in advance. Interestingly, DBSCAN correctly predicted three clusters (labeled -1, 0 and 1), though it placed 84 of the 100 *Iris virginica* and *Iris versicolor* samples in the same cluster. The MeanShift estimator, on the other hand, predicted only two clusters (labeled as 0 and 1), and placed 99 of the 100 *Iris virginica* and *Iris versicolor* samples in the same cluster:

```
In [41]: import numpy as np

In [42]: for name, estimator in estimators.items():
    ...:     estimator.fit(iris.data)
    ...:     print(f'\n{name}:')
    ...:     for i in range(0, 101, 50):
    ...:         labels, counts = np.unique(
    ...:             estimator.labels_[i:i+50], return_counts=True)
    ...:         print(f'{i}-{i+50}:')
    ...:         for label, count in zip(labels, counts):
    ...:             print(f'   label={label}, count={count}')
    ...:

KMeans:
0-50:
   label=1, count=50
50-100:
   label=0, count=48
   label=2, count=2
100-150:
   label=0, count=14
   label=2, count=36
```

---

15. We're running KMeans here on the *small* Iris dataset. If you experience performance problems with KMeans on larger datasets, consider using the MiniBatchKMeans estimator. The scikit-learn documentation indicates that MiniBatchKMeans is faster on large datasets and the results are almost as good.

```
DBSCAN:
0-50:
   label=-1, count=1
   label=0, count=49
50-100:
   label=-1, count=6
   label=1, count=44
100-150:
   label=-1, count=10
   label=1, count=40

MeanShift:
0-50:
   label=1, count=50
50-100:
   label=0, count=49
   label=1, count=1
100-150:
   label=0, count=50

SpectralClustering:
0-50:
   label=2, count=50
50-100:
   label=1, count=50
100-150:
   label=0, count=35
   label=1, count=15

AgglomerativeClustering:
0-50:
   label=1, count=50
50-100:
   label=0, count=49
   label=2, count=1
100-150:
   label=0, count=15
   label=2, count=35
```

Though these algorithms label every sample, the labels simply indicate the clusters. What do you do with the cluster information once you have it? If your goal is to use the data in supervised machine learning, typically you'd study the samples in each cluster to try to determine how they're related and label them accordingly. As we'll see in the next chapter, unsupervised learning is commonly used in deep-learning applications. Some examples of unlabeled data processed with unsupervised learning include tweets from Twitter, Facebook posts, videos, photos, news articles, customers' product reviews, viewers' movie reviews and more.

14.8 Wrap-Up

In this chapter we began our study of machine learning, using the popular scikit-learn library. We saw that machine learning is divided into two types. Supervised machine learning, which works with labeled data and unsupervised machine learning which works with unlabeled data. Throughout this chapter, we continued emphasizing visualizations using Matplotlib and Seaborn, particularly for getting to know your data.

We discussed how scikit-learn conveniently packages machine-learning algorithms as estimators. Each is encapsulated so you can create your models quickly with a small amount of code, even if you don't know the intricate details of how these algorithms work.

We looked at supervised machine learning with classification, then regression. We used one of the simplest classification algorithms, k-nearest neighbors, to analyze the Digits dataset bundled with scikit-learn. You saw that classification algorithms predicts the classes to which samples belong. Binary classification uses two classes (such as "spam" or "not spam") and multi-classification uses more than two classes (such as the 10 classes in the Digits dataset).

We performed the steps of a typical machine-learning case study, including loading the dataset, exploring the data with pandas and visualizations, splitting the data for training and testing, creating the model, training the model and making predictions. We discussed why you should partition your data into a training set and a testing set. You saw ways to evaluate a classification estimator's accuracy via a confusion matrix and a classification report.

We mentioned that it's difficult to know in advance which model(s) will perform best on your data, so you typically try many models and pick the one that performs best. We showed that it's easy to run multiple estimators. We also used hyperparameter tuning with k-fold cross-validation to choose the best value of k for the k-NN algorithm.

We revisited the time series and simple linear regression example from Chapter 10's Intro to Data Science section, this time implementing it using a scikit-learn LinearRegression estimator. Next, we used a LinearRegression estimator to perform multiple linear regression with the California Housing dataset that's bundled with scikit-learn. You saw that the LinearRegression estimator, by default, uses all the numerical features in a dataset to make more sophisticated predictions than you can with simple linear regression. Again, we ran multiple scikit-learn estimators to compare how they performed and choose the best one.

Next, we introduced an unsupervised machine learning and mentioned that it's typically accomplished with clustering algorithms. We used introduced dimensionality reduction (with scikit-learn's TSNE estimator) and used it to compress the Digits dataset's 64 features down to two for visualization purposes. This enabled us to see the clustering of the digits data.

We presented one of the simplest unsupervised machine learning algorithms, k-means clustering, and demonstrated clustering on the Iris dataset that's also bundled with scikit-learn. We used dimensionality reduction (with scikit-learn's PCA estimator) to compress the Iris dataset's four features to two for visualization purposes to show the clustering of the three *Iris* species in the dataset and their centroids. Finally, we ran multiple clustering estimators to compare their ability to label the Iris dataset's samples into three clusters.

In the next chapter, we'll continue our study of machine learning technologies with discussions of deep learning and reinforcement learning. We'll tackle some fascinating and challenging problems.

Deep Learning

Objectives

In this chapter you'll:

- Understand what a neural network is and how it enables deep learning.
- Create Keras neural networks.
- Understand Keras layers, activation functions, loss functions and optimizers.
- Use a Keras convolutional neural network (CNN) trained on the MNIST dataset to recognize handwritten digits.
- Use a Keras recurrent neural network (RNN) trained on the IMDb dataset to perform binary classification of positive and negative movie reviews.
- Use TensorBoard to visualize the progress of training deep-learning networks.
- Learn which pretrained neural networks come with Keras.
- Understand the value of using models pretrained on the massive ImageNet dataset for computer vision apps.

15.1 Introduction

One of AI's most exciting areas is **deep learning**, a powerful subset of machine learning that has produced impressive results in computer vision and many other areas over the last few years. The availability of big data, significant processor power, faster Internet speeds and advancements in parallel computing hardware and software are making it possible for more organizations and individuals to pursue resource-intensive deep-learning solutions.

Keras and TensorFlow

In the previous chapter, scikit-learn enabled you to define machine-learning models conveniently with one statement. Deep learning models require more sophisticated setups, typically connecting multiple objects, called **layers**. We'll build our deep learning models with **Keras**, which offers a friendly interface to Google's **TensorFlow**—the most widely used deep-learning library.[1] François Chollet of the Google Mind team developed Keras to make deep-learning capabilities more accessible. His book *Deep Learning with Python* is a must read.[2] Google has thousands of TensorFlow and Keras projects underway internally and that number is growing quickly.[3],[4]

---

1. Keras also serves as a friendlier interface to Microsoft's *CNTK* and the Université de Montréal's *Theano* (which ceased development in 2017). Other popular deep learning frameworks include Caffe (http://caffe.berkeleyvision.org/), Apache MXNet (https://mxnet.apache.org/) and PyTorch (https://pytorch.org/).
2. Chollet, François. *Deep Learning with Python.* Shelter Island, NY: Manning Publications, 2018.
3. http://theweek.com/speedreads/654463/google-more-than-1000-artificial-intelligence-projects-works.
4. https://www.zdnet.com/article/google-says-exponential-growth-of-ai-is-changing-nature-of-compute/.

Models

Deep learning models are complex and require an extensive mathematical background to understand their inner workings. As we've done throughout the book, we'll avoid heavy mathematics here, preferring English explanations.

Keras is to deep learning as scikit-learn is to machine learning. Each encapsulates the sophisticated mathematics, so developers need only define, parameterize and manipulate objects. With Keras, you build your models from *pre-existing* components and quickly parameterize those components to your unique requirements. This is what we've been referring to as *object-based programming* throughout the book.

Experiment with Your Models

Machine learning and deep learning are empirical rather than theoretical fields. You'll experiment with many models, tweaking them in various ways until you find the models that perform best for your applications. Keras facilitates such experimentation.

Dataset Sizes

Deep learning works well when you have lots of data, but it also can be effective for smaller datasets when combined with techniques like transfer learning[5,6] and data augmentation[7,8]. Transfer learning uses existing knowledge from a previously trained model as the foundation for a new model. Data augmentation adds data to a dataset by deriving new data from existing data. For example, in an image dataset, you might rotate the images left and right so the model can learn about objects in different orientations. In general, though, the more data you have, the better you'll be able to train a deep learning model.

Processing Power

Deep learning can require significant processing power. Complex models trained on big-data datasets can take hours, days or even more to train. The models we present in this chapter can be trained in minutes to just less than an hour on computers with conventional CPUs. You'll need only a reasonably current personal computer. We'll discuss the special high-performance hardware called GPUs (Graphics Processing Units) and TPUs (Tensor Processing Units) developed by NVIDIA and Google to meet the extraordinary processing demands of edge-of-the-practice deep-learning applications.

Bundled Datasets

Keras comes packaged with some popular datasets. You'll work with two of these datasets in the chapter's examples. You can find many Keras studies online for each of these datasets, including ones that take different approaches.

In the "Machine Learning" chapter, you worked with Scikit-learn's Digits dataset, which contained 1797 handwritten-digit images that were selected from the much larger

---

5. https://towardsdatascience.com/transfer-learning-from-pre-trained-models-f2393f124751.

6. https://medium.com/nanonets/nanonets-how-to-use-deep-learning-when-you-have-limited-data-f68c0b512cab.

7. https://towardsdatascience.com/data-augmentation-and-images-7aca9bd0dbe8.

8. https://medium.com/nanonets/how-to-use-deep-learning-when-you-have-limited-data-part-2-data-augmentation-c26971dc8ced.

MNIST dataset (60,000 training images and 10,000 test images).[9] In this chapter you'll work with the full MNIST dataset. You'll build a Keras *convolutional neural network* (CNN or convnet) model that will achieve high performance recognizing digit images in the test set. Convnets are especially appropriate for computer vision tasks, such as recognizing handwritten digits and characters or recognizing objects (including faces) in images and videos. You'll also work with a Keras *recurrent neural network*. In that example, you'll perform sentiment analysis using the IMDb Movie reviews dataset, in which the reviews in the training and testing sets are labeled as positive or negative.

Future of Deep Learning
Newer automated deep learning capabilities are making it even easier to build deep-learning solutions. These include Auto-Keras[10] from Texas A&M University's DATA Lab, Baidu's EZDL[11] and Google's AutoML[12].

15.1.1 Deep Learning Applications

Deep learning is being used in a wide range of applications, such as:

- Game playing
- Computer vision: Object recognition, pattern recognition, facial recognition
- Self-driving cars
- Robotics
- Improving customer experiences
- Chatbots
- Diagnosing medical conditions
- Google Search
- Facial recognition
- Automated image captioning and video closed captioning
- Enhancing image resolution
- Speech recognition
- Language translation
- Predicting election results
- Predicting earthquakes and weather
- Google Sunroof to determine whether you can put solar panels on your roof
- Generative applications—Generating original images, processing existing images to look like a specified artist's style, adding color to black-and-white images and video, creating music, creating text (books, poetry) and much more.

---

9. "The MNIST Database." MNIST Handwritten Digit Database, Yann LeCun, Corinna Cortes and Chris Burges. http://yann.lecun.com/exdb/mnist/.
10. https://autokeras.com/.
11. https://ai.baidu.com/ezdl/.
12. https://cloud.google.com/automl/.

15.1.2 Deep Learning Demos

Check out these four deep-learning demos and search online for lots more, including practical applications like we mentioned in the preceding section:

- DeepArt.io—Turn a photo into artwork by applying an art style to the photo. `https://deepart.io/`.

- DeepWarp Demo—Analyzes a person's photo and makes the person's eyes move in different directions. `https://sites.skoltech.ru/sites/compvision_wiki/static_pages/projects/deepwarp/`.

- Image-to-Image Demo—Translates a line drawing into a picture. `https://affinelayer.com/pixsrv/`.

- Google Translate Mobile App (download from an app store to your smartphone)—Translate text in a photo to another language (e.g., take a photo of a sign or a restaurant menu in Spanish and translate the text to English).

15.1.3 Keras Resources

Here are some resources you might find valuable as you study deep learning:

- To get your questions answered, go to the Keras team's slack channel at `https://kerasteam.slack.com`.

- For articles and tutorials, visit `https://blog.keras.io`.

- The Keras documentation is at `http://keras.io`.

- If you're looking for term projects, directed study projects, capstone course projects or thesis topics, visit arXiv (pronounced "archive," where the X represents the Greek letter "chi") at `https://arXiv.org`. People post their research papers here in parallel with going through peer review for formal publication, hoping for fast feedback. So, this site gives you access to extremely current research.

15.2 Keras Built-In Datasets

Here are some of Keras's datasets (from the module **tensorflow.keras.datasets**[13]) for practicing deep learning. We'll use a couple of these in the chapter's examples:

- **MNIST**[14] **database of handwritten digits**—Used for classifying handwritten digit images, this dataset contains 28-by-28 grayscale digit images labeled as 0 through 9 with 60,000 images for training and 10,000 for testing. We use this dataset in Section 15.6, where we study convolutional neural networks.

---

13. In the standalone Keras library, the module names begin with `keras` rather than `tensorflow.keras`.
14. "The MNIST Database." MNIST Handwritten Digit Database, Yann LeCun, Corinna Cortes and Chris Burges. `http://yann.lecun.com/exdb/mnist/`.

- **Fashion-MNIST[15] database of fashion articles**—Used for classifying clothing images, this dataset contains 28-by-28 grayscale images of clothing labeled in 10 categories[16] with 60,000 for training and 10,000 for testing. Once you build a model for use with MNIST, you can reuse that model with Fashion-MNIST by changing a few statements.

- **IMDb Movie reviews[17]**—Used for sentiment analysis, this dataset contains reviews labeled as positive (1) or negative (0) sentiment with 25,000 reviews for training and 25,000 for testing. We use this dataset in Section 15.9, where we study recurrent neural networks.

- **CIFAR10[18] small image classification**—Used for small-image classification, this dataset contains 32-by-32 color images labeled in 10 categories with 50,000 images for training and 10,000 for testing.

- **CIFAR100[19] small image classification**—Also, used for small-image classification, this dataset contains 32-by-32 color images labeled in 100 categories with 50,000 images for training and 10,000 for testing.

15.3 Custom Anaconda Environments

Before running this chapter's examples, you'll need to install the libraries we use. In this chapter's examples, we'll use the TensorFlow deep-learning library's version of Keras.[20] At the time of this writing, TensorFlow does not yet support Python 3.7. So, you'll need Python 3.6.x to execute this chapter's examples. We'll show you how to set up a *custom environment* for working with Keras and TensorFlow.

Environments in Anaconda

The Anaconda Python distribution makes it easy to create custom **environments**. These are separate configurations in which you can install different libraries and different library versions. This can help with *reproducibility* if your code depends on specific Python or library versions.[21]

The default environment in Anaconda is called the *base environment*. This is created for you when you install Anaconda. All the Python libraries that come with Anaconda are installed into the base environment and, unless you specify otherwise, any additional libraries you install also are placed there. Custom environments give you control over the specific libraries you wish to install for your specific tasks.

---

15. Han Xiao and Kashif Rasul and Roland Vollgraf, Fashion-MNIST: a Novel Image Dataset for Benchmarking Machine Learning Algorithms, arXiv, cs.LG/1708.07747.

16. `https://keras.io/datasets/#fashion-mnist-database-of-fashion-articles`.

17. Andrew L. Maas, Raymond E. Daly, Peter T. Pham, Dan Huang, Andrew Y. Ng, and Christopher Potts. (2011). Learning Word Vectors for Sentiment Analysis. The 49th Annual Meeting of the Association for Computational Linguistics (ACL 2011).

18. `https://www.cs.toronto.edu/~kriz/cifar.html`.

19. `https://www.cs.toronto.edu/~kriz/cifar.html`.

20. There's also a standalone version that enables you to choose between TensorFlow, Microsoft's *CNTK* or the Université de Montréal's *Theano* (which ceased development in 2017).

21. In the next chapter, we'll introduce Docker as another reproducibility mechanism and as a convenient way to install complex environments for use on your local computer.

Creating an Anaconda Environment

The **conda create command** creates an environment. Let's create a TensorFlow environment and name it tf_env (you can name it whatever you like). Run the following command in your Terminal, shell or Anaconda Command Prompt:[22,23]

```
conda create -n tf_env tensorflow anaconda ipython jupyterlab
    scikit-learn matplotlib seaborn h5py pydot graphviz
```

This will determine the listed libraries' dependencies, then display all the libraries that will be installed in the new environment. There are many dependencies, so this may take a few minutes. When you see the prompt:

```
Proceed ([y]/n)?
```

press *Enter* to create the environment and install the libraries.[24]

Activating an Alternate Anaconda Environment

To use a custom environment, execute the **conda activate command**:

```
conda activate tf_env
```

This affects only the current Terminal, shell or Anaconda Command Prompt. When a custom environment is activated and you install more libraries, they become part of the activated environment, not the base environment. If you open separate Terminals, shells or Anaconda Command Prompts, they'll use Anaconda's base environment by default.

Deactivating an Alternate Anaconda Environment

When you're done with a custom environment, you can return to the base environment in the current Terminal, shell or Anaconda Command Prompt by executing:

```
conda deactivate
```

Jupyter Notebooks and JupyterLab

This chapter's examples are provided only as Jupyter Notebooks, which will make it easier for you to experiment with the examples. You can tweak the options we present and re-execute the notebooks. For this chapter, you should launch JupyterLab from the ch15 examples folder (as discussed in Section 1.5.3).

15.4 Neural Networks

Deep learning is a form of machine learning that uses artificial neural networks to learn. An **artificial neural network** (or just neural network) is a software construct that operates similarly to how scientists believe our brains work. Our biological nervous systems are controlled via *neurons*[25] that communicate with one another along pathways called *synapses*[26].

---

22. Windows users should run the Anaconda Command Prompt as Administrator,
23. If you have a computer with an NVIDIA GPU that's compatible with TensorFlow, you can replace the tensorflow library with tensorflow-gpu to get better performance. For more information, see https://www.tensorflow.org/install/gpu. Some AMD GPUs also can be used with Tensor-Flow: http://timdettmers.com/2018/11/05/which-gpu-for-deep-learning/.
24. When we created our custom environment, conda installed Python 3.6.7, which was the most recent Python version compatible with the tensorflow library.
25. https://en.wikipedia.org/wiki/Neuron.
26. https://en.wikipedia.org/wiki/Synapse.

As we learn, the specific neurons that enable us to perform a given task, like walking, communicate with one another more efficiently. These neurons *activate* anytime we need to walk.[27]

Artificial Neurons

In a neural network, interconnected **artificial neurons** simulate the human brain's neurons to help the network learn. The connections between specific neurons are reinforced during the learning process with the goal of achieving a specific result. In **supervised deep learning**—which we'll use in this chapter—we aim to predict the target labels supplied with data samples. To do this, we'll train a general neural network model that we can then use to make predictions on unseen data.[28]

Artificial Neural Network Diagram

The following diagram shows a three-*layer* neural network. Each circle represents a neuron, and the lines between them simulate the synapses. The output of a neuron becomes the input of another neuron, hence the term neural network. This particular diagram shows a **fully connected network**—every neuron in a given layer is connected to *all* the neurons in the next layer:

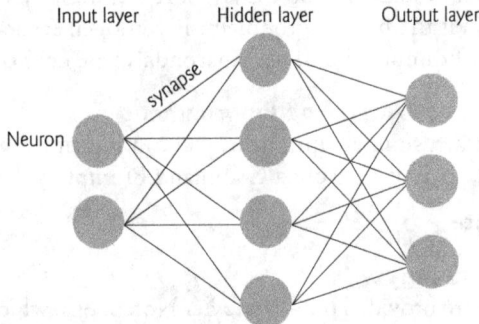

Learning Is an Iterative Process

When you were a baby, you did not learn to walk instantaneously. You learned that process *over time* with repetition. You built up the smaller components of the movements that enabled you to walk—learning to stand, learning to balance to remain standing, learning to lift your foot and move it forward, etc. And you got feedback from your environment. When you walked successfully your parents smiled and clapped. When you fell, you might have bumped your head and felt pain.

Similarly, we train neural networks iteratively over time. Each iteration is known as an **epoch** and processes every sample in the training dataset once. There's no "correct" number of epochs. This is a hyperparameter that may need tuning, based on your training data and your model. The inputs to the network are the features in the training samples. Some layers learn new features from previous layers' outputs and others interpret those features to make predictions.

---

27. https://www.sciencenewsforstudents.org/article/learning-rewires-brain.
28. As in machine learning, you can create *unsupervised* deep learning networks—these are beyond this chapter's scope.

How Artificial Neurons Decide Whether to Activate Synapses

During the training phase, the network calculates values called **weights** for every connection between the neurons in one layer and those in the next. On a neuron-by-neuron basis, each of its inputs is multiplied by that connection's weight, then the sum of those weighted inputs is passed to the neuron's **activation function**. This function's output determines which neurons to activate based on the inputs—just like the neurons in your brain passing information around in response to inputs coming from your eyes, nose, ears and more. The following diagram shows a neuron receiving three inputs (the black dots) and producing an output (the hollow circle) that would be passed to all or some of neurons in the next layer, depending on the types of the neural network's layers:

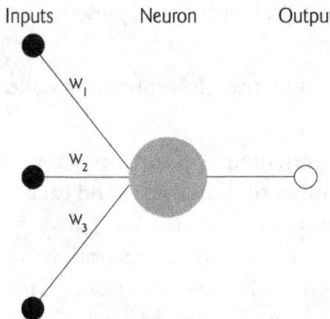

The values w_1, w_2 and w_3 are weights. In a new model that you train from scratch, these values are initialized randomly by the model. As the network trains, it tries to minimize the error rate between the network's predicted labels and the samples' actual labels. The error rate is known as the **loss**, and the calculation that determines the loss is called the **loss function**. Throughout training, the network determines the amount that each neuron contributes to the overall loss, then goes back through the layers and adjusts the weights in an effort to minimize that loss. This technique is called **backpropagation**. Optimizing these weights occurs gradually—typically via a process called **gradient descent**.

15.5 Tensors

Deep learning frameworks generally manipulate data in the form of **tensors**. A "tensor" is basically a multidimensional array. Frameworks like TensorFlow pack all your data into one or more tensors, which they use to perform the mathematical calculations that enable neural networks to learn. These tensors can become quite large as the number of dimensions increases and as the richness of the data increases (for example, images, audios and videos are richer than text). Chollet discusses the types of tensors typically encountered in deep learning:[29]

- **0D (0-dimensional) tensor**—This is one value and is known as a *scalar*.
- **1D tensor**—This is similar to a one-dimensional array and is known as a *vector*. A 1D tensor might represent a sequence, such as hourly temperature readings from a sensor or the words of one movie review.

---

29. Chollet, François. *Deep Learning with Python*. Section 2.2. Shelter Island, NY: Manning Publications, 2018.

- **2D tensor**—This is similar to a two-dimensional array and is known as a *matrix*. A 2D tensor could represent a grayscale image in which the tensor's two dimensions are the image's width and height in pixels, and the value in each element is the intensity of that pixel.

- **3D tensor**—This is similar to a three-dimensional array and could be used to represent a color image. The first two dimensions would represent the width and height of the image in pixels and the *depth* at each location might represent the red, green and blue (RGB) components of a given pixel's color. A 3D tensor also could represent a *collection* of 2D tensors containing grayscale images.

- **4D tensor**—A 4D tensor could be used to represent a *collection* of color images in 3D tensors. It also could be used to represent one video. Each frame in a video is essentially a color image.

- **5D tensor**—This could be used to represent a collection of 4D tensors containing videos.

A tensor's *shape* typically is represented as a tuple of values in which the number of elements specifies the tensor's number of dimensions and each value in the tuple specifies the size of the tensor's corresponding dimension.

Let's assume we're creating a deep-learning network to identify and track objects in 4K (high-resolution) videos that have 30 frames-per-second. Each frame in a 4K video is 3840-by-2160 pixels. Let's also assume the pixels are presented as red, green and blue components of a color. So *each frame* would be a 3D tensor containing a total of 24,883,200 elements (3840 * 2160 * 3) and each video would be a 4D tensor containing the sequence of frames. If the videos are one minute long, you'd have 44,789,760,000 elements *per tensor*!

Over 600 hours of video are uploaded to YouTube every minute[30] so, in just one minute of uploads, Google could have a tensor containing 1,612,431,360,000,000 elements to use in training deep-learning models—that's *big data*. As you can see, tensors can quickly become *enormous*, so manipulating them efficiently is crucial. This is one of the key reasons that most deep learning is performed on GPUs. More recently Google created TPUs (Tensor Processing Units) that are specifically designed to perform tensor manipulations, executing faster than GPUs.

High-Performance Processors

Powerful processors are needed for real-world deep learning because the size of tensors can be enormous and large-tensor operations can place crushing demands on processors. The processors most commonly used for deep learning are:

- NVIDIA GPUs (Graphics Processing Units)—Originally developed by companies like NVIDIA for computer gaming, GPUs are much faster than conventional CPUs for processing large amounts of data, thus enabling developers to train, validate and test deep-learning models more efficiently—and thus experiment with more of them. GPUs are optimized for the mathematical matrix operations typically performed on tensors, an essential aspect of how deep learning works "under the hood." NVIDIA's Volta Tensor Cores are specifically designed for deep learn-

---

30. https://www.inc.com/tom-popomaronis/youtube-analyzed-trillions-of-data-points-in-2018-revealing-5-eye-opening-behavioral-statistics.html.

ing.[31,32] Many NVIDIA GPUs are compatible with TensorFlow, and hence Keras, and can enhance the performance of your deep-learning models.[33]

• Google TPUs (Tensor Processing Units)—Recognizing that deep learning is crucial to its future, Google developed TPUs (Tensor Processing Units), which they now use in their Cloud TPU service, which "can provide up to 11.5 petaflops of performance in a single pod"[34] (that's 11.5 *quadrillion* floating-point operations per second). Also, TPUs are designed to be especially energy efficient. This is a key concern for companies like Google with already massive computing clusters that are growing exponentially and consuming vast amounts of energy.

15.6 Convolutional Neural Networks for Vision; Multi-Classification with the MNIST Dataset

In the "Machine Learning" chapter, we classified handwritten digits using the 8-by-8-pixel, low-resolution images from the Digits dataset bundled with Scikit-learn. That dataset is based on a subset of the higher-resolution MNIST handwritten digits dataset. Here, we'll use MNIST to explore deep learning with a **convolutional neural network**[35] (also called a **convnet** or **CNN**). Convnets are common in computer-vision applications, such as recognizing handwritten digits and characters, and recognizing objects in images and video. They're also used in non-vision applications, such as natural-language processing and recommender systems.

The Digits dataset has only 1797 samples, whereas MNIST has 70,000 labeled digit image samples—60,000 for training and 10,000 for testing. Each sample is a grayscale 28-by-28 pixel image (784 total features) represented as a NumPy array. Each pixel is a value from 0 to 255 representing the intensity (or shade) of that pixel—the Digits dataset uses less granular shading with values from 0 to 16. MNIST's labels are integer values in the range 0 through 9, indicating the digit each image represents.

The machine-learning model you used in the previous chapter produced as its output a digit image's predicted class—an integer in the range 0–9. The convnet model we'll build will perform **probabilistic classification**.[36] For each digit image, the model will output an *array* of 10 probabilities, each indicating the likelihood that the digit belongs to a particular one of the classes 0 through 9. The class with the *highest* probability is the predicted value.

Reproducibility in Keras and Deep Learning

We've discussed the importance of *reproducibility* throughout the book. In deep learning, reproducibility is more difficult because the libraries heavily parallelize operations that perform floating-point calculations. Each time operations execute, they may execute in a different order. This can produce differences in your results. Getting reproducible results in

---

31. https://www.nvidia.com/en-us/data-center/tensorcore/.
32. https://devblogs.nvidia.com/tensor-core-ai-performance-milestones/.
33. https://www.tensorflow.org/install/gpu.
34. https://cloud.google.com/tpu/.
35. https://en.wikipedia.org/wiki/Convolutional_neural_network.
36. https://en.wikipedia.org/wiki/Probabilistic_classification.

Keras requires a combination of environment settings and code settings that are described in the Keras FAQ:

```
https://keras.io/getting-started/faq/#how-can-i-obtain-reproducible-
    results-using-keras-during-development
```

Basic Keras Neural Network

A Keras neural network consists of the following components:

- A **network** (also called a **model**)—A sequence of **layers** containing the neurons used to learn from the samples. Each layer's neurons receive inputs, process them (via an *activation function*) and produce outputs. The data is fed into the network via an **input layer** that specifies the dimensions of the sample data. This is followed by **hidden layers** of neurons that implement the learning and an **output layer** that produces the predictions. The more layers you *stack*, the deeper the network is, hence the term deep learning.

- A **loss function**—This produces a measure of how well the network predicts the target values. Lower loss values indicate better predictions.

- An **optimizer**—This attempts to minimize the values produced by the loss function to tune the network to make better predictions.

Launch JupyterLab

This section assumes that you've activated the tf_env Anaconda environment you created in Section 15.3 and launched JupyterLab from the ch15 examples folder. You can either open the MNIST_CNN.ipynb file in JupyterLab and execute the code in the cells we provided, or you can create a new notebook and enter the code on your own. If you prefer, you can work at the command line in IPython, however, placing your code in a Jupyter Notebook makes it significantly easier for you to *re-execute* this chapter's examples.

As a reminder, you can reset a Jupyter Notebook and remove its outputs by selecting **Restart Kernel and Clear All Outputs...** from JupyterLab's **Kernel** menu. This terminates the notebook's execution and removes its outputs. You might do this if your model is not performing well and you want to try different hyperparameters or possibly restructure your neural network.[37] You can then re-execute the notebook one cell at a time or execute the entire notebook by selecting **Run All** from JupyterLab's **Run** menu.

15.6.1 Loading the MNIST Dataset

Let's import the **tensorflow.keras.datasets.mnist module** so we can load the dataset:

```
[1]: from tensorflow.keras.datasets import mnist
```

Note that because we're using the version of Keras built into TensorFlow, the Keras module names begin with "tensorflow.". In the standalone Keras version, the module names begin with "keras.", so keras.datasets would be used above. Keras uses *TensorFlow* to execute the deep-learning models.

The mnist module's **load_data function** loads the MNIST training and testing sets:

```
[2]: (X_train, y_train), (X_test, y_test) = mnist.load_data()
```

---

37. We found that we sometimes had to execute this menu option twice to clear the outputs.

When you call `load_data` it will download the MNIST data to your system. The function returns a tuple of two elements containing the training and testing sets. Each element is itself a tuple containing the samples and labels, respectively.

15.6.2 Data Exploration

Let's get to know the data before working with it. First, we check the dimensions of the training set images (`X_train`), training set labels (`y_train`), testing set images (`X_test`) and testing set labels (`y_test`):

```
[3]: X_train.shape
[3]: (60000, 28, 28)

[4]: y_train.shape
[4]: (60000,)

[5]: X_test.shape
[5]: (10000, 28, 28)

[6]: y_test.shape
[6]: (10000,)
```

You can see from `X_train`'s and `X_test`'s shapes that the images are higher resolution than those in Scikit-learn's Digits dataset (which are 8-by-8).

Visualizing Digits

Let's visualize some of the digit images. First, enable Matplotlib in the notebook, import Matplotlib and Seaborn and set the font scale:

```
[7]: %matplotlib inline

[8]: import matplotlib.pyplot as plt

[9]: import seaborn as sns

[10]: sns.set(font_scale=2)
```

The IPython magic

```
%matplotlib inline
```

indicates that Matplotlib-based graphics should be displayed *in the notebook* rather than in separate windows. For more IPython magics, you can use in Jupyter Notebooks, see:

```
https://ipython.readthedocs.io/en/stable/interactive/magics.html
```

Next, we'll display a randomly selected set of 24 MNIST training set images. Recall from the "Array-Oriented Programming with NumPy" chapter that you can pass a sequence of indexes as a NumPy array's subscript to select only the array elements at those indexes. We'll use that capability here to select the elements at the same indexes in both the `X_train` and `y_train` arrays. This ensures that we display the correct label for each randomly selected image.

NumPy's **choice function** (from the `numpy.random` module) randomly selects the number of elements specified in its second argument (24) from the array of values in its first argument (in this case, an array containing `X_train`'s range of indices). The function returns an array containing the selected values, which we store in index. The expressions X_train[index] and y_train[index] use index to get the corresponding elements from both arrays. The rest of this cell is the visualization code from the previous chapter's Digits case study:

```
[11]: import numpy as np
      index = np.random.choice(np.arange(len(X_train)), 24, replace=False)
      figure, axes = plt.subplots(nrows=4, ncols=6, figsize=(16, 9))

      for item in zip(axes.ravel(), X_train[index], y_train[index]):
          axes, image, target = item
          axes.imshow(image, cmap=plt.cm.gray_r)
          axes.set_xticks([])   # remove x-axis tick marks
          axes.set_yticks([])   # remove y-axis tick marks
          axes.set_title(target)
      plt.tight_layout()
```

You can see in the output below that MNIST's digit images have higher resolution than those in Scikit-learn's Digits dataset.

Looking at the digits, you can see why handwritten digit recognition is a challenge:

- Some people write "open" 4s (like the ones in the first and third rows), and some write "closed" 4s (like the one in the second row). Though each 4 has some similar features, they're all different from one another.

- The 3 in the second row looks strange—more like a merged 6 and 7. Compare this to the much clearer 3 in the fourth row.

- The 5 in the second row could easily be confused with a 6.

- Also, people write their digits at different angles, as you can see with the four 6s in the third and fourth rows—two are upright, one leans left and one leans right.

If you run the preceding snippet multiple times, you can see additional randomly selected digits.[38] You'll probably find that—if not for the labels displayed above each digit—it would be difficult for you to identify some of the digits. We'll soon see how accurately our first convnet will predict the digits in the MNIST test set.

15.6.3 Data Preparation

Recall from the "Machine Learning" chapter that Scikit-learn's bundled datasets were pre-processed into the shapes its models required. In real-world studies, you'll generally have to do some or all of the data preparation. The MNIST dataset requires some preparation for use in a Keras convnet.

Reshaping the Image Data

Keras convnets require NumPy array inputs in which each sample has the shape:

> (*width*, *height*, *channels*)

For MNIST, each image's *width* and *height* are 28 pixels, and each pixel has one *channel* (the grayscale shade of the pixel from 0 to 255), so each sample's shape will be:

> (28, 28, 1)

Full-color images with RGB (red/green/blue) values for each pixel, would have three *channels*—one channel each for the red, green and blue components of a color.

As the neural network learns from the images, it creates many more channels. Rather than shade or color, the learned channels will represent more complex features, like edges, curves and lines, that will eventually enable the network to recognize digits based on these additional features and how they're combined.

Let's reshape the 60,000 training and 10,000 testing set images into the correct dimensions for use in our convnet and confirm their new shapes. Recall that NumPy array method reshape receives a tuple representing the array's new shape:

```
[12]: X_train = X_train.reshape((60000, 28, 28, 1))

[13]: X_train.shape
[13]: (60000, 28, 28, 1)

[14]: X_test = X_test.reshape((10000, 28, 28, 1))

[15]: X_test.shape
[15]: (10000, 28, 28, 1)
```

Normalizing the Image Data

Numeric features in data samples may have value ranges that vary widely. Deep learning networks perform better on data that is scaled either into the range 0.0 to 1.0, or to a range for which the data's mean is 0.0 and its standard deviation is 1.0.[39] Getting your data into one of these forms is known as **normalization**.

---

38. If you do run the cell multiple times, the snippet number next to the cell will increment each time, as it does in IPython at the command line.

39. S. Ioffe and Szegedy, C.. "Batch Normalization: Accelerating Deep Network Training by Reducing Internal Covariate Shift." https://arxiv.org/abs/1502.03167.

In MNIST, each pixel is an integer in the range 0–255. The following statements convert the values to 32-bit (4-byte) floating-point numbers using the NumPy array method astype, then divide every element in the resulting array by 255, producing normalized values in the range 0.0–1.0:

```
[16]: X_train = X_train.astype('float32') / 255

[17]: X_test = X_test.astype('float32') / 255
```

One-Hot Encoding: Converting the Labels From Integers to Categorical Data
As we mentioned, the convnet's prediction for each digit will be an array of 10 probabilities, indicating the likelihood that the digit belongs to a particular one of the classes 0 through 9. When we evaluate the model's accuracy, Keras compares the model's predictions to the labels. To do that, Keras requires both to have the same shape. The MNIST label for each digit, however, is one integer value in the range 0–9. So, we must transform the labels into **categorical data**—that is, arrays of categories that match the format of the predictions. To do this, we'll use a process called **one-hot encoding**,[40] which converts data into arrays of 1.0s and 0.0s in which only one element is 1.0 and the rest are 0.0s. For MNIST, the one-hot-encoded values will be 10-element arrays representing the categories 0 through 9. One-hot encoding also can be applied to other types of data.

We know precisely which category each digit belongs to, so the categorical representation of a digit label will consist of a 1.0 at that digit's index and 0.0s for all the other elements (again, Keras uses floating-point numbers internally). So, a 7's categorical representation is:

```
[0.0, 0.0, 0.0, 0.0, 0.0, 0.0, 0.0, 1.0, 0.0, 0.0]
```

and a 3's representation is:

```
[0.0, 0.0, 0.0, 1.0, 0.0, 0.0, 0.0, 0.0, 0.0, 0.0]
```

The **tensorflow.keras.utils module** provides function **to_categorical** to perform one-hot encoding. The function counts the unique categories then, for each item being encoded, creates an array of that length with a 1.0 in the correct position. Let's transform y_train and y_test from one-dimensional arrays containing the values 0–9 into two-dimensional arrays of categorical data. After doing so, the rows of these arrays will look like those shown above. Snippet [21] outputs one sample's categorical data for the digit 5 (recall that NumPy shows the decimal point, but not trailing 0s on floating-point values):

```
[18]: from tensorflow.keras.utils import to_categorical

[19]: y_train = to_categorical(y_train)

[20]: y_train.shape
[20]: (60000, 10)

[21]: y_train[0]
[21]: array([ 0.,   0.,   0.,   0.,   0.,   1.,   0.,   0.,   0.,   0.],
      dtype=float32)

[22]: y_test = to_categorical(y_test)
```

40. This term comes from certain digital circuits in which a group of bits is allowed to have only one bit turned on (that is, to have the value 1). https://en.wikipedia.org/wiki/One-hot.

```
[23]: y_test.shape
[23]: (10000, 10)
```

15.6.4 Creating the Neural Network

Now that we've prepared the data, we'll configure a convolutional neural network. We begin with the Keras **Sequential** model from the **tensorflow.keras.models** module:

```
[24]: from tensorflow.keras.models import Sequential
```

```
[25]: cnn = Sequential()
```

The resulting network will execute its layers sequentially—the output of one layer becomes the input to the next. This is known as a **feed-forward network**. As you'll see when we discuss *recurrent neural networks*, not all neural network operate this way.

Adding Layers to the Network

A typical convolutional neural network consists of several layers—an *input layer* that receives the training samples, *hidden layers* that learn from the samples and an *output layer* that produces the prediction probabilities. We'll create a basic convnet here. Let's import from the **tensorflow.keras.layers module** the layer classes we'll use in this example:

```
[26]: from tensorflow.keras.layers import Conv2D, Dense, Flatten,
      MaxPooling2D
```

We discuss each below.

Convolution

We'll begin our network with a **convolution layer**, which uses the relationships between pixels that are close to one another to learn useful features (or patterns) in small areas of each sample. These features become inputs to subsequent layers.

The small areas that convolution learns from are called **kernels** or **patches**. Let's examine convolution on a 6-by-6 image. Consider the following diagram in which the 3-by-3 shaded square represents the kernel—the numbers are simply position numbers showing the order in which the kernels are visited and processed:

6-by-6 before convolution

You can think of the kernel as a "sliding window" that the convolution layer moves one pixel at a time left-to-right across the image. When the kernel reaches the right edge, the convolution layer moves the kernel one pixel down and repeats this left-to-right process. Kernels typically are 3-by-3,[41] though we found convnets that used 5-by-5 and 7-by-7 for higher-resolution images. Kernel-size is a tunable hyperparameter.

Initially, the kernel is in the upper-left corner of the original image—kernel position 1 (the shaded square) in the input layer above. The convolution layer performs mathematical calculations using those *nine* features to "learn" about them, then outputs *one* new feature to position 1 in the layer's output. By looking at features near one another, the network begins to recognize features like edges, straight lines and curves.

Next, the convolution layer moves the kernel one pixel to the right (known as the *stride*) to position 2 in the input layer. This new position *overlaps* with two of the three columns in the previous position, so that the convolution layer can learn from all the features that touch one another. The layer learns from the nine features in kernel position 2 and outputs one new feature in position 2 of the output, as in:

For a 6-by-6 image and a 3-by-3 kernel, the convolution layer does this two more times to produce features for positions 3 and 4 of the layer's output. Then, the convolution layer moves the kernel one pixel down and begins the left-to-right process again for the next four kernel positions, producing outputs in positions 5–8, then 9–12 and finally 13–16. The complete pass of the image left-to-right and top-to-bottom is called a **filter**. For a 3-by-3 kernel, the filter dimensions (4-by-4 in our sample above) will be *two less than the input dimensions* (6-by-6). For each 28-by-28 MNIST image, the filter will be 26-by-26.

The number of filters in the convolutional layer is commonly 32 or 64 when processing small images like those in MNIST, and each filter produces different results. The number of filters depends on the image dimensions—higher-resolution images have more features, so they require more filters. If you study the code the Keras team used to produce their pretrained convnets,[42] you'll find that they used 64, 128 or even 256 filters in their

41. https://www.quora.com/How-can-I-decide-the-kernel-size-output-maps-and-layers-of-CNN.
42. https://github.com/keras-team/keras-applications/tree/master/keras_applications.

first convolutional layers. Based on their convnets and the fact that the MNIST images are small, we'll use 64 filters in our first convolutional layer. The set of filters produced by a convolution layer is called a **feature map**.

Subsequent convolution layers combine features from previous feature maps to recognize larger features and so on. If we were doing facial recognition, early layers might recognize lines, edges and curves, and subsequent layers might begin combining those into larger features like eyes, eyebrows, noses, ears and mouths. Once the network learns a feature, because of convolution, it can recognize that feature anywhere in the image. This is one of the reasons that convnets are used for object recognition in images.

Adding a Convolution Layer
Let's add a **Conv2D** convolution layer to our model:

```
[27]: cnn.add(Conv2D(filters=64, kernel_size=(3, 3), activation='relu',
                     input_shape=(28, 28, 1)))
```

The Conv2D layer is configured with the following arguments:

- `filters=64`—The number of filters in the resulting feature map.

- `kernel_size=(3, 3)`—The size of the kernel used in each filter.

- `activation='relu'`—The **'relu'** (**Rectified Linear Unit) activation function** is used to produce this layer's output. `'relu'` is the most widely used activation function in today's deep learning networks[43] and is good for performance because it's easy to calculate.[44] It's commonly recommended for convolutional layers.[45]

Because this is the first layer in the model, we also pass the `input_shape=(28, 28,1)` argument to specify the shape of each sample. This automatically creates an input layer to load the samples and pass them into the Conv2D layer, which is actually the first *hidden* layer. In Keras, each subsequent layer infers its `input_shape` from the previous layer's output shape, making it easy to *stack* layers.

Dimensionality of the First Convolution Layer's Output
In the preceding convolutional layer, the input samples are 28-by-28-by-1—that is, 784 features each. We specified 64 filters and a 3-by-3 kernel size for the layer, so the output for each image is 26-by-26-by-64 for a total of 43,264 features in the feature map—a significant increase in dimensionality and an enormous number compared to the numbers of features we processed in the "Machine Learning" chapter's models. As each layer adds more features, the resulting feature maps' *dimensionality* becomes significantly larger. This is one of the reasons that deep learning studies often require tremendous processing power.

Overfitting
Recall from the previous chapter, that overfitting can occur when your model is too complex compared to what it is modeling. In the most extreme case, a model memorizes its training

---

43. Chollet, François. *Deep Learning with Python*. p. 72. Shelter Island, NY: Manning Publications, 2018.

44. https://towardsdatascience.com/exploring-activation-functions-for-neural-networks-73498da59b02.

45. https://www.quora.com/How-should-I-choose-a-proper-activation-function-for-the-neural-network.

data. When you make predictions with an overfit model, they will be accurate if new data matches the training data, but the model could perform poorly with data it has never seen.

Overfitting tends to occur in deep learning as the dimensionality of the layers becomes too large.[46,47,48] This causes the network to learn *specific* features of the training-set digit images, rather than learning the *general* features of digit images. Some techniques to prevent overfitting include training for fewer epochs, data augmentation, dropout and L1 or L2 regularization.[49,50] We'll discuss dropout later in the chapter.

Higher dimensionality also increases (and sometimes explodes) computation time. If you're performing the deep learning on CPUs rather than GPUs or TPUs, the training could become intolerably slow.

Adding a Pooling Layer

To reduce overfitting and computation time, a convolution layer is often followed by one or more layers that *reduce the dimensionality* of the convolution layer's output. A **pooling layer** *compresses* (or *down-samples*) the results by discarding features, which helps make the model more general. The most common pooling technique is called **max pooling**, which examines a 2-by-2 square of features and keeps only the maximum feature. To understand pooling, let's once again assume a 6-by-6 set of features. In the following diagram, the numeric values in the 6-by-6 square represent the features that we wish to compress and the 2-by-2 dark gray square in position 1 represents the initial pool of features to examine:

The max pooling layer first looks at the pool in position 1 above, then outputs the *maximum* feature from that pool—9 in our diagram. Unlike convolution, there's *no overlap* between pools. The pool moves by its width—for a 2-by-2 pool, the *stride* is 2. For the second pool, represented by the light gray 2-by-2 square, the layer outputs 7. For the third pool, the layer outputs 9. Once the pool reaches the right edge, the pooling layer moves the pool

---

46. https://cs231n.github.io/convolutional-networks/.
47. https://medium.com/@cxu24/why-dimensionality-reduction-is-important-dd60b5611543.
48. https://towardsdatascience.com/preventing-deep-neural-network-from-overfitting-953458db800a.
49. https://towardsdatascience.com/deep-learning-3-more-on-cnns-handling-overfitting-2bd5d99abe5d.
50. https://www.kdnuggets.com/2015/04/preventing-overfitting-neural-networks.html.

down by its height—2 rows—then continues from left-to-right. Because every group of four features is reduced to one, 2-by-2 pooling *compresses* the number of features by 75%.

Let's add a **MaxPooling2D** layer to our model:

```
[28]: cnn.add(MaxPooling2D(pool_size=(2, 2)))
```

This reduces the previous layer's output from 26-by-26-by-64 to 13-by-13-by-64.[51]

Though pooling is a common technique to reduce overfitting, some research suggests that additional convolutional layers which use larger strides for their kernels can reduce dimensionality and overfitting *without* discarding features.[52]

Adding Another Convolutional Layer and Pooling Layer

Convnets often have many convolution and pooling layers. The Keras team's convnets tend to double the number of filters in subsequent convolutional layers to enable the model to learn more relationships between the features.[53] So, let's add a second convolution layer with 128 filters, followed by a second pooling layer to once again reduce the dimensionality by 75%:

```
[29]: cnn.add(Conv2D(filters=128, kernel_size=(3, 3), activation='relu'))
```

```
[30]: cnn.add(MaxPooling2D(pool_size=(2, 2)))
```

The input to the second convolution layer is the 13-by-13-by-64 output of the first pooling layer. So, the output of snippet [29] will be 11-by-11-by-128. For odd dimensions like 11-by-11, Keras pooling layers round *down* by default (in this case to 10-by-10), so this pooling layer's output will be 5-by-5-by-128.

Flattening the Results

At this point, the previous layer's output is three-dimensional (5-by-5-by-128), but the final output of our model will be a *one-dimensional* array of 10 probabilities that classify the digits. To prepare for the one-dimensional final predictions, we first need to *flatten* the previous layer's three-dimensional output. A Keras **Flatten** layer reshapes its input to one dimension. In this case, the Flatten layer's output will be 1-by-3200 (that is, 5 * 5 * 128):

```
[31]: cnn.add(Flatten())
```

Adding a Dense Layer to Reduce the Number of Features

The layers before the Flatten layer learned digit features. Now we need to take all those features and learn the relationships among them so our model can classify which digit each image represents. Learning the relationships among features and performing classification is accomplished with fully connected **Dense** layers, like those shown in the neural network diagram earlier in the chapter. The following Dense layer creates 128 neurons (units) that learn from the 3200 outputs of the previous layer:

```
[32]: cnn.add(Dense(units=128, activation='relu'))
```

Many convnets contain at least one Dense layer like the one above. Convnets geared to more complex image datasets with higher-resolution images like ImageNet—a dataset of

---

51. Another technique for reducing overfitting is to add Dropout layers.
52. Tobias, Jost, Dosovitskiy, Alexey, Brox, Thomas, Riedmiller, and Martin. "Striving for Simplicity: The All Convolutional Net." April 13, 2015. https://arxiv.org/abs/1412.6806.
53. https://github.com/keras-team/keras-applications/tree/master/keras_applications.

over 14 million images[54]—often have several Dense layers, commonly with 4096 neurons. You can see such configurations in several of Keras's pretrained ImageNet convnets[55]— we list these in Section 15.11.

Adding Another Dense Layer to Produce the Final Output

Our final layer is a Dense layer that classifies the inputs into neurons representing the classes 0 through 9. The **softmax activation function** converts the values of these remaining 10 neurons into classification probabilities. The neuron that produces the highest probability represents the prediction for a given digit image:

```
[33]: cnn.add(Dense(units=10, activation='softmax'))
```

Printing the Model's Summary

A model's **summary method** shows you the model's layers. Some interesting things to note are the output shapes of the various layers and the number of parameters. The parameters are the *weights* that the network learns during training.[56,57] This is a relatively small network, yet it will need to learn nearly 500,000 parameters! And this is for tiny images that have less than one quarter of the resolution of the icons on most smartphone home screens. Imagine how many features a network would have to learn to process high-resolution 4K video frames or the super-high-resolution images produced by today's digital cameras. In the Output Shape, None simply means that the model does not know in advance how many training samples you're going to provide—this is known only when you start the training.

```
[34]: cnn.summary()
```

Layer (type)	Output Shape	Param #
conv2d_1 (Conv2D)	(None, 26, 26, 64)	640
max_pooling2d_1 (MaxPooling2	(None, 13, 13, 64)	0
conv2d_2 (Conv2D)	(None, 11, 11, 128)	73856
max_pooling2d_2 (MaxPooling2	(None, 5, 5, 128)	0
flatten_1 (Flatten)	(None, 3200)	0
dense_1 (Dense)	(None, 128)	409728
dense_2 (Dense)	(None, 10)	1290

```
Total params: 485,514
Trainable params: 485,514
Non-trainable params: 0
```

54. http://www.image-net.org.
55. https://github.com/keras-team/keras-applications/tree/master/keras_applications.
56. https://hackernoon.com/everything-you-need-to-know-about-neural-networks-8988c3ee4491.
57. https://www.kdnuggets.com/2018/06/deep-learning-best-practices-weight-initialization.html.

Also, note that there are no "non-trainable" parameters. By default, Keras trains *all* parameters, but it is possible to prevent training for specific layers, which is typically done when you're tuning your networks or using another model's learned parameters in a new model (a process called *transfer learning*).[58]

Visualizing a Model's Structure

You can visualize the model summary using the **plot_model function** from the module tensorflow.keras.utils:

```
[35]:  from tensorflow.keras.utils import plot_model
       from IPython.display import Image
       plot_model(cnn, to_file='convnet.png', show_shapes=True,
                  show_layer_names=True)
       Image(filename='convnet.png')
```

After storing the visualization in convnet.png, we use module IPython.display's **Image class** to show the image in the notebook. Keras assigns the layer names in the image:[59]

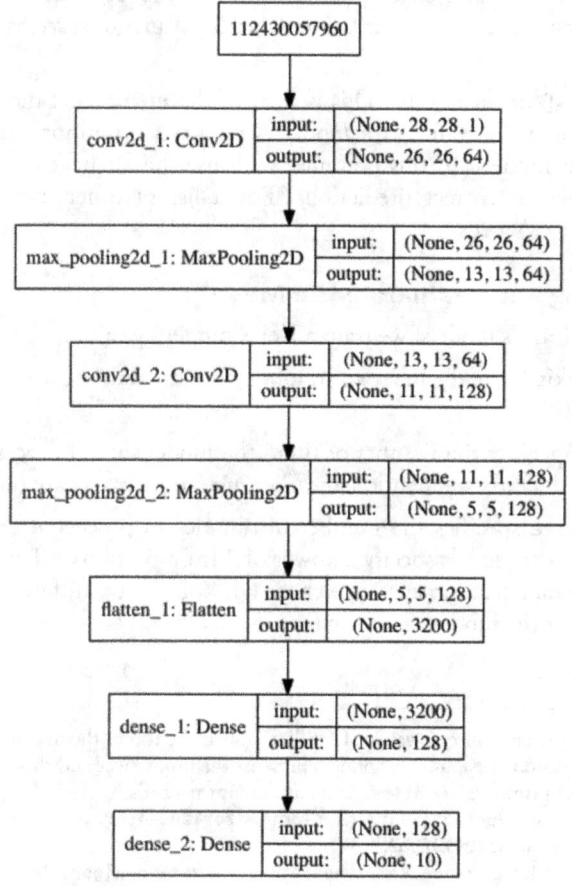

---

58. https://keras.io/getting-started/faq/#how-can-i-freeze-keras-layers.

Compiling the Model

Once you've added all the layers you complete the model by calling its **compile** method:

```
[36]: cnn.compile(optimizer='adam',
                   loss='categorical_crossentropy',
                   metrics=['accuracy'])
```

The arguments are:

- `optimizer='adam'`—The *optimizer* this model will use to adjust the weights throughout the neural network as it learns. There are many optimizers[60]—`'adam'` performs well across a wide variety of models.[61,62]

- `loss='categorical_crossentropy'`—This is the *loss function* used by the optimizer in multi-classification networks like our convnet, which will predict 10 classes. As the neural network learns, the optimizer attempts to minimize the values returned by the loss function. The lower the loss, the better the neural network is at predicting what each image is. For binary classification (which we'll use later in this chapter), Keras provides `'binary_crossentropy'`, and for regression, `'mean_squared_error'`. For other loss functions, see https://keras.io/losses/.

- `metrics=['accuracy']`—This is a list of the *metrics* that the network will produce to help you evaluate the model. Accuracy is a commonly used metric in classification models. In this example, we'll use the accuracy metric to check the percentage of correct predictions. For a list of other metrics, see https://keras.io/metrics/.

15.6.5 Training and Evaluating the Model

Similar to Scikit-learn's models, we train a Keras model by calling its **fit** method:

- As in Scikit-learn, the first two arguments are the training data and the categorical target labels.

- **epochs** specifies the number of times the model should process the entire set of training data. As we mentioned earlier, neural networks are trained iteratively.

- **batch_size** specifies the number of samples to process at a time during each epoch. Most models specify a power of 2 from 32 to 512. Larger batch sizes can decrease model accuracy.[63] We chose 64. You can try different values to see how they affect the model's performance.

---

59. The node with the large integer value 112430057960 at the top of the diagram appears to be a bug in the current version of Keras. This node represents the input layer and should say "InputLayer".
60. For more Keras optimizers, see https://keras.io/optimizers/.
61. https://medium.com/octavian-ai/which-optimizer-and-learning-rate-should-i-use-for-deep-learning-5acb418f9b2.
62. https://towardsdatascience.com/types-of-optimization-algorithms-used-in-neural-networks-and-ways-to-optimize-gradient-95ae5d39529f.
63. Keskar, Nitish Shirish, Dheevatsa Mudigere, Jorge Nocedal, Mikhail Smelyanskiy and Ping Tak Peter Tang. "On Large-Batch Training for Deep Learning: Generalization Gap and Sharp Minima." CoRR abs/1609.04836 (2016). https://arxiv.org/abs/1609.04836.

- In general, some samples should be used to *validate* the model. If you specify validation data, after each epoch, the model will use it to make predictions and display the *validation loss and accuracy*. You can study these values to tune your layers and the `fit` method's hyperparameters, or possibly change the layer composition of your model. Here, we used the **validation_split argument** to indicate that the model should reserve the *last* 10% (0.1) of the training samples for validation[64]—in this case, 6000 samples will be used for validation. If you have separate validation data, you can use the `validation_data` argument (as you'll see in Section 15.9) to specify a tuple containing arrays of samples and target labels. In general, it's better to get *randomly selected validation data*. You can use scikit-learn's `train_test_split` function for this purpose (as we'll do later in this chapter), then pass the randomly selected data with the `validation_data` argument.

In the following output, we highlighted the training accuracy (acc) and validation accuracy (val_acc) in bold:

```
[37]: cnn.fit(X_train, y_train, epochs=5, batch_size=64,
              validation_split=0.1)
Train on 54000 samples, validate on 6000 samples
Epoch 1/5
54000/54000 [==============================] - 68s 1ms/step - loss:
0.1407 - acc: 0.9580 - val_loss: 0.0452 - val_acc: 0.9867
Epoch 2/5
54000/54000 [==============================] - 64s 1ms/step - loss:
0.0426 - acc: 0.9867 - val_loss: 0.0409 - val_acc: 0.9878
Epoch 3/5
54000/54000 [==============================] - 69s 1ms/step - loss:
0.0299 - acc: 0.9902 - val_loss: 0.0325 - val_acc: 0.9912
Epoch 4/5
54000/54000 [==============================] - 70s 1ms/step - loss:
0.0197 - acc: 0.9935 - val_loss: 0.0335 - val_acc: 0.9903
Epoch 5/5
54000/54000 [==============================] - 63s 1ms/step - loss:
0.0155 - acc: 0.9948 - val_loss: 0.0297 - val_acc: 0.9927
[37]: <tensorflow.python.keras.callbacks.History at 0x7f105ba0ada0>
```

In Section 15.7, we'll introduce *TensorBoard*—a TensorFlow tool for visualizing data from your deep-learning models. In particular, we'll view charts showing how the training and validation accuracy and loss values change through the epochs. In Section 15.8, we'll demonstrate Andrej Karpathy's ConvnetJS tool, which trains convnets in your web browser and dynamically visualizes the layers' outputs, including what each convolutional layer "sees" as it learns. Also run his MNIST and CIFAR10 models. These will help you better understand neural networks' complex operations.

As the training proceeds, the `fit` method outputs information showing you the progress of each epoch, how long the epoch took to execute (in this case, each took 63–70 seconds), and the evaluation metrics for that pass. During the last epoch of this model, the accuracy reached 99.48% for the training samples (acc) and 99.27% for the validation samples (val_acc). Those are impressive numbers, given that we have not yet tried to tune the hyperparameters or tweak the number and types of the layers, which could lead to even

---

64. https://keras.io/getting-started/faq/#how-is-the-validation-split-computed.

better (or worse) results. Like machine learning, deep learning is an empirical science that benefits from lots of experimentation.

Evaluating the Model

Now we can check the accuracy of the model on data the model has not yet seen. To do so, we call the model's **evaluate method**, which displays as its output, how long it took to process the test samples (four seconds and 366 microseconds in this case):

```
[38]: loss, accuracy = cnn.evaluate(X_test, y_test)
10000/10000 [==============================] - 4s 366us/step

[39]: loss
[39]: 0.026809450998473768

[40]: accuracy
[40]: 0.9917
```

According to the preceding output, our convnet model is 99.17% accurate when predicting the labels for unseen data—and, at this point, we have not tried to tune the model. With a little online research, you can find models that can predict MNIST with nearly 100% accuracy. Try experimenting with different numbers of layers, types of layers and layer parameters and observe how those changes affect your results.

Making Predictions

The model's **predict method** predicts the classes of the digit images in its argument array (X_test):

```
[41]: predictions = cnn.predict(X_test)
```

We can check what the first sample digit should be by looking at y_test[0]:

```
[42]: y_test[0]
[42]: array([0., 0., 0., 0., 0., 0., 0., 1., 0., 0.], dtype=float32)
```

According to this output, the first sample is the digit 7, because the categorical representation of the test sample's label specifies a 1.0 at index 7—recall that we created this representation via *one-hot encoding*.

Let's check the probabilities returned by the predict method for the first test sample:

```
[43]: for index, probability in enumerate(predictions[0]):
          print(f'{index}: {probability:.10%}')
0: 0.0000000201%
1: 0.0000001355%
2: 0.0000186951%
3: 0.0000015494%
4: 0.0000000003%
5: 0.0000000012%
6: 0.0000000000%
7: 99.9999761581%
8: 0.0000005577%
9: 0.0000011416%
```

According to the output, predictions[0] indicates that our model believes this digit is a 7 with *nearly* 100% certainty. Not all predictions have this level of certainty.

Locating the Incorrect Predictions

Next, we'd like to view some of the *incorrectly* predicted images to get a sense of the ones our model has trouble with. For example, if it's always mispredicting 8s, perhaps we need more 8s in our training data.

Before we can view incorrect predictions, we need to locate them. Consider `predictions[0]` above. To determine whether the prediction was correct, we must compare the index of the largest probability in `predictions[0]` to the index of the element containing 1.0 in `y_test[0]`. If these index values are the same, then the prediction was correct; otherwise, it was incorrect. NumPy's `argmax` function determines the index of the highest valued element in its array argument. Let's use that to locate the incorrect predictions. In the following snippet, `p` is the predicted value array, and `e` is the expected value array (the expected values are the labels for the dataset's test images):

```
[44]: images = X_test.reshape((10000, 28, 28))
      incorrect_predictions = []

      for i, (p, e) in enumerate(zip(predictions, y_test)):
          predicted, expected = np.argmax(p), np.argmax(e)

          if predicted != expected:
              incorrect_predictions.append(
                  (i, images[i], predicted, expected))
```

In this snippet, we first reshape the samples from the shape (28, 28, 1) that Keras required for learning back to (28, 28), which Matplotlib requires to display the images. Next, we populate the list `incorrect_predictions` using the for statement. We `zip` the rows that represent each sample in the arrays `predictions` and `y_test`, then enumerate those so we can capture their indexes. If the `argmax` results for `p` and `e` are different, then the prediction was incorrect, and we append a tuple to `incorrect_predictions` containing that sample's index, image, the `predicted` value and the `expected` value. We can confirm the total number of incorrect predictions (out of 10,000 images in the test set) with:

```
[45]: len(incorrect_predictions)
[45]: 83
```

Visualizing Incorrect Predictions

The following snippet displays 24 of the incorrect images labeled with each image's index, predicted value (p) and expected value (e):

```
[46]: figure, axes = plt.subplots(nrows=4, ncols=6, figsize=(16, 12))

      for axes, item in zip(axes.ravel(), incorrect_predictions):
          index, image, predicted, expected = item
          axes.imshow(image, cmap=plt.cm.gray_r)
          axes.set_xticks([])   # remove x-axis tick marks
          axes.set_yticks([])   # remove y-axis tick marks
          axes.set_title(
              f'index: {index}\np: {predicted}; e: {expected}')
      plt.tight_layout()
```

Before reading the expected values, look at each digit and write down what digit you think it is. This is an important part of getting to know your data:

index: 18   index: 340   index: 460   index: 495   index: 583   index: 619
p: 8; e: 3   p: 3; e: 5   p: 9; e: 5   p: 0; e: 8   p: 7; e: 2   p: 8; e: 1

index: 625   index: 659   index: 720   index: 924   index: 947   index: 1014
p: 4; e: 6   p: 7; e: 2   p: 8; e: 5   p: 7; e: 2   p: 9; e: 8   p: 5; e: 6

index: 1062 index: 1182 index: 1226 index: 1232 index: 1260 index: 1319
p: 9; e: 3   p: 5; e: 6   p: 2; e: 7   p: 4; e: 9   p: 1; e: 7   p: 0; e: 8

index: 1393 index: 1414 index: 1522 index: 1530 index: 1611 index: 1621
p: 3; e: 5   p: 4; e: 9   p: 9; e: 7   p: 7; e: 8   p: 8; e: 3   p: 6; e: 0

Displaying the Probabilities for Several Incorrect Predictions

Let's look at the probabilities of some incorrect predictions. The following function displays the probabilities for the specified prediction array:

```
[47]: def display_probabilities(prediction):
          for index, probability in enumerate(prediction):
              print(f'{index}: {probability:.10%}')
```

Though the 8 (at index 495) in the first line of the image output looks like an 8, our model had trouble with it. As you can see in the following output, the model predicted this image as a 0, but also thought there was a 16% chance it was a 6 and a 23% chance it was an 8:

```
[48]: display_probabilities(predictions[495])
0: 59.7235262394%
1: 0.0000015465%
2: 0.8047289215%
3: 0.0001740813%
4: 0.0016636326%
5: 0.0030567855%
6: 16.1390662193%
7: 0.0000001781%
8: 23.3022540808%
9: 0.0255270657%
```

The 2 (at index 583) in the first row was predicted to be a 7 with 62.7% certainty, but the model also thought there was a 36.4% chance it was a 2:

```
[49]: display_probabilities(predictions[583])
0: 0.0000003016%
1: 0.0000005715%
```

```
2: 36.4056706429%
3: 0.0176281916%
4: 0.0000561930%
5: 0.0000000003%
6: 0.0000000019%
7: 62.7455413342%
8: 0.8310816251%
9: 0.0000114385%
```

The 6 (at index 625) at the beginning of the second row was predicted to be a 4, though that was far from certain. In this case, the probability of a 4 (51.6%) was only slightly higher than the probability of a 6 (48.38%):

```
[50]: display_probabilities(predictions[625])
0: 0.0008245181%
1: 0.0000041209%
2: 0.0012774357%
3: 0.0000000009%
4: 51.6223073006%
5: 0.0000001779%
6: 48.3754962683%
7: 0.0000000085%
8: 0.0000048182%
9: 0.0000785786%
```

15.6.6 Saving and Loading a Model

Neural network models can require significant training time. Once you've designed and tested a model that suits your needs, you can save its state. This allows you to load it later to make more predictions. Sometimes models are loaded and further trained for new problems. For example, layers in our model already know how to recognize features such as lines and curves, which could be useful in handwritten character recognition (as in the EMNIST dataset) as well. So you could potentially load the existing model and use it as the basis for a more robust model. This process is called **transfer learning**[65,66]—you transfer an existing model's knowledge into a new model. A Keras model's **save method** stores the model's architecture and state information in a format called **Hierarchical Data Format (HDF5)**. Such files use the .h5 file extension by default:

```
[51]: cnn.save('mnist_cnn.h5')
```

You can load a saved model with the **load_model function** from the tensorflow.keras.models module:

```
from tensorflow.keras.models import load_model
cnn = load_model('mnist_cnn.h5')
```

You can then invoke its methods. For example, if you've acquired more data, you could call predict to make additional predictions on new data, or you could call fit to start training with the additional data.

---

65. https://towardsdatascience.com/transfer-learning-from-pre-trained-models-f2393f124751.

66. https://medium.com/nanonets/nanonets-how-to-use-deep-learning-when-you-have-limited-data-f68c0b512cab.

Keras provides several additional functions that enable you to save and load various aspects of your models. For more information, see

```
https://keras.io/getting-started/faq/#how-can-i-save-a-keras-model
```

15.7 Visualizing Neural Network Training with TensorBoard

With deep learning networks, there's so much complexity and so much going on internally that's hidden from you that it's difficult to know and fully understand all the details. This creates challenges in testing, debugging and updating models and algorithms. Deep learning learns the features but there may be enormous numbers of them, and they may not be apparent to you.

Google provides the **TensorBoard**[67],[68] tool for visualizing neural networks implemented in TensorFlow and Keras. Just as a car's dashboard visualizes data from your car's sensors, such as your speed, engine temperature and the amount of gas remaining, a **TensorBoard dashboard** visualizes data from a deep learning model that can give you insights into how well your model is learning and potentially help you tune its hyperparameters. Here, we'll introduce TensorBoard.

Executing TensorBoard

TensorBoard monitors a folder on your system looking for files containing the data it will visualize in a web browser. Here, you'll create that folder, execute the TensorBoard server, then access it via a web browser. Perform the following steps:

1. Change to the ch15 folder in your Terminal, shell or Anaconda Command Prompt.

2. Ensure that your custom Anaconda environment tf_env is activated:

   ```
   conda activate tf_env
   ```

3. Execute the following command to create a subfolder named logs in which your deep-learning models will write the information that TensorBoard will visualize:

   ```
   mkdir logs
   ```

4. Execute TensorBoard

   ```
   tensorboard --logdir=logs
   ```

5. You can now access TensorBoard in your web browser at

   ```
   http://localhost:6006
   ```

If you connect to TensorBoard before executing any models, it will initially display a page indicating "No dashboards are active for the current data set."[69]

---

67. `https://github.com/tensorflow/tensorboard/blob/master/README.md`.
68. `https://www.tensorflow.org/guide/summaries_and_tensorboard`.
69. TensorBoard does not currently work with Microsoft's Edge browser.

The TensorBoard Dashboard

TensorBoard monitors the folder you specified looking for files output by the model during training. When TensorBoard sees updates, it loads the data into the dashboard:

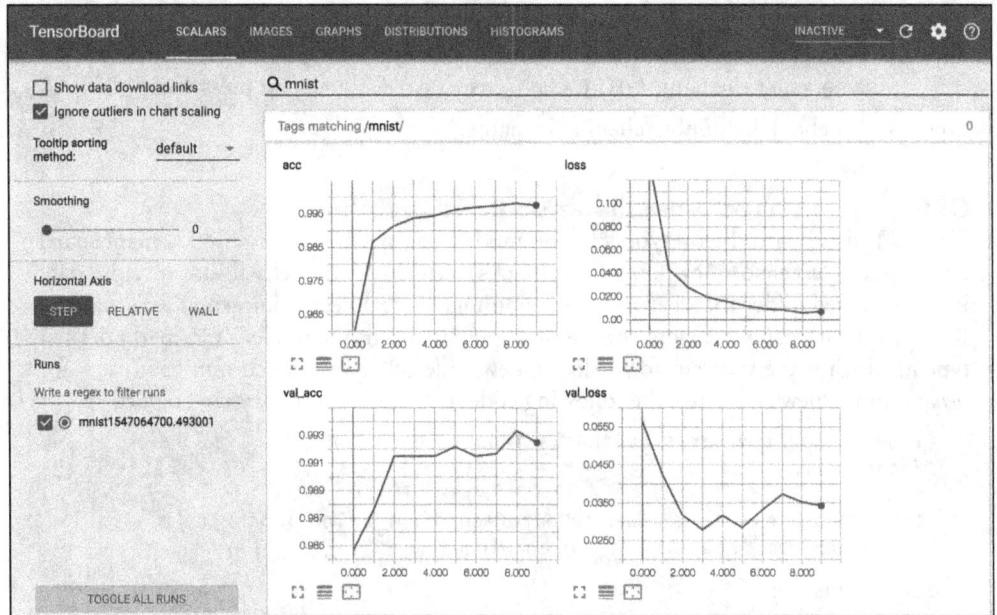

You can view the data as you train or after training completes. The dashboard above shows the TensorBoard **SCALARS** tab, which displays charts for individual values that change over time, such as the training accuracy (acc) and training loss (loss) shown in the first row, and the validation accuracy (val_acc) and validation_loss (val_loss) shown in the second row. The diagrams visualize a 10-epoch run of our MNIST convnet, which we provided in the notebook MNIST_CNN_TensorBoard.ipynb. The epochs are displayed along the x-axes starting from 0 for the first epoch. The accuracy and loss values are displayed on the y-axes. Looking at the training and validation accuracies, you can see in the first 5 epochs similar results to the five-epoch run in the previous section.

For the 10-epoch run, the training accuracy continued to improve through the 9th epoch, then decreased slightly. This might be the point at which we're starting to overfit, but we might need to train longer to find out. For the validation accuracy, you can see that it jumped up quickly, then was relatively flat for five epochs before jumping up then decreasing. For the training loss, you can see that it drops quickly, then continuously declines through the ninth epoch, before a slight increase. The validation loss dropped quickly then bounced around. We could run this model for more epochs to see whether results improve, but based on these diagrams, it appears that around the sixth epoch we get a nice combination of training and validation accuracy with minimal validation loss.

Normally these diagrams are stacked vertically in the dashboard. We used the search field (above the diagrams) to show any that had the name "mnist" in their folder name—we'll configure that in a moment. TensorBoard can load data from multiple models at once and you can choose which to visualize. This makes it easy to compare several different models or multiple runs of the same model.

Copy the MNIST Convnet's Notebook

To create the new notebook for this example:

1. Right-click the MNIST_CNN.ipynb notebook in JupyterLab's **File Browser** tab and select **Duplicate** to make a copy of the notebook.

2. Right-click the new notebook named MNIST_CNN-Copy1.ipynb, then select **Rename**, enter the name MNIST_CNN_TensorBoard.ipynb and press *Enter*.

Open the notebook by double-clicking its name.

Configuring Keras to Write the TensorBoard Log Files

To use TensorBoard, before you fit the model, you need to configure a **TensorBoard** object (module tensorflow.keras.callbacks), which the model will use to write data into a specified folder that TensorBoard monitors. This object is known as a **callback** in Keras. In the notebook, click to the left of snippet that calls the model's fit method, then type a, which is the shortcut for adding a new code cell *above* the current cell (use b for *below*). In the new cell, enter the following code to create the TensorBoard object:

```
from tensorflow.keras.callbacks import TensorBoard
import time

tensorboard_callback = TensorBoard(log_dir=f'./logs/mnist{time.time()}',
    histogram_freq=1, write_graph=True)
```

The arguments are:

- log_dir—The name of the folder in which this model's log files will be written. The notation './logs/' indicates that we're creating a new folder within the logs folder you created previously, and we follow that with 'mnist' and the current time. This ensures that each new execution of the notebook will have its own log folder. That will enable you to compare multiple executions in TensorBoard.

- histogram_freq—The frequency in *epochs* that Keras will output to the model's log files. In this case, we'll write data to the logs for every epoch.

- write_graph—When this is true, a graph of the model will be output. You can view the graph in the **GRAPHS** tab in TensorBoard.

Updating Our Call to fit

Finally, we need to modify the original fit method call in snippet 37. For this example, we set the number of epochs to 10, and we added the callbacks argument, which is a list of callback objects[70]:

```
cnn.fit(X_train, y_train, epochs=10, batch_size=64,
    validation_split=0.1, callbacks=[tensorboard_callback])
```

You can now re-execute the notebook by selecting **Kernel > Restart Kernel and Run All Cells** in JupyterLab. After the first epoch completes, you'll start to see data in TensorBoard.

---

70. You can view Keras's other callbacks at https://keras.io/callbacks/.

15.8 ConvnetJS: Browser-Based Deep-Learning Training and Visualization

In this section, we'll overview Andrej Karpathy's JavaScript-based ConvnetJS tool for training and visualizing convolutional neural networks in your web browser:[71]

```
https://cs.stanford.edu/people/karpathy/convnetjs/
```

You can run the ConvnetJS sample convolutional neural networks or create your own. We've used the tool on several desktop, tablet and phone browsers.

The ConvnetJS MNIST demo trains a convolutional neural network using the MNIST dataset we presented in Section 15.6. The demo presents a scrollable dashboard that updates dynamically as the model trains and contains several sections.

Training Stats

This section contains a **Pause** button that enables you to stop the learning and "freeze" the current dashboard visualizations. Once you pause the demo, the button text changes to **resume**. Clicking the button again continues training. This section also presents training statistics, including the training and validation accuracy and a graph of the training loss.

Instantiate a Network and Trainer

In this section, you'll find the JavaScript code that creates the convolutional neural network. The default network has similar layers to the convnet in Section 15.6. The ConvnetJS documentation[72] shows the supported layer types and how to configure them. You can experiment with different layer configurations in the provided textbox and begin training an updated network by clicking the **change network** button.

Network Visualization

This key section shows one training image at a time and how the network processes that image through each layer. Click the **Pause** button to inspect all the layers' outputs for a given digit to get a sense of what the network "sees" as it learns. The network's last layer produces the probabilistic classifications. It shows 10 squares—9 black and 1 white, indicating the predicted class of the current digit image.

Example Predictions on Test Set

The final section shows a random selection of the test set images and the top three possible classes for each digit. The one with the highest probability is shown on a green bar and the other two are displayed on red bars. The length of each bar is a visual indication of that class's probability.

15.9 Recurrent Neural Networks for Sequences; Sentiment Analysis with the IMDb Dataset

In the MNIST CNN network, we focused on stacked layers that were applied *sequentially*. Non-sequential models are possible, as you'll see here with *recurrent neural networks*. In this section, we use Keras's bundled IMDb (the Internet Movie Database) movie reviews

---

71. You also can download ConvnetJS from GitHub at `https://github.com/karpathy/convnetjs`.
72. `https://cs.stanford.edu/people/karpathy/convnetjs/docs.html`.

dataset[73] to perform **binary classification**, predicting whether a given review's sentiment is positive or negative.

We'll use a **recurrent neural network (RNN)**, which processes sequences of data, such as time series or text in sentences. The term "recurrent" comes from the fact that the neural network contains *loops* in which the output of a given layer becomes the input to that same layer in the next **time step**. In a time series, a time step is the next point in time. In a text sequence, a "time step" would be the next word in a sequence of words.

The looping in RNNs enables them to learn and remember relationships among the data in the sequence. For example, consider the following sentences we used in the "Natural Language Processing" chapter. The sentence

```
The food is not good.
```

clearly has negative sentiment. Similarly, the sentence

```
The movie was good.
```

has positive sentiment, though not as positive as

```
The movie was excellent!
```

In the first sentence, the word "good" on its own has positive sentiment. However, when *preceded by* "not," which appears earlier in the sequence, the sentiment becomes negative. RNNs take into account the relationships among the earlier and later parts of a sequence.

In the preceding example, the words that determined sentiment were adjacent. However, when determining the meaning of text there can be many words to consider and an arbitrary number of words in between them. In this section, we'll use a **Long Short-Term Memory (LSTM)** layer, which makes the neural network *recurrent* and is optimized to handle learning from sequences like the ones we described above.

RNNs have been used for many tasks including:[74,75,76]

- predictive text input—displaying possible next words as you type,
- sentiment analysis,
- responding to questions with the predicted best answers from a corpus,
- inter-language translation, and
- automated closed captioning in video.

15.9.1 Loading the IMDb Movie Reviews Dataset

The IMDb movie reviews dataset included with Keras contains 25,000 training samples and 25,000 testing samples, each labeled with its positive (1) or negative (0) sentiment. Let's import the **tensorflow.keras.datasets.imdb module** so we can load the dataset:

```
[1]: from tensorflow.keras.datasets import imdb
```

73. Maas, Andrew L. and Daly, Raymond E. and Pham, Peter T. and Huang, Dan and Ng, Andrew Y. and Potts, Christopher, "Learning Word Vectors for Sentiment Analysis," *Proceedings of the 49th Annual Meeting of the Association for Computational Linguistics: Human Language Technologies*, June 2011. Portland, Oregon, USA. Association for Computational Linguistics, pp. 142–150. http://www.aclweb.org/anthology/P11-1015.
74. https://www.analyticsindiamag.com/overview-of-recurrent-neural-networks-and-their-applications/.
75. https://en.wikipedia.org/wiki/Recurrent_neural_network#Applications.
76. http://karpathy.github.io/2015/05/21/rnn-effectiveness/.

The `imdb` module's **load_data function** returns the IMDb training and testing sets. There are over 88,000 unique words in the dataset. The `load_data` function enables you to specify the number of unique words to import as part of the training and testing data. In this case, we loaded only the top 10,000 most frequently occurring words due to the memory limitations of our system and the fact that we're (intentionally) training on a CPU rather than a GPU (because most of our readers will not have access to systems with GPUs and TPUs). The more data you load, the longer training will take, but more data may help produce better models:

```
[2]: number_of_words = 10000
```

```
[3]: (X_train, y_train), (X_test, y_test) = imdb.load_data(
         num_words=number_of_words)
```

The `load_data` function returns a tuple of two elements containing the training and testing sets. Each element is itself a tuple containing the samples and labels, respectively. In a given review, `load_data` replaces any words outside the top 10,000 with a placeholder value, which we'll discuss shortly.

15.9.2 Data Exploration

Let's check the dimensions of the training set samples (`X_train`), training set labels (`y_train`), testing set samples (`X_test`) and testing set labels (`y_test`):

```
[4]: X_train.shape
[4]: (25000,)
```

```
[5]: y_train.shape
[5]: (25000,)
```

```
[6]: X_test.shape
[6]: (25000,)
```

```
[7]: y_test.shape
[7]: (25000,)
```

The arrays `y_train` and `y_test` are one-dimensional arrays containing 1s and 0s, indicating whether each review is positive or negative. Based on the preceding outputs, `X_train` and `X_test` also appear to be one-dimensional. However, their elements actually are *lists* of integers, each representing one review's contents, as shown in snippet [9]:[77]

```
[8]: %pprint
[8]: Pretty printing has been turned OFF
```

```
[9]: X_train[123]
[9]: [1, 307, 5, 1301, 20, 1026, 2511, 87, 2775, 52, 116, 5, 31, 7, 4,
91, 1220, 102, 13, 28, 110, 11, 6, 137, 13, 115, 219, 141, 35, 221, 956,
54, 13, 16, 11, 2714, 61, 322, 423, 12, 38, 76, 59, 1803, 72, 8, 2, 23,
5, 967, 12, 38, 85, 62, 358, 99]
```

Keras deep learning models require *numeric data*, so the Keras team preprocessed the IMDb dataset for you.

---

77. Here we used the `%pprint` magic to turn off pretty printing so the following snippet's output could be displayed horizontally rather than vertically to save space. You can turn pretty printing back on by re-executing the `%pprint` magic.

Movie Review Encodings

Because the movie reviews are numerically encoded, to view their original text, you need to know the word to which each number corresponds. Keras's IMDb dataset provides a dictionary that maps the words to their indexes. Each word's corresponding value is its frequency ranking among all the words in the entire set of reviews. So the word with the ranking 1 is the most frequently occurring word (calculated by the Keras team from the dataset), the word with ranking 2 is the second most frequently occurring word, and so on.

Though the dictionary values begin with 1 as the most frequently occurring word, in each encoded review (like X_train[123] shown previously), the ranking values are *offset by 3*. So any review containing the most frequently occurring word will have the value 4 wherever that word appears in the review. Keras reserves the values 0, 1 and 2 in each encoded review for the following purposes:

- The value 0 in a review represents *padding*. Keras deep learning algorithms expect all the training samples to have the same dimensions, so some reviews may need to be expanded to a given length and some shortened to that length. Reviews that need to be expanded are padded with 0s.

- The value 1 represents a token that Keras uses internally to indicate the start of a text sequence for learning purposes.

- The value 2 in a review represents an unknown word—typically a word that was not loaded because you called load_data with the num_words argument. In this case, any review that contained words with frequency rankings greater than num_words would have those words' numeric values replaced with 2. This is all handled by Keras when you load the data.

Because each review's numeric values are offset by 3, we'll have to account for this when we decode the review.

Decoding a Movie Review

Let's decode a review. First, get the word-to-index dictionary by calling the function **get_word_index** from the tensorflow.keras.datasets.imdb module:

```
[10]: word_to_index = imdb.get_word_index()
```

The word 'great' might appear in a positive movie review, so let's see whether it's in the dictionary:

```
[11]: word_to_index['great']
[11]: 84
```

According to the output, 'great' is the dataset's 84th most frequent word. If you look up a word that's not in the dictionary, you'll get an exception.

To transform the frequency ratings into words, let's first reverse the word_to_index dictionary's mapping, so we can look up every word by its frequency rating. The following dictionary comprehension reverses the mapping:

```
[12]: index_to_word = \
          {index: word for (word, index) in word_to_index.items()}
```

Recall that a dictionary's items method enables us to iterate through tuples of key–value pairs. We unpack each tuple into the variables word and index, then create an entry in the new dictionary with the expression index: word.

The following list comprehension gets the top 50 words from the new dictionary—recall that the most frequent word has the value 1:

```
[13]: [index_to_word[i] for i in range(1, 51)]
[13]: ['the', 'and', 'a', 'of', 'to', 'is', 'br', 'in', 'it', 'i',
 'this', 'that', 'was', 'as', 'for', 'with', 'movie', 'but', 'film', 'on',
 'not', 'you', 'are', 'his', 'have', 'he', 'be', 'one', 'all', 'at', 'by',
 'an', 'they', 'who', 'so', 'from', 'like', 'her', 'or', 'just', 'about',
 "it's", 'out', 'has', 'if', 'some', 'there', 'what', 'good', 'more']
```

Note that most of these are *stop words*. Depending on the application, you might want to remove or keep the stop words. For example, if you were creating a predictive-text application that suggests the next word in a sentence the user is typing, you'd want to keep the stop words so they can be displayed as predictions.

Now, we can decode a review. We use the index_to_word dictionary's two-argument method get rather than the [] operator to get value for each key. If a value is not in the dictionary, the get method returns its second argument, rather than raising an exception. The argument i - 3 accounts for the offset in the encoded reviews of each review's frequency ratings. When the Keras reserved values 0–2 appear in a review, get returns '?'; otherwise, get returns the word with the key i - 3 in the index_to_word dictionary:

```
[14]: ' '.join([index_to_word.get(i - 3, '?') for i in X_train[123]])
[14]: '? beautiful and touching movie rich colors great settings good
 acting and one of the most charming movies i have seen in a while i
 never saw such an interesting setting when i was in china my wife
 liked it so much she asked me to ? on and rate it so other would
 enjoy too'
```

We can see from the y_train array that this review is classified as positive:

```
[15]: y_train[123]
[15]: 1
```

15.9.3 Data Preparation

The number of words per review varies, but the Keras requires all samples to have the same dimensions. So, we need to perform some data preparation. In this case, we need to restrict every review to the *same* number of words. Some reviews will need to be *padded* with additional data and others will need to be *truncated*. The **pad_sequences** utility function (module **tensorflow.keras.preprocessing.sequence**) reshapes X_train's samples (that is, its rows) to the number of features specified by the maxlen argument (200) and returns a two-dimensional array:

```
[16]: words_per_review = 200
```

```
[17]: from tensorflow.keras.preprocessing.sequence import pad_sequences
```

```
[18]: X_train = pad_sequences(X_train, maxlen=words_per_review)
```

If a sample has more features, pad_sequences truncates it to the specified length. If a sample has fewer features, pad_sequences adds 0s to the beginning of the sequence to pad it to the specified length. Let's confirm X_train's new shape:

```
[19]: X_train.shape
[19]: (25000, 200)
```

We also must reshape X_test for later in this example when we evaluate the model:

```
[20]: X_test = pad_sequences(X_test, maxlen=words_per_review)

[21]: X_test.shape
[21]: (25000, 200)
```

Splitting the Test Data into Validation and Test Data

In our convnet, we used the fit method's validation_split argument to indicate that 10% of our training data should be set aside to validate the model as it trains. For this example, we'll manually split the 25,000 test samples into 20,000 test samples and 5,000 validation samples. We'll then pass the 5,000 validation samples to the model's fit method via the argument **validation_data**. Let's use Scikit-learn's train_test_split function from the previous chapter to split the test set:

```
[22]: from sklearn.model_selection import train_test_split
      X_test, X_val, y_test, y_val = train_test_split(
          X_test, y_test, random_state=11, test_size=0.20)
```

Let's also confirm the split by checking X_test's and X_val's shapes:

```
[23]: X_test.shape
[23]: (20000, 200)

[24]: X_val.shape
[24]: (5000, 200)
```

15.9.4 Creating the Neural Network

Next, we'll configure the RNN. Once again, we begin with a Sequential model to which we'll add the layers that compose our network:

```
[25]: from tensorflow.keras.models import Sequential

[26]: rnn = Sequential()
```

Next, let's import the layers we'll use in this model:

```
[27]: from tensorflow.keras.layers import Dense, LSTM

[28]: from tensorflow.keras.layers.embeddings import Embedding
```

Adding an Embedding Layer

Previously, we used *one-hot encoding* to convert the MNIST dataset's integer labels into *categorical* data. The result for each label was a vector in which all but one element was 0. We could do that for the index values that represent our words. However, this example processes 10,000 unique words. That means we'd need a 10,000-by-10,000 array to represent all the words. That's 100,000,000 elements, and almost all the array elements would be 0. This is not an efficient way to encode the data. If we were to process all 88,000+ unique words in the dataset, we'd need an array of nearly *eight billion* elements!

To *reduce dimensionality*, RNNs that process text sequences typically begin with an **embedding layer** that encodes each word in a more compact *dense-vector representation*. The vectors produced by the embedding layer also capture the word's context—that is, how a given word relates to the words around it. So the embedding layer enables the RNN to learn word relationships among the training data.

There are also **predefined word embeddings**, such as **Word2Vec** and **GloVe**. You can load these into neural networks to save training time. They're also sometimes used to add basic word relationships to a model when smaller amounts of training data are available. This can improve the model's accuracy by allowing it to build upon previously learned word relationships, rather than trying to learn those relationships with insufficient amounts of data.

Let's create an `Embedding` layer (module `tensorflow.keras.layers`):

```
[29]: rnn.add(Embedding(input_dim=number_of_words, output_dim=128,
                        input_length=words_per_review))
```

The arguments are:

- `input_dim`—The number of unique words.

- `output_dim`—The size of each word embedding. If you load pre-existing embeddings[78] like *Word2Vec* and *GloVe*, you must set this to match the size of the word embeddings you load.

- `input_length=words_per_review`—The number of words in each input sample.

Adding an LSTM Layer

Next, we'll add an LSTM layer:

```
[30]: rnn.add(LSTM(units=128, dropout=0.2, recurrent_dropout=0.2))
```

The arguments are:

- `units`—The number of neurons in the layer. The more neurons the more the network can remember. As a guideline, you can start with a value between the length of the sequences you're processing (200 in this example) and the number of classes you're trying to predict (2 in this example).[79]

- `dropout`—The percentage of neurons to randomly disable when processing the layer's input and output. Like the pooling layers in our convnet, **dropout** is a proven technique[80,81] that reduces overfitting. Keras provides a **Dropout** layer that you can add to your models.

- `recurrent_dropout`—The percentage of neurons to randomly disable when the layer's output is fed back into the layer again to allow the network to learn from what it has seen previously.

The mechanics of how the LSTM layer performs its task are beyond the scope of this book. Chollet says: "you don't need to understand anything about the specific architecture of an LSTM cell; as a human, it shouldn't be your job to understand it. Just keep in mind what the LSTM cell is meant to do: allow past information to be reinjected at a later time."[82]

---

78. `https://blog.keras.io/using-pre-trained-word-embeddings-in-a-keras-model.html`.
79. `https://towardsdatascience.com/choosing-the-right-hyperparameters-for-a-simple-lstm-using-keras-f8e9ed76f046`.
80. Yarin, Ghahramani, and Zoubin. "A Theoretically Grounded Application of Dropout in Recurrent Neural Networks." October 05, 2016. `https://arxiv.org/abs/1512.05287`.
81. Srivastava, Nitish, Geoffrey Hinton, Alex Krizhevsky, Ilya Sutskever, and Ruslan Salakhutdinov. "Dropout: A Simple Way to Prevent Neural Networks from Overfitting." *Journal of Machine Learning Research* 15 (June 14, 2014): 1929-1958. `http://jmlr.org/papers/volume15/srivastava14a/srivastava14a.pdf`.
82. Chollet, François. *Deep Learning with Python.* p. 204. Shelter Island, NY: Manning Publications, 2018.

Adding a Dense Output Layer

Finally, we need to take the LSTM layer's output and reduce it to one result indicating whether a review is positive or negative, thus the value 1 for the units argument. Here we use the **'sigmoid'** activation function, which is preferred for binary classification.[83] It reduces arbitrary values into the range 0.0–1.0, producing a probability:

```
[31]: rnn.add(Dense(units=1, activation='sigmoid'))
```

Compiling the Model and Displaying the Summary

Next, we compile the model. In this case, there are only two possible outputs, so we use the **binary_crossentropy** loss function:

```
[32]: rnn.compile(optimizer='adam',
                   loss='binary_crossentropy',
                   metrics=['accuracy'])
```

The following is the summary of our model. Notice that even though we have fewer layers than our convnet, the RNN has nearly three times as many trainable parameters (the network's weights) as the convnet and more parameters means more training time. The large number of parameters primarily comes from the number of words in the vocabulary (we loaded 10,000) times the number of neurons in the Embedding layer's output (128):

```
[33]: rnn.summary()
```

Layer (type)	Output Shape	Param #
embedding_1 (Embedding)	(None, 200, 128)	1280000
lstm_1 (LSTM)	(None, 128)	131584
dense_1 (Dense)	(None, 1)	129

```
Total params: 1,411,713
Trainable params: 1,411,713
Non-trainable params: 0
```

15.9.5 Training and Evaluating the Model

Let's train our model.[84] Notice for each epoch that the model takes significantly longer to train than our convnet did. This is due to the larger numbers of parameters (weights) our RNN model needs to learn. We bolded the accuracy (acc) and validation accuracy (val_acc) values for readability—these represent the percentage of training samples and the percentage of validation_data samples that the model predicts correctly.

```
[34]: rnn.fit(X_train, y_train, epochs=10, batch_size=32,
              validation_data=(X_test, y_test))
Train on 25000 samples, validate on 5000 samples
Epoch 1/5
25000/25000 [==============================] - 299s 12ms/step - loss:
0.6574 - acc: 0.5868 - val_loss: 0.5582 - val_acc: 0.6964
```

---

83. Chollet, François. *Deep Learning with Python.* p.114. Shelter Island, NY: Manning Publications, 2018.
84. At the time of this writing, TensorFlow displayed a warning when we executed this statement. This is a known TensorFlow issue and, according to the forums, you can safely ignore the warning.

```
Epoch 2/5
25000/25000 [==============================] - 298s 12ms/step - loss:
0.4577 - acc: 0.7786 - val_loss: 0.3546 - val_acc: 0.8448
Epoch 3/5
25000/25000 [==============================] - 296s 12ms/step - loss:
0.3277 - acc: 0.8594 - val_loss: 0.3207 - val_acc: 0.8614
Epoch 4/5
25000/25000 [==============================] - 307s 12ms/step - loss:
0.2675 - acc: 0.8864 - val_loss: 0.3056 - val_acc: 0.8700
Epoch 5/5
25000/25000 [==============================] - 310s 12ms/step - loss:
0.2217 - acc: 0.9083 - val_loss: 0.3264 - val_acc: 0.8704
[34]: <tensorflow.python.keras.callbacks.History object at 0xb3ba882e8>
```

Finally, we can evaluate the results using the test data. Function `evaluate` returns the loss and accuracy values. In this case, the model was 85.99% accurate:

```
[35]: results = rnn.evaluate(X_test, y_test)
20000/20000 [==============================] - 42s 2ms/step

[36]: results
[36]: [0.3415240607559681, 0.8599]
```

Note that the accuracy of this model seems low compared to our MNIST convnet's results, but this is a much more difficult problem. If you search online for other IMDb sentiment-analysis binary-classification studies, you'll find lots of results in the high 80s. So we did reasonably well with our small recurrent neural network of only three layers. You might want to study some online models and try to produce a better model.

15.10 Tuning Deep Learning Models

In Section 15.9.5, notice in the `fit` method's output that both the testing accuracy (85.99%) and validation accuracy (87.04%) were significantly less than the 90.83% training accuracy. Such disparities are usually the result of overfitting, so there is plenty of room for improvement in our model.[85,86] If you look at the output of each epoch, you'll notice both the training and validation accuracy continue to increase. Recall that training for too many epochs can lead to overfitting, but it's possible we have not yet trained enough. Perhaps one hyperparameter tuning option for this model would be to increase the number of epochs.

Some variables that affect your models' performance include:

- having more or less data to train with

- having more or less to test with

- having more or less to validate with

- having more or fewer layers

- the types of layers you use

- the order of the layers

---

85. https://towardsdatascience.com/deep-learning-overfitting-846bf5b35e24.
86. https://hackernoon.com/memorizing-is-not-learning-6-tricks-to-prevent-overfit-ting-in-machine-learning-820b091dc42.

In our IMDb RNN example, some things we could tune include:

- trying different amounts of the training data—we used only the top 10,000 words
- different numbers of words per review—we used only 200,
- different numbers of neurons in our layers,
- more layers or
- possibly loading pre-trained word vectors rather than having our Embedding layer learn them from scratch.

The compute time required to train models multiple times is significant so, in deep learning, you generally do not tune hyperparameters with techniques like k-fold cross-validation or grid search.[87] There are various tuning techniques,[88,89,90,91] but one particularly promising area is automated machine learning (AutoML). For example, the Auto-Keras[92] library is specifically geared to automatically choosing the best configurations for your Keras models. Google's Cloud AutoML and Baidu's EZDL are among various other automated machine learning efforts.

15.11 Convnet Models Pretrained on ImageNet

With deep learning, rather than starting fresh on every project with costly training, validating and testing, you can use **pretrained deep neural network models** to:

- make new predictions,
- continue training them further with new data or
- transfer the weights learned by a model for a similar problem into a new model—this is called *transfer learning*.

Keras Pretrained Convnet Models
Keras comes bundled with the following pretrained convnet models,[93] each pretrained on ImageNet[94]—a growing dataset of 14+ million images:

- Xception
- VGG16
- VGG19

---

87. https://www.quora.com/Is-cross-validation-heavily-used-in-deep-learning-or-is-it-too-expensive-to-be-used.
88. https://towardsdatascience.com/what-are-hyperparameters-and-how-to-tune-the-hy-perparameters-in-a-deep-neural-network-d0604917584a.
89. https://medium.com/machine-learning-bites/deeplearning-series-deep-neural-net-works-tuning-and-optimization-39250ff7786d.
90. https://flyyufelix.github.io/2016/10/03/fine-tuning-in-keras-part1.html and https://flyyufelix.github.io/2016/10/08/fine-tuning-in-keras-part2.html.
91. https://towardsdatascience.com/a-comprehensive-guide-on-how-to-fine-tune-deep-neural-networks-using-keras-on-google-colab-free-daaaa0aced8f.
92. https://autokeras.com/.
93. https://keras.io/applications/.
94. http://www.image-net.org.

- ResNet50
- Inception v3
- Inception-ResNet v2
- MobileNet v1
- DenseNet
- NASNet
- MobileNet v2

Reusing Pretrained Models
ImageNet is too big for efficient training on most computers, so most people interested in using it start with one of the smaller pretrained models.

You can reuse just the architecture of each model and train it with new data, or you can reuse the pretrained weights. For a few simple examples, see:

```
https://keras.io/applications/
```

ImageNet Challenge
In the end-of-chapter projects, you'll research and use some of these bundled models. You'll also investigate the *ImageNet Large Scale Visual Recognition Challenge* for evaluating object-detection and image-recognition models.[95] This competition ran from 2010 through 2017. ImageNet now has a continuously running challenge on the Kaggle competition site called the *ImageNet Object Localization Challenge*.[96] The goal is to identify "all objects within an image, so those images can then be classified and annotated." ImageNet releases the current participants leaderboard once per quarter.

A lot of what you've seen in the machine learning and deep learning chapters is what the Kaggle competition website is all about. There's no obvious optimal solution for many machine learning and deep learning tasks. People's creativity is really the only limit. On Kaggle, companies and organizations fund competitions where they encourage people worldwide to develop better-performing solutions than they've been able to do for something that's important to their business or organization. Sometimes companies offer prize money, which has been as high as $1,000,000 on the famous Netflix competition. Netflix wanted to get a 10% or better improvement in their model for determining whether people will like a movie, based on how they rated previous ones.[97] They used the results to help make better recommendations to members. Even if you do not win a Kaggle competition, it's a great way to get experience working on problems of current interest.

15.12 Wrap-Up

In Chapter 16, you peered into the future of AI. Deep Learning has captured the imagination of the computer-science and data science-communities. This may be the most important AI chapter in the book.

---

95. http://www.image-net.org/challenges/LSVRC/.
96. https://www.kaggle.com/c/imagenet-object-localization-challenge.
97. https://netflixprize.com/rules.html.

We mentioned the key deep-learning platforms, indicating that Google's TensorFlow is the most widely used. We discussed why Keras, which presents a friendly interface to TensorFlow, has become so popular.

We set up a custom Anaconda environment for TensorFlow, Keras and JupyterLab, then used the environment to implement the Keras examples.

We explained what tensors are and why they're crucial to deep learning. We discussed the basics of neurons and multi-layered neural networks for building Keras deep-learning models. We considered some popular types of layers and how to order them.

We introduced convolutional neural networks (convnets) and indicated that they're especially appropriate for computer-vision applications. We then built, trained, validated and tested a convnet using the MNIST database of handwritten digits for which we achieved 99.17% prediction accuracy. This is remarkable, given that we achieved it by working with a only a basic model and without doing any hyperparameter tuning. You can try more sophisticated models and tune the hyperparameters to try to achieve better performance. We listed a variety of intriguing computer vision tasks.

We introduced TensorBoard for visualizing TensorFlow and Keras neural network training and validation. We also discussed ConvnetJS, a browser-based convnet training and visualization tool, which enables you to peek inside the training process.

Next, we presented recurrent neural networks (RNNs) for processing sequences of data, such as time series or text in sentences. We used an RNN with the IMDb movie reviews dataset to perform binary classification, predicting whether each review's sentiment was positive or negative. We also discussed tuning deep learning models and how high-performance hardware, like NVIDIA's GPUs and Google's TPUs, is making it possible for more people to tackle more substantial deep-learning studies.

Given how costly and time-consuming it is to train deep-learning models, we explained the strategy of using pretrained models. We listed various Keras convnet image-processing models that were trained on the massive ImageNet dataset, and discussed how transfer learning enables you to use these models to create new ones quickly and effectively. Deep learning is a large, complex topic. We focused on the basics in the chapter.

In the next chapter, we present the big data infrastructure that supports the kinds of AI technologies we've discussed in Chapters 12 through 15. We'll consider the Hadoop and Spark platforms for big data batch processing and real-time streaming applications. We'll look at relational databases and the SQL language for querying them—these have dominated the database field for many decades. We'll discuss how big data presents challenges that relational databases don't handle well, and consider how NoSQL databases are designed to handle those challenges. We'll conclude the book with a discussion of the Internet of Things (IoT), which will surely be the world's largest big-data source and will present many opportunities for entrepreneurs to develop leading-edge businesses that will truly make a difference in people's lives.

16

Big Data: Hadoop, Spark, NoSQL and IoT

Objectives

In this chapter you'll:

- Understand what big data is and how quickly it's getting bigger.
- Manipulate a SQLite relational database using Structured Query Language (SQL).
- Understand the four major types of NoSQL databases.
- Store tweets in a MongoDB NoSQL JSON document database and visualize them on a Folium map.
- Understand Apache Hadoop and how it's used in big-data batch-processing applications.
- Build a Hadoop MapReduce application on Microsoft's Azure HDInsight cloud service.
- Understand Apache Spark and how it's used in high-performance, real-time big-data applications.
- Use Spark streaming to process data in mini-batches.
- Understand the Internet of Things (IoT) and the publish/subscribe model.
- Publish messages from a simulated Internet-connected device and visualize its messages in a dashboard.
- Subscribe to PubNub's live Twitter and IoT streams and visualize the data.

16.1 Introduction

In Section 1.7, we introduced big data. In this capstone chapter, we discuss popular hardware and software infrastructure for working with big data, and we develop complete applications on several desktop and cloud-based big-data platforms.

Databases

Databases are critical big-data infrastructure for storing and manipulating the massive amounts of data we're creating. They're also critical for securely and confidentially maintaining that data, especially in the context of ever-stricter privacy laws such as **HIPAA** (**Health Insurance Portability and Accountability Act**) in the United States and **GDPR** (**General Data Protection Regulation**) for the European Union.

First, we'll present **relational databases**, which store **structured data** in tables with a fixed-size number of columns per row. You'll manipulate relational databases via **Structured Query Language (SQL)**.

Most data produced today is **unstructured data**, like the content of Facebook posts and Twitter tweets, or **semi-structured data** like JSON and XML documents. Twitter processes each tweet's contents into a semi-structured JSON document with lots of *metadata*, as you saw in the "Data Mining Twitter" chapter. Relational databases are not geared to the unstructured and semi-structured data in big-data applications. So, as big data evolved, new kinds of databases were created to handle such data efficiently. We'll discuss the four major types of these **NoSQL databases**—key–value, document, columnar and graph databases. Also, we'll overview **NewSQL databases**, which blend the benefits of relational and NoSQL databases. Many NoSQL and NewSQL vendors make it easy to get started with their products through free tiers and free trials, and typically in cloud-based environments that require minimal installation and setup. This makes it practical for you to gain big-data experience before "diving in."

Apache Hadoop

Much of today's data is so large that it cannot fit on one system. As big data grew, we needed distributed data storage and parallel processing capabilities to process the data more efficiently. This led to complex technologies like Apache Hadoop for distributed data processing with massive parallelism among clusters of computers where the intricate details are handled for you automatically and correctly. We'll discuss Hadoop, its architecture and how it's used in big-data applications. We'll guide you through configuring a multi-node Hadoop cluster using the Microsoft Azure HDInsight cloud service, then use it to execute a Hadoop MapReduce job that you'll implement in Python. Though HDInsight is not free, Microsoft gives you a generous new-account credit that should enable you to run the chapter's code examples without incurring additional charges.

Apache Spark

As big-data processing needs grow, the information-technology community is continually looking for ways to increase performance. Hadoop executes tasks by breaking them into pieces that do lots of disk I/O across many computers. Spark was developed as a way to perform certain big-data tasks *in memory* for better performance.

We'll discuss Apache Spark, its architecture and how it's used in high-performance, real-time big-data applications. You'll implement a Spark application using functional-style filter/map/reduce programming capabilities. First, you'll build this example using a Jupyter Docker stack that runs locally on your desktop computer, then you'll implement it using a cloud-based Microsoft Azure HDInsight multi-node Spark cluster.

We'll introduce Spark streaming for processing streaming data in mini-batches. Spark streaming gathers data for a short time interval you specify, then gives you that batch of data to process. You'll implement a Spark streaming application that processes tweets. In that example, you'll use Spark SQL to query data stored in a Spark `DataFrame` which, unlike pandas `DataFrame`s, may contain data distributed over many computers in a cluster.

Internet of Things

We'll conclude with an introduction to the Internet of Things (IoT)—billions of devices that are continuously producing data worldwide. We'll introduce the *publish/subscribe model* that IoT and other types of applications use to connect data users with data providers. First, without writing any code, you'll build a web-based dashboard using Freeboard.io and a sample live stream from the PubNub messaging service. Next, you'll simulate an Internet-connected thermostat which publishes messages to the free Dweet.io messaging service using the Python module Dweepy, then create a dashboard visualization of the data with Freeboard.io. Finally, you'll build a Python client that *subscribes* to a sample live stream from the PubNub service and dynamically visualizes the stream with Seaborn and a Matplotlib `FuncAnimation`.

Experience Cloud and Desktop Big-Data Software

Cloud vendors focus on **service-oriented architecture (SOA)** technology in which they provide "as-a-Service" capabilities that applications connect to and use in the cloud. Common services provided by cloud vendors include:[1]

"As-a-Service" acronyms (note that several are the same)	
Big data as a Service (BDaaS)	Platform as a Service (PaaS)
Hadoop as a Service (HaaS)	Software as a Service (SaaS)
Hardware as a Service (HaaS)	Storage as a Service (SaaS)
Infrastructure as a Service (IaaS)	Spark as a Service (SaaS)

You'll get hands-on experience in this chapter with several cloud-based tools. In this chapter's examples, you'll use the following platforms:

- A *free* MongoDB Atlas cloud-based cluster.

- A multi-node Hadoop cluster running on Microsoft's Azure HDInsight cloud-based service—for this you'll use the *credit* that comes with a new Azure account.

- A *free* single-node Spark "cluster" running on your desktop computer, using a Jupyter Docker-stack container.

- A multi-node Spark cluster, also running on Microsoft's Azure HDInsight—for this you'll continue using your Azure new-account *credit*.

There are many other options, including cloud-based services from Amazon Web Services, Google Cloud and IBM Watson, and the free *desktop* versions of the Hortonworks and Cloudera platforms (there also are cloud-based paid versions of these). You also could try a single-node Spark cluster running on the *free* cloud-based Databricks Community Edition. Spark's creators founded Databricks.

Always check the latest terms and conditions of each service you use. Some require you to enable credit-card billing to use their clusters. *Caution:* **Once you allocate Microsoft Azure HDInsight clusters (or other vendors' clusters), they incur costs. When you complete the case studies using services such as Microsoft Azure, be sure to delete your cluster(s) and their other resources (like storage). This will help extend the life of your Azure new-account credit.**

Installation and setups vary across platforms and over time. Always follow each vendor's latest steps. If you have questions, the best sources for help are the vendor's support capabilities and forums. Also, check sites such as stackoverflow.com—other people may have asked questions about similar problems and received answers from the developer community.

Algorithms and Data

Algorithms and data are the core of Python programming. The first few chapters of this book were mostly about algorithms. We introduced control statements and discussed algorithm development. Data was small—primarily individual integers, floats and strings.

1. For more "as-a-Service" acronyms, see https://en.wikipedia.org/wiki/Cloud_computing and https://en.wikipedia.org/wiki/As_a_service.

Chapters 5–9 emphasized *structuring* data into lists, tuples, dictionaries, sets, arrays and files.

Data's Meaning

But, what about the *meaning* of the data? Can we use the data to gain insights to better diagnose cancers? Save lives? Improve patients' quality of life? Reduce pollution? Conserve water? Increase crop yields? Reduce damage from devastating storms and fires? Develop better treatment regimens? Create jobs? Improve company profitability?

The data-science case studies of Chapters 11–15 all focused on AI. In this chapter, we focus on the big-data infrastructure that supports AI solutions. As the data used with these technologies continues growing exponentially, we want to learn from that data and do so at blazing speed. We'll accomplish these goals with a combination of sophisticated algorithms, hardware, software and networking designs. We've presented various machine-learning technologies, seeing that there are indeed great insights to be mined from data. With more data, and especially with big data, machine learning can be even more effective.

Big-Data Sources

The following articles and sites provide links to hundreds of free big data sources:

Big-data sources

"Awesome-Public-Datasets," GitHub.com,
  https://github.com/caesar0301/awesome-public-datasets.

"AWS Public Datasets," https://aws.amazon.com/public-datasets/.

"Big Data And AI: 30 Amazing (And Free) Public Data Sources For 2018," by B. Marr,
  https://www.forbes.com/sites/bernardmarr/2018/02/26/big-data-and-ai-30-amazing-and-free-public-data-sources-for-2018/.

"Datasets for Data Mining and Data Science," http://www.kdnuggets.com/datasets/index.html.

"Exploring Open Data Sets," https://datascience.berkeley.edu/open-data-sets/.

"Free Big Data Sources," Datamics, http://datamics.com/free-big-data-sources/.

Hadoop Illuminated, Chapter 16. Publicly Available Big Data Sets,
  http://hadoopilluminated.com/hadoop_illuminated/Public_Bigdata_Sets.html.

"List of Public Data Sources Fit for Machine Learning,"
  https://blog.bigml.com/list-of-public-data-sources-fit-for-machine-learning/.

"Open Data," Wikipedia, https://en.wikipedia.org/wiki/Open_data.

"Open Data 500 Companies," http://www.opendata500.com/us/list/.

"Other Interesting Resources/Big Data and Analytics Educational Resources and Research," B. Marr, http://computing.derby.ac.uk/bigdatares/?page_id=223.

"6 Amazing Sources of Practice Data Sets,"
  https://www.jigsawacademy.com/6-amazing-sources-of-practice-data-sets/.

"20 Big Data Repositories You Should Check Out," M. Krivanek,
  http://www.datasciencecentral.com/profiles/blogs/20-free-big-data-sources-everyone-should-check-out.

"70+ Websites to Get Large Data Repositories for Free,"
  http://bigdata-madesimple.com/70-websites-to-get-large-data-repositories-for-free/.

Big-data sources
"Ten Sources of Free Big Data on Internet," A. Brown, `https://www.linkedin.com/pulse/ten-sources-free-big-data-internet-alan-brown`.
"Top 20 Open Data Sources," `https://www.linkedin.com/pulse/top-20-open-data-sources-zygimantas-jacikevicius`.
"We're Setting Data, Code and APIs Free," NASA, `https://open.nasa.gov/open-data/`.
"Where Can I Find Large Datasets Open to the Public?" Quora, `https://www.quora.com/Where-can-I-find-large-datasets-open-to-the-public`.

16.2 Relational Databases and Structured Query Language (SQL)

Databases are crucial, especially for big data. In Chapter 9, we demonstrated sequential text-file processing, working with data from CSV files and working with JSON. Both are useful when *most or all* of a file's data is to be processed. On the other hand, in transaction processing we need to locate and, possibly, update an *individual* data item quickly.

A **database** is an integrated collection of data. A **database management system (DBMS)** provides mechanisms for storing and organizing data in a manner consistent with the database's format. Database management systems allow for convenient access and storage of data without concern for the internal representation of databases.

Relational database management systems (RDBMSs) store data in **tables** and define relationships among the tables. Structured Query Language (SQL) is used almost universally with relational database systems to manipulate data and perform **queries**, which request information that satisfies given criteria.[2]

Popular *open-source* RDBMSs include SQLite, PostgreSQL, MariaDB and MySQL. These can be downloaded and used *freely* by anyone. All have support for Python. We'll use SQLite, which is bundled with Python. Some popular proprietary RDBMSs include Microsoft SQL Server, Oracle, Sybase and IBM Db2.

Tables, Rows and Columns

A relational database is a logical table-based representation of data that allows the data to be accessed without consideration of its physical structure. The following diagram shows a sample Employee table that might be used in a personnel system:

	Number	Name	Department	Salary	Location
	23603	Jones	413	1100	New Jersey
	24568	Kerwin	413	2000	New Jersey
Row {	34589	Larson	642	1800	Los Angeles
	35761	Myers	611	1400	Orlando
	47132	Neumann	413	9000	New Jersey
	78321	Stephens	611	8500	Orlando

Primary key   Column

---

2. The writing in this chapter assumes that SQL is pronounced as "see-quel." Some prefer "ess que el."

The table's primary purpose is to store employees' attributes. Tables are composed of **rows**, each describing a single entity. Here, each row represents one employee. Rows are composed of **columns** containing individual attribute values. The table above has six rows. The Number column represents the **primary key**—a column (or group of columns) with a value that's *unique* for each row. This guarantees that each row can be identified by its primary key. Examples of primary keys are Social Security numbers, employee ID numbers and part numbers in an inventory system—values in each of these are guaranteed to be unique. In this case, the rows are listed in ascending order by primary key, but they could be listed in descending order or no particular order at all.

Each column represents a different data attribute. Rows are unique (by primary key) within a table, but particular column values may be duplicated between rows. For example, three different rows in the Employee table's Department column contain number 413.

Selecting Data Subsets
Different database users are often interested in different data and different relationships among the data. Most users require only subsets of the rows and columns. Queries specify which subsets of the data to select from a table. You use Structured Query Language (SQL) to define queries. For example, you might select data from the Employee table to create a result that shows where each department is located, presenting the data sorted in increasing order by department number. This result is shown below. We'll discuss SQL shortly.

```
Department       Location

413              New Jersey
611              Orlando
642              Los Angeles
```

SQLite
The code examples in the rest of Section 16.2 use the open-source SQLite database management system that's included with Python, but most popular database systems have Python support. Each typically provides a module that adheres to Python's **Database Application Programming Interface (DB-API)**, which specifies common object and method names for manipulating any database.

16.2.1 A books Database
In this section, we'll present a books database containing information about several of our books. We'll set up the database in SQLite via the Python Standard Library's **sqlite3 module**, using a script provided in the ch16 example's folder's sql subfolder. Then, we'll introduce the database's tables. We'll use this database in an IPython session to introduce various database concepts, including operations that **create**, **read**, **update** and **delete** data—the so-called **CRUD** operations. As we introduce the tables, we'll use SQL and pandas DataFrames to show you each table's contents. Then, in the next several sections, we'll discuss additional SQL features.

Creating the books Database
In your Anaconda Command Prompt, Terminal or shell, change to the ch16 examples folder's sql subfolder. The following **sqlite3 command** creates a SQLite database named

`books.db` and executes the `books.sql` SQL script, which defines how to create the database's tables and populates them with data:

```
sqlite3 books.db < books.sql
```

The notation `<` indicates that `books.sql` is input into the `sqlite3` command. When the command completes, the database is ready for use. Begin a new IPython session.

Connecting to the Database in Python

To work with the database in Python, first call `sqlite3`'s **connect function** to connect to the database and obtain a **Connection** object:

```
In [1]: import sqlite3

In [2]: connection = sqlite3.connect('books.db')
```

authors Table

The database has three tables—authors, `author_ISBN` and `titles`. The authors table stores all the authors and has three columns:

- id—The author's unique ID number. This integer column is defined as **autoincremented**—for each row inserted in the table, SQLite increases the id value by 1 to ensure that each row has a unique value. This column is the table's primary key.

- first—The author's first name (a string).

- last—The author's last name (a string).

Viewing the authors Table's Contents

Let's use a SQL query and pandas to view the authors table's contents:

```
In [3]: import pandas as pd

In [4]: pd.options.display.max_columns = 10

In [5]: pd.read_sql('SELECT * FROM authors', connection,
   ...:                index_col=['id'])
   ...:
Out[5]:
         first    last
id
1         Paul  Deitel
2       Harvey  Deitel
3        Abbey  Deitel
4          Dan   Quirk
5    Alexander    Wald
```

Pandas function **read_sql** executes a SQL query and returns a DataFrame containing the query's results. The function's arguments are:

- a string representing the SQL query to execute,

- the SQLite database's Connection object, and in this case

- an `index_col` keyword argument indicating which column should be used as the DataFrame's row indices (the author's id values in this case).

As you'll see momentarily, when `index_col` is not passed, index values starting from 0 appear to the left of the DataFrame's rows.

A SQL **SELECT** query gets rows and columns from one or more tables in a database. In the query:

```
SELECT * FROM authors
```

the **asterisk** (*) is a *wildcard* indicating that the query should get *all* the columns from the authors table. We'll discuss SELECT queries in more detail shortly.

titles Table

The titles table stores all the books and has four columns:

- isbn—The book's ISBN (a string) is this table's primary key. ISBN is an abbreviation for "International Standard Book Number," which is a numbering scheme that publishers use to give every book a unique identification number.

- title—The book's title (a string).

- edition—The book's edition number (an integer).

- copyright—The book's copyright year (a string).

Let's use SQL and pandas to view the titles table's contents:

```
In [6]: pd.read_sql('SELECT * FROM titles', connection)
Out[6]:
        isbn                                title   edition  copyright
0  0135404673        Intro to Python for CS and DS        1       2020
1  0132151006        Internet & WWW How to Program        5       2012
2  0134743350                 Java How to Program       11       2018
3  0133976890                    C How to Program        8       2016
4  0133406954    Visual Basic 2012 How to Program        6       2014
5  0134601548           Visual C# How to Program        6       2017
6  0136151574          Visual C++ How to Program        2       2008
7  0134448235                  C++ How to Program       10       2017
8  0134444302              Android How to Program        3       2017
9  0134289366            Android 6 for Programmers        3       2016
```

author_ISBN Table

The author_ISBN table uses the following columns to associate authors from the authors table with their books in the titles table:

- id—An author's id (an integer).

- isbn—The book's ISBN (a string).

The id column is a **foreign key**, which is a column in this table that matches a *primary-key* column in another table—in particular, the authors table's id column. The isbn column also is a foreign key—it matches the titles table's isbn primary-key column. A database might have many tables. A goal when designing a database is to *minimize* data *duplication* among the tables. To do this, each table represents a specific entity, and foreign keys help link the data in *multiple* tables. The primary keys and foreign keys are designated when you create the database tables (in our case, in the books.sql script).

Together the id and isbn columns in this table form a *composite primary key*. Every row in this table *uniquely* matches *one* author to *one* book's ISBN. This table contains many entries, so let's use SQL and pandas to view just the first five rows:

```
In [7]: df = pd.read_sql('SELECT * FROM author_ISBN', connection)

In [8]: df.head()
Out[8]:
   id        isbn
0   1  0134289366
1   2  0134289366
2   5  0134289366
3   1  0135404673
4   2  0135404673
```

Every foreign-key value must appear as the primary-key value in a row of another table so the DBMS can ensure that the foreign-key value is valid. This is known as the **Rule of Referential Integrity**. For example, the DBMS ensures that the id value for a particular author_ISBN row is valid by checking that there is a row in the authors table with that id as the primary key.

Foreign keys also allow *related* data in *multiple* tables to be *selected* from those tables and combined—this is known as **joining** the data. There is a **one-to-many relationship** between a primary key and a corresponding foreign key—one author can write many books, and similarly one book can be written by many authors. So a foreign key can appear *many* times in its table but only *once* (as the primary key) in another table. For example, in the books database, the ISBN 0134289366 appears in several author_ISBN rows because this book has several authors, but it appears only once as a primary key in titles.

Entity-Relationship (ER) Diagram

The following **entity-relationship (ER) diagram** for the books database shows the database's *tables* and the *relationships* among them:

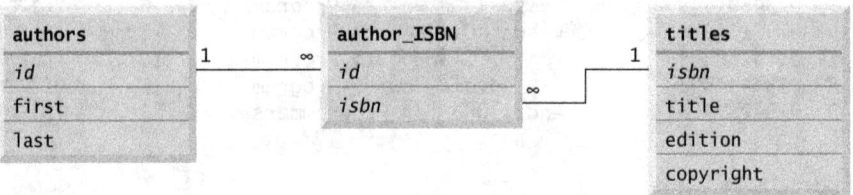

The first compartment in each box contains the table's name, and the remaining compartments contain the table's columns. The names in italic are primary keys. *A table's primary key uniquely identifies each row in the table.* Every row must have a primary-key value, and that value must be unique in the table. This is known as the **Rule of Entity Integrity**. Again, for the author_ISBN table, the primary key is the combination of both columns—this is known as a composite primary key.

The lines connecting the tables represent the *relationships* among the tables. Consider the line between authors and author_ISBN. On the authors end there's a 1, and on the author_ISBN end there's an infinity symbol (∞). This indicates a *one-to-many relationship*. For *each* author in the authors table, there can be an *arbitrary number* of ISBNs for books written by that author in the author_ISBN table—that is, an author can write *any* number of books, so an author's id can appear in multiple rows of the author_ISBN table. The relationship line links the id column in the authors table (where id is the primary key) to the id column in the author_ISBN table (where id is a foreign key). The line between the tables links the primary key to the matching foreign key.

The line between the `titles` and `author_ISBN` tables illustrates a *one-to-many rela-tionship*—one book can be written by many authors. The line links the primary key `isbn` in table `titles` to the corresponding foreign key in table `author_ISBN`. The relationships in the entity-relationship diagram illustrate that the sole purpose of the `author_ISBN` table is to provide a **many-to-many relationship** between the `authors` and `titles` tables—an author can write *many* books, and a book can have *many* authors.

SQL Keywords

The following subsections continue our SQL presentation in the context of our books database, demonstrating SQL queries and statements using the SQL keywords in the fol-lowing table. Other SQL keywords are beyond this text's scope:

SQL keyword	Description
SELECT	Retrieves data from one or more tables.
FROM	Tables involved in the query. Required in every SELECT.
WHERE	Criteria for selection that determine the rows to be retrieved, deleted or updated. Optional in a SQL statement.
GROUP BY	Criteria for grouping rows. Optional in a SELECT query.
ORDER BY	Criteria for ordering rows. Optional in a SELECT query.
INNER JOIN	Merge rows from multiple tables.
INSERT	Insert rows into a specified table.
UPDATE	Update rows in a specified table.
DELETE	Delete rows from a specified table.

16.2.2 SELECT Queries

The previous section used SELECT statements and the `*` wildcard character to get all the columns from a table. Typically, you need only a subset of the columns, especially in big data where you could have dozens, hundreds, thousands or more columns. To retrieve only specific columns, specify a comma-separated list of column names. For example, let's retrieve only the columns `first` and `last` from the `authors` table:

```
In [9]: pd.read_sql('SELECT first, last FROM authors', connection)
Out[9]:
        first    last
0        Paul   Deitel
1      Harvey   Deitel
2       Abbey   Deitel
3         Dan    Quirk
4   Alexander    Wald
```

16.2.3 WHERE Clause

You'll often select rows in a database that satisfy certain **selection criteria**, especially in big data where a database might contain millions or billions of rows. Only rows that satisfy the selection criteria (formally called **predicates**) are selected. SQL's **WHERE clause** specifies a query's selection criteria. Let's select the `title`, `edition` and `copyright` for all books with copyright years greater than 2016. String values in SQL queries are delimited by single (') quotes, as in '2016':

```
In [10]: pd.read_sql("""SELECT title, edition, copyright
    ...:                 FROM titles
    ...:                 WHERE copyright > '2016'""", connection)
Out[10]:
                             title  edition  copyright
0     Intro to Python for CS and DS       1       2020
1                Java How to Program      11       2018
2            Visual C# How to Program      6       2017
3                 C++ How to Program      10       2017
4              Android How to Program      3       2017
```

Pattern Matching: Zero or More Characters

The WHERE clause may can contain the operators <, >, <=, >=, =, <> (not equal) and LIKE. Operator **LIKE** is used for **pattern matching**—searching for strings that match a given pattern. A pattern that contains the **percent (%)** wildcard character searches for strings that have *zero or more* characters at the percent character's position in the pattern. For example, let's locate all authors whose last name starts with the letter D:

```
In [11]: pd.read_sql("""SELECT id, first, last
    ...:                 FROM authors
    ...:                 WHERE last LIKE 'D%'""",
    ...:     connection, index_col=['id'])
    ...:
Out[11]:
       first    last
id
1       Paul  Deitel
2     Harvey  Deitel
3      Abbey  Deitel
```

Pattern Matching: Any Character

An **underscore (_)** in the pattern string indicates a single wildcard character at that position. Let's select the rows of all the authors whose last names start with any character, followed by the letter b, followed by any number of additional characters (specified by %):

```
In [12]: pd.read_sql("""SELECT id, first, last
    ...:                 FROM authors
    ...:                 WHERE first LIKE '_b%'""",
    ...:     connection, index_col=['id'])
    ...:
Out[12]:
       first    last
id
3      Abbey  Deitel
```

16.2.4 ORDER BY Clause

The **ORDER BY clause** sorts a query's results into ascending order (lowest to highest) or descending order (highest to lowest), specified with ASC and DESC, respectively. The default sorting order is ascending, so ASC is optional. Let's sort the titles in ascending order:

```
In [13]: pd.read_sql('SELECT title FROM titles ORDER BY title ASC',
    ...:                        connection)
Out[13]:
                                 title
0              Android 6 for Programmers
1              Android How to Program
2                     C How to Program
3                   C++ How to Program
4       Internet & WWW How to Program
5       Intro to Python for CS and DS
6                  Java How to Program
7  Visual Basic 2012 How to Program
8              Visual C# How to Program
9             Visual C++ How to Program
```

Sorting By Multiple Columns

To sort by multiple columns, specify a comma-separated list of column names after the ORDER BY keywords. Let's sort the authors' names by last name, then by first name for any authors who have the same last name:

```
In [14]: pd.read_sql("""SELECT id, first, last
    ...:                      FROM authors
    ...:                      ORDER BY last, first""",
    ...:              connection, index_col=['id'])
    ...:
Out[14]:
          first     last
id
3         Abbey   Deitel
2        Harvey   Deitel
1          Paul   Deitel
4           Dan    Quirk
5     Alexander     Wald
```

The sorting order can vary by column. Let's sort the authors in descending order by last name and ascending order by first name for any authors who have the same last name:

```
In [15]: pd.read_sql("""SELECT id, first, last
    ...:                      FROM authors
    ...:                      ORDER BY last DESC, first ASC""",
    ...:              connection, index_col=['id'])
    ...:
Out[15]:
          first     last
id
5     Alexander     Wald
4           Dan    Quirk
3         Abbey   Deitel
2        Harvey   Deitel
1          Paul   Deitel
```

Combining the WHERE and ORDER BY Clauses

The WHERE and ORDER BY clauses can be combined in one query. Let's get the isbn, title, edition and copyright of each book in the titles table that has a title ending with 'How to Program' and sort them in ascending order by title.

```
In [16]: pd.read_sql("""SELECT isbn, title, edition, copyright
    ...:                 FROM titles
    ...:                 WHERE title LIKE '%How to Program'
    ...:                 ORDER BY title""", connection)
Out[16]:
         isbn                            title  edition  copyright
0  0134444302             Android How to Program       3       2017
1  0133976890                   C How to Program       8       2016
2  0134448235                 C++ How to Program      10       2017
3  0132151006       Internet & WWW How to Program    5       2012
4  0134743350                Java How to Program      11       2018
5  0133406954  Visual Basic 2012 How to Program      6       2014
6  0134601548          Visual C# How to Program       6       2017
7  0136151574         Visual C++ How to Program       2       2008
```

16.2.5 Merging Data from Multiple Tables: INNER JOIN

Recall that the books database's author_ISBN table links authors to their corresponding titles. If we did not separate this information into individual tables, we'd need to include author information with each entry in the titles table. This would result in storing *duplicate* author information for authors who wrote multiple books.

You can merge data from multiple tables, referred to as joining the tables, with **INNER JOIN**. Let's produce a list of authors accompanied by the ISBNs for books written by each author—because there are many results for this query, we show just the head of the result:

```
In [17]: pd.read_sql("""SELECT first, last, isbn
    ...:                 FROM authors
    ...:                 INNER JOIN author_ISBN
    ...:                     ON authors.id = author_ISBN.id
    ...:                 ORDER BY last, first""", connection).head()
Out[17]:
    first    last        isbn
0   Abbey  Deitel  0132151006
1   Abbey  Deitel  0133406954
2  Harvey  Deitel  0134289366
3  Harvey  Deitel  0135404673
4  Harvey  Deitel  0132151006
```

The INNER JOIN's **ON clause** uses a primary-key column in one table and a foreign-key column in the other to determine which rows to merge from each table. This query merges the authors table's first and last columns with the author_ISBN table's isbn column and sorts the results in ascending order by last then first.

Note the syntax authors.id *(table_name.column_name)* in the ON clause. This **qualified name** syntax is required if the columns have the same name in both tables. This syntax can be used in any SQL statement to distinguish columns in different tables that have the same name. In some systems, table names qualified with the database name can be used to perform cross-database queries. As always, the query can contain an ORDER BY clause.

16.2.6 INSERT INTO Statement

To this point, you've queried existing data. Sometimes you'll execute SQL statements that *modify* the database. To do so, you'll use a sqlite3 **Cursor** object, which you obtain by calling the Connection's **cursor** method:

```
In [18]: cursor = connection.cursor()
```

The pandas method read_sql actually uses a Cursor behind the scenes to execute queries and access the rows of the results.

The **INSERT INTO** statement inserts a row into a table. Let's insert a new author named Sue Red into the authors table by calling Cursor method **execute**, which executes its SQL argument and returns the Cursor:

```
In [19]: cursor = cursor.execute("""INSERT INTO authors (first, last)
    ...:                             VALUES ('Sue', 'Red')""")
    ...:
```

The SQL keywords INSERT INTO are followed by the table in which to insert the new row and a comma-separated list of column names in parentheses. The list of column names is followed by the SQL keyword **VALUES** and a comma-separated list of values in parentheses. The values provided must match the column names specified both in order and type.

We do not specify a value for the id column because it's an autoincremented column in the authors table—this was specified in the script books.sql that created the table. For every new row, SQLite assigns a unique id value that is the next value in the autoincremented sequence (i.e., 1, 2, 3 and so on). In this case, Sue Red is assigned id number 6. To confirm this, let's query the authors table's contents:

```
In [20]: pd.read_sql('SELECT id, first, last FROM authors',
    ...:              connection, index_col=['id'])
    ...:
Out[20]:
        first    last
id
1        Paul  Deitel
2      Harvey  Deitel
3       Abbey  Deitel
4         Dan   Quirk
5   Alexander    Wald
6         Sue     Red
```

Note Regarding Strings That Contain Single Quotes

SQL delimits strings with single quotes ('). A string containing a single quote, such as O'Malley, must have *two* single quotes in the position where the single quote appears (e.g., 'O''Malley'). The first acts as an escape character for the second. Not escaping single-quote characters in a string that's part of a SQL statement is a SQL syntax error.

16.2.7 UPDATE Statement

An **UPDATE** statement modifies existing values. Let's assume that Sue Red's last name is incorrect in the database and update it to 'Black':

```
In [21]: cursor = cursor.execute("""UPDATE authors SET last='Black'
    ...:                            WHERE last='Red' AND first='Sue'""")
```

The UPDATE keyword is followed by the table to update, the keyword **SET** and a comma-separated list of *column_name = value* pairs indicating the columns to change and their new values. The change will be applied to *every* row if you do not specify a WHERE clause. The WHERE clause in this query indicates that we should update only rows in which the last name is 'Red' and the first name is 'Sue'.

Of course, there could be multiple people with the same first and last name. To make a change to only one row, it's best to use the row's unique primary key in the WHERE clause. In this case, we could have specified:

```
WHERE id = 6
```

For statements that modify the database, the Cursor object's rowcount attribute contains an integer value representing the number of rows that were modified. If this value is 0, no changes were made. The following confirms that the UPDATE modified one row:

```
In [22]: cursor.rowcount
Out[22]: 1
```

We also can confirm the update by listing the authors table's contents:

```
In [23]: pd.read_sql('SELECT id, first, last FROM authors',
    ...:              connection, index_col=['id'])
    ...:
Out[23]:
        first    last
id
1         Paul  Deitel
2       Harvey  Deitel
3        Abbey  Deitel
4          Dan   Quirk
5    Alexander    Wald
6          Sue   Black
```

16.2.8 DELETE FROM Statement

A SQL **DELETE FROM** statement removes rows from a table. Let's remove Sue Black from the authors table using her author ID:

```
In [24]: cursor = cursor.execute('DELETE FROM authors WHERE id=6')

In [25]: cursor.rowcount
Out[25]: 1
```

The optional WHERE clause determines which rows to delete. If WHERE is omitted, all the table's rows are deleted. Here's the authors table after the DELETE operation:

```
In [26]: pd.read_sql('SELECT id, first, last FROM authors',
    ...:              connection, index_col=['id'])
    ...:
Out[26]:
        first    last
id
1         Paul  Deitel
2       Harvey  Deitel
3        Abbey  Deitel
4          Dan   Quirk
5    Alexander    Wald
```

Closing the Database
When you no longer need access to the database, you should call the Connection's **close** method to disconnect from the database:

```
connection.close()
```

SQL in Big Data

SQL's importance is growing in big data. Later in this chapter, we'll use Spark SQL to query data in a Spark DataFrame for which the data may be distributed over many computers in a Spark cluster. As you'll see, Spark SQL looks much like the SQL presented in this section.

16.3 NoSQL and NewSQL Big-Data Databases: A Brief Tour

For decades, relational database management systems have been the standard in data processing. However, they require *structured data* that fits into neat rectangular tables. As the size of the data and the number of tables and relationships increases, relational databases become more difficult to manipulate efficiently. In today's big-data world, NoSQL and NewSQL databases have emerged to deal with the kinds of data storage and processing demands that traditional relational databases cannot meet. Big data requires massive databases, often spread across data centers worldwide in huge clusters of commodity computers. According to statista.com, there are currently over 8 million data centers worldwide.[3]

NoSQL originally meant what its name implies. With the growing importance of SQL in big data—such as SQL on Hadoop and Spark SQL—NoSQL now is said to stand for "Not Only SQL." NoSQL databases are meant for unstructured data, like photos, videos and the natural language found in e-mails, text messages and social-media posts, and semi-structured data like JSON and XML documents. Semi-structured data often wraps unstructured data with additional information called **metadata**. For example, YouTube videos are unstructured data, but YouTube also maintains metadata for each video, including who posted it, when it was posted, a title, a description, tags that help people discover the videos, privacy settings and more—all returned as JSON from the YouTube APIs. This metadata adds structure to the unstructured video data, making it semi-structured.

The next several subsections overview the four NoSQL database categories—key–value, document, columnar (also called column-based) and graph. In addition, we'll overview NewSQL databases, which blend features of relational and NoSQL databases. In Section 16.4, we'll present a case study in which we store and manipulate a large number of JSON tweet objects in a NoSQL document database, then summarize the data in an interactive visualization displayed on a Folium map of the United States.

16.3.1 NoSQL Key–Value Databases

Like Python dictionaries, **key–value databases**[4] store key–value pairs, but they're optimized for distributed systems and big-data processing. For reliability, they tend to replicate data in multiple cluster nodes. Some key–value databases, such as Redis, are implemented in memory for performance, and others store data on disk, such as HBase, which runs on top of Hadoop's HDFS distributed file system. Other popular key–value databases include Amazon DynamoDB, Google Cloud Datastore and Couchbase. DynamoDB and Couchbase are **multi-model databases** that also support documents. HBase is also a column-oriented database.

---

3.   https://www.statista.com/statistics/500458/worldwide-datacenter-and-it-sites/.
4.   https://en.wikipedia.org/wiki/Key-value_database.

16.3.2 NoSQL Document Databases

A **document database**[5] stores semi-structured data, such as JSON or XML documents. In document databases, you typically add indexes for specific attributes, so you can more efficiently locate and manipulate documents. For example, let's assume you're storing JSON documents produced by IoT devices and each document contains a type attribute. You might add an index for this attribute so you can filter documents based on their types. Without indexes, you can still perform that task, it will just be slower because you have to search each document in its entirety to find the attribute.

The most popular document database (and most popular overall NoSQL database[6]) is **MongoDB**, whose name derives from a sequence of letters embedded in the word "hu**mongo**us." In an example, we'll store a large number of tweets in MongoDB for processing. Recall that Twitter's APIs return tweets in JSON format, so they can be stored directly in MongoDB. After obtaining the tweets we'll summarize them in a pandas Data-Frame and on a Folium map. Other popular document databases include Amazon DynamoDB (also a key–value database), Microsoft Azure Cosmos DB and Apache CouchDB.

16.3.3 NoSQL Columnar Databases

In a relational database, a common query operation is to get a specific column's value for every row. Because data is organized into rows, a query that selects a specific column can perform poorly. The database system must get every matching row, locate the required column and discard the rest of the row's information. A **columnar database**[7,8], also called a **column-oriented database**, is similar to a relational database, but it stores structured data in columns rather than rows. Because all of a column's elements are stored together, selecting all the data for a given column is more efficient.

Consider our authors table in the books database:

```
          first     last
id
1          Paul    Deitel
2        Harvey    Deitel
3         Abbey    Deitel
4           Dan    Quirk
5     Alexander     Wald
```

In a relational database, all the data for a row is stored together. If we consider each row as a Python tuple, the rows would be represented as (1, 'Paul', 'Deitel'), (2, 'Harvey', 'Deitel'), etc. In a columnar database, all the values for a given column would be stored together, as in (1, 2, 3, 4, 5), ('Paul', 'Harvey', 'Abbey', 'Dan', 'Alexander') and ('Deitel', 'Deitel', 'Deitel', 'Quirk', 'Wald'). The elements in each column are maintained in row order, so the value at a given index in each column belongs to the same row. Popular columnar databases include MariaDB ColumnStore and HBase.

---

5. https://en.wikipedia.org/wiki/Document-oriented_database.
6. https://db-engines.com/en/ranking.
7. https://en.wikipedia.org/wiki/Columnar_database.
8. https://www.predictiveanalyticstoday.com/top-wide-columnar-store-databases/.

16.3.4 NoSQL Graph Databases

A graph models relationships between objects.[9] The objects are called **nodes** (or **vertices**) and the relationships are called **edges**. Edges are *directional.* For example, an edge representing an airline flight points from the origin city to the destination city, but not the reverse. A **graph database**[10] stores nodes, edges and their attributes.

If you use social networks, like Instagram, Snapchat, Twitter and Facebook, consider your social graph, which consists of the people you know (nodes) and the relationships between them (edges). Every person has their own social graph, and these are interconnected. The famous "six degrees of separation" problem says that any two people in the world are connected to one another by following a maximum of six edges in the worldwide social graph.[11] Facebook's algorithms use the social graphs of their billions of monthly active users[12] to determine which stories should appear in each user's news feed. By looking at your interests, your friends, their interests and more, Facebook predicts the stories they believe are most relevant to you.[13]

Many companies use similar techniques to create recommendation engines. When you browse a product on Amazon, they use a graph of users and products to show you comparable products people browsed before making a purchase. When you browse movies on Netflix, they use a graph of users and movies they liked to suggest movies that might be of interest to you.

One of the most popular graph databases is Neo4j. Many real-world use-cases for graph databases are provided at:

```
https://neo4j.com/graphgists/
```

With most of the use-cases, sample graph diagrams produced by Neo4j are shown. These visualize the relationships between the graph nodes. Check out Neo4j's free PDF book, *Graph Databases*.[14]

16.3.5 NewSQL Databases

Key advantages of relational databases include their security and transaction support. In particular, relational databases typically use **ACID (Atomicity, Consistency, Isolation, Durability)**[15] transactions:

- *Atomicity* ensures that the database is modified only if *all* of a transaction's steps are successful. If you go to an ATM to withdraw $100, that money is not removed from your account unless you have enough money to cover the withdrawal *and* there is enough money in the ATM to satisfy your request.

- *Consistency* ensures that the database state is always valid. In the withdrawal example above, your new account balance after the transaction will reflect precisely what you withdrew from your account (and possibly ATM fees).

9.   https://en.wikipedia.org/wiki/Graph_theory.
10. https://en.wikipedia.org/wiki/Graph_database.
11. https://en.wikipedia.org/wiki/Six_degrees_of_separation.
12. https://zephoria.com/top-15-valuable-facebook-statistics/.
13. https://newsroom.fb.com/news/2018/05/inside-feed-news-feed-ranking/.
14. https://neo4j.com/graph-databases-book-sx2.
15. https://en.wikipedia.org/wiki/ACID_(computer_science).

- *Isolation* ensures that concurrent transactions occur as if they were performed sequentially. For example, if two people share a joint bank account and both attempt to withdraw money at the same time from two separate ATMs, one transaction must wait until the other completes.

- *Durability* ensures that changes to the database survive even hardware failures.

If you research benefits and disadvantages of NoSQL databases, you'll see that NoSQL databases generally do not provide ACID support. The types of applications that use NoSQL databases typically do not require the guarantees that ACID-compliant databases provide. Many NoSQL databases typically adhere to the **BASE (Basic Availability, Soft-state, Eventual consistency)** model, which focuses more on the database's availability. Whereas, ACID databases guarantee consistency when you write to the database, BASE databases provide consistency at some later point in time.

NewSQL databases blend the benefits of both relational and NoSQL databases for big-data processing tasks. Some popular NewSQL databases include VoltDB, MemSQL, Apache Ignite and Google Spanner.

16.4 Case Study: A MongoDB JSON Document Database

MongoDB is a document database capable of storing and retrieving JSON documents. Twitter's APIs return tweets to you as JSON objects, which you can write directly into a MongoDB database. In this section, you'll:

- use Tweepy to stream tweets about the 100 U.S. senators and store them into a MongoDB database,

- use pandas to summarize the top 10 senators by tweet activity and

- display an interactive Folium map of the United States with one popup marker per state that shows the state name and both senators' names, their political parties and tweet counts.

You'll use a free cloud-based MongoDB Atlas cluster, which requires no installation and currently allows you to store up to 512MB of data. To store more, you can download the MongoDB Community Server from:

```
https://www.mongodb.com/download-center/community
```

and run it locally or you can sign up for MongoDB's *paid* Atlas service.

Installing the Python Libraries Required for Interacting with MongoDB
You'll use the **pymongo library** to interact with MongoDB databases from your Python code. You'll also need the dnspython library to connect to a MongoDB Atlas Cluster. To install these libraries, use the following commands:

```
conda install -c conda-forge pymongo
conda install -c conda-forge dnspython
```

keys.py
The ch16 examples folder's TwitterMongoDB subfolder contains this example's code and keys.py file. Edit this file to include your Twitter credentials and your OpenMapQuest

key from the "Data Mining Twitter" chapter. After we discuss creating a MongoDB Atlas cluster, you'll also need to add your MongoDB connection string to this file.

16.4.1 Creating the MongoDB Atlas Cluster

To sign up for a free account go to

```
https://mongodb.com
```

then enter your email address and click **Get started free.** On the next page, enter your name and create a password, then read their terms of service. If you agree, click **Get started free** on this page and you'll be taken to the screen for setting up your cluster. Click **Build my first cluster** to get started.

They walk you through the getting started steps with popup bubbles that describe and point you to each task you need to complete. They provide default settings for their free Atlas cluster (**M0** as they refer to it), so just give your cluster a name in the **Cluster Name** section, then click **Create Cluster.** At this point, they'll take you to the **Clusters** page and begin creating your new cluster, which takes several minutes.

Next, a **Connect to Atlas** popup tutorial will appear, showing a checklist of additional steps required to get you up and running:

- **Create your first database user**—This enables you to log into your cluster.

- **Whitelist your IP address**—This is a security measure which ensures that only IP addresses you verify are allowed to interact with your cluster. To connect to this cluster from multiple locations (school, home, work, etc.), you'll need to whitelist each IP address from which you intend to connect.

- **Connect to your cluster**—In this step, you'll locate your cluster's connection string, which will enable your Python code to connect to the server.

Creating Your First Database User

In the popup tutorial window, click **Create your first database user** to continue the tutorial, then follow the on-screen prompts to view the cluster's **Security** tab and click **+ ADD NEW USER.** In the **Add New User** dialog, create a username and password. Write these down—you'll need them momentarily. Click **Add User** to return to the **Connect to Atlas** popup tutorial.

Whitelist Your IP Address

In the popup tutorial window, click **Whitelist your IP address** to continue the tutorial, then follow the on-screen prompts to view the cluster's **IP Whitelist** and click **+ ADD IP ADDRESS.** In the **Add Whitelist Entry** dialog, you can either add your computer's current IP address or allow access from anywhere, which they do not recommend for production databases, but is OK for learning purposes. Click **ALLOW ACCESS FROM ANYWHERE** then click **Confirm** to return to the **Connect to Atlas** popup tutorial.

Connect to Your Cluster

In the popup tutorial window, click **Connect to your cluster** to continue the tutorial, then follow the on-screen prompts to view the cluster's **Connect to** *YourClusterName* dialog. Connecting to a MongoDB Atlas database from Python requires a connection string. To get your connection string, click **Connect Your Application**, then click **Short SRV connec-**

tion string. Your connection string will appear below **Copy the SRV address**. Click **COPY** to copy the string. Paste this string into the keys.py file as mongo_connection_string's value. Replace "<PASSWORD>" in the connection string with your password, and replace the database name "test" with "senators", which will be the database name in this example. At the bottom of the **Connect to *YourClusterName***, click **Close**. You're now ready to interact with your Atlas cluster.

16.4.2 Streaming Tweets into MongoDB

First we'll present an interactive IPython session that connects to the MongoDB database, downloads current tweets via Twitter streaming and summarizes the top-10 senators by tweet count. Next, we'll present class TweetListener, which handles the incoming tweets and stores their JSON in MongoDB. Finally, we'll continue the IPython session by creating an interactive Folium map that displays information from the tweets we stored.

Use Tweepy to Authenticate with Twitter
First, let's use Tweepy to authenticate with Twitter:

```
In [1]: import tweepy, keys

In [2]: auth = tweepy.OAuthHandler(
   ...:     keys.consumer_key, keys.consumer_secret)
   ...: auth.set_access_token(keys.access_token,
   ...:     keys.access_token_secret)
   ...:
```

Next, configure the Tweepy API object to wait if our app reaches any Twitter rate limits.

```
In [3]: api = tweepy.API(auth, wait_on_rate_limit=True,
   ...:                  wait_on_rate_limit_notify=True)
   ...:
```

Loading the Senators' Data
We'll use the information in the file senators.csv (located in the ch16 examples folder's TwitterMongoDB subfolder) to track tweets to, from and about every U.S. senator. The file contains the senator's two-letter state code, name, party, Twitter handle and Twitter ID.

Twitter enables you to follow specific users via their numeric Twitter IDs, but these must be submitted as string representations of those numeric values. So, let's load senators.csv into pandas, convert the TwitterID values to strings (using Series method **astype**) and display several rows of data. In this case, we set 6 as the maximum number of columns to display. Later we'll add another column to the DataFrame and this setting will ensure that all the columns are displayed, rather than a few with ... in between:

```
In [4]: import pandas as pd

In [5]: senators_df = pd.read_csv('senators.csv')

In [6]: senators_df['TwitterID'] = senators_df['TwitterID'].astype(str)

In [7]: pd.options.display.max_columns = 6
```

```
In [8]: senators_df.head()
Out[8]:
   State           Name Party    TwitterHandle            TwitterID
0    AL  Richard Shelby     R       SenShelby             21111098
1    AL     Doug Jomes     D    SenDougJones  941080085121175552
2    AK  Lisa Murkowski     R    lisamurkowski             18061669
3    AK    Dan Sullivan     R  SenDanSullivan           2891210047
4    AZ         Jon Kyl     R       SenJonKyl             24905240
```

Configuring the `MongoClient`

To store the tweet's JSON as documents in a MongoDB database, you must first connect to your MongoDB Atlas cluster via a pymongo **MongoClient**, which receives your cluster's connection string as its argument:

```
In [9]: from pymongo import MongoClient
```

```
In [10]: atlas_client = MongoClient(keys.mongo_connection_string)
```

Now, we can get a pymongo **Database** object representing the senators database. The following statement creates the database if it does not exist:

```
In [11]: db = atlas_client.senators
```

Setting up Tweet Stream

Let's specify the number of tweets to download and create the TweetListener. We pass the db object representing the MongoDB database to the TweetListener so it can write the tweets into the database. Depending on the rate at which people are tweeting about the senators, it may take minutes to hours to get 10,000 tweets. For testing purposes, you might want to use a smaller number:

```
In [12]: from tweetlistener import TweetListener
```

```
In [13]: tweet_limit = 10000
```

```
In [14]: twitter_stream = tweepy.Stream(api.auth,
    ...:     TweetListener(api, db, tweet_limit))
    ...:
```

Starting the Tweet Stream

Twitter live streaming allows you to track up to 400 keywords and follow up to 5,000 Twitter IDs at a time. In this case, let's track the senators' Twitter handles and follow the senator's Twitter IDs. This should give us tweets from, to and about each senator. To show you progress, we display the screen name and time stamp for each tweet received, and the total number of tweets so far. To save space, we show here only one of those tweet outputs and replace the user's screen name with XXXXXXX:

```
In [15]: twitter_stream.filter(track=senators_df.TwitterHandle.tolist(),
    ...:     follow=senators_df.TwitterID.tolist())
    ...:
    Screen name: XXXXXXX
      Created at: Sun Dec 16 17:19:19 +0000 2018
Tweets received: 1
...
```

Class `TweetListener`

For this example, we slightly modified class `TweetListener` from the "Data Mining Twitter" chapter. Much of the Twitter and Tweepy code shown below is identical to the code you saw previously, so we'll focus on only the new concepts here:

```
1   # tweetlistener.py
2   """TweetListener downloads tweets and stores them in MongoDB."""
3   import json
4   import tweepy
5
6   class TweetListener(tweepy.StreamListener):
7       """Handles incoming Tweet stream."""
8
9       def __init__(self, api, database, limit=10000):
10          """Create instance variables for tracking number of tweets."""
11          self.db = database
12          self.tweet_count = 0
13          self.TWEET_LIMIT = limit  # 10,000 by default
14          super().__init__(api)  # call superclass's init
15
16      def on_connect(self):
17          """Called when your connection attempt is successful, enabling
18          you to perform appropriate application tasks at that point."""
19          print('Successfully connected to Twitter\n')
20
21      def on_data(self, data):
22          """Called when Twitter pushes a new tweet to you."""
23          self.tweet_count += 1  # track number of tweets processed
24          json_data = json.loads(data)  # convert string to JSON
25          self.db.tweets.insert_one(json_data)  # store in tweets collection
26          print(f'    Screen name: {json_data["user"]["name"]}')
27          print(f'     Created at: {json_data["created_at"]}')
28          print(f'Tweets received: {self.tweet_count}')
29
30          # if TWEET_LIMIT is reached, return False to terminate streaming
31          return self.tweet_count != self.TWEET_LIMIT
32
33      def on_error(self, status):
34          print(status)
35          return True
```

Previously, `TweetListener` overrode method `on_status` to receive Tweepy `Status` objects representing tweets. Here, we override the `on_data` method instead (lines 21–31). Rather than `Status` objects, `on_data` receives each tweet object's *raw JSON*. Line 24 converts the JSON string received by `on_data` into a Python JSON object. Each MongoDB database contains one or more **Collections** of documents. In line 25, the expression

```
self.db.tweets
```

accesses the `Database` object db's tweets `Collection`, creating it if it does not already exist. Line 25 uses the tweets `Collection`'s **insert_one method** to store the JSON object in the tweets collection.

Counting Tweets for Each Senator

Next, we'll perform a full-text search on the collection of tweets and count the number of tweets containing each senator's Twitter handle. To text search in MongoDB, you must create a *text index* for the collection.[16] This specifies which document field(s) to search. Each text index is defined as a tuple containing the field name to search and the index type ('text'). MongoDB's wildcard specifier ($**) indicates that every text field in a document (a JSON tweet object in our case) should be indexed for a full-text search:

```
In [16]: db.tweets.create_index([('$**', 'text')])
Out[16]: '$**_text'
```

Once the index is defined, we can use the Collection's **count_documents** method to count the total number of documents in the collection that contain the specified text. Let's search the database's tweets collection for every twitter handle in the senators_df Data-Frame's TwitterHandle column:

```
In [17]: tweet_counts = []

In [18]: for senator in senators_df.TwitterHandle:
    ...:     tweet_counts.append(db.tweets.count_documents(
    ...:         {"$text": {"$search": senator}}))
    ...:
```

The JSON object passed to count_documents in this case indicates that we're using the index named text to search for the value of senator.

Show Tweet Counts for Each Senator

Let's create a copy of the DataFrame senators_df that contains the tweet_counts as a new column, then display the top-10 senators by tweet count:

```
In [19]: tweet_counts_df = senators_df.assign(Tweets=tweet_counts)

In [20]: tweet_counts_df.sort_values(by='Tweets',
    ...:     ascending=False).head(10)
    ...:
```

```
Out[20]:
```

	State	Name	Party	TwitterHandle	TwitterID	Tweets
78	SC	Lindsey Graham	R	LindseyGrahamSC	432895323	1405
41	MA	Elizabeth Warren	D	SenWarren	970207298	1249
8	CA	Dianne Feinstein	D	SenFeinstein	476256944	1079
20	HI	Brian Schatz	D	brianschatz	47747074	934
62	NY	Chuck Schumer	D	SenSchumer	17494010	811
24	IL	Tammy Duckworth	D	SenDuckworth	1058520120	656
13	CT	Richard Blumenthal	D	SenBlumenthal	278124059	646
21	HI	Mazie Hirono	D	maziehirono	92186819	628
86	UT	Orrin Hatch	R	SenOrrinHatch	262756641	506
77	RI	Sheldon Whitehouse	D	SenWhitehouse	242555999	350

---

16. For additional details on MongoDB index types, text indexes and operators, see: https://docs.mongodb.com/manual/indexes, https://docs.mongodb.com/manual/core/index-text and https://docs.mongodb.com/manual/reference/operator.

Get the State Locations for Plotting Markers

Next, we'll use the techniques you learned in the "Data Mining Twitter" chapter to get each state's latitude and longitude coordinates. We'll soon use these to place on a Folium map popup markers that contain the names and numbers of tweets mentioning each state's senators.

The file `state_codes.py` contains a `state_codes` dictionary that maps two-letter state codes to their full state names. We'll use the full state names with geopy's Open-MapQuest geocode function to look up the location of each state.[17] First, let's import the libraries we need and the `state_codes` dictionary:

```
In [21]: from geopy import OpenMapQuest
```

```
In [22]: import time
```

```
In [23]: from state_codes import state_codes
```

Next, let's get the geocoder object to translate location names into `Location` objects:

```
In [24]: geo = OpenMapQuest(api_key=keys.mapquest_key)
```

There are two senators from each state, so we can look up each state's location once and use the `Location` object for both senators from that state. Let's get the unique state names, then sort them into ascending order:

```
In [25]: states = tweet_counts_df.State.unique()
```

```
In [26]: states.sort()
```

The next two snippets use code from the "Data Mining Twitter" chapter to look up each state's location. In snippet [28], we call the geocode function with the state name followed by `', USA'` to ensure that we get United States locations,[18] since there are places outside the United States with the same names as U.S. states. To show progress, we display each new `Location` object's string:

```
In [27]: locations = []

In [28]: for state in states:
    ...:     processed = False
    ...:     delay = .1
    ...:     while not processed:
    ...:         try:
    ...:             locations.append(
    ...:                 geo.geocode(state_codes[state] + ', USA'))
    ...:             print(locations[-1])
    ...:             processed = True
    ...:         except:  # timed out, so wait before trying again
    ...:             print('OpenMapQuest service timed out. Waiting.')
    ...:             time.sleep(delay)
    ...:             delay += .1
    ...:
```

---

17. We use full state names because, during our testing, the two-letter state codes did not always return correct locations.

18. When we initially performed the geocoding for Washington state, OpenMapQuest returned Washington, D.C.'s location. So we modified `state_codes.py` to use "Washington State" instead.

```
Alaska, United States of America
Alabama, United States of America
Arkansas, United States of America
...
```

Grouping the Tweet Counts by State
We'll use the total number of tweets for the two senators in a state to color that state on the map. Darker colors will represent the states with higher tweet counts. To prepare the data for mapping, let's use the pandas DataFrame method **groupby** to group the senators by state and calculate the total tweets by state:

```
In [29]: tweets_counts_by_state = tweet_counts_df.groupby(
    ...:     'State', as_index=False).sum()
    ...:

In [30]: tweets_counts_by_state.head()
Out[30]:
  State  Tweets
0    AK      27
1    AL       2
2    AR      47
3    AZ      47
4    CA    1135
```

The as_index=False keyword argument in snippet [29] indicates that the state codes should be values in a column of the resulting **GroupBy** object, rather than the indices for the rows. The GroupBy object's **sum** method totals the numeric data (the tweets by state). Snippet [30] displays several rows of the GroupBy object so you can see some of the results.

Creating the Map
Next, let's create the map. You may want to adjust the zoom. On our system, the following snippet creates a map in which we initially can see only the continental United States. Remember that Folium maps are interactive, so once the map is displayed, you can scroll to zoom in and out or drag to see different areas, such as Alaska or Hawaii:

```
In [31]: import folium

In [32]: usmap = folium.Map(location=[39.8283, -98.5795],
    ...:                    zoom_start=4, detect_retina=True,
    ...:                    tiles='Stamen Toner')
    ...:
```

Creating a Choropleth to Color the Map
A **choropleth** shades areas in a map using the values you specify to determine color. Let's create a choropleth that colors the states by the number of tweets containing their senators' Twitter handles. First, save Folium's us-states.json file at

> https://raw.githubusercontent.com/python-visualization/folium/mas-
> ter/examples/data/us-states.json

to the folder containing this example. This file contains a JSON dialect called **GeoJSON** (**Geographic JSON**) that describes the boundaries of shapes—in this case, the boundaries of every U.S. state. The choropleth uses this information to shade each state. For more

about GeoJSON, see http://geojson.org/.[19] The following snippets create the choropleth, then add it to the map:

```
In [33]: choropleth = folium.Choropleth(
   ...:        geo_data='us-states.json',
   ...:        name='choropleth',
   ...:        data=tweets_counts_by_state,
   ...:        columns=['State', 'Tweets'],
   ...:        key_on='feature.id',
   ...:        fill_color='YlOrRd',
   ...:        fill_opacity=0.7,
   ...:        line_opacity=0.2,
   ...:        legend_name='Tweets by State'
   ...: ).add_to(usmap)
   ...:

In [34]: layer = folium.LayerControl().add_to(usmap)
```

In this case, we used the following arguments:

- geo_data='us-states.json'—This is the file containing the GeoJSON that
  specifies the shapes to color.

- name='choropleth'—Folium displays the Choropleth as a layer over the map.
  This is the name for that layer that will appear in the map's layer controls, which
  enable you to hide and show the layers. These controls appear when you click the
  layers icon ( ) on the map.

- data=tweets_counts_by_state—This is a pandas DataFrame (or Series) containing the values that determine the Choropleth colors.

- columns=['State', 'Tweets']—When the data is a DataFrame, this is a list of
  two columns representing the keys and the corresponding values used to color the
  Choropleth.

- key_on='feature.id'—This is a variable in the GeoJSON file to which the
  Choropleth binds the values in the columns argument.

- fill_color='YlOrRd'—This is a color map specifying the colors to use to fill in
  the states. Folium provides 12 colormaps: 'BuGn', 'BuPu', 'GnBu', 'OrRd',
  'PuBu', 'PuBuGn', 'PuRd', 'RdPu', 'YlGn', 'YlGnBu', 'YlOrBr' and 'YlOrRd'.
  You should experiment with these to find the most effective and eye-pleasing
  ones for your application(s).

- fill_opacity=0.7—A value from 0.0 (transparent) to 1.0 (opaque) specifying
  the transparency of the fill colors displayed in the states.

- line_opacity=0.2—A value from 0.0 (transparent) to 1.0 (opaque) specifying
  the transparency of lines used to delineate the states.

---

19. Folium provides several other GeoJSON files in its examples folder at https://github.com/
    python-visualization/folium/tree/master/examples/data. You also can create your own at
    http://geojson.io.

- `legend_name='Tweets by State'`—At the top of the map, the `Choropleth` displays a color bar (the legend) indicating the value range represented by the colors. This `legend_name` text appears below the color bar to indicate what the colors represent.

The complete list of `Choropleth` keyword arguments is documented at:

```
http://python-visualization.github.io/folium/mod-
    ules.html#folium.features.Choropleth
```

Creating the Map Markers for Each State

Next, we'll create `Markers` for each state. To ensure that the senators are displayed in descending order by the number of tweets in each state's `Marker`, let's sort `tweet_counts_df` in descending order by the `'Tweets'` column:

```
In [35]: sorted_df = tweet_counts_df.sort_values(
    ...:     by='Tweets', ascending=False)
    ...:
```

The loop in the following snippet creates the `Markers`. First,

```
sorted_df.groupby('State')
```

groups `sorted_df` by `'State'`. A DataFrame's groupby method maintains the *original row order* in each group. Within a given group, the senator with the most tweets will be first, because we sorted the senators in descending order by tweet count in snippet [35]:

```
In [36]: for index, (name, group) in enumerate(sorted_df.groupby('State')):
    ...:     strings = [state_codes[name]]  # used to assemble popup text
    ...:
    ...:     for s in group.itertuples():
    ...:         strings.append(
    ...:             f'{s.Name} ({s.Party}); Tweets: {s.Tweets}')
    ...:
    ...:     text = '<br>'.join(strings)
    ...:     marker = folium.Marker(
    ...:         (locations[index].latitude, locations[index].longitude),
    ...:         popup=text)
    ...:     marker.add_to(usmap)
    ...:
    ...:
```

We pass the grouped `DataFrame` to `enumerate`, so we can get an index for each group, which we'll use to look up each state's `Location` in the `locations` list. Each group has a name (the state code we grouped by) and a collection of items in that group (the two senators for that state). The loop operates as follows:

- We look up the full state name in the `state_codes` dictionary, then store it in the `strings` list—we'll use this list to assemble the `Marker`'s popup text.

- The nested loop walks through the items in the `group` collection, returning each as a named tuple that contains a given senator's data. We create a formatted string for the current senator containing the person's name, party and number of tweets, then append that to the `strings` list.

- The Marker text can use HTML for formatting. We join the strings list's elements, separating each from the next with an HTML <br> element which creates a new line in HTML.

- We create the Marker. The first argument is the Marker's location as a tuple containing the latitude and longitude. The popup keyword argument specifies the text to display if the user clicks the Marker.

- We add the Marker to the map.

Displaying the Map

Finally, let's save the map into an HTML file

```
In [37]: usmap.save('SenatorsTweets.html')
```

Open the HTML file in your web browser to view and interact with the map. Recall that you can drag the map to see Alaska and Hawaii. Here we show the popup text for the South Carolina marker:

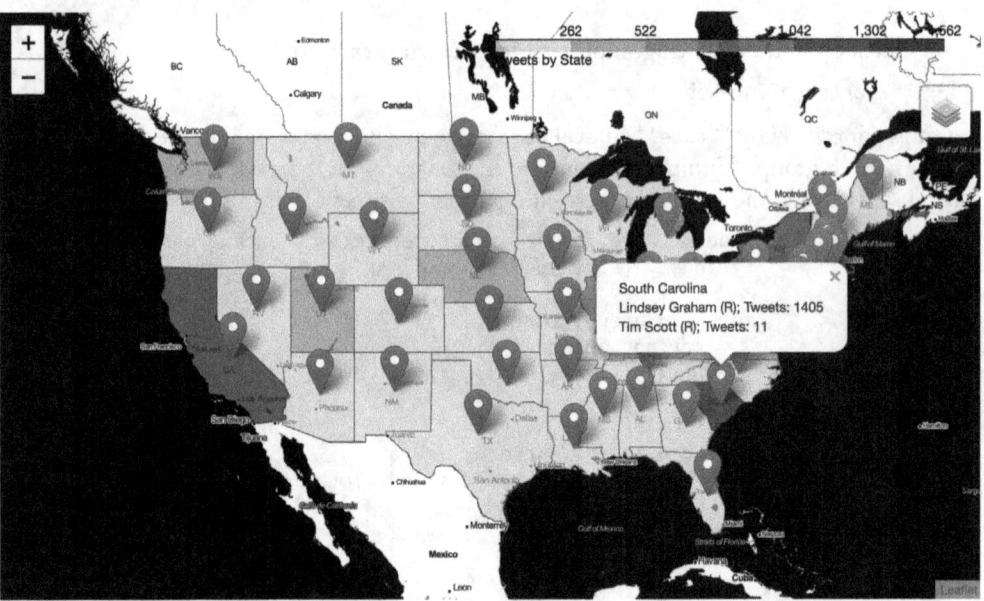

You could enhance this case study to use the sentiment-analysis techniques you learned in previous chapters to rate as positive, neutral or negative the sentiment expressed by people who send tweets ("tweeters") mentioning each senator's handle.

16.5 Hadoop

The next several sections show how Apache Hadoop and Apache Spark deal with big-data storage and processing challenges via huge clusters of computers, massively parallel processing, Hadoop MapReduce programming and Spark in-memory processing techniques. Here, we discuss Apache Hadoop, a key big-data infrastructure technology that also serves as the foundation for many recent advancements in big-data processing and an entire ecosystem of software tools that are continually evolving to support today's big-data needs.

16.5.1 Hadoop Overview

When Google was launched in 1998, the amount of online data was already enormous with approximately 2.4 million websites[20]—truly big data. Today there are now nearly two billion websites[21] (almost a thousandfold increase) and Google is handling over two trillion searches per year![22] Having used Google search since its inception, our sense is that today's responses are significantly faster.

When Google was developing their search engine, they knew that they needed to return search results quickly. The only practical way to do this was to store and index the entire Internet using a clever combination of secondary storage and main memory. Computers of that time couldn't hold that amount of data and could not analyze that amount of data fast enough to guarantee prompt search-query responses. So Google developed a **clustering** system, tying together vast numbers of computers—called **nodes**. Because having more computers and more connections between them meant greater chance of hardware failures, they also built in high levels of *redundancy* to ensure that the system would continue functioning even if nodes within clusters failed. The data was distributed across all these inexpensive "commodity computers." To satisfy a search request, all the computers in the cluster searched in parallel the portion of the web they had locally. Then the results of those searches were gathered up and reported back to the user.

To accomplish this, Google needed to develop the clustering hardware and software, including distributed storage. Google published its designs, but did not open source its software. Programmers at Yahoo!, working from Google's designs in the "Google File System" paper,[23] then built their own system. They open-sourced their work and the Apache organization implemented the system as Hadoop. The name came from an elephant stuffed animal that belonged to a child of one of Hadoop's creators.

Two additional Google papers also contributed to the evolution of Hadoop—"MapReduce: Simplified Data Processing on Large Clusters"[24] and "Bigtable: A Distributed Storage System for Structured Data,"[25] which was the basis for Apache HBase (a NoSQL key–value and column-based database).[26]

HDFS, MapReduce and YARN

Hadoop's key components are:

- **HDFS (Hadoop Distributed File System)** for storing massive amounts of data throughout a cluster, and

- **MapReduce** for implementing the tasks that process the data.

---

20. http://www.internetlivestats.com/total-number-of-websites/.
21. http://www.internetlivestats.com/total-number-of-websites/.
22. http://www.internetlivestats.com/google-search-statistics/.
23. http://static.googleusercontent.com/media/research.google.com/en//archive/gfs-sosp2003.pdf.
24. http://static.googleusercontent.com/media/research.google.com/en//archive/mapreduce-osdi04.pdf.
25. http://static.googleusercontent.com/media/research.google.com/en//archive/bigtable-osdi06.pdf.
26. Many other influential big-data-related papers (including the ones we mentioned) can be found at: https://bigdata-madesimple.com/research-papers-that-changed-the-world-of-big-data/.

Earlier in the book we introduced basic functional-style programming and filter/map/ reduce. Hadoop MapReduce is similar in concept, just on a massively parallel scale. A MapReduce task performs two steps—**mapping** and **reduction**. The mapping step, which also may include *filtering*, processes the original data across the entire cluster and maps it into tuples of key–value pairs. The reduction step then combines those tuples to produce the results of the MapReduce task. The key is how the MapReduce step is performed. Hadoop divides the data into *batches* that it distributes across the nodes in the cluster— anywhere from a few nodes to a Yahoo! cluster with 40,000 nodes and over 100,000 cores.[27] Hadoop also distributes the MapReduce task's code to the nodes in the cluster and executes the code in parallel on every node. Each node processes only the batch of data stored on that node. The reduction step combines the results from all the nodes to produce the final result. To coordinate this, Hadoop uses **YARN** ("**yet another resource negotiator**") to manage all the resources in the cluster and schedule tasks for execution.

Hadoop Ecosystem

Though Hadoop began with HDFS and MapReduce, followed closely by YARN, it has grown into a large ecosystem that includes Spark (discussed in Sections 16.6–16.7) and many other Apache projects:[28,29,30]

- **Ambari** (https://ambari.apache.org)—Tools for managing Hadoop clusters.

- **Drill** (https://drill.apache.org)—SQL querying of non-relational data in Hadoop and NoSQL databases.

- **Flume** (https://flume.apache.org)—A service for collecting and storing (in HDFS and other storage) streaming event data, like high-volume server logs, IoT messages and more.

- **HBase** (https://hbase.apache.org)—A NoSQL database for big data with "billions of rows by[31] millions of columns—atop clusters of commodity hardware."

- **Hive** (https://hive.apache.org)—Uses SQL to interact with data in data warehouses. A **data warehouse** aggregates data of various types from various sources. Common operations include extracting data, transforming it and loading (known as **ETL**) into another database, typically so you can analyze it and create reports from it.

- **Impala** (https://impala.apache.org)—A database for real-time SQL-based queries across distributed data stored in Hadoop HDFS or HBase.

- **Kafka** (https://kafka.apache.org)—Real-time messaging, stream processing and storage, typically to transform and process high-volume streaming data, such as website activity and streaming IoT data.

---

27. https://wiki.apache.org/hadoop/PoweredBy.
28. https://hortonworks.com/ecosystems/.
29. https://readwrite.com/2018/06/26/complete-guide-of-hadoop-ecosystem-components/.
30. https://www.janbasktraining.com/blog/introduction-architecture-components-hadoop-ecosystem/.
31. We used the word "by" to replace "X" in the original text.

- **Pig** (`https://pig.apache.org`)—A scripting platform that converts data analysis tasks from a scripting language called **Pig Latin** into MapReduce tasks.

- **Sqoop** (`https://sqoop.apache.org`)—Tool for moving structured, semi-structured and unstructured data between databases.

- **Storm** (`https://storm.apache.org`)—A real-time stream-processing system for tasks such as data analytics, machine learning, ETL and more.

- **ZooKeeper** (`https://zookeeper.apache.org`)—A service for managing cluster configurations and coordination between clusters.

- And more.

Hadoop Providers

Numerous cloud vendors provide Hadoop as a service, including Amazon EMR, Google Cloud DataProc, IBM Watson Analytics Engine, Microsoft Azure HDInsight and others. In addition, companies like Cloudera and Hortonworks (which at the time of this writing are merging) offer integrated Hadoop-ecosystem components and tools via the major cloud vendors. They also offer free *downloadable* environments that you can run on the desktop[32] for learning, development and testing before you commit to cloud-based hosting, which can incur significant costs. We introduce MapReduce programming in the example in the following sections by using a Microsoft cloud-based Azure HDInsight cluster, which provides Hadoop as a service.

Hadoop 3

Apache continues to evolve Hadoop. Hadoop 3[33] was released in December of 2017 with many improvements, including better performance and significantly improved storage efficiency.[34]

16.5.2 Summarizing Word Lengths in *Romeo and Juliet* via MapReduce

In the next several subsections, you'll create a cloud-based, multi-node cluster of computers using Microsoft Azure HDInsight. Then, you'll use the service's capabilities to demonstrate Hadoop MapReduce running on that cluster. The MapReduce task you'll define will determine the length of each word in RomeoAndJuliet.txt (from the "Natural Language Processing" chapter), then summarize how many words of each length there are. After defining the task's mapping and reduction steps, you'll submit the task to your HDInsight cluster, and Hadoop will decide how to use the cluster of computers to perform the task.

16.5.3 Creating an Apache Hadoop Cluster in Microsoft Azure HDInsight

Most major cloud vendors have support for Hadoop and Spark computing clusters that you can configure to meet your application's requirements. Multi-node cloud-based clus-

---

32. Check their significant system requirements first to ensure that you have the disk space and memory required to run them.
33. For a list of features in Hadoop 3, see `https://hadoop.apache.org/docs/r3.0.0/`.
34. `https://www.datanami.com/2018/10/18/is-hadoop-officially-dead/`.

ters typically are *paid* services, though most vendors provide free trials or credits so you can try out their services.

We want you to experience the process of setting up clusters and using them to perform tasks. So, in this Hadoop example, you'll use Microsoft Azure's HDInsight service to create cloud-based clusters of computers in which to test our examples. Go to

```
https://azure.microsoft.com/en-us/free
```

to sign up for an account. Microsoft requires a credit card for identity verification.

Various services are always free and some you can continue to use for 12 months. For information on these services see:

```
https://azure.microsoft.com/en-us/free/free-account-faq/
```

Microsoft also gives you a credit to experiment with their *paid* services, such as their HDInsight Hadoop and Spark services. Once your credits run out or 30 days pass (whichever comes first), you cannot continue using paid services unless you authorize Microsoft to charge your card.

Because you'll use your new Azure account's credit for these examples,[35] we'll discuss how to configure a low-cost cluster that uses less computing resources than Microsoft allocates by default.[36] **Caution: Once you allocate a cluster, it incurs costs whether you're using it or not. So, when you complete this case study, be sure to delete your cluster(s) and other resources, so you don't incur additional charges.** For more information, see:

```
https://docs.microsoft.com/en-us/azure/azure-resource-manager/
    resource-group-portal
```

For Azure-related documentation and videos, visit:

- `https://docs.microsoft.com/en-us/azure/`—the Azure documentation.
- `https://channel9.msdn.com/`—Microsoft's Channel 9 video network.
- `https://www.youtube.com/user/windowsazure`—Microsoft's Azure channel on YouTube.

Creating an HDInsight Hadoop Cluster

The following link explains how to set up a cluster for Hadoop using the Azure HDInsight service:

```
https://docs.microsoft.com/en-us/azure/hdinsight/hadoop/apache-
    hadoop-linux-create-cluster-get-started-portal
```

While following their **Create a Hadoop cluster** steps, please note the following:

- In *Step 1*, you access the Azure portal by logging into your account at

    ```
    https://portal.azure.com
    ```

- In *Step 2*, **Data + Analytics** is now called **Analytics**, and the HDInsight icon and icon color have changed from what is shown in the tutorial.

---

35. For Microsoft's latest free account features, visit `https://azure.microsoft.com/en-us/free/`.
36. For Microsoft's recommended cluster configurations, see `https://docs.microsoft.com/en-us/azure/hdinsight/hdinsight-component-versioning#default-node-configuration-and-virtual-machine-sizes-for-clusters`. If you configure a cluster that's too small for a given scenario, when you try to deploy the cluster you'll receive an error.

- In *Step 3*, you must choose a cluster name that does *not* already exist. When you enter your cluster name, Microsoft will check whether that name is available and display a message if it is not. You must create a password. For the **Resource group**, you'll also need to click **Create new** and provide a group name. Leave all other settings in this step as is.

- In *Step 5*: Under **Select a Storage account**, click **Create new** and provide a storage account name containing only lowercase letters and numbers. Like the cluster name, the storage account name must be unique.

When you get to the **Cluster summary** you'll see that Microsoft initially configures the cluster as **Head (2 x D12 v2), Worker (4 x D4 v2)**. At the time of this writing, the estimated cost-per-hour for this configuration was $3.11. This setup uses a total of 6 CPU nodes with 40 cores—far more than we need for demonstration purposes.

You can edit this setup to use fewer CPUs and cores, which also saves money. Let's change the configuration to a four-CPU cluster with 16 cores that uses less powerful computers. In the **Cluster summary:**

1. Click **Edit** to the right of **Cluster size**.

2. Change the **Number of Worker** nodes to 2.

3. Click **Worker node size**, then **View all**, select **D3 v2** (this is the minimum CPU size for Hadoop nodes) and click **Select**.

4. Click **Head node size**, then **View all**, select **D3 v2** and click **Select**.

5. Click **Next** and click **Next** again to return to the **Cluster summary**. Microsoft will validate the new configuration.

6. When the **Create** button is enabled, click it to deploy the cluster.

It takes 20–30 minutes for Microsoft to "spin up" your cluster. During this time, Microsoft is allocating all the resources and software the cluster requires.

After the changes above, our estimated cost for the cluster was $1.18 per hour, based on *average* use for similarly configured clusters. Our actual charges were less than that. If you encounter any problems configuring your cluster, Microsoft provides HDInsight chat-based support at:

```
https://azure.microsoft.com/en-us/resources/knowledge-center/
    technical-chat/
```

16.5.4 Hadoop Streaming

For languages like Python that are not natively supported in Hadoop, you must use **Hadoop streaming** to implement your tasks. In Hadoop streaming, the Python scripts that implement the mapping and reduction steps use the **standard input stream** and **standard output stream** to communicate with Hadoop. Usually, the standard input stream reads from the keyboard and the standard output stream writes to the command line. However, these can be *redirected* (as Hadoop does) to read from other sources and write to other destinations. Hadoop uses the streams as follows:

- Hadoop supplies the input to the mapping script—called the **mapper**. This script reads its input from the standard input stream.

- The mapper writes its results to the standard output stream.

- Hadoop supplies the mapper's output as the input to the reduction script—called the **reducer**—which reads from the standard input stream.

- The reducer writes its results to the standard output stream.

- Hadoop writes the reducer's output to the Hadoop file system (HDFS).

The mapper and reducer terminology used above should sound familiar to you from our discussions of functional-style programming and filter, map and reduce in the "Sequences: Lists and Tuples" chapter.

16.5.5 Implementing the Mapper

In this section, you'll create a mapper script that takes lines of text as input from Hadoop and maps them to *key–value pairs* in which each key is a word, and its corresponding value is 1. The mapper sees each word individually so, as far as it is concerned, there's only one of each word. In the next section, the reducer will summarize these key–value pairs by key, reducing the counts to a single count for each key. By default, Hadoop expects the mapper's output and the reducer's input and output to be in the form of key–value pairs separated by a *tab*.

In the mapper script (`length_mapper.py`), the notation `#!` in line 1 tells Hadoop to execute the Python code using `python3`, rather than the default Python 2 installation. This line must come before all other comments and code in the file. At the time of this writing, Python 2.7.12 and Python 3.5.2 were installed. Note that because the cluster does not have Python 3.6 or higher, you cannot use f-strings in your code.

```
1   #!/usr/bin/env python3
2   # length_mapper.py
3   """Maps lines of text to key-value pairs of word lengths and 1."""
4   import sys
5
6   def tokenize_input():
7       """Split each line of standard input into a list of strings."""
8       for line in sys.stdin:
9           yield line.split()
10
11  # read each line in the the standard input and for every word
12  # produce a key-value pair containing the word, a tab and 1
13  for line in tokenize_input():
14      for word in line:
15          print(str(len(word)) + '\t1')
```

Generator function `tokenize_input` (lines 6–9) reads lines of text from the standard input stream and for each returns a list of strings. For this example, we are not removing punctuation or stop words as we did in the "Natural Language Processing" chapter.

When Hadoop executes the script, lines 13–15 iterate through the lists of strings from `tokenize_input`. For each list (`line`) and for every string (`word`) in that list, line 15 outputs a key–value pair with the word's length as the key, a tab (`\t`) and the value 1, indicating that there is one word (so far) of that length. Of course, there probably are many words of that length. The MapReduce algorithm's reduction step will summarize these key–value pairs, reducing all those with the same key to a single key–value pair with the total count.

16.5.6 Implementing the Reducer

In the reducer script (`length_reducer.py`), function `tokenize_input` (lines 8–11) is a generator function that reads and splits the key–value pairs produced by the mapper. Again, the MapReduce algorithm supplies the standard input. For each line, `tokenize_input` strips any leading or trailing whitespace (such as the terminating new-line) and yields a list containing the key and a value.

```
1  #!/usr/bin/env python3
2  # length_reducer.py
3  """Counts the number of words with each length."""
4  import sys
5  from itertools import groupby
6  from operator import itemgetter
7
8  def tokenize_input():
9      """Split each line of standard input into a key and a value."""
10     for line in sys.stdin:
11         yield line.strip().split('\t')
12
13 # produce key-value pairs of word lengths and counts separated by tabs
14 for word_length, group in groupby(tokenize_input(), itemgetter(0)):
15     try:
16         total = sum(int(count) for word_length, count in group)
17         print(word_length + '\t' + str(total))
18     except ValueError:
19         pass  # ignore word if its count was not an integer
```

When the MapReduce algorithm executes this reducer, lines 14–19 use the **groupby** function from the **itertools module** to group all word lengths of the same value:

- The first argument calls `tokenize_input` to get the lists representing the key–value pairs.

- The second argument indicates that the key–value pairs should be grouped based on the element at index 0 in each list—that is, the key.

Line 16 totals all the counts for a given key. Line 17 outputs a new key–value pair consisting of the word and its total. The MapReduce algorithm takes all the final word-count outputs and writes them to a file in HDFS—the Hadoop file system.

16.5.7 Preparing to Run the MapReduce Example

Next, you'll upload files to the cluster so you can execute the example. In a Command Prompt, Terminal or shell, change to the folder containing your mapper and reducer scripts and the `RomeoAndJuliet.txt` file. We assume all three are in this chapter's `ch16` examples folder, so be sure to copy your `RomeoAndJuliet.txt` file to this folder first.

Copying the Script Files to the HDInsight Hadoop Cluster

Enter the following command to upload the files. Be sure to replace *YourClusterName* with the cluster name you specified when setting up the Hadoop cluster and press *Enter* only after you've typed the entire command. The colon in the following command is required and indicates that you'll supply your cluster password when prompted. At that prompt, type the password you specified when setting up the cluster, then press *Enter*:

```
scp length_mapper.py length_reducer.py RomeoAndJuliet.txt
    sshuser@YourClusterName-ssh.azurehdinsight.net:
```

The first time you do this, you'll be asked for security reasons to confirm that you trust the target host (that is, Microsoft Azure).

Copying RomeoAndJuliet into the Hadoop File System

For Hadoop to read the contents of RomeoAndJuliet.txt and supply the lines of text to your mapper, you must first copy the file into Hadoop's file system. First, you must use ssh[37] to log into your cluster and access its command line. In a Command Prompt, Terminal or shell, execute the following command. Be sure to replace *YourClusterName* with your cluster name. Again, you'll be prompted for your cluster password:

```
ssh sshuser@YourClusterName-ssh.azurehdinsight.net
```

For this example, we'll use the following Hadoop command to copy the text file into the already existing folder /examples/data that the cluster provides for use with Microsoft's Azure Hadoop tutorials. Again, press *Enter* only when you've typed the entire command:

```
hadoop fs -copyFromLocal RomeoAndJuliet.txt
    /example/data/RomeoAndJuliet.txt
```

16.5.8 Running the MapReduce Job

Now you can run the MapReduce job for RomeoAndJuliet.txt on your cluster by executing the following command. For your convenience, we provided the text of this command in the file yarn.txt with this example, so you can copy and paste it. We reformatted the command here for readability:

```
yarn jar /usr/hdp/current/hadoop-mapreduce-client/hadoop-streaming.jar
    -D mapred.output.key.comparator.class=
        org.apache.hadoop.mapred.lib.KeyFieldBasedComparator
    -D mapred.text.key.comparator.options=-n
    -files length_mapper.py,length_reducer.py
    -mapper length_mapper.py
    -reducer length_reducer.py
    -input /example/data/RomeoAndJuliet.txt
    -output /example/wordlengthsoutput
```

The **yarn command** invokes the Hadoop's YARN ("yet another resource negotiator") tool to manage and coordinate access to the Hadoop resources the MapReduce task uses. The file hadoop-streaming.jar contains the Hadoop streaming utility that allows you to use Python to implement the mapper and reducer. The two -D options set Hadoop properties that enable it to sort the final key–value pairs by key (KeyFieldBasedComparator) in descending order numerically (-n; the minus indicates descending order) rather than alphabetically. The other command-line arguments are:

---

37. Windows users: If ssh does not work for you, install and enable it as described at https:// blogs.msdn.microsoft.com/powershell/2017/12/15/using-the-openssh-beta-in-windows-10-fall-creators-update-and-windows-server-1709/. After completing the installation, log out and log back in or restart your system to enable ssh.

- -files—A comma-separated list of file names. Hadoop copies these files to every node in the cluster so they can be executed locally on each node.

- -mapper—The name of the mapper's script file.

- -reducer—The name of the reducer's script file

- -input—The file or directory of files to supply as input to the mapper.

- -output—The HDFS directory in which the output will be written. If this folder already exists, an error will occur.

The following output shows some of the feedback that Hadoop produces as the MapReduce job executes. We replaced chunks of the output with ... to save space and bolded several lines of interest including:

- The total number of "input paths to process"—the 1 source of input in this example is the RomeoAndJuliet.txt file.

- The "number of splits"—2 in this example, based on the number of worker nodes in our cluster.

- The percentage completion information.

- File System Counters, which include the numbers of bytes read and written.

- Job Counters, which show the number of mapping and reduction tasks used and various timing information.

- Map-Reduce Framework, which shows various information about the steps performed.

```
packageJobJar: [] [/usr/hdp/2.6.5.3004-13/hadoop-mapreduce/hadoop-stream-
ing-2.7.3.2.6.5.3004-13.jar] /tmp/streamjob2764990629848702405.jar tmp-
Dir=null
...
18/12/05 16:46:25 INFO mapred.FileInputFormat: Total input paths to pro-
cess : 1
18/12/05 16:46:26 INFO mapreduce.JobSubmitter: number of splits:2
...
18/12/05 16:46:26 INFO mapreduce.Job: The url to track the job: http://
hn0-paulte.y3nghy5db2kehav5m0opqrjxcb.cx.internal.cloudapp.net:8088/
proxy/application_1543953844228_0025/
...
18/12/05 16:46:35 INFO mapreduce.Job:  map 0% reduce 0%
18/12/05 16:46:43 INFO mapreduce.Job:  map 50% reduce 0%
18/12/05 16:46:44 INFO mapreduce.Job:  map 100% reduce 0%
18/12/05 16:46:48 INFO mapreduce.Job:  map 100% reduce 100%
18/12/05 16:46:50 INFO mapreduce.Job: Job job_1543953844228_0025 complet-
ed successfully
18/12/05 16:46:50 INFO mapreduce.Job: Counters: 49
        File System Counters
            FILE: Number of bytes read=156411
            FILE: Number of bytes written=813764
...

        Job Counters
            Launched map tasks=2
            Launched reduce tasks=1
...
```

```
       Map-Reduce Framework
              Map input records=5260
              Map output records=25956
              Map output bytes=104493
              Map output materialized bytes=156417
              Input split bytes=346
              Combine input records=0
              Combine output records=0
              Reduce input groups=19
              Reduce shuffle bytes=156417
              Reduce input records=25956
              Reduce output records=19
              Spilled Records=51912
              Shuffled Maps =2
              Failed Shuffles=0
              Merged Map outputs=2
              GC time elapsed (ms)=193
              CPU time spent (ms)=4440
              Physical memory (bytes) snapshot=1942798336
              Virtual memory (bytes) snapshot=8463282176
              Total committed heap usage (bytes)=3177185280
   ...
   18/12/05 16:46:50 INFO streaming.StreamJob: Output directory: /example/
   wordlengthsoutput
```

Viewing the Word Counts

Hadoop MapReduce saves its output into HDFS, so to see the actual word counts you must look at the file in HDFS within the cluster by executing the following command:

```
hdfs dfs -text /example/wordlengthsoutput/part-00000
```

Here are the results of the preceding command:

```
18/12/05 16:47:19 INFO lzo.GPLNativeCodeLoader: Loaded native gpl library
18/12/05 16:47:19 INFO lzo.LzoCodec: Successfully loaded & initialized
native-lzo library [hadoop-lzo rev b5efb3e531bc1558201462b8ab15bb412f-
fa6b89]
1         1140
2         3869
3         4699
4         5651
5         3668
6         2719
7         1624
8         1062
9         855
10        317
11        189
12        95
13        35
14        13
15        9
16        6
17        3
18        1
23        1
```

Deleting Your Cluster So You Do Not Incur Charges

Caution: Be sure to delete your cluster(s) and associated resources (like storage) so you don't incur additional charges. In the Azure portal, click **All resources** to see your list of resources, which will include the cluster you set up and the storage account you set up. Both can incur charges if you do not delete them. Select each resource and click the **Delete** button to remove it. You'll be asked to confirm by typing yes. For more information, see:

```
https://docs.microsoft.com/en-us/azure/azure-resource-manager/
    resource-group-portal
```

16.6 Spark

In this section, we'll overview Apache Spark. We'll use the Python **PySpark library** and Spark's functional-style filter/map/reduce capabilities to implement a simple word count example that summarizes the word counts in *Romeo and Juliet*.

16.6.1 Spark Overview

When you process truly big data, performance is crucial. Hadoop is geared to disk-based batch processing—reading the data from disk, processing the data and writing the results back to disk. Many big-data applications demand better performance than is possible with disk-intensive operations. In particular, fast streaming applications that require either real-time or near-real-time processing won't work in a disk-based architecture.

History

Spark was initially developed in 2009 at U. C. Berkeley and funded by DARPA (the Defense Advanced Research Projects Agency). Initially, it was created as a distributed execution engine for high-performance machine learning.[38] It uses an **in-memory architecture** that "has been used to sort 100 TB of data 3X faster than Hadoop MapReduce on 1/10th of the machines"[39] and runs some workloads up to 100 times faster than Hadoop.[40] Spark's significantly better performance on batch-processing tasks is leading many companies to replace Hadoop MapReduce with Spark.[41,42,43]

Architecture and Components

Though it was initially developed to run on Hadoop and use Hadoop components like HDFS and YARN, Spark can run standalone on a single computer (typically for learning and testing purposes), standalone on a cluster or using various cluster managers and distributed storage systems. For resource management, Spark runs on Hadoop YARN, Apache Mesos, Amazon EC2 and Kubernetes, and it supports many distributed storage systems, including HDFS, Apache Cassandra, Apache HBase and Apache Hive.[44]

---

38. https://gigaom.com/2014/06/28/4-reasons-why-spark-could-jolt-hadoop-into-hyperdrive/.
39. https://spark.apache.org/faq.html.
40. https://spark.apache.org/.
41. https://bigdata-madesimple.com/is-spark-better-than-hadoop-map-reduce/.
42. https://www.datanami.com/2018/10/18/is-hadoop-officially-dead/.
43. https://blog.thecodeteam.com/2018/01/09/changing-face-data-analytics-fast-data-displaces-big-data/.
44. http://spark.apache.org/.

At the core of Spark are **resilient distributed datasets (RDDs)**, which you'll use to process distributed data using functional-style programming. In addition to reading data from disk and writing data to disk, Hadoop uses replication for fault tolerance, which adds even more disk-based overhead. RDDs eliminate this overhead by remaining in memory—using disk only if the data will not fit in memory—and by not replicating data. Spark handles fault tolerance by remembering the steps used to create each RDD, so it can rebuild a given RDD if a cluster node fails.[45]

Spark distributes the operations you specify in Python to the cluster's nodes for parallel execution. Spark streaming enables you to process data as it's received. Spark Data-Frames, which are similar to pandas DataFrames, enable you to view RDDs as a collection of named columns. You can use Spark DataFrames with Spark SQL to perform queries on distributed data. Spark also includes **Spark MLlib** (the Spark Machine Learning Library), which enables you to perform machine-learning algorithms, like those you learned in Chapters 14 and 15. We'll use RDDs, Spark streaming, DataFrames and Spark SQL in the next few examples.

Providers

Hadoop providers typically also provide Spark support. In addition to the providers listed in Section 16.5, there are Spark-specific vendors like Databricks. They provide a "zero-management cloud platform built around Spark."[46] Their website also is an excellent resource for learning Spark. The paid Databricks platform runs on Amazon AWS or Microsoft Azure. Databricks also provides a free Databricks Community Edition, which is a great way to get started with both Spark and the Databricks environment.

16.6.2 Docker and the Jupyter Docker Stacks

In this section, we'll show how to download and execute a Docker stack containing Spark and the PySpark module for accessing Spark from Python. You'll write the Spark example's code in a Jupyter Notebook. First, let's overview Docker.

Docker

Docker is a tool for packaging software into **containers** (also called **images**) that bundle *everything* required to execute that software across platforms. Some software packages we use in this chapter require complicated setup and configuration. For many of these, there are preexisting Docker containers that you can download for free and execute locally on your desktop or notebook computers. This makes Docker a great way to help you get started with new technologies quickly and conveniently.

Docker also helps with *reproducibility* in research and analytics studies. You can create custom Docker containers that are configured with the versions of every piece of software and every library you used in your study. This would enable others to recreate the environment you used, then reproduce your work, and will help you reproduce your results at a later time. We'll use Docker in this section to download and execute a Docker container that's preconfigured to run Spark applications.

---

45. https://spark.apache.org/research.html.
46. https://databricks.com/product/faq.

Installing Docker
You can install Docker for Windows 10 Pro or macOS at:

```
https://www.docker.com/products/docker-desktop
```

On Windows 10 Pro, you must allow the "Docker for Windows.exe" installer to make changes to your system to complete the installation process. To do so, click **Yes** when Windows asks if you want to allow the installer to make changes to your system.[47] Windows 10 Home users must use Virtual Box as described at:

```
https://docs.docker.com/machine/drivers/virtualbox/
```

Linux users should install Docker Community Edition as described at:

```
https://docs.docker.com/install/overview/
```

For a general overview of Docker, read the **Getting started** guide at:

```
https://docs.docker.com/get-started/
```

Jupyter Docker Stacks
The Jupyter Notebooks team has preconfigured several Jupyter "Docker stacks" containers for common Python development scenarios. Each enables you to use Jupyter Notebooks to experiment with powerful capabilities without having to worry about complex software setup issues. In each case, you can open JupyterLab in your web browser, open a notebook in JupyterLab and start coding. JupyterLab also provides a **Terminal window** that you can use in your browser like your computer's Terminal, Anaconda Command Prompt or shell. Everything we've shown you in IPython to this point can be executed using IPython in JupyterLab's Terminal window.

We'll use the jupyter/pyspark-notebook Docker stack, which is preconfigured with everything you need to create and test Apache Spark apps on your computer. When combined with installing other Python libraries we've used throughout the book, you can implement most of this book's examples using this container. For more about the available Docker stacks, visit:

```
https://jupyter-docker-stacks.readthedocs.io/en/latest/index.html
```

Run Jupyter Docker Stack
Before performing the next step, ensure that JupyterLab is not currently running on your computer. Let's download and run the jupyter/pyspark-notebook Docker stack. To ensure that you do not lose your work when you close the Docker container, we'll attach a local file-system folder to the container and use it to save your notebook—Windows users should replace \ with ^. :

```
docker run -p 8888:8888 -p 4040:4040 -it --user root \
    -v fullPathToTheFolderYouWantToUse:/home/jovyan/work \
    jupyter/pyspark-notebook:14fdfbf9cfc1 start.sh jupyter lab
```

---

47. Some Windows users might have to follow the instructions under **Allow specific apps to make changes to controlled folders** at https://docs.microsoft.com/en-us/windows/security/threat-protection/windows-defender-exploit-guard/customize-controlled-folders-exploit-guard.

The first time you run the preceding command, Docker will download the Docker container named:

```
jupyter/pyspark-notebook:14fdfbf9cfc1
```

The notation ":14fdfbf9cfc1" indicates the specific jupyter/pyspark-notebook container to download. At the time of this writing, 14fdfbf9cfc1 was the newest version of the container. Specifying the version as we did here helps with *reproducibility*. Without the ":14fdfbf9cfc1" in the command, Docker will download the *latest* version of the container, which might contain different software versions and might not be compatible with the code you're trying to execute. The Docker container is nearly 6GB, so the initial download time will depend on your Internet connection's speed.

Opening JupyterLab in Your Browser

Once the container is downloaded and running, you'll see a statement in your Command Prompt, Terminal or shell window like:

```
Copy/paste this URL into your browser when you connect for the first
time, to login with a token:
        http://(bb00eb337630 or 127.0.0.1):8888/?token=
            9570295e90ee94ecef75568b95545b7910a8f5502e6f5680
```

Copy the long hexadecimal string (the string on your system will differ from this one):

```
9570295e90ee94ecef75568b95545b7910a8f5502e6f5680
```

then open http://localhost:8888/lab in your browser (localhost corresponds to 127.0.0.1 in the preceding output) and *paste* your token in the **Password or token** field. Click **Log in** to be taken to the JupyterLab interface. If you accidentally close your browser, go to http://localhost:8888/lab to continue your session.

When running in this Docker container, the work folder in the **Files** tab at the left side of JupyterLab represents the folder you attached to the container in the docker run command's -v option. From here, you can open the notebook files we provide for you. Any new notebooks or other files you create will be saved to this folder by default. Because the Docker container's work folder is connected to a folder on your computer, any files you create in JupyterLab will remain on your computer, even if you decide to delete the Docker container.

Accessing the Docker Container's Command Line

Each Docker container has a command-line interface like the one you've used to run IPython throughout this book. Via this interface, you can install Python packages into the Docker container and even use IPython as you've done previously.

Open a separate Anaconda Command Prompt, Terminal or shell and list the currently running Docker containers with the command:

```
docker ps
```

The output of this command is wide, so the lines of text will likely wrap, as in:

```
CONTAINER ID       IMAGE                                              COMMAND
        CREATED          STATUS            PORTS
    NAMES
f54f62b7e6d5          jupyter/pyspark-notebook:14fdfbf9cfc1    "tini -g --
/bin/bash"  2 minutes ago     Up 2 minutes      0.0.0.0:8888->8888/tcp
    friendly_pascal
```

In the last line of our system's output under the column head NAMES in the third line is the name that Docker randomly assigned to the running container—friendly_pascal—the name on your system will differ. To access the container's command line, execute the following command, replacing *container_name* with the running container's name:

```
docker exec -it container_name /bin/bash
```

The Docker container uses Linux under the hood, so you'll see a Linux prompt where you can enter commands.

The app in this section will use features of the NLTK and TextBlob libraries you used in the "Natural Language Processing" chapter. Neither is preinstalled in the Jupyter Docker stacks. To install NLTK and TextBlob enter the command:

```
conda install -c conda-forge nltk textblob
```

Stopping and Restarting a Docker Container
Every time you start a container with docker run, Docker gives you a new instance that does *not* contain any libraries you installed previously. For this reason, you should keep track of your container name, so you can use it from another Anaconda Command Prompt, Terminal or shell window to stop the container and restart it. The command

```
docker stop container_name
```

will shut down the container. The command

```
docker restart container_name
```

will restart the container. Docker also provides a GUI app called Kitematic that you can use to manage your containers, including stopping and restarting them. You can get the app from https://kitematic.com/ and access it through the Docker menu. The following user guide overviews how to manage containers with the tool:

```
https://docs.docker.com/kitematic/userguide/
```

16.6.3 Word Count with Spark
In this section, we'll use Spark's filtering, mapping and reducing capabilities to implement a simple word count example that summarizes the words in *Romeo and Juliet*. You can work with the existing notebook named RomeoAndJulietCounter.ipynb in the Spark-WordCount folder (into which you should copy your RomeoAndJuliet.txt file from the "Natural Language Processing" chapter), or you can create a new notebook, then enter and execute the snippets we show.

Loading the NLTK Stop Words
In this app, we'll use techniques you learned in the "Natural Language Processing" chapter to eliminate stop words from the text before counting the words' frequencies. First, download the NLTK stop words:

```
[1]: import nltk
     nltk.download('stopwords')
[nltk_data] Downloading package stopwords to /home/jovyan/nltk_data...
[nltk_data]   Package stopwords is already up-to-date!
[1]: True
```

Next, load the stop words:

```
[2]: from nltk.corpus import stopwords
     stop_words = stopwords.words('english')
```

Configuring a SparkContext

A **SparkContext** (from module pyspark) object gives you access to Spark's capabilities in Python. Many Spark environments create the SparkContext for you, but in the Jupyter pyspark-notebook Docker stack, you must create this object.

First, let's specify the configuration options by creating a **SparkConf** object (from module pyspark). The following snippet calls the object's **setAppName** method to specify the Spark application's name and calls the object's **setMaster** method to specify the Spark cluster's URL. The URL 'local[*]' indicates that Spark is executing on your local computer (as opposed to a cloud-based cluster), and the asterisk indicates that Spark should run our code using the same number of *threads* as there are cores on the computer:

```
[3]: from pyspark import SparkConf
     configuration = SparkConf().setAppName('RomeoAndJulietCounter')\
                               .setMaster('local[*]')
```

Threads enable a single node cluster to execute portions of the Spark tasks *concurrently* to simulate the parallelism that Spark clusters provide. When we say that two tasks are operating concurrently, we mean that they're both making progress at once—typically by executing a task for a short burst of time, then allowing another task to execute. When we say that two tasks are operating in *parallel*, we mean that they're executing simultaneously, which is one of the key benefits of Hadoop and Spark executing on cloud-based clusters of computers.

Next, create the SparkContext, passing the SparkConf as its argument:

```
[4]: from pyspark import SparkContext
     sc = SparkContext(conf=configuration)
```

Reading the Text File and Mapping It to Words

You work with a SparkContext using functional-style programming techniques, like filtering, mapping and reduction, applied to a **resilient distributed dataset (RDD)**. An RDD takes data stored throughout a cluster in the Hadoop file system and enables you to specify a series of processing steps to transform the data in the RDD. These processing steps are *lazy* (Chapter 5)—they do not perform any work until you indicate that Spark should process the task.

The following snippet specifies three steps:

- SparkContext method **textFile** loads the lines of text from RomeoAndJuliet.txt and returns it as an **RDD** (from module pyspark) of strings that represent each line.

- RDD method **map** uses its lambda argument to remove all punctuation with TextBlob's strip_punc function and to convert each line of text to lowercase. This method returns a new RDD on which you can specify additional tasks to perform.

- RDD method **flatMap** uses its lambda argument to map each line of text into its words and produces a single list of words, rather than the individual lines of text. The result of flatMap is a new RDD representing all the words in *Romeo and Juliet*.

```
[5]: from textblob.utils import strip_punc
     tokenized = sc.textFile('RomeoAndJuliet.txt')\
                    .map(lambda line: strip_punc(line, all=True).lower())\
                    .flatMap(lambda line: line.split())
```

Removing the Stop Words
Next, let's use RDD method **filter** to create a new RDD with no stop words remaining:

```
[6]: filtered = tokenized.filter(lambda word: word not in stop_words)
```

Counting Each Remaining Word
Now that we have only the non-stop-words, we can count the number of occurrences of each word. To do so, we first map each word to a tuple containing the word and a count of 1. This is similar to what we did in Hadoop MapReduce. Spark will distribute the reduction task across the cluster's nodes. On the resulting RDD, we then call the method **reduceByKey**, passing the operator module's add function as an argument. This tells method reduceByKey to *add* the counts for tuples that contain the same word (the key):

```
[7]: from operator import add
     word_counts = filtered.map(lambda word: (word, 1)).reduceByKey(add)
```

Locating Words with Counts Greater Than or Equal to 60
Since there are hundreds of words in *Romeo and Juliet*, let's filter the RDD to keep only those words with 60 or more occurrences:

```
[8]: filtered_counts = word_counts.filter(lambda item: item[1] >= 60)
```

Sorting and Displaying the Results
At this point, we've specified all the steps to count the words. When you call RDD method **collect**, Spark initiates all the processing steps we specified above and returns a list containing the final results—in this case, the tuples of words and their counts. From your perspective, everything appears to execute on one computer. However, if the SparkContext is configured to use a cluster, Spark will divide the tasks among the cluster's worker nodes for you. In the following snippet, sort in descending order (reverse=True) the list of tuples by their counts (itemgetter(1)).

The following snippet calls method collect to obtain the results and sorts those results in descending order by word count:

```
[9]: from operator import itemgetter
     sorted_items = sorted(filtered_counts.collect(),
                            key=itemgetter(1), reverse=True)
```

Finally, let's display the results. First, we determine the word with the most letters so we can right-align all the words in a field of that length, then we display each word and its count:

```
[10]: max_len = max([len(word) for word, count in sorted_items])
      for word, count in sorted_items:
          print(f'{word:>{max_len}}: {count}')
[10]:   romeo: 298
         thou: 277
       juliet: 178
          thy: 170S
        nurse: 146
```

```
   capulet: 141
      love: 136
      thee: 135
     shall: 110
      lady: 109
     friar: 104
      come: 94
   mercutio: 83
      good: 80
  benvolio: 79
     enter: 75
        go: 75
      i'll: 71
    tybalt: 69
     death: 69
     night: 68
  lawrence: 67
       man: 65
      hath: 64
       one: 60
```

16.6.4 Spark Word Count on Microsoft Azure

As we said previously, we want to expose you to both tools you can use for free and real-world development scenarios. In this section, you'll implement the Spark word-count example on a Microsoft Azure HDInsight Spark cluster.

Create an Apache Spark Cluster in HDInsight Using the Azure Portal
The following link explains how to set up a Spark cluster using the HDInsight service:

```
https://docs.microsoft.com/en-us/azure/hdinsight/spark/apache-spark-
    jupyter-spark-sql-use-portal
```

While following the **Create an HDInsight Spark cluster** steps, note the same issues we listed in the Hadoop cluster setup earlier in this chapter and for the **Cluster type** select **Spark**.

Again, the default cluster configuration provides more resources than you need for our examples. So, in the **Cluster summary**, perform the steps shown in the Hadoop cluster setup to change the number of worker nodes to 2 and to configure the worker and head nodes to use **D3 v2** computers. When you click **Create**, it takes 20 to 30 minutes to configure and deploy your cluster.

Install Libraries into a Cluster
If your Spark code requires libraries that are not installed in the HDInsight cluster, you'll need to install them. To see what libraries are installed by default, you can use ssh to log into your cluster (as we showed earlier in the chapter) and execute the command:

```
/usr/bin/anaconda/envs/py35/bin/conda list
```

Since your code will execute on multiple cluster nodes, libraries must be installed on *every* node. Azure requires you to create a Linux shell script that specifies the commands to install the libraries. When you submit that script to Azure, it validates the script, then executes it on every node. Linux shell scripts are beyond this book's scope, and the script must be hosted on a web server from which Azure can download the file. So, we created an install script for you that installs the libraries we use in the Spark examples. Perform the following steps to install these libraries:

1. In the Azure portal, select your cluster.

2. In the list of items under the cluster's search box, click **Script Actions**.

3. Click **Submit new** to configure the options for the library installation script. For the **Script type** select **Custom**, for the **Name** specify `libraries` and for the **Bash script URI** use:

   `http://deitel.com/bookresources/IntroToPython/install_libraries.sh`

4. Check both **Head** and **Worker** to ensure that the script installs the libraries on all the nodes.

5. Click **Create**.

When the cluster finishes executing the script, if it executed successfully, you'll see a green check next to the script name in the list of script actions. Otherwise, Azure will notify you that there were errors.

Copying `RomeoAndJuliet.txt` to the HDInsight Cluster

As you did in the Hadoop demo, let's use the `scp` command to upload to the cluster the `RomeoAndJuliet.txt` file you used in the "Natural Language Processing" chapter. In a Command Prompt, Terminal or shell, change to the folder containing the file (we assume this chapter's `ch16` folder), then enter the following command. Replace *YourClusterName* with the name you specified when creating your cluster and press *Enter* only when you've typed the entire command. The colon is required and indicates that you'll supply your cluster password when prompted. At that prompt, type the password you specified when setting up the cluster, then press *Enter*:

```
scp RomeoAndJuliet.txt sshuser@YourClusterName-ssh.azurehdinsight.net:
```

Next, use `ssh` to log into your cluster and access its command line. In a Command Prompt, Terminal or shell, execute the following command. Be sure to replace *YourClusterName* with your cluster name. Again, you'll be prompted for your cluster password:

```
ssh sshuser@YourClusterName-ssh.azurehdinsight.net
```

To work with the `RomeoAndJuliet.txt` file in Spark, first use the `ssh` session to copy the file into the cluster's Hadoop's file system by executing the following command. Once again, we'll use the already existing folder `/examples/data` that Microsoft includes for use with HDInsight tutorials. Again, press *Enter* only when you've typed the entire command:

```
hadoop fs -copyFromLocal RomeoAndJuliet.txt
    /example/data/RomeoAndJuliet.txt
```

Accessing Jupyter Notebooks in HDInsight

At the time of this writing, HDInsight uses the *old* Jupyter Notebook interface, rather than the newer JupyterLab interface shown earlier. For a quick overview of the old interface see:

```
https://jupyter-notebook.readthedocs.io/en/stable/examples/Notebook/
    Notebook%20Basics.html
```

To access Jupyter Notebooks in HDInsight, in the Azure portal select **All resources**, then your cluster. In the **Overview** tab, select **Jupyter notebook** under **Cluster dashboards**. This opens a web browser window and asks you to log in. Use the username and password you specified when setting up the cluster. If you did not specify a username, the default is `admin`. Once you log in, Jupyter displays a folder containing PySpark and Scala subfolders. These contain Python and Scala Spark tutorials.

Uploading the `RomeoAndJulietCounter.ipynb` Notebook

You can create new notebooks by clicking **New** and selecting PySpark3, or you can upload existing notebooks from your computer. For this example, let's upload the previous section's `RomeoAndJulietCounter.ipynb` notebook and modify it to work with Azure. To do so, click the **Upload** button, navigate to the ch16 example folder's SparkWordCount folder, select `RomeoAndJulietCounter.ipynb` and click **Open**. This displays the file in the folder with an **Upload** button to its right. Click that button to place the notebook in the current folder. Next, click the notebook's name to open it in a new browser tab. Jupyter will display a **Kernel not found** dialog. Select **PySpark3** and click **OK**. Do not run any cells yet.

Modifying the Notebook to Work with Azure

Perform the following steps, executing each cell as you complete the step:

1. The HDInsight cluster will not allow NLTK to store the downloaded stop words in NLTK's default folder because it's part of the system's protected folders. In the first cell, modify the call `nltk.download('stopwords')` as follows to store the stop words in the current folder (`'.'`):

   ```
   nltk.download('stopwords', download_dir='.')
   ```

   When you execute the first cell, `Starting Spark application` appears below the cell while HDInsight sets up a `SparkContext` object named `sc` for you. When this task is complete, the cell's code executes and downloads the stop words.

2. In the second cell, before loading the stop words, you must tell NLTK that they're located in the current folder. Add the following statement after the `import` statement to tell NLTK to search for its data in the current folder:

   ```
   nltk.data.path.append('.')
   ```

3. Because HDInsight sets up the `SparkContext` object for you, the third and fourth cells of the original notebook are not needed, so you can delete them. To do so, either click inside it and select **Delete Cells** from Jupyter's **Edit** menu, or click in the white margin to the cell's left and type dd.

4. In the next cell, specify the location of `RomeoAndJuliet.txt` in the underlying Hadoop file system. Replace the string `'RomeoAndJuliet.txt'` with the string

   ```
   'wasb:///example/data/RomeoAndJuliet.txt'
   ```

   The notation `wasb:///` indicates that `RomeoAndJuliet.txt` is stored in a Windows Azure Storage Blob (WASB)—Azure's interface to the HDFS file system.

5. Because Azure currently uses Python 3.5.x, it does not support f-strings. So, in the last cell, replace the f-string with the following older-style Python string formatting using the string method **format**:

   ```
   print('{:>{width}}: {}'.format(word, count, width=max_len))
   ```

You'll see the same final results as in the previous section.

Caution: Be sure to delete your cluster and other resources when you're done with them, so you do not incur charges. For more information, see:

```
https://docs.microsoft.com/en-us/azure/azure-resource-manager/
    resource-group-portal
```

Note that when you delete your Azure resources, *your notebooks will be deleted as well.* You can download the notebook you just executed by selecting **File > Download as > Notebook (.ipynb)** in Jupyter.

16.7 Spark Streaming: Counting Twitter Hashtags Using the pyspark-notebook Docker Stack

In this section, you'll create and run a Spark streaming application in which you'll receive a stream of tweets on the topic(s) you specify and summarize the top-20 hashtags in a bar chart that updates every 10 seconds. For this purpose of this example, you'll use the Jupyter Docker container from the first Spark example.

There are two parts to this example. First, using the techniques from the "Data Mining Twitter" chapter, you'll create a script that streams tweets from Twitter. Then, we'll use Spark streaming in a Jupyter Notebook to read the tweets and summarize the hashtags.

The two parts will communicate with one another via networking **sockets**—a low-level view of *client/server networking* in which a *client* app communicates with a *server* app over a network using techniques similar to file I/O. A program can read from a socket or write to a socket similarly to reading from a file or writing to a file. The socket represents one endpoint of a connection. In this case, the *client* will be a Spark application, and the *server* will be a script that receives streaming tweets and sends them to the Spark app.

Launching the Docker Container and Installing Tweepy
For this example, you'll install the Tweepy library into the Jupyter Docker container. Follow Section 16.6.2's instructions for launching the container and installing Python libraries into it. Use the following command to install Tweepy:

```
pip install tweepy
```

16.7.1 Streaming Tweets to a Socket

The script `starttweetstream.py` contains a modified version of the `TweetListener` class from the "Data Mining Twitter" chapter. It streams the specified number of tweets and sends them to a socket on the local computer. When the tweet limit is reached, the script closes the socket. You've already used Twitter streaming, so we'll focus only on what's new. Ensure that the file `keys.py` (in the `ch16` folder's `SparkHashtagSummarizer` subfolder) contains your Twitter credentials.

Executing the Script in the Docker Container
In this example, you'll use JupyterLab's Terminal window to execute `starttweetstream.py` in one tab, then use a notebook to perform the Spark task in another tab. With the Jupyter pyspark-notebook Docker container running, open

```
http://localhost:8888/lab
```

in your web browser. In JupyterLab, select **File > New > Terminal** to open a new tab containing a **Terminal**. This is a Linux-based command line. Typing the `ls` command and pressing *Enter* lists the current folder's contents. By default, you'll see the container's work folder.

To execute `starttweetstream.py`, you must first navigate to the `SparkHashtagSummarizer` folder with the command[48]:

```
cd work/SparkHashtagSummarizer
```

You can now execute the script with the command of the form

```
ipython starttweetstream.py number_of_tweets search_terms
```

where *number_of_tweets* specifies the total number of tweets to process and *search_terms* one or more space-separated strings to use for filtering tweets. For example, the following command would stream 1000 tweets about football:

```
ipython starttweetstream.py 1000 football
```

At this point, the script will display `"Waiting for connection"` and will wait until Spark connects to begin streaming the tweets.

`starttweetstream.py` import **Statements**
For discussion purposes, we've divided `starttweetstream.py` into pieces. First, we import the modules used in the script. The Python Standard Library's **socket module** provides the capabilities that enable Python apps to communicate via sockets.

```
1   # starttweetstream.py
2   """Script to get tweets on topic(s) specified as script argument(s)
3      and send tweet text to a socket for processing by Spark."""
4   import keys
5   import socket
6   import sys
7   import tweepy
8
```

Class `TweetListener`
Once again, you've seen most of the code in class `TweetListener`, so we focus only on what's new here:

- Method `__init__` (lines 12–17) now receives a `connection` parameter representing the socket and stores it in the `self.connection` attribute. We use this socket to send the hashtags to the Spark application.

- In method `on_status` (lines 24–44), lines 27–32 extract the hashtags from the Tweepy `Status` object, convert them to lowercase and create a space-separated string of the hashtags to send to Spark. The key statement is line 39:

  ```
  self.connection.send(hashtags_string.encode('utf-8'))
  ```

  which uses the `connection` object's **send** method to send the tweet text to whatever application is reading from that socket. Method send expects as its argument

---

48. Windows users should note that Linux uses / rather than \ to separate folders and that file and folder names are case sensitive.

a sequence of bytes. The string method call encode('utf-8') converts the string to bytes. Spark will automatically read the bytes and reconstruct the strings.

```python
 9  class TweetListener(tweepy.StreamListener):
10      """Handles incoming Tweet stream."""
11
12      def __init__(self, api, connection, limit=10000):
13          """Create instance variables for tracking number of tweets."""
14          self.connection = connection
15          self.tweet_count = 0
16          self.TWEET_LIMIT = limit  # 10,000 by default
17          super().__init__(api)  # call superclass's init
18
19      def on_connect(self):
20          """Called when your connection attempt is successful, enabling
21          you to perform appropriate application tasks at that point."""
22          print('Successfully connected to Twitter\n')
23
24      def on_status(self, status):
25          """Called when Twitter pushes a new tweet to you."""
26          # get the hashtags
27          hashtags = []
28
29          for hashtag_dict in status.entities['hashtags']:
30              hashtags.append(hashtag_dict['text'].lower())
31
32          hashtags_string = ' '.join(hashtags) + '\n'
33          print(f'Screen name: {status.user.screen_name}:')
34          print(f'    Hashtags: {hashtags_string}')
35          self.tweet_count += 1  # track number of tweets processed
36
37          try:
38              # send requires bytes, so encode the string in utf-8 format
39              self.connection.send(hashtags_string.encode('utf-8'))
40          except Exception as e:
41              print(f'Error: {e}')
42
43          # if TWEET_LIMIT is reached, return False to terminate streaming
44          return self.tweet_count != self.TWEET_LIMIT
45
46      def on_error(self, status):
47          print(status)
48          return True
49
```

Main Application

Lines 50–80 execute when you run the script. You've connected to Twitter to stream tweets previously, so here we discuss only what's new in this example.

Line 51 gets the number of tweets to process by converting the command-line argument sys.argv[1] to an integer. Recall that element 0 represents the script's name.

```python
50  if __name__ == '__main__':
51      tweet_limit = int(sys.argv[1])  # get maximum number of tweets
```

Line 52 calls the socket module's **socket function**, which returns a socket object that we'll use to wait for a connection from the Spark application.

```
52    client_socket = socket.socket()  # create a socket
53
```

Line 55 calls the socket object's **bind method** with a tuple containing the hostname or IP address of the computer and the port number on that computer. Together these represent where this script will wait for an initial connection from another app:

```
54        # app will use localhost (this computer) port 9876
55        client_socket.bind(('localhost', 9876))
56
```

Line 58 calls the socket's **listen method**, which causes the script to *wait* until a connection is received. This is the statement that prevents the Twitter stream from starting until the Spark application connects.

```
57        print('Waiting for connection')
58        client_socket.listen()  # wait for client to connect
59
```

Once the Spark application connects, line 61 calls socket method **accept**, which accepts the connection. This method returns a tuple containing a new socket object that the script will use to communicate with the Spark application and the IP address of the Spark application's computer.

```
60        # when connection received, get connection/client address
61        connection, address = client_socket.accept()
62        print(f'Connection received from {address}')
63
```

Next, we authenticate with Twitter and start the stream. Lines 73–74 set up the stream, passing the socket object connection to the TweetListener so that it can use the socket to send hashtags to the Spark application.

```
64        # configure Twitter access
65        auth = tweepy.OAuthHandler(keys.consumer_key, keys.consumer_secret)
66        auth.set_access_token(keys.access_token, keys.access_token_secret)
67
68        # configure Tweepy to wait if Twitter rate limits are reached
69        api = tweepy.API(auth, wait_on_rate_limit=True,
70                         wait_on_rate_limit_notify=True)
71
72        # create the Stream
73        twitter_stream = tweepy.Stream(api.auth,
74            TweetListener(api, connection, tweet_limit))
75
76        # sys.argv[2] is the first search term
77        twitter_stream.filter(track=sys.argv[2:])
78
```

Finally, lines 79–80 call the **close** method on the socket objects to release their resources.

```
79        connection.close()
80        client_socket.close()
```

16.7.2 Summarizing Tweet Hashtags; Introducing Spark SQL

In this section, you'll use Spark streaming to read the hashtags sent via a socket by the script `starttweetstream.py` and summarize the results. You can either create a new notebook and enter the code you see here or load the `hashtagsummarizer.ipynb` notebook we provide in the ch16 examples folder's `SparkHashtagSummarizer` subfolder.

Importing the Libraries

First, let's import the libraries used in this notebook. We'll explain the pyspark classes as we use them. From `IPython`, we imported the `display` module, which contains classes and utility functions that you can use in Jupyter. In particular, we'll use the `clear_output` function to remove an existing chart before displaying a new one:

```
[1]: from pyspark import SparkContext
     from pyspark.streaming import StreamingContext
     from pyspark.sql import Row, SparkSession
     from IPython import display
     import matplotlib.pyplot as plt
     import seaborn as sns
     %matplotlib inline
```

This Spark application summarizes hashtags in 10-second batches. After processing each batch, it displays a Seaborn barplot. The IPython magic

```
%matplotlib inline
```

indicates that Matplotlib-based graphics should be displayed in the notebook rather than in their own windows. Recall that Seaborn uses Matplotlib.

We've used several IPython magics throughout the book. There are many magics specifically for use in Jupyter Notebooks. For the complete list of magics see:

```
https://ipython.readthedocs.io/en/stable/interactive/magics.html
```

Utility Function to Get the SparkSession

As you'll soon see, you can use **Spark SQL** to query data in resilient distributed datasets (RDDs). Spark SQL uses a Spark **DataFrame** to get a table view of the underlying RDDs. A **SparkSession** (module `pyspark.sql`) is used to create a `DataFrame` from an RDD.

There can be only one SparkSession object per Spark application. The following function, which we borrowed from the *Spark Streaming Programming Guide*,[49] defines the correct way to get a SparkSession instance if it already exists or to create one if it does not yet exist:[50]

---

49. `https://spark.apache.org/docs/latest/streaming-programming-guide.html#dataframe-and-sql-operations`.

50. Because this function was borrowed from the *Spark Streaming Programming Guide*'s **DataFrame and SQL Operations** section (`https://spark.apache.org/docs/latest/streaming-programming-guide.html#dataframe-and-sql-operations`), we did not rename it to use Python's standard function naming style, and we did not use single quotes to delimit strings.

```
[2]: def getSparkSessionInstance(sparkConf):
         """Spark Streaming Programming Guide's recommended method
            for getting an existing SparkSession or creating a new one."""
         if ("sparkSessionSingletonInstance" not in globals()):
             globals()["sparkSessionSingletonInstance"] = SparkSession \
                 .builder \
                 .config(conf=sparkConf) \
                 .getOrCreate()
         return globals()["sparkSessionSingletonInstance"]
```

Utility Function to Display a Barchart Based on a Spark DataFrame

We call function display_barplot after Spark processes each batch of hashtags. Each call clears the previous Seaborn barplot, then displays a new one based on the Spark DataFrame it receives. First, we call the Spark DataFrame's **toPandas** method to convert it to a pandas DataFrame for use with Seaborn. Next, we call the **clear_output function** from the IPython.display module. The keyword argument wait=True indicates that the function should remove the prior graph (if there is one), but only once the new graph is ready to display. The rest of the code in the function uses standard Seaborn techniques we've shown previously. The function call sns.color_palette('cool', 20) selects twenty colors from the Matplotlib 'cool' color palette:

```
[3]: def display_barplot(spark_df, x, y, time, scale=2.0, size=(16, 9)):
         """Displays a Spark DataFrame's contents as a bar plot."""
         df = spark_df.toPandas()

         # remove prior graph when new one is ready to display
         display.clear_output(wait=True)
         print(f'TIME: {time}')

         # create and configure a Figure containing a Seaborn barplot
         plt.figure(figsize=size)
         sns.set(font_scale=scale)
         barplot = sns.barplot(data=df, x=x, y=y
                               palette=sns.color_palette('cool', 20))

         # rotate the x-axis labels 90 degrees for readability
         for item in barplot.get_xticklabels():
             item.set_rotation(90)

         plt.tight_layout()
         plt.show()
```

Utility Function to Summarize the Top-20 Hashtags So Far

In Spark streaming, a **DStream** is a sequence of RDDs each representing a mini-batch of data to process. As you'll soon see, you can specify a function that is called to perform a task for every RDD in the stream. In this app, the function count_tags will summarize the hashtag counts in a given RDD, add them to the current totals (maintained by the SparkSession), then display an updated top-20 barplot so that we can see how the top-20 hashtags are changing over time.[51] For discussion purposes, we've broken this function

---

51. When this function gets called the first time, you might see an exception's error message display if no tweets with hashtags have been received yet. This is because we simply display the error message in the standard output. That message will disappear as soon as there are tweets with hashtags.

into smaller pieces. First, we get the SparkSession by calling the utility function getSparkSessionInstance with the SparkContext's configuration information. Every RDD has access to the SparkContext via the context attribute:

```
[4]: def count_tags(time, rdd):
         """Count hashtags and display top-20 in descending order."""
         try:
             # get SparkSession
             spark = getSparkSessionInstance(rdd.context.getConf())
```

Next, we call the RDD's map method to map the data in the RDD to **Row** objects (from the pyspark.sql package). The RDDs in this example contain tuples of hashtags and counts. The Row constructor uses the names of its keyword arguments to specify the column names for each value in that row. In this case, tag[0] is the hashtag in the tuple, and tag[1] is the total count for that hashtag:

```
         # map hashtag string-count tuples to Rows
         rows = rdd.map(
             lambda tag: Row(hashtag=tag[0], total=tag[1]))
```

The next statement creates a Spark DataFrame containing the Row objects. We'll use this with Spark SQL to query the data to get the top-20 hashtags with their total counts:

```
         # create a DataFrame from the Row objects
         hashtags_df = spark.createDataFrame(rows)
```

To query a Spark DataFrame, first create a *table view*, which enables Spark SQL to query the DataFrame like a table in a relational database. Spark DataFrame method **createOrReplaceTempView** creates a temporary table view for the DataFrame and names the view for use in the from clause of a query:

```
         # create a temporary table view for use with Spark SQL
         hashtags_df.createOrReplaceTempView('hashtags')
```

Once you have a table view, you can query the data using Spark SQL.[52] The following statement uses the SparkSession instance's sql method to perform a Spark SQL query that selects the hashtag and total columns from the hashtags table view, orders the selected rows by total in descending (desc) order, then returns the first 20 rows of the result (limit 20). Spark SQL returns a new Spark DataFrame containing the results:

```
         # use Spark SQL to get top 20 hashtags in descending order
         top20_df = spark.sql(
             """select hashtag, total
                from hashtags
                order by total, hashtag desc
                limit 20""")
```

---

52. For details of Spark SQL's syntax, see https://spark.apache.org/sql/.

Finally, we pass the Spark DataFrame to our `display_barplot` utility function. The hashtags and totals will be displayed on the *x*- and *y*-axes, respectively. We also display the time at which `count_tags` was called:

```
        display_barplot(top20_df, x='hashtag', y='total', time=time)
    except Exception as e:
        print(f'Exception: {e}')
```

Getting the SparkContext

The rest of the code in this notebook sets up Spark streaming to read text from the start-tweetstream.py script and specifies how to process the tweets. First, we create the Spark-Context for connecting to the Spark cluster:

```
[5]: sc = SparkContext()
```

Getting the StreamingContext

For Spark streaming, you must create a **StreamingContext** (module pyspark.streaming), providing as arguments the SparkContext and how often in seconds to process batches of streaming data. In this app, we'll process batches every 10 seconds—this is the *batch interval*:

```
[6]: ssc = StreamingContext(sc, 10)
```

Depending on how fast data is arriving, you may wish to shorten or lengthen your batch intervals. For a discussion of this and other performance-related issues, see the Performance Tuning section of the *Spark Streaming Programming Guide*:

> https://spark.apache.org/docs/latest/streaming-programming-
>   guide.html#performance-tuning

Setting Up a Checkpoint for Maintaining State

By default, Spark streaming does not maintain state information as you process the stream of RDDs. However, you can use Spark **checkpointing** to keep track of the streaming state. Checkpointing enables:

- fault-tolerance for restarting a stream in cases of cluster node or Spark application failures, and

- stateful transformations, such as summarizing the data received so far—as we're doing in this example.

StreamingContext method **checkpoint** sets up the checkpointing folder:

```
[7]: ssc.checkpoint('hashtagsummarizer_checkpoint')
```

For a Spark streaming application in a cloud-based cluster, you'd specify a location within HDFS to store the checkpoint folder. We're running this example in the local Jupyter Docker image, so we simply specified the name of a folder, which Spark will create in the current folder (in our case, the ch16 folder's SparkHashtagSummarizer). For more details on checkpointing, see

> https://spark.apache.org/docs/latest/streaming-programming-
>   guide.html#checkpointing

Connecting to the Stream via a Socket

`StreamingContext` method **socketTextStream** connects to a socket from which a stream of data will be received and returns a `DStream` that receives the data. The method's arguments are the hostname and port number to which the `StreamingContext` should connect—these must match where the `starttweetstream.py` script is waiting for the connection:

```
[8]: stream = ssc.socketTextStream('localhost', 9876)
```

Tokenizing the Lines of Hashtags

We use functional-style programming calls on a `DStream` to specify the processing steps to perform on the streaming data. The following call to `DStream`'s **flatMap** method tokenizes a line of space-separated hashtags and returns a new `DStream` representing the individual tags:

```
[9]: tokenized = stream.flatMap(lambda line: line.split())
```

Mapping the Hashtags to Tuples of Hashtag-Count Pairs

Next, similar to the Hadoop mapper earlier in this chapter, we use `DStream` method **map** to get a new `DStream` in which each hashtag is mapped to a hashtag-count pair (in this case as a tuple) in which the count is initially 1:

```
[10]: mapped = tokenized.map(lambda hashtag: (hashtag, 1))
```

Totaling the Hashtag Counts So Far

`DStream` method **updateStateByKey** receives a two-argument `lambda` that totals the counts for a given key and adds them to the prior total for that key:

```
[11]: hashtag_counts = tokenized.updateStateByKey(
          lambda counts, prior_total: sum(counts) + (prior_total or 0))
```

Specifying the Method to Call for Every RDD

Finally, we use `DSteam` method **foreachRDD** to specify that every processed RDD should be passed to function `count_tags`, which then summarizes the top-20 hashtags so far and displays a barplot:

```
[12]: hashtag_counts.foreachRDD(count_tags)
```

Starting the Spark Stream

Now, that we've specified the processing steps, we call the `StreamingContext`'s **start** method to connect to the socket and begin the streaming process.

```
[13]: ssc.start()  # start the Spark streaming
```

The following shows a sample barplot produced while processing a stream of tweets about "football." Because football is a different sport in the United States and the rest of the world the hashtags relate to both American football and what we call soccer—we grayed out three hashtags that were not appropriate for publication:

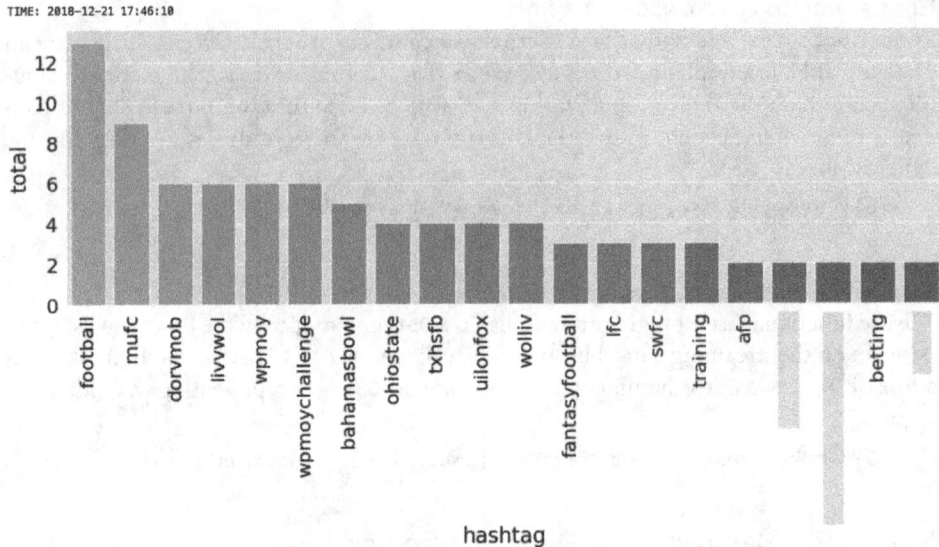

16.8 Internet of Things and Dashboards

In the late 1960s, the Internet began as the ARPANET, which initially connected four universities and grew to 10 nodes by the end of 1970.[53] In the last 50 years, that has grown to billions of computers, smartphones, tablets and an enormous range of other device types connected to the Internet worldwide. *Any* device connected to the Internet is a "thing" in the Internet of Things (IoT).

Each device has a unique Internet protocol address (IP address) that identifies it. The explosion of connected devices exhausted the approximately 4.3 billion available IPv4 (Internet Protocol version 4) addresses[54] and led to the development of IPv6, which supports approximately 3.4×10^{38} addresses (that's a lot of zeros).[55]

"Top research firms such as Gartner and McKinsey predict a jump from the 6 billion connected devices we have worldwide today, to 20–30 billion by 2020."[56] Various predictions say that number could be 50 billion. Computer-controlled, Internet-connected devices continue to proliferate. The following is a small subset IoT device types and applications.

---

53. https://en.wikipedia.org/wiki/ARPANET#History..
54. https://en.wikipedia.org/wiki/IPv4_address_exhaustion.
55. https://en.wikipedia.org/wiki/IPv6.
56. https://www.pubnub.com/developers/tech/how-pubnub-works/.

IoT devices		
activity trackers—Apple Watch, FitBit, …	healthcare—blood glucose monitors for diabetics, blood pressure monitors, electrocardiograms (EKG/ECG), electroencephalograms (EEG), heart monitors, ingestible sensors, pacemakers, sleep trackers, …	smart home—lights, garage openers, video cameras, doorbells, irrigation controllers, security devices, smart locks, smart plugs, smoke detectors, thermostats, air vents
Amazon Dash ordering buttons		tsunami sensors
Amazon Echo (Alexa), Apple HomePod (Siri), Google Home (Google Assistant)		tracking devices
appliances—ovens, coffee makers, refrigerators, …	sensors—chemical, gas, GPS, humidity, light, motion, pressure, temperature, …	wine cellar refrigerators
driverless cars		wireless network devices
earthquake sensors		

IoT Issues

Though there's a lot of excitement and opportunity in IoT, not everything is positive. There are many security, privacy and ethical concerns. Unsecured IoT devices have been used to perform distributed-denial-of-service (DDOS) attacks on computer systems.[57] Home security cameras that you intend to protect your home could potentially be hacked to allow others access to the video stream. Voice-controlled devices are always "listening" to hear their trigger words. This leads to privacy and security concerns. Children have accidentally ordered products on Amazon by talking to Alexa devices, and companies have created TV ads that would activate Google Home devices by speaking their trigger words and causing Google Assistant to read Wikipedia pages about a product to you.[58] Some people worry that these devices could be used to eavesdrop. Just recently, a judge ordered Amazon to turn over Alexa recordings for use in a criminal case.[59]

This Section's Examples

In this section, we discuss the **publish/subscribe model** that IoT and other types of applications use to communicate. First, without writing any code, you'll build a web-based dashboard using Freeboard.io and subscribe to a sample live stream from the PubNub service. Next, you'll simulate an Internet-connected thermostat which publishes messages to the free Dweet.io service using the Python module Dweepy, then create a dashboard visualization of it with Freeboard.io. Finally, you'll build a Python client that subscribes to a sample live stream from the PubNub service and dynamically visualizes the stream with Seaborn and a Matplotlib FuncAnimation.

16.8.1 Publish and Subscribe

IoT devices (and many other types of devices and applications) commonly communicate with one another and with applications via **pub/sub (publisher/subscriber) systems**. A **publisher** is any device or application that sends a message to a cloud-based service, which in turn sends that message to all **subscribers**. Typically each publisher specifies a topic or

57. https://threatpost.com/iot-security-concerns-peaking-with-no-end-in-sight/131308/.
58. https://www.symantec.com/content/dam/symantec/docs/security-center/white-papers/istr-security-voice-activated-smart-speakers-en.pdf.
59. https://techcrunch.com/2018/11/14/amazon-echo-recordings-judge-murder-case/.

channel, and each subscriber specifies one or more **topics** or **channels** for which they'd like to receive messages. There are many pub/sub systems in use today. In the remainder of this section, we'll use PubNub and Dweet.io. You also should investigate Apache Kafka—a Hadoop ecosystem component that provides a high-performance publish/subscribe service, real-time stream processing and storage of streamed data.

16.8.2 Visualizing a PubNub Sample Live Stream with a Freeboard Dashboard

PubNub is a pub/sub service geared to real-time applications in which any software and device connected to the Internet can communicate via small messages. Some of their common use-cases include IoT, chat, online multiplayer games, social apps and collaborative apps. PubNub provides several live streams for learning purposes, including one that simulates IoT sensors (Section 16.8.5 lists the others).

One common use of live data streams is visualizing them for monitoring purposes. In this section, you'll connect PubNub's live simulated sensor stream to a Freeboard.io web-based dashboard. A car's dashboard visualizes data from your car's sensors, showing information such as the outside temperature, your speed, engine temperature, the time and the amount of gas remaining. A web-based dashboard does the same thing for data from various sources, including IoT devices.

Freeboard.io is a cloud-based dynamic dashboard visualization tool. You'll see that, without writing any code, you can easily connect Freeboard.io to various data streams and visualize the data as it arrives. The following dashboard visualizes data from three of the four simulated sensors in the PubNub simulated IoT sensors stream:

Courtesy of freeboard™, brought to you by Bug Labs, Inc. (`https://freeboard.io`, `https://buglabs.net`)

For each sensor, we used a **Gauge** (the semicircular visualizations) and a **Sparkline** (the jagged lines) to visualize the data. When you complete this section, you'll see the **Gauges** and **Sparklines** frequently moving as new data arrives multiple times per second.

In addition to their paid service, Freeboard.io provides an open-source version (with fewer options) on GitHub. They also provide tutorials that show how to add *custom plug-ins*, so you can develop your own visualizations to add to their dashboards.

Signing up for Freeboard.io
For this example, register for a Freeboard.io 30-day trial at

```
https://freeboard.io/signup
```

Once you've registered, the **My Freeboards** page appears. If you'd like, you can click the **Try a Tutorial** button and visualize data from your smartphone.

Creating a New Dashboard
In the upper-right corner of the **My Freeboards** page, enter `Sensor Dashboard` in the **enter a name** field, then click the **Create New** button to create a dashboard. This displays the dashboard designer.

Adding a Data Source
If you add your data source(s) before designing your dashboard, you'll be able to configure each visualization as you add it:

1. Under **DATASOURCES**, click **ADD** to specify a new data source.
2. The **DATASOURCE** dialog's **TYPE** drop-down list shows the currently supported data sources, though you can develop plug-ins for new data sources as well.[60] Select **PubNub**. The web page for each PubNub sample live stream specifies the **Channel** and **Subscribe key**. Copy these values from PubNub's Sensor Network page at `https://www.pubnub.com/developers/realtime-data-streams/sensor-network/`, then insert their values in the corresponding **DATASOURCE** dialog fields. Provide a **NAME** for your data source, then click **SAVE**.

Adding a Pane for the Humidity Sensor
A Freeboard.io dashboard is divided into panes that group visualizations. Multiple panes can be dragged to rearrange them. Click the **+ Add Pane** button to add a new pane. Each pane can have a title. To set it, click the wrench icon on the pane, specify `Humidity` for the **TITLE**, then click **SAVE**.

Adding a Gauge to the Humidity Pane
To add visualizations to a pane, click its + button to display the **WIDGET** dialog. The **TYPE** drop-down list shows several built-in widgets. Choose **Gauge**. To the right of the **VALUE** field, click **+ DATASOURCE**, then select the name of your data source. This displays the available values from that data source. Click **humidity** to select the humidity sensor's value. For **UNITS**, specify %, then click **SAVE**. This displays the new visualization, which immediately begins showing values from the sensor stream.

Notice that the humidity value has four digits of precision to the right of the decimal point. PubNub supports JavaScript expressions, so you can use them to perform calculations or format data. For example, you can use JavaScript's function `Math.round` to round the humidity value to the closest integer. To do so, hover the mouse over the gauge and click its wrench icon. Then, insert `"Math.round("` before the text in the **VALUE** field and `")"` after the text, then click `SAVE`.

Adding a Sparkline to the Humidity Pane
A **sparkline** is a line graph without axes that's typically used to give you a sense of how a data value is changing over time. Add a sparkline for the humidity sensor by clicking the

---

60. Some of the listed data sources are available only via Freeboard.io, not the open source Freeboard on GitHub.

humidity pane's + button, then selecting Sparkline from the **TYPE** drop-down list. For the **VALUE**, once again select your data source and **humidity**, then click **SAVE**.

Completing the Dashboard

Using the techniques above, add two more panes and drag them to the right of the first. Name them **Radiation Level** and **Ambient Temperature**, respectively, and configure each pane with a **Gauge** and **Sparkline** as shown above. For the **Radiation Level** gauge, specify `Millirads/Hour` for the **UNITS** and 400 for the **MAXIMUM**. For the **Ambient Temperature** gauge, specify `Celsius` for the **UNITS** and 50 for the **MAXIMUM**.

16.8.3 Simulating an Internet-Connected Thermostat in Python

Simulation is one of the most important applications of computers. We used simulation with dice rolling in earlier chapters. With IoT, it's common to use simulators to test your applications, especially when you do not have access to actual devices and sensors while developing applications. Many cloud vendors have IoT simulation capabilities, such as IBM Watson IoT Platform and IOTIFY.io.

Here, you'll create a script that simulates an Internet-connected thermostat publishing periodic JSON messages—called dweets—to dweet.io. The name "dweet" is based on "tweet"—a dweet is like a tweet from a device. Many of today's Internet-connected security systems include temperature sensors that can issue low-temperature warnings before pipes freeze or high-temperature warnings to indicate there might be a fire. Our simulated sensor will send dweets containing a location and temperature, as well as low- and high-temperature notifications. These will be `True` only if the temperature reaches 3 degrees Celsius or 35 degrees Celsius, respectively. In the next section, we'll use freeboard.io to create a simple dashboard that shows the temperature changes as the messages arrive, as well as warning lights for low- and high-temperature warnings.

Installing Dweepy

To publish messages to dweet.io from Python, first install the Dweepy library:

```
pip install dweepy
```

The library is straightforward to use. You can view its documentation at:

```
https://github.com/paddycarey/dweepy
```

Invoking the simulator.py Script

The Python script `simulator.py` that simulates our thermostat is located in the ch16 example folder's iot subfolder. You invoke the simulator with two command-line arguments representing the number of total messages to simulate and the delay in seconds between sending dweets:

```
ipython simulator.py 1000 1
```

Sending Dweets

The `simulator.py` is shown below. It uses random-number generation and Python techniques that you've studied throughout this book, so we'll focus just on a few lines of code that publish messages to dweet.io via Dweepy. We've broken apart the script below for discussion purposes.

By default, `dweet.io` is a public service, so any app can publish or subscribe to messages. When publishing messages, *you'll want to specify a unique name for your device.* We used `'temperature-simulator-deitel-python'` (line 17).[61] Lines 18–21 define a Python dictionary, which will store the current sensor information. Dweepy will convert this into JSON when it sends the dweet.

```
1   # simulator.py
2   """A connected thermostat simulator that publishes JSON
3   messages to dweet.io"""
4   import dweepy
5   import sys
6   import time
7   import random
8
9   MIN_CELSIUS_TEMP = -25
10  MAX_CELSIUS_TEMP = 45
11  MAX_TEMP_CHANGE = 2
12
13  # get the number of messages to simulate and delay between them
14  NUMBER_OF_MESSAGES = int(sys.argv[1])
15  MESSAGE_DELAY = int(sys.argv[2])
16
17  dweeter = 'temperature-simulator-deitel-python'  # provide a unique name
18  thermostat = {'Location': 'Boston, MA, USA',
19                'Temperature': 20,
20                'LowTempWarning': False,
21                'HighTempWarning': False}
22
```

Lines 25–53 produce the number of simulated message you specify. During each iteration of the loop, we

- generate a random temperature change in the range –2 to +2 degrees and modify the temperature,

- ensure that the temperature remains in the allowed range,

- check whether the low- or high-temperature sensor has been triggered and update the thermostat dictionary accordingly,

- display how many messages have been generated so far,

- use Dweepy to send the message to dweet.io (line 52), and

- use the `time` module's `sleep` function to wait the specified amount of time before generating another message.

```
23  print('Temperature simulator starting')
24
25  for message in range(NUMBER_OF_MESSAGES):
26      # generate a random number in the range -MAX_TEMP_CHANGE
27      # through MAX_TEMP_CHANGE and add it to the current temperature
28      thermostat['Temperature'] += random.randrange(
29          -MAX_TEMP_CHANGE, MAX_TEMP_CHANGE + 1)
```

---

61. To truly guarantee a unique name, `dweet.io` can create one for you. The Dweepy documentation explains how to do this.

```
30
31          # ensure that the temperature stays within range
32          if thermostat['Temperature'] < MIN_CELSIUS_TEMP:
33              thermostat['Temperature'] = MIN_CELSIUS_TEMP
34
35          if thermostat['Temperature'] > MAX_CELSIUS_TEMP:
36              thermostat['Temperature'] = MAX_CELSIUS_TEMP
37
38          # check for low temperature warning
39          if thermostat['Temperature'] < 3:
40              thermostat['LowTempWarning'] = True
41          else:
42              thermostat['LowTempWarning'] = False
43
44          # check for high temperature warning
45          if thermostat['Temperature'] > 35:
46              thermostat['HighTempWarning'] = True
47          else:
48              thermostat['HighTempWarning'] = False
49
50          # send the dweet to dweet.io via dweepy
51          print(f'Messages sent: {message + 1}\r', end='')
52          dweepy.dweet_for(dweeter, thermostat)
53          time.sleep(MESSAGE_DELAY)
54
55   print('Temperature simulator finished')
```

You do not need to register to use the service. On the first call to dweepy's **dweet_for function** to send a dweet (line 52), dweet.io creates the device name. The function receives as arguments the device name (dweeter) and a dictionary representing the message to send (thermostat). Once you execute the script, you can immediately begin tracking the messages on the dweet.io site by going to the following address in your web browser:

```
https://dweet.io/follow/temperature-simulator-deitel-python
```

If you use a different device name, replace "temperature-simulator-deitel-python" with the name you used. The web page contains two tabs. The **Visual** tab shows you the individual data items, displaying a sparkline for any numerical values. The **Raw** tab shows you the actual JSON messages that Dweepy sent to dweet.io.

16.8.4 Creating the Dashboard with Freeboard.io

The sites dweet.io and freeboard.io are run by the same company. In the dweet.io webpage discussed in the preceding section, you can click the **Create a Custom Dashboard** button to open a new browser tab, with a default dashboard already implemented for the temperature sensor. By default, freeboard.io will configure a data source named Dweet and auto-generate a dashboard containing one pane for each value in the dweet JSON. Within each pane, a text widget will display the corresponding value as the messages arrive.

If you prefer to create your own dashboard, you can use the steps in Section 16.8.2 to create a data source (this time selecting Dweepy) and create new panes and widgets, or you can you modify the auto-generated dashboard.

Below are three screen captures of a dashboard consisting of four widgets:

- A **Gauge** widget showing the current temperature. For this widget's **VALUE** setting, we selected the data source's Temperature field. We also set the **UNITS** to Celsius and the **MINIMUM** and **MAXIMUM** values to -25 and 45 degrees, respectively.

- A **Text** widget to show the current temperature in Fahrenheit. For this widget, we set the **INCLUDE SPARKLINE** and **ANIMATE VALUE CHANGES** to **YES**. For this widget's **VALUE** setting, we again selected the data source's Temperature field, then added to the end of the **VALUE** field

    * 9 / 5 + 32

  to perform a calculation that converts the Celsius temperature to Fahrenheit. We also specified Fahrenheit in the **UNITS** field.

- Finally, we added two **Indicator Light** widgets. For the first **Indicator Light**'s **VALUE** setting, we selected the data source's LowTempWarning field, set the **TITLE** to Freeze Warning and set the **ON TEXT** value to LOW TEMPERATURE WARNING—**ON TEXT** indicates the text to display when value is true. For the second **Indicator Light**'s **VALUE** setting, we selected the data source's HighTempWarning field, set the **TITLE** to High Temperature Warning and set the **ON TEXT** value to HIGH TEMPERATURE WARNING.

Courtesy of freeboard™, brought to you by Bug Labs, Inc.
(https://freeboard.io, https://buglabs.net)

16.8.5 Creating a Python PubNub Subscriber

PubNub provides the pubnub Python module for conveniently performing pub/sub operations. They also provide seven sample streams for you to experiment with—four real-time streams and three simulated streams:[62]

---

62. https://www.pubnub.com/developers/realtime-data-streams/.

- Twitter Stream—provides up to 50 tweets-per-second from the Twitter live stream and does not require your Twitter credentials.

- Hacker News Articles—this site's recent articles.

- State Capital Weather—provides weather data for the U.S. state capitals.

- Wikipedia Changes—a stream of Wikipedia edits.

- Game State Sync—simulated data from a multiplayer game.

- Sensor Network—simulated data from radiation, humidity, temperature and ambient light sensors.

- Market Orders—simulated stock orders for five companies.

In this section, you'll use the **pubnub module** to subscribe to their simulated Market Orders stream, then visualize the changing stock prices as a Seaborn barplot, like:

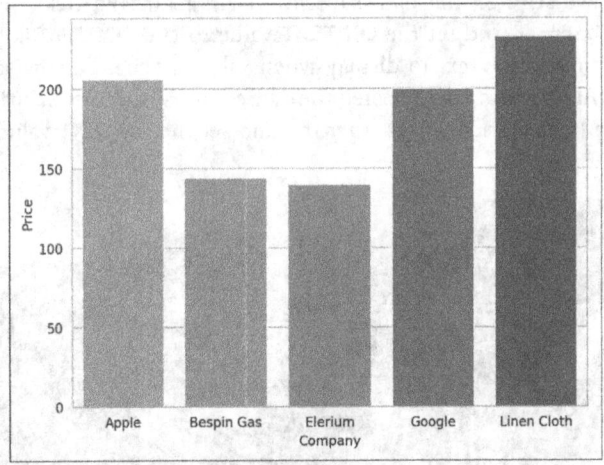

Of course, you also can publish messages to streams. For details, see the pubnub module's documentation at https://www.pubnub.com/docs/python/pubnub-python-sdk.

To prepare for using PubNub in Python, execute the following command to install the latest version of the pubnub module—the '>=4.1.2' ensures that at a minimum the 4.1.2 version of the pubnub module will be installed:

```
pip install "pubnub>=4.1.2"
```

The script stocklistener.py that subscribes to the stream and visualizes the stock prices is defined in the ch16 folder's pubnub subfolder. We break the script into pieces here for discussion purposes.

Message Format

The simulated Market Orders stream returns JSON objects containing five key–value pairs with the keys 'bid_price', 'order_quantity', 'symbol', 'timestamp' and 'trade_type'. For this example, we'll use only the 'bid_price' and 'symbol'. The PubNub client returns the JSON data to you as a Python dictionary.

Importing the Libraries

Lines 3–13 import the libraries used in this example. We discuss the PubNub types imported in lines 10–13 as we encounter them below.

```
1   # stocklistener.py
2   """Visualizing a PubNub live stream."""
3   from matplotlib import animation
4   import matplotlib.pyplot as plt
5   import pandas as pd
6   import random
7   import seaborn as sns
8   import sys
9
10  from pubnub.callbacks import SubscribeCallback
11  from pubnub.enums import PNStatusCategory
12  from pubnub.pnconfiguration import PNConfiguration
13  from pubnub.pubnub import PubNub
14
```

List and DataFrame Used for Storing Company Names and Prices

The list companies contains the names of the companies reported in the Market Orders stream, and the pandas DataFrame companies_df is where we'll store each company's last price. We'll use this DataFrame with Seaborn to display a bar chart.

```
15  companies = ['Apple', 'Bespin Gas', 'Elerium', 'Google', 'Linen Cloth']
16
17  # DataFrame to store last stock prices
18  companies_df = pd.DataFrame(
19      {'company': companies, 'price' : [0, 0, 0, 0, 0]})
20
```

Class SensorSubscriberCallback

When you subscribe to a PubNub stream, you must add a listener that receives status notifications and messages from the channel. This is similar to the Tweepy listeners you've defined previously. To create your listener, you must define a subclass of SubscribeCallback (module pubnub.callbacks), which we discuss after the code:

```
21  class SensorSubscriberCallback(SubscribeCallback):
22      """SensorSubscriberCallback receives messages from PubNub."""
23      def __init__(self, df, limit=1000):
24          """Create instance variables for tracking number of tweets."""
25          self.df = df  # DataFrame to store last stock prices
26          self.order_count = 0
27          self.MAX_ORDERS = limit  # 1000 by default
28          super().__init__()  # call superclass's init
29
30      def status(self, pubnub, status):
31          if status.category == PNStatusCategory.PNConnectedCategory:
32              print('Connected to PubNub')
33          elif status.category == PNStatusCategory.PNAcknowledgmentCategory:
34              print('Disconnected from PubNub')
35
```

```
36    def message(self, pubnub, message):
37        symbol = message.message['symbol']
38        bid_price = message.message['bid_price']
39        print(symbol, bid_price)
40        self.df.at[companies.index(symbol), 'price'] = bid_price
41        self.order_count += 1
42
43        # if MAX_ORDERS is reached, unsubscribe from PubNub channel
44        if self.order_count == self.MAX_ORDERS:
45            pubnub.unsubscribe_all()
46
```

Class SensorSubscriberCallback's __init__ method stores the DataFrame in which each new stock price will be placed. The PubNub client calls overridden method status each time a new status message arrives. In this case, we're checking for the notifications that indicate that we've subscribed to or unsubscribed from a channel.

The PubNub client calls overridden method message (lines 36–45) when a new message arrives from the channel. Lines 37 and 38 get the company name and price from the message, which we print so you can see that messages are arriving. Line 40 uses the DataFrame method at to locate the appropriate company's row and its 'price' column, then assign that element the new price. Once the order_count reaches MAX_ORDERS, line 45 calls the PubNub client's unsubscribe_all method to unsubscribe from the channel.

Function Update

This example visualizes the stock prices using the animation techniques you learned in Chapter 6's Intro to Data Science section. Function update specifies how to draw one animation frame and is called repeatedly by the FuncAnimation we'll define shortly. We use Seaborn function barplot to visualize data from the companies_df DataFrame, using its 'company' column values on the x-axis and 'price' column values on the y-axis.

```
47    def update(frame_number):
48        """Configures bar plot contents for each animation frame."""
49        plt.cla()  # clear old barplot
50        axes = sns.barplot(
51            data=companies_df, x='company', y='price', palette='cool')
52        axes.set(xlabel='Company', ylabel='Price')
53        plt.tight_layout()
54
```

Configuring the Figure

In the main part of the script, we begin by setting the Seaborn plot style and creating the Figure object in which the barplot will be displayed:

```
55    if __name__ == '__main__':
56        sns.set_style('whitegrid')  # white background with gray grid lines
57        figure = plt.figure('Stock Prices')  # Figure for animation
58
```

Configuring the FuncAnimation and Displaying the Window

Next, we set up the FuncAnimation that calls function update, then call Matplotlib's show method to display the Figure. Normally, this method blocks the script from continuing until you close the Figure. Here, we pass the block=False keyword argument to allow the script to continue so we can configure the PubNub client and subscribe to a channel.

```
59    # configure and start animation that calls function update
60    stock_animation = animation.FuncAnimation(
61        figure, update, repeat=False, interval=33)
62    plt.show(block=False)  # display window
63
```

Configuring the PubNub Client

Next, we configure the PubNub subscription key, which the PubNub client uses in combination with the channel name to subscribe to the channel. The key is specified as an attribute of the PNConfiguration object (module pubnub.pnconfiguration), which line 69 passes to the new PubNub client object (module pubnub.pubnub). Lines 70–72 create the SensorSubscriberCallback object and pass it to the PubNub client's add_listener method to register it to receive messages from the channel. We use a command-line argument to specify the total number of messages to process.

```
64    # set up pubnub-market-orders sensor stream key
65    config = PNConfiguration()
66    config.subscribe_key = 'sub-c-4377ab04-f100-11e3-bffd-02ee2ddab7fe'
67
68    # create PubNub client and register a SubscribeCallback
69    pubnub = PubNub(config)
70    pubnub.add_listener(
71        SensorSubscriberCallback(df=companies_df,
72            limit=int(sys.argv[1] if len(sys.argv) > 1 else 1000))
73
```

Subscribing to the Channel

The following statement completes the subscription process, indicating that we wish to receive messages from the channel named 'pubnub-market-orders'. The execute method starts the stream.

```
74    # subscribe to pubnub-sensor-network channel and begin streaming
75    pubnub.subscribe().channels('pubnub-market-orders').execute()
76
```

Ensuring the Figure Remains on the Screen

The second call to Matplotlib's show method ensures that the Figure remains on the screen until you close its window.

```
77    plt.show()  # keeps graph on screen until you dismiss its window
```

16.9 Wrap-Up

In this chapter, we introduced big data, discussed how large data is getting and discussed hardware and software infrastructure for working with big data. We introduced traditional relational databases and Structured Query Language (SQL) and used the sqlite3 module to create and manipulate a books database in SQLite. We also demonstrated loading SQL query results into pandas DataFrames.

We discussed the four major types of NoSQL databases—key–value, document, columnar and graph—and introduced NewSQL databases. We stored JSON tweet objects as documents in a cloud-based MongoDB Atlas cluster, then summarized them in an interactive visualization displayed on a Folium map.

We introduced Hadoop and how it's used in big-data applications. You configured a multi-node Hadoop cluster using the Microsoft Azure HDInsight service, then created and executed a Hadoop MapReduce task using Hadoop streaming.

We discussed Spark and how it's used in high-performance, real-time big-data applications. You used Spark's functional-style filter/map/reduce capabilities, first on a Jupyter Docker stack that runs locally on your own computer, then again using a Microsoft Azure HDInsight multi-node Spark cluster. Next, we introduced Spark streaming for processing data in mini-batches. As part of that example, we used Spark SQL to query data stored in Spark DataFrames.

The chapter concluded with an introduction to the Internet of Things (IoT) and the publish/subscribe model. You used Freeboard.io to create a dashboard visualization of a live sample stream from PubNub. You simulated an Internet-connected thermostat which published messages to the free dweet.io service using the Python module Dweepy, then used Freeboard.io to visualize the simulated device's data. Finally, you subscribed to a PubNub sample live stream using their Python module.

Thanks for reading *Python for Programmers*. We hope that you enjoyed the book and that you found it entertaining and informative. Most of all we hope you feel empowered to apply the technologies you've learned to the challenges you'll face in your career.

Index

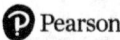

"Helps readers leverage the large number of existing libraries to **accomplish tasks with minimal code.** Concepts are accompanied by rich Python examples that readers can adapt to implement their own solutions to data science problems. I like that **cloud services** are used."
—**David Koop, Assistant Professor, U-Mass Dartmouth**

"I enjoyed the **OOP** chapter—**doctest unit testing** is nice because you can have the test in the actual docstring so things are traveling together. The line-by-line explanations of the **static and dynamic visualizations** of the die rolling example are just great." —**Daniel Chen, Data Scientist, Lander Analytics**

"A lucid exposition of the **fundamentals of Python and Data Science.** Thanks for pointing out seeding the random number generator for **reproducibility.** I like the use of **dictionary and set comprehensions** for succinct programming. 'List vs. Array Performance: Introducing %timeit' is convincing on why one should use **ndarrays.** Good **defensive programming.** Great section on **Pandas Series and DataFrames**—one of the clearest expositions that I have seen. The section on **data wrangling** is excellent. **Natural Language Processing** is an excellent chapter! I **learned a tremendous amount** going through it."
—**Shyamal Mitra, Senior Lecturer, University of Texas**

"I like the discussion of **exceptions** and **tracebacks.** I really liked the **Data Mining Twitter** chapter; it focused on a **real data source** and brought in a lot of techniques for analysis (e.g., **visualization, NLP**). I like that the Python modules helped hide some of the complexity. **Word clouds** look cool."
—**David Koop, Assistant Professor, U-Mass Dartmouth**

"**I love the book!** The **examples** are definitely a **high point.**" —**Dr. Irene Bruno, George Mason University**

"I was very excited to see this book. I like its **focus on data science** and a **general purpose language** for writing useful data science programs. The **data science portion distinguishes this book** from most other introductory Python books." —**Dr. Harvey Siy, University of Nebraska at Omaha**

"I've learned a lot in this review process, discovering the exciting field of AI. I've liked the **Deep Learning** chapter, which has left me amazed with the things that have already been achieved in this field."
—**José Antonio González Seco, Consultant**

"An impressive **hands-on approach** to programming meant for **exploration** and **experimentation.**"
—**Elizabeth Wickes, Lecturer, School of Information Sciences, University of Illinois at Urbana-Champaign**

"I was impressed at how easy it was to get started with **NLP using Python.** A meaningful overview of **deep learning** concepts, using **Keras.** I like the **streaming example.**" —**David Koop, Assistant Professor, U-Mass Dartmouth**

"Really like the use of **f-strings**, instead of the older string-formatting methods. Seeing how easy **TextBlob** is compared to base **NLTK** was great. I never made **word clouds with shapes** before, but I can see this being a motivating example for people getting started with **NLP.** I'm **enjoying the case-study chapters** in the latter parts of the book. They are **really practical.** I really enjoyed working through all the **Big Data** examples, especially the **IoT** ones."
—**Daniel Chen, Data Scientist, Lander Analytics**

"I really liked the live **IPython input-output.** The thing that I like most about this product is that it is a Deitel & Deitel book (I'm a big fan) that covers Python." —**Dr. Mark Pauley, University of Nebraska at Omaha**